LEARN Excel 97 through EXCEL 2007 FROM MR EXCEL

377 Excel Mysteries Solved

Bill Jelen

Holy Macro! Books
13386 Judy Ave NW, Uniontown OH 44685

Learn Excel 97 through Excel 2007 from MrExcel

© 2007 by Bill Jelen

Printed in USA by Malloy

Third Printing: Nov.2009

SUSTAINABLE FORESTRY INITIATIVE — Certified Fiber Sourcing — Label applies to the text stock — www.sfiprogram.org

Author: Bill Jelen

Editors: Kitty Jarrett

Interior Design: Cass White

Cover Design: Shannon Mattiza, 6Ft4 Productions

Illustrations: Bob DAmico, Millenium Design Group

Cover Photo: Dallas Wallace, Paramount Photo

Interior Design: Paragon Prepress, Inc.

Published by: Holy Macro! Books, PO Box 82, Uniontown OH 44685

Distributed by Independent Publishers Group

ISBN 978-1-932802-27-6

Library of Congress Control Number: 2007922378

TABLE OF CONTENTS

DEDICATION

Dedicated to every person who has ever asked a question at one of my Power Excel seminars.

ABOUT THE AUTHOR

In 1989, Bill Jelen took a job in a finance department to maintain a very expensive reporting tool. When he discovered on day one that this new tool did not work, he began to learn how to use a $299 spreadsheet program in ways no sane person would ever think to use it. To the manager who hired him, he now wants to admit that all the reports that allegedly came out of the $50K 4th GL reporting tool from 1989 through 1994 really were actually produced with Lotus 1-2-3 and, later, Excel.

Thinking he was the smartest spreadsheet guy he knew, Jelen launched MrExcel.com in 1998 and quickly learned that while he knew everything about taking 50,000 rows of mainframe data and turning them into a summary report, there were many people using Excel in many different ways. To all of the people who mailed in questions back in 1998 and 1999, Jelen thanks them for honing his spreadsheet skills. He now admits that he initially knew the answers to none of their questions, but secretly researched the answer before replying to their e-mails.

Today, MrExcel Consulting provides custom VBA solutions to hundreds of clients around the English speaking world. The MrExcel.com Web site continues to provide answers to 30,000 questions a year. In fact, with 250,000 answers archived, it is likely that the answer to nearly any Excel question has already been posted on the Web site's message board.

Jelen enjoys getting out to teach a Power Excel seminars. There are so many features in Excel, that Jelen has never taught a seminar without learning something new from someone in the audience who reveals some new technique or shortcut. Mostly, though, Jelen learns what Excel annoyances are driving people crazy. The questions in this book are the types of questions Jelen hears over and over.

Jelen is the author of 18 books on Excel. You can see him regularly on The Lab with Leo Laporte on TechTV Canada and Google Video. He has produced over 500 episodes of the Learn Excel from MrExcel video podcast.

Jelen lives outside Akron, Ohio with his wife Mary Ellen, sons, Josh and Zeke, and two dogs.

ACKNOWLEDGMENTS

This book and its predecessor have been honed by hundreds of people. More than 6 million chapters of the previous edition were downloaded. More than 250 podcasts were produced and downloaded by thousands each day. I've discussed tips in my Power Excel seminars for thousands of people. Along the way, people have added comments, suggestions, and new tips to make the book better.

This edition was edited by Kitty Jarrett. Cass White did the layout. Suat Ozgur provided countless macros to help format the text. Lora White provided production help and proofreading. The previous edition was edited by Linda Delonais, with special advice from Kat Chamberlin. Shannon Mattiza provided a great cover and publicity materials.

Some of the people who sent in suggestions are James Afflitto, Paul Allen, Andres Alvear, Loren Anderson, Neil Appleton, Ilia Asafiev, Doug Bailey, David Baker, Cliff Barnett, Wolfgang Bartel, Bill Bentley, A. Besis, Ron Binder, Alan Brady, Derek Brown, Alan Brown, Daniel Burke, Price Chadwick, Phil Chamberlain, Ronnie Chio, Richard Clapp, Dave Connors, Mark A Davis, Vlad De Rosa, Patrick Delange, Rob Donaldson, Adrian Early, Bryan Enos, Roger Evangelista, Nora Fazio, Linda Foster, Margarita George, Mark Grint, Sue Hartman, Peter Harvest, G. Russell Hauf, Dermot Hayes, Rich Herbert, Andrew Hinton, Steve Hocking, Mike Howlett, John Hulls, Odd Inge Halvorsen, Jerry Jacobson, Rick Johnson, Andrew Jones, David Komisar, Howard Krams, Ann LaSasso, Mark Leskowitz, Bei Lin, Sérgio Nuno Pedro Lopes, Stuart Luxmore, Carl MacKinder, Al Marsella, Giles Martin, Real Mayer, Wendy McCann, Bethany McCrea, Bill McDiarmid, James McKay, Henning Mikkelsen, Dan Miller, Richard Miller, Dan Miller, Mark Miller, Terry Moorehouse, Shawn Nelson, Susan Nicholls, Richard Oldcorn, Milind Padhye, E. Phillips, Pete Pierron, Bill Polen, Dave Poling, Brenton Prior, Blaine Raddon, Jerry Ransom, Bill Robertson, Julie Rohmann, Dave Rosenberger, Peter Rutter, Marty Ryerson, Dion Sanchez, Ricardo Santiago, Julie Scheels, Randal L. Schwartz, Ashokan Selliah, Wayne Shelton, Don Smith, Clay Sullivan, Bill Swearer, Brian Taylor, Sarah Thomas, Denise Thomson, Paul van den Berg, Dinesh Vijaywargiay, Tim Wang, Susan Wells, John Wendell, Douglas A. Wesney, and Bill Wood. Thanks to them and the many others who offered cool tips during a seminar.

Before the book went to print, I formed an advisory board of people to read and review the book. This global cross section provided excellent feedback. For example, around the world, the symbol that I call a pound sign (#) is also known as a hash sign or a number sign. In England, a pound sign is a currency symbol (£). Feedback from advisors indicated that my use of the term pound sign would cause confusion internationally. So, in this book, you will hear about number signs when the column is not wide enough for a value. This is just one example of hundreds of tweaks suggested by the advisory council. Thanks to the advisory council members: Paul Allen, Mr. Loren Anderson, Apostolos H. Besis from Greece, Wolfgang Bartel, Tim Bene, Ron Binder, Graham Booth, Derek Brown from Basingstoke UK, Andres Cabello, Mark Chambers, Natalie Chapman, Jack Chopper, Richard Clapp, Patrick Delange, Bill Fuhrmann, Marc Gershberg, Cheri Grady of Seneca MO, Peter Harvest, Karen Havens, Dermot Hayes, Andrew Hinton, Steve Hocking, Howard Kaplan from Personal Computer Training Services of LI, Ari Kornhauser, Stuart Luxmore, Al Marsella, Matt, Susan Miller-Wells, Terry Moorehouse, Susan Nichols, Dara Nolan, Dolores Oddo, Richard Oldcorn from Sydney, Jeremy Oosthuizen, Stephen Pike from Beyond Reporting, Bill Polen, Sandra Renker, Bill Robertson, Julie Rohmann, Dion Sanchez, Lorna A. Saunders, Bryony Seume, Sarah Thomas, Mark Tittley, Mr. Andrew Tucker, Rebecca Weing, and Dick Yalmokas.

I always thank Dan Bricklin and Bob Frankston for inventing the spreadsheet in the first place. Without them, the computer industry would not be where it is today. At Microsoft, David Gainer and his team keep adding new features to Excel. Thanks to those folks who dramatically improved Excel 2007.

Thanks to the entire crew at The Lab with Leo, including Leo Laporte, Matt Harris, Mike Lazazzera, Sean Carruthers, Ryan Yewell, and Kate Abraham.

Tracy Syrstad managed MrExcel Consulting while I was writing this book. My sister Barb Jelen likely packed and shipped the book if you ordered it directly from MrExcel.com.

Thanks to Josh Jelen, Zeke Jelen, and Mary Ellen Jelen!

FOREWORD

I am a comic book superhero.

At least, I play one at work. As the mighty man of macro, I have the coolest job in town: playing MrExcel, the smartest guy in the world of spreadsheets.

Well, yes, that is a lot of hype. I am not really MrExcel. In fact, there are so many different ways to do the same thing in Excel that I am frequently shown up by one of my own students. Of course, I then appropriate that tip and use it as my own!

I have incorporated some of these discoveries in a pretty cool 3.5-hour seminar titled Power Excel Tips. This is amazing stuff—like pivot tables, filters, and automatic subtotals. I love to be in front of a room full of accountants who use Excel 40+ hours a week and get oohs and ahhhs within the first few minutes. I have to tell you, if you can make a room full of CPAs ooh and ahh, you know that you've got some good karma going. At that point, I know it will be a laugh-filled session and a great morning.

One of these classes, which I was presenting at the Greater Akron Chamber, provided the Genesis moment for this book. One of the questions from the audience was about something fairly basic. As I went through the explanation, the room was silent as everyone sat in rapt attention. People were interested in this basic tip because it was something that affected their lives every day. It didn't involve anything cool. It was just basic Excel stuff. But it was basic Excel stuff that a room full of pretty bright people had never figured out.

Think about how most of us learned Excel. We started a new job where they wanted us to use Excel. They showed us the basics of moving around a spreadsheet and sent us on our way. We were lucky to get 5 minutes of training on the world's most complex piece of software!

Here is the surprising part of this deal. With only 5 minutes of training, you can use Excel 40 hours a week and be productive. Isn't that cool? A tiny bit of training, and you can do 80% of what you need to do in Excel.

The problem, though, is that there are lots of cool things you never learned about. Microsoft and Lotus were locked in a bitter battle for market share in the mid-1990s. In an effort to slay one another, each succeeding version of Excel or Lotus 1-2-3 offered incredibly powerful new features. This stuff is still lurking in there, but you would never know to even look for it. My experience tells me that the average Excel user is still doing things the slow way. If you learn a just couple of these new tips, you could save 2 hours per week.

This book talks about 377 of the most common and irritating problems in Excel. You will find each of these 377 items (which you have been stumbling over ever since your "5 minutes of training") followed by the solution or solutions you need to solve that problem. A lot of these topics stem from questions sent my way in seminars I've taught. They may not be the coolest tips in the whole world, but if you master even half of these concepts, you will be smarter than 95% of the other Excellers in the world and will certainly save yourself several hours per week.

Each of the 377 topics in this book presents a problem and its solution. There are plenty of books that go through all of Excel's menus in a serial fashion. The trouble with those books is that you have no clue what to look up when you are having a problem. No one at my dinner table has ever used the word concatenation, so why would anyone ever think of looking up that word when they want to join a first name in column A with the last name in column B?

Despite its size, this book is a quick read. You can probably skim all 377 topics in a couple of hours to get a basic idea of what is in here. When you face a similar situation, you can find the appropriate topic, apply it to your own problem, and you should be all set.

This book takes a different approach than others I have tried to use. I am MrExcel, but I am hopelessly clueless with PhotoShop. Wow! This is an intimidating program. I own a ton of books on PhotoShop. There must be a bazillion toolbars in there. Most books I pick up tell me to press the XYZ button on the ABC toolbar. I can't even begin to figure out where that toolbar is. I hate those books. So, my philosophy here is to explain the heck out of things. If you find a topic in this book in which I tell you to do something without explaining how to do it, please send me an e-mail to yell at me for not being clear.

How to Use This Book

Each topic starts with a problem and then provides a strategy for solving the problem. Some topics may offer additional details, alternate strategies, results, gotchas, and other elements, as appropriate to the topic. Each chapter wraps up with a summary and a list of any Excel commands or functions used in the chapter. Finally, at the end of each topic, you'll find a section labeled "Excel 97-2003." If you are using Excel 97, Excel 2000, Excel 2002 from Office XP or Excel 2003, you can easily do the techniques in this book. Most of the dialogs look the same, but getting to them may require different commands. Each topic's directions include the Excel 2007 commands. To complete the same task in an earlier version of Excel, use the commands listed in the Excel 97-2003 section.

In Excel 2007, Microsoft has organized the ribbon into a series of tabs: the Home tab, the Insert tab, the Page Layout tab, and so on. Within each tab, Microsoft has organized icons into various groups. On the Home tab, for example, there are groups for Clipboard, Font, Alignment, Number, Styles, Cells, and Editing. In this book, if I want you to choose the Delete icon from the Cells group on the Home tab of the ribbon, I say, "Choose Home – Delete." The other option is to say "Choose Home – Cells – Delete," but you never actually choose Cells; it is merely a label, so I generally do not mention the group when I write about a command.

Gotcha: When you are working on a chart, Excel adds three new tabs under the Chart Tools heading, as shown in Figure 1. (These tabs do not appear when you are not working with charts.) You might see Excel Help referring to the "Chart Tools | Design tab". I won't don't do this. There can only be only one Design, Layout, or Format tab available at any given time. If the topic is talking about charts, I am going to assume that you are actually working on a chart, and I will refer to the Layout tab instead of the Chart Tools | Layout tab.

Figure 1

This book refers to the Design, Layout and Format tabs.

Gotcha: Some of the icons on the ribbon tabs have two parts: the main icon and a dropdown. You can see the dividing line between the two parts only when you hover the mouse over the icon. When you need to click the icon itself, this book uses the name of the icon. For example, when you need to select the Paste icon from the Home tab, the text says to choose Home – Paste. When you need to select something from a dropdown under an icon, the text specifies dropdown; for example, when you need to select Paste Values from the Paste dropdown, this book tells you to choose Home – Paste dropdown – Paste Values.

In addition to the tabs across the ribbon, many dialog boxes contain a number of tabs. For example, if you click the Print Titles icon on the Page Layout tab, Excel displays the Page Setup dialog, which has four tabs as shown in Figure 2. If I want you to choose the Header/Footer tab of the dialog, I might write, "Select Page Layout – Print Titles – Header/Footer – Custom Header." Or, I might say, "From the Page Layout tab of the ribbon, select Print Titles. In the Page Setup dialog, choose the Header/Footer tab and then click Custom Header."

Figure 2

Select Page Layout – Print Titles – Header/Footer – Custom Header.

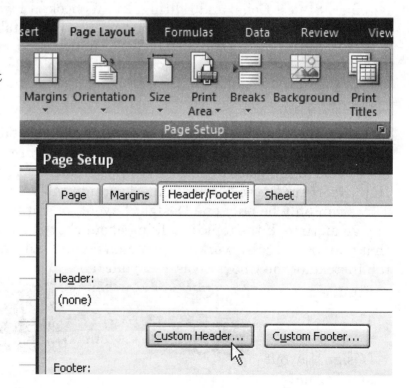

Gotcha: In newer dialog boxes, Excel has abandoned tabs across the top and used a left navigation instead. This is particularly true in the Formatting dialog, in the Excel Options dialog, and in the Trust Center dialog. For such dialogs, I sometimes write to "choose Fill from the left pane of the Format Data Series dialog," but I also sometimes write "Choose Layout – Format Selection – Fill – No Fill." In this case, Layout is the ribbon tab, Format Selection is the icon, Fill is the name of the category along the left pane, and No Fill is the option to choose.

Figure 2

Use the Page
Layout tab
of the ribbon
to get to this
dialog box.

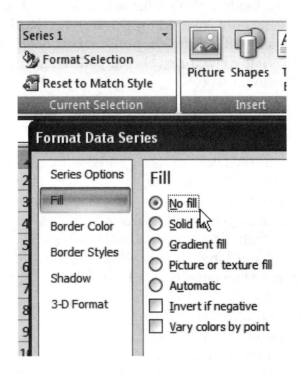

I hate books where the text refers to a figure that is on the next two-page spread. In the interest of readability, I've chosen to allow white space at the bottom of the right-hand page if it will allow the text and figure to remain together. This is a conscious decision. I'm not trying to pad the page count or increase the cost of paper in the book. I believe this layout maximizes the ease of use of the book. I'm also getting to the point in life where I can't see as well as I used to. Rather than show you the entire Excel window, I zoom in and show only the relevant portion of the screen in the figures. This will make the figures big enough to see.

This book uses the term press to refer to keyboard keys (for example, "press Enter," "press F2"). It uses the term click to refer to buttons and other items you click onscreen (for example, "click OK," "click the Paste icon"). It uses the term select or choose to refer to selections from the ribbon and option buttons and check boxes within dialogs (for example, "select the Home tab," "select the No Fill option").

Additional Resources

The files used in the production of this book are available for download at www.mrexcel.com/learn2007files.html. All 277 topics in the original edition were eventually covered on the free MrExcel podcast. I suspect that by the end of 2008, all the chapters in this book will also be covered by the podcast. Visit www.mrexcel.com/podcast.shtml for details on how to get the podcasts for free.

Quick Start - If You are New to Excel

If you consider yourself new to Excel and don't know where to start, here are some great topics for you. You will find that they are arranged from really easy to less easy.

- See headings as you scroll - Page 57
- Use the Fill Handle to enter months - Page 68
- Get finished worksheets from Office Online - Page 43
- Fit a report to one page wide - Page 68
- Excel as a calculator - Page 284
- Total without formulas - Page 177
- Entering formulas - Page 236
- Plot your Excel data on a map - Page 885
- Mix formatting within a cell - Page 39
- Join two text columns - Page 184
- Excel can read to you - Page 126
- Calculate a loan payment - Page 224
- Add a dropdown to a cell - Page 890
- Discover new functions - Page 232
- Make a formula always point at a particular cell - Page 148
- Calculate a % of total - Page 294
- Match records with VLOOKUP - Page 367
- Add hundreds of subtotals at once - Page 441
- Summarize a data set in 6 clicks - Page 536

Quick Start - For Power Excellers

If you think you know Excel really well, I bet you will find some gems in these topics:
*   Amazing way to paste values - Page 108
*   Copy just the subtotals - Page 447
*   See worksheets from the same workbook side by side - Page 73
*   Never change your margins again - Page 82
*   Back into an answer - Page 226
*   Formula to put worksheet name in a cell - Page 210
*   Trace formulas - Page 331
*   Automatically import web data each day - Page 655
*   Add new data to a chart - Page 710
*   Paste a live picture of cells - Page 830
*   See key cells from many worksheets in one place - Page 835
*   Track negative time - Page 359
*   Quickly rearrange columns - Page 740
*   Total just the filtered rows - Page 254
*   Supercharge your formulas - Page 399
*   Generate reports for every customer without a macro - Page 571

Quick Start - Excel 2007 Only

Here are a few amazing new features in Excel 2007:
*   Sort red cells to the top - Page 426
*   Keep favorites in the Recent Documents List - Page 46
*   Help your manager visualize numbers - Page 857
*   Use Document Themes - Page 681
*   Draw business diagrams - Page 788
*   Get SmartArt content from cells - Page 812

PART 1

THE EXCEL ENVIRONMENT

FIND ICONS ON THE RIBBON

Problem: The new ribbon user interface might be great for people new to Excel, but I knew the old Excel perfectly well. Why did Microsoft put pivot tables on the Insert tab instead of the Data tab, where they belong?

Strategy: You can use one of many available third-party tools to assist with the transition.

At MrExcel.com, I offer a free tip card that maps each item on the Excel 2003 menu to a tab on the Excel 2007 ribbon. If you have a color printer, download the card and print it for free.

Lin Jie was the first to solve the Excel 2007 ribbon confusion. His Classic Excel Menu add-in will add a new menu tab to the Excel 2007 ribbon. This tab replicates the Excel 2003 menu. The add-in sells for $16.95. Versions are also available for Word 2007 and PowerPoint 2007.

Figure 4

The Classic Excel Menu add-in brings the File, – Edit, – View, – and Insert menus back to Excel 2007.

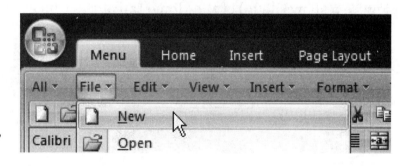

The second impressive utility is the Toolbar Toggle add-in. This add-in offers a lite version similar to the Classic Excel Menu add-in and also offers a full-featured utility that brings back the Excel 2003 menu and toolbars, as well as the ability to customize the toolbars. If you were a fan of customizing toolbars in Excel 2003, you will love the functionality of this product.

With both of these add-ins, you can work in the Excel 2003 menu, and then switch over to the Excel 2007 menu when you need to access new features.

Find links to these utilities as well as any others that become available at www.mrexcel.com/excel2007.html.

Summary: You can ease the transition to Excel 2007's ribbon interface by using a third-party solution.

GO WIDE

Problem: I can't find anything on the Excel 2007 ribbon.

Strategy: Invest in a wide-screen monitor. The Office 2007 experience dramatically improves at a 1440x900 resolution.

When you reduce the size of the Excel window, Excel automatically starts consolidating ribbon options into smaller icons and then groups. Figure 5 shows detail of the Home tab of the ribbon at normal size.

Figure 5

On a typical monitor, Excel uses many icons.

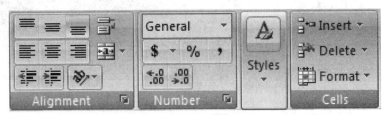

If the Excel window gets smaller, more and more icons are grouped into dropdown menus, as shown in Figure 6.

Figure 6

The icons are grouped into dropdowns at smaller window sizes.

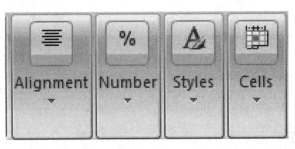

If you open Excel 2007 on a 1440x900 monitor, as shown in Figure 7, you will be able to see more icons, as well as descriptive text for many of the icons. In Figure 7, for example, the Wrap Text icon (which has never existed in previous versions of Excel) is now labeled.

Figure 7

On a wide-screen monitor, you can see more icons instead of dropdowns.

The price of widescreen monitors has dropped in recent years. In the summer of 2007, I found widescreen monitors on sale at the office supply chains for around $159. Purchasing one of these monitors is a worthwhile investment to help make your Office 2007 experience better. Not only does a widescreen monitor make the ribbon easier to work with, but it enables you to see 21 normal-sized worksheet columns.

Additional Details: If you reduce the Excel window down to about four columns wide, Microsoft assumes that you can not possibly be working in something that small, and it hides the ribbon completely. (see Figure 8)

Figure 8

When the window is smaller than four columns wide, the ribbon disappears completely.

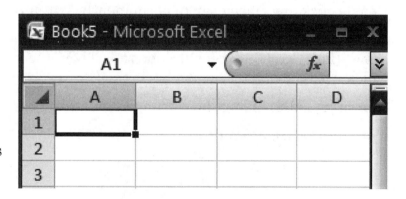

Summary: You can make your Excel window as wide as possible to see the full set of ribbon icons.

MINIMIZE THE RIBBON TO MAKE EXCEL FEEL A BIT MORE LIKE EXCEL 2003

Problem: The ribbon is taking up a lot of real estate at the top of my screen. It distracts me. I spend 99% of my Excel time in the grid, so I don't need to see the ribbon all the time.

Strategy: You can minimize the ribbon, reducing it to a simple line of Home, Insert, Page Layout, Formulas, and so on, as shown in Figure 9.

Figure 9

You can minimize the ribbon to a single line.

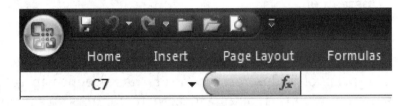

To minimize the ribbon, you can either press Ctrl+F1 or right-click anywhere on the ribbon and then choose Minimize the Ribbon.

Additional Details: When you either click a ribbon tab with the mouse or use an Excel 2007 shortcut key, the ribbon will temporarily reappear. When you select the command from the ribbon, it will minimize again.

Double-click any ribbon tab to permanently exit minimized mode.

Alternate Strategy: Excel also offers a full screen mode. If you choose View – Full Screen, Excel will hide the ribbon, the ribbon tabs, and the Quick Access toolbar. You can press the Esc key to exit this mode.

Summary: Minimizing the ribbon frees up more space for the grid.

Commands Discussed: Minimize the Ribbon; Ctrl+F1; View – Full Screen

THE OFFICE DEVELOPMENT TEAM LIKES
THE ARTIST FORMERLY KNOWN AS PRINCE

Problem: I've searched all the ribbon tabs, but I cannot find a Print icon or a Save icon. What happened to all my File menu favorites?

Strategy: The round circle to the left of the Home tab is what was the File menu in earlier versions of Excel. Many important commands are hidden behind this nameless menu item (see Figure 10).

Figure 10

Menu items like Save are hidden behind this icon.

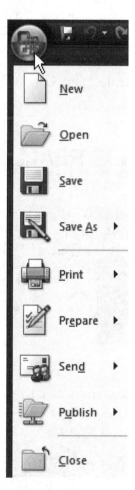

I had the opportunity to use five different beta versions of Excel 2007. For the first several versions, the round icon was a menu named File.

Somewhere along the line, someone at Microsoft decided to replace the word File with an unintelligible symbol.

It wouldn't be so bad if nothing important were behind the symbol. But important tasks such as Save, Print, Close, and Excel Options are in this menu formerly known as File.

I've checked out a few books on Excel 2007. Some are calling this the Orb. Some are calling it File or Start. My rule is to refer to this menu as the Office Icon. In this book, if I say to use Office Icon – Close, I am telling you to use the Close option on the Office Icon menu.

Additional Details: The very first time you open Excel 2007, the Office Icon pulses from white to orange. Did you notice this? This was Microsoft's only indication that there is something important under the icon.

Summary: Important items are under the Office Icon, the menu formerly known as File.

THE PASTE ICON IS REALLY TWO ICONS

Problem: When I click Paste, Excel 2007 does a regular paste instead of offering to paste only values. What's the deal?

Figure 11

The Paste icon on the Home ribbon tab.

Strategy: Many icons on the ribbon have an upper half and a lower half, but you can see the dividing line only if you hover above the icon (see Figure 12).

Figure 12

Click the upper half of the icon to paste.

You can click the upper half of Paste to invoke the Paste command. The lower half leads to a larger menu with various paste options, as shown in Figure 13.

Figure 13

Click the lower half of the icon to access a menu.

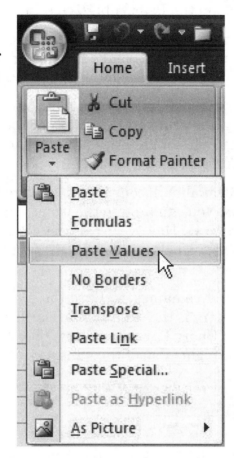

When you need to click the Paste icon, this book says to select Home – Paste. When you need to select something from the Paste dropdown, such as Paste Values, this book tells you to select Home – Paste dropdown – Paste Values.

Additional Details: In addition to Paste, several other icons have an upper (icon) half and a lower (dropdown) half:

·   The Insert icon on the Home tab

·   The Delete icon on the Home tab

·   The Pivot Table icon on the Insert tab

- The AutoSum icon on the Formulas tab

- The Macros icon on the View tab

- The Options icon on the PivotTable Tools Options tab

Ironically, the bottom half of the Options icon leads to a menu where one of the choices is Options. I have to shake my head in Microsoft's direction when I write "Choose Options – Options dropdown – Options."

Additional Details: Excel 2007 introduces a new control called the gallery. The Cell Styles gallery on the Home tab of the ribbon is one example. Many other examples of galleries appear when you are working with charts or SmartArt graphics.

A gallery has a row of thumbnail icons and three arrows along the right edge. The theory is that you can browse the icons one row at a time, using the up and down arrows. However, I almost always tell you to open the gallery. This means to click the bottom arrow to see all the selections.

Gallery controls do not have names, so I use the group name. In Figure 14, for example, the gallery is the only item in the Chart Layouts group. I would say, "Open the Chart Layouts gallery." This means to click the bottom arrow along the right edge of the gallery.

Figure 14

Click the bottom button to open the gallery.

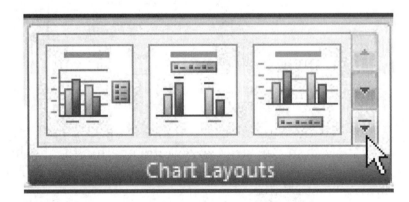

When you click the bottom arrow icon, the entire gallery opens, revealing many more thumbnails (see Figure 15).

Figure 15

You can now see all the thumbnails in the gallery.

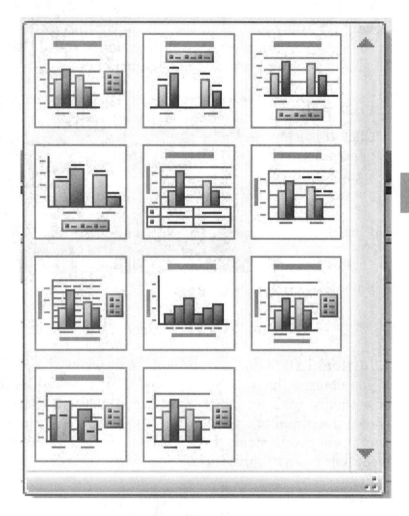

Summary: The Excel 2007 interface is made up of many new controls, from the ribbon to detailed dropdowns to complicated dialogs. You can easily navigate this interface when you understand how to read the directions in this book.

USE DIALOG LAUNCHERS
TO ACCESS THE EXCEL 2003 DIALOG

Problem: I just want to go back to using the Excel 2003 dialogs.

Strategy: Many groups in the ribbon contain a tiny icons called dialog launchers. You can click an icon to return to the old-style dialogs. Figure 16 shows an example of a dialog launcher.

Figure 16

Click this icon to access a legacy-style dialog.

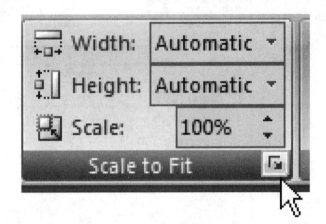

Additional Details: It is difficult to describe the dialog launcher icon. If you enlarge the icon, you can see that it looks like the top-left corner of a square with an arrow pointing down and to the right. Figure 17 shows the detail of this icon. I am sure there is some artistic rationale why these pixels mean "take me back to the old dialog that I know and love," but I can't figure it out.

Figure 17

Dialog launch-er detail.

Summary: If you want to use the Excel 2003 dialogs in Excel 2007, watch for dialog launcher icons throughout the ribbon groups.

MAKE YOUR MOST-USED ICONS ALWAYS VISIBLE

Problem: With the ribbon, I can only see one-seventh of the icons at any one time. I find that I spend a lot of time on the Data tab, but I annoyingly have to keep switching back to the Home tab. Does Microsoft really think this is better?

Strategy: Microsoft provided the Quick Access toolbar to address this problem. You can add your favorite icons to the Quick Access toolbar and then, because the Quick Access toolbar is always visible, you can invoke your most-used icons without having to switch ribbon tabs so frequently.

The Quick Access toolbar starts out as a small bar with the icons Save, Undo, and Redo. It initially appears above the ribbon, just to the right of the Office Icon, as shown in Figure 18.

Part I

Figure 18

The Quick Access toolbar starts with three icons.

If you right-click the Quick Access toolbar, you can choose to move it below the ribbon (see Figure 19). This gets your most used icons closer to the grid and provides room for a few more icons.

Figure 19

Right-click to move the Quick Access Toolbar below the ribbon.

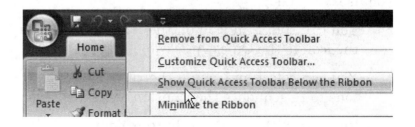

When you find yourself using a ribbon icon frequently, you can right-click the icon and choose Add to Quick Access Toolbar, as shown in Figure 20. This is the easiest way to customize the Quick Access toolbar.

Figure 20

Add your favorite icons to the Quick Access toolbar.

Gotcha: Some of the icons look similar to one another when moved to the Quick Access toolbar. For example, both Goal Seek and Scenario Manager use a green crystal ball icon. To figure out which is which, you need to hover over an icon to see its ToolTip (see Figure 21).

Figure 21

Some icons are ambiguous.

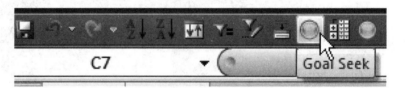

Additional Details: You can right-click the Quick Access toolbar and choose Customize Quick Access Toolbar to reach the full-featured dialog shown in Figure 22. The dialog offers a dropdown of categories on the left. Below this dropdown is a list of icons from the category. Here's how you use this dialog:

- You can select an icon on the left and click the Add button to add the icon to the Quick Access toolbar.

- You can select an icon on the right and click the Up or Down buttons to re-sequence the icons on the Quick Access toolbar.

- You can click the Reset button near the bottom to undo all your customizations and restore the Quick Access toolbar to the initial three buttons.

- You can use the top-right dropdown to say that certain icons should be assigned to the current workbook. Most Quick Access toolbar icons apply to every workbook. However, you can have 10 icons for every workbook and then add 3 additional icons for each specific workbook. The 10 global icons appear first, followed by the 3 local icons.

- You can organize your icons into logical groups and then add a separator between groups. To do this, you click the <Separator> item at the top of the left list and then click Add to add a vertical line between icons.

- You should pay particular attention to the category Commands Not in the Ribbon. If one of your favorite Excel 2003 or earlier commands is in this category, Microsoft completely left it out of the ribbon. The only way to access the command is by adding it to the Quick Access toolbar.

Part
I

Figure 22

This dialog offers many more Quick Access Toolbar options.

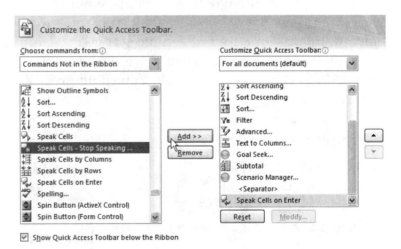

Summary: You can customize the Quick Access toolbar to have your favorite icons always available.

Commands Discussed: Customize the Quick Access Toolbar

THE ALT KEYSTROKES STILL WORK IN 2007 (IF YOU TYPE THEM SLOWLY ENOUGH)

Problem: I can't find anything on the Excel 2007 ribbon. I used to use a lot of keyboard shortcuts. For example, I often used Alt+E+I+J to invoke Edit – Fill – Justify. Microsoft completely eliminated the Edit menu, so what shortcuts do I use now?

Strategy: Your old keystrokes still work; you just have to invoke them a bit more slowly than usual. In Excel 2003, the top-level menus are File, Edit, View, Insert, Format, Tools, Data, Window, and Help, and one letter of each menu item is underlined, indicating the shortcut key to use with Alt. If you press Alt+E, you will open the Edit menu. If you press Alt+I, you will open the Insert menu.

Figure 23 shows the old Insert menu, where you can see that many of the menu items have underlined letters. You can choose a menu item by continuing pressing its underlined letter. For example, you could press Alt+I+E to insert cells. You could press Alt+I+R to insert rows. You could press Alt+I+C to insert columns. You could press Alt+I+N+D to perform Insert – Name – Define.

Figure 23

Use Alt+I to open the Insert menu in Excel 2003.

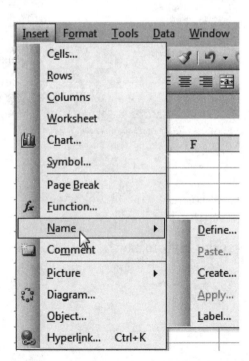

Many people who use Excel regularly memorize a few of these keyboard shortcuts. My favorites, for example, are Alt+E+S+V for Edit – Paste Special – Values, Alt+O+C+A for Format – Column – AutoFit Selection, and Alt+E+I+J for Edit – Fill – Justify.

In Excel 2007, any Excel 2003 keyboard shortcuts you memorized between the Edit and Window menus continue to work. A few of the keyboard shortcuts from the File menu still work, but others do not.

To use an Excel 2003 shortcut, you press Alt and the first letter rapidly. If you press Alt and E, V, I, O, T, D, or W, Excel will display a ToolTip above the ribbon that says Office 2003 Access Key. At this point, you can continue typing the rest of the Excel 2003 menu shortcut. In Figure 24, the ToolTip shows that Alt+E+I has been typed, which is two-thirds of the shortcut to reach Edit – Fill – Justify.

Figure 24

Type the old Alt shortcuts, and Excel will acknowledge with this message.

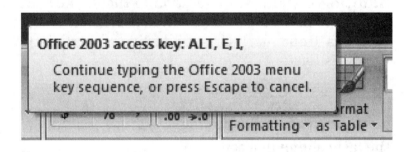

When you type the final bit of the shortcut, Excel closes the ToolTip and performs the command.

Gotcha: Excel doesn't provide any feedback about what command you are typing. In Excel 2003, you could look at the Data menu to learn what to do after typing Alt+D, but Excel 2007 doesn't offer this feature.

Gotcha: It takes Excel a fraction of a second to display the ToolTip. I find that I have to pause briefly after typing Alt plus the first keystroke. For example, if I rapidly type Alt+O+C+A to invoke Format – Column – AutoFit Selection, about half the time, Excel thinks that I typed Format – AutoFormat. It seems that while Excel is busy displaying the ToolTip, the fact that I typed C doesn't make it into the keyboard buffer. If you slow down slightly, the Excel 2003 menu keys will work more reliably. (It's ironic that we have to work more slowly in Excel 2007, isn't it?)

Gotcha: The old keyboard shortcut Alt+H to open Help does not work in Excel 2007. Microsoft decided that Alt+H would open the Home tab in all its products, so people who used to use the menu shortcuts for Help are sunk. (Although… there wasn't that much helpful on the old Help menu. I can't imagine anyone memorizing Alt+HA to open the Help – About dialog.) The F1 keystroke still invokes help.

Gotcha: Only some of the keystrokes from the old File menu continue to work. Alt+F opens the Office Icon, where you are supposed to use the Excel 2007 shortcut keys. The big three continue to work: Alt+F+O is File – Open, Alt+F+N is File – New. Alt+F+C is File – Close. However, beyond that, you will find differences. In Excel 2003, using Alt+F+W would save a workspace. In Excel 2007, the same keystrokes take you to the Print fly-out menu. Go figure.

Additional Details: In addition to the Alt key shortcuts, the Ctrl key combinations from previous versions of Excel still work: Ctrl+B is Bold, Ctrl+I is Italic, Ctrl+U is Underline, Ctrl+C is Copy, Ctrl+X is Cut, Ctrl+V is Paste.

In addition, any keystrokes that you use while working in the grid continue to work. Ctrl+Down Arrow moves to the last row in the current region. Ctrl+* selects the current region, the End+Right Arrow moves to the last column in a contiguous range.

The Function keys continue to work as well. F2 edits the current cell. F4 repeats the last command or adds dollar signs to the last reference when you're entering a formula. F11 continues to create a chart in one click, and the new Alt+F1 will create the same chart as an embedded object.

Summary: If you memorized the old Alt keyboard shortcuts to access the Excel 2003 menu, you're in luck: Most of them continue to work in Excel 2007.

USE NEW KEYBOARD SHORTCUTS
TO ACCESS THE RIBBON

Problem: I never learned the Excel 2003 menu shortcuts. I would like to be able to use the keyboard to access some of the most-used Excel 2007 commands.

Strategy: The keyboard shortcuts for Excel 2007 allow you to access almost everything on the ribbon and Quick Access toolbar. While the Quick Access toolbar shortcuts are subject to change, the ribbon shortcuts are predictable and worth learning.

You can use the Alt key to access the ribbon tabs. Excel labels the Office Icon with the letter F and each tab of the ribbon with a different letter. In Figure 25, you can see that the letters H, N, P, M, and A will allow you to access different tabs of the ribbon. The Quick Access toolbar shortcuts are numbers 1 through 9, and then they start using two digits. You can type Alt plus one of these letters to switch to a particular ribbon tab.

Figure 25

Press Alt to show the keyboard shortcuts for selecting a ribbon tab.

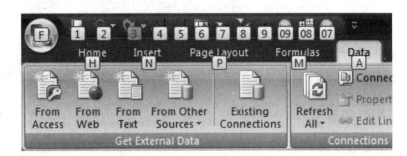

After pressing Alt+H, Excel draws in new shortcut keys to access all of the commands on the Home tab. In Figure 26, you can see that C is Copy, F+P is Format Painter, and F+O is the dialog launcher for the Clipboard group.

Figure 26

Next, type a letter to switch to a ribbon tab and Excel shows the keyboard shortcuts for that tab.

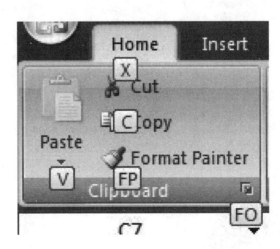

Some of these keyboard shortcuts are somewhat obvious; for example, F+P stands for Format Painter and A+L is for Align Left. Other keyboard shortcuts make sense in a historical context; for example, Ctrl+V has meant Paste for 20 years, so it seems natural to use V for Paste. Some of the shortcuts don't seem to have any rhyme or reason; I have no idea why 5 is supposed to make you think of Increase Indent.

Figure 27

Some short-cuts make sense; others do not.

In some cases, a keyboard shortcut leads to a new menu. Typing V actually opens the Paste dropdown. You then have to type S to access Paste Special. Thus, you could memorize that Alt+H+V+S is the Excel 2007 shortcut to access Paste Special.

Figure 28

Alt+H+V+S is Paste Special.

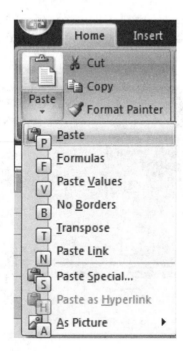

Additional Details: Each transient tab of the ribbon has a two-letter shortcut. For example, J+C is the Design tab when the Chart Tools tabs are displayed (see Figure 29).

Figure 29

Transient tabs usually get two-letter abbreviations.

The keyboard shortcut for a gallery will open the gallery. You can then use arrow keys to navigate through the gallery.

A few commands in Excel 2003 were difficult to reach with the keyboard shortcuts. In Excel 2007, you should be able to reach every command by using the keyboard.

Gotcha: Although it makes sense to memorize keyboard shortcuts for the ribbon, it does not make sense to do so for the Quick Access toolbar. Every computer's Quick Access toolbar will be different, and your Quick Access toolbar will be different if you customize. Although you can invoke Quick Access toolbar commands with the keyboard, it's probably not worth your time and effort to memorize them.

Summary: Excel 2007 offers a new keyboard shortcut system that is similar to the Excel 2003 system in many ways.

THE BLUE QUESTION MARK IS HELP

Problem: What happened to the Help menu? Where is Clippy, the annoying animated Office Assistant?

Strategy: In Excel 2007, Help is the blue question mark near the top right of the Excel window. Microsoft rewrote most Help topics in Excel 2007, and many are actually helpful. As always, the F1 key is the shortcut for help.

Figure 30

Help.

Clippy (aka the Office Assistant) has been fired. At last report, he was seen digging ditches in California.

Figure 31

Clippy will not bother you any more.

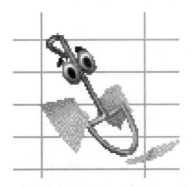

Everything else that used to be on the Help menu has moved to the Resources category in the Excel Options dialog. To find it, select Office Icon – Excel Options. In the Excel Options dialog, you choose Resources from the left navigation pane.

Figure 32

The rest of the Help menu is in the Excel Options dialog.

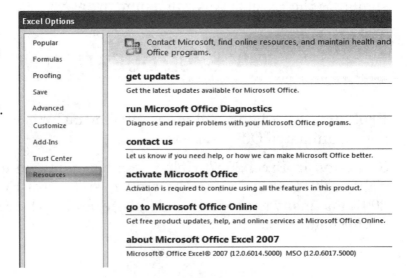

Summary: Click the blue question mark to open Excel 2007 Help.

Commands Discussed: F1; Office Icon – Excel Options – Resources

ALL COMMANDS START AT THE TOP (EXCEPT FOR 2 CONTROLS AT THE BOTTOM)

Problem: Microsoft is trying to get away from floating toolbars. In Excel 2003, I could float toolbars right near my work area. The task pane would often appear at the right side of the screen. Microsoft sold the ribbon as easier to use because we always know to start any command at the top of the screen. So, what are those icons in the lower-right corner for (see Figure 33)?

Figure 33

Control zoom and view in the lower right.

Strategy: The icons in the lower-right corner of the screen control the zoom and switch between Normal view, Page Break Preview, and the new Page Layout view.

The zoom slider gives you one-click access to change the zoom from 10% up to 400%. This is easier to use than the old Zoom dropdown on the Standard toolbar. You just click the + icon at the right to increase the zoom in 10% increments. You click the – icon at the left to decrease the zoom in 10% increments, or you can simply drag the zoom slider to any spot along the continuum.

As in past versions of Excel, the quickest way to zoom in Excel 2007 is to use the wheel mouse. You hold down the Ctrl key while you scroll the wheel on your mouse forward to zoom in or backward to zoom out.

At a 400% zoom, you can get an ultra-close look at the detail of Excel's High-Low-Close stock chart to see that they really don't draw the left-facing Open symbol (see Figure 34).

Figure 34

At 400% zoom, you can see tiny details in charts.

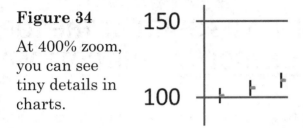

At a 10% zoom, you can get a view of hundreds of pages at once. The tiny screenshot in Figure 35 shows more than 21,000 cells.

Figure 35

At 10% zoom, you can see an overview of an entire document.

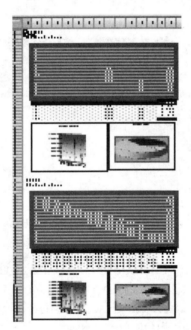

The other three buttons in the lower-right corner of the screen switch between Normal view, Page Break Preview, and the new Layout view. You can read about the cool new Layout view in "How to Print Page Numbers at the Bottom of Each Page" on page 66.

Summary: Excel 2007 offers new methods for controlling zoom and selecting different screen views.

WHAT HAPPENED TO TOOLS – CUSTOMIZE?

Problem: Where is the Excel 2003 Customize command? I loved customizing my toolbars, adding new toolbars, and so on.

Strategy: You will be disappointed. Microsoft removed this functionality from inside Excel. It is still possible to customize the ribbon, but you have to be a programmer to do it. Eventually, third-party tools will appear that will allow you to customize the ribbon. One such tool, Toolbar Toggle, already lets you customize a special version of the menu. More tools will undoubtedly follow. See www.mrexcel.com/classicexcelmenu. html for the latest details on these products.

Part I

Microsoft only gives you control over the color scheme used for the ribbon. To change from Blue to Silver to Black, you select Office Icon – Excel Options. In the Popular category of the Excel Options dialog, you choose the Color Scheme dropdown (see Figure 36).

Figure 36

Microsoft removed the powerful Customize dialog and replaced it with these three options.

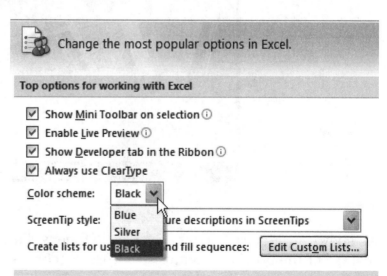

Summary: The inability to drag and drop icons on the ribbon is a major disappointment in Excel 2007.

WHAT HAPPENED TO TOOLS – OPTIONS?

Problem: Where is the Excel 2003 Options command? Did Microsoft simplify the 13-tabbed Options dialog in Excel 2007?

Strategy: Instead of Options, Microsoft now provides an Excel Options dialog. You access it by clicking the Excel Options button, at the bottom right of the Office Icon menu (see Figure 37).

Figure 37

Access Excel Options from the Office Icon menu.

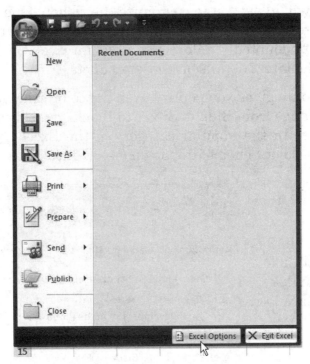

As shown in Figure 38, the new Excel Options dialog has 9 categories instead of the previous 13 tabs. It incorporates most settings that used to be in the Options dialog, plus Tools – AutoCorrect, Tools – Macro – Security, Tools – Add-Ins, and many options from the old Help menu.

In what seems like a confusing move, Excel took a few options from the old General tab, combined them with some new options, and moved them to the Popular category in the Excel Options dialog.

The Advanced category in Excel 2007 offers 10 different sections. You will find that many of the former tabs from the Excel 2003 Options dialog have moved to the Advanced category in Excel 2007. Instead of flipping from tab to tab to tab in Excel 2003, you can scroll through the long list of Advanced options in Excel 2007.

Figure 38

The new Excel Options dialog has 9 categories instead of 13 tabs.

Excel Options

- Popular
- Formulas
- Proofing
- Save
- Advanced
- Customize
- Add-Ins
- Trust Center
- Resources

Part I

The following table maps the Excel 2003 Options dialog tabs to the Excel 2007 Excel Options dialog categories:

Excel 2003 Tab	Excel 2007 Excel Options Dialog Category
View	Advanced (Groups 4 through 6)
Calculation	Formulas and Advanced (Group 6)
Edit	Advanced (Groups 1 and 2)
General	Popular and Advanced (Group 9)
Transition	Advanced (Group 10)
Custom Lists	Popular
Charts	Advanced (Group 4)
Color	Save
International	Advanced (Group 1)
Save	Save
Error Checking	Proofing
Spelling	Proofing
Security	Removed from the dialog; select File – Save As, click the Tools button, and choose the General category

The final four categories in the Excel Options dialog do not correspond to the Excel 2003 Options dialog:

- Customize: For adding icons to the Quick Access toolbar
- Add-Ins: For managing add-ins (similar to Tools – Add-Ins in Excel 2003)
- Trust Center: For managing security and much more
- Resources: For non-Help choices from the Excel 2003 Help menu

Summary: The Options dialog has been redesigned for Excel 2007. You access the new Excel Options dialog by selecting Office Icon – Excel Options.

Commands Discussed: Office Icon – Excel Options; Office Icon – Save As

Excel 97-2003: The Excel Options dialog incorporates Tools – Options, Tools – Customize, Tools – Add-Ins, and Tools – Autocorrect

WHERE ARE MY MACROS?

Problem: Did Microsoft abandon the macro facility? Where are the buttons to record a new macro, run a macro, and so on? How do I get to the Visual Basic Editor?

Strategy: Due to beta tester outcry, Microsoft reluctantly added three macro options to the extreme right end of the View tab. You use the Macros dropdown to view macros, record a macro, or use relative references while recording a macro (see Figure 39).

Figure 39

A small subset of macro commands are available on the View tab.

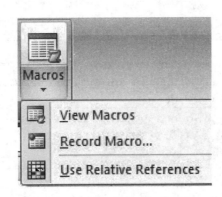

To access the rest of the macro functionality, you need to enable a hidden ribbon tab by selecting Office Icon – Excel Options – Popular – Show Developer Tab in the Ribbon (see Figure 40).

Figure 40

Microsoft disabled the Developer tab by default.

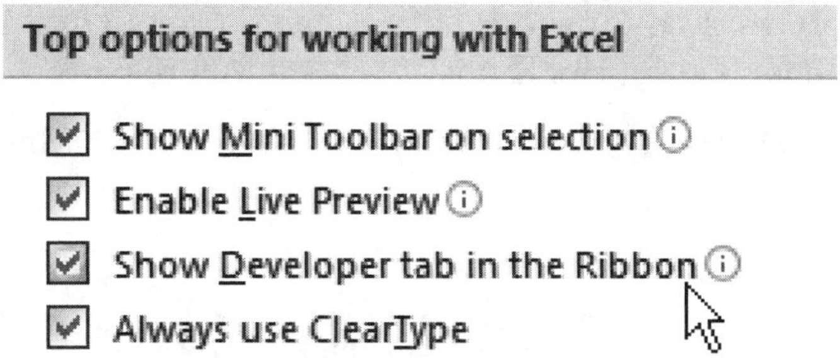

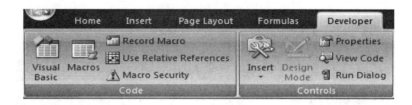

The Developer tab offers macro commands, buttons from the former Forms toolbar and Control Toolbox, and XML settings (see Figure 41).

Figure 41

Anyone writing macros will want to enable the Developer tab.

The Developer tab offers macro commands, buttons from the former Forms toolbar and Control Toolbox, and XML settings (see Figure 41).

Additional Details: When you are recording a macro, instead of seeing the Stop Recording icon floating above the Excel window, you now see it in the lower-left corner of the Excel window (see Figure 42).

Figure 42

The Stop Recording button is now on the status bar.

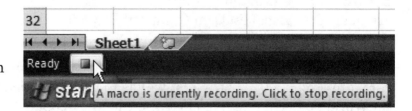

The same area of the status bar includes a Record Macro button when you are not recording a macro. However, because there is not a Relative

References button, you cannot effectively record macros without using either the View tab or the Developer tab of the ribbon.

Summary: Microsoft is making it harder to use macros in Excel.

Commands Discussed: Office Icon – Excel Options – Popular – Show Developer Tab in the Ribbon; View – Macros

Excel 97-2003: Tools – Macro – Record New Macro; Tools – Macro – Macros

WHY DO I HAVE ONLY 65,536 ROWS?

Problem: Hey! Microsoft said that the grid in Excel 2007 was massively large—1.1 million rows by 16,384 columns. I opened my favorite Excel file, and I have only 65,536 rows. What's going on?

Figure 43

Your last cell is IV65536 instead of XFD1048576.

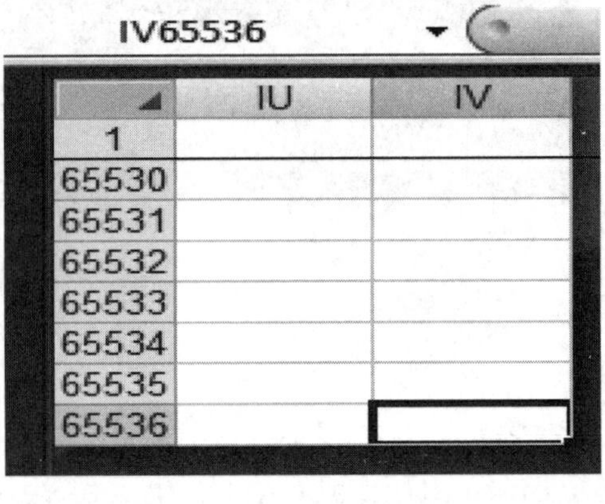

Strategy: Files created in Excel 2003 and stored with an .xls extension are opened in Excel 2007 in Compatibility mode. In this mode, you can only access the original grid size.

If you will not be using this file in Excel 2003 anymore, you should convert it to Excel 2007. The safest way is to use Office Icon – Save As – Excel Workbook. You have to close the file and reopen it in order to access the extra rows.

Now, Excel does offer a Convert command on the Office Icon menu. When you select Office Icon – Convert, Excel will update the file, save the file, close the file, and reopen the file. However, the Convert command also deletes the original .xls version of the file! I am not convinced that I want Excel deleting my original files, so I recommend using the Office Icon – Save As – Excel Workbook method instead.

Figure 44

The Convert command deletes your original file.

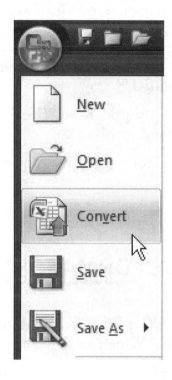

Results: After you use either Office Icon – Save As – Excel Workbook or Office Icon –Convert, you will be able to access all 17 billion cells on Sheet1, all the way out to XFD1048576.

Figure 45

Save the file, close the file, open the file, and you can access all cells.

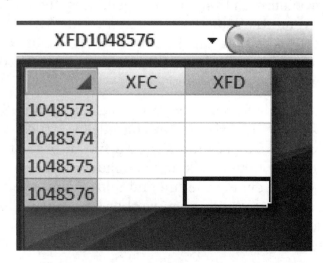

Additional Details: Excel 2007's larger grid introduces an interesting problem. In Excel 2003, you might have a spreadsheet with named ranges such as TAX97, ROI2008, and so on. In Excel 2007, these names are now actual cell addresses! If you open a workbook that had these names defined and then convert to Excel 2007, Excel will change the named range to _ROI2008 (with an underscore). While most of your formulas will update, any functions that use the INDIRECT function or VBA code might need to be manually updated.

Summary: You have to explicitly update an Excel 2003 file to Excel 2007 before you can access beyond row 65,536.

Commands Discussed: Office Icon – Save As – Excel Workbook; Office Icon – Convert

Functions Discussed: =INDIRECT()

WHICH FILE FORMAT SHOULD I USE?

Problem: I've been using .xls files for years. What are these new .xlsx, .xlsm, .xlsb, and .xlam file types? Which should I use?

Strategy: Excel 97-2003 typically stored files in a proprietary binary format. There are problems inherent with that format. For one thing, if a few bits get corrupted, you might lose all the data in the file. In addition, it is difficult for third-party programs to create binary .xls files.

Another problem was that the old .xls binary file format could not handle data beyond row 65,536. So, the new .xlsb file format is a proprietary binary file format that can handle the 17 billion cells in Excel 2007. However, this is not the default file format in Excel 2007. Microsoft has created something even better.

The new .xlsm file format is an amazing file format. The entire spreadsheet is saved as a series of text-based XML files, and then that collection of files is zipped into a single file in order to save disk space. You can actually take a look at the insides of an .xlsm file. In Windows Explorer, if you rename the file and add a .zip extension, you can then open the file using WinZip or any other zip utility. This is a fairly exciting advancement because it means people will be able to use third-party tools to generate Excel files without having Excel on their computers.

You can tell that security issues have taken a grip on the people at Microsoft. They've introduced a new file format that guarantees that there will be no macros inside. The .xlsx file format uses the same zipped file structure as .xlsm but deletes any macros in the file. As someone who uses macros all the time, I think this is a silly file format. I guess if you plan on doing everything manually in Excel and if you never have any plans to learn how to dramatically increase your efficiency with Excel, then you could adopt the .XLSX file format. Actually, if you fit into this category, you could use Microsoft Works, Star Office, or Google Spreadsheets.

.xlam is another new file format. Developers can deliver Excel add-ins in this file format.

In case you are working in an office where many people still use legacy versions of Excel, you can always use the Save As command to save an Excel 2007 file as an Excel 97-2003 file format. Excel actually supports saving to 24 different file formats, including CSV, DIF, SLK, and other specialized formats.

Additional Details: You will probably choose one file type and stick with it. I've been using .xlsm files without issue for over a year. If you decide on one format, you can tell Excel to always use that file format. To do so, you select Office Icon – Excel Options, and in the left pane of the Excel Options dialog, you choose the Save category. From the top dropdown, you select your favorite file format, as shown in Figure 46.

Figure 46

Choose a default file format.

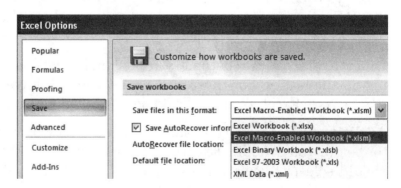

Gotcha: Like many accountants, I look forward to Walt Mossberg's review of the new Office suite in the Wall Street Journal. When reviewing Excel 2007, Walt actually suggested setting this dropdown to save workbooks as Excel 97-2003 files. If you follow Walt's advice, you will never be able to use the big grid, new data visualizations, new functions, or improved pivot tables.

Summary: Excel introduces four new file formats that enable all kinds of new possibilities: .xlsx, .xlsm, .xlsb, and .xlam.

Commands Discussed: Office Icon – Excel Options – Save – Save Files in This Format

SHARE FILES WITH PEOPLE WHO ARE STILL USING EXCEL 97 THROUGH EXCEL 2003

Problem: One of my customers is still using Excel 2003. Are there any issues to be aware of when sharing files with him?

Strategy: There are two strategies you can use in this situation. If your customer is using Excel 2002 or Excel 2003, you can ask him to install the free file converter from Microsoft. The Microsoft Office Compatibility Pack for Word, Excel, and PowerPoint 2007 Formats will allow the customer to open any of the new file formats in his version of Excel. He can also make changes to the file and save it back as an Excel 2007 file format. The utility works amazingly well. To install the utility in Excel 2003, your customer simply needs to try to open an .xlsm file in Excel 2003. Excel will offer to download and install the utility for him. He will need an Internet connection.

Unfortunately, some customers are technologically challenged and won't install the utility. For those customers, you will have to use Office Icon – Save As – Excel 97-2003 Workbook.

Additional Details: To ensure that your file will work as you want it to, before you send an Excel 2007 file to an Excel 2003 computer, you should select Office Icon – Prepare – Run Compatibility Checker, as shown in Figure 47.

Figure 47

This utility will check for compatibility problems.

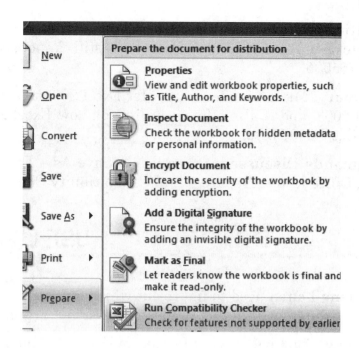

As shown in Figure 48, Excel will report major and minor problems. Minor problems are identified as a "Minor Loss of Fidelity." You can usually skip these. Major problems are identified as a "Significant Loss of Functionality." You should use the Find links to locate the cells with these major problems.

Figure 48

While you can ignore the minor issues, you need to pay attention to major issues.

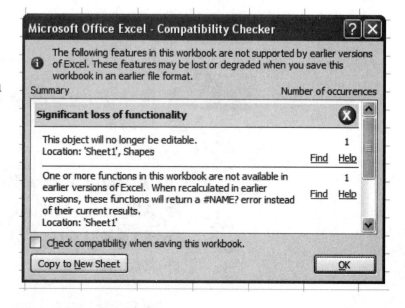

Additional Details: Although the Compatibility Pack will allow Excel 2003 to open Excel 2007 files, Excel 2003 still cannot access data beyond cell IV65536.

Summary: Microsoft offers a way for Excel 2007 to save files for use in Excel 2003, and it also offers a utility to allow Excel 2003 to open and save Excel 2007 files.

Commands Discussed: Office Icon – Save As – Excel 97-2003 Workbook; Office Icon – Prepare – Run Compatibility Checker

USE LIVE PREVIEW

Problem: I often need to figure out which font to use and want to preview the different styles on a chart or SmartArt graphic.

Strategy: The Live Preview feature in Excel 2007 makes choosing from a gallery very easy. You just select a range in Excel and then open the Font dropdown. When you hover over a font name in the list, Excel will show you the spreadsheet in that font.

Figure 49

Hover over a font to see a preview.

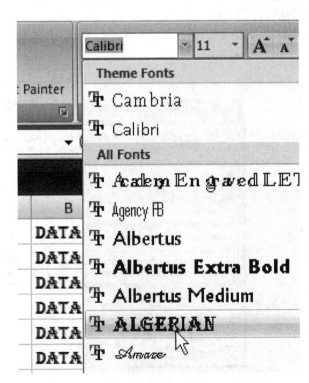

Note that the change is not permanent in the worksheet. You can continue hovering over new fonts, and Excel will show you a preview of the font (see Figure 50).

Figure 50

Preview other fonts by hovering over them.

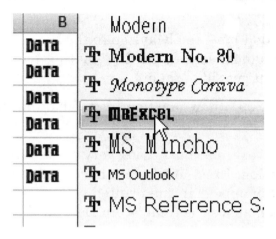

When you find a font that looks good, you can click the font name to select it. Excel will then apply the font to the selected range.

Additional Details: Many galleries besides the Font dropdown offer Live Preview. It is likely that even more galleries will inherit this feature in future versions of Excel.

Gotcha: Live Preview is memory intensive. You can turn off the feature if your computer doesn't have the processing power to handle it. Select Office Icon – Excel Options – Popular – Enable Live Preview.

Summary: Live Preview allows you to quickly see the effects of many formatting changes in Excel.

Commands Discussed: Office Icon – Excel Options – Popular – Enable Live Preview

GET QUICK ACCESS TO FORMATTING OPTIONS USING THE MINI TOOLBAR

Problem: Why do I have to always go to the top of the window to reach formatting commands? I loved having floating toolbars in Excel 2003. Why did Microsoft get rid of them?

Strategy: Excel 2007 offers one floating toolbar, but it is elusive. Here's how you use it:

1) Select some text in a chart. Look very closely above and to the right of the selection. Excel draws in a nearly invisible Mini toolbar. (It may not even appear in the printed version of this book.) Look for the Bold icon above the final "a" in Data in Figure 51.

Figure 51

The Mini tool-bar starts out nearly invisible.

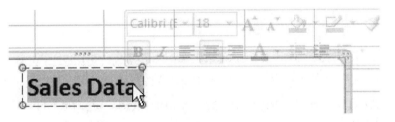

2) Move the mouse toward the Mini toolbar. The Mini toolbar will become more visible and will be available for use (see Figure 52).

Figure 52

Move the mouse toward the toolbar, and it will solidify.

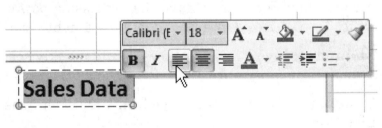

Gotcha: If you generally select text by dragging the mouse from right to left, you will never see the mini toolbar. I used Excel for months without ever causing it to appear.

Additional Details: If you move the mouse toward the Mini toolbar and then away, the Mini toolbar will solidify and then disappear. You can keep making it appear and disappear, but if you eventually get a certain number of pixels away from the toolbar, Excel will hide the toolbar until you reselect the data.

Additional Details: The Mini toolbar will appear often in Word. In order for it to appear in an Excel cell, you have to select only a portion of the characters in the cell. In this case, you will see an abbreviated version of the Mini toolbar.

You can also cause the Mini toolbar to appear if you select cells and right-click.

Summary: The Mini toolbar puts 22 commands in close proximity to your mouse.

MIX FORMATTING IN A SINGLE CELL

Problem: I'd like to use strikethrough on the text in part of a cell. Is this possible?

Strategy: You can apply different formatting to certain characters in a cell.

You select the cell and then press F2 or double-click the cell. Select characters with the mouse or by using the arrow keys in combination with the Shift key. You can then apply formatting. Many icons on the Home tab of the ribbon are enabled. Any formatting shortcut keys, such as Ctrl+5 for strikethrough, will work. If you need to apply superscript or subscript, you use the Format Cells dialog by pressing Ctrl+1 or click the dialog launcher in the bottom-right corner of the Font group.

Figure 53 shows a variety formatting applied to part of a cell.

Figure 53

Format a subset of characters in a cell.

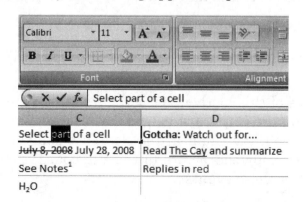

Gotcha: In addition to the character formatting, you can apply other formatting to the entire cell. For example, in C5, you can safely apply italic or underline to the cell without removing the bold from the first word. However, if you apply bold to the entire cell, Excel will not remember that you started with just the first word bold. You can not use the Bold icon on the entire cell to toggle back to the formatting shown in the figure.

Gotcha: If you later use the Justify command, the internal formatting will be lost.

Summary: You can mix font formatting within a cell.

Commands Discussed: Home – Format – Format Cells

Excel 97-2003: Format – Cells

COPY THE CHARACTERS FROM A CELL INSTEAD OF COPYING AN ENTIRE CELL

Problem: I need to copy from Excel to Outlook. Microsoft applies weird formatting to the values when I paste to Outlook. Instead of getting just the text, it almost seems like Outlook is wrapping the cell value in a table.

Strategy: If you have a single cell to copy and want to grab just the characters from the cell, you follow these steps:

1)   Select the cell. Put the cell in Edit mode by pressing F2.

2)   Select all the characters in the cell by pressing Ctrl+A.

3)   Press Ctrl+C to copy.

4)   Paste to another application. Excel will not try to place the text in a table.

An advantage of this method is that characters copied to the Clipboard will remain on the Clipboard longer than cells copied to the Clipboard. If you copy a cell, the Clipboard is cleared when you press Esc or save the file. If you copy characters to the Clipboard, they will stay on the Clipboard after these events.

Alternate Strategy: If you have several cells to copy, you can just copy and paste the cells. After you paste to Outlook, a Paste Options icon will appear. You can open the icon and choose Keep Text Only to convert the table to text (see Figure 54).

Figure 54

Override the annoying table formatting.

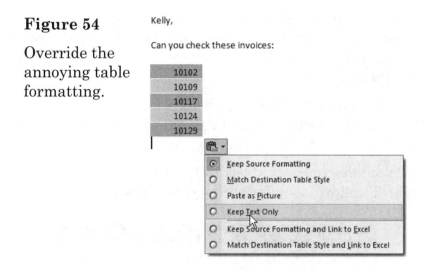

Kelly,
Can you check these invoices:
10102
10109
10117
10124
10129
Keep Source Formatting
Match Destination Table Style
Paste as Picture
Keep Text Only
Keep Source Formatting and Link to Excel
Match Destination Table Style and Link to Excel

After converting the pasted cells to text, you will have plain text that appears as if you simply typed the values (see Figure 55)

Figure 55

You are left with plain text.

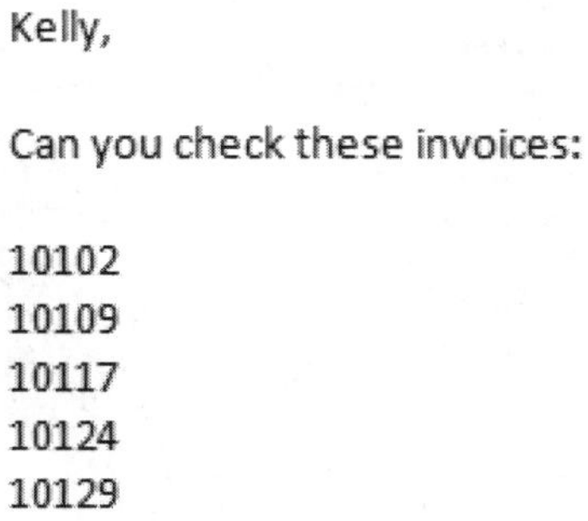

Kelly,
Can you check these invoices:
10102
10109
10117
10124
10129

Summary: Instead of copying an entire cell, you can copy the characters from the cell.

Commands Discussed: Ctrl+A; Ctrl+C

I AM A LOBBYIST WRITING POLICY PAPERS FOR THE WHITE HOUSE

Problem: I was so embarrassed when some computer guru discovered that I left my name in the Document Properties dialog. The press traced that press release from the White House back to my lobbying firm. Who knew that Excel stored secret hidden information?

Strategy: There are dozens of places where data can get hidden in Excel. The new Document Inspector can find 90% of them. Before you try to pass your work off as someone else's work, try to cover your tracks.

To look for hidden data in your workbook, select Office Icon – Prepare – Inspect Document. Excel will look for all the data shown in Figure 56.

Figure 56

Excel helps sneaky people cover their tracks.

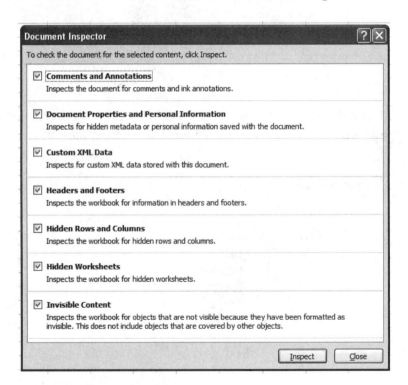

Gotcha: The Document Inspector finds a lot of hidden data, but not all hidden data. For example, if you hid data by formatting with a white font, or if you used the ;;; custom number format, it will not detect either of these. Further, some personal information might be stored in the Manage Names dialog. The Document Inspector will not discover this information.

Summary: Will you actually sleep better knowing that the Document Inspector will protect you 90% of the time?

Commands Discussed: Office Icon – Prepare – Inspect Document

MY MANAGER WANTS ME TO CREATE A NEW EXPENSE REPORT FROM SCRATCH

Problem: My manager wants me to design a new expense report completely from scratch. It seems intimidating to create this report from scratch.

Strategy: There are hundreds of free prebuilt documents available to registered owners of Excel 2007, so "starting from scratch" isn't as frightening as it might seem. When you select Office Icon – New and then select a category from the list at the left, Excel will show you all the available documents. To use a document, you click the thumbnail and choose Download (see Figure 57).

Figure 57

Get free prebuilt worksheets from the New Workbook dialog.

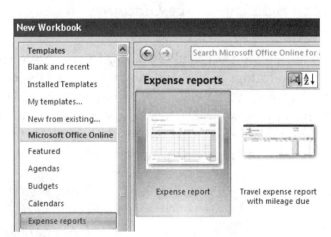

Additional Details: The variety of documents available in Excel 2007 is amazing. For instance, choose More Categories from the left, and you

can access identification cards, games, fantasy football trackers, score-cards, and tournament brackets. Before you design a new form, see if Excel has such a form already available.

Gotcha: This feature is available only to people who own legitimate copies of Office 2007. If you are using a pirated version, you cannot access the templates.

Summary: The Excel 2007 New Workbook dialog offers hundreds of prebuilt forms from Office Online.

Commands Discussed: Office Icon – New

Excel 97-2003: File – New – Templates on Office Online

INCREASE THE NUMBER OF DOCUMENTS IN THE RECENT DOCUMENTS LIST

Problem: I routinely open the same 50 workbooks. The Office Icon menu shows only the last 10 workbooks that I opened or saved. It sure would be nice if it showed more workbooks.

Strategy: Good news! You can increase the Recent Documents list (located on the right side of the Office Icon menu) from 10 to 50 workbooks.

You select Office Icon – Excel Options. In the Advanced category of the Excel Options dialog, you scroll down to the Display group. The first item in that group is Show This Number of Recent Documents. Use the spin button to increase to 50, as shown in Figure 58. This is a dramatic improvement over Excel 2003, where the list started with four entries and could contain as many as nine entries.

Figure 58

Increase the recent documents list up to 50 entries.

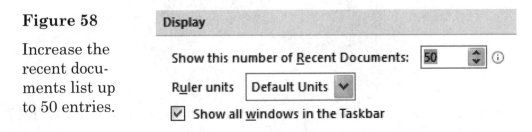

Results: The Office Icon will show up to the last 50 files that you opened, as shown in Figure 59.

Figure 59

The most recent document is at the top of the list.

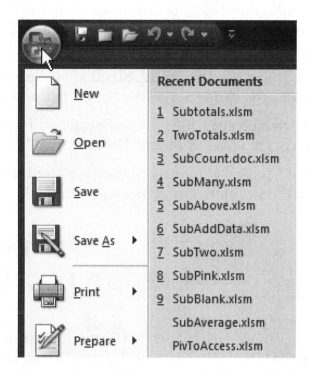

Additional Details: The Recent Documents list in Excel 2007 works better than the Recently Used File List in Excel 2003. The old list worked fine for files opened through File – Open, but it failed to note files that were opened by double-clicking in Windows Explorer. In Excel 2007, the Recent Documents list will note files that are opened through Windows Explorer or even files opened through a macro.

Gotcha: Although you can specify for the Recent Documents list to show up to 50 files, the number of files it can actually show is limited by your available screen space. If you have a 1440x900 monitor, as suggested in "Go Wide" on page 4, you will have room for only about 36 files. Excel will not add a second column nor a scrollbar to the Recent Documents to show more files.

Gotcha: If you are snooping around in files that you should not be looking at, the Recent Documents list can be problematic. The operation of the list changed since Excel 2003. It used to be that you could delete file 5 from the list by changing the setting to 4 files and then back to 9 files.

This would clear items 5 through 9 from the list. An "improvement" in Excel 2007 is that if you change the setting from 50 to 5 and then back to 50, Excel will immediately return to showing the last 50 items in the list. If you are trying to hide your trail, you have to set the setting back to 0 files. This is the only way to delete the file list from the cache.

Summary: To have the Office Icon menu show more than the last few workbooks used, you can increase the option to up to 50 workbooks.

Commands Discussed: Office Icon – Excel Options – Advanced – Display – Show This Number of Recent Documents

Excel 97-2003: Tools – Options– General – Recently Used File List (although the setting is limited to 9 files instead of 50).

KEEP FAVORITES IN
THE RECENT DOCUMENTS LIST

Problem: I routinely open more than 50 workbooks, but there are a few favorite files that I have to open all the time. Does Excel have a Favorites list, like Internet Explorer?

Strategy: Excel does not have a Favorites list, but you can ensure that certain files remain in the Recent Documents list. To do so, you need to open a file you want to appear in the Recent Documents list on the Office Icon menu. At the right side of the Office Icon menu, a gray pushpin will appear. When you click this pushpin, it changes to green, and the perspective changes so that it appears that the pushpin is pushed into the page (see Figure 60).

Figure 60

Pin a file to the list.

1	Regression.xlsm
2	F9Test.xlsm
3	DateDisplay.xlsm
4	CalcPctTotal.xlsm
5	CalcRunning.xlsm
6	Exponent.xlsm

Results: The selected files will remain on the Recent Documents list, although they may move to new locations as you open new files.

Additional Details: To unpin an item, you click the green pushpin. It will change back to a gray pushpin. Even though this file may not be in the recent 50 files, it will continue to remain on the list until it eventually falls off the end of the list.

Summary: You can specify to keep certain files on the Recent Documents list.

I'VE SEARCHED EVERYWHERE. WHERE IS THE SAVE WORKSPACE COMMAND?

Problem: Where is the Save Workspace command? It used to be on the File menu, but it isn't in the Office Icon menu now. Where did Microsoft move this command? I'm tired of clicking on all 47 ribbon tabs, trying to find commands.

Strategy: Here is a great trick for finding the location of any command:

1) Right-click the Quick Access toolbar and choose Customize Quick Access Toolbar.

2) In the Choose Commands From dropdown, choose All Commands (the third item in the list). After a few moments, Excel will provide an alphabetical list of all Excel commands.

3) Scroll through the alphabetical list to find your command.

4) When you locate the command, hover over it. Excel will show you a ToolTip with the path to the command, with the menu options separated by pipe characters (|). In Figure 61, the ToolTip indicates that you should look for Save Workspace in the Window group of the View tab.

Figure 61

Excel guides you to the correct tab.

Unlike the convention I use in this book, the ToolTip shows the group name after the ribbon tab. Although you don't actually click on Window, you can use the Window name to narrow down where on the ribbon tab to begin looking. In Figure 62, the mouse pointer is noting the Window name. The Save Workspace command is located above Window and to the right.

Figure 62

Oh! So that's where they moved it.

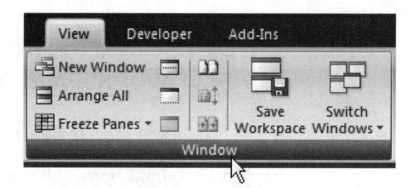

Gotcha: If you hover over a command in the Choose Commands From dropdown and it says Commands Not in the Ribbon (see Figure 63), Microsoft considered this command too obscure to add to the ribbon. However, you can add it to the Quick Access toolbar if you need to use it. (See "Make Your Most-Used Icons Always Visible" on page 13.)

Figure 63

Microsoft should make a ribbon tab of all the commands not in the ribbon.

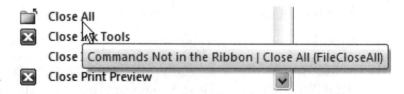

Summary: If you can't find a particular command, you can hover over the command in the Customize tab of the Excel Options dialog to find the current location on the ribbon.

Commands Discussed: Office Icon – Excel Options – Customize

USE A WORKSPACE TO REMEMBER WHAT WORKBOOKS TO OPEN

Problem: I need to open the same four files in order to prepare a weekly report. It is tedious to open all these workbooks.

Strategy: You can open the workbook files and save them as a workspace. Follow these steps:

1) Open the workbooks.

2) (Optional) If you want the workbooks to always appear in a particular arrangement, select View – Arrange to arrange the workbooks in a certain tiled pattern, such as the one shown in Figure 64.

Figure 64

The workspace remembers the files and their arrangement.

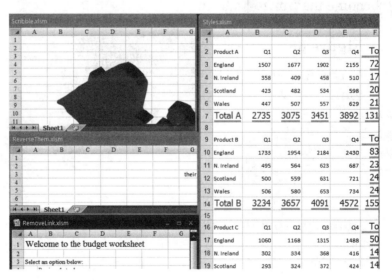

3) Select View – Save Workspace. Give the workspace file a name, such as MyFiles. As shown in Figure 65, note that the file saved will have an .xlw extension instead of .xlsm. The MyFiles.xlw workspace will appear as a recent document in the Office Icon menu.

Figure 65

Excel uses an .xlw extension.

4) Close Excel and open MyFiles.xlw. All four workbooks will open at once and be arranged as you set them up in step 2.

Gotcha: This workspace does not actually store the files but only points to them. If you were to move one of the files to a new folder by using Windows Explorer, Excel would not be able to open that file. Similarly, if you rename one of the files by Windows Explorer, Excel will not be able to locate the file.

Gotcha: I am not a big fan of arranging documents in a tiled pattern. I keep all my files maximized and use Ctrl+Tab to switch among them. I still use workspaces to have Excel quickly open several files. However, because all my files were maximized, Excel will arrange them in a cascaded pattern. You simply click the Maximize button in the upper-right corner of the active workbook (see Figure 66), and all the workbooks will become maximized again.

Figure 66

Maximize button.

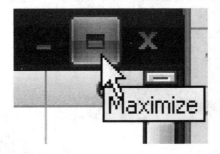

Summary: To reduce the time it takes to open the same set of workbooks over and over, you can use View – Save Workspace after opening the workbooks and then name the workspace.

Commands Discussed: View – Save Workspace

Excel 97-2003: File – Save Workspace

CLOSE ALL OPEN WORKBOOKS

Problem: I have 22 Excel Workbooks open. I want to keep Excel open but close all the workbooks. Excel 2007 does not have a Close All icon on the ribbon, and selecting Office Icon – Close 22 times can get monotonous.

Strategy: You can add a Close All button to your Quick Access toolbar. Follow these steps:

1) Right-click the Quick Access toolbar and choose Customize Quick Access Toolbar.

2) In the left dropdown, choose Commands Not in the Ribbon.

3) Find the Close All item in the left list. Select Close All. Click the Add button to add the icon to the Quick Access toolbar. Click OK to close the Excel Options dialog.

Results: The Close All icon will be available on the Quick Access toolbar. When you click this icon, Excel will still individually ask you about any unsaved documents. However, it is a faster way of closing all open workbooks than manually closing each one.

Gotcha: The Close and Close All icons look the same in the Quick Access toolbar (see Figure 67). While I used to suggest adding a Close icon to the toolbar, it is true that the X in the upper-right corner of Excel does essentially the same thing as the Close icon. In previous versions of Excel, you could tell Excel to display an icon along with the caption to solve this problem. But Microsoft removed that ability in Excel 2007.

Figure 67

Close and
Close All look
similar.

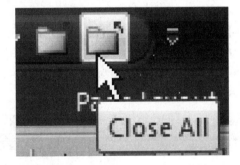

Summary: Close All is not available on the ribbon, but you can add a Close All icon to your Quick Access toolbar to save time.

Commands Discussed: Office Icon – Excel Options -- Customize

Excel 97-2003: In Excel 97-2003, you can hold down the Shift key and then open the File menu; the place where the Close command normally is located is replaced by Close All.

AUTOMATICALLY MOVE THE CELL POINTER IN A DIRECTION AFTER ENTERING A NUMBER

Problem: If I type a number and then press a direction arrow key, Excel will enter the number and move the cell pointer in the direction of the arrow key. However, if I am using the numeric keypad, it is much more convenient to use the Enter key on the numeric keypad than to use the arrow keys. By default, Excel will move the cell pointer down one cell when I press Enter. When entering data in a worksheet such as the one shown in Figure 68, is there a way to have Excel automatically move the cell pointer to the next cell to the right after each entry?

Figure 68

Move right instead of down.

	A	B	C	D	E	F	G	H
1	Region	Jan	Feb	Mar	Apr	May	Jun	Jul
2	City of London	432	754	136	302	91	194	89
3	Barking and Dagenham	95	238	183	713	601	772	559
4	Barnet	590	643	564	87	325	295	413
5	Bexley	454	657	455	354	542		
6	Brent							
7	Bromley							

Strategy: You can select Office Icon – Excel Options. On the Advanced tab of the Excel Options dialog, you select the first setting, "After Pressing Enter, Move Selection Direction," and choose Right from its drop-down, as shown in Figure 69.

Figure 69

Excel offers this option.

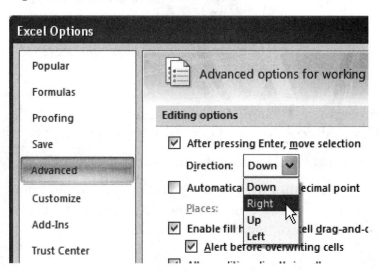

Results: The cursor will automatically move one cell to the right every time you press the Enter key.

Summary: You can have the cell pointer move in any direction after you press Enter by changing a setting on the Advanced tab of the Excel Options dialog.

Commands Discussed: Office Icon – Excel Options – Advanced

Excel 97-2003: Tools – Options – Edit

Part
I

RETURN TO THE FIRST COLUMN
AFTER TYPING THE LAST COLUMN

Problem: I learned in "Automatically Move the Cell Pointer in a Direction After Entering a Number" how to set up the cell pointer to move right after I press Enter. This works great. I just typed figures for Q1, Q2, Q3, and Q4 (see Figure 70). So I can quickly enter all four quarters, is there any way to make Excel jump to cell B3 after I type in cell E2?

Figure 70

Can Excel jump to the first column in the next row?

	A	B	C	D	E	F
1	Region	Q1	Q2	Q3	Q4	
2	City of London	1322	587	896	1121	
3	Barking and Dagenham					
4	Barnet					
5	Bexley					
6	Brent					

Strategy: Yes! Here's what you do:

1) Select Office Icon – Excel Options.

2) On the Advanced tab of the Excel Options dialog, select the first setting, After Pressing Enter, Move Selection Direction, and choose Right from its dropdown. Click OK.

3) Select the range before you start typing the data. For example, in Figure 70, you might select B3:E99. Although you have selected a rectangular range, B3 is the active cell.

4) Type 123 and press Enter. Excel will move to B4.

5)   Repeat this to fill in the numbers for Q2, Q3, and Q4. When you press Enter in cell E3, Excel will move to B4 (see Figure 71).

Figure 71

Excel will jump to B4 after you press Enter in E3.

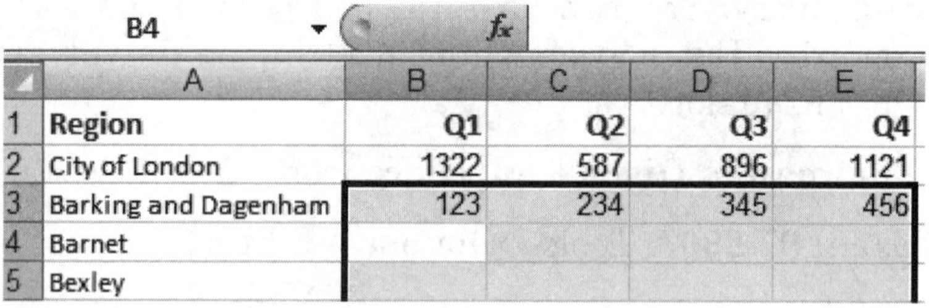

	A	B	C	D	E
1	Region	Q1	Q2	Q3	Q4
2	City of London	1322	587	896	1121
3	Barking and Dagenham	123	234	345	456
4	Barnet				
5	Bexley				

Alternate Strategy: There is another way to handle this situation, although it's not as straightforward as the method just described. Whereas the method just described requires you to use Right as the Move Selection Direction, this strategy requires that setting to be set to Down:

1)   Select Office Icon – Excel Options.

2)   On the Advanced tab of the Excel Options dialog, select the first setting, After Pressing Enter, Move Selection Direction, and choose Down from its dropdown. Click OK.

3)   Select cell B5. Type a value and press Tab. Excel will jump to C5.

4)   Type a value for Q2 and press Tab. Excel will jump to D5.

5)   Type a value for Q3 and press Tab. Excel will jump to E5.

6)   Type a value for Q4 and press Enter. Excel will jump back to cell B6!

I have no idea how Excel knows how to do this. Apparently, Microsoft programmed in a bit of logic to remember the first column you tabbed out of. When you switch from Tab to Enter, Excel will jump down one row and back to that column. Amazing.

Summary: Select the data range before typing data. Excel will automatically jump to the next row after you type the last column.

Commands Discussed: Office Icon – Excel Options – Advanced

Excel 97-2003: Tools – Options – Edit

ENTER DATA IN A CIRCLE
(OR ANY OTHER PATTERN)

Problem: I need to fill out a form in which the data fields jump all over the place. I start in cell H1, then jump to H5, then E4, then B2, and so on. Figure 72 shows the sequence of fields I have to fill out.

Figure 72

You need to enter data in a bizarre sequence.

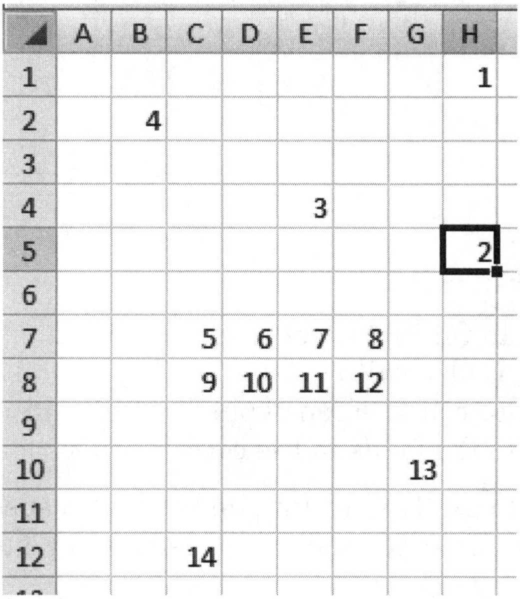

◢	A	B	C	D	E	F	G	H
1								1
2		4						
3								
4					3			
5								2
6								
7			5	6	7	8		
8			9	10	11	12		
9								
10							13	
11								
12		14						

Strategy: You can use the method described in "Return to the First Column After Typing the Last Column" to solve this problem. The solution relies on the fact that Excel can remember the sequence in which you select cells. Follow these steps:

1) For now, ignore cell 1. Click in cell 2.

2) Hold down the Ctrl key and click cell 3.

3) Keep holding down the Ctrl key while you select cell 4, 5, 6, and so on, in order. (Yes, it absolutely matters that you select the cells in the correct order.)

4) After you select the last cell, keep holding down the Ctrl key and select cell 1.

5) Click the mouse in the Name box (the area to the left of the formula bar that shows an address like H1) and type MyData (see Figure 73). Press Enter. Nothing will happen. The Name box will return to saying H1.

Figure 73

Name the se-
lected range.

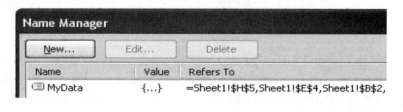

6) Save the file.

When you need to fill in the cells, select the Name box dropdown and choose MyData. Cell 1 will be selected. Type a value and press Enter. Excel will jump to cell 2. Keep typing values and pressing Enter, and Excel will jump to the fields in the correct order.

Additional Details: This technique works because Excel defines the named range as a specific sequence of cells (see Figure 74).

Figure 74

Excel defines
the name as
a sequence of
cells.

Name Manager		
New...	Edit...	Delete
Name	Value	Refers To
MyData	{...}	=Sheet1!$H$5,Sheet1!$E$4,Sheet1!$B$2,

Summary: By selecting cells in sequence and naming the range, you can enter data in any pattern.

Commands Discussed: Name box

Excel 97-2003: Name box

HOW TO SEE HEADINGS
AS YOU SCROLL AROUND A REPORT

Problem: I have a spreadsheet that has headings at the top, (Figure 75). I want to scroll through the data and always see the headings.

Figure 75

In this spreadsheet, you need to see the headings in row 3 when you scroll to row 876.

▲	A	B	C	D	E
1	**Sales Report - 2008**				
2					
3	**Rep**	**Customer**	**Product**	**Sales**	**Revenue**
4	Joe	RST Company	GHI	624	55536
5	Mary	EFG Pty Ltd	GHI	605	53845
6	Dan	TUV Company	DEF	733	65237
7	Dan	CDE GMbH	XYZ	634	56426
8	Bob	BCD Corporation	ABC	795	70755
9	Dan	CDE Pty Ltd	ABC	447	39783
10	Mary	NOP LLC	ABC	627	55803

Part
I

Strategy: You can use the Freeze Panes command on the View tab. In order to make the Freeze Panes command work, you must place the cell pointer in the correct location before using the command.

In the spreadsheet shown in Figure 75 it would be really handy to have rows 1 through 3 always visible while you scroll. Here's how you make that happen:

1) Place the cell pointer in cell A4, as shown in Figure 76. You're going to use the Freeze Panes command, which will freeze all visible rows above the cell pointer and all visible columns to the left of the cell pointer. If you place the cell pointer on the heading for column A, you will not freeze any columns, only the rows.

Figure 76

Everything visible above and to the left of the active cell will be frozen.

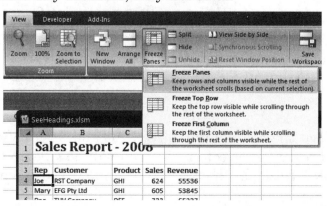

2) With the cell pointer in cell A4, select View – Freeze Panes – Freeze Panes. A solid horizontal line will be drawn between rows 3 and 4. As you scroll down past row 30, you will always be able to see the heading rows, as shown in Figure 77.

Figure 77

As you scroll, the headings remain visible.

	A	B	C	D	E
1	**Sales Report - 2008**				
2					
3	**Rep**	**Customer**	**Product**	**Sales**	**Revenue**
19	Dan	KLM Company	XYZ	661	58829
20	Mary	GHI Company	GHI	654	58206
21	Joe	NOP, LLC	GHI	593	52777
22	Dan	ABC GMbH	GHI	553	49217

Additional Details: To turn off this feature, go to the View tab and select Freeze Panes – Unfreeze Panes. The Unfreeze Panes menu item is visible only after you have frozen the panes.

You can maximize the number of rows visible by freezing a single row. For example, here's how you freeze only row 3:

1) If necessary, unfreeze the panes by selecting View – Freeze Panes – Unfreeze Panes.

2) Place the cell pointer in the last visible row in the window. Press the Down Arrow key twice to force rows 1 and 2 to scroll above the window. Row 3 is now the first visible row, as shown in Figure 78.

Figure 78

Unfreeze and scroll A1 and A2 out of view.

	A	B	C
3	**Rep**	**Customer**	**Product**
4	Joe	RST Company	GHI
5	Mary	EFG Pty Ltd	GHI
6	Dan	TUV Company	DEF

3) Place the cell pointer in cell A4 and select View – Freeze Panes – Freeze Panes command. You will now be able to scroll with only row 3 frozen at the top of the window, as shown in Figure 79.

Figure 79

Only row 3 is frozen.

3	Rep	Customer	Product	Sales	Revenue
34	Bob	JKL, Inc.	XYZ	691	61499
35	Dan	WXY, Inc.	XYZ	681	60609
36	Dan	BCD Corporation	ABC	575	51175
37	Bob	LMN GMbH	ABC	647	57583

Summary: You can use the View – Freeze Panes – Freeze Panes command to keep certain rows visible at the top of the window as you scroll through the data.

Commands Discussed: : View – Freeze Panes – Freeze Panes; View – Freeze Panes – Unfreeze Panes

Excel 97-2003: Window – Freeze Panes

See Also: "How to See Both Headings and Row Labels as You Scroll Around a Report," "How to Print Titles at the Top of Each Page"

HOW TO SEE HEADINGS AND ROW LABELS AS YOU SCROLL AROUND A REPORT

Problem: I have a wide spreadsheet. As shown in Figure 80, there are headings at the top of the spreadsheet, and there are several columns of labels at the left side of the spreadsheet. I also have monthly sales figures that extend far to the right. I need to be able to scroll through the sales figures while always seeing both the headings at the top and the labels at the left of the spreadsheet.

Figure 80

You want to see columns A:F as you scroll right.

	A	B	C	D	E	F	G	H	I	J
1	OurCo LLC									
2	Sales Report by Month, Customer and Region									
3	12 Months Ending 12/31/2008									
4										
5	Country	Region	District	Sales Rep	Customer	Product	Jan	Feb	Mar	Q1
6	USA	West	No. California	Joe	RST Company	GHI	37	44	26	107
7	Australia	Australia	Australia	Mary	EFG Pty Ltd	GHI	40	92	72	204
8	USA	Central	Chicago	Dan	TUV Company	DEF	86	55	74	215
9	Germany	Germany	Germany	Dan	CDF GMbH	XYZ	73	20	5	98

Strategy: You can use the Freeze Panes command on the View tab. To make the Freeze Panes command work, you must place the cell pointer in the correct location before using the command.

In the spreadsheet shown in Figure 80, you might want row 5 and columns A through F to be visible at all times. Then, you could scroll through the monthly figures and always be able to see the customer information in the left columns and the month name information in row 5. Here's how you make it happen:

1)   Scroll the worksheet so that cell A5 is in the upper left visible corner. You could try to do this with the scrollbars or the arrows, but this method will always work:

-    Scroll A5 out of view by pressing PgDn a few times and the Tab key a few times.

-    Press the F5 key to bring up the Go To dialog.

-    Enter A5 in the Reference box and press Enter. Cell A5 will now be the first visible cell in the window.

2)   Place the cell pointer in cell G6. Select View – Freeze Panes – Freeze Panes. You will see a solid line between columns F and G and between rows 5 and 6.

Results: As shown in Figure 81, as you scroll through the table data, you can now always see the row and column headings.

Figure 81

When you scroll right or down, you can still see the identifying labels.

	A	B	C	D	E	F	S	T	U
5	Country	Region	District	Sales Rep	Customer	Product	Oct	Nov	Dec
46	Australia	Australia	Australia	Bob	VWX Pty Ltd	ABC	0	10	11
47	USA	East	New England	Bob	ABC Company	DEF	86	49	72
48	USA	West	No. California	Bob	XYZ Company	DEF	54	95	2
49	France	France	France	Dan	XYZ S.A.	GHI	85	56	92
50	Australia	Australia	Australia	Mary	CDE Pty Ltd	GHI	45	32	92
51	Germany	Germany	Germany	Bob	NOP GMbH	GHI	94	96	68

Gotcha: In Figure 81, rows 1 through 4 cannot be viewed. You can use the Go To dialog or the arrow keys to move the cell pointer to those cells. You can then see the value of the selected cell in the formula bar.

Gotcha: If you have many columns frozen at the left of the report and then make those columns wider, it is possible that the entire window will be filled with the frozen columns. In this situation, the arrow keys will move the cell pointer to other cells that you cannot see. The address bar and the formula bar will show you the active cell, but you cannot see it. You need to either make the frozen columns less wide or use the View – Freeze Panes – Unfreeze Panes command to unfreeze the panes.

Summary: You can use the View – Freeze Panes – Freeze Panes command to keep certain rows and columns visible at the top of the window as you scroll through the data. It is critical that you place the cell pointer in the first cell that is not to be frozen before invoking the command.

Part
I

Commands Discussed: View – Freeze Panes – Freeze Panes; Home – Find & Select – Go To Special

Excel 97-2003: Window – Freeze Panes; Edit – Go To

See Also: "How to See Headings as You Scroll Around a Report," "How to Print Titles at the Top of Each Page"

HOW TO PRINT TITLES
AT THE TOP OF EACH PAGE

Problem: I have a report that has 90 rows of data (see Figure 82). I want to have the title rows print at the top of each printed page.

Figure 82

You want to repeat the titles and headings at the top of each printed page.

▲	A	B	C	D	E
1	**XYZ Corporation**				
2	**Sales by Rep & Day**				
3	**January 2008**				
4					
5	Sales Rep	Date	Quota	Sales	Over Quota
6	Joe	1/2/2008	800	666	0
7	Dan	1/2/2008	800	1290	490
8	Mary	1/2/2008	800	896	96
9	Joe	1/3/2008	800	559	0
10	Dan	1/3/2008	800	192	0
11	Mary	1/3/2008	800	703	0
12	Joe	1/4/2008	800	1131	331

Strategy: Printing options are controlled on the fourth tab of the Page Setup dialog box. You can jump to this tab of the dialog by using the Print Titles icon on the Page Layout tab. In this case, you want rows 1 through 5 to print at the top of each page.

1) Select Print Titles. The Sheet tab of the Page Setup dialog will be displayed (see Figure 83).

Figure 83

You control what rows to repeat at the top of the page by using the Sheet tab of the Page Setup dialog.

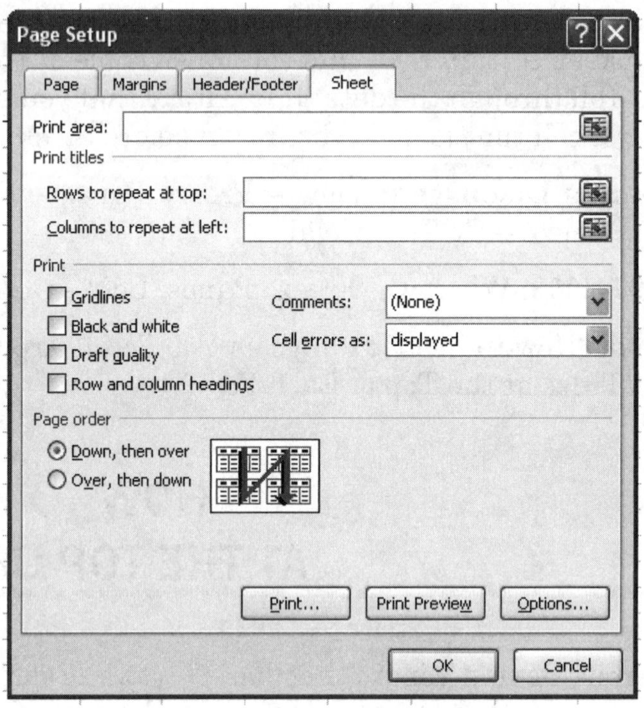

2) In order to have rows 1 through 5 repeated at the top of each page, enter 1:5 in the Rows to Repeat at Top box. Click Print Preview to ensure that the results are what you desire.

Alternate Strategy: Rather than type 1:5 in the text box, you could click the reference icon on the right side of the box.

This will shrink the Page Setup dialog box to just the Page Setup – Rows to Repeat at Top dialog, as shown in Figure 84. You can now use the mouse to select rows 1 through 5. Choose the icon at the right side of this dialog to return to the complete Page Setup dialog box.

Figure 84

Shrink the dialog and point to the rows using the mouse.

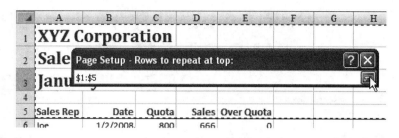

Alternate Strategy: If the rows you want to repeat at the top are visible behind the dialog box, as shown in Figure 85, use the mouse to highlight them while the cell pointer is in the Rows to Repeat at Top text box.

Figure 85

If the dialog box is not in the way, select the rows without shrinking the dialog.

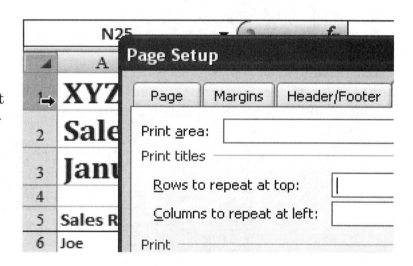

Summary: You can select Page Layout – Print Titles to have titles and headings appear at the top of every page.

Commands Discussed: Page Layout – Print Titles

Excel 97-2003: File – Page Setup – Sheet

See Also: "How to Print Page Numbers at the Bottom of Each Page" on page 66.

PRINT A LETTER AT THE TOP OF PAGE 1 AND REPEAT HEADINGS AT THE TOP OF EACH SUBSEQUENT PAGE

Problem: I am sending out a worksheet that contains a letter followed by a lengthy report (see Figure 86). I would like the headings to appear at the top of each page after the first page. I don't want the headings to appear at the top of the letter on the first page.

Figure 86

You want to make the headings from row 19 appear at the top of page 2 and beyond.

	A	B	C	D	E	F	G	H	I	J	K	L	M	N	O
1	**Welcome to the 2008-2009 Budget Process**														
2															
3	Dear Manager,														
4															
5	This Excel workbook contains all of the worksheets that you need to complete in order														
6	to produce your forecast for our next fiscal year. The data below shows your actual sales														
7	by SKU for your region. You should build a sales forecast for the next year and then														
8	break the data out by month.														
9															
10	Your forecast should be sent to your regional VP for review no later than noon on														
11	March 12. Thank you for your attention to the forecast process.														
12															
13				Sincerely,											
14															
15				Joe Smith											
16				Director of Operations Analysis											
17				(330) 555-1212											
18															
19	SKU	Prior Sales	Planned Sales	Apr	May	Jun	Jul	Aug	Sep	Oct	Nov	Dec	Jan	Feb	Mar
20	S-001	562													
21	S-002	142													
22	S-003	451													
23	S-004	534													

Strategy: You control printing options on the Sheet tab of the Page Setup dialog box. If you specify that a row in the middle of the print range should be repeated at the top of the pages, it will not begin repeating until the next page. Here's how it works:

1) Select Page Layout – Print Titles. Excel will display the Sheet tab of the Page Setup dialog, as shown in Figure 87.

2) Enter 19:19 in the Rows to Repeat at Top text box (Figure 87). Excel will print row 19 at the top of each page after page 1.

Figure 87

Specify a row in the middle of the print range as the row to repeat at the top of each page.

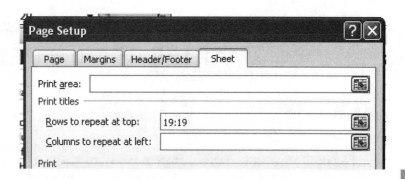

Results: The headings do not print at the top of page 1, but they do print at the top of pages 2 and beyond. Figure 88 shows the first two pages in Page Layout mode at 40% zoom.

Figure 88

The headings from row 19 start repeating on page 2.

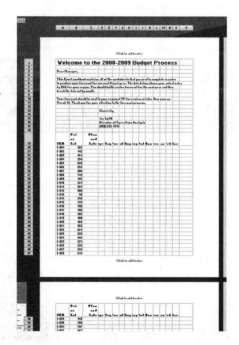

Summary: The number you enter in the Rows to Repeat at Top text box does not have to be at the top of the print range. If your selection is in the middle of the print range, the headings will print only on subsequent pages.

Commands Discussed: Page Layout – Print Titles

Excel 97-2003: File – Page Setup.

HOW TO PRINT PAGE NUMBERS AT THE BOTTOM OF EACH PAGE

Problem: I am printing a lengthy report, and I want the pages to be numbered.

Strategy: There is a convoluted new way to specify headers and footers in Excel 2007. This method is undoubtedly cool, but it requires more steps than the old method:

1) Ensure that your document is in Page Layout mode by clicking the middle of the three icons next to the zoom slider in the lower-right corner of the document window (see Figure 89). Excel will show your worksheet in virtual pages.

Figure 89

Use Page Layout mode.

2) Scroll to the bottom of the first virtual page. Look for the area in the bottom center of the page with the words "Click to add footer." Hover over this area, and a box will appear illustrating the position for the center footer. You can also hover to the left or right of this area to access the left or right footer. Click in a footer area. A new ribbon tab, Header & Footer Tools, will appear (Figure 90).

Figure 90

The new header and footer tools are powerful but difficult to locate.

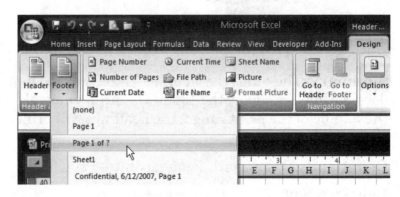

3) From the Footer dropdown, select Page 1 of ?. Excel will add a footer such as Page 1 of 10 at the bottom of each page.

4) Click outside the header or footer area to close the Header & Footer Tools tab.

Alternate Strategy: You can also build headers and footers the same way as you did in Excel 2003: If you display the Page Layout tab of the ribbon, a small icon (called a dialog launcher) appears in the lower-right corner of the Page Setup group (see Figure 17 on page 12). You click this icon to display the Page Setup dialog, and then you click the Header/Footer tab and make the appropriate settings.

Additional Details: You can also customize left, center, and right headers as you do the footers.

Also, new in Excel 2007, you can specify different footers for the first page and different footers for odd vs. even pages. You control these settings in the Options area of the Header & Footer Tools Design tab of the ribbon.

Gotcha: Sometimes the footer text will crash into the data from the report. If you have adjusted the lower margin to 0.5 inch, you should adjust the footer margin to 0.25 inch to prevent this condition.

Summary: You can customize the header and footer to contain a page number, the total number of printed pages, the file name, or any custom text you like. There are left, center, and right headers and footers.

Commands Discussed: Page Layout mode; Header & Footer Tools Design commands

Excel 97-2003: File – Page Setup Header/Footer tab (Page Layout mode was not available before Excel 2007.)

See Also: "How to Print Titles at the Top of Each Page"

Part I

HOW TO MAKE A WIDE REPORT FIT TO ONE PAGE WIDE BY MANY PAGES TALL

Problem: After I create a wide report, it prints four pages wide, as shown in Figure 91. How do I make it print one page wide?

Figure 91

Have you taped together four pages of a report into one wide report?

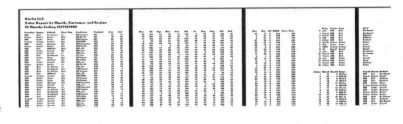

Strategy: Ultimately, you will set the Scale to Fit settings to print to one page wide by any number of pages tall. Before you can do that, you should follow these steps:

1) Eliminate extra columns from the print range. Because this worksheet has some lookup tables beyond column X that you do not want to print, highlight columns A through X and select Page Layout – Print Area – Set Print Area.

2) Set long headings on two lines rather than one. For example, Sales Rep in cell D5 could be on two lines to save width in the column. In cell C5, type Sales, press Alt+Enter, and type Rep. Do the same thing for Prior Year in X5.

3) Make the columns narrower. Select the data in A5:X130 and then select Home – Format – AutoFit Column Width. **Gotcha:** The AutoFit command does not deal well with cells in which Alt+Enter was used, as in step 2. You therefore have to manually adjust the column width of columns D and X.

4) Change the orientation to Landscape by selecting Page Layout – Orientation – Landscape.

5) Adjust the margins by selecting Page Layout – Margins – Custom Margins. On the Margins tab of the Page Setup dialog, set the top,

left, and right margins at 0.25 inch. Adjust the bottom to 0.5 inch and the footer margin to 0.25 inch

6) On the Page Layout tab, open the Width dropdown in the Scale to Fit group. Choose 1 page. (This is much easier than using the Page Setup dialog, as discussed in the following alternate strategy.)

Results: The report will fit on one page wide and three pages tall.

Alternate Strategy: You can use the Page Layout dialog to indicate that the report should fit to one page wide by <blank> pages tall. On the Page Layout tab of the ribbon, click the dialog launcher in the lower-right corner of the Page Setup group. Choose the Page tab of the Page Setup dialog. Choose Fit To. Leave the first spin button at 1 Page(s) Wide. Using your mouse, highlight the 1 in the spin button for Tall. After the 1 is highlighted, press Delete to leave this entry completely blank. Before Excel 2007, you followed this rather convoluted process to create a setting equivalent to step 6 above.

Summary: The secret to having the report constrained to one page wide and any number of pages tall is to leave the Height setting in Scale to Fit as Automatic (in Excel 2007) or blank (in Excel 97-2003).

Commands Discussed: Page Layout – Print Area – Set Print Area; Home – Format – AutoFit Column Width; Page Layout – Margins – Custom Margins; Page Layout – Width – Scale to Fit

Excel 97-2003: File – Print Area – Set Print Area; Format – Column – AutoFit Selection; File – Page Setup (Because Automatic was not available before Excel 2007, you have to use the Page Setup dialog method described in the alternate strategy.)

See Also: "How to Fit a Multiline Heading into One Cell" on p. 414

ARRANGE WINDOWS TO SEE
TWO OR MORE OPEN WORKBOOKS

Problem: I have two workbooks open. One workbook contains a list of airport codes and their respective cities. In the other workbook, I am building a list of recommended packing items for students going on a seven-city tour. Currently, I am shifting back and forth between the workbooks, using Ctrl+Tab every time I forget an airport code. It would be cool if I could see the airport codes from Figure 92 at the same time I'm working on the other workbook

Figure 92

You keep referring to this worksheet.

	A	
1	Code	City
2	ABE	Allentown, PA
3	ABI	Abilene, TX
4	ABK	Kabri Dar, Ethiopia
5	ABL	Ambler, AK
6	ABM	Bamaga, Australia
7	ABQ	Albuquerque, NM

Strategy: You can select View – Arrange All. The Arrange Windows dialog will appear, giving you four Arrange options, as shown in Figure 93. Select Vertical and click OK to see the two worksheets side by side

Figure 93

Arrange all open workbooks in vertical windows.

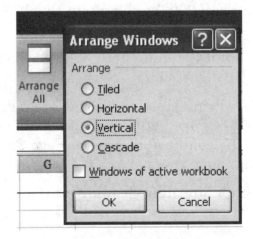

Results: As shown in Figure 94, you will see both windows, side by side. The window with the darker toolbar is the active window. Any data entry will occur in the active cell of that workbook.

Figure 94

Both work-books are vis-ible simultane-ously.

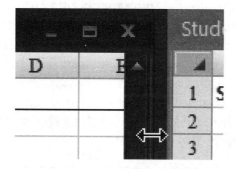

You can resize the window widths by hovering your mouse at the right edge of the left workbook. The cell pointer changes to a two-headed hori-zontal arrow, as shown in Figure 95. Click and drag the edge of the left window until you have the proper width.

Part I

Figure 95

Drag the edge to a new width.

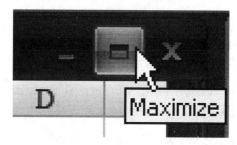

Repeat for the left edge of the right workbook.

To go back to full screen mode, click the Maximize icon (see Figure 96) at the top of one workbook.

Figure 96

Return to full screen mode.

Gotcha: If you have additional workbooks open, they will also appear side by side. The side-by-side display works fine for 2 or 3 workbooks but would not work for 20 open workbooks because each workbook would be too narrow to see

Additional Details: Starting in Excel 2003, a new command makes it possible to scroll two open workbooks simultaneously. As shown in Figure 97, you use the View Side by Side icon on the View tab of the ribbon.

Figure 97

Scroll two workbooks simultaneously.

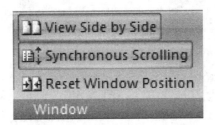

Gotcha: If you are comparing two workbooks that are supposed to be similar, it is likely that someone added some rows to one workbook or the other. When you initially turn on View Side by Side, the workbooks will be synchronized so that when you see row 150 in the first workbook, you will see row 150 in the second workbook. However, if someone inserted 10 rows in the original workbook, you might need row 150 of the original workbook to line up with row 140 of the second workbook. Follow these steps to correct the problem:

1) In the View tab of the ribbon, turn off Synchronous Scrolling by clicking the second icon in Figure 97.

2) Press the Down Arrow key until row 140 is at the top of the left window. In the right window, press the Down Arrow key until row 150 is at the top of that window.

3) Choose the Synchronous Scrolling icon again to force the workbooks to scroll together. Now, when you move down in either workbook, both workbooks will scroll together.

Summary: Arranging windows in a vertical fashion allows you to view two different workbooks at the same time.

Commands Discussed: View – Arrange All; View – View Side by Side; View – Synchronous Scrolling

Excel 97-2003: Window – Arrange; Window – Compare Side by Side (Excel 2003 only)

WHY IS THERE A ":2" AFTER MY WORKBOOK NAME IN THE TITLE BAR?

Problem: Without any apparent reason, a ":2" appeared after the spreadsheet name in the title bar of my spreadsheet (see Figure 98). What is this and what caused it?

Figure 98

Why the :2?

ColonTwo.xlsm:2		
◢	A	B
1	**Account Codes**	
2		
3	1010	QRS

Strategy: This annoying thing got turned on when you accidentally chose View – New Window. This setting applies to the workbook and persists from one usage of Excel to the next, so it is possible that the :2 showed up months ago and has been stuck there ever since. You will notice that you appear to have two copies of the same workbook open in the Switch Windows dropdown menu, as shown in Figure 99.

Figure 99

The workbook is open twice?

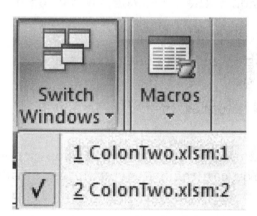

Switch Windows ▾   Macros ▾

1 ColonTwo.xlsm:1

✓ 2 ColonTwo.xlsm:2

To remove the :2, switch to the :2 version of the workbook and click the Close Window (X) icon to close that window, as shown in Figure 100.

Figure 100

Click the Close Window icon.

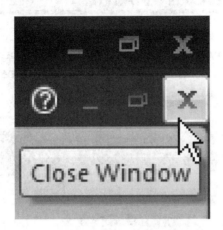

You might worry that this will close the workbook without saving. Instead, it will close the second window of the workbook and both the :2 and :1 will be removed from the title bar. The workbook will remain open.

Additional Details: Is there ever a time that you would want to use this feature? Is it useful to have two versions of the workbook? Yes. Let's say that you want to see both Sheet1 and Sheet2 of the workbook at the same time. Follow these steps:

1)   Select View – New Window.

2)   In the :2 version of the workbook, switch to Sheet2.

3)   Select View – Arrange All.

4)   In the Arrange Windows dialog, choose Windows of Active Workbook and Vertical. Click OK.

You will now be able to view two different sheets of the same workbook, side by side.

Summary: The :2 usually appears when you accidentally choose View – New Window. You can remove it, but in certain instances, it can be useful.

Commands Discussed: View – New Window; View – Arrange All

Excel 97-2003: Window – New Window; Window – Arrange

HAVE EXCEL ALWAYS OPEN CERTAIN WORKBOOK(S)

Problem: I always use Excel to work on a particular workbook. Every time that I open Excel, I want this workbook to open automatically

Strategy: You can place the file you want to always open (or a shortcut to the file) in the XLStart folder, which is generally found in the %AppData%\Microsoft\Excel\ folder. Anything in this folder will automatically start when Excel starts.

Alternate Strategy: You can specify one folder to act as an additional XLStart folder. Follow these steps:

1)   Move the Excel workbook or workbooks to a new folder.

     Excel will try to open every file in this folder, so make sure you do not have other files in it.

2)   Open Excel. Select Office Icon – Options.

3)   Click Advanced in the left pane of the Excel Options dialog.

4)   Scroll down to the General section. Enter the path to the folder from step 1 in the At Startup, Open All Files In text box, as shown in Figure 101.

Figure 101

Any workbooks in this path open every time you open Excel.

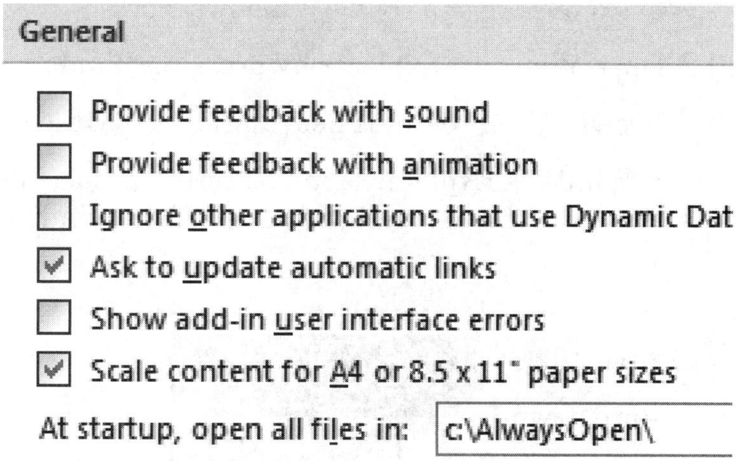

General
☐ Provide feedback with sound
☐ Provide feedback with animation
☐ Ignore other applications that use Dynamic Dat
☑ Ask to update automatic links
☐ Show add-in user interface errors
☑ Scale content for A4 or 8.5 x 11" paper sizes
At startup, open all files in: `c:\AlwaysOpen\`

Alternate Strategy: Another strategy is to use a command-line switch, as discussed in "Set Up Excel Icons to Open a Specific File on Startup."

Summary: Excel will automatically open all files in the XLStart folder or in one additional alternate startup folder that you specify.

Commands Discussed: Office Icon – Options

Excel 97-2003: Tools – Options – General (In Excel 2000 and earlier, the field was labeled "Alternate Startup File Location.")

See Also: "Set Up Excel Icons to Open a Specific File on Startup"

SET UP EXCEL ICONS TO OPEN A SPECIFIC FILE ON STARTUP

Problem: I routinely use the same five files in my job. I want a series of five icons on my Desktop so I can easily open these five files.

Strategy: You can use a startup switch in the shortcut. Excel offers startup switches to open a specific file, to open a file as read-only, to suppress the startup screen, or to specify an alternate default file location. Follow these steps.

1)   Minimize all open windows by pressing Windows+M. (The Windows key is usually located between the left Ctrl and Alt keys. It has a picture of a flying Windows icon.)

2)   Open Windows Explorer by pressing Windows+E.

3)   Browse to %ProgramFiles%\Microsoft Office\Office12.

4)   If Windows Explorer is in full screen mode, click the Restore Down button in the upper-right corner of the window, as shown in Figure 102.

Figure 102

Restore down.

5) Using the mouse, grab the title bar of the Windows Explorer window and move it so you can see part of the Desktop.

6) Find the Excel icon in Windows Explorer. Right-click and drag it to the Desktop.

7) Choose Create Shortcuts Here from the menu that appears when you release the right mouse button (see Figure 103)

Figure 103

Copy the icon to the Desktop.

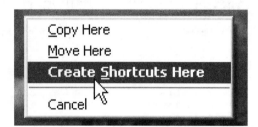

8) Close Windows Explorer.

9) On the Desktop, right-click the new Shortcut to Excel icon and choose Properties.

10) In the Properties dialog, choose the General tab.

11) Change the name in the top text box to something meaningful. If this icon will be used to open the Sales file, for example, a short name like Sales would work.

12) On the Shortcut tab, locate the Target field. As you can see in Figure 104, this field contains the complete path and file name to EXCEL. EXE, with the path and file name enclosed in quotation marks. (The Target field is not big enough to display the entire path, so you must click in the field and press the End key in order to see the end of the entry.)

Figure 104

Press the End key to see the end of the field.

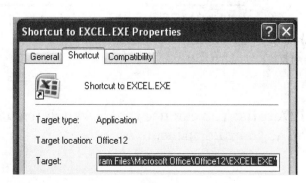

13) After the final quote in the Target field, type a space and the start-up switch. If you use multiple startup switches, enter a space before each one:

To open a file in read-only mode, use the /R switch, followed by the complete path and file name, as shown in Figure 105.

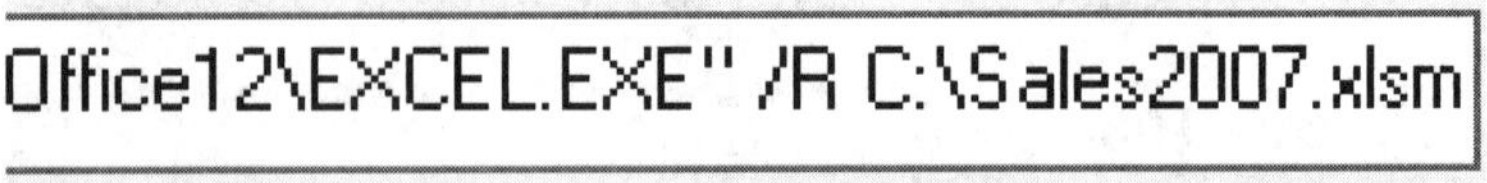

Figure 105

Separate multiple switches with spaces.

```
Office12\EXCEL.EXE" /R C:\Sales2007.xlsm
```

To open a file in normal mode, leave out the /R switch. Just have a space followed by the path and file name, as shown in Figure 106.

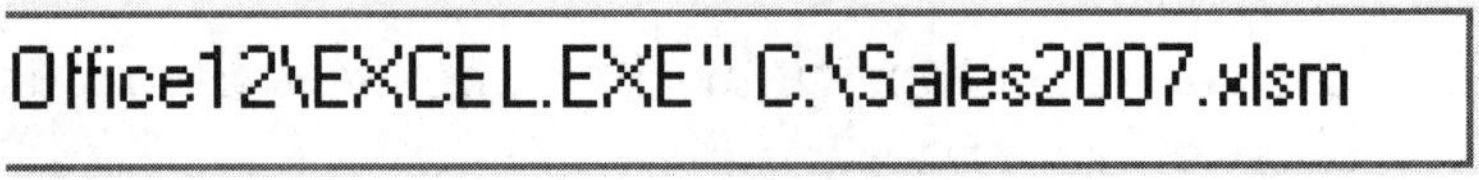

Figure 106

Open a specific file in normal mode.

```
Office12\EXCEL.EXE" C:\Sales2007.xlsm
```

Gotcha: If you start Excel normally, select Office Icon – Open, and browse to the C:\ folder, subsequent Open or Save As dialogs will start in the C:\ folder. Frustratingly, neither of the above switches will change the current path to the folder as the open file. In order to do that, use the /P switch with the same path as your file, as shown in Figure 107.

Figure 107

Change the current path.

```
e12\EXCEL.EXE" C:\Sales2007.xlsm /P C:\
```

Additional Details: You can use the /E switch to suppress the Excel splash screen as your file opens.

Summary: You can customize your shortcut to Excel to open a specific file or to use a specific path as the current folder.

Excel 97-2003: In step 3, browse to the appropriate path:

*   For Excel 2003: %ProgramFiles%\Microsoft Office\Office11

*   For Excel 2002: %ProgramFiles%\Microsoft Office\Office10

*   For Excel 2000: %ProgramFiles%\Microsoft Office\Office

USE A MACRO TO FURTHER CUSTOMIZE STARTUP

Part I

Problem: Every time I open a workbook, I would like to put the file in Data Form mode, as shown in Figure 108, or invoke another Excel menu as the file opens.

Figure 108

The data form is increasingly difficult to find in Excel 2007.

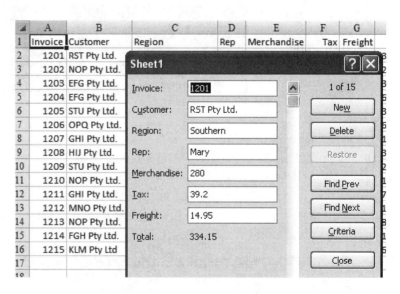

Strategy: Startup switches can only do so many things. You will have to use a Workbook_Open macro in order to force Excel into Data Form mode. Follow these steps:

1)   Select Office Icon – Excel Options.

2) Choose Popular from the left pane of the Excel Options dialog. Select the third item, Show Developer Tab in the Ribbon.

3) Choose Trust Center from the left pane of the Excel Options dialog. Click the Trust Center Settings button.

4) Choose Macro Settings in the left pane of the Trust Center. Choose Disable All Macros with Notification.

5) Click OK twice to return to Excel.

6) Open your workbook.

7) Press Alt+F11 to open the VBA Editor. (**Gotcha:** The Microsoft Natural Multimedia keyboard does not support the use of Alt+function keys. You might have to use Developer – Visual Basic, instead.)

8) Press Ctrl+R to show the Project Explorer in the upper-left corner. You should see something that looks like VBAProject (Your Book-Name) in the Project Explorer, as shown in Figure 109.

Figure 109

Expand the project.

9) If there is a + to the left of this entry, press the + to expand it. You will see a folder underneath, called Microsoft Excel Objects. If there is a + to the left of this entry, press the + to expand it, also. You will now see one entry for each worksheet, plus an entry called ThisWorkbook.

10) Right-click ThisWorkbook and choose View Code from the context menu.

11) Copy these three lines of code to the large white code window:

```
Private Sub Workbook_Open()
    ActiveSheet.ShowDataForm
End Sub
```

12) Press Alt+Q to return to Excel.

13) Select Office Icon – Save As – Excel Macro-Enabled Workbook.

14) Close the file.

15) Open the file. The information bar tells you that macros have been disabled.

16) Select Options – Enable This Content. The data form will open.

Alternate Strategy: To prevent Excel from automatically disabling macros, you can save the file in a trusted location. Follow these steps:

1) In Windows Explorer, create a new folder such as C:\MyTrusted-Files\.

2) In Excel, select Office Icon – Excel Options.

3) In the left pane of the Excel Options dialog, choose Trust Center and click the Trust Center Settings button.

4) In the left pane of the Trust Center, choose Trusted Locations. Click the Add New Location button.

5) Click the Browse button. Navigate to C:\MyTrustedFiles\ and click OK. Click OK to close the Microsoft Office Trusted Location dialog.

6) Save your workbook in the C:\MyTrustedFiles\ folder. When you open the workbook, the Workbook_Open macro will run automatically.

Gotcha: The data form used to be an option on the Excel 2003 Data menu. It is not an option on the Excel 2007 ribbon. To invoke this command in the Excel 2007 user interface, you can either press Alt+D+O or add the command to your Quick Access toolbar.

Additional Details: The simple Workbook_Open macro invokes a Menu command. It is possible to build highly complex macros that would control literally anything. For a primer on macros, consult *VBA and Macros for Microsoft Excel 2007* from Que Publishing.

Summary: You can customize your shortcut to Excel to open a specific file or to use a specific path as the current folder.

Excel 97-2003: Choose Tools – Macro – Security – Medium and then continue with steps 6–12. Save the file.

Part
I

CONTROL SETTINGS FOR EVERY NEW WORKBOOK AND WORKSHEET

Problem: Every time I start a new workbook or insert a new worksheet, I always make the same customizations, such as setting print scaling to fit to one page wide, setting certain margins, adding a "Page 1 of n" footer to the worksheet (see Figure 110), making the heading row bold, and so forth. How can I have these settings applied to every new workbook or worksheet?

Figure 110

If you always use the same heading, add it to the default workbook template.

Strategy: Two files control the defaults for new workbooks and inserted worksheets. You can easily customize a blank workbook to contain your favorite settings and then save the file as book.xlt and sheet.xlt. Then, any time you either click the New Workbook icon or select the Insert – Worksheet command, the new book or sheet will inherit the settings from these files. Follow these steps to create book.xlt:

1) In Excel, open a new blank workbook by choosing Office Icon – New.

2) Customize the workbook as you like. Feel free to make adjustments to any of the following:
   - Page layout settings
   - The print area
   - Cell styles
   - Formatting commands on the Home tab
   - Data – Validation settings
   - The number and type of sheets in the workbook
   - The window view options from the View tab

3) Decide where you want to save the file. This can be either in the XLStart folder (generally C:\Program Files\Microsoft Office\Offi-ce*nn*\XLStart) or in the alternate startup folder. (See "Have Excel Always Open Certain Workbooks" on page 75.)

4) Select Office Icon – Save As – Other Formats.

5) In the Save As dialog, open the Save as Type dropdown and choose Excel Template (*.xltx), as shown in Figure 111.

Part I

Figure 111

Change the
Save as Type
to a template.

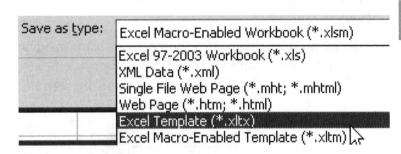

6) Browse to the XLStart folder you specified in step 3.

7) Save the file as book.xltx.

Results: All subsequent new workbooks will inherit the settings from the book.xltx file.

Additional Details: You should also set up a workbook with one worksheet and save this workbook as sheet.xlt. All inserted worksheets will inherit the settings from this file.

Summary: Rather than constantly setting the same settings for all new workbooks, you can save your favorite settings in either book.xlt or sheet.xlt in the XLStart folder. All new workbooks will inherit these settings.

Excel 97-2003: Specify the alternate startup folder in Tools – Options – General, save the file as an Excel Template (*.xlt), and use book.xlt and sheet.xlt as the file names.

OPEN A COPY OF A WORKBOOK

Problem: I have a workbook called invoice.xls. I want to keep the original file unchanged and save each new version as a new workbook. However, I tend to forget to use Save As, so I often overwrite this workbook.

Strategy: When using the Open command, you can specify that you want to open the file as a copy. Here's how you take advantage of this option:

1) Instead of clicking the Open button to open a file, click the dropdown arrow next to the Open button. Choose Open as Copy, as shown in Figure 112. The file that opens will be named Copy (1) of invoice. xlsm.

Figure 112

Open as copy to prevent accidentally saving over the original.

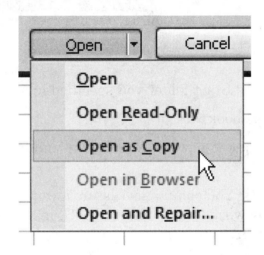

2) Select Office Icon – Save As to save the file with a new name. Note that even if you forget to use Save As, at least you will not overwrite the original invoice.xls.

Summary: To open a copy of a workbook, instead of choosing the Open button, you can use the dropdown arrow next to the Open button and choose Open as Copy.

Commands Discussed: Office Icon – Open as Copy; Office Icon – Save As

Excel 97-2003: File – Open

OPEN A SAVED FILE WHOSE NAME
YOU CANNOT RECALL

Problem: I created and saved a file last Wednesday. It is no longer in my recently used file list on the Office Icon menu, and I can't remember its name. How do I find and open it?

Strategy: You can use the Details icon to find the files you saved last Wednesday. Follow these steps:

Part
I

1) Select Office Icon – Open. From the open dropdown, choose the Details icon, as shown in Figure 113.

Figure 113

Choosing Details provides a list that can be sorted by date.

2) You can now see file names as well as dates and times of the last save. Sort by date by clicking the Date Modified header, as shown in Figure 114. The first click will sort in either ascending or descending order.

Figure 114

Click a heading to toggle from ascending to descending and back.

Type	Date Modified ▼
Microsoft Of…	6/14/2007 8:49 AM
Microsoft Of…	6/13/2007 7:09 AM
Microsoft Of…	6/13/2007 7:09 AM
Microsoft Of…	6/13/2007 6:32 AM

3) Use the scrollbar to go to the top of the list. If the top contains old files, click the Date Modified header again to sort in descending order. You can now scroll back to last Wednesday to find the file.

Summary: You can use the Details mode of the open dropdown to sort files by date, time, or name.

Commands Discussed: Office Icon – Open

Excel 97-2003: File – Open

EXCEL 2007'S OBSESSION WITH SECURITY HAS DESTROYED LINKED WORKBOOKS

Problem: It used to be easy to set up a link between one workbook and another workbook. The only problem occurred when I sent Book2.xls and the recipient did not have access to Book1.xls. People would have to deal with the rather innocuous message shown in Figure 115.

Figure 115

The update links message from the last decade.

Instead of giving you an Update Links message, Excel 2007 gives you a security warning, along with the offer "Help Protect Me From Unknown Content" (see Figure 116). Help protect me? Are they serious? Ooooh... this workbook is going to pull last year's budget total from a closed workbook. I don't think I can look.

Figure 116

I'm terrified that the linked number might be...a five.

Strategy: I spent a good hour trying to figure out how to have Excel 2007 simply ask the question, "Do you want to update the links or not?" There is no way to get this question. I talked to the folks on the Excel team and, indeed, if you tell Excel to ask the question, the question is going to come in the form shown in Figure 116.

Yes, if you tell Excel to ask, it "asks" by telling you that the links are disabled. You have to convince Joe, the VP of Marketing, to actually click the Options button and then click Enable. Joe can easily *ignore* the question and just start working with out-of-date data. Frankly, this is more dangerous than whatever Excel was trying to protect you from.

It is easy for me, because I don't have a VP of Marketing that I have to deal with. I feel bad for you, though, because there are a lot of Excel rookies in those higher ranks, and they really want an excuse to not have to fill out their budgets. This new link system just fans the flames.

Here are your options (aside from staying with Excel 2003). If you choose Office Icon – Excel Options – Trust Center – Trust Center Settings – External Content, you have the three choices shown in Figure 117. Apparently the person who wrote this screen didn't get the memo that the middle option should have been "Completely freak out Joe in Marketing by telling him that there is a security risk in his workbook and offer to help protect him by not giving him the current numbers from the server."

Figure 117

The prompt
appears as a
Security Alert.

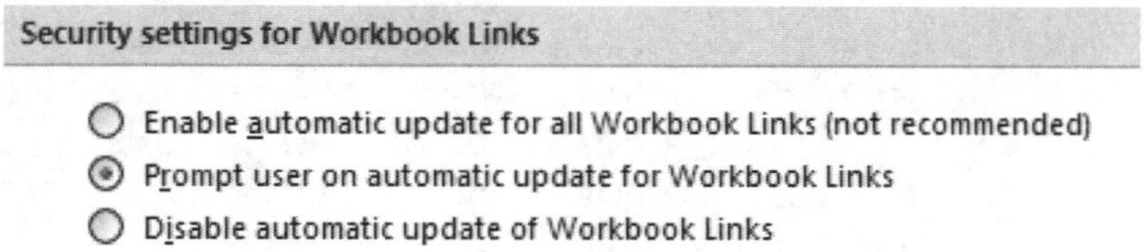

Security settings for Workbook Links

○ Enable automatic update for all Workbook Links (not recommended)
◉ Prompt user on automatic update for Workbook Links
○ Disable automatic update of Workbook Links

If you choose option 1, Excel will update the links without asking. If you choose option 2, you get the security warning that the recipient can ignore. If you choose option 3, the links won't update.

Before you send the workbook to Joe, you might as well visit the Trust Center and make the decision for Joe. If Joe has network access to the linked files, choose the unrecommended option 1. If Joe doesn't have access, choose option 3.

Summary: The security warning message in Excel 2007 is completely misrepresentative. Unlike in Excel 2003, where the person had to choose Link or Don't Link, Joe in Marketing is free to start working with unlinked data and claim he never saw the question.

Commands Discussed: Office Icon – Excel Options – Trust Center

I NAVIGATE BY SLIDING THE SCROLLBAR AND NOW THE SLIDER HAS BECOME TINY

Problem: I have a worksheet with two or three screens of data (see Figure 118). I can easily grab the vertical scrollbar and move to the top of the data set. Something happened, and now the huge scrollbar slider has become really tiny. Further, if I move it just one pixel, instead of jumping to the next screen of data, Excel will move to row 4500.

Figure 118

The slider will take you to the last row with data.

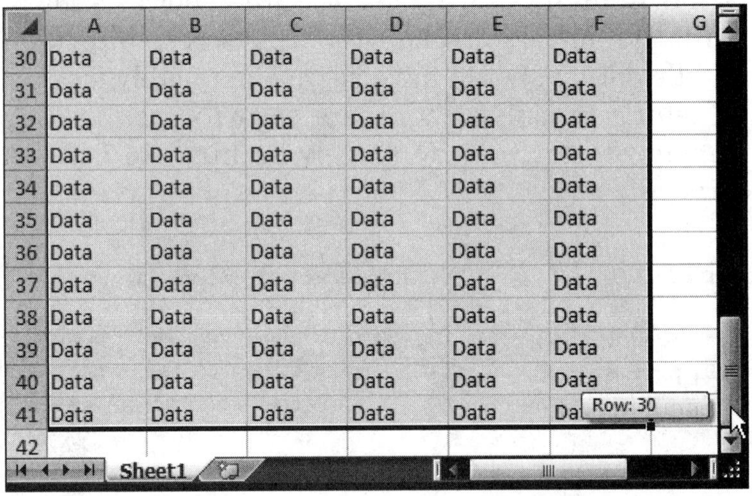

Strategy: Someone pressed End+Down Arrow key to move to row 1048576. This causes the scrollbar slider to become tiny, as shown in Figure 119.

Figure 119

Because you (accidentally?) went to the last row, the slider is tiny.

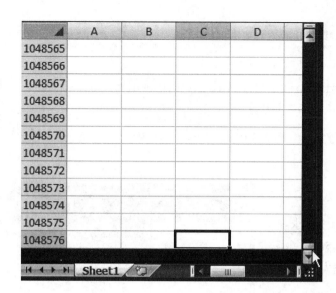

You can often restore the size of the slider by moving it completely to the top of the spreadsheet. If this does not work, then there is one rogue cell way below your data that has become activated. Perhaps someone pressed the Spacebar or applied text formatting or something. Follow these steps:

1) Note the last row that you believe to contain data.

2) Press the End key and then press the Home key. Excel will jump to the intersection of the last active row and the last active column. This row is usually way beyond the row that you believe to be the last row.

3) Delete all rows from the bottom of your data set to the rogue last row.

4) Save the workbook. The scrollbar slider will return to full size.

Saving the workbook is the key. Even after you delete the extra rows, Excel will not restore the size of the workbook. In past editions of Excel, copying the worksheet was enough, but in Excel 2007, the scrollbar will not resize until you save the workbook.

Summary: A stray bit of formatting or a spacebar can sometimes activate a cell that is far below your data. This will cause the scrollbar slider to become so small that it is no longer useful.

SEND AN EXCEL FILE AS AN ATTACHMENT

Problem: I need to send my currently open Excel workbook as an attachment to an Outlook e-mail message.

Strategy: You can select Office Icon – Send – E-Mail, as shown in Figure 120.

Figure 120

Send a workbook as an attachment.

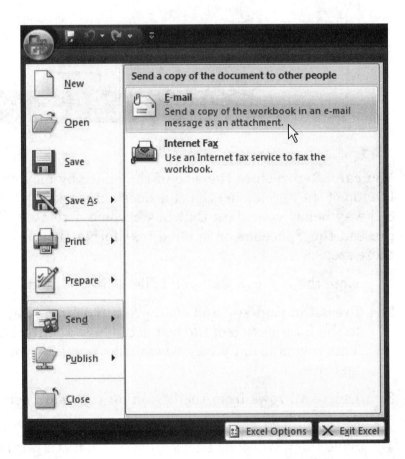

Excel will open something that looks a lot like the Outlook Send Mail dialog, as shown in Figure 121. Fill out the addressee list and the subject line and click Send.

Figure 121

Even though this looks like Outlook, it is not.

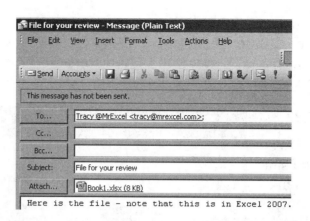

Gotcha: Although this looks like Outlook, it is actually an Excel version of the dialog. While this dialog is displayed, you cannot access other Outlook e-mails. This can be a problem. What if you receive a file from someone not in your address book, edit the file, and then need to send it back? You will find that you need to access the original e-mail to get the sender's e-mail address, but you cannot switch to another e-mail message until you've sent this one.

The solution is to click the Save icon in the Standard toolbar of the e-mail dialog. Then click the Close Window (X) icon in the upper-right corner of the window. The unfinished e-mail will be saved from Excel to the Outlook inbox, and you will be returned to Excel. You can now safely switch back to the original Outlook e-mail to get the address.

Additional Details: In previous versions of Excel, you had the option to send the current worksheet in the body of an e-mail. This option enabled you to send a worksheet to a recipient who did not have Excel. That original command is still in Excel, you can customize the Quick Access toolbar and find the icon in the Commands Not in the Ribbon section, as shown in Figure 122.

Figure 122

This option was not popular, but it can be useful.

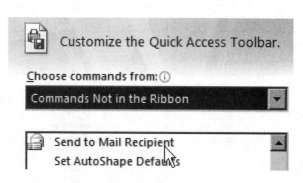

An even better option would be to download the Save as PDF/XPS add-in from Office Online. This utility will let you send a workbook as a PDF or an XPS document. After you install the add-in, new options will be added to the menu shown in Figure 123.

Figure 123

Send the Excel workbook as a PDF file. This allows people without Excel to see the document. By the way, XPS is Microsoft's new format that competes with PDF.

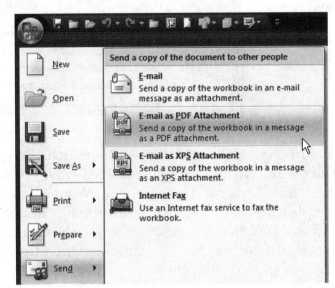

Summary: To send an Excel file without leaving Excel, you can select Office Icon – Send – E-Mail.

Commands Discussed: Office Icon – Send – E-Mail

Excel 97-2003: File – Send To – Mail Recipient (as Attachment).

SAVE EXCEL DATA AS A TEXT FILE

Problem: I am working with the Excel file shown in Figure 124. I need to produce a file for another application to read, but that application can read only .txt files.

Figure 124

You need to export to a text file.

	A	B	C	D	E	F	G	H
1	Region	Product	Date	Customer	Quantity	Revenue	COGS	Profit
2	East	XYZ	31-Dec-07	Ford	1000	22810	10220	12590
3	Central	DEF	1-Jan-08	Verizon	100	2257	984	1273
4	East	ABC	1-Jan-08	Verizon	500	10245	4235	6010

Strategy: You have a couple options. Typically, the other application will either want the columns to be separated by a fixed number of spaces or separated by commas. Files with columns separated by commas are called comma-separated values, or CSV, files. CSV files are easier to create than space-separated files. Here's how you create a CSV file:

1) Select Office Icon – Save As – Other Formats. In the Save as Type dropdown, choose CSV (Comma delimited) (*.csv), as shown in Figure 125.

Part
I

Figure 125

Use the Save as Type dropdown.

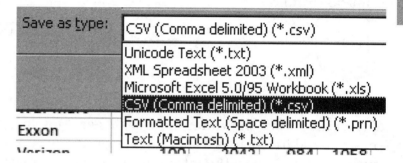

2) Click the Save button. Important: Only the current worksheet is saved in the CSV file. If you have multiple worksheets in the workbook, save each worksheet separately. Excel will generally warn you that you are saving the file in a format that will leave out incompatible features, as shown in Figure 126.

Figure 126

In step 3, you can re-save the file as Excel to keep the compatible features.

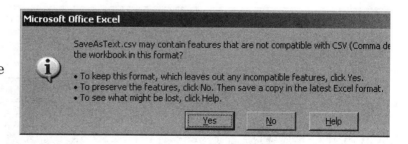

3) After saving the file as CSV, use Save As to save the file as an Excel file.

Results: Figure 127 shows the created file as it appears when edited with Notepad. Pay particular attention to the "Molson, Inc" entry. Because cell D5 already contained a comma, Excel was smart enough to surround Molson, Inc with quotation marks, as shown in Figure 127.

Figure 127

Excel adds quotation marks around a cell that contains a comma.

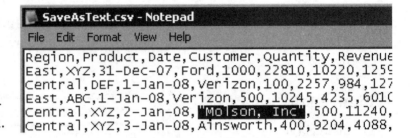

Gotcha: The dates in column C are written to the file in the same format as they were shown on the worksheet. Most programs will not understand a date such as 1-Jan-04. Check the documentation of the program that will import the information, and if you need to, format column C to appear as mm/dd/yyyy before exporting to CSV.

Alternate Strategy: Another option is to create a file in which each field is supposed to take a fixed number of characters. You might need to use this method to produce a file which is to be imported by another application. In this case, the other application will usually give you a file specification for you to follow. It might indicate the following:

Field Name	Start	Length	Decimals
Region	1	12	
Product	13	10	
Date	23	10	
Customer	33	20	
Quantity	53	8	0
Revenue	61	10	2
Cost	71	10	2
Profit	81	10	2

In this case, you follow these steps:

1) Go through the columns in the worksheet, resetting the column widths. If the other program expects the Region field to be 12 characters wide, for example, select column A and then choose Home – Format – Column Width and set the Column Width text box to 12, as shown in Figure 128.

Figure 128

Set the column widths to match the required file specification.

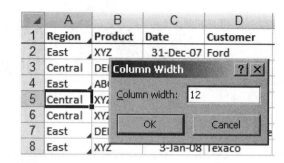

2) Format the dates as specified by the other system. Make sure the Revenue, Cost, and Profit columns show two decimal places. The other system probably will not want field headings, so delete row 1.

3) Select Office Icon – Save As – Other Formats. In the Save as Type dropdown, select Formatted Text (Space Delimited).

Gotcha: Excel changes the file name so that it has a .prn extension. Even if you try to change the extension to .txt here, Excel will still save the file with the extension .prn. It is best to leave it as .prn and then rename it in Windows Explorer.

4) When Excel warns you that you will lose features if you have multiple sheets, click Yes.

Figure 129 shows the resulting file, viewed in Notepad.

Figure 129

Data is neatly aligned in columns.

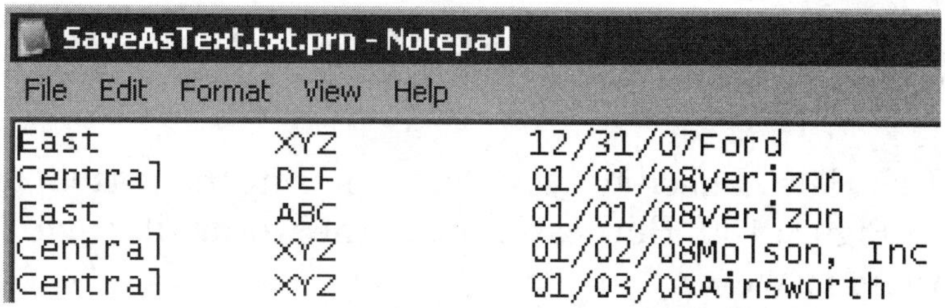

Summary: You can easily export Excel data to a text file. Before exporting, you need to determine whether the receiving system needs CSV or text formatted using spaces.

Commands Discussed: Office Icon – Save As – Other Formats

Excel 97-2003: File – Save As

USE A LASER PRINTER
TO HAVE EXCEL CALCULATE FASTER

Problem: How can I speed up my Excel calculations?

Strategy: Believe it or not, Excel uses your print driver to draw the screen. Having an HP LaserJet as your default printer can enable Excel operations to finish in one-fourth the time it takes if you have a cheap inkjet driver as the default. If response time is critical, you can download and install the printer driver for an HP LaserJet and set it as your default printer during calculations. You don't need to actually have an HP LaserJet—you just need the driver.

Gotcha: If you don't actually have an HP LaserJet printer hooked to your computer, you will have to refrain from using the Printer icon and instead print by selecting Office Icon – Print and choosing a non-default printer.

Summary: Using an HP LaserJet driver during Excel calculations can speed up your Excel operations time.

Commands Discussed: Office Icon – Print

USE EXCEL AS A WORD PROCESSOR

Problem: I need to type some notes at the bottom of a report, as shown in Figure 130. How can I make the words fill each line as if I had typed them in Word?

Figure 130

The disclaimer needs to fit in columns A through G.

	A	B	C	D	E	F	G	H	I
21									
22	This prospectus includes forward-looking statements.								
23	All statements other than statements of historical facts contained in this pr								
24	including statements regarding our future financial position, business strateg								
25	and objectives of management for future operations, are forward-looking st								
26	The words "believe", "may", "will", "estimate", "continue", "anticipate", "in								
27	events and financial trends that we believe may affect our financial condition								
28	financial needs.								

Strategy: You can select Fill dropdown – Justify. The Fill dropdown now appears in the Editing group of the Home tab of the ribbon. Follow these steps:

1) To have the words fill columns A through G, select a range such as A22:G35. Include enough extra blank rows in the selection to handle the text after word wrapping (see Figure 131).

Figure 131

The number of columns in your selection determines the length of each line.

	A	B	C	D	E	F	G
21							
22	This prospectus includes forward-looking statements						
23	All statements other than statements of historical fac						
24	including statements regarding our future financial po						
25	and objectives of management for future operations,						
26	The words "believe", "may", "will", "estimate", "co						
27	events and financial trends that we believe may affe						
28	financial needs.						
29							
30							

2) Select Home – Fill dropdown – Justify. (The Fill dropdown now appears in the Editing group of the Home tab. As shown in Figure 132, it might appear only as a blue down-arrow icon.)

Figure 132

Select Justify from the Fill dropdown of the Editing group on the Home tab.

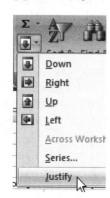

Results: Excel will rearrange the text to fill each row, as shown in Figure 133.

Figure 133

Text is re-flowed to fit the width of the selection.

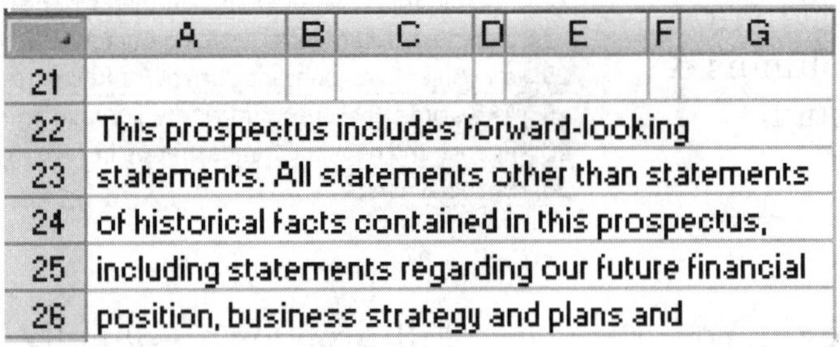

	A	B	C	D	E	F	G
21							
22	This prospectus includes forward-looking						
23	statements. All statements other than statements						
24	of historical facts contained in this prospectus,						
25	including statements regarding our future financial						
26	position, business strategy and plans and						

Gotcha: If you have a few words in bold in one cell, this formatting will be lost.

Gotcha: If you later change the widths of columns A:G, you will have to use the Justify command again to force the data to fit.

Gotcha: Do not use this method if any of your cells contain more than 255 characters. Excel will silently truncate those cells to 255 characters without any notice!

Alternate Strategy: You can also use a text box to solve this problem. You simply click the Text box icon on the Insert tab, draw a text box to fill columns A through G, and paste your text into the text box. You can then format the text box to hide its border: Select the text box and on the Drawing Tools Format tab, select Shape Outline – None.

Additional Details: In Excel 2007, you can give a text box multiple columns. To do so, you select the text box. On the Drawing Tools Format tab, you click the dialog launcher icon in the bottom-right corner of the Shape Styles group to display the Format Shape dialog. In the left pane, you choose Text Box. Then you click on Columns and specify two columns, with separation between them of 0.1". The top of Figure 134 shows the result.

Summary: When you need to add a bit of text to an Excel worksheet, you can use the Justify command to make the range look as if it was created with a word processor.

Figure 134

New in Excel 2007, text boxes can support multiple columns.

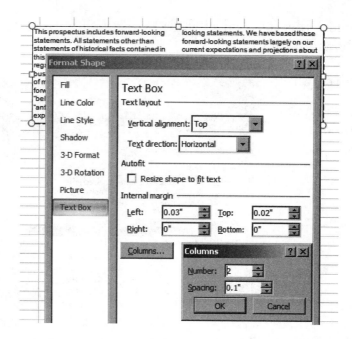

Commands Discussed: Home – Fill dropdown – Justify; Drawing Tools Format – Shape Outline – None; Drawing Tools Format – dialog launcher – Text Box – Columns

Excel 97-2003: Edit – Fill – Justify. The text box icon was on the Drawing toolbar. After adding the text box, Ctrl+right-click the border of the text box, choose Format Text Box, and on the Colors and Lines tab, open the Line Color dropdown and choose No Line. The two-column text box was not available in prior versions of Excel.

ADD WORD TO EXCEL

Problem: I need to type a three-page document at the end of my Excel data. I don't want to use a text box or the Justify command with all that text.

Strategy: You can use the full power of Word in Excel. While you are typing the document, you can put all of the Word menus right in the Excel menu. Follow these steps:

1) Place the cell pointer in the top-left cell where the text should start.

2)   Select Insert – Object. Excel will display the Object dialog box, as shown in Figure 135.

Figure 135

Insert a Word document in Excel.

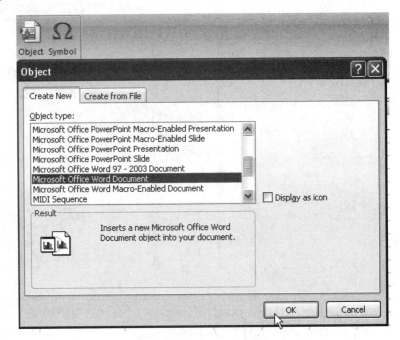

3)   Choose Microsoft Office Word Document. Click OK.

4)   Type your document in the frame. You can use the resize handles in the corner of the frame to make the document as wide and tall as necessary. Notice that while you are editing the document, the Excel ribbon is replaced with the Word ribbon (see Figure 136).

Figure 136

Those are ribbon tabs from Word at the top.

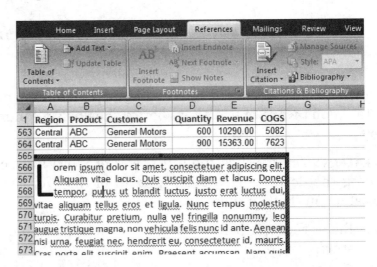

5) Click outside the document. The text automatically appears with a border. To remove the border, right-click the border and choose Format Object. In the Colors and Lines tab of the Format Object dialog, open the Line Color dropdown and choose No Line (see Figure 137).

Figure 137

Remove the border from the text.

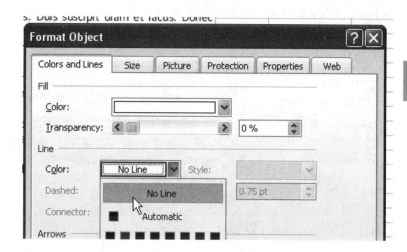

Additional Details: In addition to using Word in Excel, you can also use PowerPoint or Access. At a recent MVP Summit at Microsoft, Nick Hodge, one of the British MVPs, joked about a set of add-ins that Microsoft had created to help people using Excel. He noted the add-ins were: Word, PowerPoint, and Access (Which caused the rest of the Excel MVP's to laugh). As you've seen in this topic, you have the ability to add Word menus right into Excel, so Nick may be right!

Additional Details: In case you would ever find yourself typing in Microsoft Word, you can insert an Excel table in the Word document by using Insert – Object.

Summary: You can add Word, PowerPoint, or Access into Excel to get the functionality you need.

Commands Discussed: Insert – Object

SPELL CHECK A REGION

Problem: I want to spell check the notes at the bottom of a report (see Figure 138), but I don't want to spell check the customer names in the report. How can I accomplish this?

A
B
C
D
E
F
G
22
23 This prospectus includes forward-looking statem
24 contained in this prospectus, including statemen
25 and plans and objectives of management for futu
26 "believe", "may", "will", "estimate", "continue", "a

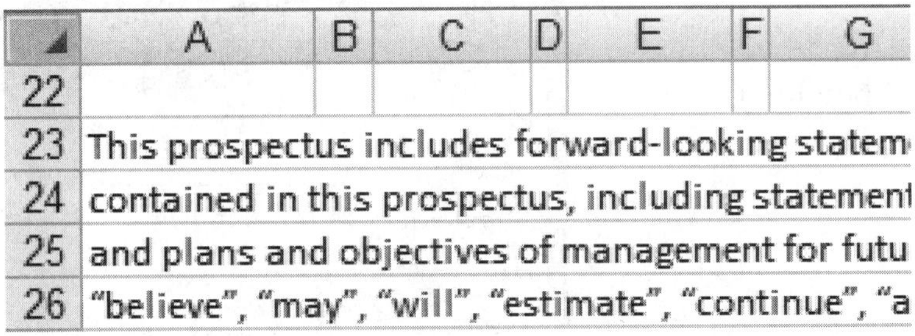

Figure 138

You want to check spelling in a portion of the spreadsheet.

Strategy: You can select the region to be spell checked and then choose Review – Spelling, as shown in Figure 139. (Or press F7, the Spelling shortcut key).

ABC
Spelling
Research
Thesaurus
Translate
Proofing

Figure 139

Select multiple cells before invoking the Spelling command.

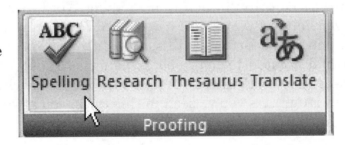

Results: Excel will spell check just the selected cells, as shown in Figure 140.

Microsoft Office Excel
The spelling check is complete for the selected cells.
OK

Figure 140

Excel will check only the selected range.

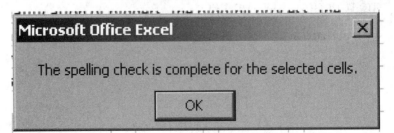

Gotcha: If you indicate to spell check a single cell, Excel will expand your selection to the entire worksheet. To get around this problem, you can select the desired cell and any one adjacent cell. When you have two or more cells selected, Excel will check only the selection.

Summary: To spell check only a part of your worksheet, you can select the area to be checked and then select Review – Spelling or press the F7 key.

Commands Discussed: Review – Spelling; F7 key

Excel 97-2003: Tools – Spelling

Part
I

TRANSLATE WITH EXCEL

Problem: I have a client whose German subsidiary sent me an Excel file. The headings are in German. I need to figure out what each column means.

Strategy: Excel 2007 added a translation interface to the Review tab of the ribbon. This interface is based on WorldLingo.com, and although the translations are not perfect, they can give you a general idea of the meaning of a passage or paragraph. Here's how it works:

1) Select a cell that contains text you want to translate.

2) Select Review – Translate, as shown in Figure 141. The Research task pane appears along the right side of the window.

Figure 141

Choose text in a cell and click Translate.

3) In the From dropdown, choose German.

4) In the To dropdown, choose English. In a few moments, a rough translation will appear in the Research pane (see Figure 142).

Figure 142

A rough translation will appear.

Additional Details: The Research pane offers a link to Translation Options. The Translation Options dialog allows you to prevent translation between certain languages. If you have a rogue employee who is addicted to ordering Italian shoes on company time, perhaps you would want to turn off the Italian to English language pair. The dialog also allows you to choose the translation service to use for any given language. However, at press time, Microsoft only offers WorldLingo for translations.

Summary: Excel provides a rough translation utility.

Commands Discussed: Review – Translate

Excel 97-2003: There was no Translate command.

USE HYPERLINKS TO CREATE AN OPENING MENU FOR A WORKBOOK

Problem: I have designed a budget workbook that has various worksheets. Managers throughout the company need to use it, but some of the managers are not entirely comfortable with Excel. A navigation tool would help them get through the worksheet.

Strategy: You can make your first worksheet a menu with hyperlinks. Here's how:

Part
I

1) Insert an opening worksheet called Menu. Add an entry for each section of the workbook, as shown in Figure 143.

Figure 143

The cells in B will become clickable hyperlinks.

▲	A	B	C	D	E
1	Welcome to the budget worksheet				
2					
3	Select an option below:				
4		Review Actuals			
5		Enter Forecast			
6		Submit to Corporate			
7					

2) In order to add a hyperlink that enables a manager to click the cell and jump to the section, select cell B4 and then select Insert – Hyperlink or press Ctrl+K. Initially, the Insert Hyperlink dialog will default to linking to an existing file or Web page, as shown in Figure 144.

Figure 144

Excel assumes that you want to link to an external Web page.

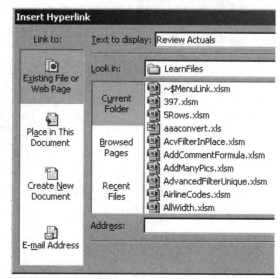

3) On the left side of the dialog, choose the second option, Place in This Document. The dialog changes to show you all the worksheets in the document, as shown in Figure 145.

Figure 145

Choose Place in This Document to specify a sheet and cell address.

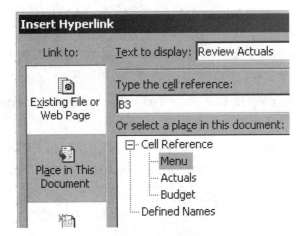

4) Choose a worksheet, choose a cell address, and click OK.

5) Optionally, click the ScreenTip button and provide friendly text that will appear when someone hovers over the link.

Figure 146

Provide friendly text that will appear when someone hovers over the link.

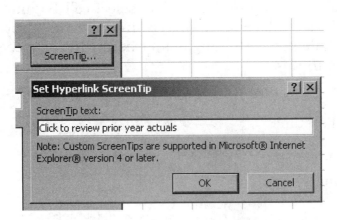

Gotcha: If you don't provide ScreenTip text, Excel will display a rather verbose ToolTip (see Figure 147) that will distract managers.

Figure 147

If you don't specify a ScreenTip, Excel uses this default ToolTip.

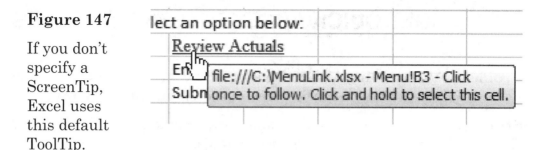

Results: The cell becomes a clickable hyperlink. Clicking on the link will take the manager to the Actuals worksheet.

Additional Details: Be sure to provide a hyperlink on the Actuals worksheet to take the manager back to the menu, as shown in Figure 148.

Figure 148

Provide a friendly way to return to the menu.

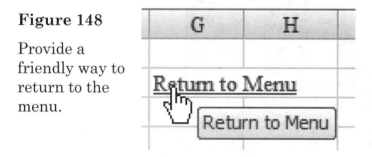

Additional Details: You cannot select a hyperlinked cell by clicking it. You can select an adjacent cell and use an arrow key to get into the cell, or you can click and hold on a cell that contains a hyperlink. To edit an existing hyperlink, you use the Insert – Hyperlink command again or right-click the cell and choose Edit Hyperlink.

See Also: "Remove Hyperlinks Inserted by Excel" on page 819

Summary: You can make Excel less intimidating for other people by adding hyperlinks to provide simple navigation around the workbook.

Commands Discussed: Insert – Hyperlink

GET QUICK ACCESS TO PASTE VALUES

Problem: After reading MrExcel books, I find myself routinely using Paste – Values. Is there a quicker way to access this functionality?

Strategy: Aren't you glad you're using these cool features all the time? Excel 2007 gives you an even faster way to go.

In Excel 2007, the Paste icon on the Home tab of the ribbon contains a top half and a bottom half. If you click the bottom half, you get a drop-down, which this book refers to as the Paste dropdown. Open the Paste dropdown and choose Paste Values (see Figure 149). From the Paste dropdown you also have other options, such as Formulas, No Borders, Transpose, and Paste Link.

Figure 149

Select Home – Paste drop-down – Paste Values

In Excel 97-2003, you would typically copy a range of formulas and then select Edit – Paste Special – Values. You choose Paste Special from the Paste dropdown to access the traditional Paste Special dialog shown in Figure 150.

Figure 150

Select Home – Paste drop-down – Paste Special to access the familiar dialog.

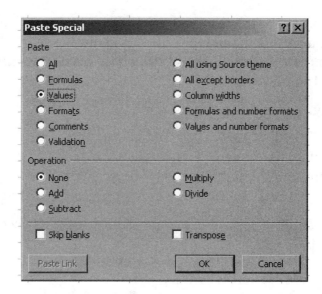

Alternate Strategy: There is an *amazing* alternative method for converting formulas to values. I learned this method from someone in the second row of a seminar I conducted in Columbus, Indiana.

Most of the time when you want to paste values, you have to copy the range to the Clipboard. However, the amazing alternative method does not require you to copy the data. Follow these steps to try it out.

1) Select the range containing the formulas you want to paste.

2) Right-click-and-hold the right border of the selection.

3) Drag right one column.

4) Drag left one column

5) When you release the right mouse button, choose Copy Here as Values Only from the context menu (see Figure 151).

Figure 151

The strangest accidental click in the history of the world?

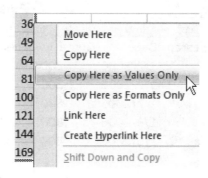

I was amazed to learn this new trick. I have probably used Paste Values over a hundred thousand times, but this method is radically quicker and easier. You can right-click-and-drag any border in any direction to get the menu to appear.

Summary: You can use various commands in the Paste dropdown to get quick access to the most popular Paste options.

Commands Discussed: Home – Paste dropdown – Paste Special -- Values; Home – Paste dropdown – Paste Values; Copy Here as Values Only

Excel 97-2003: The Paste Values menu item is accessed from a tiny dropdown to the right of the Paste icon in the Standard toolbar.

QUICKLY COPY A FORMULA
TO ALL ROWS OF DATA

Problem: I have a worksheet with 5,000 rows of data (see Figure 152). I often enter a formula in a new column and need to copy it down to all of the rows. I try to do this by dragging the fill handle. But as I try to drag, Excel starts accelerating faster and faster. Before I know it, I've overshot row 5,000 and find myself at row 8,000. After grumbling a bit, I start dragging back up. Again, Excel starts accelerating. After 1,000 rows, the cell pointer is moving somewhere close to the speed of sound, and I find that I've overshoot row 5,000 by 2,000. I end up going down and up, down and up. I call this frustrating process the "fill handle dance." Is there a way to stop the madness?

Figure 152

You want to copy this formula down to all rows of your data set.

	E2			f_x	=MAX(D2-C2,0)	
	A	B	C	D	E	
1	Salesrep	Date	Quota	Sales	Over Quota	
2	Joe	1/2/2006	800	666	0	
3	Dan	1/2/2006	800	1290		
4	Mary	1/2/2006	800	896		
5	Joe	1/3/2006	800	559		
6	Dan	1/3/2006	800	192		

Strategy: You can very quickly copy a formula down to all the rows by double-clicking the fill handle. Excel will copy the formula down until it encounters a blank cell in column D.

The fill handle is the square dot in the lower-right corner of the cell pointer box. When you hover your mouse over the fill handle, the cell pointer changes to a plus, as shown in Figure 153.

Figure 153

The square dot is the fill handle.

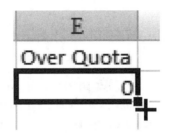

How does Excel decide how far to copy the formula? In the most common arrangement, you have data in the cell to the left of the formula (for example, cell D2). In this arrangement, Excel will copy the formula down until it comes to the first row with a blank cell in the column to the left. If there is no data in D2, but there is data in F2, Excel will copy down to the first blank cell in column F.

What if there are 10 cells starting D2 and 20 cells starting in F2? The column to the left will win; Excel will copy the data from E2:E11. In addition, a cell that trumps both D2 and F2 is the cell immediately underneath the formula. If E3 is non-blank, you can double-click, and Excel will copy the formula down until it comes to the first blank cell in column E.

Gotcha: Sometimes the data to the left of your formula is particularly sparse. You might have name in A, address in B, an address line 2 in C and a formula to be copied in D. Since not everyone has an apartment or suite number, there are many gaps in column C. But, everyone has an address in column B. One cool trick is to temporarily hide column C. Now, column B is the visible column to the left of column D and Excel will copy the formula to the bottom.

Summary: You can double-click the fill handle to quickly copy a formula down to all cells in a range of data.

ENTER A SERIES OF MONTHS, DAYS, OR MORE BY USING THE FILL HANDLE

Problem: I need to create a new worksheet. My first task is to enter the 12 month names across row 1. Is there a faster way than typing them all?

Strategy: You type the first value and drag that cell's fill handle to the right or down. Follow these steps:

1) Type January in cell B1. If you now press the Enter key, Excel will normally move the cell pointer to B2. You can press Enter and then press the Up Arrow key to move back to B1, or you can simply press Ctrl+Enter to accept the cell value and stay in the current cell.

2) The square dot in the lower right corner of the cell is the fill handle. Click it and drag right or down. As you drag, a ToolTip will show you the value that will be entered in each cell (see Figure 154).

Figure 154

As you drag the fill handle, a ToolTip will show the values that will be filled.

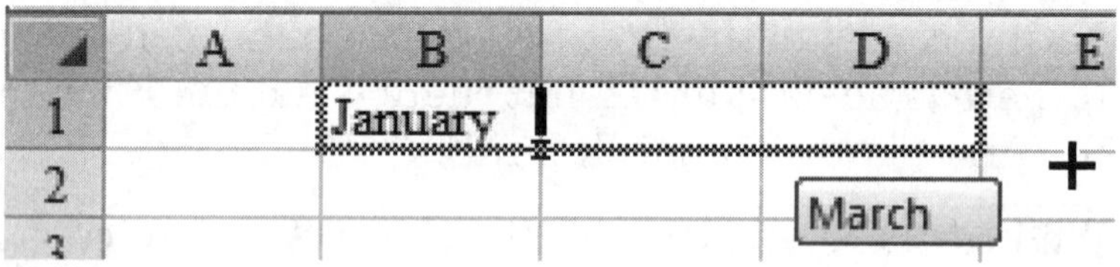

◢	A	B	C	D	E
1		January			
2				March	+
3					

3) When you release the mouse button, Excel will fill the series with month names.

Additional Details: Excel can extend many other built-in series in addition to month names:

- Jan will extend to Feb, Mar, and so on.
- Monday will extend to Tue, Wed, and so on.
- Q1 will extend to Q2, Q3, Q4, Q1. (Also Qtr 1 or Quarter 1)
- 1st period will extend to 2nd period, 3rd period, and so on.
- Today's date (press Ctrl+;) will extend to tomorrow's date.

Gotcha: Excel can extend many built-in series, but can it count 1, 2, 3, and so on? If you enter 1 in cell B1 and drag the fill handle down, what do you think you will get? 1, 2, 3. What will you actually get? 1, 1, 1.

Many people tell me to enter 1 in B1, 2 in B2, select B1:B2 and drag the fill handle. While this works, there is a faster way: You can enter 1 in B1 and then hold down the Ctrl key while you drag the fill handle. Excel will fill with 1, 2, 3, and so on. Somehow, the Ctrl key tells Excel to reverse the usual result. Normally, Excel would extend the series of a cell that contains a date. If you want to force Excel to copy the date instead, you could Ctrl+click the fill handle.

Additional Details: If you forget to hold down Ctrl, you can open the Auto Fill Options dropdown that appears at the end of the range (see Figure 155). You can select Fill Series and then change the 1, 1, 1, 1, 1 to 1, 2, 3, 4, 5.

Figure 155

If you fail to hold down Ctrl, you can change the series of 1s to 1, 2, 3 by using this icon.

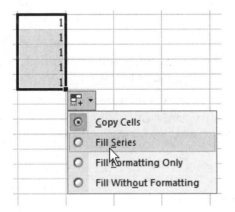

Gotcha: The Fill Options icon can be difficult to dismiss. This is particularly annoying if it is covering up data. The Esc key will not make it go away. One fast way to dismiss the icon is to resize a column on the worksheet.

If you need to fill odd numbers, you can enter 1 in B1 and 3 in B2. Select B1:B2 and drag the fill handle.

There are other fill possibilities as well. One cool option is Fill Weekdays. You enter a starting date in a cell, place the cell pointer in that cell, right-click, and drag the fill handle down several cells. A ToolTip will indicate that you are filling the series with daily dates. When you release the mouse button, you will have several options to choose from, as shown in Figure 156. You can select Fill Weekdays to fill in only Monday through Friday.

Figure 156

Right-click and drag the fill handle to access these options.

Additional Details: The fill handle is a shortcut to default settings you can also get by selecting Home – Fill – Series. You can enter a value in a cell, select that cell, and choose Home – Fill – Series to display a dialog where you can specify any type of series. As shown in Figure 157, the dialog will fill every third number from 1 to 99, down a column starting with the active cell.

Figure 157

Use the Series dialog to build any conceivable series.

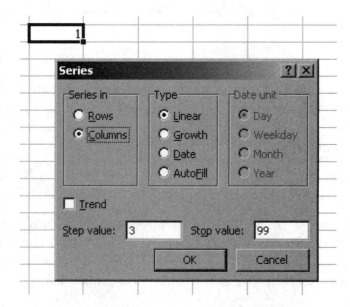

Summary: You can use the fill handle to quickly fill a row or column with a built-in series of data.

Commands Discussed: Home – Fill – Series

Excel 97-2003: Edit – Fill – Series

HAVE THE FILL HANDLE FILL YOUR LIST OF PART NUMBERS

Part I

Problem: Sure, the fill handle is good for filling months, days, and sequential numbers. But what about the really annoying lists I have to type all the time at work? I have to type lists of product lines, company regions, sales rep names, and even bagel flavors.

Strategy: No matter what job you do, you probably have some annoying list of items that you have to type over and over. You can add your list of items to the Custom Lists tab of the Excel Options dialog. You can then fill items from the defined custom lists by using the fill handle.

Say that you work at the Bigger Better Bagel Co., and you constantly need to type the flavors of bagels, as shown in Figure 158. Here's how you can simplify this task;

Figure 158

Get ready to type this list for the last time.

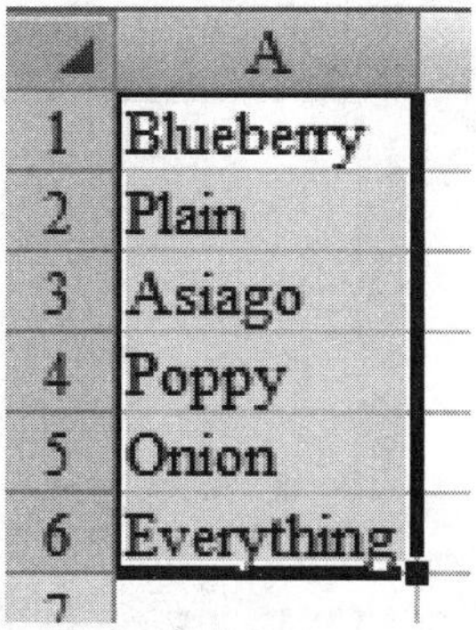

◢	A
1	Blueberry
2	Plain
3	Asiago
4	Poppy
5	Onion
6	Everything
7	

1)   Either enter the list in a blank section of the worksheet or find a worksheet with the existing list and select the range. Either way, make sure the list is selected before going to step 2.

2) Choose Office Icon – Excel Options. You should be looking at the Popular category. Click the Edit Custom List button as shown in Figure 159.

Figure 159

Find the Edit Custom Lists button in the Excel Options dialog.

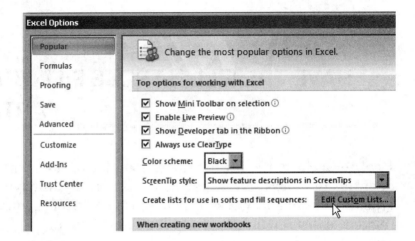

3) As shown in Figure 160, in the Custom Lists dialog, the Import List from Cells text box (to the left of the Import button) should already contain the range address that you selected in Step 1. If it is not, click the Refers To icon at the right edge of the text box and select the range that contains your list.

Figure 160

Import the list from a range.

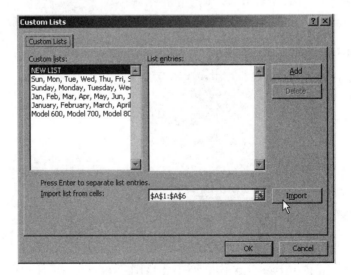

4) Click the Import button. The list of values will be added as a new custom list, as shown in Figure 161. (Note that if you later change the flavors in this list, you can edit the list in this dialog. Make sure to click the Add button to commit the changes.).

Figure 161

You've successfully added a new custom list.

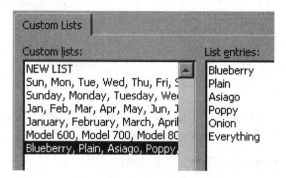

5) After you add the custom list, you can type any item from the list in a cell and then drag the fill handle. Excel will fill in the remaining items from the list (see Figure 162).

Figure 162

Type one item and drag the fill handle.

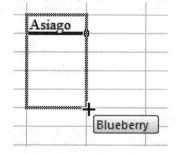

Additional Details: Say that you want to store a list of names, and the first name in the list is a really long name, such as John Jacob Jingleheimer Schmidt. Rather than having to type this name to start the list, you could make the first item in the list the heading. So, perhaps you could type Class1 or MktgDept and drag the fill handle to get the correct list.

Additional Details: Custom lists are stored in your computer's registry. It is therefore very difficult to transfer a list from one computer to another. One method is as follows:

Part
I

1) Set up a custom sort using your custom list. (See How to Sort a Report into a Custom Sequence on page 422)

2) Move the workbook to the new computer.

3) Do a sort on the new computer. In the Order column, select Custom Lists. Click Add.

Since the above process is fairy convoluted, it might be easier to copy the lists into a blank workbook on the old computer, and then import the lists on the new computer.

Summary: You can create a custom list so that you will then be able to easily fill that list on your computer.

Commands Discussed: Office Icon – Excel Options – Edit Custom Lists.

Excel 97-2003: Tools – Options – Custom Lists; Data – Sort – Options – First Key Sort Order

QUICKLY TURN A RANGE ON ITS SIDE

Problem; I have a column that contains 20 department names going down a column (see Figure 163). I need to build a spreadsheet with those names going across row 1.

Figure 163

This list needs to be horizontal instead of vertical.

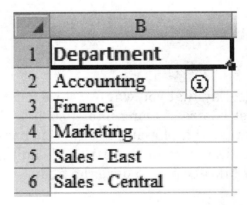

Strategy: You can use Home – Paste dropdown – Transpose to turn the range on its side. Here's how:

1) Highlight the department names in column A.

2) Select Edit – Copy to copy the cells to the Clipboard.

3) Move the cell pointer to a blank area of the worksheet (for example, cell C1 in this example).

4) Select Home – Paste dropdown – Transpose.

Results: The department numbers are transposed so that they fill cells C1 to Z1.

Gotcha: The columns you paste to will not automatically resize to fit the data. To fix this problem, you can select the appropriate range (in this case, C1:Z1) and then choose Home – Format – AutoFit Column Width.

Additional Details: You can also use Home – Paste dropdown – Transpose to convert a horizontal row of numbers into a column. In addition, you can use it to turn a rectangular range on its side. In Figure 164, for example, range A1:D4 was transposed to range A6:D9.

Figure 164

You can turn a rectangular range on its side.

	A	B	C	D
1		Sales	COGS	Profit
2	Jan	10000	5400	4600
3	Feb	11000	5900	5100
4	Mar	12000	6500	5500
5				
6		Jan	Feb	Mar
7	Sales	10000	11000	12000
8	COGS	5400	5900	6500
9	Profit	4600	5100	5500

Summary: Using Home – Paste dropdown – Transpose is useful for quickly turning a range of values on its side.

Commands Discussed: Home – Paste – Transpose

Excel 97-2003: Edit – Paste Special – Transpose

STOP EXCEL FROM AUTOCORRECTING CERTAIN WORDS

Problem: Every time I type the name of my WYA Division, as shown in Figure 165, Excel changes "WYA" to "WAY," as shown in Figure 166. It is impossible to type WYA without entering it as a formula: ="W"&"Y"&"A".

Figure 165

WYA until...

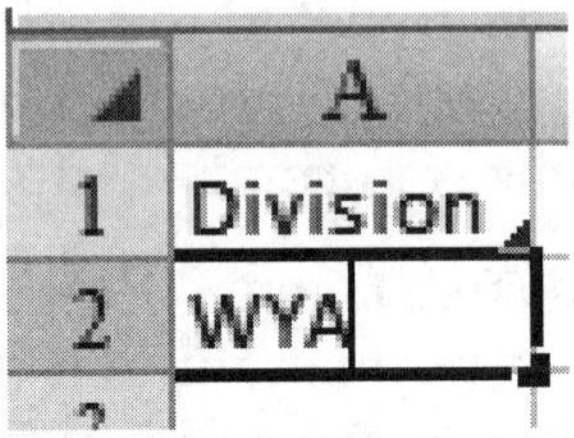

◢	A
1	Division
2	WYA

Figure 166

...you type a space or press Enter.

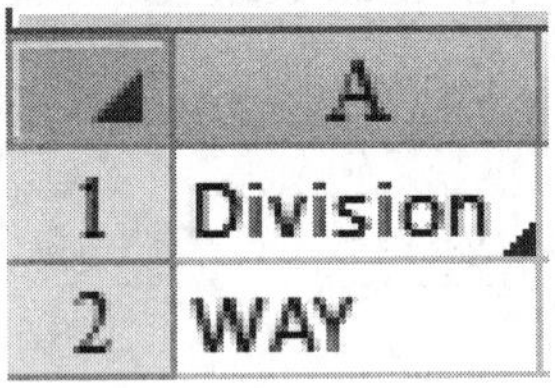

◢	A
1	Division
2	WAY

Strategy: To help correct common mis-typings, Excel has a large list of words that are automatically replaced as you type. This is a good feature, unless you routinely have to type one of the words that Excel thinks is wrong. Luckily, you can edit this list rather than turning it off. Here's how:

1) Select Office Icon – Excel Options – Proofing.

2) Click the AutoCorrect Options button.

3) On the AutoCorrect dialog, go to the AutoCorrect tab.

4) Scroll down the Replace Text as You Type section until you find the entry for replacing WYA with WAY. Select that line and click Delete, as shown in Figure 167.

Figure 167

Delete any
replacements
that cause
problems.

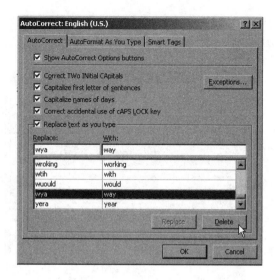

Summary: You can edit how Excel will autocorrect words without turning off the feature by clicking to AutoCorrect Options in the Excel Options dialog and then removing the selected lines from the Replace Text as You Type list.

See Also: "Use AutoCorrect to Enable a Shortcut"

Commands Discussed: Office Icon – Excel Options – Proofing – Auto-Correct Options

Excel 97-2003: Tools – AutoCorrect Options

USE AUTOCORRECT TO ENABLE A SHORTCUT

Problem: I work for John Jacob Jingleheimer Schmidt. It is frustrating to type this name continuously. How can I save time?

Strategy: You can set up an AutoCorrect entry to replace JJJS with John Jacob Jingleheimer Schmidt. Here's how:

1)   Select Office Icon – Excel Options – Proofing.

2)   Click the AutoCorrect Options button.

3)   On the AutoCorrect dialog, go to the AutoCorrect tab.

4)   In the Replace section, type JJJS. In the With section, type the complete name. Click Add, as shown in Figure 168.

Figure 168

Add your own shortcut as an AutoCorrect option.

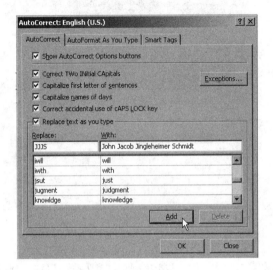

Results: When you type JJJS in a cell, as shown in Figure 169, and then type a space or press Enter, Excel will replace your text with the complete text specified in the AutoCorrect list, as shown in Figure 170.

Figure 169

Type the shortcut...

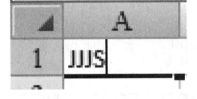

Figure 170

...and a space to invoke the correction.

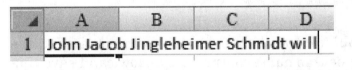

Additional Details: If you sometimes need to use the abbreviation and sometimes need to spell out the words, then set up JJJS> to be the shortcut for spelling out the words. Then, when you type JJJS, the intials will appear. When you type JJJS>, the words will appear.

Summary: You can use AutoCorrect to add a shortcut for a long or difficult word.

See Also: "Stop Excel From AutoCorrecting Certain Words" on p. 120

Commands Discussed: Office Icon – Excel Options – Proofing – Auto-Correct Options

Excel 97-2003: Tools – AutoCorrect Options

WHY WON'T THE TRACK CHANGES FEATURE WORK IN EXCEL?

Problem: After I select Review – Track Changes – Highlight Changes, I cannot insert cells. What's going on?

Strategy: Track Changes is a great feature in Word. However, when you turn on Track Changes in Excel, Microsoft automatically makes your workbook a shared workbook (see Figure 171).

Figure 171

Tracking changes shares the workbook.

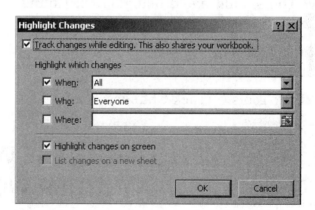

The shared workbook function in Excel has so many limitations that it is nearly impossible to use. When you share a workbook, you cannot do any of the following tasks:

- Insert blocks of cells
- Delete worksheets
- Merge or unmerge cells
- Change conditional formatting or data validation

- Create charts
- Insert drawing objects, hyperlinks, or scenarios
- Use automatic subtotals
- Use pivot tables
- Record or edit macros
- Enter CSE or array formulas
- Use data tables

It is possible that a novice Excel user might never use these features. It is even possible that before you bought this book, you never used them. However, sharing a workbook makes it virtually unusable for an intermediate Excel user. There is no strategy to get around this. Unless your changes will involve only radically simple worksheet changes, you should avoid the Track Changes and Share Workbooks options.

Alternate Strategy: Google Spreadsheet can easily allow multiple people to edit the same spreadsheet. Currently, this application can only handle worksheets with up to 10,000 cells. It is possible to open the Excel file in Google Spreadsheet, have a joint editing session, then save back to Excel.

Summary: You should avoid using Track Changes and Share Workbooks in Excel.

Commands Discussed: Review – Track Changes – Highlight Changes; Review – Share Workbooks

Excel 97-2003: Tools – Track Changes; Tools – Share Workbooks

COPY CELLS FROM ONE WORKSHEET TO MANY OTHER WORKSHEETS

Problem: I have 12 monthly worksheets in a workbook. I've made changes to January and now need to copy those changes to the other 11 worksheets. Is there an easy way?

Strategy: After you've successfully made changes to January, you can follow these steps:

1) Select the January worksheet. Hold down the Shift key and select the December worksheet. Alternatively, right-click the Janu-

ary sheet tab and choose Select All Sheets. Excel will select all 12 worksheets and make the January worksheet the active sheet.

Note: If your changes are in a middle sheet, such as April, then the process is different. First, click the April worksheet. Next, Shift+click the December sheet, and then Ctrl+click the January, February, and March sheets.

2)   Select the cells you want to copy. If the cells are not adjacent to one another, select the first range and then hold down Ctrl while selecting the remaining ranges.

3)   Select Home – Fill – Across Worksheets, as shown in Figure 172.

Figure 172

Find the Fill icon in the Editing group.

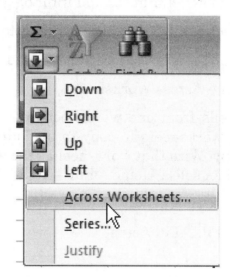

4)   From the Fill Across Worksheets dialog, as shown in Figure 173, select whether to copy values, formats, or both.

Figure 173

You could also use this command to copy formatting to all sheets.

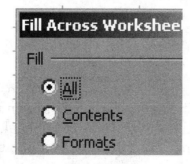

5)   Right-click any sheet tab and select Ungroup.

Gotcha: If you fail to ungroup, any changes you make to the active worksheet will be made to all worksheets.

Additional Details: Home – Fill – Across Worksheets is fairly difficult to use. You have to be able to group sheets and then make the sheet with the changes to copy the active (top) sheet. The steps listed here are designed to help select all sheets. If you need to copy from March to only June, September, and December, however, you might do this:

1)   Select March to make it the active sheet.

2)   Hold down Ctrl and select June to add it to the group.

3)   Hold down Ctrl and select September to add it to the group.

4)   Hold down Ctrl and select December to add it to the group.

5)   Select Home – Fill – Across Worksheets.

Summary: To copy cells from one worksheet to several other worksheets, you select the worksheets to copy to, including the worksheet that has the data to copy. With that worksheet as the active sheet, select the data to copy and then select Home – Fill – Across Worksheets.

Commands Discussed: Home – Fill – Across Worksheets

Excel 97-2003: Edit – Fill – Fill Across Worksheets

HAVE EXCEL TALK TO YOU

Problem: I have many numbers to enter, but I am notoriously bad at keying data. How can I get my numbers into Excel accurately?

Strategy: You can verify your typing by having Excel's speech utility speak each number as you complete an entry.

Before trying the Speech option, you need to go to the Windows Control Panel and choose Speech. The available voices are on the Text to Speech tab. Windows XP offered Microsoft Sam, LH Michael, and LH Michelle. While they were all annoying, I've found Michelle to be the least annoying. In Windows Vista, the voice is dramatically improved. Preview the voices and choose the one that is the least annoying to you. If you want to, change the speed of the voice.

In my Power Excel seminars, I frequently show this trick as both a useful tool for proofreading and a great April Fool's Day prank: You can turn on the Speech option on a co-worker's computer and then hide the icons. Despite my efforts at popularizing it, either this feature wasn't used by enough people or it was too annoying. In Excel 2007, the feature was banished to the Commands Not on the Ribbon category in the Quick Access toolbar customization dialog. To use the Text to Speech option in Excel 2007, you have to add the icons to the Quick Access toolbar. To do so, follow these steps:

1)   Right-click the ribbon and choose Customize the Quick Access Toolbar.

2)   In the left dropdown, choose Commands Not in the Ribbon.

3)   Scroll down to the icons that start with S. Locate and click on Speak Cells. (see Figure 174)

Figure 174

Move the top five icons to the Quick Access toolbar.

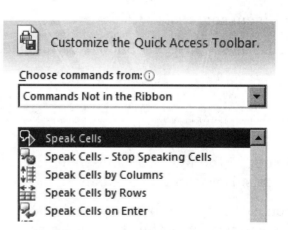

Click the Add>> button five times to move the Speak Cells icons to the Quick Access toolbar.

You can now select a range of cells and click the Speak Cells icon. Excel will read you the cells, so you can focus on the original paper from which you're keying the data.

Gotcha: If you accidentally select a million cells and ask Excel to speak the cells, you can click the Stop Speaking Cells icon to stop Excel from reading the cells. (I've worked for a couple managers who should have had this button on their forehead.)

Additional Details: You can choose whether Excel should read a rectangular range column by column or row by row by using the Speak Cells by Columns or Speak Cells by Rows icons.

The Speak on Enter icon is a fun icon. Imagine that your co-worker heads out to lunch on April Fool's Day. You could add the Speak on Enter icon to the Quick Access toolbar, turn on this feature, and then remove the icon from the Quick Access toolbar. Your co-worker returns from lunch, starts typing, and is perplexed to find that the computer starts repeating everything he types, reminiscent of the computer on *Star Trek*.

Gotcha: Be careful if you have kids in middle school. I showed some this feature, and they very quickly demonstrated that Excel knows how to say all words, including bad ones!

Summary: Excel's Text to Speech tools can help you verify your data entry or drive a co-worker batty.

Commands Discussed: Speak Cells

Excel 97-2003: Tools – Speech – Show Text to Speech Toolbar

ENTER SPECIAL SYMBOLS

Problem: I work in the music business, and I routinely have to enter copyright symbols. How can I do so easily?

Strategy: You can enter (c) followed by a space as a shortcut for the © symbol. You can use (r) as the shortcut for the registered trademark symbol, ®. For other special symbols, you can use Insert – Symbol to display the Symbol dialog, as shown in Figure 175.

Figure 175

This dialog offers many symbols.

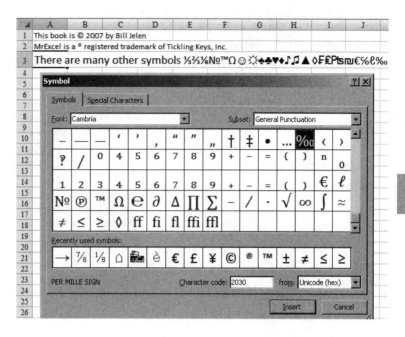

You simply select any symbol from the Symbol dialog and choose Insert to type the symbol in the cell.

Summary: To insert symbols in a worksheet, you use Insert – Symbol.

Commands Discussed: Insert – Symbol

FIND TEXT ENTRIES

Problem: I suspect that there are cells in my data that contain text numbers instead of numbers. I know that numbers entered as text cause a variety of problems. For example, although a formula such as =E3+E4 will include the text number in E3, most functions, such as SUM or AVERAGE, will ignore the text cells. Text versions of a number will sort to a different place than numeric versions. If I use a MATCH or VLOOKUP function, a text version of 3446 will not match a numeric version of 3446. How can I find text entries that need to be converted to numbers?

Strategy: In versions before Excel 2002, there was no easy way to visually locate these cells. In versions of Excel from Excel 2002 through Excel 2007, these text cells, as well as a variety of other potential errors, are noted by a dark green triangle in the upper-left corner of the cell. As shown in Figure 176, cells C3, E2, E3, E4, and E5 have triangles in their upper-left corners because they are text entries that look like numbers

Figure 176

Some cells contain text that looks like numbers.

	A	B	C	D	E
1	Invoice	Rep	Customer	Product	Sales
2	1041	Chaz	1183	ABC	216
3	1086	Amy	3446	DEF	150
4	1089	Deb	2506	DEF	127
5	1070	Amy	9484	XYZ	111
6	1061	Amy	4056	DEF	349
7	1047	Amy	5719	XYZ	345
8	1101	Ben	7142	ABC	345
9	1102	Chaz	8695	DEF	342

E3 — fx '150

Instead of looking for those little triangles, here's an easier way to locate all the text entries so you can convert them to numbers:

1) Select the entire range of data by selecting one cell and then pressing Ctrl+*.

2) Select Home – Find & Select – Go To Special. Excel will display the Go To Special dialog.

3) Select Constants and Text, as shown in Figure 177. In the process, deselect the three options Numbers, Logicals, and Errors.

Figure 177

Choose Constants and Text.

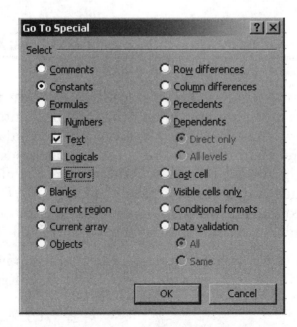

Results: All the text entries will be highlighted, as shown in Figure 178.

Figure 178

Any highlighted numbers are really text.

◢	A	B	C	D	E
1	Invoice	Rep	Customer	Product	Sales
2	1041	Chaz	1183	ABC	216
3	1086	Amy	3446	DEF	150
4	1089	Deb	2506	DEF	127

Part I

Additional Details: There are a number of ways to convert these cells from text to numbers. The easiest way is to get all the text cells in one contiguous range. If you can sort the data by column E descending, all the text entries will sort to the top of the list.

In Excel 2002 and newer versions, you can convert a contiguous range of text numbers. To do so, you use the Caution (exclamation point) dropdown and select Convert to Number. This method works only if the top-left cell in your selection contains a number stored as text.

Figure 179

Use the Caution dropdown to convert text to numbers.

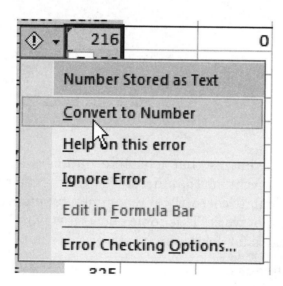

For earlier versions of Excel, you can use the following trick:

1) Enter a zero in a blank cell.

2)   Copy the cell with the zero by using Ctrl+C.

3)   Highlight the text cells.

4)   Choose Edit – Paste Special. In the Paste Special dialog that appears, select Values and Add and then click OK (see Figure 180).

Adding a zero to the text cells will cause them to be converted to real numbers.

Figure 180

Copy a zero to the Clipboard and then add it to the text numbers.

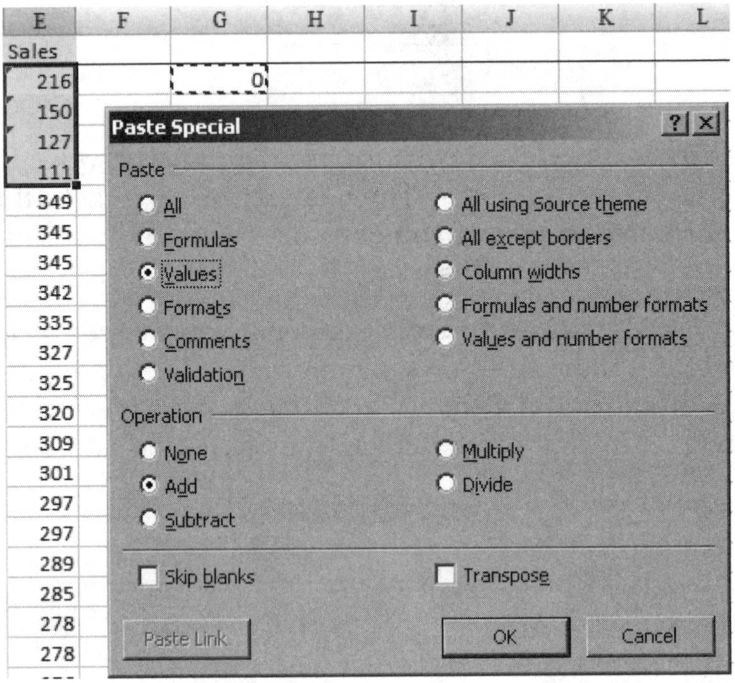

Summary: Text entries that look like numbers are a very confusing aspect of Excel. Formulas that directly refer to a cell that contains a text number will calculate correctly, but common functions such as SUM and AVERAGE will not work. This topic shows a way to locate text cells and a couple strategies for correcting them.

Commands Discussed: Home – Find & Select – Go To Special; Home – Paste – Paste Special

Excel 97-2003: Edit – Go To Special; Edit – Paste Special

WHAT DO ALL THE TRIANGLES MEAN?

Problem: In "Find Text Entries," you described the green triangles. What are the red triangles and purple triangles that sometimes appear in my worksheets (see Figure 181)? I've always wondered about those.

Figure 181

This worksheet is littered with green, red, and purple triangles.

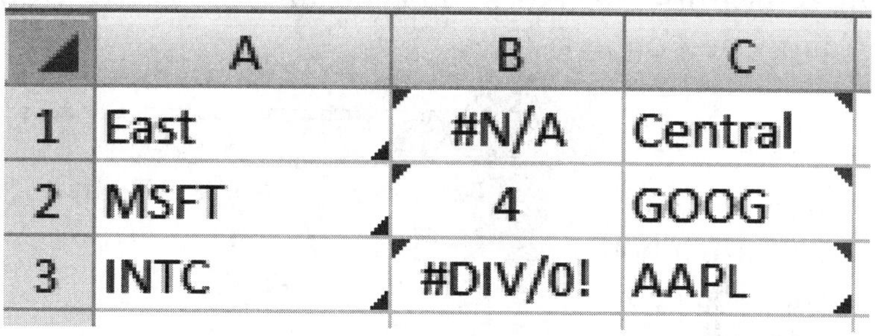

	A	B	C
1	East	#N/A	Central
2	MSFT	4	GOOG
3	INTC	#DIV/0!	AAPL

Strategy: Each color of triangle serves a different purpose.

The purple triangles in the lower-right corners of cells are SmartTag indicators. They often appear when you type a stock symbol in capital letters. If you have MapPoint installed, they also appear over certain geographic headings. As shown in Figure 182, if you select a cell with a purple triangle and open the I icon that appears, Excel will offer to insert a stock quote or a MapPoint map. You might have other SmartTags installed on your computer. For information about turning off Smart-Tags, see "Why Does Excel Mark All Cost Cells with an Indicator?" on page 888.

Figure 182

Do you find it odd that Microsoft fails to recognize Google's symbol?

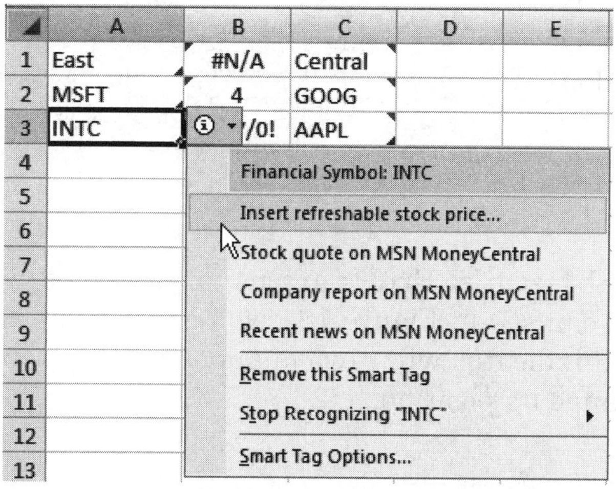

	A	B	C	D	E
1	East	#N/A	Central		
2	MSFT	4	GOOG		
3	INTC	ⓘ ▾ /0!	AAPL		
4					
5		Financial Symbol: INTC			
6		Insert refreshable stock price...			
7		Stock quote on MSN MoneyCentral			
8		Company report on MSN MoneyCentral			
9		Recent news on MSN MoneyCentral			
10		Remove this Smart Tag			
11		Stop Recognizing "INTC" ▸			
12		Smart Tag Options...			
13					

The red triangles in the top-right corners of cells are comment indicators. Where you see one of these, someone used Review – New Comment to add a bit of explanatory text to a cell. If you hover over a red indicator, Excel will display the comment, as shown in Figure 183. If the red indicators are bothering you, you can use Office Icon – Excel Options – Advanced – Display – For Cells with Comment, Show No Comments or Indicators. For more information, see "Leave Helpful Notes with Cell Comments" on page 749.

Figure 183

Red indicators are a note that someone added.

	A	B	C	D	E
1	East	#N/A	Central		
2	MSFT	4	GOOG		
3	INTC	#DIV/0!	AAPL		
4					
5					

Bill:
You'll have to manually link this to GOOG stock info!!

The final indicator is the green triangle in the top left of a cell. This indicator appears whenever Excel thinks you might have made an error. Figure 184 shows the complete list of errors. You can control which errors are flagged by selecting Office Icon – Excel Options – Formulas – Error Checking.

Figure 184

Control error checking in the Excel Options dialog.

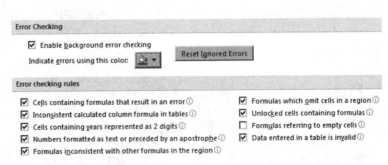

Error Checking

☑ Enable background error checking

Indicate errors using this color: [Reset Ignored Errors]

Error checking rules

☑ Cells containing formulas that result in an error ⓘ
☑ Inconsistent calculated column formula in tables ⓘ
☑ Cells containing years represented as 2 digits ⓘ
☑ Numbers formatted as text or preceded by an apostrophe ⓘ
☑ Formulas inconsistent with other formulas in the region ⓘ

☑ Formulas which omit cells in a region ⓘ
☑ Unlocked cells containing formulas ⓘ
☐ Formulas referring to empty cells ⓘ
☑ Data entered in a table is invalid ⓘ

Additional Details: Errors are usually flagged with green triangles, but as you can see in Figure 184, you can change the color used to flag errors. The indicator will always appear in the top left of the cell; you cannot change its position.

Summary: An array of triangles may litter your worksheet. Depending on your personal preference, you can turn them off or you can learn what they mean and take advantage of the help they offer.

Commands Discussed: Office Icon – Excel Options; Review – New Comment

Excel 97-2003: Tools – Error Checking – Options; Insert – Comment

See Also: "Why Does Excel Mark All Cost Cells with an Indicator?" (p. 888), "Leave Helpful Notes with Cell Comments" (p. 749)

WHY CAN'T EXCEL FIND A NUMBER?

Problem: The Excel Find and Replace dialog drives me crazy. I always have to worry about settings in the Options area. In the worksheet shown in Figure 185, I told Excel to look for values instead of formulas. I searched for the invoice amount 1630.17, but Excel cannot find the value. But then when I sort the data, there is a value of 1630.17 (in cell C15). How can Excel be so bad at finding numbers? Is this a floating-point arithmetic problem again?

Figure 185

Hey, Excel! Try looking under the mouse pointer.

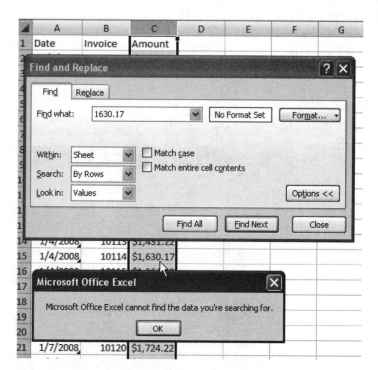

Strategy: You've pointed out a lot of the problems with Find and Replace. Let's take a quick review to uncover some of the problems. First, when you select Home – Find & Select – Find, Excel presents the simplified version of the Find and Replace dialog shown in Figure 186.

Figure 186

This simple Find will rarely work. Always click Options.

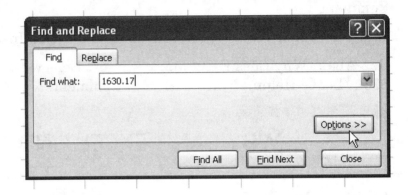

There are important settings hiding behind the Options button. These settings will often cause a Find to fail. Say that you have a calculation for sales tax in column D. Cell D3 shows 70.81 as the result of a formula. By default, Excel is searching the formulas instead of the values. If you tried the Find shown in Figure 187, Excel could find 0.06 (contained in the formula) but would not find 70.81.

Figure 187

By default, Excel searches the text of the formulas.

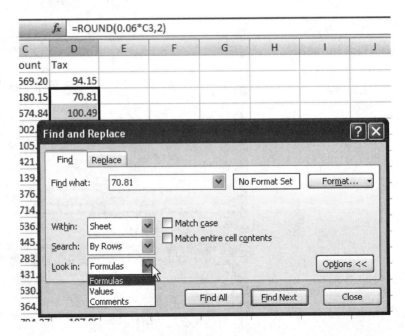

Searching the text of the formulas is a bit annoying. How often do you say to yourself, "Wow, I wonder in which cell I used the SQRTPI function?" But even more annoying are the other settings, such as Match Case and Match Entire Cell Contents. These settings can be useful, but if you happened to change them at 8:04 a.m. today and haven't closed Excel since then, even though you've opened and closed 40 other workbooks and are working on something completely different, Excel will remember that previous setting. You will often get stung by a strange setting left behind earlier in the day, or even a setting changed when a macro tried to use the Find command with Match Entire Cell Contents turned on.

To solve the problem in Figure 187, change Look In from Formulas to Values. Excel has no problem finding the cells with a result of 70.81.

So why can't Excel see the 1630.17 value? Excel is displaying cell C15 with a currency symbol and a comma, and in order to find the cell, you have to search for $1,630.17! In Figure 188, Excel correctly finds cell C15. Because Excel's forte is numbers, it's rather disappointing that Excel works like this. But when you understand it, you can work around it.

Figure 188

Search for $1,630.17, and Excel will find the match.

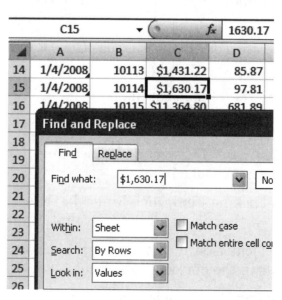

Additional Details: People often ask how they can search through all sheets in a workbook. You do this by changing the Within dropdown from Sheet to Workbook.

Additional Details: Amazingly, Excel can find cells that are displaying as number signs (#) instead of numbers. In Figure 189, many values are too wide for the column.

Figure 189

The column isn't wide enough.

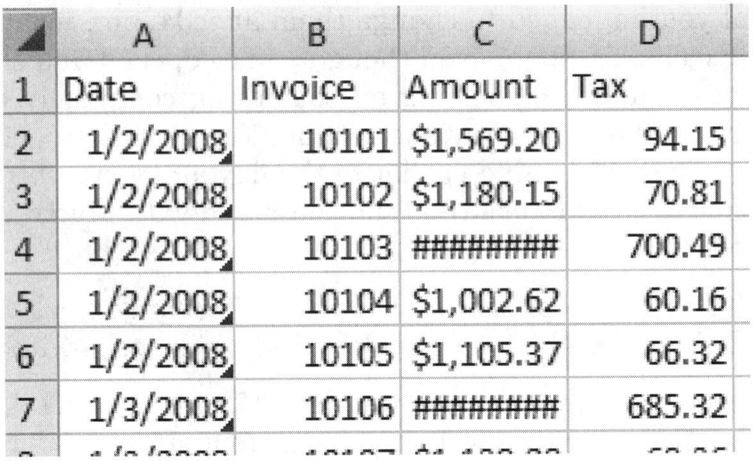

◢	A	B	C	D
1	Date	Invoice	Amount	Tax
2	1/2/2008	10101	$1,569.20	94.15
3	1/2/2008	10102	$1,180.15	70.81
4	1/2/2008	10103	########	700.49
5	1/2/2008	10104	$1,002.62	60.16
6	1/2/2008	10105	$1,105.37	66.32
7	1/3/2008	10106	########	685.32

Now, any sane person would make the column wider or turn on Shrink to Fit, but Excel allows you to perform the following rather crazy set of steps:

1) Select the range of numbers. Press Ctrl+F to display the Find dialog.

2) Type ### in the Find What dialog.

3) If the dialog is not showing the options, click the Options button.

4) Ensure that Look In is set to Values and that Match Entire Cell Contents is not checked.

5) Instead of clicking Find, click Find All. Excel adds a new section to the dialog, with a list of all the cells that contain ###.

6) While the focus is still on the dialog, click Ctrl+A. This will select all the cells in the bottom of the Find All dialog (see Figure 190).

You can now format just the selected cells. For example, you could choose fewer decimals or a smaller font size, or you could choose to display the numbers in thousands.

Figure 190

Use Find
All and then
Ctrl+A to se-
lect the results
of the Find.

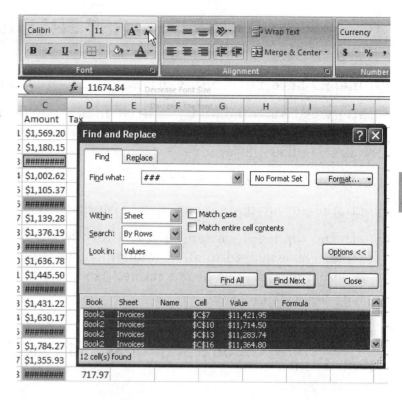

Gotcha: In Step 6, you are supposed to press Ctrl+A to select all of the found cells. Be careful that the focus is on the dialog box before pressing Ctrl+A. For example, if you change the font size, the focus would switch to the worksheet, even though the dialog is still displayed. Pressing Ctrl+A at this point would select all cells in the worksheet instead of just the matching cells. To reestablish focus on the dialog box, you need to click the title bar of the Find and Replace dialog.

Summary: Excel's Find function offers many maddening options. If you are trying to find a number, you need to type the number exactly as it is displayed.

Commands Discussed: Home – Find & Select – Find

Excel 97-2003: Edit – Find

GET FREE EXCEL HELP

Problem: I have a question which is not answered in this book.

Strategy: A large community of Excel fans are available at the MrExcel.com message board. Collectively, they answer over 30,000 questions each year. Follow these steps:

1) Browse to www.MrExcel.com

2) In the left navigation bar, choose Message Board

3) In the top right corner, click the link to Register. Registration is free. The site used to allow anonymous postings, but it became too confusing when two people named "anonymous" started participating in a conversation.

Figure 191

Register once.

4) As you register, a question asks you to confirm that you are 13 or older. Please choose this appropriately, or you will not be able to post.

5) Click the appropriate forum. Most Excel questions, including macro programming questions, should go in the Excel Questions forum. (Figure 192)

Figure 192

Choose the forum.

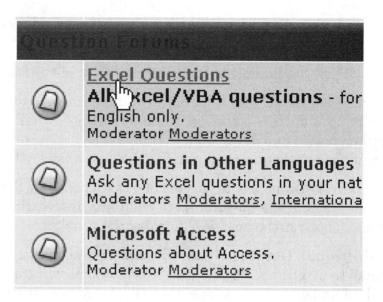

6) Click the New Topic icon.

Figure 193

Start a new topic.

7) Use a meaningful subject. "Pivot Table Calculated Fields" is a good subject. "Help" or "Please Help" is not a good subject.

8) Type your question. Read over the question to make sure that someone who has not been dealing with your spreadsheet for the last hour can get a good sense of the meaning. If it would help to

see the spreadsheet, post a copy of the spreadsheet using Colo's tool (See Additional Detail, below).

9)   Click the Submit button at the bottom of the form.

Within a minute, your question will appear in the forum. Other readers will check out the question. Usually within 15 minutes, someone will either post a clarifying question or a suggestion on how to proceed. If someone asks a question, provide the best answer that you can.

Usually, within a few iterations of questions, you will have your answer. Sometimes, if the question is particularly interesting, a discussion will break out over the best way to solve the problem.

Additional Details: At the bottom of the message board, there are links to utilities. Colo provided a utility that will copy a range of an Excel spreadsheet and render it as HTML code that can be pasted in the message board.

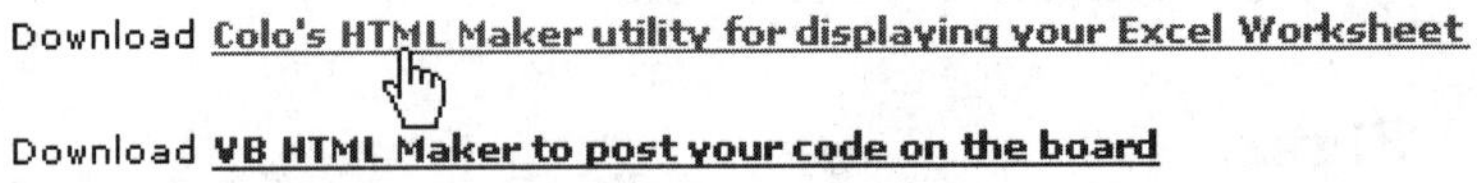

Figure 194

Colo's utility for posting a view of your spreadsheet.

Download Colo's HTML Maker utility for displaying your Excel Worksheet

Download VB HTML Maker to post your code on the board

Additional Details: Over 250,000 answers are archived and searchable. Before posting your question, spend a few minutes searching to see if the problem has already been solved.

Summary: A community of people can answer your Excel questions.

PART 2

CALCULATING WITH EXCEL

COPY A FORMULA
THAT CONTAINS RELATIVE REFERENCES

Problem: I have 5,000 rows of data. After entering a formula to calculate gross profit percent for the first row, as shown in Figure 195, how do I copy the formula down to other rows?

Figure 195

After building a formula, copy it to all rows.

	G2				fx =IF(E2>0,1-F2/E2,"NA")	
	B	C	D	E	F	G
1	Product	Date	Quantity	Unit Price	Unit Cost	GP%
2	XYZ	1/1/04	10000	22.81	10.22	55.2%
3	DEF	1/2/04	1000	22.57	9.84	
4	ABC	1/2/04	5000	20.49	8.47	

Part II

Strategy: All of the cell references in the Figure 195 formula are known as relative references. The amazing thing about Excel is that when you copy a formula, all of the relative cell references are automatically adjusted. If you copy a formula from row 2 down to row 3, as shown in Figure 196, then every relative reference pointing at row 2 will change to point to row 3.

Figure 196

E2 changes to E3, and F2 changes to F3.

	G3				fx =IF(E3>0,1-F3/E3,"NA")	
	B	C	D	E	F	G
1	Product	Date	Quantity	Unit Price	Unit Cost	GP%
2	XYZ	1/1/04	10000	22.81	10.22	55.2%
3	DEF	1/2/04	1000	22.57	9.84	56.4%

So, the solution to the problem is simply to copy the formula down to all the other rows. A shortcut for doing this is to select the cell and then double-click the fill handle to copy the formula down to all rows with values in the adjacent column. The fill handle is the square dot in the lower right corner of the selection rectangle.

Additional Details: Relative references will move in all four directions. In Figure 197, for example, if you copy the formula in cell F7 to E6, the referenced cell will change from D3 to C2.

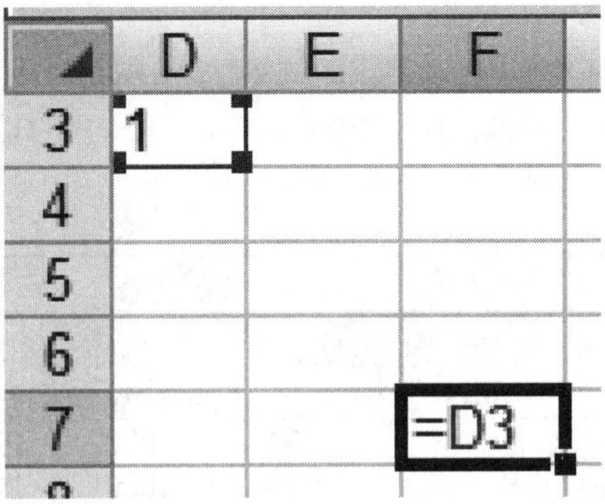

Figure 197

The formula in F2 points to D3.

In Figure 198, you can see how the formula copied from F7 to E6:G8 will change.

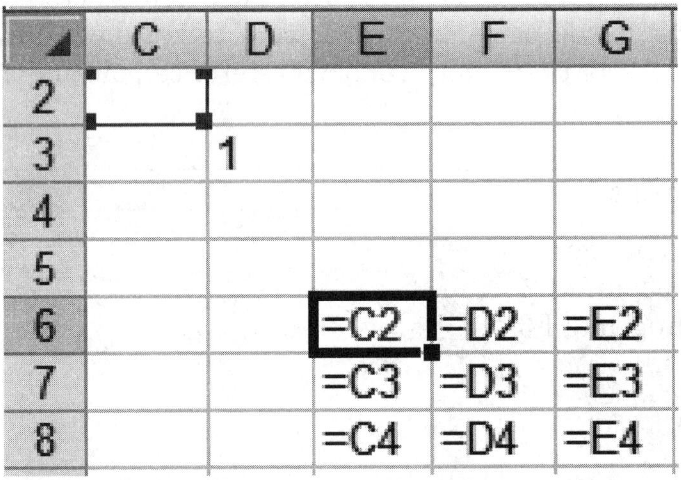

Figure 198

The reference to D3 changes to C2.

Additional Details: Figure 198 was shot in Show Formulas mode. To enter Show Formulas mode, press Ctrl+`. (On a U.S. keyboard the grave accent is on the same key as the tilde, ~, just below the Esc key.) To toggle back to regular mode, press Ctrl+` again.

Gotcha: It is possible to copy a formula so that it will point to a cell that does not exist. As shown in Figure 199, what would happen if you copied C4 to B3?

Figure 199

Cell C4 points to the top row of the spreadsheet.

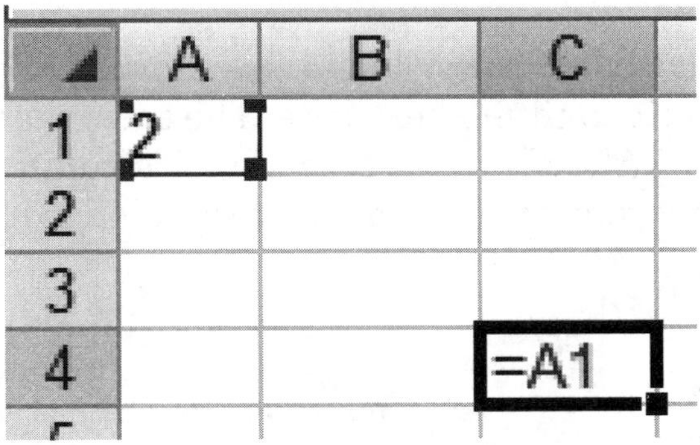

◢	A	B	C
1	2		
2			
3			
4			=A1

The reference to A1 would have to point to the cell one row above and one column to the left of A1. That cell does not exist, so Excel will return a #REF error, as shown in Figure 200.

Figure 200

The cell reference wants to point to row zero, but because it doesn't exist, you get a reference error.

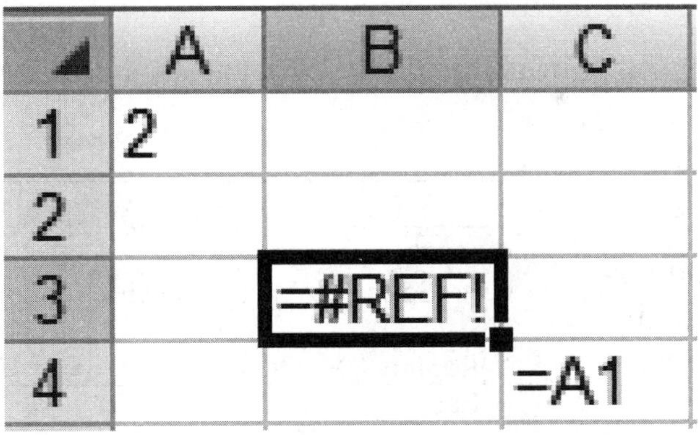

◢	A	B	C
1	2		
2			
3		=#REF!	
4			=A1

Summary: In Excel, you can enter a formula in one place and copy it to many other places, and it will miraculously still work. This is because a regular cell reference, such as B1, is a relative reference.

COPY A FORMULA
WHILE KEEPING ONE REFERENCE FIXED

Problem: I have 5,000 rows of data. As shown in Figure 201, each row contains a quantity and the unit price. The sales tax rate for all orders is shown in cell C1. After I enter a formula to calculate the total with sales tax in the first row, how do I copy the formula down to other rows??

Figure 201

This formula works in row 4....

	F4				f_x	=ROUND((D4*E4)*C1,2)

	A	B	C	D	E	F
1	Sales Tax Factor:		106.5%			
2						
3	Region	Product	Date	Qty	Unit Price	Total
4	East	XYZ	1/1/04	4	22.81	97.17
5	Central	DEF	1/2/04	10	22.57	
6	East	ABC	1/2/04	8	20.49	
7	Central	XYZ	1/3/04	8	22.48	

If I copy the formula in F4 to F5, I get an invalid result, as shown in Figure 202.

Figure 202

...but the formula fails in all other rows.

	F5				f_x	=ROUND((D5*E5)*C2,2)

	A	B	C	D	E	F
1	Sales Tax Factor:		106.5%			
2						
3	Region	Product	Date	Qty	Unit Price	Total
4	East	XYZ	1/1/04	4	22.81	97.17
5	Central	DEF	1/2/04	10	22.57	0.00
6	East	ABC	1/2/04	8	20.49	

Look at the formula in the formula bar in Figure 202. As I copy the formula, the references to D4 and E4 changed as expected. However, the reference to C1 moved to C2. I need to find a way to copy this formula and always have the formula reference C1.

Note: This may be the most important technique in the entire book. I once had a manager who entered every formula in every data set by hand. I didn't have the heart to tell him there was an easier way.

Strategy: You need to indicate to Excel that the reference to C1 in the formula is absolute. You do this by inserting a dollar sign before the C and before the 1 in the formula. For example, you would change the formula in F4 to =ROUND((D4*E4)*$C$1,2).

As you copy this formula down to other rows in your data set, the portion that refers to $C$1 will continue to point at $C$1, as shown in Figure 203.

Figure 203

The dollar signs in the C1 reference ensure that it always points to C1.

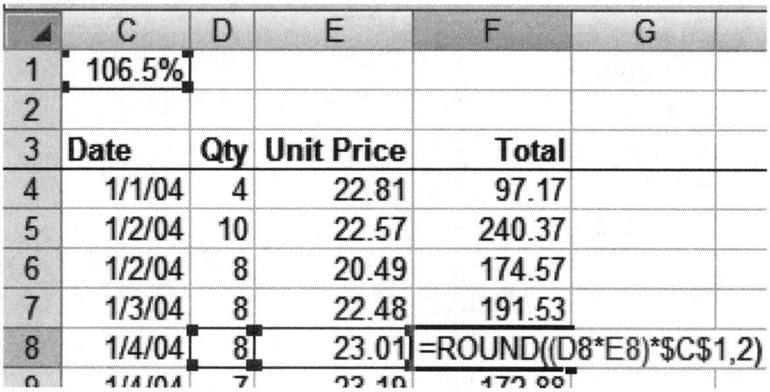

	C	D	E	F	G
1	106.5%				
2					
3	Date	Qty	Unit Price	Total	
4	1/1/04	4	22.81	97.17	
5	1/2/04	10	22.57	240.37	
6	1/2/04	8	20.49	174.57	
7	1/3/04	8	22.48	191.53	
8	1/4/04	8	23.01	=ROUND((D8*E8)*$C$1,2)	
9	1/4/04	7	23.10	172.88	

Part II

Additional Details: See "Create a Multiplication Table" on page 150 to learn the effect of using just one dollar sign in a reference instead of two. Read "Simplify the Entry of Dollar Signs in Formulas" on page 154 to learn a cool shortcut for entering the dollar signs automatically.

Summary: Entering dollar signs in a reference will lock the reference and make it absolute. No matter where you copy the formula, it will continue to point to the original cell.

Functions Discussed: =ROUND()

See Also: "Create a Multiplication Table" (p. 150), "Simplify the Entry of Dollar Signs in Formulas" (p. 154)

CREATE A MULTIPLICATION TABLE

Problem: I want to create a multiplication table to help my kids in school. In Figure 204, I want to be able to enter a single formula in cell B2 that I can copy to the entire table.

Figure 204

Can one formula always point to row 1 and column 1?

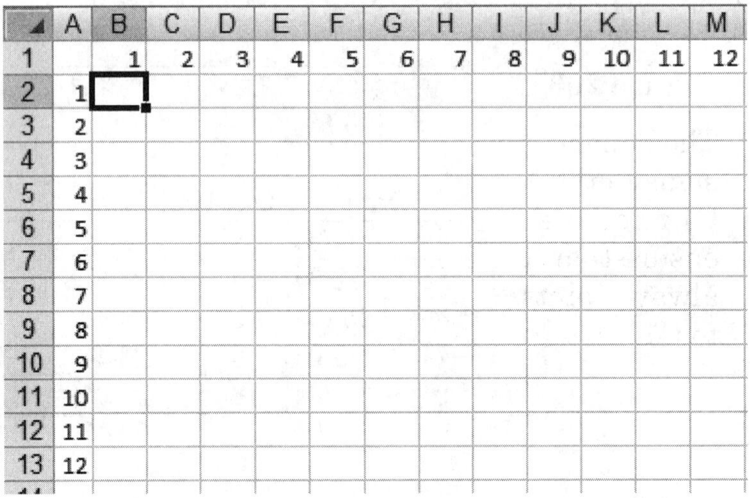

Strategy: In "Copy a Formula While Keeping One Reference Fixed," you learned how to use an absolute reference, such as $C$1, so that Excel would not change from column C or row 1 as it copied the formula. To create a multiplication table, you need to use a mixed reference. A mixed reference, such as $A2, will lock the formula to column A while allowing the row to change. A mixed reference, such as B$1, will lock the row to row 1 while allowing the column to change.

The formula you need for the multiplication table is a formula that will multiply whatever is in row 1 above the cell by whatever is in column A to the left of the cell.

To have a reference that always points to row 1, you use something in the format of B$1. To have a reference that points to column A, you use a reference in the format of $A2.

1)   As shown in Figure 205, enter the formula =$A2*B$1 in B2.

Figure 205

Multiply column A by row 1.

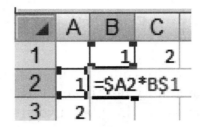

2)   Copy the formula in B2 to the entire range.

Result: Excel will always properly multiply column A by row 1, as shown in Figure 206.

Part II

Figure 206

=$A13*M$1 creates the multiplication table.

M13							f_x	=$A13*M$1			
	A	B	C	D	E	F	G	H	I	J	K	L	M
1		1	2	3	4	5	6	7	8	9	10	11	12
2	1	1	2	3	4	5	6	7	8	9	10	11	12
3	2	2	4	6	8	10	12	14	16	18	20	22	24
4	3	3	6	9	12	15	18	21	24	27	30	33	36
5	4	4	8	12	16	20	24	28	32	36	40	44	48
6	5	5	10	15	20	25	30	35	40	45	50	55	60
7	6	6	12	18	24	30	36	42	48	54	60	66	72
8	7	7	14	21	28	35	42	49	56	63	70	77	84
9	8	8	16	24	32	40	48	56	64	72	80	88	96
10	9	9	18	27	36	45	54	63	72	81	90	99	108
11	10	10	20	30	40	50	60	70	80	90	100	110	120
12	11	11	22	33	44	55	66	77	88	99	110	121	132
13	12	12	24	36	48	60	72	84	96	108	120	132	144

Summary: Using a single dollar sign in a cell reference will create a mixed reference. Only the row or column will be fixed as you copy the formula.

See Also: "Copy a Formula While Keeping One Reference Fixed" (p. 148), "Simplify the Entry of Dollar Signs in Formulas" (p. 154)

CALCULATE A SALES COMMISSION

Problem: The VP of sales in my company has dreamed up the most convoluted sales plan in the history of the world. Rather than just paying the reps a straight commission, this plan involves paying a base rate and a 2% bonus based on the product sold, and a monthly profit sharing bonus. For the spreadsheet shown in Figure 207, I need to create a formula that can be copied to all rows and all months.

Figure 207

Perhaps the VP of sales designed the commission plan to test your knowledge of Excel!

	A	B	C	D	E	F	G	H	I	J
1	Base Rate	2%		Bonus Factor:	102%	100%	104%			
2										
3						SALES			COMMISSION	
4										
5	Rep	Product	Prod Rate	Customer	Jan	Feb	Mar	Jan	Feb	Mar
6	Jones	ABC	5%	General Motors	15205	9039	13768			
7	Jones	DEF	8%	Molson, Inc.	18716	7023	9876			
8	Doe	DEF	8%	Verizon	11560	12456	15853			

Strategy: This formula will contain all four reference types: relative, mixed, the other mixed, and absolute. While entering the first formula in H6, you want to base the commission calculation on the January sales in E6. As you copy the formula from January to February, you want the E6 reference to be able to change to F6. As you copy the formula down to other rows, you want the E6 to change to E7, E8, and so on. Thus, the E6 portion of the formula needs to be a relative reference and will have no dollar signs.

You multiply the sales by the base rate in B1. As you copy the formula to other months and rows, it always needs to point to B1. Thus, you need to use dollar signs before the B and before the 1: $B$1.

To incorporate the product bonus, you need to multiply sales by the product rate in column C. All the months in row 6 have to refer to C6. All the months in row 7 have to refer to C7. Thus, you need a mixed reference where column C is locked; use the address of $C6.

Finally, to address the monthly profit sharing bonus, the entire commission calculation is multiplied by the bonus factor shown in row 1. The

January commission calculation uses the factor in E1. The February factor is in F1. The March factor is in G1. In this case, you need to allow the formula to point to different columns but always to row 1. This requires a mixed reference of E$1.

Now that you have the four components of the formula, you can enter this formula in E6: =E6*($B$1+$C6)*E$1 (see Figure 208).

Figure 208

The formula in E6 contains one of each type of reference.

	A	B	C	D	E	F	G	H	I	J
	PMT				=E6*($B$1+$C6)*E$1					
1	Base Rate	2%		Bonus Factor:	102%	100%	104%			
2										
3						SALES			COMMISSION	
4										
5	Rep	Product	Prod Rate	Customer	Jan	Feb	Mar	Jan	Feb	Mar
6	Jones	ABC	5%	General Motors	15205	9039	13768	=E6*($B$1+$C6)*E$1		

Part II

Result: As shown in Figure 209, you have created a single formula that can be copied to all columns and rows of your data set.

Figure 209

When you copy the formula, it points to the correct cells.

	A	B	C	D	E	F	G	H	I	J
	J7				=G7*($B$1+$C7)*G$1					
1	Base Rate	2%		Bonus Factor:	102%	100%	104%			
2										
3						SALES			COMMISSION	
4										
5	Rep	Product	Prod Rate	Customer	Jan	Feb	Mar	Jan	Feb	Mar
6	Jones	ABC	5%	General Motors	15205	9039	13768	1086	632.7	1002
7	Jones	DEF	8%	Molson, Inc.	18716	7023	9876	1909	702.3	1027

Summary: The concept of relative, absolute, and mixed references is one of the most important concepts in Excel. Being able to use the right reference will allow you to create a single formula that can be copied everywhere.

SIMPLIFY THE ENTRY OF DOLLAR SIGNS IN FORMULAS

Problem: It is a pain to type the dollar signs in complex formulas such as the formula shown in Figure 210. How can I make this job easier?

Figure 210

Typing dollar signs is a pain.

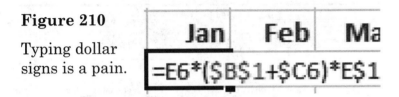

Press the F4 key as you are entering a formula to toggle a reference through the four possible reference types. Here's an example of how to use it:

1) As shown in Figure 211, start to type the formula =E6*(B1.

Figure 211

Type B1 without $.

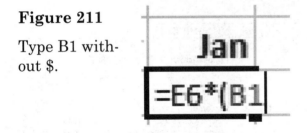

2) Immediately after you type B1, press the F4 key. Excel will insert both dollar signs in the B1 reference, as shown in Figure 212.

Figure 212

F4 affects the reference next to the insertion character.

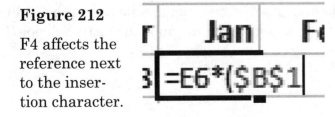

3) Press the F4 key again. Excel changes the reference from an absolute reference to a mixed reference, with the row portion of the reference locked, as shown in Figure 213.

Figure 213

Next, F4 locks just the row.

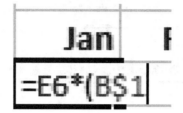

4) Press the F4 key again. Excel changes the reference to a mixed reference, with the column portion of the reference locked, as shown in Figure 214.

Part II

Figure 214

Next, F4 locks just the column.

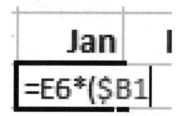

5) Press the F4 key once more. Excel changes the reference back to a relative reference, as shown in Figure 215.

Figure 215

Eventually, F4 returns to a relative reference.

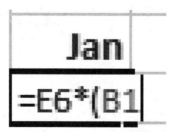

Here are the steps for entering the complex formula shown in Figure 210:

1) Type =E6*(B1.

2) Press the F4 key once.

3)   Type +C6.

4)   Press the F4 key three times. Your formula will now appear as shown in Figure 216.

Figure 216

Press F4 three times to lock the column.

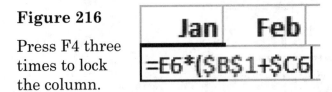

5)   Type)*E1, as shown in Figure 217.

Figure 217

To lock the row, press F4 twice.

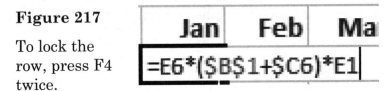

6)   Press the F4 key twice to change E1 to a reference with the row locked, as shown in Figure 218.

Figure 218

E$1 always points to row 1, three columns to the left.

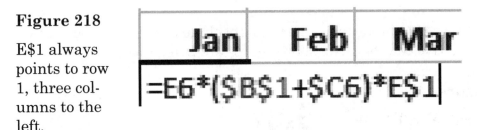

7)   Press Ctrl+Enter to accept the formula without moving the cell pointer to the next cell, as shown in Figure 219.

Figure 219

Ctrl+Enter to keep the cell pointer in the current cell.

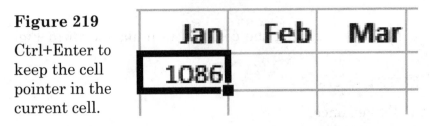

8) Use the mouse to grab the fill handle (the square dot in the lower-right corner of the cell) and drag it to the right by two cells, as shown in Figure 220.

Figure 220

Drag the fill handle to the right.

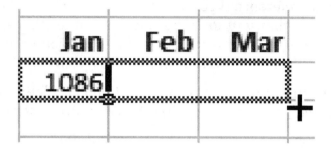

Excel will copy the formula from January to the other two months, as shown in Figure 221.

Part II

Figure 221

The formula is copied to all columns.

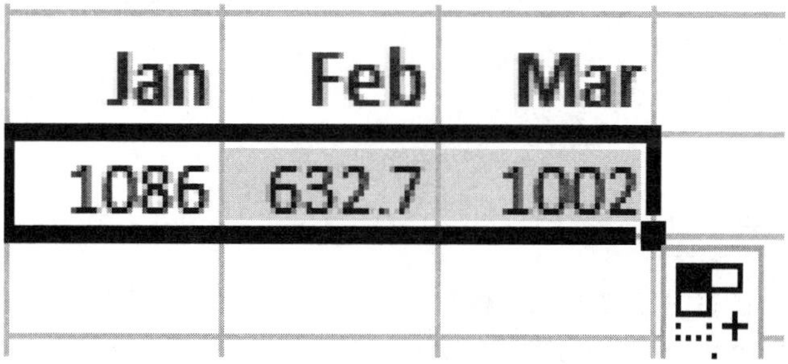

Jan	Feb	Mar
1086	632.7	1002

9) Double-click the fill handle. Excel will copy the three cells down to all the rows that contain data, as shown in Figure 222.

Figure 222

Double-click the fill handle to copy the formula down.

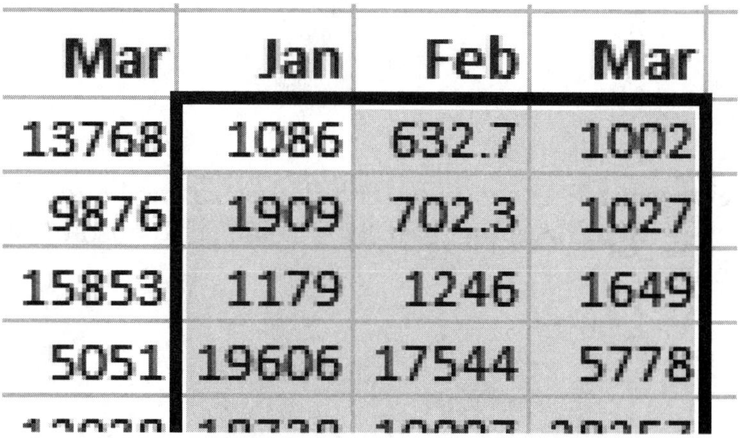

Mar	Jan	Feb	Mar
13768	1086	632.7	1002
9876	1909	702.3	1027
15853	1179	1246	1649
5051	19606	17544	5778

Additional Details: You might find mixed references confusing. As you work on building the first formula, you might know that you need to point to C7. Enter C7 in the formula and then use F4 to toggle between the various reference types. Say to yourself, "Okay, there is a dollar sign before the C that will lock the column and let the row change. Is that what I need?" As long as you say this to yourself without your lips moving, your officemates won't think any less of you.

Further Information: If you did not add the dollar signs as you typed the formula, you can still use the F4 trick later. Here's how:

1)   Use the mouse to highlight the proper reference in the formula bar, as shown in Figure 223.

Figure 223

Highlight a cell reference in the formula bar.

2)   Press the F4 key to toggle the highlighted reference through the four reference styles, as shown in Figure 224.

Figure 224

Press F4 to toggle through the four reference styles.

Summary: You can use the F4 key to easily add dollar signs to a reference in order to toggle it from relative to absolute to mixed to the other mixed.

LEARN R1C1 REFERENCING
TO UNDERSTAND FORMULA COPYING

Problem: All of a sudden, the column letters along the top of my spreadsheet have been replaced by numbers, as shown in Figure 225. None of the formulas I enter will work. What's wrong?

Figure 225

Why is column B now column 2?

R6C4	▼		f_x	=R[-1]C+RC[-1]-RC[

◢	1	2	3	4	5
1	Loan	8,000		Term	
2	Rate	5%		Pmt	$350.9
3					
4	#	Pmt Amt	Interest	Balance	
5				8,000	
6	1	$350.97	33.33333	$7,682.36	
7	2	$350.97	32.00984	$7,363.40	

Part II

Strategy: Relax. There are two ways of naming cells, and in this case, someone has turned on the R1C1 style of addressing. To return to the normal A1 style of cell addressing, select Office Icon – Excel Options – Formulas. Uncheck the R1C1 Reference Style check box (see Figure 226).

Figure 226

This setting affects all workbooks.

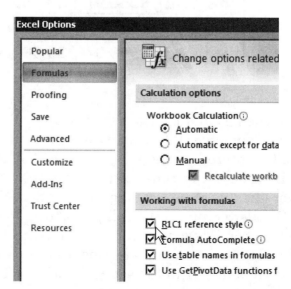

But wait. While you are here, you can learn something fascinating about spreadsheets. In the topic "Copy a Formula That Contains Relative References," I say that it's miraculous that Excel can automatically change a formula as you copy it. If you take a couple of minutes to learn about this other method of cell addressing, you will understand that it may not be so amazing after all.

When Dan Bricklin and Bob Frankston invented VisiCalc, they used the A1 style of cell naming. When Mitch Kapor started selling Lotus 1-2-3, he used the same style. When Microsoft came out with its first spreadsheet product, Microsoft Multiplan, it used a very different method of cell addressing, known as R1C1. In the Microsoft system, the rows are numbered just as in the A1 system. However, the columns are also numbered. Each cell is given a name, such as "R4C8," which stands for the cell at row 4, column 8. This is the cell that you and I know as H4.

In the R1C1 style, the formulas are interesting. Look at the A1-style formula shown in cell D6 in Figure 227.

Figure 227

Consider the formula in D6.

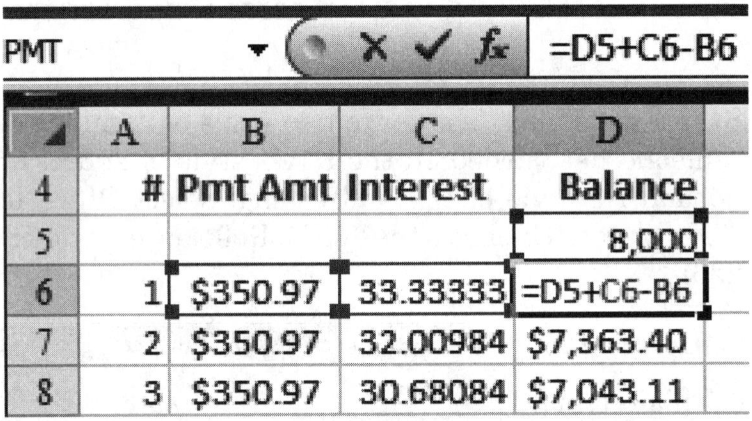

| PMT | ▼ | ✕ ✓ *fx* | =D5+C6-B6 |

◢	A	B	C	D
4		#	Pmt Amt	Interest	Balance
5				8,000
6		1	$350.97	33.33333	=D5+C6-B6
7		2	$350.97	32.00984	$7,363.40
8		3	$350.97	30.68084	$7,043.11

The formula in the formula bar says =D5+C6-B6. But think about this formula in plain language. What it really means is "Take the cell just above me, add the interest in the cell just to the left of me, and subtract the payment in the cell two cells to the left of me." Formulas in R1C1 style are rather like this plain language description. If you want to enter a formula in D6 that points to the cell just above, for example, you use =R[-1]C. The number in square brackets after the R indicates to how many rows ahead or back you are referring. In this case, row 5 is one row above row 6, so you put a -1 in the square brackets. There is no number after the C portion of the address, which means you are referring to the same column as the cell that contains the formula.

To refer to a cell that is two cells to the left of the cell with the formula, you use =RC[-2].

As shown in Figure 228, the formula from Figure 168 can be restated in R1C1 style as follows: =R[-1]C+RC[-1]-RC[-2].

Figure 228

When you get the hang of them, R1C1 formulas are intuitive.

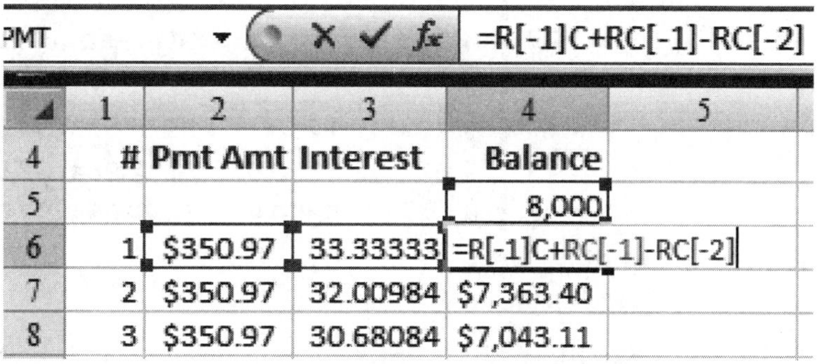

PMT	▼	●	✗ ✓	fx	=R[-1]C+RC[-1]-RC[-2]

◢	1	2	3	4	5
4		# Pmt Amt	Interest	Balance	
5				8,000	
6	1	$350.97	33.33333	=R[-1]C+RC[-1]-RC[-2]	
7	2	$350.97	32.00984	$7,363.40	
8	3	$350.97	30.68084	$7,043.11	

Part II

All relative references in R1C1 style have a number in square brackets—either after the R or after the C or both.

It is very interesting to see how this style handles absolute addresses. As shown in Figure 229, the A1 style formula in B6 is an absolute formula that always points to cell E2. The formula in A1 style is =$E$2.

Figure 229

An absolute reference in A1 style. Are the dollar signs really that intuitive?

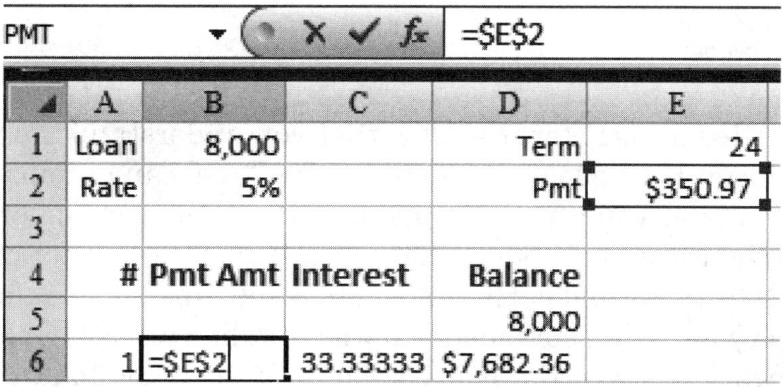

PMT	▼	●	✗ ✓	fx	=$E$2

◢	A	B	C	D	E
1	Loan	8,000		Term	24
2	Rate	5%		Pmt	$350.97
3					
4	#	Pmt Amt	Interest	Balance	
5				8,000	
6	1	=$E$2	33.33333	$7,682.36	

To enter a similar absolute reference in R1C1 style, you do not include square brackets in the address. As shown in Figure 230, the formula =R2C5 will always point to cell E2.

Figure 230

R2C5 is Row 2, Column 5.

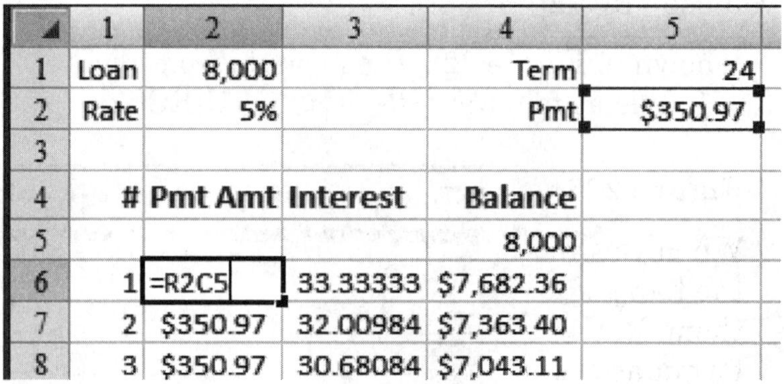

◢	1	2	3	4	5
1	Loan	8,000		Term	24
2	Rate	5%		Pmt	$350.97
3					
4	#	Pmt Amt	Interest	Balance	
5				8,000	
6	1	=R2C5	33.33333	$7,682.36	
7	2	$350.97	32.00984	$7,363.40	
8	3	$350.97	30.68084	$7,043.11	

It is also possible to have mixed references. Flip back to Figure 205, for example. Figure 231 shows that formula in R1C1 style.

Figure 231

This row, column 1 (RC1) times row 1 of this column (R1C).

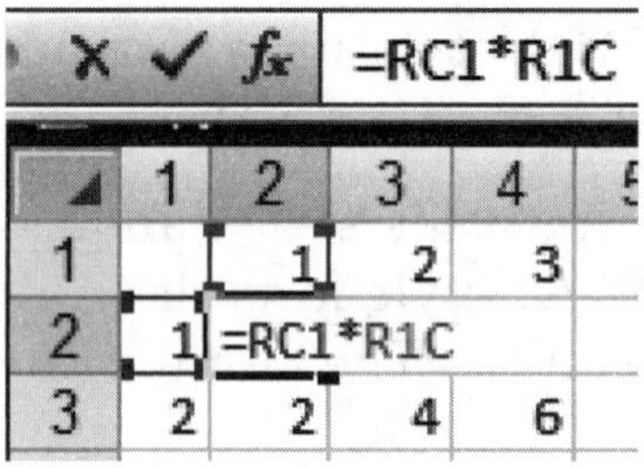

| X ✓ fx | =RC1*R1C |

◢	1	2	3	4	5
1		1	2	3	
2	1	=RC1*R1C			
3	2	2	4	6	

Additional Details: Now that you understand the basics of R1C1-style formulas, you can appreciate how Excel can automatically change a formula as you copy it. Remember that Microsoft invented this method for its Multiplan product. Lotus 1-2-3 was the dominant spreadsheet in the late 1980s and early 1990s. Microsoft was battling for market share. Everyone using spreadsheets was familiar with the A1 style. No one would want to learn the R1C1 style in order to switch to Microsoft. So, in its Excel product, Microsoft developed an elaborate system to actually store the formulas in R1C1 style but to translate the R1C1 formulas to A1 style to make it easier for all the Lotus fans to understand.

By default, Microsoft starts with A1-style addressing. However, remember from Figure 226 that you are just one check mark away from switching to R1C1-style addressing.

To really see R1C1 in its glory, examine the amortization table example in Formula View mode. (Press Ctrl+` to toggle into Formula View mode.) Figure 232 shows Formula View mode in A1 style. As you can see, every formula in column D is different.

Figure 232

Isn't it a miracle that Excel changes every formula from row to row?

	#	Pmt Amt	Interest	Balance
4				
5				=B1
6	1	=$E$2	=D5*$B$2/12	=D5+C6-B6
7	=1+A6	=$E$2	=D6*$B$2/12	=D6+C7-B7
8	=1+A7	=$E$2	=D7*$B$2/12	=D7+C8-B8
9	=1+A8	=$E$2	=D8*$B$2/12	=D8+C9-B9
10	=1+A9	=$E$2	=D9*$B$2/12	=D9+C10-B10
11	=1+A10	=$E$2	=D10*$B$2/12	=D10+C11-B11

Figure 233 shows the Formula View mode in R1C1 style.

Figure 233

In R1C1 style, every formula is identical to the one above it.

#	Pmt Amt	Interest	Balance
			=R[-4]C[-2]
1	=R2C5	=R[-1]C[1]*R2C2/12	=R[-1]C+RC[-1]-RC[-2]
=1+R[-1]C	=R2C5	=R[-1]C[1]*R2C2/12	=R[-1]C+RC[-1]-RC[-2]
=1+R[-1]C	=R2C5	=R[-1]C[1]*R2C2/12	=R[-1]C+RC[-1]-RC[-2]
=1+R[-1]C	=R2C5	=R[-1]C[1]*R2C2/12	=R[-1]C+RC[-1]-RC[-2]
=1+R[-1]C	=R2C5	=R[-1]C[1]*R2C2/12	=R[-1]C+RC[-1]-RC[-2]

In A1 style, it seems *amazing* that Excel can change a reference from D10 to D11 when the formula is copied down. However, look closely at the formulas in each row of rows 7 and higher in the R1C1 style shown in Figure 233. Each formula in a column is identical to the formula located just above it!

While VisiCalc and Lotus 1-2-3 made the formula replication seem amazing because of their A1 reference style, if the Multiplan invention of R1C1 style had taken hold, it would not seem amazing at all because, in fact, every formula is exactly identical as you copy it down through the rows. Microsoft actually had a better system. Just as Beta was superior to VHS but fell by the wayside due to market share, Microsoft's superior R1C1 style lost its battle, and Microsoft chose A1 style as the default in Excel.

If you ever plan on writing VBA macros in Excel, it is important that you understand the R1C1 style of formulas. For general use in Excel, you never really need to totally understand the R1C1 style, but it is interesting to see how Microsoft's R1C1 style is actually better than A1 when you're copying formulas in a spreadsheet.

Summary: You should learn R1C1-style formulas to better understand how Excel replicates formulas across a worksheet.

Commands Discussed: Office Icon – Excel Options – Formulas

Excel 97-2003: Tools – Options -- General

CREATE EASIER-TO-UNDERSTAND FORMULAS WITH NAMED RANGES

Problem: As you can see in Figure 234, my worksheet contains several different formulas. How can I create easier-to-understand formulas?

Figure 234

This formula is not very intuitive.

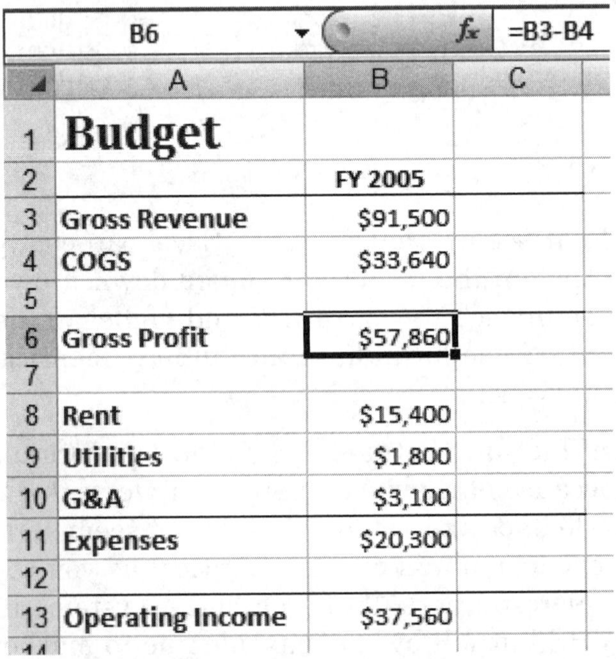

	B6	▼	f_x	=B3-B4
◢	A		B	C
1	**Budget**			
2			**FY 2005**	
3	**Gross Revenue**		$91,500	
4	**COGS**		$33,640	
5				
6	**Gross Profit**		$57,860	
7				
8	**Rent**		$15,400	
9	**Utilities**		$1,800	
10	**G&A**		$3,100	
11	**Expenses**		$20,300	
12				
13	**Operating Income**		$37,560	

Strategy: It would be easier to understand the results if each component of every formula were named for what it represented and not just for the cell it came from. You can therefore use named ranges to make formulas easier to understand:

1) Select cell B3. In the Name box (the area to the left of the formula bar), type Revenue and press Enter, as shown in Figure 235.

Figure 235

Type Revenue in the Name Box and press Enter.

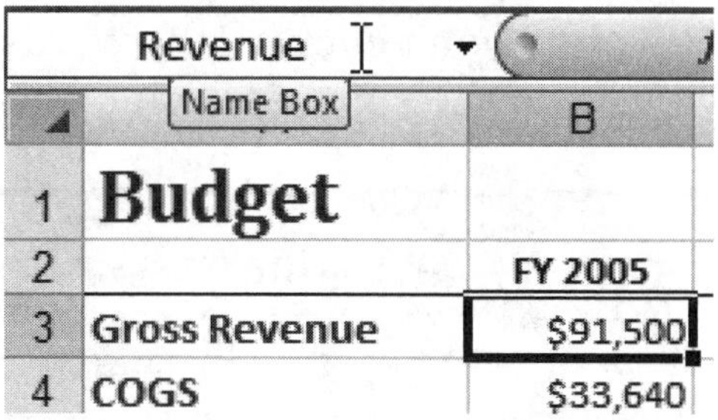

	A	B
1	**Budget**	
2		FY 2005
3	**Gross Revenue**	$91,500
4	**COGS**	$33,640

2) Select cell B4. Click in the Name box, type COGS, and press Enter.

3) Clear the formula in B6. Reenter the formula and use the mouse to select the cells. Type =. Using the mouse, touch B3. Type -. Using the mouse, touch B4. Excel will enter the formula as =Revenue-COGS, as shown in Figure 236. This is easier to understand than a typical formula.

Figure 236

For novice Excellers, this formula is easier to comprehend than one with many confusing numbers and letters.

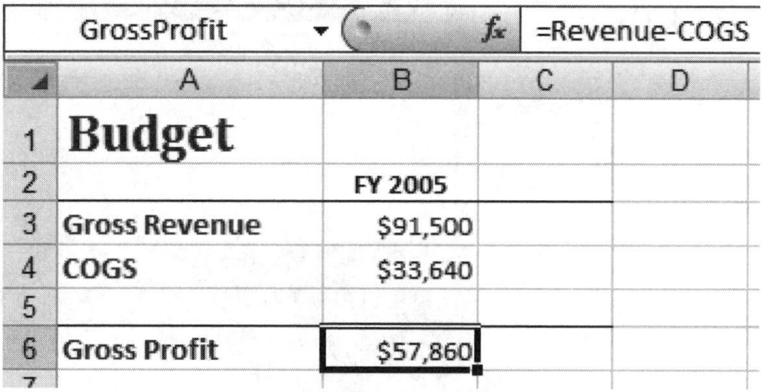

GrossProfit f_x =Revenue-COGS

	A	B	C	D
1	**Budget**			
2		FY 2005		
3	**Gross Revenue**	$91,500		
4	**COGS**	$33,640		
5				
6	**Gross Profit**	$57,860		
7				

Gotcha: You need a lot of foresight to use this technique. In order to have this work automatically, you are supposed to be smart enough to create the range names before you enter the formula. However, most people create a formula first and then decide to make the worksheet easier to understand. To assign range names after creating formulas, follow these steps:

1) Select Formulas – Define Name dropdown – Apply Names, as shown in Figure 237. **Gotcha:** Don't click on the words Define Name; click on the dropdown icon to the right of Define Name.

Figure 237

Apply Names is hidden in the Define Name drop-down.

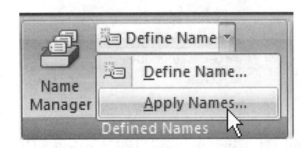

2) Select all the names you want to apply, as shown in Figure 238.

Figure 238

Select multiple names and click OK.

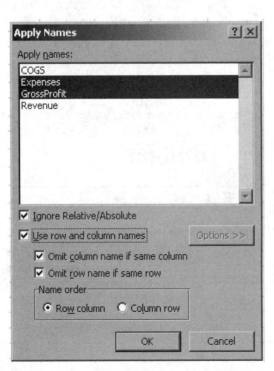

Results: A formula like =B6-B11 will be updated to =GrossProfit-Expenses, as shown in Figure 239.

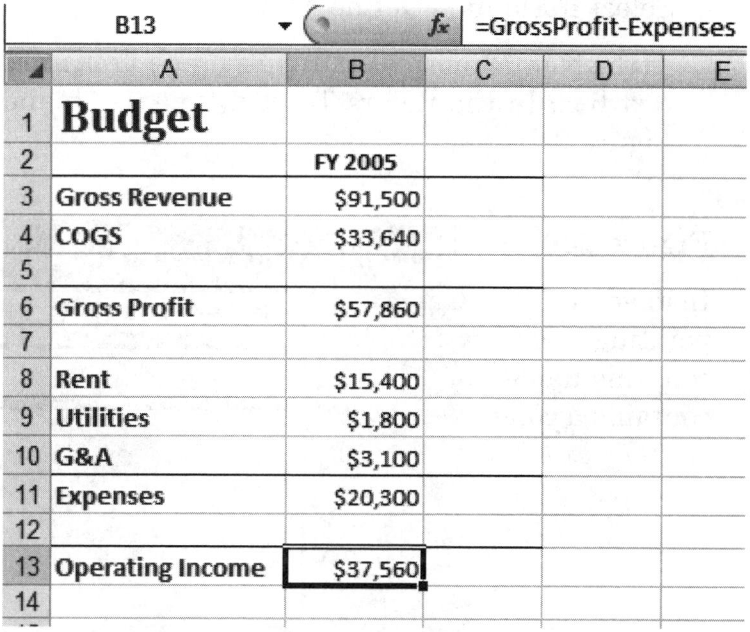

Figure 239

Excel rewrites formulas to use the selected names.

B13				f_x	=GrossProfit-Expenses	
	A	B	C	D	E
1	**Budget**				
2		**FY 2005**			
3	Gross Revenue	$91,500			
4	COGS	$33,640			
5					
6	Gross Profit	$57,860			
7					
8	Rent	$15,400			
9	Utilities	$1,800			
10	G&A	$3,100			
11	Expenses	$20,300			
12					
13	Operating Income	$37,560			
14					

Part II

Summary: To create plain language formulas, you assign a range name to each cell in a formula and use the mouse when entering the formula. To assign range names to a formula after the fact, you use Formulas – Define Name dropdown – Apply Names.

Commands Discussed: Formulas – Define Name dropdown – Apply Names

Excel 97-2003: Insert – Name – Apply

USE NAMED CONSTANTS TO STORE NUMBERS

Problem: I've seen how to assign a name to a cell. Is it also possible to assign a name to a constant? That could be useful for a number, such as a local sales tax rate, that changes periodically.

Strategy: Yes, you can assign names to constants. To do so, you follow these steps:

1)   Select Formula – Define Name.

2)   In the New Name dialog, type a name such as SalesTax in the Name text box. In the Refers To box, type 0.065 and then click OK (see Figure 240).

Figure 240

Instead of pointing to a cell, this name contains a constant.

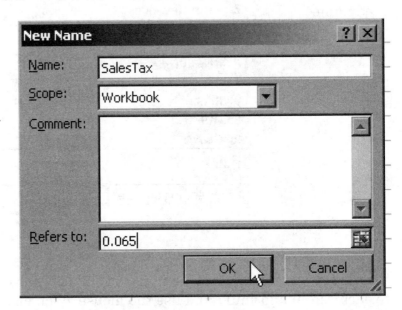

3)   In this workbook, you can now use a formula such as =SalesTax*D2, as shown in Figure 241.

Figure 241

Use the defined name in a formula.

	E2		▼	fx	=SalesTax*D2	
◢	A	B	C	D	E	F
1	Item	Qty	Price	Total	Tax	
2	PR197	100	1.54	154	10.01	

4)   If the tax rate changes later, select Formulas – Name Manager. In the Name Manager, select the constant's name and click Edit (see Figure 242). Change the value stored in the name.

Figure 242

To change a
name later,
use the Name
Manager.

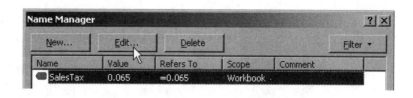

Summary: To name a constant in a workbook, you use Formulas – Define Name, type in the name of the constant, and then define the constant in the Refers To box.

Commands Discussed: Formulas – Define Names, Formulas – Name Manager

Excel 97-2003: Insert – Name – Define.

Part
II

ASSIGN A NAME TO A FORMULA

Problem: I use the same formula thousands of times on 20 worksheets (see Figure 243). Every time I want to change the formula, I have to edit all 20 sheets. Is there a way to make a formula variable so I can change it in just one place?

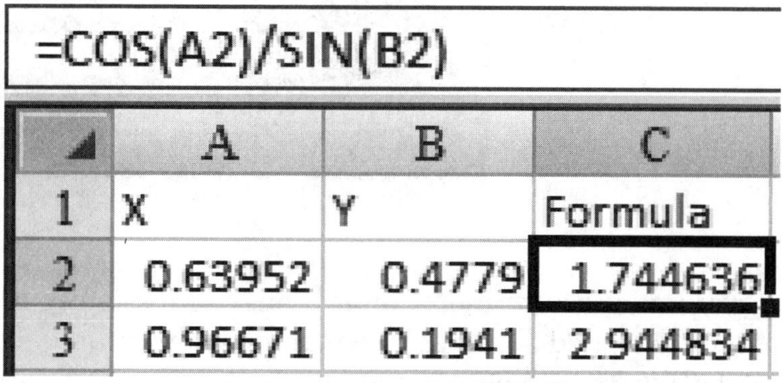

Figure 243

You have thousands of instances of this formula on 20 worksheets.

=COS(A2)/SIN(B2)

	A	B	C
1	X	Y	Formula
2	0.63952	0.4779	1.744636
3	0.96671	0.1941	2.944834

Strategy: You can assign a name to the formula.

Think about what you do when you set up a named range. For instance, you could assign the name MyData to cell D1, as shown in Figure 244.

Figure 244

Usually a name refers to a cell.

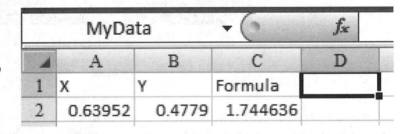

However, when you look at the definition of this name in the Names Manager dialog (which you open by selecting Formulas – Name Manager – Edit), you will see that MyData is really equal to a formula called =Sheet1!$D$1, as shown in Figure 245.

Figure 245

A named range is really a formula that points to a range.

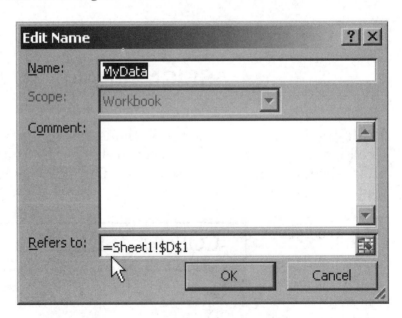

If you understand this, then it is easy to make the leap that any formula can be assigned a name. For example, you could define a formula named GlobalFormula. Then, when you enter =GlobalFormula in the thousand cells on each of the 20 sheets, they will each inherit the formula from GlobalFormula.

Gotcha: Remember the topic "Learn R1C1 Referencing to Understand Formula Copying"? If you were using R1C1-style addressing, then all the formulas in column C would be identical, as shown in Figure 246, and assigning the same formula to all the cells would be an easy task.

Figure 246

If R1C1 had won over A1, this would be simple.

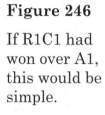
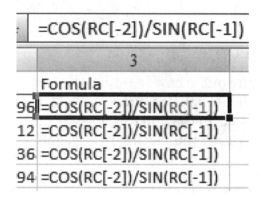

However, people don't tend to use R1C1-style references, so you will have to build this formula the hard way. In A1-style references, each formula is different in each cell, as shown in Figure 247.

Figure 247

In A1 style, every formula is different.

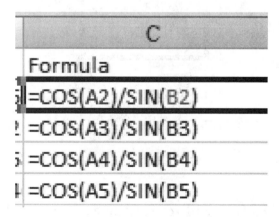

If you want GlobalFormula to be =COS(A2), you cannot just write that. You need to develop a formula that takes the COS function of the cell two cells to the left of the current cell. This is possible, but it requires a whole bunch of new functions that you might never have used before.

Consider the INDIRECT() function. =INDIRECT("A2") will return the value that is in A2. When you try to use the results of an INDIRECT function in another calculation, it always helps to put the INDIRECT function inside a SUM function, as shown here:

=SUM(INDIRECT("A2"))

So, if you wanted to take the cosine of A2, you could use the following formula:

=COS(SUM(INDIRECT("A2")))

The next trick to figure out is how to return the text of A2 to refer to a cell. To do this, you use the ADDRESS function. =ADDRESS(2,1) will return the text A2 because A2 is in the 2nd row, first column. =ADDRESS(52,26) would return Z52 because this is the fifty-second row, twenty-sixth column.

Is there a function that will return the row number of the cell that contains the formula? Yes. The ROW function will return the row number of the cell that contains the formula, as shown in Figure 248.

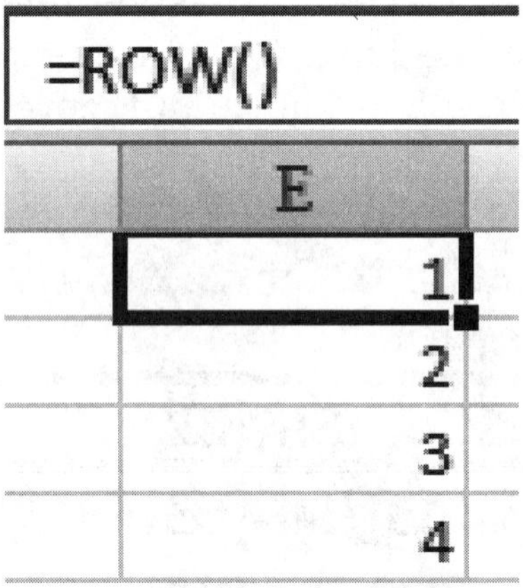

Figure 248

The ROW function will return the row number of the cell that contains the formula.

Similarly, =COLUMN() will return the column number of the cell that contains the formula, as shown in Figure 249.

Figure 249

COLUMN will return the current column number.

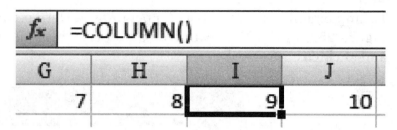

So, you could write a formula that returns the name of the cell, like the one shown in Figure 250.

Figure 250

ADDRESS can return a cell address.

	A	B	C	D	E	F	G
1	$A$1	$B$1	$C$1	$D$1	$E$1	$F$1	
2	$A$2	$B$2	$C$2	$D$2	$E$2	$F$2	
3	$A$3	$B$3	$C$3	$D$3	$E$3	$F$3	
4	$A$4	$B$4	$C$4	$D$4	$E$4	$F$4	

E1   fx =ADDRESS(ROW(),COLUMN())

Part II

To return the address of a cell two columns to the left of the current cell, you add a -2 after the COLUMN() function, as shown in Figure 251.

Figure 251

Adjust the formula to point two columns to the left.

C1   fx =ADDRESS(ROW(),COLUMN()-2)

	A	B	C	D	E	F	G	H
1			$A$1	$B$1	$C$1	$D$1		
2			$A$2	$B$2	$C$2	$D$2		
3			$A$3	$B$3	$C$3	$D$3		

Therefore, you use the following formula in order to take the cosine of the cell two cells to the left of the cell containing the formula:

=COS(SUM(INDIRECT(ADDRESS(ROW(),COLUMN()-2))))

The actual current formula is =COS(A2)/SIN(A2). This is the formula you would use:

=COS(SUM(INDIRECT(ADDRESS(ROW(),COLUMN()-2))))/ SIN(SUM (INDIRECT(ADDRESS(ROW(),COLUMN()-1))))

To implement this, you choose Formulas – Define Name. As shown in Figure 252, in the New Name box, you type a name, type the formula, and click OK.

Figure 252

Assign this formula to a name.

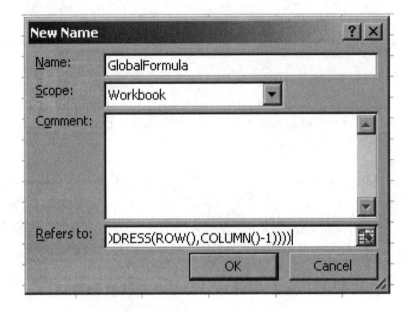

Results: A name is added to the Workbook Names. The name is assigned your formula, as shown in Figure 253.

Figure 253

The name appears in the Name Manager.

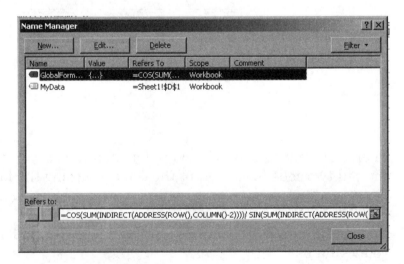

Now, in any cell in the workbook, you can use the formula =GlobalFormula, as shown in Figure 254.

Figure 254

Enter =Global-
Formula.

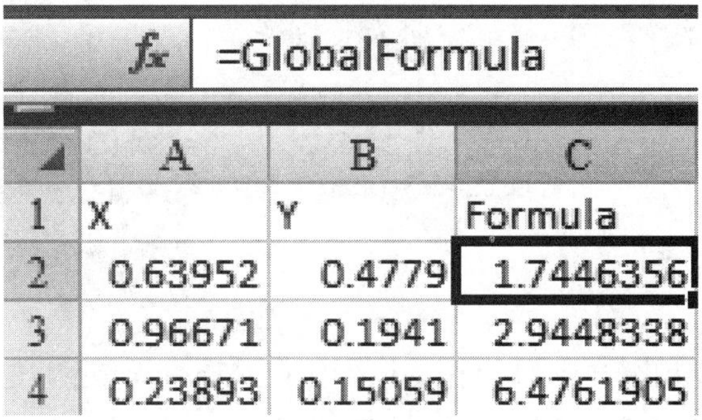

f_x	=GlobalFormula	
A	B	C
1	X	Y	Formula
2	0.63952	0.4779	1.7446356
3	0.96671	0.1941	2.9448338
4	0.23893	0.15059	6.4761905

Additional Details: Any time you need to change the formula, you can simply edit it in the Name Manager.

Gotcha: The Refers To box in the Edit Name dialog is one of the most maddening things in all of Excel. Editing a formula in that box is sometimes difficult. For example, if you want to change the final 1 to a 2 (in order to refer to B instead of A), you will have to highlight the 1, as shown in Figure 255, and type a 2.

Figure 255

Select the
1 and then
change it to a
2.

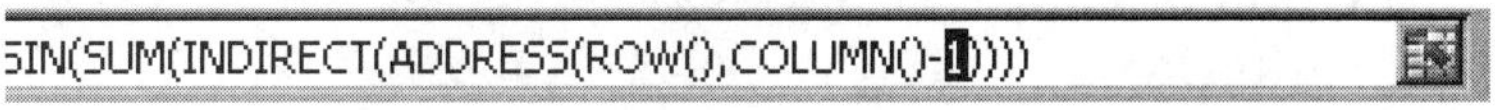

`SIN(SUM(INDIRECT(ADDRESS(ROW(),COLUMN()-1))))`

If you attempt to use the Left Arrow key or Right Arrow key to move through the formula, Excel will insert a cell address to the left or right of the current cell. For example, in Figure 256, I've placed the cell pointer after the word Indirect.

Figure 256

Randomly
click in the
reference box.

Refers to: `=COS(SUM(INDIRECT,ADDR`

Part
II

One press of the Left Arrow key will insert +Sheet1!$B$2 in the formula, as shown in Figure 257.

Figure 257

Arrow to a new character, Excel inserts cell addresses!

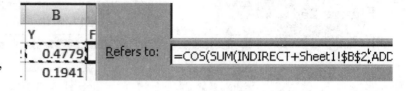

The main problem with this is that sometimes the formula is so long that you cannot see the end of it in the Refers To box. When you try to click near the end of the field and press the Right Arrow key, you end up adding references to the formula.

One solution is to click early in the formula and drag all the way to the end. This forces Excel to scroll to the end of the formula, as shown in Figure 258.

Figure 258

To move to the end of the formula, you could use the mouse to select all characters.

A better solution is to press the F2 key, which is a toggle that changes the status bar from Edit to Enter (see Figure 259). When the status bar says Edit, you can use the arrow keys to move through the Refers To box without inserting cell addresses. If you attempt to use a navigation key while in Enter mode, the status bar indicator changes to Point. You can press F2 again to exit Point mode.

Figure 259

Press F2 to toggle the indicator in the status bar.

Summary: Named formulas can save the day, although they can be incredibly complex.

Commands Discussed: Formulas – Define Name; Formulas – Name Manager

Excel 97-2003: Insert – Name – Define

Functions Discussed: =COS(), =SIN()

TOTAL WITHOUT USING A FORMULA

Problem: My manager called on the telephone, asking for the total sales of a particular product. I need to quickly find a total. Is there a faster way than entering a formula?

Strategy: While you're on the phone with your manager, you can highlight the numbers in question, as shown in Figure 260. The QuickSum indicator in the status bar will show the total of the highlighted cells.

Figure 260

Select numeric cells, and the total appears in the status bar.

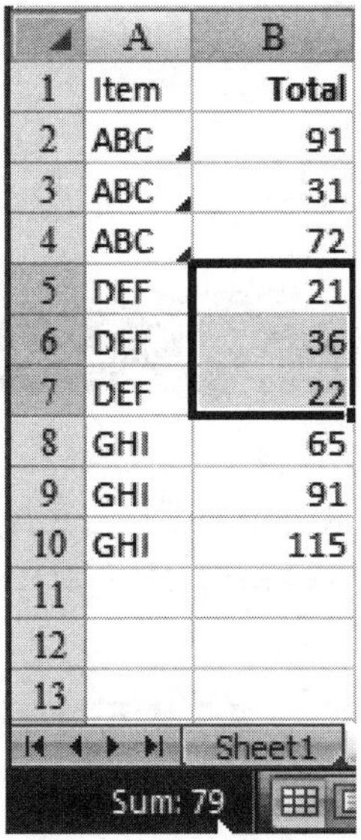

	A	B
1	Item	Total
2	ABC	91
3	ABC	31
4	ABC	72
5	DEF	21
6	DEF	36
7	DEF	22
8	GHI	65
9	GHI	91
10	GHI	115
11		
12		
13		

Sheet1

Sum: 79

Additional Details: New in Excel 2007, the status bar can simultaneously show a count, a numeric count, a sum, and so on. You can right-click the status bar and choose the statistics you would like to show (see Figure 261).

Figure 261

Choose which statistics to show.

Gotcha: In prior versions of Excel, it is possible to turn off the status bar. If the status bar is not visible at the bottom of your screen after selecting a range of numeric cells, select View – Status Bar from the Excel 2003 menu. You cannot turn off the status bar in Excel 2007.

Gotcha: The Average, Numerical Count, and Sum parts of the status bar will ignore text entries within the selection. In Figure 262, for example, Sum and Numerical Count only factor in B2:B3.

Figure 262

Count, Numerical Count, and Sum will ignore text cells.

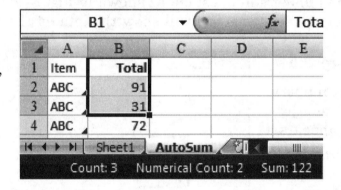

However, as shown in Figure 263, if one of the highlighted cells is an error such as #N/A, the Sum and Average statistics will not appear in the status bar.

Figure 263

An error cell will cause the Sum statistic to disappear.

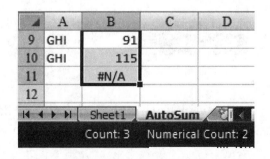

Sometimes, when you are trying to find a lone #N/A within a column, it is fastest to start at the top of the column, hold down the Shift key, and start pressing PgDn. As soon as the Sum statistic disappears, you know that you have recently paged past the first #N/A error. (With 1 million rows, it might be faster to use Home – Find & Select – Go To Special – Errors.)

Summary: The QuickSum feature in the status bar will show the total, average, count, and other statistics for the selected cells.

Excel 97-2003: The status bar could show only one statistic at a time. You could choose the statistic by right-clicking the status bar. You could also turn on or off the status bar by selecting View – Status Bar.

ADD TWO COLUMNS
WITHOUT USING FORMULAS

Problem: I've prepared a summary of sales by rep for the month. Due to an accounting glitch, someone gave me a similar file with additional sales made on the last day of the month, as shown in Figure 264. I need to add the new sales to the old sales. There is no need to keep the original two columns of partial month's sales.

Figure 264

Add column H
to column B.

	A	B	C	D	E	F	G	H
1	XYZ Co - Commission Statement for June							
2								
3	Sales Rep	Sales	Comm %	Commission	Base	Salary		New Sales
4	George Wa	13,125	5%	656.25	1000	1,656.25		609
5	John Adam	11,706	5%	585.30	1000	1,585.30		983
6	Thomas Jef	14,513	5%	725.65	1000	1,725.65		205
7	James Mad	6,857	4%	274.28	1000	1,274.28		536
8	James Mon	6,247	4%	249.88	1000	1,249.88		355
9	John Quinc	10,646	5%	532.30	1000	1,532.30		269
10	Andrew Jac	8,640	4%	345.60	1000	1,345.60		795
11	Martin Var	14,864	5%	743.20	1000	1,743.20		215
12	William He	14,105	5%	705.25	1000	1,705.25		676
13	John Tyler	10,387	5%	519.35	1000	1,519.35		877
14	James K. Po	5,400	4%	216.00	1000	1,216.00		78
15	Zachary Ta	5,380	4%	215.20	1000	1,215.20		214
16	Millard Fil	8,578	4%	343.12	1000	1,343.12		943
17	Franklin Pi	7,233	4%	289.32	1000	1,289.32		60
18	James Buch	13,612	5%	680.60	1000	1,680.60		795
19	Abraham Li	13,904	5%	695.20	1000	1,695.20		871
20	Andrew Joh	5,084	4%	203.36	1000	1,203.36		10
21	Ulysses S. (	14,077	5%	703.85	1000	1,703.85		203
22	Rutherford	15,534	5%	776.70	1000	1,776.70		894
23	Total	199,892		9,460.41	19000	28,460.41		

Strategy: You can copy the new values in column H and use Home – Paste dropdown – Paste Special – Add to add the values to column B. Follow these steps:

1) Select H4:H22. Select Home – Copy to copy the cells to the Clipboard.

2) Move the cell pointer to B4. Select Home – Paste dropdown – Paste Special. (Don't select the large Paste icon; instead, choose the dropdown below the icon.)

3) As shown in Figure 265, in the Paste Special dialog box, choose the Add option in the Operation section. Optionally, also choose Values in the Paste section in order to preserve the formatting in column B. Click OK.

Figure 265

Choose Values and Add.

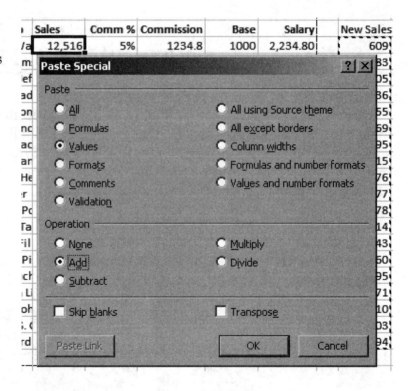

Results: As shown in Figure 266, the new sales values from column H are added to the values in column B. You can safely delete column H.

Figure 266

Excel adds the range on the Clipboard to column B.

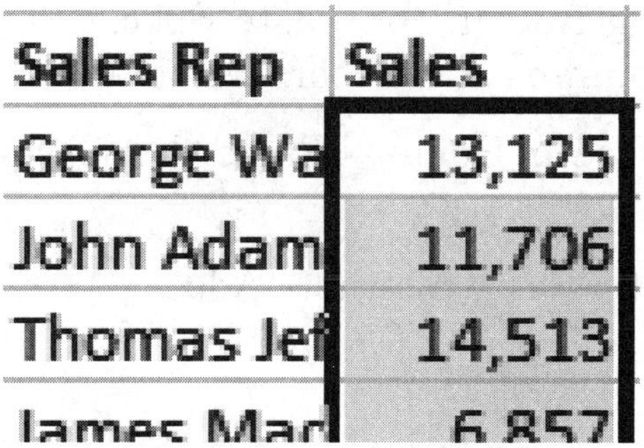

Sales Rep	Sales
George Wa	13,125
John Adam	11,706
Thomas Jef	14,513
James Mad	6,857

Gotcha: If column B is properly formatted and the temporary data in H is not formatted, the default Paste All option will cause the formats in column B to be lost. You should therefore consider choosing both Values and Add in the Paste Special dialog.

Additional Details: The technique described here for selecting Add in the Paste Special dialog has an interesting effect if you add cells to a range that contains a formula. Amazingly, Excel handles it correctly. For example, in Figure 267, cell D4 contains a formula.

Figure 267

Before pasting, this cell contains a formula.

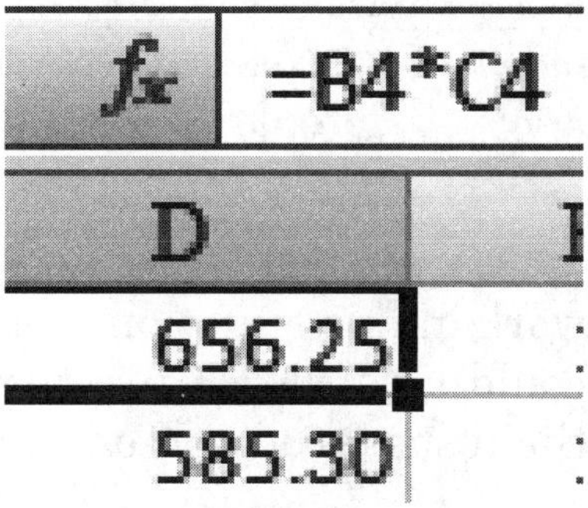

f_x | =B4*C4

D	
656.25	:
585.30	:

If you select Add in the Paste Special dialog to add a value to this formula, Excel changes the formula to add the value, as shown in Figure 268.

Figure 268

After Paste Special Add, Excel modifies the formula.

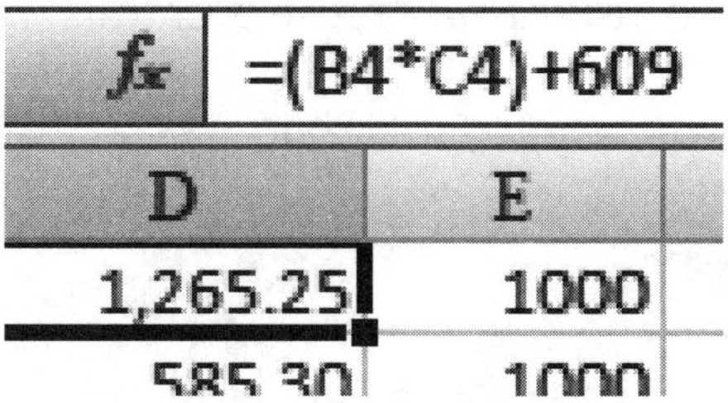

f_x | =(B4*C4)+609

D	E
1,265.25	1000
585.30	1000

Summary: Selecting Add in the Paste Special dialog is useful when you're adding two columns of numbers without using a formula.

Commands Discussed: Home – Paste dropdown – Paste Special – Add

Excel 97-2003: Edit – Paste Special – Add

HOW TO CALCULATE SALES IN EXCESS OF A QUOTA

Problem: In the spreadsheet shown in Figure 269, I need to enter a formula to calculate the excess of sales over quota on a record-by-record basis. How do I do it?

Figure 269

It seems as if an IF function would solve this.

▲	A	B	C	D	E
1	Salesrep	Date	Quota	Sales	Over Quota
2	Joe	1/1/2008	800	666	
3	Dan	1/1/2008	800	1290	
4	Mary	1/1/2008	800	896	

A couple functions would work in this situation. For instance, you could use an IF function. You could give the IF function a logical test and specify one calculation if the test is true and one calculation if the test is false.

If the sales value is greater than the quota, the IF function would return the result of sales (D2) minus the quota (C2). If the sales did not exceed the quota, the IF function would return a 0.

The syntax for the IF function is =IF(*logical test, value if true, value if false*). Thus, as shown in Figure 270, the formula would be:

=IF(D2>C2,D2-C2,0)

Figure 270

=IF(D2>C2,D2-C2,0)

Most people
would use an
IF to solve
this.

	A	B	C	D	E
1	Salesrep	Date	Quota	Sales	Over Quota
2	Joe	1/1/2008	800	666	0
3	Dan	1/1/2008	800	1290	490
4	Mary	1/1/2008	800	896	96

Alternate Strategy: Instead of using IF, you can use the MAX function. One parameter to the MAX function in this example will be D2-C2. This number will be either positive or negative, as shown in column F in Figure 271.

Figure 271

F2   *fx* =D2-C2

Is there a
good way to
keep only the
positive values
from F?

	A	B	C	D	E	F
1	Salesrep	Date	Quota	Sales	Over Quota	Temp
2	Joe	1/1/2008	800	666		-134
3	Dan	1/1/2008	800	1290		490
4	Mary	1/1/2008	800	896		96
5	Joe	1/2/2008	800	559		-241

To keep only the positive numbers, you can ask Excel to calculate the larger of either the calculation in F or zero. This works because the maximum of 0 and a positive number is the positive number. The maximum of 0 and a negative number is 0. As shown in Figure 272, using =MAX() is slightly shorter and quicker than entering the =IF() function.

Figure 272

E2   *fx* =MAX(D2-C2,0)

Ask for the
maximum of
the calculation
and 0 to return
only positive
values.

	A	B	C	D	E	F
1	Salesrep	Date	Quota	Sales	Over Quota	
2	Joe	1/1/2008	800	666	0	
3	Dan	1/1/2008	800	1290	490	
4	Mary	1/1/2008	800	896	96	
5	Joe	1/2/2008	800	559	0	

Summary: To find only positive results of a calculation, you can use either the =IF() or =MAX(Calc, 0) function. Either will work. Using =MAX is slightly better. Similarly, you can use =MIN(Calc,0) to find only negative values.

Functions Discussed: =IF(); =MAX(); =MIN()

HOW TO JOIN TWO TEXT COLUMNS

Problem: As you can see in Figure 273, I have data with first names in column A and last names in column B. I want to merge these two columns into one column.

Figure 273

You want to join A2 and B2 into a single cell.

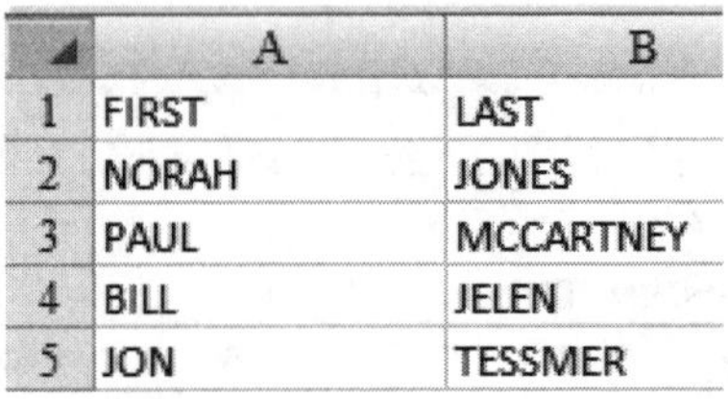

	A	B
1	FIRST	LAST
2	NORAH	JONES
3	PAUL	MCCARTNEY
4	BILL	JELEN
5	JON	TESSMER

Strategy: You can use the ampersand (&) as a concatenation operator in a formula in column C. You change the formulas in column C to values before deleting columns A and B. These are the steps:

1) In cell C2, enter the formula =A2&B2, as shown in Figure 274.

Figure 274

Use & to concatenate. How many people actually use the word concatenation?

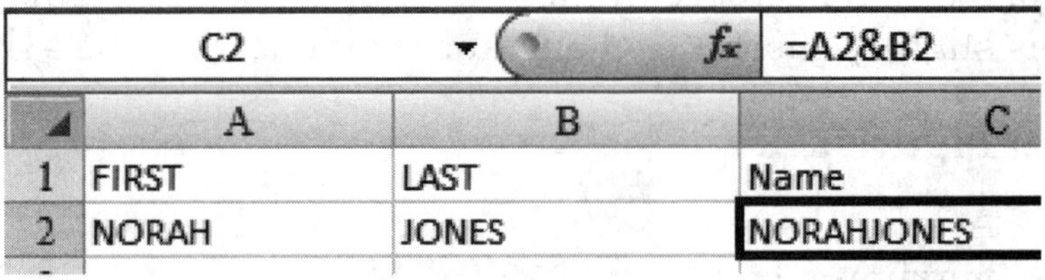

C2			f_x	=A2&B2

	A	B	C
1	FIRST	LAST	Name
2	NORAH	JONES	NORAHJONES

2) To insert a space between the first name and the last name, join cell A2, a space in quotes, and cell B2, using the formula =A2&" "&B2.

3) Copy the formula down to all the cells in the range, as shown in Figure 275.

Figure 275

Join A2, a space, and B2.

	C2		f_x =A2&" "&B2	
	A	B	C	
1	FIRST	LAST	Name	
2	NORAH	JONES	NORAH JONES	
3	PAUL	MCCARTNEY	PAUL MCCARTNEY	
4	BILL	JELEN	BILL JELEN	
5	JON	TESSMER	JON TESSMER	

Additional Details: To convert NORAH JONES to Norah Jones, you use the PROPER function. =PROPER(A2&" "&B2) will convert the names to proper case, as shown in Figure 276. This will work for all your names except names with interior capitals, such as Paul McCartney or Dave VanHorn. After using the PROPER function, you will have to manually fix any names that have interior capital letters. (Some people suggest entering the last name as Mc Cartney, with a space to prevent this problem.) Note: If you like PROPER, consider UPPER and LOWER to convert text to upper or lower case.

Figure 276

There are also UPPER and LOWER functions.

	A	B	C
1	FIRST	LAST	Name
2	NORAH	JONES	Norah Jones
3	PAUL	MCCARTNEY	Paul Mccartney
4	BILL	JELEN	Bill Jelen

Gotcha: If you delete columns A and B while column C still contains formulas, all the formulas will change to #REF! errors, as shown in Figure 277. This tells you that you have a formula that points to cells(s) that are no longer there. You can immediately press Ctrl+Z to undo the deletion.

Figure 277

Delete A and B, the live formulas in C will change to #REF! errors.

	A2		f_x =PROPER(#REF!&" "&#REF!)		
	A	B	C	D	E
1	Name				
2	#REF!				
3	#REF!				
4	#REF!				
5	#REF!				

Part II

To work around this situation, you first convert all the formulas in column C to values. Follow these steps:

1) Select the data in column C.

2) Press Ctrl+C to copy the data to the Clipboard.

3) Without changing the selection, select Home – Paste dropdown – Paste Special.

4) In the Paste Special dialog box, choose Values and then click OK, as shown in Figure 278. Excel converts column C from live formulas to static values.

Figure 278

Convert formulas to values.

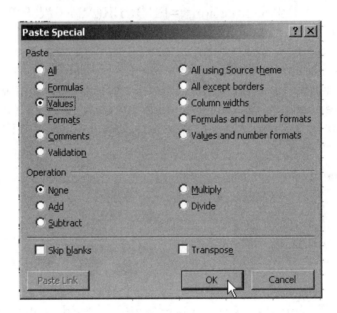

5) You can now delete columns A and B.

Summary: The ampersand (&) is the concatenation character, which you use to join text cells with other text cells or with literal values in a formula.

Commands Discussed: Home – Paste dropdown – Paste Special

Functions Discussed: =PROPER(); =UPPER(); =LOWER()

Excel 97-2003: Edit – Paste Special

See Also: "Get Quick Access to Paste Values" on page 108

JOIN TEXT WITH A DATE OR CURRENCY

Problem: I just learned about concatenation, and I'm trying to join text with currency and with a date. As you can see in cell B13 of Figure 279, when I attempt to join both date and currency with text, the currency loses the dollar sign and the date appears as a strange number. What am I doing wrong?

Figure 279

The formula in B13 fails miserably.

| | B13 | | | | f_x | ="Please remit "&E11&" before "&F1+F3 |

▲	A	B	C	D	E	F	G
1	INVOICE				Date:	6/18/2008	
2							
3					Net:	30	
4							
5		Quantity	Item	Unit Price	Total		
6		62	S97	64.08	$3,972.96		
7		76	S43	39.91	3,033.16		
8		83	S99	45.72	3,794.76		
9		27	S53	41.66	1,124.82		
10		57	S67	53.5	3,049.50		
11				TOTAL	$14,975.20		
12							
13		Please remit 14975.2 before 39647					
14							

Strategy: Excel internally stores dates as numbers and relies on the number format to display the number as a date. In the formula, you can use the TEXT function to convert a date or a number into text with a particular numeric format. For example, the formula =TEXT(F1+F3,"mm/dd/yyyy") would produce the text 07/18/2008. Thanks to the variety of custom number formats, you could also use =TEXT(F1+F3,"dddd, mmmm d, yyyy") to create the text Friday, July 18, 2008.

Additional Details: If you are not sure of the actual custom number format codes, you can query them from any existing cell. Here's an example:

1) Select cell E11.

2) Press Ctrl+1 to display the Format Cells dialog.

3) Click the Number tab and then select the Custom category. Excel
    will show the actual code used to generate the format in that cell.

4) Highlight those characters, press Ctrl+C to copy to the Clipboard,
    and paste into the TEXT function (see Figure 280).

Figure 280

To see what
the numeric
format is set
to for any cell,
display For-
mat Cells and
choose the
Custom cat-
egory.

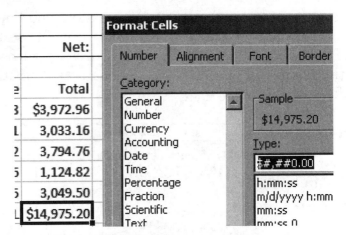

5) Change the formula in B13 to =“Please remit “&TEXT(E11,”$#,##
    0.00”)&” before “&TEXT(F1+F3,”dddd, mmmm d, yyyy”), as shown
    in Figure 281.

Figure 281

Use the TEXT
function to
control how
dates and
currency are
joined with
text.

f_x ="Please remit "&TEXT(E11,"$#,##0.00")&" before "&
TEXT(F1+F3,"dddd, mmmm d, yyyy")

	A	B	C	D	E	F
1	INVOICE				Date:	6/18/2008
2						
3					Net:	30
4						
5		Quantity	Item	Unit Price	Total	
6		62	S30	64.08	$3,972.96	
7		76	S63	39.91	3,033.16	
8		83	S54	45.72	3,794.76	
9		27	S47	41.66	1,124.82	
10		57	S11	53.5	3,049.50	
11				TOTAL	$14,975.20	
12						
13		Please remit $14,975.20 before Friday, July 18, 2008				

Additional Details: Excel stores dates as the number of days elapsed since January 1, 1900 (on a PC), or since January 1, 1904 (on a Mac). The 39647 shown in cell B13 of Figure 279 corresponds to July 18, 2008. While this is a fascinating bit of information (if you are Cliff Claven), I've never had a manager call and ask, "Hey, how many days after January 1, 1900, is that receivable due?" This method makes it easy for Excel to calculate differences between two dates.

Summary: When you need to concatenate text with a date or currency or any other formatted value, you use the TEXT function.

Functions Discussed: =TEXT()

HOW TO SORT ON ONE PORTION OF AN ACCOUNT ID

Problem: My company assigns an account ID to every customer. One portion of the account ID contains useful information, such as a parent company code. In Figure 282, for example, the first three digits of the account are used to identify an office. How can I sort on the basis of a portion of the account ID?

Figure 282

In this bad data design, the first three characters of column A indicate an office.

	A	B	C	D	E	F
1	Account	Product	Jan	Feb	Mar	Q1
2	4010	XYZ	37	82	12	131
3	4021	ABC	89	20	69	178
4	4030	XYZ	73	90	62	225
5	4030	ABC	55	26	23	104
6	4030	GHI	33	0	25	58

Strategy: You can insert a new column and use the LEFT function to isolate the necessary digits from the Account field. Here's how:

1) In the blank column, such as G, enter a heading such as Key.

2) In cell G2, enter the formula =LEFT(A2,3), as shown in Figure 283. This indicates that the new field should contain just the three left-most characters in the Account field. Note that Excel also offers the RIGHT function to isolate the rightmost characters.

Figure 283

Get the first three charac-ters.

G2						f_x	=LEFT(A2,3)
	A	B	C	D	E	F	G
1	Account	Product	Jan	Feb	Mar	Q1	Key
2	4010	XYZ	37	82	12	131	401
3	4021	ABC	89	20	69	178	

3) Double-click the fill handle in cell G2 to copy the formula down to all the rows in your data set. (The fill handle is the black square dot in the lower-right corner of the cell pointer.)

4) To change the formulas in column G to values, highlight all the cells in column G if they are not still selected after using the fill handle in step 3. Press Ctrl+C to copy. Choose Home – Paste drop-down – Paste Values, as shown in Figure 284.

Figure 284

Select the Paste drop-down to access this menu.

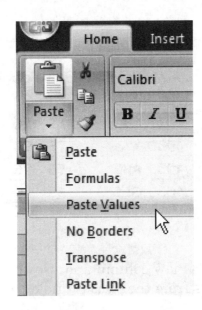

Results: A certain portion of the Account field is now available in a new column. You can now use data tools, such as Sort, Filter, or Subtotal, to isolate certain offices.

When you need to isolate a portion of the characters in another column, you can do so by creating a temporary column.

Commands Discussed: Home – Paste dropdown – Paste Values

Functions Discussed: =LEFT(), =RIGHT()

Excel 92-2003: Edit – Paste Special – Values

See Also: "How to Isolate the Center Portion of an Account ID", "How to Isolate Everything Before a Dash in a Column By Using Functions"

Part
II

HOW TO ISOLATE
THE CENTER PORTION OF AN ACCOUNT ID

Problem: My company assigns an account ID in the format SSS-XX-YYYY, as shown in Figure 285. I need to isolate the XX portion of the account ID in order to subtotal or sort the data.

Figure 285

Use a formula to extract the middle of the account ID.

	A	B	C	D	E	F
1	Account	Product	Jan	Feb	Mar	Q1
2	668-50-3295	XYZ	93	94	85	272
3	844-50-3736	XYZ	99	69	76	244
4	672-50-8695	XYZ	36	96	94	226
5	109-50-7003	ABC	80	66	70	216
6	423-50-9810	DEF	86	55	74	215

Strategy: You can insert a new column and use the MID function to isolate the necessary digits from the Account field.

The MID function takes three arguments: (1) a cell that contains a text value, (2) the character number where you want the result to start, and (3) the length of the result.

In a well-formed account number, such as 123-45-6789, you can predict that the start of the second segment will always be in the fifth character position and the length of the second segment is always two characters. Therefore, you can follow these steps:

1) In a blank column, such as column G, enter a heading such as Key.

2) In cell G2, enter the formula =MID(A2,5,2).

3) Copy the formula down to all rows, as shown in Figure 286.

Figure 286

Grab the middle characters, starting at position 5, for a length of 2.

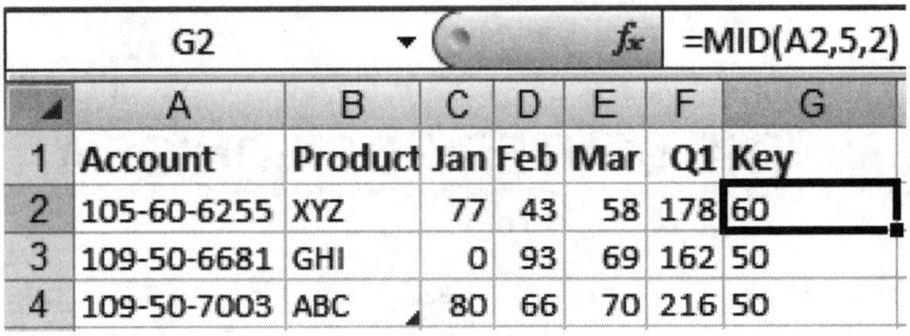

	G2					f_x	=MID(A2,5,2)
	A	B	C	D	E	F	G
1	Account	Product	Jan	Feb	Mar	Q1	Key
2	105-60-6255	XYZ	77	43	58	178	60
3	109-50-6681	GHI	0	93	69	162	50
4	109-50-7003	ABC	80	66	70	216	50

Additional Details: In order to capture the final four digits of the account number, you could either use =MID(A2,8,4) or =RIGHT(A2,4).

Results: You can now sort by the new column and add subtotals based on the Account field.

Summary: When you need to isolate a portion of the characters in another column, you can do so by creating a temporary column.

Functions Discussed: =MID(); =RIGHT()

See Also: "How to Sort on One Segment of an Account ID", "How to Isolate Everything Before a Dash in a Column By Using Functions"

HOW TO ISOLATE EVERYTHING BEFORE A DASH IN A COLUMN BY USING FUNCTIONS

Problem: A vendor has given me the Excel worksheet shown in Figure 287. As you can see, one field has a manufacturer code, a dash, and a part number. I need to isolate the manufacturer code in a new column, but the manufacturer codes are not always the same length.

Figure 287

You need the left characters, up to but not including the dash.

◢	A	B	C	D	E
1	Item	Jan	Feb	Mar	Q1
2	KO-4679855	93	94	85	272
3	CISCO-85590	99	69	76	244
4	TLXN-859	36	96	94	226

Strategy: You can use the FIND function to locate the character position of the dash in the manufacturer code. You can then use that result minus one in the LEFT function to isolate the manufacturer code.

The FIND function requires two arguments. The first argument is the text that you are trying to locate. In this case, you are trying to locate a dash, so you should include the dash in quotation marks. The second argument is the location of the cell that contains the text to search. Here's how the process works:

1) Enter =FIND("-",A2) in cell F2.

2) Copy this formula down to all the other cells, as shown in Figure 288. The 3 in cell F2 indicates that the dash is located in the third character position of cell A2. The 6 in cell F3 indicates that the dash is in the sixth position of cell A3.

Figure 288

The 3 says the dash is the 3rd character in A2.

F2				▼		f_x	=FIND("-",A2)

◢	A	B	C	D	E	F	G
1	Item	Jan	Feb	Mar	Q1	Find	
2	KO-4679855	93	94	85	272	3	
3	CISCO-85590	99	69	76	244	6	

3) To isolate the manufacturer code, you need a number that is one less than the number in column F, so in cell G2, enter the formula =LEFT(A2,F2-1), as shown in Figure 289.

4) Double-click the fill handle to copy this formula down to all cells.

Figure 289

The FIND function provides information for the LEFT function.

	A	B	C	D	E	F	G
							G2 =LEFT(A2,F2-1)
1	Item	Jan	Feb	Mar	Q1	Find	Manufacturer
2	KO-4679855	93	94	85	272	3	KO
3	CISCO-85590	99	69	76	244	6	CISCO

Alternate Strategy: You do not need to enter the formulas in two different columns. You could instead use the following formula in cell F2:

=LEFT(A2,FIND("-",A2)-1)

Additional Details: After the formula has isolated the manufacturer code, you change the formulas to values, as described in "How to Sort on One Segment of an Account ID."

Results: You can now sort by the new column and add subtotals based on this field.

Summary: When you need to isolate a portion of the characters in another column, you can do so by creating a temporary column.

Functions Discussed: =FIND(); =LEFT()

See Also: "How to Sort on One Segment of an Account ID" (p. 189)

HOW TO USE FUNCTIONS TO ISOLATE EVERYTHING AFTER A DASH IN A COLUMN

Problem: A vendor has given me the Excel worksheet shown in Figure 290. One field has a manufacturer code, a dash, and a part number. I need to isolate the part number in a new column, but the manufacturer codes are not always the same length.

Figure 290

Grab everything after the dash.

◢	A	B	C	D	E
1	**Item**	**Jan**	**Feb**	**Mar**	**Q1**
2	KO-4679855	93	94	85	272
3	CISCO-85590	99	69	76	244
4	TLXN-859	36	96	94	226

Strategy: You can use the MID function to extract a portion of text from the middle of the text. The MID function requires three arguments: =MID(*Cell with Text, Character Number to Start, Number of Characters*). You can use the FIND function to locate the dash in the item number and start at one character to the right. You can use the LEN function to figure out how long the text is.

The FIND function requires two arguments. The first argument is the text that you are trying to locate. In this case, you are trying to locate a dash, so you should include the dash in quotation marks. The second argument is the location of the cell that contains the text to search. Here's how the process works:

1) Enter =FIND("-",A2) in cell F2.

2) Copy this formula down to all the other cells, as shown in Figure 291. The 3 in cell F2 indicates that the dash is located in the third character position of cell A2.

Figure 291

The 3 in F2 indicates that the dash is the third character in A2.

| F2 | | | | | | f_x | =FIND("-",A2) |

◢	A	B	C	D	E	F	G	H
1	**Item**	**Jan**	**Feb**	**Mar**	**Q1**	**Find**		
2	KO-4679855	93	94	85	272	3		
3	CISCO-85590	99	69	76	244	6		
4	TLXN-859	36	96	94	226	5		

3) To isolate the part number, you need to start one character to the right of the dash, so start your formula with =MID(A2,F2+1).

4) To figure out how many characters there are in the part number, in cell G2, enter the formula =LEN(A2).

5) Copy this formula down to all rows, as shown in Figure 292. The LEN function will tell you the total number of characters in cell A2. Cell G2 tells you that there are 10 characters in A2. If the dash is in the third position, then you want to grab (G2-F2) characters, or (10-3), which means seven characters.

Figure 292

LEN tells you the total number of characters in A2.

| | G2 | | | | | f_x | =LEN(A2) |

◢	A	B	C	D	E	F	G
1	Item	Jan	Feb	Mar	Q1	Find	Length
2	KO-4679855	93	94	85	272	3	10
3	CISCO-85590	99	69	76	244	6	11

6) In cell H2, enter the formula =MID(A2,F2+1,G2-F2), as shown in Figure 293. In plain language, this tells Excel to extract characters from A2. Excel should start at the character after the result in F2 and continue for a length of (G2-F2) characters.

Figure 293

Use the MID function.

| | H2 | | | | | f_x | =MID(A2,F2+1,G3-F2) |

◢	A	B	C	D	E	F	G	H
1	Item	Jan	Feb	Mar	Q1	Find	Length	Item
2	KO-4679855	93	94	85	272	3	10	4679855
3	CISCO-85590	99	69	76	244	6	11	85590

In this case, it is much more difficult to enter the formula in one column instead of three columns. This is because the result of the FIND function is used twice in the H2 formula. In order to build a single formula, you will enter the FIND function twice in that formula. As shown in Figure 294, you could skip the intermediate formulas and enter the following formula in F2:

=MID(A2,FIND("-",A2)+1,LEN(A2)-FIND("-",A2))

See "Combine Intermediate Formulas into a Mega-Formula" on page 204 for an easy way to combine intermediate formulas.

Figure 294

Combine the intermediate steps into a single formula.

=MID(A2,FIND("-",A2)+1,LEN(A2)-FIND("-",A2))

◢	A	B	C	D	E	F
1	Item	Jan	Feb	Mar	Q1	Item
2	KO-4679855	93	94	85	272	4679855
3	CISCO-85590	99	69	76	244	85590

Alternate Strategy: Rather than calculating a specific lenth, you could specify a value that is large enough to grab a part number of any conceivable length. =MID(A2,F2+1,50) will return characters starting at position 4 through the end of the cell (provided the part number is less than 54 characters).

Summary: You can use a combination of LEN and FIND functions to locate the proper position for the LEFT, MID, and RIGHT functions.

Functions Discussed: =FIND(); =MID(); =LEN()

HOW TO USE FUNCTIONS TO ISOLATE EVERYTHING AFTER THE SECOND DASH IN A COLUMN

Problem: A vendor gave me a file that contains a three-segment part number, as shown in Figure 295. Each segment is separated by a dash, and the length of each segment could be any number of characters. How do I find the second or third segment?

Figure 295

Isolate the second or third segment.

◢	A	B	C	D	E
1	Item	Jan	Feb	Mar	Q1
2	KO-4679855-A34	93	94	85	272
3	CISCO-85590-B7	99	69	76	244
4	TLXN-859-A3	36	96	94	226
5	KO-9694625-B95	80	66	70	216
6	KO-3664228-A52	86	55	74	215

Part II

Strategy: There is an optional third argument in the FIND function that tells Excel to start looking after a certain character position in the text. In this case, to find the second dash, you want Excel to start looking after the location of the first dash. Here's what you do:

1) As in the prior examples, use =FIND("-",A2) in cell F2 to locate the first dash.

2) Enter =FIND("-",A2,F2+1) in cell G2, as shown in Figure 296. The F2+1 parameter tells Excel that you want to find a dash starting at the fourth character position of cell A2.

Figure 296

The 3rd argument gives the position in which FIND should start looking.

G2				fx	=FIND("-",A2,F2+1)

	A	B	C	D	E	F	G	H
1	Item	Jan	Feb	Mar	Q1	Dash 1	Dash 2	Item 1
2	KO-4679855-A34	93	94	85	272	3	11	
3	CISCO-85590-B7	99	69	76	244	6	12	

3) Enter =LEFT(A2,F2-1) in H2. This formula locates the first segment of the part number.

4) Enter =MID(A2,F2+1,G2-F2-1) in I2. This formula locates the middle segment of the part number.

5) To get the right segment of the part number, use the RIGHT function. (Just like the LEFT function, the RIGHT function requires a cell and the number of characters from the right side of the item number.) To find the number of characters, use =LEN(A2)-G2. So enter the formula =RIGHT(A2,LEN(A2)-G2) in J2 (Figure 297).

Figure 297

Use RIGHT to find the third segment.

J2				fx	=RIGHT(A2,LEN(A2)-G2)

	A	F	G	H	I	J
1	Item	Dash 1	Dash 2	Item 1	Item 2	Item 3
2	KO-4679855-A34	3	11	KO	4679855	A34
3	CISCO-85590-B7	6	12	CISCO	85590	B7
4	TLXN-859-A3	5	9	TLXN	859	A3

Gotcha: With all these formulas, you are trusting that the vendor always included two dashes in the item number. If there is an item number that does not have a second dash, the second FIND function will return a #VALUE! error, leading to errors in the calculation for the second and third items. Before converting formulas to values and deleting the original part number, you need to sort the data in descending order by column F and then sort in descending order by column G. As shown in Figure 298, any #VALUE! errors will sort to the top of the data set so you can easily locate and correct them.

Figure 298

The formulas create an error if there is only one dash.

◢	A	F	G	H	I	J
1	Item	Dash 1	Dash 2	Item 1	Item 2	Item 3
2	KO-4679855	3	#VALUE!	KO	#VALUE!	#VALUE!
3	CISCO-85590-B7	6	12	CISCO	85590	B7

Part II

Summary: By using combinations of FIND, LEN, MID, LEFT, and RIGHT, you can parse nearly any data imaginable.

Functions Discussed: =FIND(); =LEN(); =MID(); =LEFT(); =RIGHT()

HOW TO SEPARATE A PART NUMBER INTO THREE COLUMNS

Problem: A vendor gave me a file that contains three-segment item numbers (with the segments separated by dashes), as shown in Figure 299. The FIND function makes my head hurt, but I need to break the part number into three columns. What do I do?

Figure 299

There is an easy way to break the item number cell into three cells.

◢	A	B	C	D	E
1	Item	Jan	Feb	Mar	Q1
2	KO-4679855-A34	93	94	85	272
3	CISCO-85590-B7	99	69	76	244
4	TLXN-859-A3	36	96	94	226
5	KO-9694625-B95	80	66	70	216

Strategy: You can use the Text to Columns command on the Data tab to parse the item number. Follow these steps:

1) Copy the item number to the right side of your data in column F. The Text to Columns command will fill several columns to the right of the original column. Make sure you have plenty of blank columns.

2) Select the entire range of data in column F. Place the cell pointer in F2. Press the End key. While holding down the Shift key, press the Down Arrow key to select the entire range. (Or press F2 and then press Shift+Ctrl+Down Arrow).

3) Select Data – Text to Columns. The Convert Text to Columns Wizard will work on either data that is delimited or on data that has a fixed width to each segment.

4) Because the data in this example is delimited by a dash, in step 1 of the wizard, leave the radio button on the Delimited setting (see Figure 300). Click Next.

Figure 300

The dash in the part number is a delimiter.

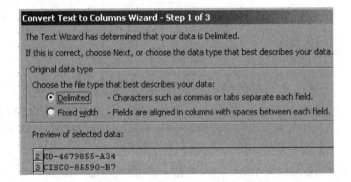

5) By default, step 2 of the wizard assumes that the data is delimited by a tab, so uncheck the Tab check box. As shown in Figure 301, other standard choices are commas, spaces, and semicolons.

Figure 301

Dashes are not a delimiter choice.

Note that dash is not in the list. Check the Other check box. In the Other text box, enter a dash. As shown in Figure 302, the Data Preview window will show the data in three columns. Click Next.

Figure 302

Use the Other field.

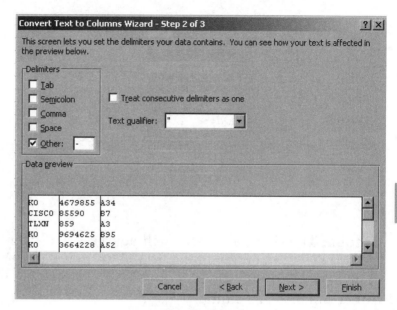

6)   In step 3 of the wizard, if desired, specify the data type of the columns. Unless you have dates, the General type is okay. Note that if you want to preserve any leading zeros in the second segment of the item number, you should choose the heading of that field and change it from General to Text, as shown in Figure 303. Click Finish.

Figure 303

Use Text only when you have to preserve leading zeros.

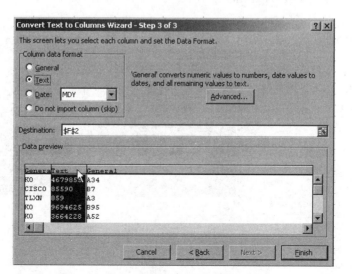

Results: The original column F has been overwritten with the first portion of the result. New columns G and H contain the second and third segments of the item number, as shown in Figure 304.

Figure 304

You've parsed column A into three new columns.

F	G	H
Item		
KO	4679855	A34
CISCO	85590	B7
TLXN	859	A3
KO	9694625	B95

Gotcha: The General format will aggressively attempt to convert anything that is remotely similar to a date to a date. For example, a part number of 5-5055 will be imported as May 1, 5055. A fraction such as 1/4 will be imported as January 4 of the current year. If your data includes dashes or slashes, use the Text format.

Gotcha: A very strange anomaly will appear for the remainder of this Excel session. If you later open a Notepad file, copy data that contains dashes, and attempt to paste to Excel, Excel will automatically split the data into columns where the dash is located, as shown in Figure 305 and Figure 306. This can be a very handy feature if you are expecting it, but it can be a very puzzling situation if you are not.

Figure 305

Copy from an e-mail or Notepad.

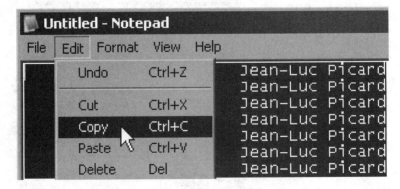

Figure 306

Paste to Excel
and the data is
automatically
parsed by the
same delimiter
used in Figure
302.

Jean	Luc Picard
Jean	Luc Picard
Jean	Luc Picard
Jean	Luc Picard

Gotcha: You should avoid using the Text option in step 3 of the wizard
unless it is absolutely necessary. In addition to preserving leading zeros,
the Text option will change the format of that column to text. When you
try to enter a formula in that column, as shown in Figure 307, you will
get the formula instead of the answer. To solve this problem, you have
to select the column, press Ctrl+1 to format cells, and select Number.
Then you select General or any other numeric format other than text.
You then have to go back and reenter the formulas in order to have them
calculate.

Part II

Figure 307

After you use
Text in step 3
of the wizard,
the column is
poisoned and
won't accept
formulas.

F	G	
Item		
KO	4679855	A34
CISCO	85590	B7
	=2+2	
TLXN	859	A3

Additional Details: Excel will walk you through the Text to Columns
wizard when you open a .txt file. However, if you open a .csv file, Excel will automatically open the file without allowing you to choose field
types. If you find that you are losing leading zeroes when you open a .csv
file, simply rename the file from .csv to .txt in Windows Explorer before
you open the file.

Summary: If your data is set up with consistent delimiters, using the Convert Text to Columns Wizard is a fast way to parse data.

See Also: "Deal with Data Where Each Record Takes Five Physical Rows" on page 526

Commands Discussed: Data – Text to Columns

Excel 97-2003: Data – Text to Columns

COMBINE INTERMEDIATE FORMULAS INTO A MEGA-FORMULA

Problem: When I need to build a complex calculation, I sometimes need to build several intermediate formulas to help figure out the problem. When these columns are working, can I combine the logic from the intermediate formulas into a single formula? For example, in the example in "How to use Functions to Isolate Everything After the Second Dash in a Column," I ended up with five calculation columns, but the intermediate calculations to locate Dash1 and Dash2 are not actually necessary in the print out.

Figure 308

Can you change the calculations in D:F so you can delete B:C?

	E2				f_x	=MID(A2,B2+1,C2-B2-1)
◢	A	B	C	D	E	F
1	Item	Dash 1	Dash 2	Item 1	Item 2	Item 3
2	KO-4679855-A34	3	11	KO	4679855	A34
3	CISCO-85590-B7	6	12	CISCO	85590	B7
4	TLXN-859-A3	5	9	TLXN	859	A3

Strategy: You can select characters in the formula bar and copy them to the Clipboard with Ctrl+C. When you copy an entire cell, you introduce many complexities, including the problem that you cannot paste this cell into the middle of a formula or into the Replace dialog. Instead, by copying characters from the formula bar, you have regular text on the Clipboard and can either paste into another formula or in the Replace dialog. Here's what you do:

1) In Figure 308, the formula in E2 contains two occurrences of cell B2. You want to replace the reference in B2 with the formula from cell B2. Select cell B2. In the formula bar, click the mouse after the equal sign and drag to the end of the formula, as shown in Figure 309. Press Ctrl+C to copy these characters to the Clipboard. Exit Edit mode by pressing the Esc key.

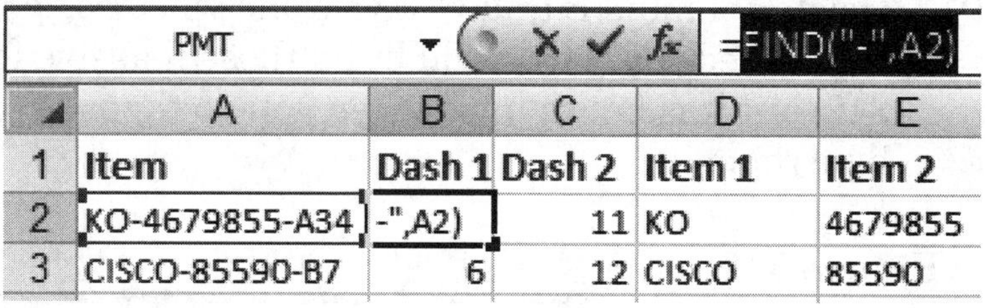

Figure 309

Select all but the equals sign in B2.

PMT	▼	X ✓ *fx*	=FIND("-",A2)

◢	A	B	C	D	E
1	Item	Dash 1	Dash 2	Item 1	Item 2
2	KO-4679855-A34	-",A2)	11	KO	4679855
3	CISCO-85590-B7	6	12	CISCO	85590

2) Select cell E2. In the formula bar, highlight the first occurrence of B2 as shown in Figure 310.

Figure 310

Select the characters B2 in the formula.

=MID(A2,B2+1,C2-B2-1)

3) Press Ctrl+V to paste the formula from B2 in place of the characters B2 in the E2 formula.

4) Select the second instance of the characters B2 in the formula in cell E2, as shown in Figure 311.

Figure 311

Select the characters B2 in your formula.

=MID(A2,FIND("-",A2)+1,C2-B2-1)

5) Press Ctrl+V to paste the B2 formula into E2.

6) B2 also appears in the C2 and D2 formulas. Paste the Clipboard contents into C2 and D2.

7) Repeat steps 1–3, using the formula in C2. Paste these characters into E2 and F2.

8) Copy the new formulas in D2:F2 down to all rows of the data set.

9) Delete columns B and C. Everyone who sees your spreadsheet will be amazed that you could build those massive formulas (see Figure 312) but it is not so hard when you do them in pieces and then combine them.

Figure 312

After several copy and paste operations, you will eliminate the intermediate columns.

`=MID(A2,FIND("-",A2)+1,FIND("-",A2,FIND("-",A2)+1)-FIND("-",A2)-1)`

	A	B	C	D	E	F
1	Item	Item 1	Item 2	Item 3		
2	KO-4679855-A34	KO	4679855	A34		
3	CISCO-85590-B7	CISCO	85590	B7		

Alternate Strategy: Instead of following the steps just outlined, you can use the Replace dialog to combine the intermediate formulas into mega-formulas. Follow these steps:

1) Select cell B2. In the formula bar, use the mouse to select everything from immediately after the equals sign to the end of the formula. Press Ctrl+C to copy those characters to the Clipboard. Press the Esc key to exit the formula bar.

2) Select cells C2:F2. **Gotcha:** Make sure this selection contains two cells, even if you are only working on a single formula! If you select two or more cells, the Replace All command will work only within the selection. If you select only one cell, the Replace All command will extend to all 17 billion cells in the worksheet.

3) Select Home – Find & Select – Replace or Ctrl+H.

4) In the Find What box, type B2.

5) Tab to the Replace With box. Press Ctrl+V. Excel will copy the characters from the B2 formula into the dialog.

6) Click the Options button.

7) Make sure the Look In dropdown is set to Formulas. Make sure that Match Entire Cell Contents is unchecked, as shown in Figure 313. (If you start a new Excel session, both of these settings will be correct. However, the dialog remembers the settings from the last find and replace you did earlier in the current session, so it is always worth your time to click the Options button to make sure these settings are correct.)

Figure 313

Replace references to B2 with the formula from B2.

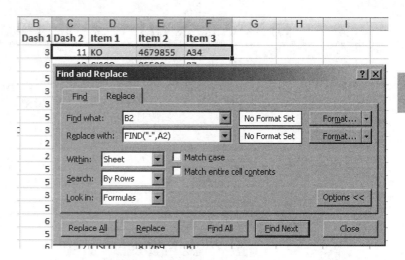

Part II

8) Click Replace All. Excel will remove the reference to B2 from the selected cells and replace it with the characters from B2.

9) Repeat step 1 for cell C2.

10) Repeat steps 2–8 for cells D2:F2. Excel will replace any reference to C2 in D2:F2.

11) Copy the new formulas from D2:F2 down to all rows.

12) Delete columns A and B.

Depending on how many times B2 and C2 are referenced, using Find and Replace might be faster than using the copy and paste method.

Gotcha: Be careful that your target formulas don't contain references that contain some other form of B2 and C2, such as B20 or C210909. If your formulas do contain such references, when you replace B2, Excel will blindly put the B2 formula where the characters B2 appear in B20.

Summary: By copying characters from the formula bar, you can use Paste or Find and Replace to combine intermediate formulas into a mega-formula.

Commands Discussed: Home – Copy; Home – Paste; Home – Find & Select – Replace

Excel 97-2003: Edit – Copy; Edit – Paste; Edit – Replace.

CHANGE SMITH, JANE TO JANE SMITH

Problem: As shown in Figure 314, I have a column of names in last name, first name style. How can I convert the data to first name last name?

Figure 314

Flip last name and first name.

	A	B	CITY, S
1	NAME	ADDRESS	CITY, S
2	SMITH, JANE	625 Johnson Road	George
3	ATKINS, ERIN	995 Hill Circle	Midwa
4	VAUGHN, WILLIAM	226 Franklin Circle	City, N
5	LEWIS, MARIAN	647 Sycamore Circle	Frankli
6	MELTON, CARL	1394 Ash Circle	Bloomi
7	ELLIS, DOUGLAS	552 College Blvd.	Barring

Strategy: While you could do this in many steps, using Text to Columns and then a concatenation formula, a single large formula would also solve the problem. To begin, you need to insert a blank column after column A to hold the calculation.

=FIND(",",A2) will locate the comma within the value in column A. In Smith, Jane, the comma is the sixth character, so the FIND function would return a 6.

The first name starts two characters after the result of the FIND function. It extends to the end of the text. You can use the MID function to isolate the first name. The MID function requires some text, a starting location, and a length. If you ask for more characters than are in the text, then Excel will return from the starting position to the end of the text. For example, if you ask for 50 characters, Excel will handle any first name that has 50 characters or less. Therefore, you use =MID(A2, FIND(",",A2)+2,50).

The last name is always the leftmost characters, so you can use =LEFT(A2,FIND(",",A2)-1).

To join the first name and last name together, you concatenate the function for the first name, a space in quotes, and the function for the last name. You need to be sure to leave the = sign off the LEFT function because you don't prefix the function with an equals sign when it occurs in the middle of the formula.

If you want the text in uppercase and lowercase, you need to wrap the entire function in the PROPER function. As shown in Figure 315, the formula is =PROPER(MID(A2,FIND(",",A2)+2,50)&" "&LEFT(A2,FIND(",",A2)-1)).

Part
II

Figure 315

The formula in column B achieves the result.

=PROPER(MID(A2,FIND(",",A2)+2,50)&" "&LEFT(A2,FIND(",",A2)-1))		
	A	B	C
1	NAME	NAME	ADDRESS
2	SMITH, JANE	Jane Smith	625 Johnson Road
3	ATKINS, ERIN	Erin Atkins	995 Hill Circle
4	VAUGHN, WILLIAM	William Vaughn	226 Franklin Circle
5	LEWIS, MARIAN	Marian Lewis	647 Sycamore Circle

Gotcha: Before deleting column A, you need to convert column B to values. You select the formulas in B, press Ctrl+C to copy, and select Home – Paste dropdown – Paste Values to convert the formulas to their current values.

Summary: Using the FIND function to locate the comma provides arguments for the LEFT and MID function.

Commands Discussed: Home – Paste dropdown – Paste Values

Functions Discussed: =FIND(); =MID(); =LEFT(); =PROPER()

Excel 97-2003: Edit – Paste Special – Values

ADD THE WORKSHEET NAME AS A TITLE

Problem: I have 12 worksheets, labeled January through December. Is there a formula that will put a worksheet name in a cell?

Strategy: You can parse the sheet name from the CELL function.

The CELL function can return a variety of information about the top-left cell in a reference. =CELL("Col",A1) will tell you that A1 is in column 1. For this particular problem, =CELL("FileName",A1) will return the path, filename, and worksheet name of a saved workbook, as shown in Figure 316.

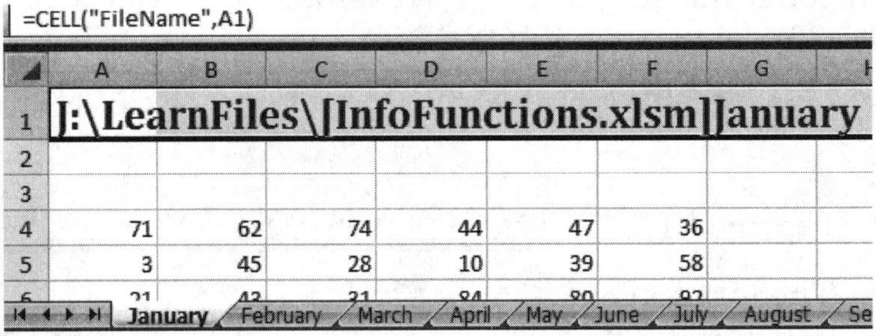

Figure 316

The CELL function returns the path, filename and worksheet name.

To isolate the sheet name, you look for the right square bracket by using the FIND function. Then you use that location plus 1 as the start position for the MID function.

In Figure 317, the formula =MID(CELL("FileName",A1),FIND("]",CELL("FileName",A1)+1,25) returns the worksheet name. Note that the final 25 argument is any number large enough to handle the longest sheet name you've used.

Figure 317

Isolate the
worksheet
name from the
path.

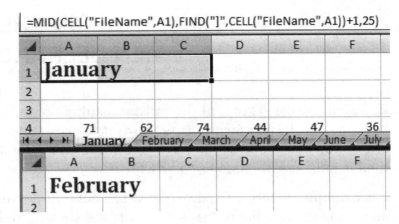

=MID(CELL("FileName",A1),FIND("]",CELL("FileName",A1))+1,25)

Gotcha: The reference argument is optional. Indeed, if you entered =CELL("FileName"), you would initially get the same result. However, if you leave off the reference, Excel will calculate the information for the last cell that was changed. This means that if you enter a number in February, all 12 worksheets will have the title February. There might be times when knowing the last cell to be changed is useful, but this is not one of them.

Additional Details: If you need to insert just the worksheet path in a cell, you can use =INFO("Directory") instead of trying to parse it from the CELL function.

Gotcha: The INFO function used to be able to return several bits of information about memory available, total memory, and so on. While these arguments were accepted in Excel 2003, they were never correct. In Excel 2007, Excel will return #N/A if you use the INFO function to return available memory.

Summary: You can add a worksheet name to a cell by using the CELL function.

Functions Discussed: =CELL(); =INFO(); =FIND(); =MID()

AVOID #REF! ERRORS
WHEN DELETING COLUMNS

Problem: Excel is great at computing results. Sometimes, I only need to keep the results of a formula, and I want to erase the columns the calculation was based on. If I delete a column used in the formula, however, the formula result changes to #REF!.

For example, where I used to work, someone in our marketing department was given a list of leads from a trade show. The Excel file had the area codes in one column and the telephone numbers in another column. There were several thousand leads. Someone in marketing was retyping all the telephone numbers in order to get the area code and phone number in one cell, as shown in Figure 318.

Figure 318

Someone new to Excel might try typing the phone numbers in a new column.

	H	I	J
	Area Code	Telephone	New Data
	817	555-1097	(817) 555-1097
	214	555-0273	(214) 555-0273
	403	555-8833	(403) 555-8833
	. . .	--- ----	/-- -/ --- ----

As shown in Figure 319, I showed this person how to use a formula to quickly convert all 5,000 telephone numbers to the format she wanted.

Figure 319

Use an ampersand to join text.

	f_x	="("&H2&") "&I2

	H	I	J
	Area Code	Telephone	New Data
	817	555-1097	(817) 555-1097
	214	555-0273	(214) 555-0273

I started to walk away, whistling a little tune because I had just saved someone a whole lot of typing. I had just about reached the door of the marketing department when I heard a scream. Because column J contained the information she needed, she had deleted columns H and I. However, column J was still a live formula, and Excel no longer knew how to calculate the results in J. And because cells referenced in the formula had been deleted, all the telephone numbers that were in column J now showed the #REF! error, as shown in Figure 320. How do I get around this problem?

Figure 320

The live formula changes to an error if you delete columns H and I.

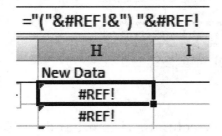

Part II

Strategy: Immediately hit Ctrl+Z to undo the delete and get the source columns back. Next, you will copy the formulas and use Paste Special to paste the cells as values instead of formulas.

1) With the cell pointer in cell J2, hold down the Shift key while you type the End key and then the Down Arrow key. This will select the entire contiguous range of cells in column J.

2) From the ribbon, select Home – Copy to copy the cells to the clipboard.

3) Without changing the selection, select Home – Paste dropdown – Paste Values as shown in Figure 321.

Figure 321

Paste values to replace the formulas with their current value.

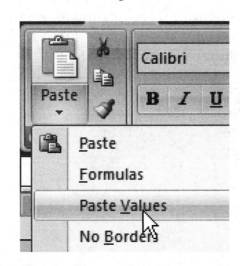

Results: The telephone numbers in column J are converted from formulas to the results of those formulas. You can verify this by noting the value instead of a formula in the formula bar, as shown in Figure 322.

Figure 322

The formula bar no longer contains a value.

	J
(817) 555-1097	

	J
ɔne	New Data
97	(817) 555-1097
73	(214) 555-0273

You can now safely delete columns H and I and the telephone numbers in column J will not change to #REF! errors.

Summary: Using the Paste Values technique is essential to becoming proficient in Excel. It will convert a range of formulas to the current value of the formula. You can then safely delete the source columns.

Commands Discussed: Home – Copy; Home – Paste dropdown – Paste Values; Quick Access Toolbar – Undo

Excel 97-2003: Edit – Copy; Edit – Paste Special; Edit – Undo

CREATE RANDOM NUMBERS

Problem: I want to create a range of random numbers in order to illustrate a concept in a class. As shown in Figure 323, I want to fill in random numbers in columns C through E.

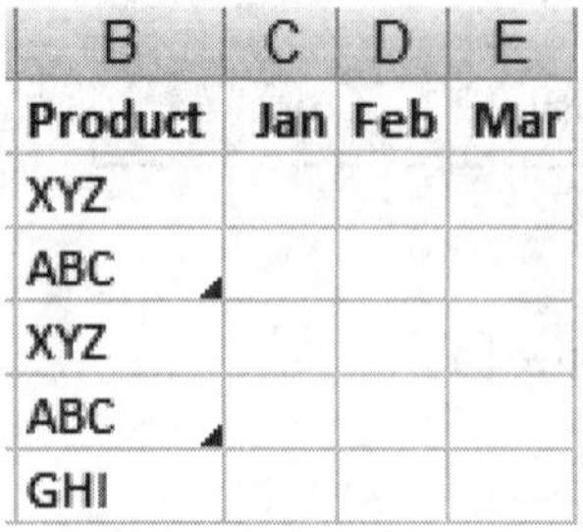

Figure 323

Fill C:E with random numbers between 1 and 99.

B	C	D	E
Product	Jan	Feb	Mar
XYZ			
ABC			
XYZ			
ABC			
GHI			

Strategy: You use the RANDBETWEEN function. This function will return a random integer between lower and upper limits. Specifically, in this case, you use =RANDBETWEEN(1,99), as shown in Figure 324.

Figure 324

Random numbers between 1 and 99.

=RANDBETWEEN(1,99)

Product	Jan	Feb	Mar
XYZ	16	67	60
ABC	81	88	47
XYZ	54	92	5

Alternate Strategy: Excel also offers the RAND function, which will return a decimal between 0 and 0.9999999. Instead of using the formula =RANDBETWEEN(1,99), you could use =INT(RAND()*99)+1.

Part
II

Additional Details: Every time you press F9 or enter a new value in the worksheet, the random numbers will change. You might want to change the formulas to values to freeze the random numbers. To do this, you select the range of random numbers, press Home – Copy, and then select Home – Paste dropdown – Paste Values to convert formulas to numbers.

Gotcha: These are actually pseudo-random numbers. If you are perfoming complex modeling involving thousands of numbers, patterns may emerge.

Summary: You can use the RANDBETWEEN function to return random numbers.

Commands Discussed: Home – Paste dropdown – Paste Values

Functions Discussed: =INT(); =RAND(), =RANDBETWEEN

Excel 97-2003: Before Excel 2007, there were 89 functions that were not in the core Excel product but were in the Analysis Toolpak add-in. This add-in was installed on every computer but not activated by default. Because RANDBETWEEN was one of the functions in the Analysis Toolpak, this function sometimes returned a NAME error in previous versions of Excel. If that happened to you, you could select Tools – Add-ins and then check the box next to Analysis Toolpak. Then, you would re-enter the formula, and the RANDBETWEEN function would work.

CREATE RANDOM NUMBERS
TO SEQUENCE A CLASS OF STUDENTS

Problem: The students in my class must present an oral book report. Rather than have them go alphabetically, as shown in Figure 325, I want to randomly sequence them. How can Excel help me do that?

Figure 325

Alex always has to go first.

	A
1	**Student**
2	Alex
3	Amy
4	Ashley
5	Athena
6	Brandon
7	Cassie

Strategy: You can use the RAND function in column B and then sort by column B. Follow these steps:

1) Enter the heading Sequence in B1.

2) Select cells B2:B22. Enter =RAND() and press Ctrl+Enter. Each student will be assigned a random decimal between 0 and 1, as shown in Figure 326.

Figure 326

Assign a random number to each student.

f_x	=RAND()

Student	**B** Sequence	C
Alex	0.38356	
Amy	0.60439	
Ashley	0.28143	

3) Select a single cell in column B and click the AZ button on the Data tab of the ribbon. The list will be sorted in a random sequence.

Gotcha: The data is sorted, and then column B is recalculated. It will appear that the new figures in column B are not in ascending order, as shown in Figure 327. This is because the sort was based on the previous values in column B.

Figure 327

Students are sorted based on values in Figure 326, and then column B is recalculated.

	f_x	=RAND()
Student	B Sequence	
Ron	0.85924	
Rowen	0.16577	
Davis	0.03056	
Megan	0.70774	

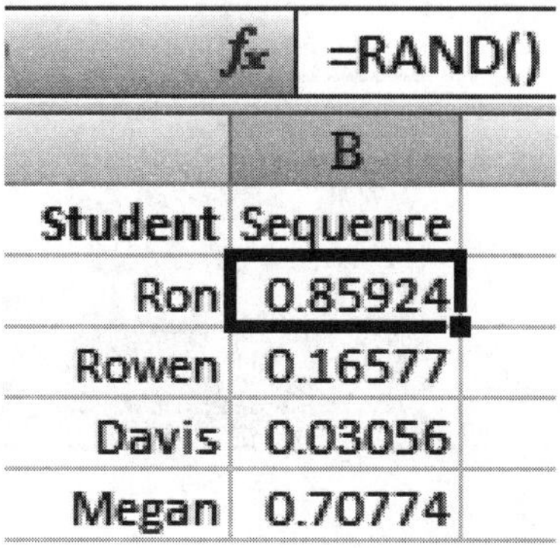

4) You can now delete column B.

Additional Details: If you want to fill column B with sequential numbers, you can enter 1 in B2 and 2 in B3. Then you highlight these two cells and double-click the fill handle to extend the series to your entire data set.

Summary: You can use the RAND function to provide a column of data to fairly and randomly sort a list.

Functions Discussed: =RAND()

PLAY DICE GAMES WITH EXCEL

Problem: My Monopoly set is missing the dice. How can I create a spreadsheet that will simulate randomly rolling two dice?

Strategy: You can use the RANDBETWEEN function and clever spreadsheet formatting to simulate two or more dice. Follow these steps:

1) Select cell B2. Select Home – Format – Row Height. Set the row height to 41, as shown in Figure 328.

Figure 328

A row height of 41 will make cell B2 basically a square.

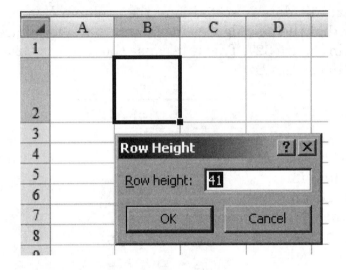

2) In cell B2, enter the formula =RANDBETWEEN(1,6).

3) With cell B2 selected, click the Center and Middle Align buttons on the Home tab of the ribbon.

Figure 329

Middle Align is a new icon on the Home tab of the ribbon.

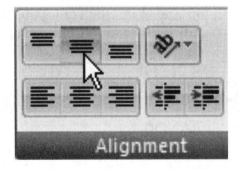

4) In the Font group of the Home tab, choose the Bold icon. Select 24 point from the font size dropdown.

5) Choose Thick Box Border from the Border dropdown, as shown in Figure 330.

Figure 330

Add a thick
border.

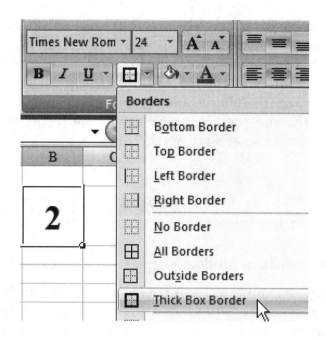

6)   Copy cell B2 and paste it to cell D2. As shown in Figure 331, you
      will have the two dice required for Monopoly.

Figure 331

Copy B2 to
make addition-
al dice.

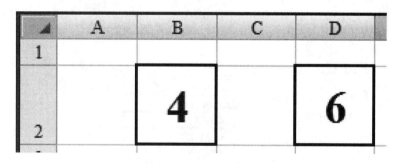

Results: You will have one die in cell B2 and another in cell D2. Every
time you press the F9 key, you will have a new roll of the dice.

Summary: You can use the RANDBETWEEN function and worksheet
formatting to create a dice simulation.

Commands Discussed: Various formatting commands on the Home
tab

Functions Discussed: =RANDBETWEEN()

Excel 97-2003: Many of the Excel 2007 Home tab formatting icons are on the Excel 2003 formatting toolbar. However, Align Middle was not in the toolbar by default; you had to select Format – Cells – Alignment – Vertical – Center. If the RANDBETWEEN function returns a NAME error, select Tools – Addins, add a check mark next to the Analysis Toolpak, click OK, and then press F9 to calculate the worksheet. Alternatively, you could use =INT(RAND()*6)+1.

CREATE RANDOM LETTERS

Problem: Instead of random numbers, I need to create random letters.

Strategy: The capital letter A is character number 65. You can use the =CHAR(65) function to produce an A. Thus, to produce a random character between A and Z, you would want to produce a random number between 65 and 90 and use it as the argument to the CHAR function.

If you forget that A is character 65, you can enter =CODE("A") in any blank cell. Excel will return the character code.

To generate random numbers between 65 and 90, you use =RANDBE-TWEEN(65,90) as shown in Figure 332.

Figure 332

Generate random letters.

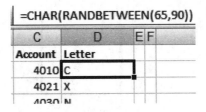

Additional Details: In my seminars, I might use customers in the form of ABC, Inc. In order to generate these names, I start with a random letter between A and X. To do this, follow these steps:

1)   In cell G2, enter the formula =RANDBETWEEN(65,88).

2)   In cell H2, enter the formula =CHAR(G2)&CHAR(G2+1)&CHAR(G2+2).

3)   In a blank area of the worksheet, enter a table with some different company name suffixes. For example, in Figure 333, my table

is in K2:K8. Note that each suffix either begins with a comma or a space.

The function called INDEX has three parameters: =INDEX(*SomeRange, WhichRow, WhichColumn*). In this case, you always want *SomeRange* to be $K$2:$K$8. You want *WhichRow* to be a random integer between 1 and 7. You always want *WhichColumn* to be 1.

4)   In cell I2, enter the formula =H2&INDEX(K$2:K$8,INT(RAND()*7) +1,1).

5)   Copy G2, H2, and I2 down to all the rows where you need data.

Results: As shown in Figure 333, you have a column of random company names.

Figure 333

Random company names.

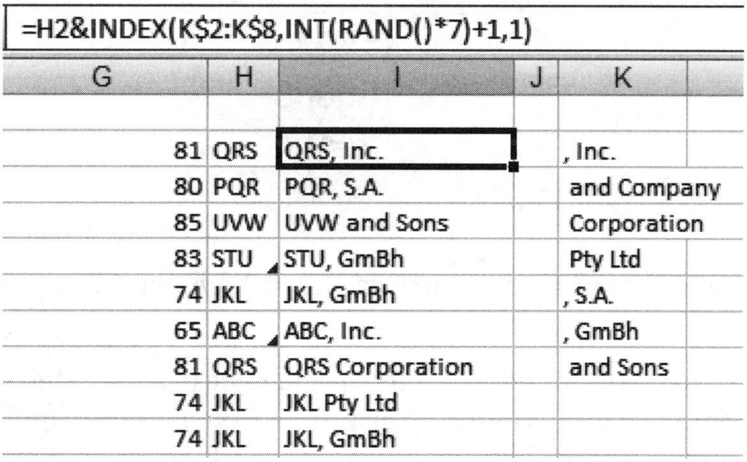

	=H2&INDEX(K$2:K$8,INT(RAND()*7)+1,1)				
G	H	I	J	K	
81	QRS	QRS, Inc.		, Inc.	
80	PQR	PQR, S.A.		and Company	
85	UVW	UVW and Sons		Corporation	
83	STU	STU, GmBh		Pty Ltd	
74	JKL	JKL, GmBh		, S.A.	
65	ABC	ABC, Inc.		, GmBh	
81	QRS	QRS Corporation		and Sons	
74	JKL	JKL Pty Ltd			
74	JKL	JKL, GmBh			

Summary: The RANDBETWEEN() function can generate random letters as well as numbers when it is used in conjunction with the CHAR function.

Functions Discussed: =CHAR(); =CODE(); =INDEX(); =RANDBE-TWEEN()

Excel 97-2003: Analysis Toolpak; =CHAR(INT(RAND()*26)+65)

CONVERT NUMBERS TO TEXT

Problem: I have a field that can contain numbers and text. I need the numeric entries to sort with the text entries. However, Excel always sorts the numeric entries to the top of the list, followed by the text entries, as shown in Figure 334.

Figure 334

Random company names.

	A
1	Style
2	5500
3	6000
4	7000
5	5500A
6	6000B
7	7000A

Strategy: This is a rare case in which you need to convert numeric entries to text entries.

If you were building this spreadsheet from scratch, you could select column A, select Home – Format – Format Cells, and then format the column as text. This would allow all future entries to automatically be converted to text. However, converting cells to have a text format does *not* retroactively convert numbers to text.

Another option would be to edit each cell that contains a number. To do this, you select the cell, press F2 to edit the cell, press Home to move to the beginning of the cell, and type an apostrophe. Then you press Enter to move to the next cell. This could get very tedious with more than a few cells to change.

The good news is that there is an easier method for converting all the entries in a column to text:

1) Select all the data in a column. Select Data – Text to Columns. In step 1 of the Convert Text to Columns Wizard, indicate that your data is fixed width.

2) In step 2 of the wizard, if you have any vertical lines drawn in the Data Preview section as shown in Figure 335, double-click to remove them.

Figure 335

Double-click any errant lines to remove them.

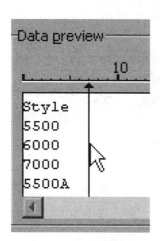

3) In step 3 of the wizard, choose Text as the column data format.

4) Click Finish. The column will be converted to text.

Gotcha: In prior versions of Excel, in this situation, you cannot sort using the AZ button. You must select Data – Sort. After you click OK to sort, you will get the Sort Warning dialog, so you need to choose to sort numbers and numbers stored as text separately.

Alternate Strategy: You could also insert a temporary column with the formula =TEXT(A2,"@").

Summary: You can select Data – Text to Columns to convert a column to text.

Commands Discussed: Data – Text to Columns; Data – Sort

CALCULATE A LOAN PAYMENT

Problem: I am considering buying a car. I want to calculate the loan payment, as shown in Figure 336.

Figure 336

Set up the price, term, and interest rate.

◢	A	B
1		
2	Price	25000
3	Term	60
4	Rate	5.25%
5		
6	Pmt	

Strategy: To calculate your car loan payment, you can use the PMT function. Follow these steps:

1) Enter price, term in months, and annual percentage rate in cells A2:B4, as shown in Figure 336. The PMT function has three required arguments: the interest rate, the number of payments in the loan, and the original loan amount.

    Gotcha: The interest rate must be entered as a percentage. If you are planning on monthly payments (which is normal), you have to divide the annual percentage rate by 12.

    Gotcha: In financial terms, the bank is loaning you $25,000—a positive amount coming to you. Thus, the payments that you make to the bank are really a negative amount—money leaving your wallet. For this reason, the result of the PMT function will be negative. However, you can precede the PMT function with a minus sign in order to return a positive payment amount.

2) Enter the formula =-PMT(B4/12,B3,B2) in cell B6 (see Figure 337).

Figure 337

The PMT function calculates the monthly payment.

=-PMT(B4/12,B3,B2)

◢	A	B
1		
2	Price	25000
3	Term	60
4	Rate	5.25%
5		
6	Pmt	$474.65
7		

Summary: The PMT function is great at calculating loan payments.

Functions Discussed: =PMT()

Part
II

CALCULATE MANY SCENARIOS FOR LOAN PAYMENTS

Problem: I am considering buying a car. I used "Calculate a Loan Payment" to calculate a loan payment. Now I want to do some what-if scenarios in order to see various options of increasing or decreasing the term or price. How can Excel help me with this?

Strategy: You follow the same setup described in "Calculate a Loan Payment." Then you copy cells B2:B6 and plug in different numbers for the price and/or term, as shown in Figure 338.

Figure 338

Copy so that you can play what-if analyses.

◢	A	B	C	D	E	F	G
1							
2	Price	25000	25000	25000	29000	29000	29000
3	Term	60	48	54	60	66	72
4	Rate	5.25%	5.25%	5.25%	5.25%	5.25%	5.25%
5							
6	Pmt	$474.65	$578.57	$520.81	$550.59	$506.83	$470.41

Summary: This is an area where Excel shines. After you have entered the formulas for one loan model, you can easily copy and create many more loan models.

BACK INTO AN ANSWER USING GOAL SEEK

Problem: I've determined that I want to obtain a 48-month loan for a car. The interest rate is 5%. I want to find out what loan amount would result in a $490 monthly payment. As shown in Figure 339, a $25,000 loan results in a $575.73 payment.

Figure 339

Find a price to yield a $490 payment.

`=-PMT(B4/12,B3,B2)`

	A	B
1		
2	Price	25000
3	Term	48
4	Rate	5%
5		
6	Pmt	$575.73
7		

Strategy: Although Excel has a financial function, PV, to determine the present value, it is easier to use the Goal Seek command on the Data tab. Here's how:

1) Select Data – What-if Analysis – Goal Seek. This will bring up the Goal Seek dialog.

2) As shown in Figure 340, indicate that you want to set cell B6 to $490 by changing cell B2.

Figure 340

Indicate which cell Excel should change to arrive at the answer.

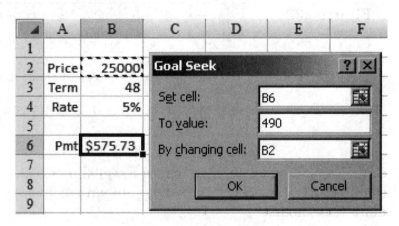

In a simple case like this one, Goal Seek will almost always succeed. Excel will play the higher/lower game until it hones in on an answer. Within a second, it will report back that it found a solution, as shown in Figure 341.

Figure 341

Excel finds the price to yield the desired payment.

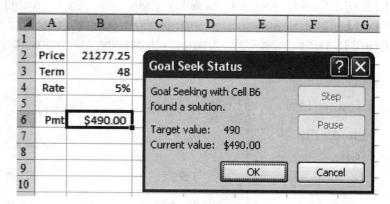

3) To accept the solution, click OK. To revert to the original value, click Cancel.

Results: Thanks to Goal Seek, you find that you can afford to borrow $21,277.25.

Additional Details: The formulas are still live after you use Goal Seek. You can continue to change terms, rates, and prices to calculate new payments.

Gotcha: When there is not a linear relationship between the two cells, Goal Seek may fail to find a solution.

Summary: The Goal Seek command is great for solving certain equations backward.

Commands Discussed: Data – What-if Analysis – Goal Seek

Excel 97-2003: Tools – Goal Seek

CREATE AN AMORTIZATION TABLE

Problem: I know it is easy to figure out a monthly payment using PMT. I would like to see my loan balance after each month's payment. How can I build an amortization table based on the information shown in Figure 342 that shows the projected principal, interest, and balance after each month?

Figure 342

Add an amortization table.

◢	A	B
1	Price	29995
2	Term	60
3	Rate	5.50%
4	Payment	$572.94

Strategy: You can use PPMT and IPMT to build this amortization table. Here's how:

1) In a blank section of the worksheet, add the column headings Payment, Date, Principal, Interest, and Balance.

2) Ensure that the formula for Balance in the first row points to the price in B1.

3) In the next row of the table, enter the number 1 for Payment. Ctrl+drag the fill handle to fill in the proper number of payments.

4) Enter the first payment date for the Date. Right-click+drag the fill handle to the last row. When you release the mouse button, choose Fill Months.

5) Enter the PPMT function, using the proper absolute references, so that you can copy the function to column D to be used for IPMT. The syntax is =PPMT(rate, per, nper, pv, [fv], [type]). The only difference from the PMT function is the addition of the period number as the second argument.

6) In C8, type =PPMT(. The rate is B3/12, but after clicking on B3, press the F4 key to add the dollar signs. Type /12 and a comma. Click on the first payment number. Press the F4 key three times so that a dollar sign appears before the column number. Type a comma. Click on the Term in B2 and press F4. Type a comma. Type a minus sign and click on the price in B1. Press F4 and type the closing parenthesis. The whole formula, as you can see in Figure 343, is =PPMT($B$3/12,$A8,$B$2,-$B$1).

7) Copy this formula to the Interest Payment column. Edit the formula and change PPMT to IPMT. Use the F2 key or double click the cell in order to edit the formula. Alternatively, select the cell. Use the mouse to select the first P in PPMT in the formula bar. Type an I to change to IPMT.

8) For the Balance formula, use the previous balance minus this month's principal payment. In Figure 343, this would be =E7-C8.

9) Select the three cells that contain the principal, interest, and balance calculations. Double-click the fill handle to copy the formulas for all months.

Results: Your table will be complete, as shown in Figure 343.

Figure 343

Copy the formulas to create the table.

=PPMT($B$3/12,$A8,$B$2,-$B$1)

	A	B	C	D	E
1	Price	29995			
2	Term	60			
3	Rate	5.50%			
4	Payment	$572.94			
5					
6	Payment	Date	Principal	Interest	Balance
7					29995
8	1	7/1/2008	$435.46	$137.48	$29,559.54
9	2	8/1/2008	$437.46	$135.48	$29,122.08
10	3	9/1/2008	$439.46	$133.48	$28,682.62

Additional Details: To test that the table is correct, scroll to the last row. You should see that the balance reaches zero with the last payment (see Figure 344).

Figure 344

If your table is correct, the balance should reach zero for the last payment.

=E66-C67

	A	B	C	D	E
1	Price	29995			
2	Term	60			
3	Rate	5.50%			
4	Payment	$572.94			
5					
6	Payment	Date	Principal	Interest	Balance
61	54	12/1/2012	$554.89	$18.05	$3,383.16
62	55	1/1/2013	$557.43	$15.51	$2,825.72
63	56	2/1/2013	$559.99	$12.95	$2,265.74
64	57	3/1/2013	$562.55	$10.38	$1,703.18
65	58	4/1/2013	$565.13	$7.81	$1,138.05
66	59	5/1/2013	$567.72	$5.22	$570.33
67	60	6/1/2013	$570.33	$2.61	$0.00
68					

Summary: You can use the PPMT and IPMT functions to calculate principal and interest for any period of a loan.

Functions Discussed: =PPMT(); =IPMT()

GET HELP ON ANY FUNCTION WHILE ENTERING A FORMULA

Problem: There are hundreds of functions available in Excel. Sometimes I remember that I need to use a particular function, but I cannot remember the sequence of the arguments in the function.

Strategy: In Excel 2002 and later, if you type the equal sign followed by the function and the opening parenthesis, a ToolTip will appear reminding you of the order of the arguments. Any arguments in square brackets are optional. The argument in bold (see Figure 345) is the argument you need to type next.

Figure 345

The ToolTip lists the arguments.

◢	A	B	C	D
1	Price	25000		
2	Rate	5.90%		
3	Payment	-425		
4				
5	Term	=NPER(		
6		NPER(rate, pmt, pv, [fv], [type])		

Alternate **Strategy:** If you are using Excel 2000 or if you need more help than the ToolTip's abbreviations (for example, pmt, pv) give you, you can use the Function Arguments dialog. To do so, you type the equals sign followed by the function name and the opening parenthesis, and then you press Ctrl+A to display the Function Arguments dialog box, as shown in Figure 346.

Figure 346

Notice the help for the current argument at the bottom.

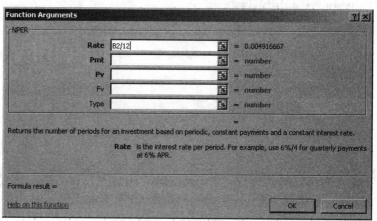

The Function Arguments dialog box shows the order of the arguments. Arguments in bold are required. The other arguments are optional. As you click into each text box in the dialog box, the text at the bottom describes that argument in detail.

If you still need more help, you can click the hyperlink at the bottom of the dialog box, which leads to the complete help topic for this function.

As you enter the value for each argument, the Function Arguments dialog box will calculate the results of that argument. After you have entered all the required arguments, the Function Wizard will display the result of the function, as shown in Figure 347. You can consider whether this result is a reasonable number before accepting the formula.

Figure 347

The solution appears at bottom right.

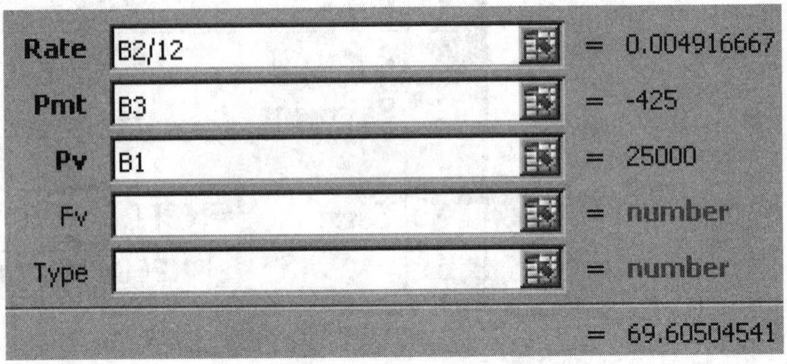

Rate	B2/12	= 0.004916667
Pmt	B3	= -425
Pv	B1	= 25000
Fv		= number
Type		= number
		= 69.60504541

The formula result indicates that if you want to pay $425 per month for a $25,000 car, you will be paying for 69.6 months. This seems about right, so click OK.

Results: You've entered a fairly complex function without having to remember its details.

Summary: You can use the Ctrl+A shortcut after entering the opening parenthesis of a function to display the Function Arguments dialog box.

DISCOVER NEW FUNCTIONS USING THE FX BUTTON

Problem: There are hundreds of functions available in Excel. I know that I want to find a function to calculate a car payment, but I have no clue which function might do this.

Strategy: To find a function, you can click the Insert Function (fx) button. This button is always available to the left of the formula bar, and it appears 12 additional times in Excel 2007, mostly on the Formulas tab. Figure 348 shows three instances of the fx button. You can click this button to bring up the Insert Function dialog.

Figure 348

Three of the 13 instances of fx.

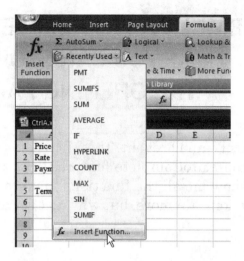

By default, the Insert Function dialog lists the most recently used functions. All of Excel's functions are categorized into these categories: Financial, Date & Time, Math & Trig, Statistical, Lookup & Reference, Database, Text, Logical, Information, Cube, and Engineering. It can be difficult to correctly guess the category. SUM is a Math & Trig function, yet AVERAGE is a Statistical function. Rather than browse each category, you can type a few words in the search box and click Go. Excel will show you the relevant functions to choose from, as shown in Figure 349.

Figure 349

Search for a function.

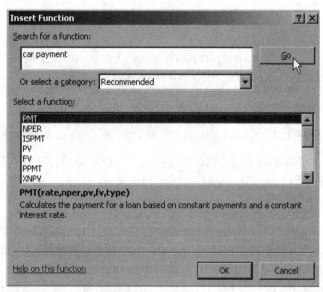

Summary: You can click the fx button to more easily find a function.

YES, FORMULA AUTOCOMPLETE IS COOL, IF YOU CAN STOP ENTERING THE OPENING PARENTHESES

Problem: At an Excel launch event, the Microsoft rep showed off the amazing new Formula AutoComplete feature. I can just type =RA in a cell, and Excel will show me all the functions that start with RA. I don't have to type my functions anymore, but why do I get an error every time I try to do this?

Figure 350

Yes, Formula AutoComplete is cool.

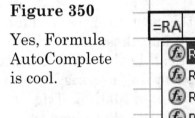
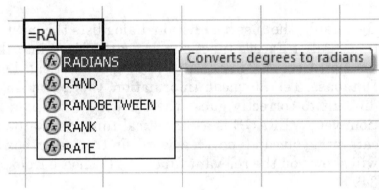

Strategy: Watch the parentheses! AutoComplete types the opening parenthesis, but not the closing parenthesis.

Here is how you're supposed to use AutoComplete:

1) Type =RA. Excel displays a list of five functions.

2) Use the down arrow to move to RANDBETWEEN. Excel will show a ToolTip to indicate that the function will return a random number between the numbers you specify.

3) Press the Tab key to accept the function and move to the arguments. I was used to using the Tab key here because I've been using AutoComplete in VBA for a while. However, many people try to press Enter here, which leads to a #NAME? error. After you press the Tab key, Excel fills in the function name and the opening parenthesis, as shown in Figure 351.

Figure 351

Press Tab to finish typing the selected function name.

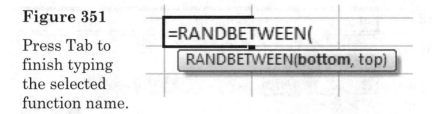

Gotcha: I don't want to sound ungrateful, but Microsoft types the opening parenthesis for you. I cannot seem to break the habit of typing the opening parenthesis myself. Going back to the days of typing @SUM(, or even typing =SUM(, my fingers automatically type the opening parenthesis. I cannot type =RANDBETWEEN(without typing an opening parenthesis. Here, let me try a few more: =VLOOKUP(=AVERAGE(=TRIM(=MID(=ROMAN(. My brain is simply hard-wired to type that opening parenthesis. I don't even consciously think about typing the parenthesis. It simply just gets typed.

So, as you can guess, every time I use AutoComplete, I get an error saying that I've typed too many parentheses (see Figure 352).

Figure 352

Too many opening parentheses.

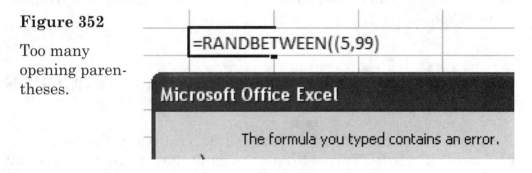

I don't have a good solution for this, other than trying to retrain yourself not to type the opening parenthesis.

Additional Details: AutoComplete can also fill in table field names for those who have embraced the new table functionality and are entering formulas in table syntax (see Figure 353).

Figure 353

I can't even
learn to stop
typing the pa-
rentheses and
you want me
to learn this??

	D	E	F	G	H	I
	rofit ▼	GP% ▼				
	11386.83	=Table1[[#This Row],[Profit]]/Table1[				
	4458.16					
	6372					
	4053.82					
	5641.1					
	5100.81					
	4984.65					
	13887.58					
	6831.33					
	4926.95					
	7749.39					

=Table1[[#This Row],[Profit]]/Table1[

Region
Revenue
Cost
Profit
GP%
#All
#Data
#Headers
#Totals
#This Row

Summary: Formula AutoComplete feature, which is new in Excel 2007, enters the opening parenthesis for you.

See Also: "Use Table Functionality to Simplify Copying of Formulas" on page 256

THREE METHODS OF ENTERING FORMULAS

Problem: I have heard that there are three basic ways of entering simple formulas in Excel. I'd like to enter formulas faster, and I suspect that knowing the three ways of entering simple formulas will help me. For example, in the worksheet shown in Figure 354, I want to calculate total cost in E3 as the case quantity in B3 multiplied by the unit cost in C3.

Figure 354

Multiply B3 by
C3.

⊿	A	B	C	D	E
1					
2	Item	Case Pack	Unit Cost	Unit Price	Total Cost
3	ABC	6	6.06	11.95	
4	DEF	6	6.18	13.45	
5	GHI	24	8.35	17.65	
6	JKL	1	1.53	2.95	
7	MNO	24	4.16	8.65	
8	PQR	1	2.71	5.65	

Strategy: One way to make this calculation is to simply type the formula:

1) Put the cell pointer in E3 and type =b3*c3, as shown in Figure 355, and then press Enter.

Figure 355

This method takes only seven keystrokes.

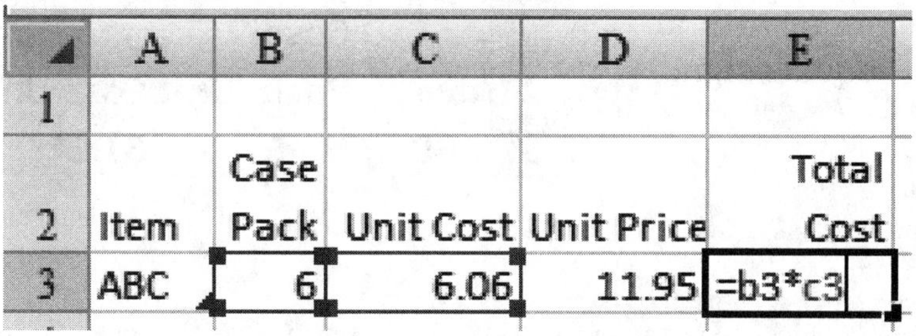

◢	A	B	C	D	E
1					
2	Item	Case Pack	Unit Cost	Unit Price	Total Cost
3	ABC	6	6.06	11.95	=b3*c3

Part II

2) The formula will calculate. You will see the original formula in the formula bar above E1. The worksheet will show the result of the calculation, as shown in Figure 356.

Figure 356

Press Enter.

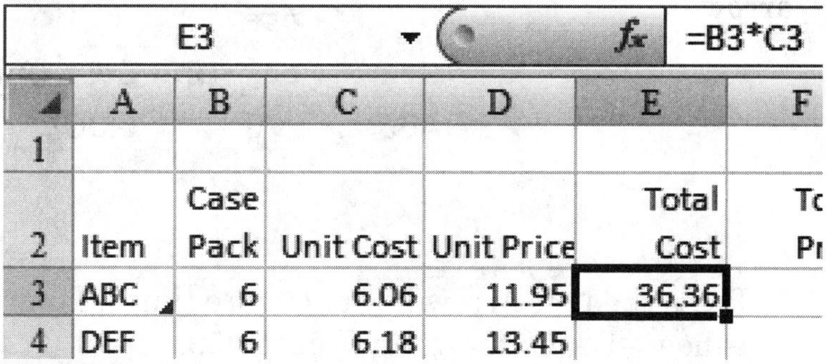

E3				▼	f_x	=B3*C3

◢	A	B	C	D	E	F
1						
2	Item	Case Pack	Unit Cost	Unit Price	Total Cost	Tc Pr
3	ABC	6	6.06	11.95	36.36	
4	DEF	6	6.18	13.45		

Additional Details: This method is great for short functions that require only a few keystrokes. However, this method gets complicated when you are dealing with complex formulas.

Alternate Strategy: Another way to enter calculations is to use the arrow keys. Anyone who was using spreadsheets in the days of Lotus 1-2-3 often used this method. When you have mastered this method, it is very fast and very intuitive. Here's how it works:

1) Move the cell pointer to E3 and type an equals sign to let Excel know that you are about to enter a formula (see Figure 357).

Figure 357

Start a formula with an equals sign.

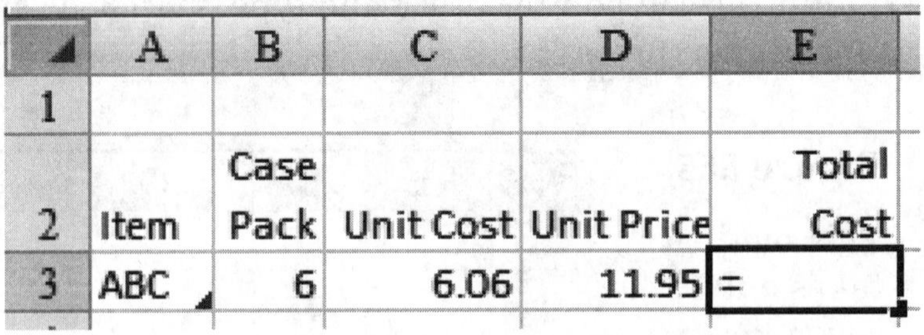

◢	A	B	C	D	E
1					
2	Item	Case Pack	Unit Cost	Unit Price	Total Cost
3	ABC	6	6.06	11.95	=

2) Press the Left Arrow key. As shown in Figure 358, a dotted border surrounds the cell to the left of E3. Excel starts to build the formula =D3.

Figure 358

Press the left arrow.

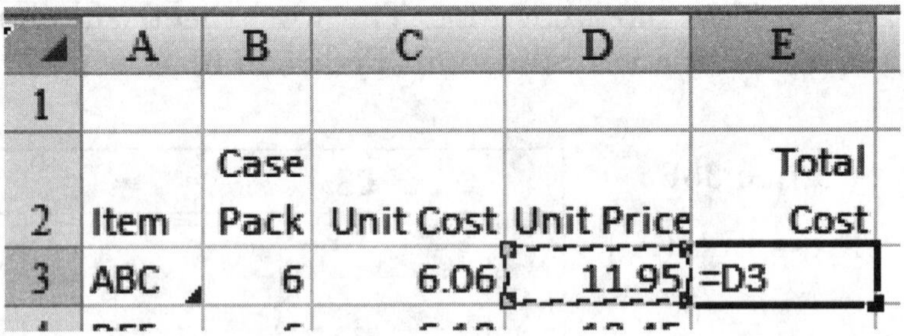

◢	A	B	C	D	E
1					
2	Item	Case Pack	Unit Cost	Unit Price	Total Cost
3	ABC	6	6.06	11.95	=D3

3) Press the Left Arrow key two more times. Your provisional formula is now =B3, as shown in Figure 359.

Figure 359

Press left arrow two more times.

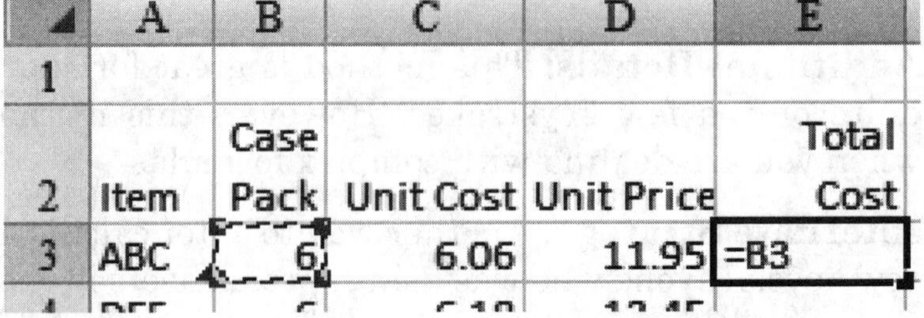

◢	A	B	C	D	E
1					
2	Item	Case Pack	Unit Cost	Unit Price	Total Cost
3	ABC	6	6.06	11.95	=B3

4) Press * on either the keyboard or the numeric keypad. The dotted border will disappear from B3 and be replaced by a solid-colored border, as shown in Figure 360. Pressing any operator key, such as +, -, *, or /, tells Excel that you are moving on to the next part of the formula.

Figure 360

Typing an operator returns the focus to the original cell.

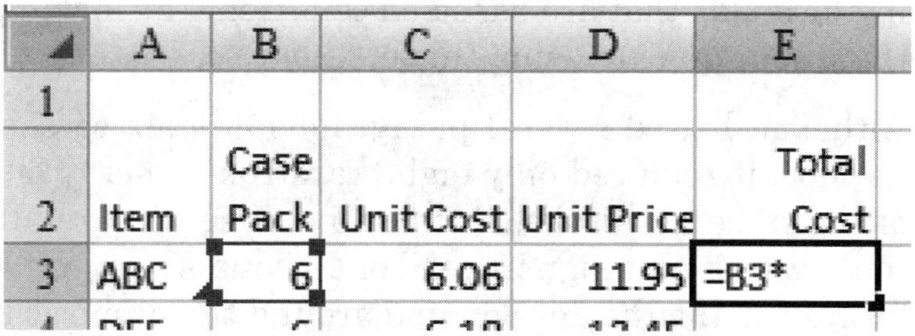

	A	B	C	D	E
1					
2	Item	Case Pack	Unit Cost	Unit Price	Total Cost
3	ABC	6	6.06	11.95	=B3*

5) Press the Left Arrow key. The dotted border reappears. You now have a provisional formula of =B3*D3, as shown in Figure 361. This isn't quite right, yet, but you're getting close.

Figure 361

Press the Left Arrow key to begin moving toward C3.

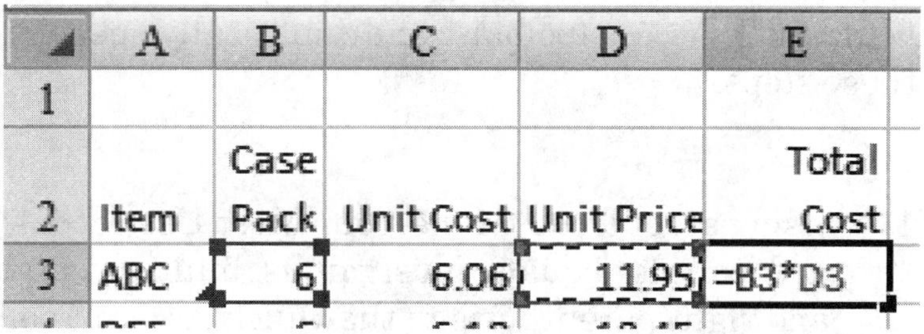

	A	B	C	D	E
1					
2	Item	Case Pack	Unit Cost	Unit Price	Total Cost
3	ABC	6	6.06	11.95	=B3*D3

6) Press the Left Arrow key one more time. As shown in Figure 362, the provisional formula is now correct.

Figure 362

Press the Left Arrow key once more to arrive at C3.

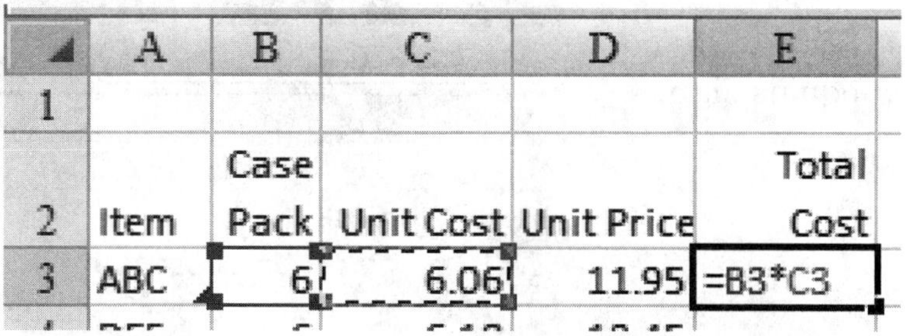

	A	B	C	D	E
1					
2	Item	Case Pack	Unit Cost	Unit Price	Total Cost
3	ABC	6	6.06	11.95	=B3*C3

7) Press Enter. The formula will calculate. You will see the original formula in the formula bar above E1. The worksheet will show the result of the calculation.

Additional Details: With this method, you never have to type cell references. You merely point to them using the arrow keys. If you are building formulas that are based on cells near the formula cell, you can enter them very quickly using this method.

Although I used several paragraphs and six screen shots to show this method, it required only eight keystrokes, many of which were repeats of the same keystroke. Further, because you are allowed to start a formula with a plus sign instead of an equals sign, you can enter the entire formula using the keys on and around the numeric keypad on a desktop computer (that is, +←←←*←←Enter).

Alternate Strategy: Another way to enter calculations in Excel is to use the mouse. Normally, people use the keyboard to type the equals sign, math operators, and enter and the mouse to click on cell references. Moving your hand from the mouse to the keyboard takes a lot of time and dramatically slows the entry of formulas. Adding a few icons to your Quick Access toolbar can dramatically speed formula entry. Follow these steps.

1) Using steps from "Make Your Most Used Icons Visible" on page 13, add icons for equals, plus, minus, multiply, divide, left parenthesis, and right parenthesis to the Quick Access Toolbar. These icons are found in the "Commands Not in the Ribbon" category.

2) Start in cell E3. Click the equals sign icon. This tells Excel that you are about to enter a formula. (see Figure 363)

Figure 363

Start with an equals sign.

▲	A	B	C	D	E
1					
2	Item	Case Pack	Unit Cost	Unit Price	Total Cost
3	ABC	6	6.06	11.95	=

3) Using the mouse, touch cell B3. Excel starts to build your formula, as shown in Figure 364.

Figure 364

Touch the first reference with the mouse.

◢	A	B	C	D	E
1					
2	Item	Case Pack	Unit Cost	Unit Price	Total Cost
3	ABC	6	6.06	11.95	=B3

4) Click the * icon.

5) Click on cell C3. The provisional formula now looks correct, as shown in Figure 365.

Figure 365

Type an asterisk.

◢	A	B	C	D	E
1					
2	Item	Case Pack	Unit Cost	Unit Price	Total Cost
3	ABC	6	6.06	11.95	=B3*C3
4	DEE	5	5.18	13.45	

6) Click the green checkmark to complete the formula. (Figure 366) The formula will calculate. You will see the original formula in the formula bar above E1. The worksheet will show the result of the calculation.

Figure 366

Complete the formula.

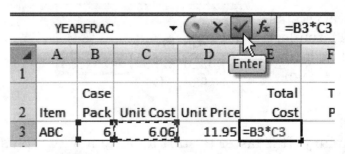

Summary: There are three basic methods for entering formulas in Excel. Using the easiest method for the situation can radically improve your efficiency.

START A FORMULA WITH = OR +

Problem: Every Excel formula has to start with an equals sign. Now that I am entering formulas using arrow keys, I think it's a pain to type the equals sign.

Strategy: In order to make the transition from Lotus 1-2-3 to Excel less painful, Microsoft allows you to start a formula with the + sign. Because there is a huge plus key on the numeric keypad of most desktop computers, it is often easier to start the formula with plus than with equals, especially if you're entering the rest of your formula using arrow keys. You simply type the plus sign and your formula, as shown in Figure 367.

Figure 367

Start your formula with a plus sign.

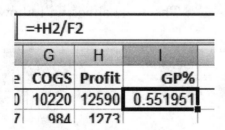

Gotcha: After you press the Enter key, Excel will edit the formula to add an equals sign before the initial plus. This will cause people to ask why you are using =+2+2 instead of just =2+2 (see Figure 368).

Figure 368

Excel accepts the formula, but adds an equals sign.

	=+H2/F2	
G	H	I
COGS	**Profit**	**GP%**
10220	12590	0.551951
984	1273	

Summary: It is faster to start a formula with a plus sign than with an equals sign.

USE AUTOSUM TO QUICKLY ENTER A TOTAL FORMULA

Problem: I have the Excel data shown in Figure 369, and I need to total the rows quickly.

Figure 369

Add total formulas.

	A	B	C	D	E	F
1	Item	Q1	Q2	Q3	Q4	Total
2	ABC	91	92	22	83	
3	DEF	31	41	17	33	
4	GHI	72	63	82	64	
5	JKL	21	98	4	90	
6	MNO	36	81	52	35	
7	PQR	22	90	87	75	
8	STU	65	85	72	34	
9	VWX	91	40	41	6	
10	Total					
11						

Part II

Strategy: You can use the AutoSum button on the Home tab or Formulas tab. The AutoSum button is a Greek letter sigma, as shown in Figure 370.

Figure 370

The odd-shaped E is a Greek letter sigma, which is the math symbol for totaling.

Here's how you use AutoSum to add a total formula:

1) Place the cell pointer in cell B10. Click the AutoSum button, as shown in Figure 371. Excel analyzes your data and predicts that

you want to total the range of numbers above the cell pointer. Excel proposes the provisional formula =SUM(B2:B9).

Figure 371

Excel proposes a formula.

	A	B
1	Item	Q1
2	ABC	91
3	DEF	31
4	GHI	72
5	JKL	21
6	MNO	36
7	PQR	22
8	STU	65
9	VWX	91
10	Total	=SUM(B2:B9)

2) Review the range in the proposed formula, if needed. When the range is correct, press Enter to accept the formula. Excel displays the total, as shown in Figure 372.

Figure 372

Build a sum formula with two clicks.

B10 f_x =SUM(B2:B9)

	A	B	C	D	E	F
1	Item	Q1	Q2	Q3	Q4	Tot
2	ABC	91	92	22	83	
3	DEF	31	41	17	33	
4	GHI	72	63	82	64	
5	JKL	21	98	4	90	
6	MNO	36	81	52	35	
7	PQR	22	90	87	75	
8	STU	65	85	72	34	
9	VWX	91	40	41	6	
10	Total	429				

3) With the mouse, drag the fill handle (the square dot in the lower-right corner of the cell pointer) to the right to include cells C10 through F10 and then release the mouse button. The formula will be copied to all five columns.

Additional Details: You can use Alt+= instead of clicking the AutoSum button.

Gotcha: Blank cells in the sum range will cause AutoSum to exclude cells above the blank cell.

Alternate Strategy: Select the range of numbers plus the blank cell where the total should go. Click AutoSum. Excel will fill in the total formula without requiring you to press Enter.

Summary: The AutoSum button is a powerful tool for quickly entering a total formula.

Functions Discussed: =SUM()

AUTOSUM DOESN'T ALWAYS PREDICT MY DATA CORRECTLY

Problem: When I use the AutoSum button, Excel sometimes predicts the wrong range of data to total. In Figure 373, for example, AutoSum worked fine in F2 and F3, but in cell F4, Excel thought I wanted to total the rows above F4. How do I enter the correct range?

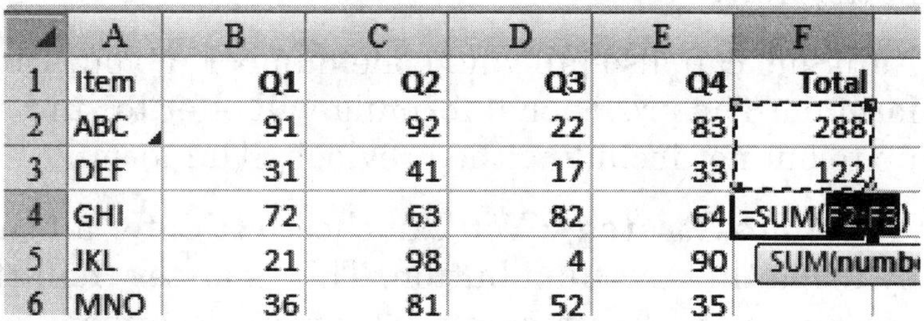

Figure 373

When given a choice between totaling a row or a column, Excel chooses the column.

◢	A	B	C	D	E	F
1	Item	Q1	Q2	Q3	Q4	Total
2	ABC	91	92	22	83	288
3	DEF	31	41	17	33	122
4	GHI	72	63	82	64	=SUM(F2:F3)
5	JKL	21	98	4	90	SUM(numb
6	MNO	36	81	52	35	

Strategy: After you press the AutoSum button, the provisional range address is highlighted in the provisional formula. Using your mouse, you highlight the correct range.

AutoSum will work correctly in F2 and F3. It will predict that you want to sum the data in that row. However, in cell F4, Excel has a choice: either sum the two cells in that column or the four cells in the row. Excel always chooses to sum the two cells above in this situation.

After you press the AutoSum button, note that F2:F3 is highlighted in the formula. This allows you to enter the correct range. There are three methods:

- With the mouse, highlight B4:E4 and press Enter.

- With the keyboard, type B4:E4.

- Using the arrow keys, press the Left Arrow key to move to E4. While holding down the Shift key, press the Left Arrow key three times to highlight B4:E4, as shown in Figure 374.

Figure 374

Use the arrow keys to select the correct range.

▲	A	B	C	D	E	F
1	Item	Q1	Q2	Q3	Q4	Total
2	ABC	91	92	22	83	288
3	DEF	31	41	17	33	122
4	GHI	72	63	82	64	=SUM(B4:E4)

Additional Details: The problem described in this section will always happen in the third and fourth rows of the data. When you try to use the AutoSum button in F6 and beyond, Excel will correctly sum all the data in that row.

AutoSum can also fail when one number in your range contains a SUM formula. The provisional formula will offer to sum a formula extending up to but not including the previous SUM formula.

Alternate Strategy: You can choose to enter all the totals at one time by using the AutoSum button. This is faster than the methods just described and will eliminate the problem described. Follow these steps:

1) Highlight the entire range that needs a SUM formula, as shown in Figure 375.

Figure 375

Select the entire range.

▲	A	B	C	D	E	F
1	Item	Q1	Q2	Q3	Q4	Total
2	ABC	91	92	22	83	
3	DEF	31	41	17	33	
4	GHI	72	63	82	64	
5	JKL	21	98	4	90	
6	MNO	36	81	52	35	
7	PQR	22	90	87	75	
8	STU	65	85	72	34	
9	VWX	91	40	41	6	
10	Total	429	590	377	420	

2)   Press the AutoSum button. Excel makes a prediction and fills in the total formulas automatically, as shown in Figure 376. Excel does not show the provisional formula, so check one formula to see that it is correct.

Figure 376

Excel fills in all the totals without displaying a provisional formula.

| F2 | | | | | fx | =SUM(B2:E2) |

▲	A	B	C	D	E	F
1	Item	Q1	Q2	Q3	Q4	Total
2	ABC	91	92	22	83	288
3	DEF	31	41	17	33	122
4	GHI	72	63	82	64	281
5	JKL	21	98	4	90	213
6	MNO	36	81	52	35	204
7	PQR	22	90	87	75	274
8	STU	65	85	72	34	256
9	VWX	91	40	41	6	178
10	Total	429	590	377	420	1816

Gotcha: Headings that contain dates or numeric years can really cause problems for AutoSum. Excel will usually get fooled into including the heading in the sum. Be extra cautious when using AutoSum in these situations. In Figure 377, for example, Excel incorrectly included the headings in row 1.

Figure 377

Excel will incorrectly assume the headings should be in the total.

| B10 | | | | | fx | =SUM(B1:B9) |

▲	A	B	C	D	E	F
1	Item	2006	2007	2008	2009	Tot
2	ABC	1	1	1	1	
3	DEF	1	1	1	1	
4	GHI	1	1	1	1	
5	JKL	1	1	1	1	
6	MNO	1	1	1	1	
7	PQR	1	1	1	1	
8	STU	1	1	1	1	
9	VWX	1	1	1	1	
10	Total	2014	2015	2016	2017	
11						

There is an amazing workaround. You can select the cells to be totaled plus one extra row and one extra column, as shown in Figure 378.

Figure 378

Select an extra row and an extra column.

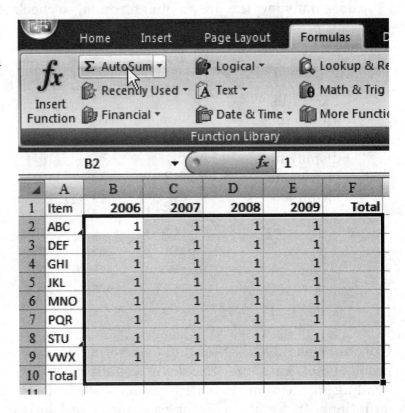

When you click the AutoSum button, Excel correctly adds SUM formulas in the total row and total column (see Figure 379).

Figure 379

Add all the totals in one click.

	A	B	C	D	E	F
		B10		fx	=SUM(B2:B9)	
1	Item	2006	2007	2008	2009	Total
2	◈	1	1	1	1	4
3	DEF	1	1	1	1	4
4	GHI	1	1	1	1	4
5	JKL	1	1	1	1	4
6	MNO	1	1	1	1	4
7	PQR	1	1	1	1	4
8	STU	1	1	1	1	4
9	VWX	1	1	1	1	4
10	Total	8	8	8	8	32
11						

Summary: The AutoSum function does not always correctly predict the range to be totaled, but it is easy to use the mouse or keyboard to show Excel the correct range.

Functions Discussed: =SUM()

USE THE AUTOSUM BUTTON TO ENTER AVERAGES, MIN, MAX, AND COUNT

Problem: I often enter totals formulas, but in this case, I need to enter an average formula (see Figure 380). How can I do it quickly?

Figure 380

Average the readings.

◢	A	B
4	Time	Reading
5	1:00 AM	86.2
6	1:05 AM	86.22
7	1:10 AM	86.21
8	1:15 AM	86.26
9	1:20 AM	86.24
10	1:25 AM	86.31
11	1:30 AM	86.33
12	1:35 AM	86.33
13	1:40 AM	86.43
14	1:45 AM	86.61
15	1:50 AM	86.88
16	1:55 AM	87.18
17	Average	
18		

Strategy: You use the dropdown arrow located next to the AutoSum button, as shown in Figure 381. Instead of selecting Sum, you select the Average option.

Figure 381

The AutoSum dropdown offers additional functions.

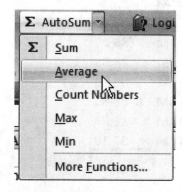

Excel enters a provisional average formula, as shown in Figure 382.

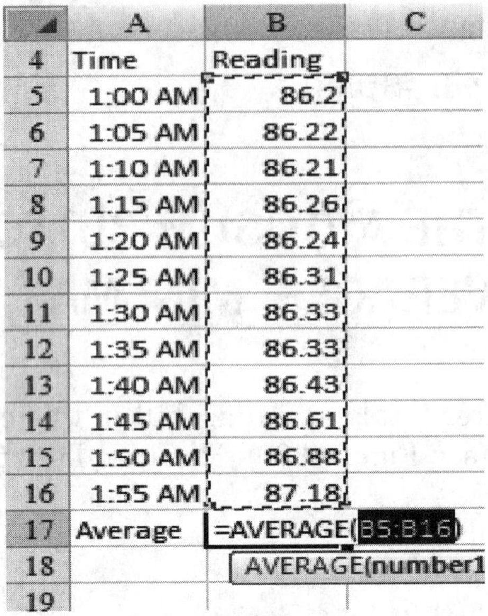

Figure 382

As with Au-
toSum, make
sure the pro-
visional range
Excel suggests
is correct.

◢	A	B	C
4	Time	Reading	
5	1:00 AM	86.2	
6	1:05 AM	86.22	
7	1:10 AM	86.21	
8	1:15 AM	86.26	
9	1:20 AM	86.24	
10	1:25 AM	86.31	
11	1:30 AM	86.33	
12	1:35 AM	86.33	
13	1:40 AM	86.43	
14	1:45 AM	86.61	
15	1:50 AM	86.88	
16	1:55 AM	87.18	
17	Average	=AVERAGE(B5:B16)	
18		AVERAGE(number1	
19			

If Excel correctly analyzes your data, as shown in Figure 383, you press
Enter to accept the formula.

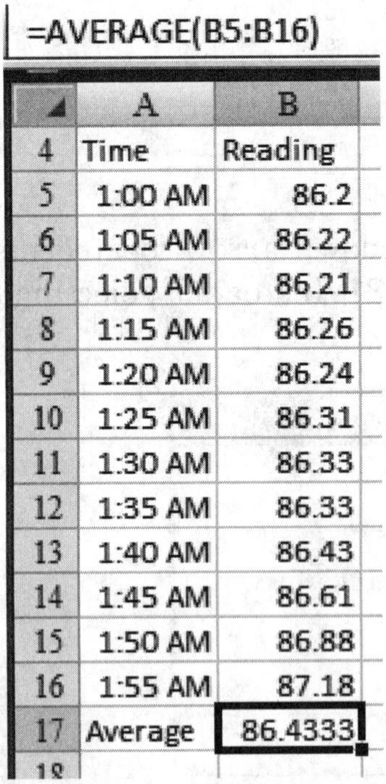

Figure 383

It takes three
clicks to enter
this formula.

=AVERAGE(B5:B16)

◢	A	B
4	Time	Reading
5	1:00 AM	86.2
6	1:05 AM	86.22
7	1:10 AM	86.21
8	1:15 AM	86.26
9	1:20 AM	86.24
10	1:25 AM	86.31
11	1:30 AM	86.33
12	1:35 AM	86.33
13	1:40 AM	86.43
14	1:45 AM	86.61
15	1:50 AM	86.88
16	1:55 AM	87.18
17	Average	86.4333
18		

Additional Details: Excel does *not* remember the last setting of the AutoSum button. If you do an average and then use just the AutoSum button, it will return to using a SUM formula.

Additional Details: You can use other options on the AutoSum dropdown as follows:

- The Max option returns the largest numeric value.

- The Min option returns the smallest numeric value.

- The Count option will count the number of numeric entries in the list.

Summary: The dropdown arrow next to the AutoSum function offers access to finding the average, min, max, or count of a range.

Functions Discussed: =AVERAGE(); =MIN(); =MAX(); =COUNT()

THE COUNT OPTION OF THE AUTOSUM DROPDOWN DOESN'T APPEAR TO WORK

Problem: I am using the Count option from the AutoSum dropdown on the toolbar, but it does not appear to provide consistent results. In Figure 384, for example, cells B11 and C11 both contain counts of the cells in rows 2 through 10 of each column. One function indicates that there are nine entries; the other function indicates that there are only two. Clearly, both columns have nine entries. What is the problem?

Figure 384

Why does Excel think the count is two?

fx	=COUNT(B2:B10)	
	A	B	C
1		Purchase Order	Amount
2		A12345	878.31
3		05J123	566.41
4		WMJ987	165.91
5		9878	115.97
6		KJHK98	788.5
7		87-9878	890.7
8		34H8987	665.17
9		87888	161.94
10		H12354	681.09
11	Count:	2	9

Strategy: The COUNT function will count only numeric entries. If you need to count all entries, you have to use the COUNTA function. One solution is to edit the formula in B2 by adding an A after the T in COUNT. The other method is to enter the formula correctly in the first place. Here's what you do:

1) Put the cell pointer in B11. Select AutoSum dropdown – More Functions, as shown in Figure 385. There are hundreds of functions available, and it can be difficult to remember where a function is; for example, you don't know if COUNTA is in the Math & Trig section or somewhere else.

Figure 385

The AutoSum dropdown can lead to more functions.

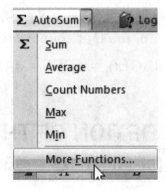

2) In the Search for a Function box, type the words "count text" then click Go. Excel will propose possible functions, as shown in Figure 386.

Figure 386

Type a few words and click Go.

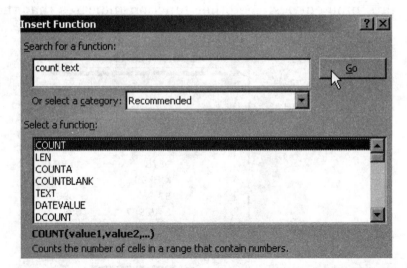

3) Scroll through the list of functions that Excel returns related to the COUNT function. (Note that a description of the selected function appears below the list.) When you find the COUNTA function, click on it and then click OK. Excel will analyze your data and predict the range that you want to use. However, Excel is not good at predicting data when the range contains numeric and alphanumeric entries. The Function Arguments dialog box appears. In this particular case, as shown in Figure 387, Excel assumes that you only want to use COUNTA on the range B9:B10.

Figure 387

Excel guessed the range incorrectly.

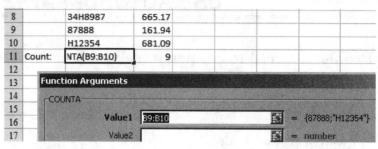

Part II

4) If you can see the data on the worksheet, use the mouse and highlight the correct range. If the range is behind the dialog, click the Reference icon at the right edge of the text box. Then highlight the correct range. Alternatively, you can drag the dialog box until your range is completely visible.

5) Click OK in the Function Arguments dialog to accept the formula.

Results: As shown in Figure 388, the COUNTA function returns the desired value.

Figure 388

COUNTA returns the expected result.

f_x	=COUNTA(B2:B10)	
A	B	C
1	Purchase Order	Amount
2	A12345	878.31
3	05J123	566.41
4	WMJ987	165.91
5	9878	115.97
6	KJHK98	788.5
7	87-9878	890.7
8	34H8987	665.17
9	87888	161.94
10	H12354	681.09
11 Count:	9	9

Additional Details: COUNTA will not count blank cells. You use COUNTBLANK to return the number of empty cells in a range.

Summary: The COUNT function does not count text entries in a list, so you need to use the COUNTA function instead.

Functions Discussed: =COUNT(); =COUNTA(), =COUNTBLANK()

USE AUTOSUM AFTER FILTERING

Problem: I need to total only the visible cells in the filtered data set shown in Figure 389.

Figure 389

Apply a filter first, then select the first blank cell below the data.

	A	B	C	D	E	F
1						
2						
3	Region ▼	Produ ▼	Invoi ▼	Customer	Quant ▼	Reven ▼
79	West	ABC	Feb-08	Air Canada	300	5859
134	Central	XYZ	Mar-08	Air Canada	200	4948
291	West	XYZ	Jul-08	Air Canada	800	17856
421	East	DEF	Sep-08	Air Canada	100	2358
570						
571						
572						

Strategy: You can use the AutoSum icon after applying a filter. Normally, the AutoSum icon inserts a SUM function. When you apply a filter and then use AutoSum, Excel will insert a SUBTOTAL function instead. This function will ignore rows hidden by the Filter command. Follow these steps:

1) Choose a cell in your data set. Select Data – Filter.

2) Apply a filter to at least one column. Open the Customer dropdown and choose one customer.

3) Select the first visible cell beneath your data. In Figure 389, the last visible row is 421, but the next blank cell is in row 570.

4) Click the AutoSum icon and press Enter. Excel inserts a SUB-TOTAL function that shows the total revenue for Air Canada as $31,021 (see Figure 390). The formula uses the correct syntax to skip rows hidden by the filter.

Figure 390

Excel inserts the SUBTO-TAL function.

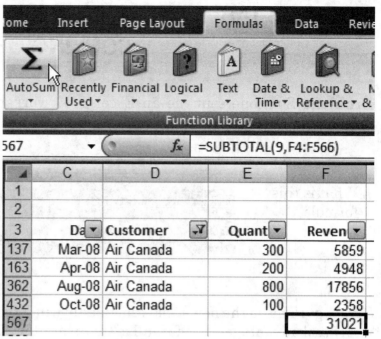

When you choose a different customer from the filter dropdown, the SUBTOTAL function will show the total for that customer's records. In Figure 391, the total for Compaq is $39,250.

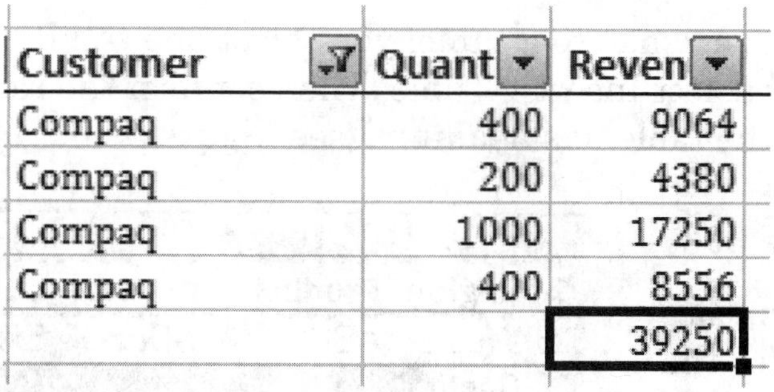

Figure 391

The total will show only the rows selected by the filter.

Customer	Quant	Reven
Compaq	400	9064
Compaq	200	4380
Compaq	1000	17250
Compaq	400	8556
		39250

Summary: You can click the AutoSum icon after applying a filter in order to see the total of the filtered rows.

Functions Discussed: =SUBTOTAL()

USE TABLE FUNCTIONALITY TO SIMPLIFY COPYING OF FORMULAS

Problem: Someone sent me an Excel 2007 worksheet with a bizarre formula, as shown in Figure 392. What is this?

Figure 392

What is this formula?

=Table1[[#This Row],[Profit]]/Table1[[#This Row],[Revenue]]					
D	E	F	G	H	I
stomer	Quant	Reven	CO	Pro	G
ord	1000	22810	10220	12590	55%
erizon	100	2257	984	1273	56%
erizon	500	10245	4235	6010	59%

Strategy: This is the new table functionality in Excel 2007. Tables offer many cool advantages, but formulas that point to tables may initially be confusing.

Think about how many spreadsheets you've seen that have a row of headings at the top and then one row per record. Probably 90% of my worksheets have this structure. Microsoft added new logic to help deal with these spreadsheets.

To convert a range to a table, you select one cell in the range and press Ctrl+T or select Insert – Table. Then confirm the range of the table and whether the table has headings (see Figure 393).

Figure 393

Confirm the range for the table.

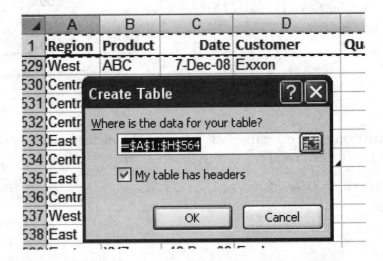

After you click OK and select one cell in the table, Excel will immediately take several actions. It will format the table, add Filter dropdowns to each heading, and display the Table Tools Design tab of the ribbon.

The most amazing feature of tables is their ability to propagate formulas. Follow these steps to add a new column to the table with a calculation:

1) Go to the blank heading cell next to the table, cell I1 (see Figure 394).

Figure 394

Select a blank cell next to the table.

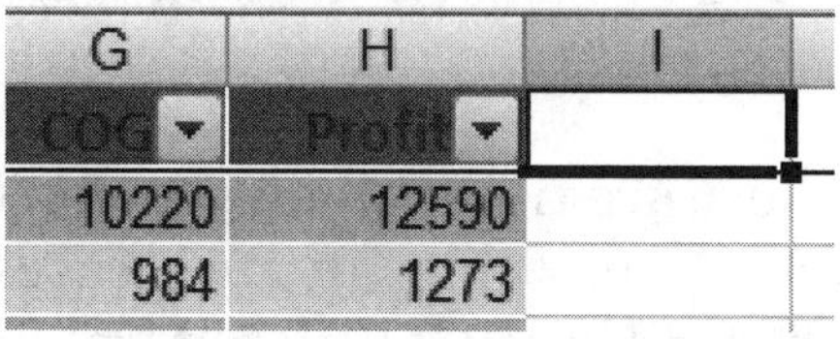

G	H	I
COG ▾	Profit ▾	
10220	12590	
984	1273	

Part
II

2) Type a heading and press Enter. Excel will format the new column to match the rest of the table.

Figure 395

Excel will automatically extend the table to the new column.

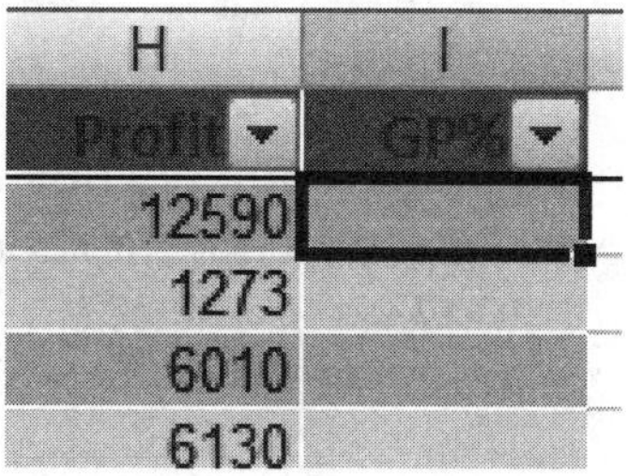

H	I
Profit ▾	GP% ▾
12590	
1273	
6010	
6130	

3) Format cell I2 as a percentage. I used to enter the formula first and then format the cell, but as you will see in step 5, you want to format the cell first.

4) In I2, enter a formula. Type the equals sign. Click on Profit in H2. Type the forward slash (/) for division. Click on Revenue in F2. Excel will enter new nomenclature for the formula, as shown in Figure 396.

Figure 396

Excel will build this syntax.

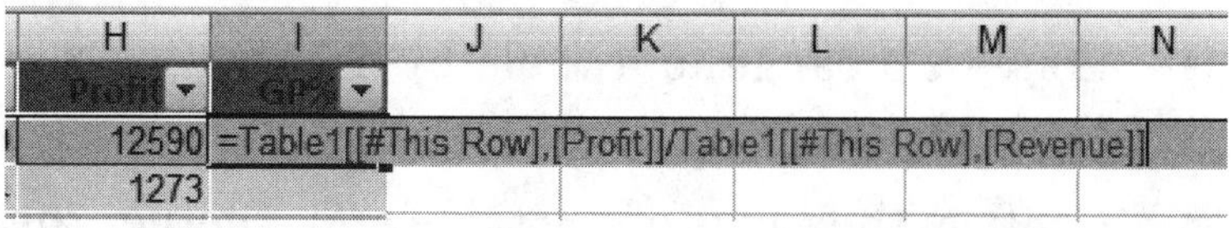

H	I	J	K	L	M	N
Profit ▾	GP% ▾					
12590	=Table1[[#This Row],[Profit]]/Table1[[#This Row],[Revenue]]					
1273						

5) Press the Enter key. Excel will automatically copy the formula down to all the rows of the table.

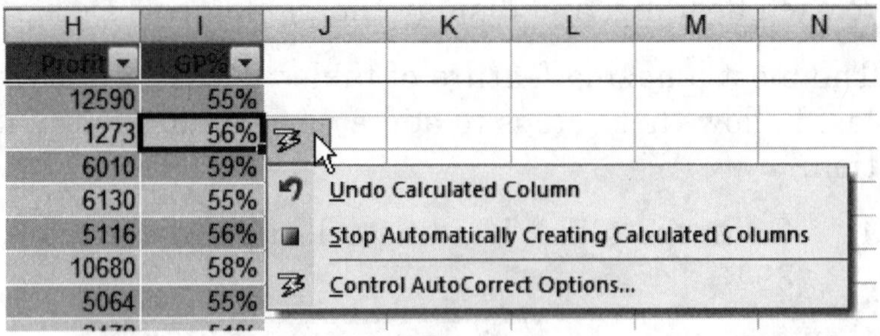

Figure 397

Excel will copy the formulas to all rows of the table.

Additional Details: There are times when you don't want Excel to copy the formula to all rows of your table. In such cases, you can open the AutoCorrect icon and choose Undo Calculated Column.

Summary: Excel's table functionality provides a new formula nomenclature. The big benefit is that the formula is automatically copied to all rows of the data set.

Commands Discussed: Insert – Table

Excel 97-2003: Excel 2003 introduced the concept of a list. You would use Ctrl+L in Excel 2003 to define a list. This method of copying the formula to all cells is new in Excel 2007.

RENAME YOUR TABLES

Problem: Is a formula such as =SUM(Table1[Revenue]) supposed to be meaningful?

Strategy: When you create a table by pressing Ctrl+T, Excel gives the table a generic name, such as Table1, Table2, and so on. If you rename the table, the formulas will start to make more sense. Here's what you do:

1) Convert a range to a table by selecting one cell in the range and pressing Ctrl+T.

2) Confirm the range of the table and whether the table has headings. Click OK and select one cell in the table. Excel will immediately

take several actions. It will format the table, add Filter dropdowns to each heading, and display the Table Tools Design tab of the ribbon.

3)   Click in the Table Name field in the Properties group in the Design ribbon and type a new name for the table. A name such as SalesData might be more meaningful than Table1.

Figure 398

Rename the table.

Results: Excel will rewrite any formulas that point to the table to use the new table name. For example, it will change the =SUM(Table1[Revenue]) you asked about to =SUM(SalesData[Revenue]).

Summary: You can rename your tables to make the formulas more self-explanatory.

Commands Discussed: Table Tools Design – Table Name

Excel 97-2003: This feature is new in Excel 2007.

USE SIMPLE REFERENCES IN A TABLE

Problem: I'm sorry. It doesn't seem like =Table2[[#This Row]],[Profit]]/Table2[[#This Row[,[Revenue]] is any easier to understand than =H2/F2. (see Figure 399)

Figure 399

Table nomenclature doesn't appear simpler.

fx	=SalesData[[#This Row],[Profit]]/SalesData[[#This Row],[Revenue]]					
	D	E	F	G	H	I
1	Customer	Quant	Reven	CO	Pro	I
2	Ford	1000	22810	10220	12590	55%
3	Verizon	100	2257	984	1273	56%

Strategy: Because you used the mouse to enter the formula, Excel built the table using something called fully qualified structured references. There is a simpler version of the structured reference style. In fact, if you start typing the formula, Excel will help you build the simplified version. Follow these steps:

1) Select cell I2, the first cell in the calculated column.

2) Type an equals sign and an open square bracket. Excel offers a list of fields in the table, as shown in Figure 400. Select Profit and press Tab.

Figure 400

Type an open square bracket, and Excel will list the fields.

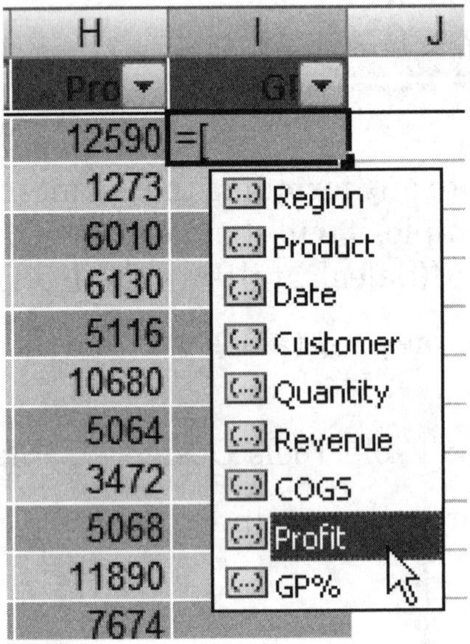

3) Type the closing square bracket.

4) Type the forward slash (/) for division and the open square bracket for the next field. Excel offers a list of fields.

5) As shown in Figure 401, choose Revenue and press Tab.

Figure 401

Select the next field.

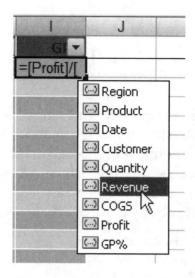

Part
II

6) Type the closing square bracket and press Enter. Excel will finish the formula and copy it down to all rows, as shown in Figure 402.

Figure 402

Excel finishes a simpler formula.

	F	G	H	I
f_x =[Profit]/[Revenue]				
	Reven ▼	CO ▼	Pro ▼	G ▼
	22810	10220	12590	55%
	2257	984	1273	56%
	10245	4235	6010	59%

Results: =[Profit]/[Revenue] is a simplified reference that refers to the current row of the table.

Additional Details: Structured references do not use named ranges. This is a brand new formula syntax for Excel 2007.

Gotcha: Previous versions of Excel offered a rarely used feature called natural language formulas. These have been removed in Excel 2007. If you were a fan of natural language formulas, you need to convert your spreadsheets to use structured references instead.

Summary: In a table, using a simplified formula reference allows you to use heading names instead of cell references.

Excel 97-2003: This feature is new in Excel 2007.

AUTOMATICALLY NUMBER
A LIST OF EMPLOYEES

Problem: I work in human resources, and I have a list of employees, separated by department. As shown in Figure 403, I have a numeric sequence in column A and the employees' names in column B. Every time the company hires or fires an employee, I have to manually renumber all the employees. How can I make this job easier?

Figure 403

Numbering the employees manually is an HR nightmare.

◢	A	B	C	D
1		Marketing Department		
2	1	George Washington		
3	2	Thomas Jefferson		
4	3	James Madison		
5	4	Ronald Reagan		
6	5	James Monroe		
7				
8		Human Resources		
9	6	John Quincy Adams		
10	7	Andrew Jackson		
11	8	Martin Van Buren		
12	9	William Henry Harrison		
13				
14		Manufacturing		
15	10	John Tyler		

Strategy: You can replace the numbers in column A with a formula that will count the entries in column B. The formula should count from the current row all the way up to row 1.

The COUNT function will not work because it only counts numeric entries. You need to use the COUNTA function and keep in mind the following points:

- The range that should be counted should extend from B1 to the current row.

- The notation to always use B1 is B$1.

Here's what you do:

1) Enter the formula =COUNTA(B$1:B2) in cell A2 (see Figure 404).

Figure 404

Count from B1 to the current row.

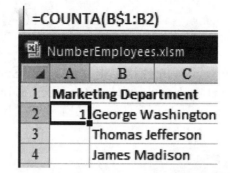

When you copy this formula down a row, the range that is counted will extend from B1 to B3, as shown in Figure 405. This is because the B2 portion of the formula is a relative reference that is allowed to change as the formula is copied. The dollar sign in the B$1 reference tells Excel that when you copy the formula, it should always refer to row 1.

Part II

Figure 405

The range now extends from B1 to B3.

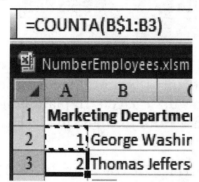

2) Copy the formula down to all the names in your list. They will be numbered just as when you typed in the names in manually.

Results: When an employee leaves the company, you can simply delete the row, and all of the later rows will be renumbered. When you hire a new person, you can insert a blank row, enter the new hire's name, and then copy any formula from another cell in A to the new row.

Summary: While this is a specific example, the concept of using a range as an argument where only one portion of the range contains an absolute reference is a common solution to keeping a running total of all cells above the current row.

Functions Discussed: =COUNT(); =COUNTA()

RANK SCORES

Problem: I have four writers working on a project. Each week, I need to report how many pages they have written toward their goal, as shown in Figure 406. I wish I had a formula that could rank them in high-to-low order.

Figure 406

Rank the scores.

◢	G	H
22		Pages
23	Tessa	145.614
24	Josh	247.968
25	Ashley	86.6364
26	Lee	96.5883

Strategy: If you are not concerned about ties, you can use the RANK function. This function requires two arguments; the cell to be ranked and the range in which to rank the cell. In plain language, you are asking the function to assign a rank to the value in H23 among all values in H23:H26.

As shown in Figure 407, in cell F23, you use =RANK(H23,$H$23:$H$26). Note that the H23:H26 range in the second parameter is in absolute reference style, as indicated by the dollar signs. This means the formula can be easily copied to each name in the list.

Figure 407

Assign a rank.

=RANK(H23,H$23:H$26)

◢	F	G	H
22	Rank		Pages
23	2	Tessa	145.614
24	1	Josh	247.968
25	4	Ashley	86.6364
26	3	Lee	96.5883

Additional Details: The formula =RANK(H23,$H$23:$H$26) will rank the values in high-to-low order. Sometimes you might need to rank in a low-to-high fashion. Golf is one such instance. In such cases, you can specify an optional third parameter to RANK to specify the order. Using a third parameter of 1 will force the rank results to be reported in low-to-high order: =RAND(H23,$H$23:$H$26,1).

Summary: The RANK function is useful for producing a ranking by using a formula.

Functions Discussed: =RANK()

See Also: "Rank a List Without Ties," "Sorting with a Formula"

Part
II

SORTING WITH A FORMULA

Problem: In "Rank Scores," I learned how to use the RANK function to find the relative rank order of four writers (refer to Figure 406). Now I want to use a formula to produce a sorted list of the writers in high-to-low sequence.

Strategy: In cells F28 through F31, you enter the numbers 1 through 4, as shown in Figure 408. Then you use the VLOOKUP function to return the name in column G and the pages in column H.

Figure 408

Set up a new table with numbers 1 through 4.

=VLOOKUP($F28,$F$23:$H$26,2,FALSE)

	F	G	H	I
22	Rank		Pages	
23	2	Tessa	145.614	
24	1	Josh	247.968	
25	4	Ashley	86.6364	
26	3	Lee	96.5883	
27				
28	1	Josh		
29	2			
30	3			
31	4			

In plain language, in this example, you are asking Excel to look for the value in F28 in the first column of the range F23:H26. When Excel finds an exactly matching value, it returns the name in the second column of the lookup range. VLOOKUP, which stands for vertical lookup, has four parameters:

- The first parameter is the value you are trying to match. In the case of cell G28, you would be looking for the value in F28. You write this as $F28 so that you can copy the formula to column H without rewriting that parameter.

- The second parameter is the database range containing rows and columns of data. The key value you are looking up must be in the first column of the range. In this case, the range would be $F$23:$H$26. Note that you use dollar signs before both the column letters and row numbers in order to keep the database range absolute as you copy the formula.

- The third parameter tells Excel the column from which you want to return the answer. For the name in column G, it is column 2 of the range F23:H26. For the page count in column H, it is column 3 of the range F23:H26.

- The fourth parameter tells Excel whether you will allow a close match. If your original data is not sorted, you are required to specify an exact match. For the fourth parameter, you use TRUE for a close match and FALSE for an exact match.

Follow these steps to create a formula that will produce a sorted list of the writers in high-to-low sequence:

1) Enter the formula =VLOOKUP($F28,$F$23:$H$26,2,FALSE) in G28 (see Figure 320).

2) Copy cell G28 to H28. The result in H28 will also be Josh because the third argument in the formula is pointing to column 2 of the table.

3) Edit the H28 formula in the formula bar to change the third parameter from column 2 to column 3. The result in H28 will now contain the number of pages written by Josh, as shown in Figure 409.

Figure 409

Use VLOOK-UP to return the name and pages for the person ranked #1.

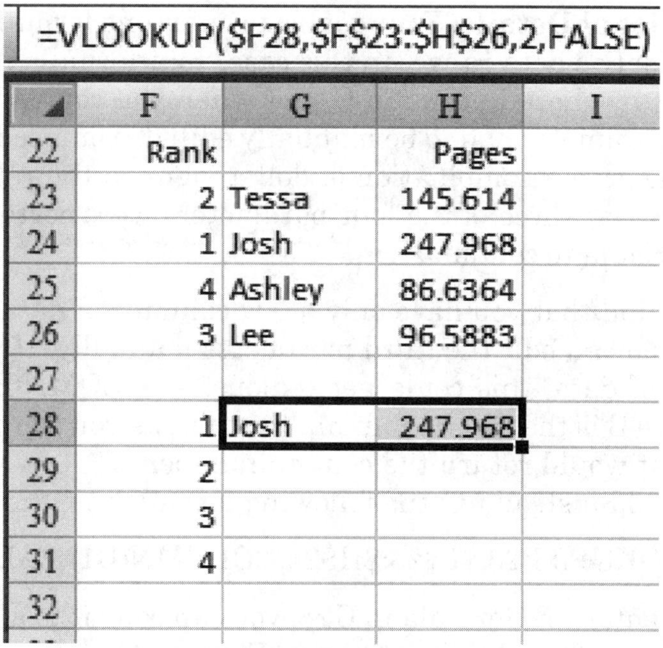

=VLOOKUP($F28,$F$23:$H$26,2,FALSE)

	F	G	H	I
22	Rank		Pages	
23	2	Tessa	145.614	
24	1	Josh	247.968	
25	4	Ashley	86.6364	
26	3	Lee	96.5883	
27				
28	1	Josh	247.968	
29	2			
30	3			
31	4			
32				

4) Copy G28:H28 down to the next three rows. You will now have a sorted list of the data, as shown in Figure 410.

Figure 410

Rows 28-31 are now a sorted version of the original data.

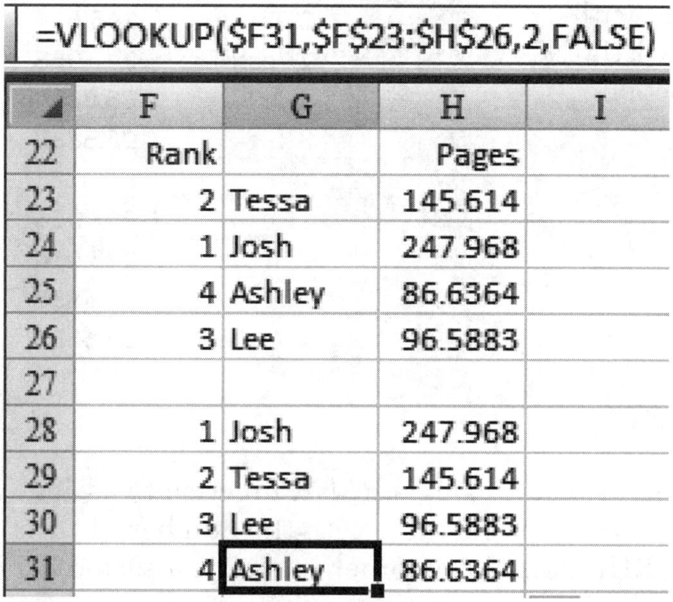

=VLOOKUP($F31,$F$23:$H$26,2,FALSE)

	F	G	H	I
22	Rank		Pages	
23	2	Tessa	145.614	
24	1	Josh	247.968	
25	4	Ashley	86.6364	
26	3	Lee	96.5883	
27				
28	1	Josh	247.968	
29	2	Tessa	145.614	
30	3	Lee	96.5883	
31	4	Ashley	86.6364	

Part
II

Additional Details: Your goal is to enter one formula that you can copy to the entire data range. In this case, your formula in G28 could be copied to anywhere in column G, but when you copied it to column H, the third parameter had to be manually edited. You needed to plan ahead to use the proper combination of dollar signs in the references in order to ensure that three of the four parameters were correct when you copied the formula to column H.

If you find that you have only a few columns of data in an example like this, you can edit the third parameter manually. If you have many columns of data, this could get tedious. =COLUMN(B1) would return 2 because B is the second column. Further, as you copy this formula to the right, it would return the column number of C1, which is 3, and so on. You could instead use the following formula in G28:

=VLOOKUP($F28,$F$23:$H$26,COLUMN(B1),FALSE)

If you enter this formula in G28, you can copy it to all rows and columns of your results table, as shown in Figure 411.

Figure 411	=VLOOKUP($F28,$F$23:$H$26,COLUMN(B1),FALSE)				

Replace the third argument with a COLUMN function.

◢	F	G	H	I	J
22	Rank		Pages		
23	2	Tessa	145.614		
24	1	Josh	247.968		
25	4	Ashley	86.6364		
26	3	Lee	96.5883		
27					
28	1	Josh	247.968		
29	2	Tessa	145.614		
30	3	Lee	96.5883		
31	4	Ashley	86.6364		
32					

Summary: After using a RANK function to assign rank values to a list, you can use a second table with the numbers 1 through n and a series of VLOOKUP formulas in order to return a sorted list of the data.

Functions Discussed: =VLOOKUP(); =COLUMN(); =RANK()

See Also: "Rank Scores" on page 264

RANK A LIST WITHOUT TIES

Problem: I have found that the RANK function behaves strangely when there are ties. For example, with RANK, it is possible to have a list where two people are ranked second and no one is ranked third. In Figure 412, for example, Dora and Jerry are ranked second, each with 90 units produced. Next is Harry with 86 units. Harry will receive a rank of 4.

Figure 412

Both records that are tied have the same rank.

`=RANK(B4,$B$4:$B$13)`

▲	A	B	C	]
1	Widget Production			
2				
3	Name	Total	Rank	
4	Ashley	80	6	
5	Bill	80	6	
6	Carl	92	1	
7	Dora	90	2	
8	Ed	79	8	
9	Fred	78	9	
10	Gary	84	5	
11	Harry	86	4	
12	Inez	70	10	
13	Jerry	90	2	
14				

Part II

If I am later going to use lookup functions to sort the employees by productivity, having two people ranked as #2 and no one ranked as #3 is not a good situation. My formulas in columns F and G reflect the fact that when I designed this spreadsheet, I counted on there being one employee at each rank from 1 to 10. Because Excel did not assign anyone to a rank of #3 or #7, Jerry and Bill do not show up in the list, as shown in Figure 413.

Figure 413

With no one ranked third, the VLOOKUP function fails.

`=INDEX($A$4:$A$13,MATCH(E6,$C$4:$C$13,FALSE),1)`

	A	B	C	D	E	F	G
1	Widget Production				Widget Production		
2							
3	Name	Total	Rank		Rank	Name	Total
4	Ashley	80	6		1	Carl	92
5	Bill	80	6		2	Dora	90
6	Carl	92	1		3	#N/A	#N/A
7	Dora	90	2		4	Harry	86
8	Ed	79	8		5	Gary	84
9	Fred	78	9		6	Ashley	80
10	Gary	84	5		7	#N/A	#N/A
11	Harry	86	4		8	Ed	79
12	Inez	70	10		9	Fred	78
13	Jerry	90	2		10	Inez	70

Strategy: In this case, you absolutely want the list in A4:A13 to be ranked without ties. The generally accepted solution may seem rather convoluted, but it works. In plain language, the formula in column C will say, "Give me the rank of this value, plus 1 for every row above me that has an identical score." As shown in Figure 414, you can accomplish this with the following formula:

=RANK(B4,$B$4:$B$13)+COUNTIF(B$3:B3,B4)

Figure 414

This formula returns no ties.

`=RANK(B4,$B$4:$B$13)+COUNTIF(B$3:B3,B4)`

	A	B	C	D	E	F	G
1	Widget Production				Widget Production		
2							
3	Name	Total	Rank		Rank	Name	Total
4	Ashley	80	6		1	Carl	92
5	Bill	80	7		2	Dora	90
6	Carl	92	1		3	Jerry	90
7	Dora	90	2		4	Harry	86
8	Ed	79	8		5	Gary	84
9	Fred	78	9		6	Ashley	80
10	Gary	84	5		7	Bill	80
11	Harry	86	4		8	Ed	79
12	Inez	70	10		9	Fred	78
13	Jerry	90	3		10	Inez	70

As you copy this formula down, the first parameter of COUNTIF will expand to include B3 down to the row above the current row. Thus, in cell C13, the formula will be as follows:

=RANK(B13,$B$4:$B$13)+COUNTIF(B$4:B12,B13)

The COUNTIF portion of the formula will count how many rows above the current row have an identical score. For each row above that is a tie, 1 gets added to the current row. This causes Bill to be ranked seventh instead of sixth. It may not be fair that Ashley appears before Bill, but in the summary report, anyone can notice that they have a tie.

Summary: You can add a COUNTIF function to the RANK function in order to prevent ties.

Functions Discussed: =RANK(); =COUNTIF()

Part
II

ADD COMMENTS TO A FORMULA

Problem: I spent a great deal of time perfecting the formula shown in Figure 415. I would like to leave myself notes about it.

Figure 415

Six months from now, will you remember what COUNTIF does?

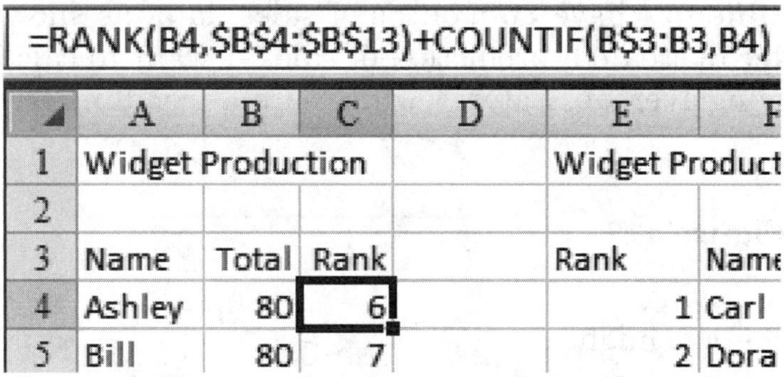

=RANK(B4,$B$4:$B$13)+COUNTIF(B$3:B3,B4)

▲	A	B	C	D	E	F
1	Widget Production				Widget Product	
2						
3	Name	Total	Rank		Rank	Name
4	Ashley	80	6		1	Carl
5	Bill	80	7		2	Dora

Strategy: An old Lotus 1-2-3 function—the N function—is still available in Excel. It turns out that N of a number is the number and N of any text is zero. Thus, you can add several N functions to a formula without changing the result, provided that they contain text.

Thus, if you have figured out some obscure formula, you can leave yourself notes about it right in the formula, as shown in Figure 416.

Figure 416

Add your comment as text in the N() function.

| | =RANK(B4,$B$4:$B$13)+N("The first part of the formula returns a rank, but ties are given the same value")+COUNTIF(B$3:B3,B4)+N("The CountIf finds any cells in the rows above this row that match this row. For each row that matches, 1 is added to the rank. This ensures that the second occurence of a tie is given a one-higher ranking.")+N("For more details, see page 232 of the MrExcel book") |

▲	A	B	C	D	E	F	G	H
1	Widget Production				Widget Production			
2								
3	Name	Total	Rank		Rank	Name	Total	
4	Ashley	80	6		1	Carl	92	
5	Bill	80	7		2	Dora	90	

Summary: For particularly complicated formulas, leave yourself detailed comments.

Functions Discussed: =N()

CALCULATE A MOVING AVERAGE

Problem: I have 36 months of sales data, as shown in Figure 417. In order to create a prediction of sales, I want to calculate a three-month moving average. Later, I will create a trendline from the moving average.

Figure 417

A moving average might reveal a trend in this fluctuating data.

▲	A	B
1		Sales
2	Jan-03	10,123
3	Feb-03	10,558
4	Mar-03	9,982
5	Apr-03	11,547
6	May-03	11,090
7	Jun-03	11,607

Strategy: You need two months of history before you can begin calculating a three-month moving average. When you have that, follow these steps:

1)   In cell C4, enter the formula =AVERAGE(B2:B4). Note that when you enter this formula, Excel will be concerned because the formula will ignore similar data in cell B5. In this case, you are smarter than Excel, so you can use the Caution (exclamation point) dropdown to tell Excel to ignore the error, as shown in Figure 418.

Figure 418

In this case, you can ignore Excel's warning that the formula omits adjacent cells.

	A	B	C	D	E
		Sales	Mov. Avg		
1		Sales	Mov. Avg		
2	Jan-03	10,123			
3	Feb-03	10,558			
4	Mar-03		10,221		
5	Apr-03	1			
6	May-03	1	Formula Omits Adjacent Cells		
7	Jun-03	1	Update Formula to Include Cells		
8	Jul-03	1	Help on this error		
9	Aug-03	1			
10	Sep-03	1	Ignore Error		
11	Oct-03	1	Edit in Formula Bar		
12	Nov-03	1			
13	Dec-03	1	Error Checking Options...		

Formula bar: =AVERAGE(B2:B4)

2)   Double-click the fill handle in C4 to copy the formula down to the rest of your data set.

Results: Moving averages are good if the underlying data has spikes in the sales. It is difficult for an automatic system to predict spikes. A moving average smoothes these spikes out of the system, as shown in Figure 419. A forecast based on the moving average line may be more accurate than a forecast based on the original data.

Figure 419

The three month moving average shows a forecastable trend.

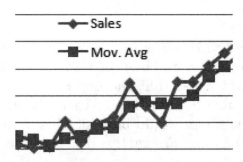

Sales
Mov. Avg

Summary: Use the AVERAGE function to create a three-month moving average to be used for forecasting.

Functions Discussed: =AVERAGE()

CALCULATE A TRENDLINE FORECAST

Problem: I have the monthly historical sales data shown in Figure 420. I want to predict future sales by month.

Figure 420

Predict how many will be sold in July.

	A	B	C
1	MoNumber	Month	Sales
2	1	Mar-03	10,221
3	2	Apr-03	10,696
4	3	May-03	10,873
5	4	Jun-03	11,415
6	5	Jul-03	11,562

Strategy: You can use the least-squares method to fit the sales data to a trendline. Excel offers a function called LINEST that will calculate the formula for the trendline.

You might remember from math class that a trendline is represented by this formula:

$$y = mx + b$$

In this example, y is the revenue for the month, m is the slope of the line, x is the month number, and b is the y-intercept. If you were to look at the data, you might guess that the prediction for a given month is $10,000 + Month number x $400. In this case, the value for b would be 10,000, and the value for m would be 400. This is just my wild guess; Excel can calculate the number exactly.

LINEST is a very special function. Instead of returning one number, it actually returns two (or more) numbers as the result.

Figure 421, shows the wrong way to enter the LINEST function. If you select a single cell and enter =LINEST(C2:C35), it will return a single number.

Figure 421

You can see in the results section at the lower right corner of this image that Excel wants to return two answers: 204 and 10248.

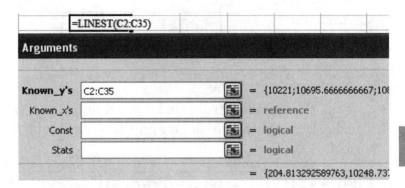

Part II

Entering the formula the wrong way returns a single answer of 204.8133, as shown in Figure 422. The first time you do this, you might wonder how the number 204.81 could describe a line.

Figure 422

How can one number describe a line?

	A	B	C	D	E
	MoNumber	Month	Sales		=LINEST(C2:C35)
1	MoNumber	Month	Sales		
2	1	Mar-03	10,221		204.8132926
3	2	Apr-03	10,696		
4	3	May-03	10,873		

It turns out that Excel really wants to return two numbers from the function. Here's the trick:

1)   Select two cells that are side by side.

2) Begin to enter the function in the first cell, as shown in Figure 423.

Figure 423

Select two cells and start to enter the function in the first cell.

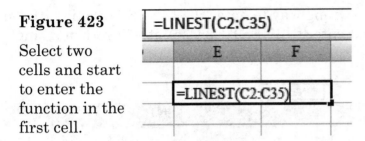

3) Type the closing parenthesis and then press Ctrl+Shift+Enter. Excel returns both the slope and the y-intercept, as shown in Figure 424.

Figure 424

The results appear in 2 cells.

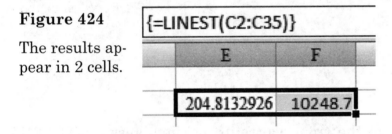

4) Fill in headings, as shown in Figure 425. In column D, enter a formula to calculate the predicted sales trendline. The formula is the intercept in F2 plus the slope in E2 times this row's month number.

Figure 425

Use the results of the LINEST to predict sales.

	D2			f_x	=$F$2+$E$2*A2	
	A	B	C	D	E	F
1	MoNumber	Month	Sales	Prediction	Slope	Intercept
2	1	Mar-03	10,221	10,454	204.8132926	10248.7
3	2	Apr-03	10,696	10,658		
4	3	May-03	10,873	10,863		
5	4	Jun-03	11,415	11,068		

You will now be able to graph columns B:D to show how well the prediction matches the historical actuals.

Additional Details: When the data along one axis of your data contains dates, it is best to delete the heading in the upper-left corner of your data set before creating the chart. You clear cell B1, select B1:D47, and select Insert – Line – Line with Markers. As shown in Figure 426, the resulting chart shows that the predicted trendline comes fairly close to the actuals. You can also see that the formula predicts that you will be selling almost $20,000 per month one year from now.

Figure 426

Plot actuals
vs. prediction
to visualize
if the sales
match a trend.

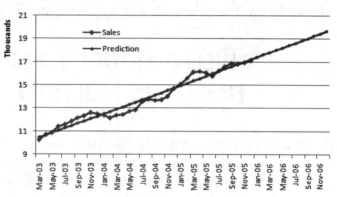

Gotcha: When you select two cells for the LINEST function, they must be side by side. If you try to select two cells that are one above the other, you will just get two copies of the slope.

Alternate Strategy: A different method is to use the INDEX function to pluck a specific answer from the array.

=INDEX(LINEST(C2:C35),1,1) will return the first element from the array, as shown in Figure 427. This is the slope.

=INDEX(LINEST(C2:C35),1,2) will return the second element from the array. This is the y-intercept.

Figure 427

Use the IN-
DEX function
to return 1
value from an
array of an-
swers.

=INDEX(LINEST(C2:C35),1,1)

	E	F	G
	068		
	273	Slope	204.813
	478	Y-Intercept	10248.7
	682		
	887		

Summary: The LINEST function will automate the process of performing a least-squares method to fit a line to a series of actual sales. Because the function returns multiple values, you have to use care when entering. Either enter it in multiple cells with the Ctrl+Shift+Enter key combination or use the INDEX function to extract values.

Functions Discussed: =LINEST(); =INDEX()

See Also: "Add a Trendline to a Chart" on page 711.

BUILD A MODEL TO PREDICT SALES BASED ON MULTIPLE REGRESSION

Problem: I run an ice cream stand. After 10 days of sales, I discovered that each day, I would either make a lot of money or nearly go broke. As I analyzed sales, I began to feel that temperature and rain might be two important determining factors in how much money I make. On rainy or cool days, fewer people buy ice cream.

I set up the table in Figure 428, which shows each day's sales, temperature, and whether it rained.

Figure 428

Sales swing wildly from day to day.

▲	A	B	C
1	Sally's Ice Cream Stand		
2			
3	Temperature	Rain	Sales
4	64	1	$28
5	95	0	$270
6	74	1	$48
7	84	1	$68
8	94	1	$88
9	75	0	$150
10	56	0	$36
11	85	0	$210
12	65	0	$90
13	55	1	$10

Based on the data I've collected, how can I determine the relationship between sales, temperature, and rainfall?

Strategy: You need to do a multiple regression. After a multiple regression, you will have a formula that predicts sales like this:

$Y = m1x1 + m2x2 + b$

Sales = Temperature x M1 + Rain x M2 + b

The LINEST function can return the values M1, M2, and b that best describe your sales model. Here's what you do:

1) LINEST is going to return three values, so select a range of three cells that are side by side, as shown in Figure 429. The first argument is the range of known sales figures. The second argument is the range of temperatures and rainfall.

Figure 429

Select three cells for the formula.

Rain	Temperature	Y Intercept
=LINEST(C4:C13,A4:B13)		

2) Press Ctrl+Shift+Enter to calculate the array formula.

3) As shown in Figure 430, enter a prediction formula in column D to see how well the regression calculation describes sales. The results are so-so. The prediction in D6 is right on the mark. The predictions in D11 and D12 are off by $20 each—an error of 10%.

Figure 430

Add the y-intercept from H4, the temperature factor from G4 times column A and the rain factor from F4 times column B.

D4				f_x =$H$4+($G$4*A4)+($F$4*B4)

	C	D	E	F	G	H
1						
2						
3	Sales	Prediction		Rain	Temperature	Y Intercept
4	$28	$8		-98.8	4	-149.6
5	$270	$230				
6	$48	$48				
7	$68	$88				
8	$88	$128				
9	$150	$150				
10	$36	$74				
11	$210	$190				
12	$90	$110				
13	$10	-$28				

4) To get the additional statistics that LINEST can return to show how well the results match reality, add a fourth argument: TRUE. Be sure to enter the function in a five-row range, as shown in Figure 431.

Figure 431

Use five rows and enough columns to handle a slope for each variable plus the intercept.

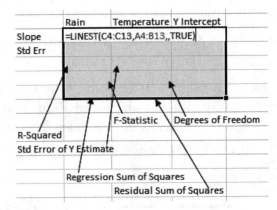

	Rain	Temperature	Y Intercept
Slope	=LINEST(C4:C13,A4:B13,,TRUE)		
Std Err			

F-Statistic   Degrees of Freedom

R-Squared
Std Error of Y Estimate

Regression Sum of Squares
Residual Sum of Squares

5) Press Ctrl+Shift+Enter. You will get the results shown in Figure 432.

Figure 432

Excel performs the regression and provides statistics.

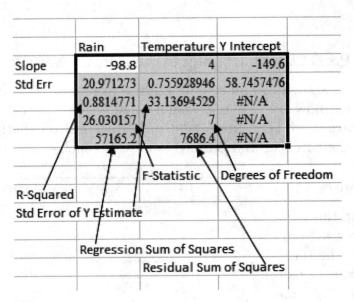

	Rain	Temperature	Y Intercept
Slope	-98.8	4	-149.6
Std Err	20.971273	0.755928946	58.7457476
	0.8814771	33.13694529	#N/A
	26.030157	7	#N/A
	57165.2	7686.4	#N/A

F-Statistic   Degrees of Freedom

R-Squared
Std Error of Y Estimate

Regression Sum of Squares
Residual Sum of Squares

I only somewhat paid attention in statistics class, but I know that a key statistical indicator is the R-squared value. It ranges from 0 to 1, where 1 is a perfect match, and 0 is a horrible match. The 0.88 value here confirms that the prediction model is pretty good but not perfect.

Additional Details: Regression models try to force actual results into a straight-line formula. The fact is that life may not fit in a straight-line formula. Because I created the spreadsheet used here, I know that the actual data in the ice cream model uses the formula (Temperature – 50) x $2 if raining and (Temperature – 50) x $6 if not raining. In this example, Sally was correct that ice cream sales are dependent on rain and temperature, but even a powerful regression engine could not predict the absolutely correct formula.

Alternate Strategy: The Analysis ToolPak still offers tools to do Regression, as well as testing correlation, exponential smoothing, create histograms, generate random numbers, create samples, and more. You have to enable the add-in first. Choose Office Icon – Excel Options – Add-Ins. At the bottom of the dialog, choose Excel Add-Ins from the Manage dropdown and click Go. Add a checkmark next to Analysis ToolPak and click OK.

Part
II

You will now have a Data Analysis icon on the right side of the Data ribbon tab. Click the icon and Excel offers a list of tools. Although some of these tools offer older dialog boxes that really need updating, they can often produce far more detailed results. The Regression tool creates charts of the residuals, Anova analysis, and tables of statistics about the regression, as shown in Figure 433.

Figure 433

The Analysis ToolPak offers a variety of statistical tools.

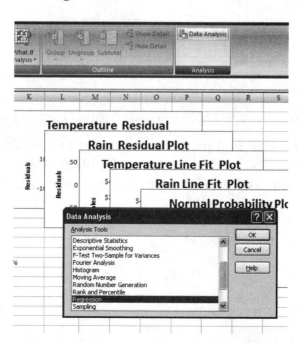

Gotcha: The results from the ToolPak are not live formulas! They are a one-time snapshot. If you change the underlying data, you will have to run the analysis tool again.

Summary: The LINEST function will automate the process of performing a least-squares method to fit a line to a series of actual sales using multifactor regression.

Functions Discussed: =LINEST()

USE F9 IN THE FORMULA BAR
TO TEST A FORMULA

Problem: I have a complex formula that does not appear to be providing the correct result. As shown in Figure 434, the formula has multiple terms, and I am not sure which part is not working correctly

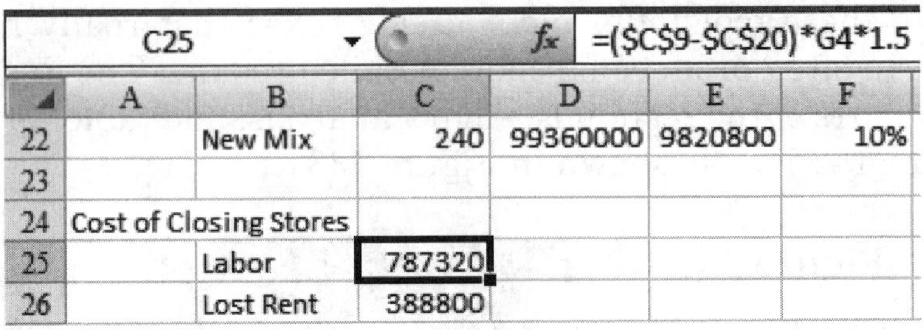

Figure 434

Troubleshoot this formula.

	C25		▼	f_x	=($C$9-$C$20)*G4*1.5	
◢	A	B	C	D	E	F
22		New Mix	240	99360000	9820800	10%
23						
24	Cost of Closing Stores					
25		Labor	787320			
26		Lost Rent	388800			

Strategy: You can use F9 to test a formula. Here's how:

1) Select cell C25 and press F2 to put the cell in Edit mode, as shown in Figure 435. In this mode, each cell reference in the formula is color coded. The $C$9 text in the formula is blue, and the outline around C9 is blue.

Figure 435

In Edit mode, the formula references are color coded.

▲	A	B	C	D	E	F	G	H
1	Section 1: Historical Trends (Per Month)							
2								
3		Store Type	Size	Rent	Sales	Profit	Labor	Net
4		Regular	1200	2400	12456	6228	6480	-2652
5		BigBox	2600	5200	34500	17250	8640	3410
6								
7	Section 2: Number of Stores							
8								
9		Regular	81					
10		BigBox	184					
11								
12	Section 3: Analysis of Profitability of Current Store Mix							
13			Sales	Net Profit	NP%			
14		Total Chain	8.8E+07	4951536	5.6%			
15		Regular	1.2E+07	-2577744	-21.3%			
16		Big Box	7.6E+07	7529280	9.9%			
17								
18	Section 4: Profit Projections with a New Mix of Stores							
19				Sales	Profit	NP%		
20		Regular	0	0	0			
21		BigBox	240	99360000	9820800			
22		New Mix	240	99360000	9820800	10%		
23								
24	Cost of Closing Stores							
25		Labor	=($C$9-$C$20)*G4*1.5					
26		Lost Rent	388800					

2) To selectively calculate just a portion of the formula, as shown in Figure 436, use the mouse to highlight a portion of the formula.

Figure 436

Select part of the formula.

=($C$9-$C$20)*G4*1.5

3) Press the F9 key. As shown in Figure 437, the highlighted portion of the formula will be replaced with the current result of the formula.

Figure 437

Press F9 to calculate the highlighted portion.

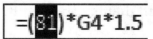

=(81)*G4*1.5

Additional Details: If you press F9 without selecting anything, it will calculate the entire formula and replace it in the result, as shown in Figure 438.

Figure 438

Press F9 to calculate the entire formula.

Summary: Placing a cell containing a formula in edit mode, selecting part of the formula, and hitting the F9 key will verify that the selected part of the formula is correct.

Commands Discussed: F2 with a selected cell; F9 in the edit mode.

QUICK CALCULATOR

Problem: I need to find a quick answer to a mathematical problem, and I don't have a calculator. Can Excel help?

Strategy: You can use Excel as a simple calculator. Follow these steps:

1) Go to a blank cell.

2) Type an equals sign.

3) Enter a calculation, as shown in Figure 439.

Figure 439

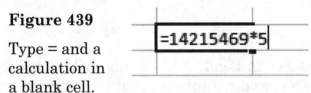

Type = and a calculation in a blank cell.

4) Press the F9 key. Excel will display the result, as shown in Figure 440.

Figure 440

The result.

5)   Press the Esc key to clear the cell.

Summary: You can use Excel as a quick calculator by selecting a blank cell, typing an equals sign, typing a calculation problem, and then pressing F9.

Commands Discussed: F9

WHEN ENTERING A FORMULA, YOU GET THE FORMULA INSTEAD OF THE RESULT

Problem: When entering a formula, Excel shows me the formula in the cell instead of the result, as shown in Figure 441.

Figure 441

Excel displays the formula.

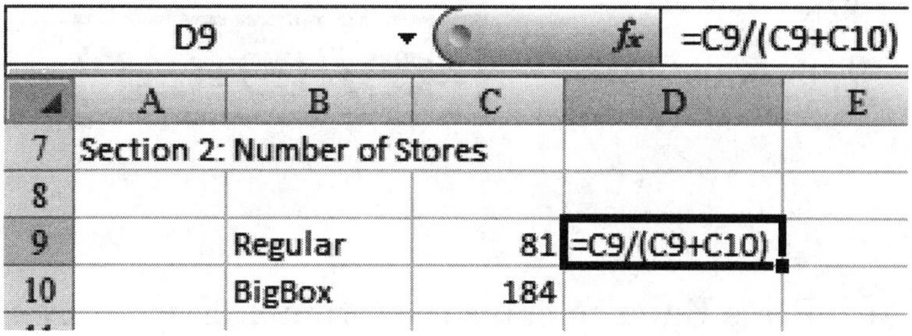

D9			f_x	=C9/(C9+C10)
◢	A	B	C	D	E
7	Section 2: Number of Stores				
8					
9		Regular	81	=C9/(C9+C10)	
10		BigBox	184		

Strategy: There are three possible problems in this case.

Possibility 1: As shown in Figure 442, you may have forgotten to start the formula with an equals sign. Follow these steps to correct the formula:

1)   Select the cell and press F2 to edit the cell, as shown in Figure 442.

Figure 442

Press F2 to edit the cell.

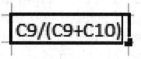
C9/(C9+C10)

2)   Press the Home key to move the cell pointer to the start of the for-
     mula, as shown in Figure 443.

Figure 443

Press Home.

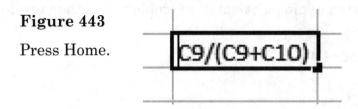

3)   If there is an apostrophe at the beginning of the cell, press Delete
     key to delete the leading apostrophe. (Your Lotus Transition set-
     tings determine wither your cell starts with an apostrophe.) Type
     the = sign, as shown in Figure 444.

Figure 444

Type =.

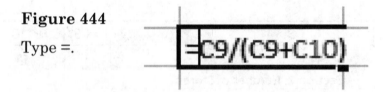

4)   Press Enter to enter the formula. Excel shows the result shown in
     Figure 445.

Figure 445

Finish the
formula with
Enter.

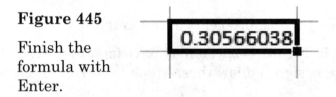

Gotcha: Typically, in a cell with general formatting, Excel will right-
align numbers and left-align text. Because you forgot to hit the Equal
sign, Excel thinks you have a text cell and even after converting to a
valid formula, the result might be left-aligned. Hit the Align Right icon
in the Home tab, as shown in Figure 446.

Figure 446

You might need to right-align the number.

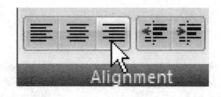

Possibility 2: The cell might have been assigned the numeric format @, which is the code for a text cell. The maddening part of this problem is that this format can get set even without you knowing it. A column can inherit a text format if you import a text file and use the text setting for the import. Here's how you fix this problem:

Part
II

1) Select the problematic cell. Press Ctrl+1; the Format Cells dialog will appear.

2) Confirm that the cell has a Text format assigned, as shown in Figure 447.

Figure 447

The Format Cells dialog shows that the cell is formatted as text.

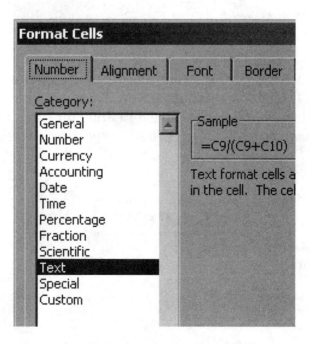

3) As shown in Figure 448, change the cell to any format other than Text.

Figure 448

Change to any format other than text.

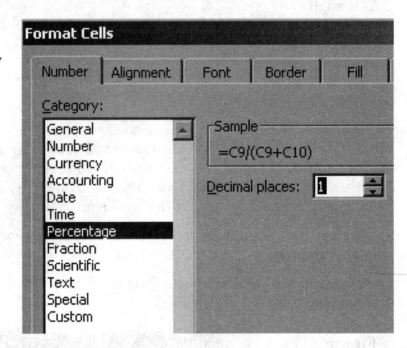

4) This does not fix the formula! Edit the cell using the F2 key. If your Lotus Transition settings are off, there is no apostrophe before the formula as shown in Figure 449 and you can simply type Enter. If your transition settings are on, type Home, Delete, and then Enter.

Figure 449

You have to edit and reenter the formula.

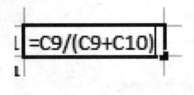

Results: Excel will display the result of the formula, as shown in Figure 450.

Figure 450

Finally, Excel will show the result of the formula.

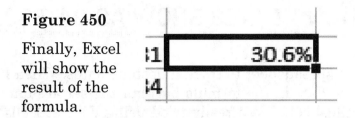

Possibility 3: The third possibility, which is the least likely, is that you are in Show Formulas mode, as shown in Figure 451. In this mode, all the cells that have formulas show their formulas.

Figure 451

In Show Formulas mode, Excel displays the formulas instead of their results.

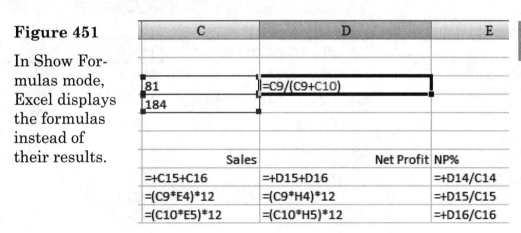

To fix this problem, you press Ctrl+` to toggle in and out of Show Formulas mode. (On U.S. keyboards, this character is below the Esc key, on the same key as the tilde.)

Summary: When a cell shows a formula rather than a result, there are three possible reasons: (1) You forgot to start the formula with an equals (=) sign, (2) the cell is not formatted for numeric data, or (3) the worksheet is in Show Formula mode.

Commands Discussed: F2; Ctrl+`

WHY DON'T DATES SHOW AS DATES?

Problem: I use a simple spreadsheet to track milestone dates. When I select a cell, I can see the date in the formula bar, but the serial number appears in the spreadsheet. I've already tried using Format Cells to specify that this cell contains a date. So why don't the dates show as dates?

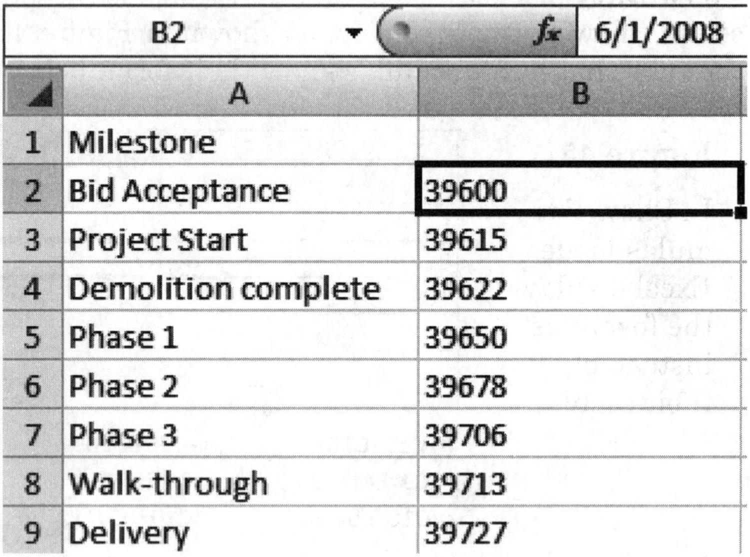

Figure 452

A date appears in the formula bar, but a serial number appears in the worksheet.

	A	B
	B2	fx 6/1/2008
1	Milestone	
2	Bid Acceptance	39600
3	Project Start	39615
4	Demolition complete	39622
5	Phase 1	39650
6	Phase 2	39678
7	Phase 3	39706
8	Walk-through	39713
9	Delivery	39727

Strategy: You have inadvertently entered Show Formulas mode, a troubleshooting mode that allows you to see all the formulas in the worksheet. For some reason, in this mode, Excel decides to show you the serial number behind the date instead of the date itself.

You press Ctrl+` to show the dates again, as shown in Figure 453. Many people use Ctrl+Tab to flip between open workbooks, and it is very easy to accidentally press Ctrl+` instead of Ctrl+Tab because the ` key is immediately above the Tab key on many keyboards.

Figure 453

Press Ctrl+` to exit Show Formulas mode.

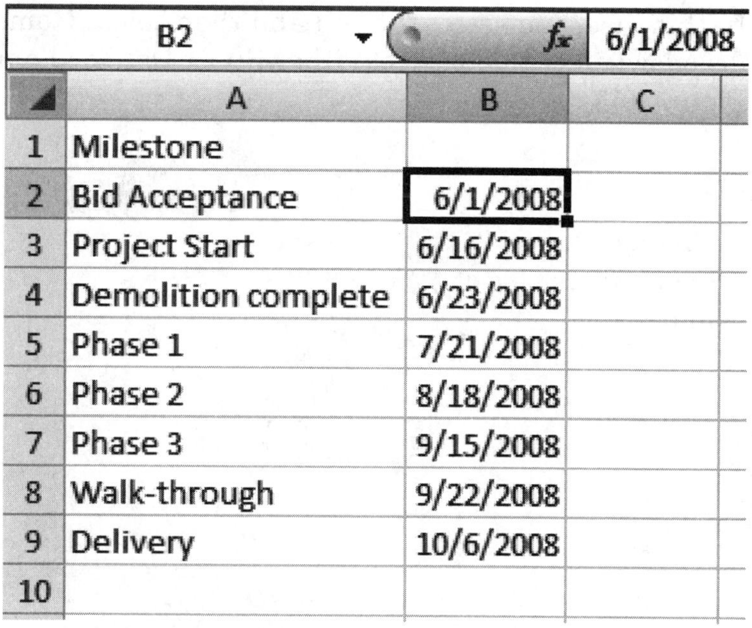

	A	B	C
1	Milestone		
2	Bid Acceptance	6/1/2008	
3	Project Start	6/16/2008	
4	Demolition complete	6/23/2008	
5	Phase 1	7/21/2008	
6	Phase 2	8/18/2008	
7	Phase 3	9/15/2008	
8	Walk-through	9/22/2008	
9	Delivery	10/6/2008	
10			

B2   ▾ f_x 6/1/2008

Part
II

Additional Details: Excel stores dates as the number of days elapsed since January 1, 1900. Assuming that you are reading this book in the 2007–2009 timeframe, whenever you see a number in the 39000–41000 range, you might be seeing a date cell that is not formatted as a date.

Alternate Strategy: A similar problem is that sometimes, you might enter a function that should return a date. The formula bar will show the formula, and the worksheet cell will show the serial number (see Figure 454).

Figure 454

Here, the cell shows a serial number but the formula bar doesn't show the date.

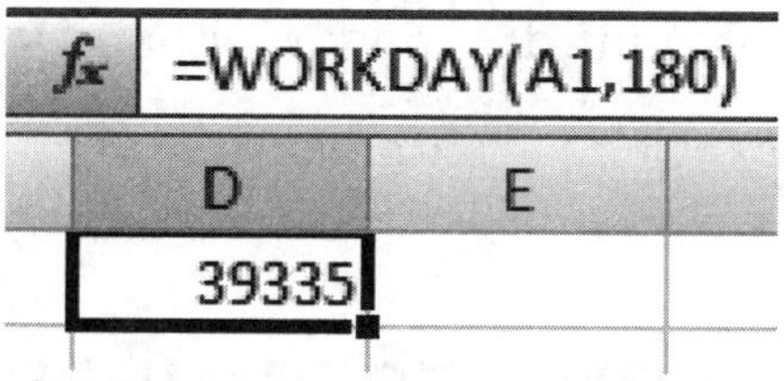

f_x =WORKDAY(A1,180)

D	E
39335	

In this case, you select the cell and then select Home – Number Format dropdown. Then you select either Short Date or Long Date, as shown in Figure 455.

Figure 455

Change from General format.

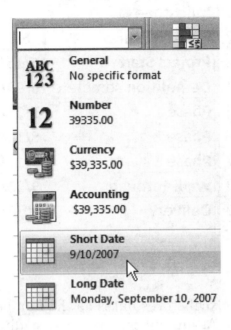

Excel will then display the formula result as a date.

Summary: Dates routinely show up as a number in the 30000-40000 range. Either exiting Show Formulas mode or formatting the cell as a date will usually correct the problem.

Commands Used: Ctrl+`; Home – Number Format dropdown – Short Date; Home – Number Format dropdown – Long Date

Excel 97-2003: Format – Cells – Number – Date

HANDLE LONG FORMULAS IN THE NEW EXCEL 2007 FORMULA BAR

Problem: When I type long formulas, they tend to spill out of the formula bar and cover part of the grid. This is particularly annoying when

I select a cell in row 1 because the formula covers the value from the formula.

Strategy: In Excel 2007, you can expand or collapse the formula bar. If you choose to expand the formula bar (with Ctrl+Shift+U), the grid actually shifts downward so that you can see the formula bar and the cell in the grid.

In Figure 456, the formula bar is collapsed. You see only the first line of the formula.

='January 2008 (2)'!G14+'January 2008 (3)'!F7+'January 2008 (4)'!I9+'January 2008 (5)'!
E
F
G
H
I
J
K
L
M
1593.03

Figure 456

You can scroll through the formula bar one line at a time.

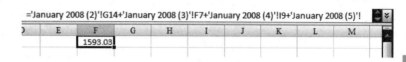

If you press Ctrl+Shift+U or click the double-down arrow icon at the right edge of the formula bar, Excel will shift the grid down and show more lines of the formula, as shown in Figure 457.

='January 2008 (2)'!G14+'January 2008 (3)'!F7+'January 2008 (4)'!I9+'January 2008 (5)'!
H6*'January 2008 (6)'!I9+'January 2008 (7)'!H11/'January 2008 (8)'!G9-AVERAGE(
'January 2008 (9)'!G7:H9)+'January 2008 (10)'!G11-'January 2008 (11)'!G3
E
F
G
H
I
J
K
L
M
1593.03

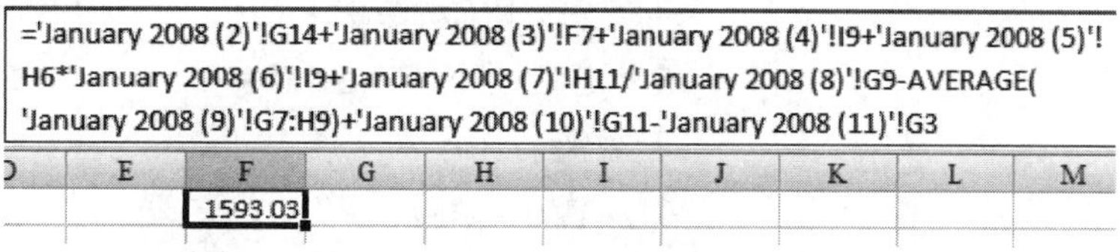

Figure 457

Excel will lower row 1 to make room for the larger formula bar.

Gotcha: With a particularly long formula, you might still have to scroll through the expanded formula bar.

Summary: You can expand the formula bar, and Excel 2007 will prevent it from covering any numbers in the grid.

Excel 97-2003: This feature is new in Excel 2007.

CALCULATE A PERCENTAGE OF TOTAL

Problem: The spreadsheet shown in Figure 458 lists a number of customers with revenue, with a total at the bottom. I want to express each customer as a percentage of the total.

Figure 458

Add percentage of total to each customer.

	A	B
1	Customer	Revenue
2	Ainsworth	2,308,900
3	Exxon	2,907,800
4	Ford	2,522,600
5	General Motors	3,145,200
6	IBM	1,693,000
7	Lucent	265,100
8	Molson, Inc	2,519,100
9	Nortel Networks	1,564,200
10	P&G	245,100
11	SBC Communications	290,100
12	Sears Canada	240,500
13	Shell Canada	292,500
14	Sun Life Financial	1,994,200
15	Verizon	1,636,700
16	Wal-Mart	3,490,000
17	Total	25,115,000

Strategy: Divide each row's sales by the total cell. Follow these steps:

1) Select a cell next to the first revenue cell.

2) Type an equals sign. Press the Left Arrow key.

3) Type the forward slash (/) sign. Press the Left Arrow key. Press the End key. Press the Down Arrow key. Your cell pointer should now be on the total cell.

4) Press the F4 key. The formula bar should now show B2/$B$17, as shown in Figure 459.

Figure 459

Make sure the reference to the total cell is an absolute reference.

◢	A	B	C
1	Customer	Revenue	% of Total
2	Ainsworth	2,308,900	=B2/$B$17
3	Exxon	2,907,800	
4	Ford	2,522,600	

5) Press Ctrl+Enter to enter the formula and stay in the current cell. Format the calculation as a percentage by using the % icon on the Home ribbon tab.

6) To use the format 9.2% (that is, one decimal place) instead of 9%, choose the Increase Decimal icon, as shown in Figure 460.

Figure 460

Format as a percentage and adjust the decimals.

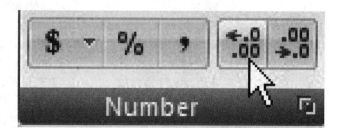

7) In cell C2, double-click the fill handle to copy the formula down to the other rows.

8) Add the heading % of Total in cell C1.

Part II

Additional Details: The key element of this procedure is pressing the F4 key to add dollar signs to the reference for the total row. As you copy the formula from C2 to C16, the formula is always going to compare the revenue in the current row to the total revenue in row 17, as shown in Figure 461.

Figure 461

The formula should divide the current row's sales by the total.

C16		=B16/$B$17
A	B	C
1 Customer	Revenue	% of Total
2 Ainsworth	2,308,900	9.2%
3 Exxon	2,907,800	11.6%
4 Ford	2,522,600	10.0%
5 General Motors	3,145,200	12.5%
6 IBM	1,693,000	6.7%
7 Lucent	265,100	1.1%
8 Molson, Inc	2,519,100	10.0%
9 Nortel Networks	1,564,200	6.2%
10 P&G	245,100	1.0%
11 SBC Communications	290,100	1.2%
12 Sears Canada	240,500	1.0%
13 Shell Canada	292,500	1.2%
14 Sun Life Financial	1,994,200	7.9%
15 Verizon	1,636,700	6.5%
16 Wal-Mart	3,490,000	13.9%
17 Total	25,115,000	100.0%

Summary: Creating a percentage of total is a common task in Excel. Being able to quickly enter an initial formula that can be copied to all cells is a good technique to have in your skill set.

CALCULATE A RUNNING PERCENTAGE OF TOTAL

Problem: I have a report of revenue by customer, sorted in descending order, as shown in Figure 462. Management consultants often argue that it's important to concentrate the best team on the 20% of the customers who provide 80% of the company's revenue. How can I calculate a cumulative running percentage of the total so I can determine which 20% of customers to focus on?

Figure 462

Calculate a running percentage of total.

	A	B
1	Customer	Revenue
2	Wal-Mart	3,490,000
3	General Motors	3,145,200
4	Exxon	2,907,800
5	Ford	2,522,600
6	Molson, Inc	2,519,100
7	Ainsworth	2,308,900
8	Sun Life Financial	1,994,200
9	IBM	1,693,000
10	Verizon	1,636,700
11	Nortel Networks	1,564,200
12	Shell Canada	292,500
13	SBC Communications	290,100
14	Lucent	265,100
15	P&G	245,100
16	Sears Canada	240,500
17		
18	Total	25,115,000

Part II

Strategy: I hate solutions that require two different formulas, but the intuitive solution to this problem is one of them. You will need one formula for cell C2 and a different formula for cells C3 and below. Here's what you do:

1) In cell C2, enter the formula =B2/$B$18. Format the result as a percentage with one decimal place.

2) Copy C2 to just the next cell, either by dragging the fill handle down one cell or using Ctrl+C and then Ctrl+V.

3) Press F2 to edit cell C3.

4) Type a plus sign and touch cell C2. Press Ctrl+Enter (see Figure 463).

Figure 463

Make B18 be absolute by adding the dollar signs.

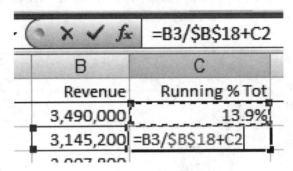

5) Double-click the fill handle in C3 to copy this formula down to all the other cells. (Note that you do not want this formula to be added to your total row. As shown in Figure 462, the data set was purposely set up with the total row and the data separated by a blank row in order to prevent this formula from copying to the total row.)

Alternate **Strategy:** If you absolutely want to produce this total with a single formula, you could use the formula =SUM(B2:B$2)/B$18 in C2 and copy it down, as shown in Figure 464. This works because the range B2:B$2 is an interesting reference: It says to add up everything from the current row to the top row. This formula seems a bit less intuitive, so you might prefer the method shown earlier.

Figure 464

It is less intuitive, but this formula will work in the entire range.

	A	B	C
	C2		f_x =SUM(B2:B$2)/B$18
1	Customer	Revenue	Running % Tot
2	Wal-Mart	3,490,000	13.9%
3	General Motors	3,145,200	26.4%
4	Exxon	2,907,800	38.0%

Summary: The formula for a running percentage of the total is a common analysis tool. You have two different options for calculating the running percentage.

USE THE ^ SIGN FOR EXPONENTS

Problem: I have a room that is 10 feet x 10 feet x 10 feet. How do I find the volume of the cube?

Strategy: The formula for volume is width x length x height. In this case, it is 10 x 10 x 10, or 10^3. In Excel, the caret symbol (also known as "the little hat," or "the symbol when you press Shift 6") is used to indicate exponents. Here's how you use it to find the volume of your room:

1)   In cell B2, enter 10.

2)   In cell B3, enter the formula =B2^3.

The result will be 1,000 cubic feet of volume in the room, as shown in Figure 465.

Part
II

Figure 465

The caret raises a number to a power.

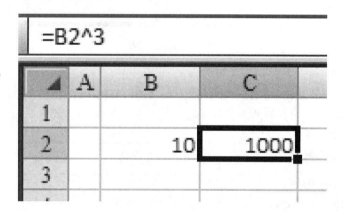

Summary: Use a caret to calculate exponents.

RAISE A NUMBER TO A FRACTION TO FIND THE SQUARE OR THIRD ROOT

Problem: Excel offers a SQRT function to find the square root of a number. What do I do if I need to figure out the third root or the fourth root of a number?

Strategy: You can raise a number to a fraction to find a root. To find the square root of a number, you can raise the number to the 1/2 power. To find the cube root of a number, you can raise the number to the 1/3 power. To find the eighth root of a number, you can raise the number to the 1/8 power.

Let's look at several examples.

If you need to find the square root, you can use the SQRT function, as shown in Figure 466.

Figure 466

Excel offers a built-in function for square roots.

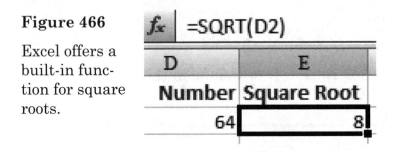

Figure 467 shows how you raise the same number to the one-half (1/2) power.

Figure 467

Raising to a fraction takes the root.

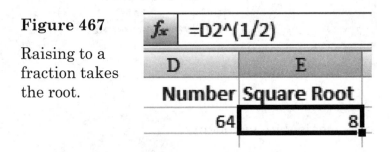

Instead of raising to the 1/2 power, you can get the same effect by raising the number to 0.5, as shown in Figure 468.

Figure 468

Raising to the 0.5 power is the same as raising to the 1/2 power.

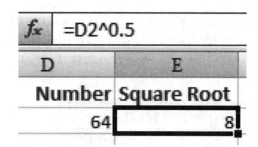

To find the cube root of a number, you can raise the number to the one-third (1/3) power, as shown in Figure 469.

Figure 469

For cube roots, raise to the 1/3 power.

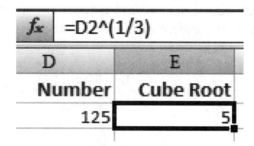

To find the fourth root of a number, you raise the number to either the one-fourth (1/4) or 0.25 power, as shown in Figure 470 and Figure 471.

Figure 470

Raise to the 1/4 power.

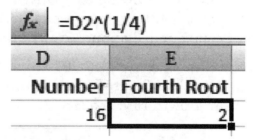

Figure 471

Raise to the 0.25 power.

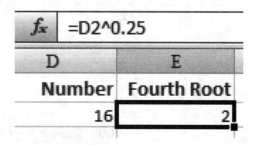

You can find any root in the same way: To find the nth root, you simply raise the number to the 1/n power. For example, to find the 17th root of a number, you raise it to the one-seventeenth (1/17) power, as shown in Figure 472.

Figure 472

Find the *n*th root by raising to 1/*n*.

f_x	=D2^(1/17)
D	**E**
Number	**17th Root**
1197964098	3.42

Summary: Although Excel only offers a function for a square root, you can use the technique of raising to a fractional power in order to determine any root of a number.

Commands Discussed: Exponent operator

Functions Discussed: =SQRT()

CALCULATE A GROWTH RATE

Problem: I work for a quickly growing company. In the first year, we had $970,000 in sales. In the fifth year, we had $6,175,000 in sales. I need to determine our compounded annual growth rate.

Strategy: Sales in the fifth year are 6,175/970 higher than in the first year. The formula for growth is (Year5/Year1) – 100%. So, as shown in Figure 473, the five-year growth rate is 537%

Figure 473

Find the five-year growth rate.

D6		f_x	=(B6/B2)-1

	A	B	C	D
1				
2	Year 1	970,000		
3	Year 2	2,250,000		
4	Year 3	4,580,000		
5	Year 4	5,850,000		
6	Year 5	6,175,000	Growth Year 1 - Year 5	537%

However, a compounded growth rate is a number, x, that will calculate like this:

Year1 * (100% + x) * (100% + x) * (100% + x) * (100% + x) = Year5

This is the same as:

Year1 * (100% + x)^4 = Year5

So, in order to calculate x, you have to be able to find the fourth root of (Year5/Year1). The formula to find the fourth root is to raise the number to the 1/4 power. Thus, as shown in Figure 474, the formula to calculate the compounded growth rate is:

(Year5/Year1)^(1/4)-100% = x

Figure 474

Find the nth root by raising to 1/n.

	D6			f_x	=(B6/B2)^(1/4)-100%
	A	B	C	D	E
1					
2	Year 1	970,000			
3	Year 2	2,250,000			
4	Year 3	4,580,000			
5	Year 4	5,850,000	Growth Year 1 - Year 5	537%	
6	Year 5	6,175,000	Compounded Growth	59%	
7					

Part II

As you can see in Figure 474, the compounded growth rate is 59%.

Summary: Compounded growth rates are common calculations that require you to raise a number to a fractional power.

Commands Discussed: Exponent operator

FIND THE AREA OF A CIRCLE

Problem: I need to order pizza for my department's staff meeting. The pizza place has two deals. I can buy three medium (12") pizzas for $15 or two large (16") pizzas for $16. Which is the better deal?

Strategy: You will have to figure out the area of a 12" pizza vs. the area of a 16" pizza. The formula for the area of a circle is pi * r^2 (where r is the radius).

The radius of a pizza is one-half the diameter. If you enter the diameter of the pizza in B2, the radius is =B2/2.

Pi is a Greek letter that represents 3.141592654. Excel offers the PI function to return this number, as shown in Figure 475. It is a lot easier to remember =PI() than the many digits in 3.141592654.

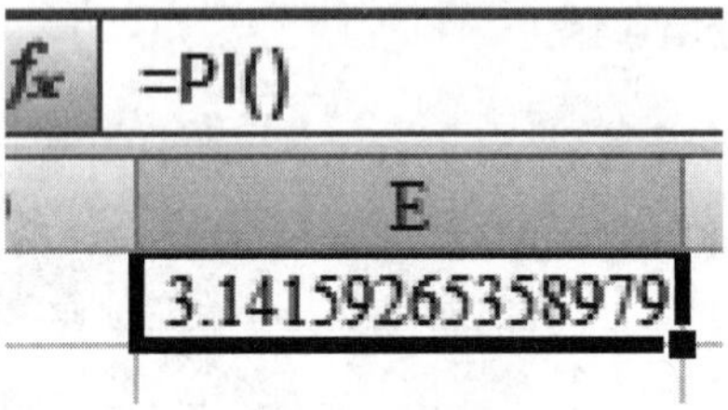

Figure 475

=PI() returns the value of pi to 15-digit precision.

f_x	=PI()
	E
	3.14159265358979

Here's how you determine which is the better pizza deal:

1)   Set up a worksheet. In cell B2, enter the diameter of the pizza.

2)   In cell C2, calculate the radius as =B2/2, as shown in Figure 476.

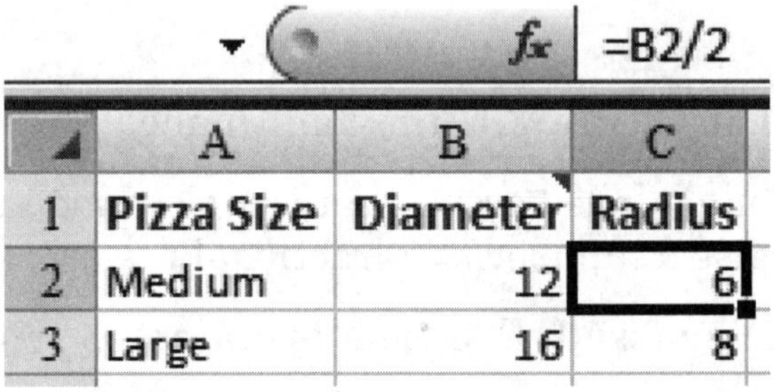

Figure 476

A 16" pie has a radius of 8.

		f_x	=B2/2
◢	**A**	**B**	**C**
1	Pizza Size	Diameter	Radius
2	Medium	12	6
3	Large	16	8

3)   In cell D2, calculate the area of the pizza in square inches, using =PI()*C2^2, as shown in Figure 477.

Figure 477

Area is pi
times radius
squared.

fx	=PI()*C2^2

▲	A	B	C	D
1	Pizza Size	Diameter	Radius	Area
2	Medium	12	6	113.0973355
3	Large	16	8	201.0619298

4) In column E, enter the quantity of pizzas.

5) Calculate the total square inches in column F by using =E2*D2, as shown in Figure 478.

Part
II

Figure 478

Figure the
total amount
of pizza.

fx	=E2*D2

D	E	F
Area	Quantity	Total Square Inches
113.0973355	3	339.2920066
201.0619298	2	402.1238597

6) Enter the cost for the special in column G. In column H, calculate the dollars per square inch of pizza, using =G2/F2, as shown in Figure 479.

Figure 479

Cost per
square inch.

H2	fx	=G2/F2

F	G	H
Total Square Inches	Cost	Cost/Sq Inch
339.2920066	$15.00	$0.0442
402.1238597	$16.00	$0.0398

Results: From a purely mathematical point of view, the special with two large pizzas is a slightly better deal, pricing the pizza at 3.98 cents per square inch.

Additional Details: My seventh-grade math teacher, Mr. Irwin, would like me to mention, for the sake of completeness, that the circumference of the pizza is pi times the diameter. That would be =PI()*B2, as shown in Figure 480.

Figure 480

Circumference of a circle.

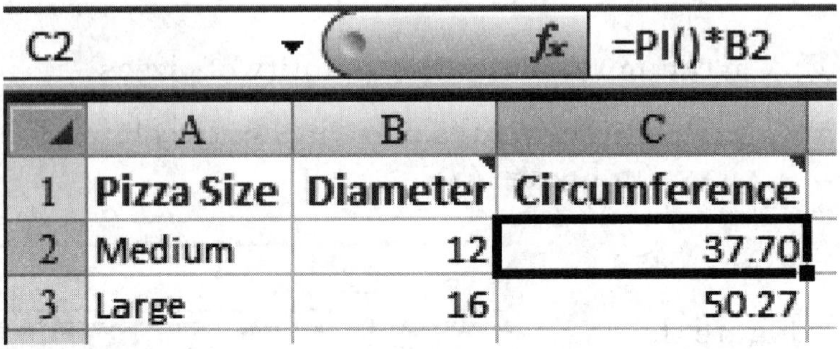

▲	A	B	C
			C2 fx =PI()*B2
1	Pizza Size	Diameter	Circumference
2	Medium	12	37.70
3	Large	16	50.27

Summary: To calculate the area of a circle, use the PI function multiplied by the radius squared.

Functions Discussed: =PI()

FIGURE OUT LOTTERY PROBABILITY

Problem: The Super Lotto jackpot is $8 million this week. Should I play?

Strategy: It depends on how many numbers are in the game. You need to figure out the number of possible combinations in the game.

You can use the COMBIN function as follows to figure out the number of possible combinations for games in which you choose 6 of 40, 44, 48, and so on numbers:

1) Set up a spreadsheet with the number of balls in the lotto game (40, 44, 48, and so on) in cell A2.

2) In cell B2, identify how many numbers you need to select correctly.

3) Enter the formula =COMBIN(A2,B2) in cell C2, as shown in Figure 481.

Figure 481

Combinations of choosing 6 numbers from 40, 44, 48, and so on numbers.

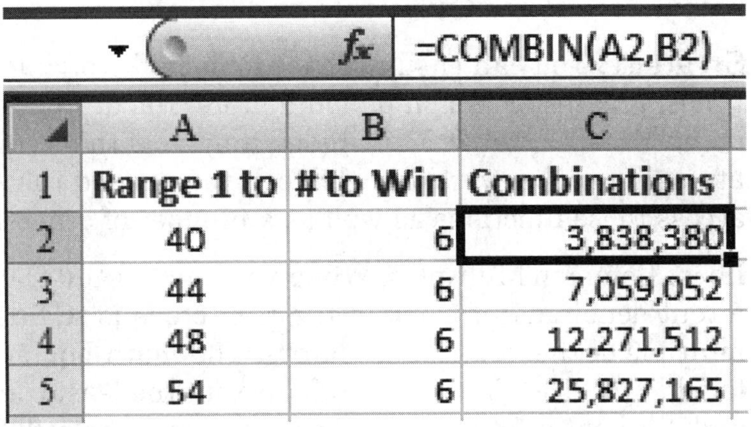

| | f_x | =COMBIN(A2,B2) |

▲	A	B	C
1	Range 1 to	# to Win	Combinations
2	40	6	3,838,380
3	44	6	7,059,052
4	48	6	12,271,512
5	54	6	25,827,165

Part II

If your state lottery game requires you to select 6 numbers out of 40, then the odds against you winning are 3.83 million to 1. For a $1 bet and an $8 million payout, the odds are in your favor.

For a game with 44 numbers, the odds are 7 million to 1. This payoff is only slightly in your favor.

For games with 48 or 54 numbers, the payout is not worth the long odds of the game.

Additional Details: COMBIN figures combinations. Here, the sequence in which the balls are drawn is not relevant. If you had a game in which you had to match both the numbers and the order in which they were drawn, you would want to use the PERMUT function to find the number of permutations of drawing 6 numbers in sequence out of 40.

Summary: You use the COMBIN function or the PERMUT function to figure out the number of combinations or permutations.

Functions Discussed: =COMBIN(); =PERMUT().

HELP YOUR KIDS WITH THEIR MATH

Problem: My kids have math homework, and I want to check their answers. They are doing least common multiples, greatest common denominators, Roman numerals, and factorials.

Strategy: You can easily solve problems involving least common multiples, greatest common denominators, roman numerals, and factorials using Excel. Excel 2007 includes functions that can help in these situations. In earlier versions of Excel, you needed the Analysis Toolpak to access these functions as well as a number of others.

Least Common Multiples: When you have to add fractions that have different denominators, one of the first steps is to find the least common multiple of the two denominators. The math homework asks your kids to add 3/26 + 3/4. You want to figure out the least common multiple of 26 and 4, so enter 26 in one cell and 4 in another cell. The formula to find the least common multiple is =LCM(A2:B2), as shown in Figure 482.

Figure 482

Calculating the least common multiple helps when adding fractions.

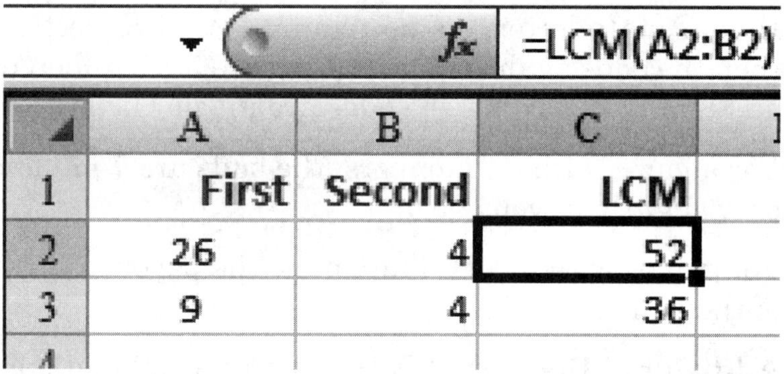

You can now have your kids change 3/26 to 6/52 and 3/4 to 39/52. Expressing the problem as 39/52 + 6/52 makes it easy to see that the answer is 45/52.

Note: In Excel 2007, many functions such as LCM can handle up to 255 numbers as arguments. In prior versions of Excel, the functions could handle only 29 numbers.

Greatest Common Denominators: This time, the problem is 2/9 + 2/4. The LCM of 9 and 4 is 36 as shown in row 3 of Figure 482. You can change 2/9 to 8/36 and 2/4 to 18/36. The problem then becomes 8/36 + 18/36. The answer is 26/36. However, can the fraction 26/36 be further reduced? You need to find the greatest common denominator of 26 and 36. To do so, you use the GCD function =GCD(A2:B2), as shown in Figure 483. Because the answer is greater than 1, your 26/36 answer can be reduced by dividing both the numerator and denominator by 2; 26/36 is the same as 13/18.

Figure 483

Calculate greatest common denominators as a step toward reducing fractions.

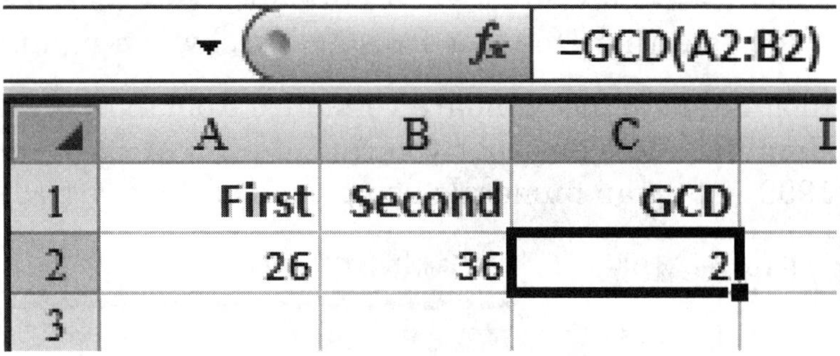

	A	B	C	I
	First	Second	GCD	
1				
2	26	36	2	
3				

f_x =GCD(A2:B2)

Part II

Roman Numerals: Your kids are supposed to use Roman numerals to express the year that each person in the family was born. To do this, you can use the ROMAN function, as shown in Figure 484.

Figure 484

Use ROMAN to convert to Roman numerals.

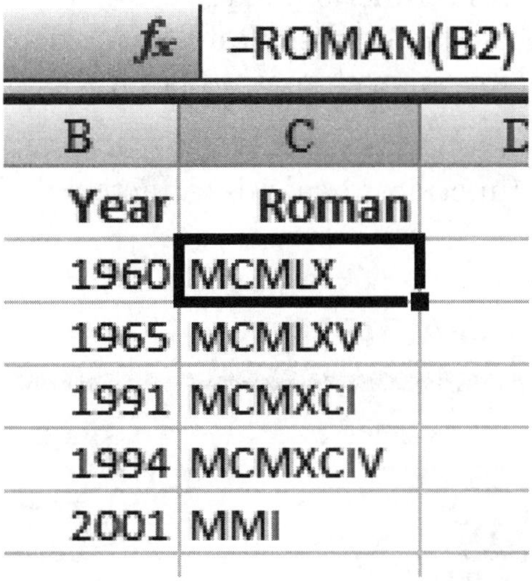

f_x =ROMAN(B2)

B	C	D
Year	Roman	
1960	MCMLX	
1965	MCMLXV	
1991	MCMXCI	
1994	MCMXCIV	
2001	MMI	

The ROMAN function will work with numbers from 1 to 3,999. If you omit an optional second argument, you will get classic Roman numerals, as shown in Figure 484.

Calculating Roman numerals is fairly obscure. Other than middle school students and Latin teachers, who has to do this? The NFL commissioner needs to calculate future Super Bowl numbers. The people who do movie credits need to figure out the information to use in the copyright line. Excel wasn't invented when Foreigner IV was released and I somehow doubt that that Holy See fires up Excel when naming the next pope.

In addition to the standard version of Roman numerals, Excel offers four simplified versions that you can use. Figure 485 compares the number 1999 in Roman numerals using each of the five styles.

Figure 485

Excel offers more concise Roman numerals.

=ROMAN($E$2,F1)

	E	F	G	H	I	J
1		0	1	2	3	4
2	1999	MCMXCIX	MLMVLIV	MXMIX	MVMIV	MIM

Factorials: The last obscure function you need to help with the math homework is the factorial function, FACT. A factorial is a number multiplied by every integer between itself and 1. To write 5 factorial, you use the number followed by an exclamation point. So, for example, 5! is 5 x 4 x 3 x 2 x 1, or 120.

You use the FACT function to calculate factorials as shown in Figure 486.

Figure 486

The factorial of 5 is 5 x 4 x 3 x 2 x 1, or 120.

=FACT(B14)

	A	B	C
13		Number	Fact
14		5	120
15		7	5040
16		8	40320
17		10	3628800

Summary: If you had had Excel in seventh grade, math would have been a lot easier.

Functions Discussed: =LCM(); =GCD(); =ROMAN(); =FACT()

Excel 97-2003: LCM, GCD, ROMAN, and FACT require the Analysis Toolpak to be installed in prior versions of Excel. Select Tools – Add-Ins and then check the box next to Analysis Toolpak.

MEASURE THE ACCURACY
OF A SALES FORECAST

Part II

Problem: I handle forecasting for my company. I collect forecasts from the sales reps and attempt to turn them into a production plan for the manufacturing plant. Can Excel help me with this chore?

Strategy: A lot of forecasting professionals measure forecast error as (Forecast–Actual)/Forecast, as shown in Figure 487.

Figure 487

Most forecasters agree that (Forecast-Actual)/Forecast is the measure of error.

E2 f_x =(C2-D2)/C2

	A	B	C	D	E
1	Product	Customer	Forecast	Actual	FC Err %
2	DEF	Wal-Mart	300	270	10%
3	XYZ	Molson, Inc	100	130	-30%
4	XYZ	Ainsworth	400	0	100%
5	ABC	Ainsworth	0	400	#DIV/0!
6	ABC	General Motors	100	100	0%
7	DEF	Wal-Mart	800	800	0%

However, there are two kinds of problems in forecasting. If you forecast 400 units and the order does not show up, then the manufacturing plant has 400 sets of material on hand and nowhere to send them. Inventory goes up. This is bad. On the other side, if you forecast 0 units and an order for 400 shows up, the plant has to scramble and start buying material on the gray market. This means the product cost could double and your profits go away. This is also bad.

You need a formula for forecast accuracy that treats both of these situations as equally bad. You take the absolute value of (Forecast-Actual) and divide by the larger of the forecasts or actuals. To calculate forecast accuracy using my formula, you follow these steps:

1) Whether the forecast was high or low, the error is always a positive number, so calculate the absolute error on a product-by-product basis. Use the ABS function to returns the absolute value of a number (see Figure 488).

Figure 488

Figure out the absolute size of the error.

=ABS(C2-D2)

C	D	F
Forecast	**Actual**	**Error**
300	270	30
100	130	30
400	0	400

2) Calculate the divisor (which is what I call the "Size of the opportunity to mess up"). Missing a 1,000-unit sale is much worse than missing a 2-unit sale. As shown in Figure 489, for column G, use the MAX function to find what is larger: forecast or actuals.

Figure 489

How bad is it if the forecast is wrong?

=MAX(C2:D2)

C	D	F	G
Forecast	**Actual**	**Error**	**Divisor**
300	270	30	300
100	130	30	130
400	0	400	400
0	400	400	400
100	100	0	100

3) Calculate the error percentage by dividing F2/G2, as shown in Figure 490.

Figure 490

Calculate error percentage.

`=F2/G2`

C	D	F	G	H
Forecast	**Actual**	**Error**	**Divisor**	**Error %**
300	270	30	300	10%
100	130	30	130	23%
400	0	400	400	100%
0	400	400	400	100%
100	100	0	100	0%

As shown in Figure 491, the traditional forecast error calculation is in E. The forecast error calculation you just did is in H. Sometimes these two forecasts are the same. Overall, though, because my calculation takes into account the negative effect of an unforecasted order showing up, my error percentage will be higher (and, I feel, more meaningful).

Figure 491

Is H a better measure of accuracy than E?

`=F12/G12`

	C	D	E	F	G	H
1	**Forecast**	**Actual**	**FC Err %**	**Error**	**Divisor**	**Error %**
2	300	270	10%	30	300	10%
3	100	130	-30%	30	130	23%
4	400	0	100%	400	400	100%
5	0	400	#DIV/0!	400	400	100%
6	100	100	0%	0	100	0%
7	800	800	0%	0	800	0%
8	500	1000	-100%	500	1000	50%
9	900	922	-2%	22	922	2%
10	800	850	-6%	50	850	6%
11	400	450	-13%	50	450	11%
12	4300	4922	-14%	1482	5352	28%

Summary: This started out as a tutorial on using ABS and MAX functions but turned into a sermon on the best way to calculate forecast accuracy. Note that I am currently the only person I know who calculates accuracy this way. When I bounce it off the pros at forecasting conventions, they reject this method. So, if you are doing forecasting, use this method at your own risk.

Functions Discussed: =ABS(); =MAX()

ROUND PRICES TO THE NEXT HIGHEST $5

Problem: I handle pricing for a company, and I have a spreadsheet that shows my cost per SKU (see Figure 492). My manager tells me to take the current manufacturing cost for each item, multiply by 2, add $3, and then round up to the next highest multiple of 5.

Figure 492

Calculate a list price from the manufacturing cost.

◢	A	B
1	SKU	Mfg Cost
2	A409	209.03
3	A322	157.98
4	A356	18.97
5	A460	88.38

Strategy: The first portion of this calculation is fairly easy. The formula in C2 shows the manufacturing cost multiplied by 2 with an additional $3, as shown in Figure 493.

Figure 493

Getting close to the list price is simple.

	f_x	=B2*2+3

◢	A	B	C
1	SKU	Mfg Cost	Part 1
2	A409	209.03	421.06
3	A322	157.98	318.96
4	A356	18.97	40.94
5	A460	88.38	179.76

To round up to the nearest $5, you can use the CEILING function. This function takes one number and the number to round up to. For example, =CEILING(421,5) will result in 425, as shown in Figure 494. Note that with CEILING, the answer is always higher than the original number.

Figure 494

CEILING will round up to a multiple.

	f_x	=CEILING(C2,5)

◢	A	B	C	D
1	SKU	Mfg Cost	Part 1	List Price
2	A409	209.03	421.06	425
3	A322	157.98	318.96	320
4	A356	18.97	40.94	45
5	A460	88.38	179.76	180

Additional Details: Excel also has a FLOOR function. With the FLOOR function, the number would be rounded down to the nearest multiple of 5.

Summary: The CEILING function will round a number up to the nearest increment.

Functions Discussed: =CEILING(); =FLOOR()

Excel 97-2003: Both CEILING and FLOOR require the Analysis Toolpak to be installed in prior versions of Excel. Select Tools – Add-Ins and then check the box next to Analysis Toolpak.

ROUND TO THE NEAREST NICKEL WITH MROUND

Problem: I know I can use the ROUND function to round to the nearest dollar or penny. How do I round to the nearest nickel or quarter?

Strategy: You can use the MROUND function. This function will round a number to the nearest multiple of the second argument. To round to the nearest nickel, as shown in Figure 495, you use =MROUND(B2,0.05). To round to the nearest quarter, you use =MROUND(B2,0.25).

Figure 495

Round to the nearest 0.05.

`=MROUND(B2,0.05)`

◢	A	B	C
1	Cost	Calc	Round
2	17.79	27.36923	27.35
3	8.54	13.13846	13.15
4	11.7	18	18
5	9.31	14.32308	14.3
6	17.51	26.93846	26.95

Additional Details: Unlike MROUND, the ROUND function's second argument points to the number of decimal places of precision. =ROUND(B2,2) will round to two decimal places, and =ROUND(B2,-1) will round to the nearest $10. Excel also offers ROUNDUP and ROUNDDOWN, in case you need to round in a particular direction.

Gotcha: Both arguments in the MROUND function must have the same sign. This can be difficult; you may have a mixture of positive and negative values. The SIGN function will return either a 1 or -1, based on the sign of a number. If there is a possibility that the first argument might be negative, you can multiply the second argument by SIGN of the first argument. In the worksheet shown in Figure 496, cell C4 fails with =MROUND(B9,0.05). The corrected formula in C9 uses =MROUND(B9,0.05*SIGN(B9)). This rounds C9 to the nearest -0.05 and rounds C10 to the nearest 0.05.

Figure 496

If your numbers might be negative, the second argument for MROUND should be negative.

=MROUND(B9,0.05*SIGN(B9))		

	A	B	C
1	MROUND WITH NEGATIVE		
2			
3	Cost	Calc	Round
4	-4.85	-7.46154	#NUM!
5	8.54	13.13846	13.15
6	11.7	18	18
7			
8	Cost	Calc	Round
9	-4.85	-7.46154	-7.45
10	8.54	13.13846	13.15
11	11.7	18	18

Summary: Excel offers the MROUND function to round to a certain multiple.

Functions Discussed: =MROUND(); =ROUND(); =SIGN(); =ROUNDUP(); =ROUNDDOWN()

WHY IS THIS PRICE SHOWING $27.85000001 CENTS?

Problem: I have a worksheet in which I expect the cells to show dollars and cents. For some reason, a price in the formula bar is showing a few millionths of a cent (see Figure 497).

Figure 497

Why the millionths of a cent?

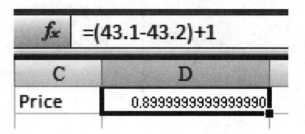

Strategy: These stray values can happen due to something called floating-point arithmetic. Whereas you think in 10s, computers actually calculate with 2s, 4s, 8s, and 16s. Excel has to convert your prices to 16s, do the math, and then present it to you in tenths. A simple number like 0.1 in a base-10 system is actually a repeating number in binary.

Sometimes seemingly bizarre rounding errors creep in. There is one quick solution, but you have to be careful when using it:

1) Format your prices to have two decimal places, as shown in Figure 498. Use either the Format Cells dialog or the Decrease Decimal icon.

Figure 498

Use Format Cells to specify that only two decimal places should be displayed.

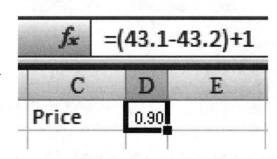

Part
II

2)   Select Office Icon – Excel Options. In the Excel Options dialog (see Figure 499), select Advanced and then select Set Precision as Displayed from the When Calculating section. Excel will immediately truncate all values to only the number of decimal places shown.

Figure 499

Truncate all numbers in the workbook to the number of decimals displayed.

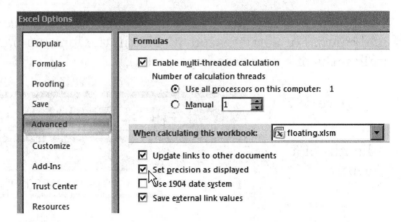

Gotcha: There is neither an Undo command nor any other way to regain those last numbers. However, Excel will warn you that your data will permanently lose accuracy, as shown in Figure 500.

Figure 500

Because there is no Undo, Excel will present this warning.

Summary: If you have annoying floating-point errors in your data, you can turn on Set Precision as Displayed. You should exercise caution when using this option, however, because it will permanently change the values of all numbers in your workbook.

Commands Discussed: Office Icon – Excel Options – Advanced –Set Precision as Displayed

Excel 97-2003: Tools – Options – Calculate – Precision as Displayed

YOU CHANGE A CELL IN EXCEL
BUT THE FORMULAS DO NOT CALCULATE

Problem: Sometimes when I change a cell in Excel, the formulas do not calculate. For example, in Figure 501, cell C2 indicates that two plus two is not four.

Figure 501

Excel stopped calculating.

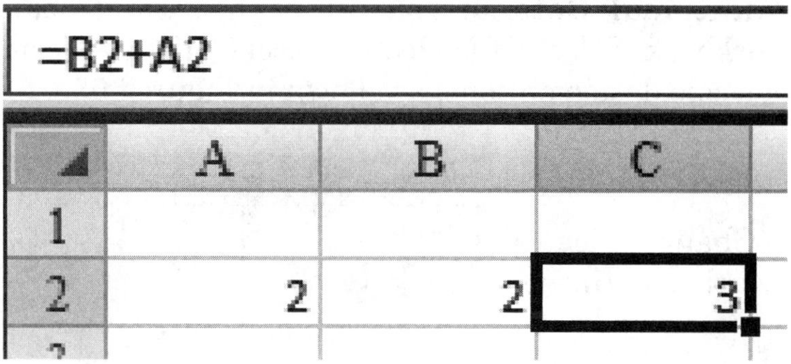

◢	A	B	C
1			
2	2	2	3

=B2+A2

Strategy: In this case, someone has put the worksheet in Manual calculation mode. You can try pressing F9 to calculate, as shown in Figure 502.

Figure 502

Excel will start calculating.

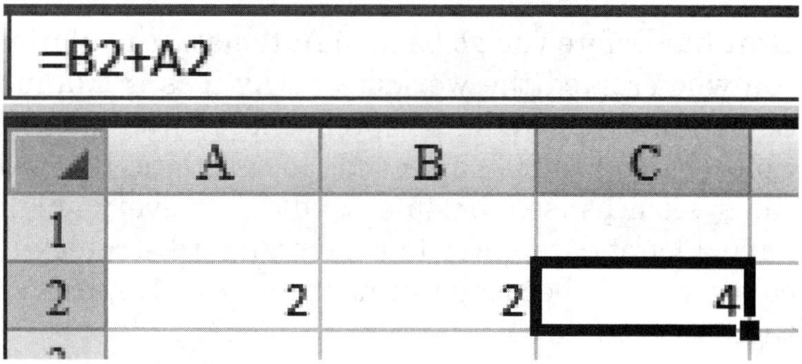

=B2+A2

◢	A	B	C
1			
2	2	2	4

Pressing F9 will have the following results:

- Pressing F9 will recalculate all cells that have changed since the last calculation, plus all formulas that depend on those cells in all open workbooks.

- For quicker calculation, use Shift+F9. This will limit the calculation to the current worksheet.

- For thorough calculation, use Ctrl+Alt+F9. This will calculate all formulas in all open workbooks, whether Excel thinks they have changed or not.

- Pressing Ctrl+Shift+Alt+F9 rebuilds the list of dependent formulas and then does a thorough calculation.

Additional Details: You can change the Calculation Options for a workbook. Select Office Icon – Excel Options – Formulas to see the various calculation options, as shown in Figure 503.

Figure 503

Change calculation settings.

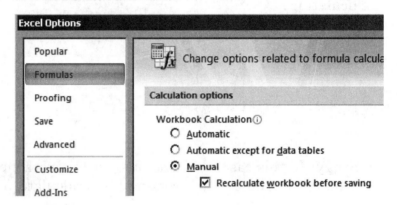

Gotcha: Before you go back to Automatic calculation mode, ask the person who created the worksheet why it is in Manual calculation mode. Sometimes you will find a spreadsheet with tens of thousands of calculations that takes 30–45 seconds to calculate. It is very frustrating when the system pauses for 45 seconds after every single data entry. If you have a lot of data entry to do, a standard strategy is to use Manual calculation mode because in this mode, you can make several changes and then press F9 to calculate.

Summary: Excel offers a Manual calculation mode. If you have a spreadsheet that takes too long to calculate after every data entry, you might consider using Manual calculation mode temporarily, doing the data entry, and then switching back to Automatic calculation mode.

Commands Discussed: F9; Office Icon – Excel Options – Formulas

Excel 97-2003: Tools – Options – Calculate

USE PARENTHESES TO CONTROL THE ORDER OF CALCULATIONS

Problem: In what order does Excel perform calculations? For example, is 2+3*4 equal to 20 or 14?

Strategy: In Excel, if you do not use parentheses, the default order of calculations is as follows:

1. Unary minus operation

2. Exponents

3. Multiply and divide, left to right

4. Add and subtract, left to right

Thus, with the formula =5+4*-5^3/6, Excel will do the following:

1. Figure unary minus on -5.

2. Raise -5 to the third power (-5*-5*-5 = -125).

3. Do division and multiplication from left to right (4*-125 is -500. Then -500/6 is -83.3).

4. Add 5 (-83.3 + 5 is -78.3).

The answer will be -78.3.

You can control the order of operations by using parentheses. For example, the formula =(5+4)*-(5^(1/2)) will yield the answer-20.1246, as shown in Figure 504.

Figure 504

Change the order of calculation by using parentheses.

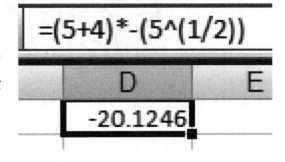

Additional Details: In math class, you may have been taught that if you need to nest parentheses, start from the inside and work your way out, using regular parentheses, then square brackets, and then curly braces. In math class, you might have written:

{(5+4)*[-5*(3/6)]}+3

Forget all that. In Excel, you use regular parentheses throughout.

((5+4)*(-5*(3/6)))+3

When you get the formula error message, as shown in Figure 505, it is almost always because you've missed a closing parenthesis somewhere.

Figure 505

Missing parentheses cause this error.

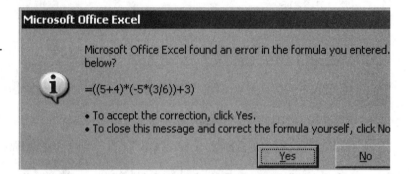

As you enter or edit a formula, when you type a closing parenthesis, Excel bolds the corresponding opening parenthesis. However, this bolded condition lasts for only a moment and disappears before you can figure out what is going on. For example, Figure 506 was taken during the fleeting moment when the first and eighth parentheses were in bold.

Figure 506

Excel highlights matching parentheses, but only for a fraction of a second.

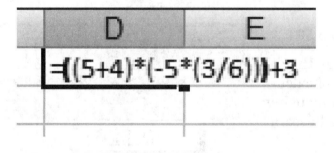

If you're dealing with a very confusing formula with many sets of parentheses, use this technique to sort out which one is missing:

1)   Highlight the formula in the formula bar.

2)   Press Ctrl+C to copy the formula.

3)   Paste it to a blank Notepad or Wordpad window and print.

4)   Use different colors of highlighters to match up the various sets of parentheses until you find the extra parenthesis.

Summary: Excel uses a default order for its calculations. You can place parentheses in a formula to force Excel to change the order of calculations.

BEFORE DELETING A CELL,
FIND OUT IF OTHER CELLS RELY ON IT

Problem: I am about to delete a section of a worksheet that I believe is no longer being used. However, I know that if I delete the cell, and some other far-off range relies on the cell, the far-off range will change to the dreaded #REF! error. How can I determine if any other range refers to this cell?

Strategy: You can select the cell that you are considering for deletion and then select Formulas – Trace Dependents, as shown in Figure 507. (*Dependents* are other cells that rely on the current cell for calculation.)

Figure 507

The Formula Auditing tools are easier to find in Excel 2007 than in prior versions.

Blue arrows will draw from the active cell out to any dependents. In Figure 508, for example, you can see that cell F4 is used to calculate H4.

Figure 508

Excel draws blue arrows to any dependents on the current worksheet.

	A B	D	E	F	G	H
1	Section 1: Historical Trends (Per Month)					
2						
3	Store Type	Rent	Sales	Profit	Labor	Net
4	Regular	2400	12456	6228	6480	-2652
5	BigBox	5200	34500	17250	8640	3410
6						

If a dependent is on another worksheet, Excel will draw a black arrow to the other worksheet icon, as shown in Figure 509.

Figure 509

This icon indicates that at least one dependent is on another worksheet.

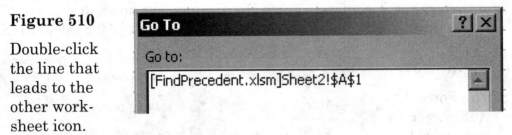

If you double-click the line that leads to the other worksheet icon in Figure 509, Excel will show you a list of the off-sheet dependents (see Figure 510).

Figure 510

Double-click the line that leads to the other worksheet icon.

Go To	? X
Go to:	
[FindPrecedent.xlsm]Sheet2!$A$1	

Additional Details: If you immediately click Trace Dependents, Excel will draw arrows from each of the dependent cells to their dependent cells. In Figure 511, you can see that F4 is used to calculate H4, and H4 is used to calculate D15 and E20.

Figure 511

Trace Dependents multiple times to follow how the value works its way through the spreadsheet.

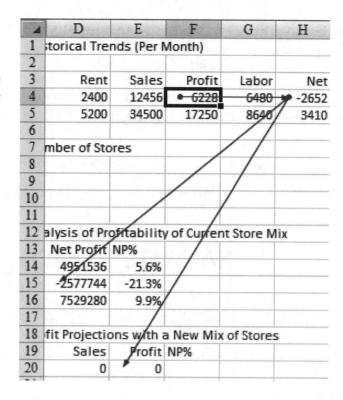

If you immediately ask to Trace Dependents several times in a row, you will see all of the formulas that would change to #REF! if you delete cell C4.

You also have a big mess on your spreadsheet! To get rid of all arrows, choose Tools – Formula Auditing – Remove All Arrows.

Additional Information: If you think that there are no cells that use the current cell and you are right, then Excel will give you the message shown in Figure 512.

Figure 512

When you see this message, it is safe to delete the original cell.

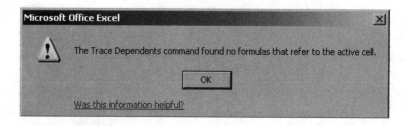

Gotcha: Some advanced functions such as =INDIRECT("F" & D4/600) might be pointing to your target cell and will not be detected by the Trace Dependents command.

Summary: To determine if a cell can be deleted without affecting any other formulas, select the cell, and then select Formulas – Trace Dependents.

Commands Discussed: Formulas – Trace Dependents

Excel 97-2003: Tools – Formula Auditing – Trace Dependents

NAVIGATE TO EACH PRECEDENT

Problem: A tip of the hat to Howard Krams in New York for this tip. Howard uses massive spreadsheets with formulas that have a dozen precedents. (A cell's precedents are the cells that are referenced in the cell's formula.) He discovered an obscure way to navigate to each precedent on the current worksheet.

Strategy: This trick works only if you turn off in-cell editing, and it works as follows:

1) Select Office Icon – Excel Options and then select Advanced and look in the Editing Options group. Uncheck the option for Allow Editing in Cells. You can then go to any cell that contains a formula, as shown in Figure 513.

Figure 513

You want to navigate to each precedent.

	f_x	=(E30/C4)^(D4/D5)+D14-E21*E16+Sheet2!C5

	A	B	C	D	E	F	G
31							
32			Big Formula	3980883.2			
33							

2) Double-click a cell that contains a formula. Excel will move to the first cell in the original formula. In this case, as shown in Figure 514, that is cell E30, just a couple rows up.

Figure 514

Press Enter to visit the next precedent.

	A	B	C	D	E
30	Bottom Line				3693144
31					
32			Big Formula	3980883.2	

3) Press the Enter key, and Excel will navigate to the next cell in the original formula. This will be cell C4, near the top of the worksheet. Excel will scroll so that you can see cell C4. You might be able to see that Excel has actually selected all of the precedent cells.

4) Continue pressing Enter to continue cycling through the precedents.

Gotcha: This feature was added to Excel back in Excel version 4. That was the last Excel version with only one worksheet in a workbook. At that time, Microsoft had never dreamt of supporting precedents on other worksheets. So you cannot use this technique to navigate to precedents on other sheets.

Shameless Commercial: When Howard pointed out this feature, he asked what it would take to actually make it work for any and all sheets. MrExcel Consulting wrote a TracePrecedents utility for Howard that does a great job of tracing precedents, as shown in Figure 515.

Part II

Figure 515

The Trace Precedents add-in finds off-sheet precedents.

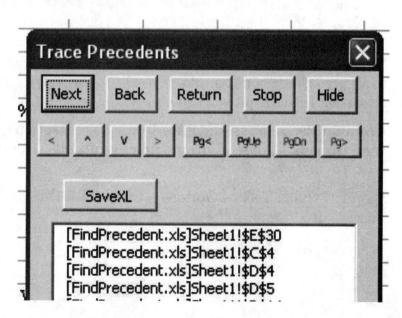

```
[FindPrecedent.xls]Sheet1!$E$30
[FindPrecedent.xls]Sheet1!$C$4
[FindPrecedent.xls]Sheet1!$D$4
[FindPrecedent.xls]Sheet1!$D$5
```

The TracePrecedents utility lists all the precedents, even precedents on other worksheets and in other open workbooks. You can use Next/Prev to move a particular precedent to the middle of the screen. If you need to be able to track precedents, write to MrExcel Consulting to buy this utility.

Additional Details: Turning off in-cell editing is a steep price to pay for the use of technique. You could instead select the original cell and use Home – Find & Select – Go To Special. As shown in Figure 516, in the Go To Special dialog, you then choose Precedents, choose Direct Only or All Levels, and click OK. Excel will select all precedent cells. You can press Enter to move from precedent to precedent.

Figure 516

Use Go To Special to select precedents of the current cell.

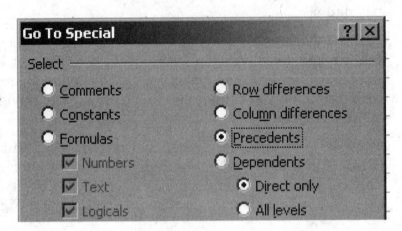

Summary: There is an obscure feature in Excel that lets you navigate to all precedents of a formula. It works fairly well for navigating to precedents on the current worksheet.

Commands Discussed: Office Icon – Excel Options – Advanced – Editing Options – Allow Editing Directly in Cells; Home – Find & Select – Go To

Excel 97-2003: Tools – Options – Edit – Edit Directly in Cell; Edit – Go To Special

CALCULATE A FORMULA IN SLOW MOTION

Problem: I am trying to trace how a formula is calculating. What should I do?

Strategy: If you have Excel 2002 or a later version, you'll want to use a cool new tool on the Formula Auditing menu called Evaluate Formula. You select the cell that contains the formula you want to examine. Then you select Formulas – Evaluate Formula.

The Evaluate Formula dialog shows the formula. The first item to be calculated is underlined, as shown in Figure 517. Click Evaluate to calculate the underlined portion of the formula.

Part II

Figure 517

The under-
lined term will
be evaluated
next.

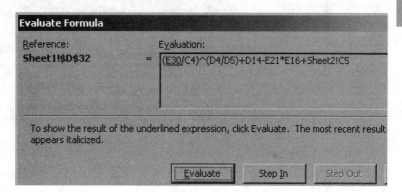

With each click of Evaluate, Excel will calculate the underlined portion and show the results in italics. It will underline the next step in the calculation. Figure 518 shows what the Evaluate Formula dialog looks like after you click Evaluate the second time: Excel has revealed that C4 is 1200 (in italics). It is about to calculate the first division in parentheses.

Figure 518

The item in
italics was the
most recent
item evalu-
ated.

Additional Details: Any time the next term to be calculated is a cell reference, you can click the Step In button to evaluate the formula in that cell. As shown in Figure 519, it is possible to use Step In for several levels. After you see the formula for D14, you can click Step In to see the formula for D15.

Figure 519

Click Step In to see the formula in the next cell reference.

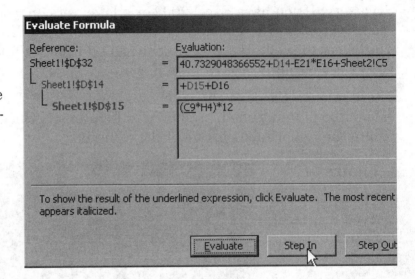

You click Step Out to close the most recent detail level and go back one level.

Summary: The Evaluate Formula dialog is a great tool for times when you are convinced that Excel is giving you the wrong answer. It can often help you discover that you had an incorrect assumption about the order of operations that Excel would use. The dialog gives you a great appreciation for just how much work Excel does every time you enter a formula because it allows you to watch the calculation happen in slow motion.

Excel 2007: Formulas – Evaluate Formula

Excel 97-2003: Excel 2002-2003, Tools – Formula Auditing – Evaluate Formula; this command was not available in earlier versions.

WHICH CELLS FLOW INTO THIS CELL?

Problem: I have a large formula, and I would like to visually see how the cell is calculated.

Strategy: One way to handle this is to select the cell and then press F2 to edit the cell. As shown in Figure 520, all the references in the formula will light up with different colors. If the precedent cell is in the visible portion of the window, the cell will be surrounded by a box of the same color as the formula.

Figure 520

Excel will colorcode the referenced cells.

12	Section 3: Analysis of Profitability of Current Store Mix			
13		Sales	Net Profit	NP%
14	Total Chair	88283232	4951536	5.6%
15	Regular	12107232	-2577744	-21.3%
16	Big Box	76176000	7529280	9.9%
17				
18	Section 4: Profit Projections with a New Mix of Stores			
19			Sales	Profit	NP%
20	Regular	0	0	0
21	BigBox	240	99360000	9820800
22	New Mix	240	99360000	9820800	10%
23					
24	Cost of Closing Stores			
25	Labor	787320		
26	Lost Rent	388800		
27				Year 1	Year 2	Ye
28	Increased Profit from New Stores			4869264	4869264	4!
29	Costs in year 1			1176120	0	
30	Bottom Line			3693144	4869264	4!
31					
32		Big Formula	=(E30/C4)^(D4/D5)+D14-E21*E16-		

You can't tell in this black-and-white book, but in the formula bar, cell E30 is a bright blue; the box around cell E30 is a matching blue. Cell C4 is a dark green; you cannot see C4 in the visible worksheet, but if you could, you would see a matching dark green cell. Cell D14 is a light green in the formula bar; the box around D14 is a matching green. Any terms that point to an off-sheet reference appear in black in the formula bar.

Alternate **Strategy:** If you need a more permanent view of the calculations than pressing F2 gives you, you can use the Formula Auditing menu to draw blue arrows from all the precedent cells. To do so, you select cell D32 and then select Formulas – Trace Precedents. Excel will draw blue arrows from all the cells that are referenced in the D32 formula. As shown near the bottom left of Figure 521, the arrow from the other worksheet icon indicates that at least one reference is on another worksheet. Double-click the arrow to see a list of those off-sheet precedents.

Figure 521

Trace Precedents shows the cells that are used in the current formula.

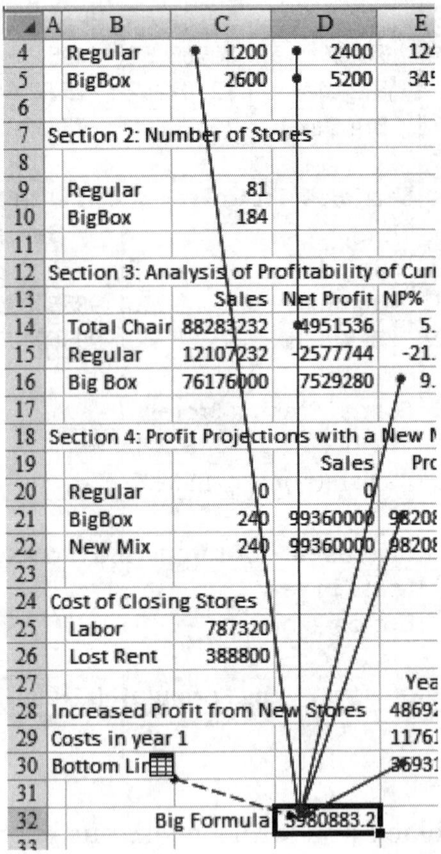

If you click Trace Precedents enough times, Excel will trace the precedents of all the arrowed cells. After a few iterations of the command, you will see that nearly all the cells factor in to the calculation, as shown in Figure 522.

Figure 522

Click Trace Precedents again to trace the precedents of the prec- edents.

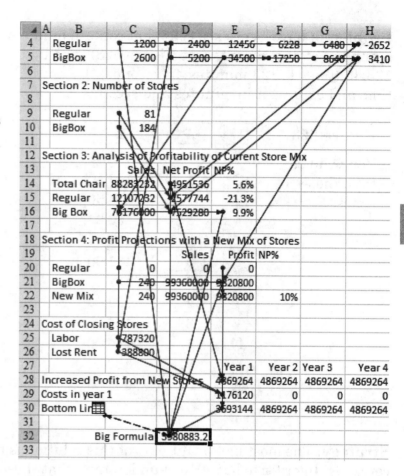

Part
II

To remove all the arrows, choose Formulas –Remove Arrows.

Summary: Tracing precedents gives you a quick visual view of all the cells that are used to calculate a formula.

Commands Discussed: Formulas – Trace Precedents; Formulas –Remove Arrows

Excel 97-2003: Tools – Auditing – Trace Precedents; Tools – Auditing – Remove All Arrows

TOTAL MINUTES THAT EXCEED AN HOUR

Problem: I have a series of cells that contain minutes and seconds from a number of experiments (see Figure 523). The times are in the format 123:45 (that is, 123 minutes 45 seconds). I want to be able to total the time and express it in minutes and seconds.

Figure 523

You want to total these times.

◢	A	B
1	Trial	Time
2	1	123:40
3	2	234:56
4	3	180:02
5	4	129:04
6	5	132:00
7	6	131:00
8	7	172:00
9	8	174:00
10	9	140:00
11	10	153:00
12	11	145:00

Strategy: The most important part of this solution is to enter the times correctly. In order to have Excel understand that these are minutes and seconds, time should be entered with a leading zero for hours.

1) Enter 0:123:40, as shown in Figure 524.

Figure 524

Enter the time with a leading 0: for hours.

◢	A	B
1	Trial	Time
2	1	0:123:40
3	2	

2)   Press Enter to accept the cell. Excel will change the value to a decimal portion of a day, as shown in Figure 525.

Figure 525

Excel displays the time as a decimal portion of a day.

◢	A	B
1	Trial	Time
2	1	0.08588
3	2	

3)   Select the cell and then select Home – Format dropdown – Format Cells (or press Ctrl+1).

4)   On the Number tab, click the Custom category. Excel will indicate that the current format is General. In the Type box, change the Custom format from General to [m]:ss, as shown in Figure 526. (The square brackets tell Excel to display minutes in excess of an hour.) You will see in the Sample box that the entry is now formatted with just minutes and seconds. .

Figure 526

Use a custom format of [m]:ss.

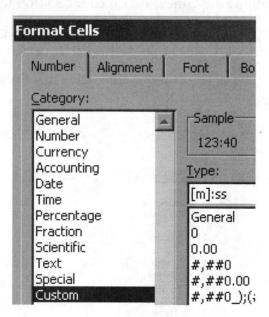

5) Click OK to close the Format Cells box. Your entry in B2 will appear correctly. Note that in the formula bar in Figure 527, Excel thinks that 123 minutes is 2:03 a.m. That is because 123 minutes after midnight is 2:03 a.m.

Figure 527

Even though the cells appears with minutes, the formula bar shows time of day.

f_x	2:03:40 AM

◢	A	B
1	Trial	Time
2	1	123:40
3	2	

6) Copy the numeric formatting from B2 to the rest of the cells in the table. To do so, place the cell pointer in B2. Press Ctrl+C to Copy. Highlight B3:B14. Select Home – Paste dropdown – Paste Special. In the Paste Special box, select Formats and then click OK.

7) Enter the remaining times, using the 0:234:56 format.

8) When you are done entering all the time entries, place the cell pointer in the cell that is to contain the total (in this case, B13).

9) In the Home tab of the ribbon, click the AutoSum button, as shown in Figure 528.

Figure 528

The Greek letter sigma is the AutoSum icon.

◢	A	B
1	Trial	Time
2	1	123:40
3	2	234:56
4	3	180:02
5	4	129:04
6	5	132:00
7	6	131:00
8	7	172:00
9	8	174:00
10	9	140:00
11	10	153:00
12	11	145:00
13	Total	

10) When Excel proposes the formula =SUM(B2:B12), press Enter because it is correct.

11) Verify that the correct total appears, as shown in Figure 529.

Figure 529

When the times are entered correctly, Excel's SUM function works properly.

fx	=SUM(B2:B12)

◢	A	B
1	Trial	Time
2	1	123:40
3	2	234:56
4	3	180:02
5	4	129:04
6	5	132:00
7	6	131:00
8	7	172:00
9	8	174:00
10	9	140:00
11	10	153:00
12	11	145:00
13	Total	1714:42

Part
II

Gotcha: Be very careful that the total cell is formatted with the custom format [m]:ss. If you instead select the built-in time format mm:ss, Excel will show you only the minutes in excess of whole hours. In the example shown here, 1714 minutes is 28 hours 34 minutes. So, with the wrong number format, you would see only 34 minutes 42 seconds (see Figure 530).

Figure 530

Using a built-in number format displays the wrong answer.

◢	A	B
1	Trial	Time
2	1	123:40
3	2	234:56
4	3	180:02
5	4	129:04
6	5	132:00
7	6	131:00
8	7	172:00
9	8	174:00
10	9	140:00
11	10	153:00
12	11	145:00
13	Total	34:42

Additional Details: As shown in Figure 531, you use the AVERAGE function in B14 to find the average time: =AVERAGE(B2:B12)

Figure 531

Other functions such as AVERAGE will work correctly.

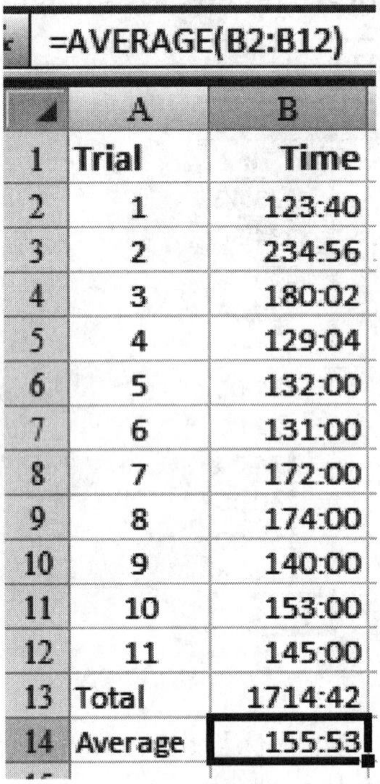

	=AVERAGE(B2:B12)	
	A	B
1	Trial	Time
2	1	123:40
3	2	234:56
4	3	180:02
5	4	129:04
6	5	132:00
7	6	131:00
8	7	172:00
9	8	174:00
10	9	140:00
11	10	153:00
12	11	145:00
13	Total	1714:42
14	Average	155:53

Summary: The formula to total a column of time entries is intuitive. However, using the proper numeric formats to allow the formula to work is rather complex. The key is to use a custom number format with square brackets around the m. Also, you need to enter the times using 0 for the hours.

Commands Discussed: Home – Format dropdown – Format Cells – Numeric; Ctrl+1

Excel 97-2003: Format – Cells – Numeric

Functions Discussed: =SUM(); =AVERAGE()

CONVERT TEXT TO MINUTES AND SECONDS

Problem: Someone in another department set up a spreadsheet that contains hundreds of time values. However, instead of using Excel time formats, he entered each cell as text, as shown in Figure 532. How can I convert the text entries to real Excel times?

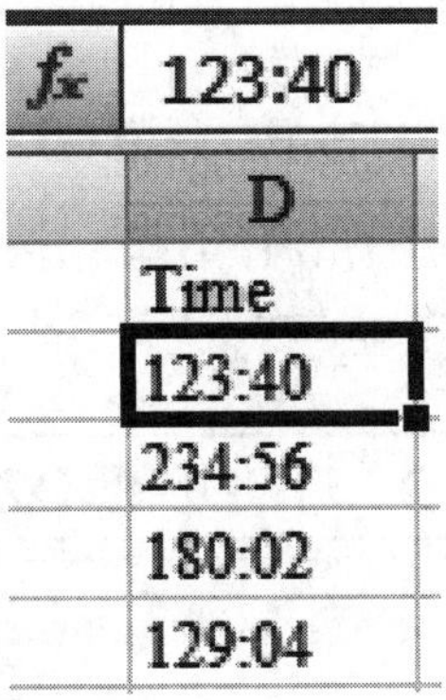

Figure 532

The formula bar gives a subtle clue that these are not real times.

f_x	123:40

	D
	Time
	123:40
	234:56
	180:02
	129:04

Strategy: You can use the TIME function, which requires three arguments: *hours*, *minutes*, and *seconds*. The function can handle normal times; for example, =TIME(1,23,40) will return 1:23 a.m. with 40 seconds. It can also handle strange times; for example, =TIME(0,123,40) represents 123 minutes 40 seconds, as shown in the first cell in Figure 533. Here's how you use TIME:

1) Enter the TIME function in a temporary column next to your data. If there is already data in column E, insert a new column E.

2) Select the cells in the new column and format them with the proper custom number format. In this case, you need the [m]:ss format discussed in "Total Minutes That Exceed an Hour."

3) Create a formula that will parse the minutes and seconds from the text entry. You do so by using a series of nested functions:

• =FIND(":",D2) will find and tell you the location of the colon in the text entry. This result minus 1 can be used as the second parameter of the =LEFT function in the next step.

- =LEFT(D2,FIND(":",D2)-1) will return just the minutes portion of the entry in D2. This function can be used for the *minutes* argument of the TIME function.

- =RIGHT(D2,2) will return just the seconds portion of the entry in D2. This parameter can be used as the *seconds* parameter of the TIME function.

Therefore, as shown in Figure 533, enter the following formula in cell E2:

=TIME(0,LEFT(D2,FIND(":",D2)-1),RIGHT(D2,2))

This will have Excel return a time with 0 hours and the proper number of minutes and seconds from the text entry.

Figure 533

Parse the minutes and seconds from the text.

=TIME(0,LEFT(D2,FIND(":",D2)-1),RIGHT(D2,2))				
D	E	F	G	H
Time				
123:40	123:40			
234:56				

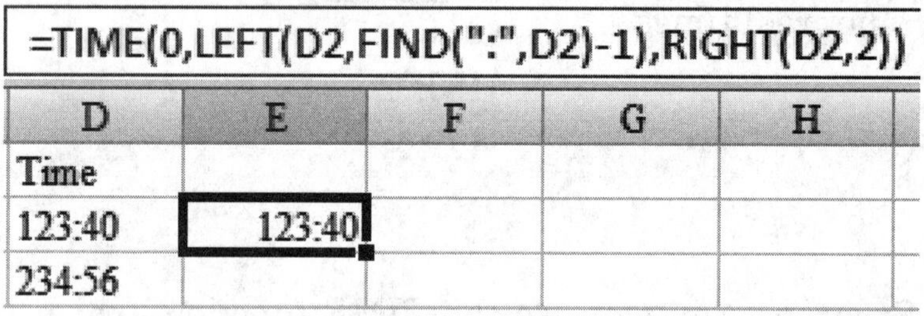

4) Double-click the fill handle in cell E2 to copy the formula down to all the rows in column D that contain data.

Additional Details: Before you can delete column D, you need to change the times in column E from formulas to values. First, you highlight the cells in column E. Then you use Ctrl+C to copy. Without changing the selection, you select Home – Paste dropdown – Paste Values.

Summary: The TIME(*hours,minutes,seconds*) function is very useful for converting text entries to real times. It is critical to have times and dates entered as real Excel times and dates instead of text if you want to do any math with the entries.

Commands Discussed: Home – Paste dropdown – Paste Values

Excel 97-2003: Format – Cells – Numeric; Edit – Paste Special – Values

Functions Discussed: =TIME(); =LEFT(); =RIGHT()

CONVERT TEXT TO HOURS, MINUTES, AND SECONDS

Problem: Someone in yet another department set up a spreadsheet with hundreds of time values. (Maybe my company should buy all these people this book.) However, instead of using Excel time formats, she entered each cell as text with hours, minutes, seconds, and AM or PM, as shown in Figure 534 . How can I convert these text entries to real Excel times? (To try this, enter a leading apostrophe before the time.)

Figure 534

Time stored as text.

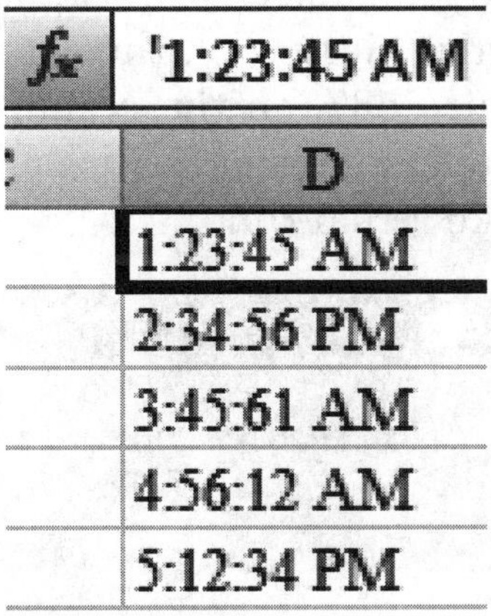

f_x	'1:23:45 AM

	D
	1:23:45 AM
	2:34:56 PM
	3:45:61 AM
	4:56:12 AM
	5:12:34 PM

Strategy: Here's how you convert the text entries to real Excel times:

1)   Use the =TIMEVALUE() function in a nearby blank column. As shown in Figure 535, this function requires one argument: a text value that looks like a valid time.

Figure 535

This function will work when the text is formatted to look like a time.

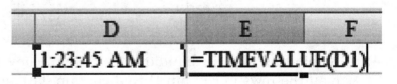

D	E	F
1:23:45 AM	=TIMEVALUE(D1)	

2) Press Enter to accept the formula. Do not be alarmed. Excel will normally display the result as the decimal portion of one day, as shown in Figure 536.

Figure 536

Correct answer; wrong formatting.

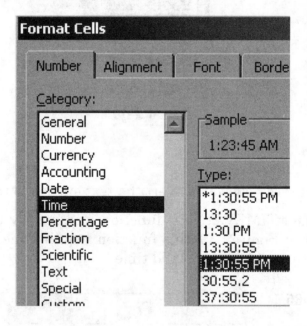

=TIMEVALUE(D1)

D	E
1:23:45 AM	0.05815972

3) Select the cell. Press Ctrl+1 to display the Format Cells dialog box. (The 1 on the numeric keypad does not work; use the 1 at the top of the keyboard. You can also right-click the cell and choose Format Cells.) As shown in Figure 537, on the Number tab, choose Time and then select an appropriate format. Click OK. The result of the formula will now look like a real time.

Figure 537

Choose a built-in time format.

4) Double-click the fill handle in cell E1 to copy the formula down to all the rows in column D that contain data, as shown in Figure 538.

Figure 538

Copy the formula.

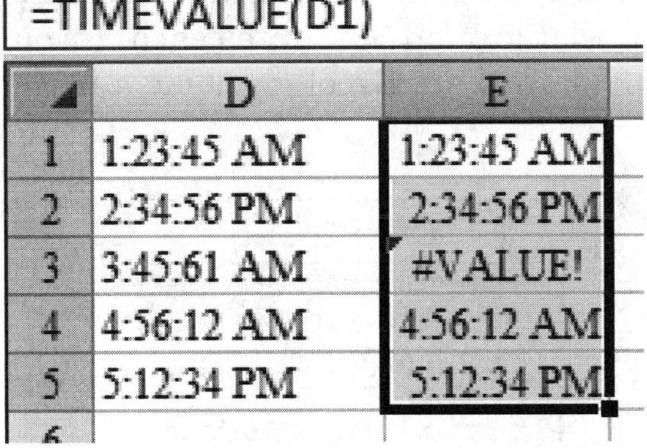

=TIMEVALUE(D1)

◢	D	E
1	1:23:45 AM	1:23:45 AM
2	2:34:56 PM	2:34:56 PM
3	3:45:61 AM	#VALUE!
4	4:56:12 AM	4:56:12 AM
5	5:12:34 PM	5:12:34 PM
6		

Gotcha: Beware; the TIMEVALUE function cannot convert an invalid time. As shown in cell D3 in Figure 538, someone entered a time with 61 seconds. Although the TIME function can handle 61 seconds, the TIMEVALUE function cannot. You need to scan through the results, looking for #VALUE! errors before changing the formulas to values.

Additional Details: Before you can delete column D, you need to change the times in column E from formulas to values. To do so, you highlight the cells in column E. Then you press Ctrl+C to copy. Without changing the selection, you select Home – Paste dropdown – Paste Values.

Summary: The TIMEVALUE function can convert text entries to real times. It is critical to have times and dates entered as real Excel times and dates instead of text if you want to do any math with the entries.

Commands Discussed: Ctrl+1; Home – Paste dropdown – Paste Values

Excel 97-2003: Format – Cells – Number; Edit – Paste Special – Values

Functions Discussed: =TIMEVALUE()

CONVERT TIMES FROM H:MM TO M:SS

Problem: I entered the results of a running challenge for the students in my gym class. The results ranged from 2 minutes 35 seconds to 3 minutes 15 seconds. When I total the times, something is clearly wrong. If I have 11 students at around 3 minutes each, I would expect an answer around 33 minutes. Instead, Excel gives me a total of 7:42, as shown in Figure 539.

Figure 539

How did approximately 30 minutes change to 7 hours?

| f_x | =SUM(B2:B12) |

◢	A	B
1	Runner	Time
2	Andy	2:35
3	Bob	3:01
4	Carol	2:41
5	David	2:56
6	Ed	3:15
7	Frank	2:56
8	Gerry	2:32
9	Hank	3:04
10	Isabel	2:51
11	John	2:49
12	Kevin	3:02
13	Total	7:42

Strategy: Although you thought that you were entering 2 minutes 35 seconds, if you place the cell pointer in B2 and examine the formula bar, you will notice that Excel thought you meant 2 hours 35 minutes, as shown in Figure 540.

Figure 540

The formula bar shows that this is 2 hours 35 minutes.

| f_x | 2:35:00 AM |

◢	A	B
1	Runner	Time
2	Andy	2:35
3	Bob	3:01

One solution is to reenter all the values, using the format 0:02:35. This is probably the fastest method for 11 entries, but if you have hundreds of entries, there is a better way: You can use a series of nested functions to extract the hour and minute from the incorrect entry and then use those results in the TIME function. Here's how:

1)   As shown in Figure 541, in column D, use the =HOUR(B2) function to return the portion of the time before the colon.

Figure 541

Extract the hour.

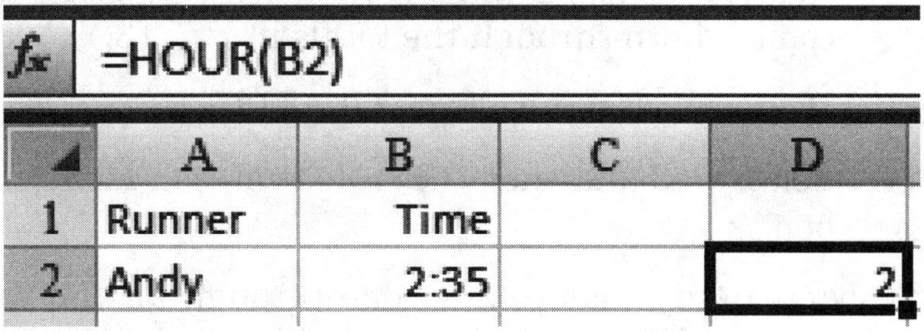

f_x	=HOUR(B2)			
	A	B	C	D
1	Runner	Time		
2	Andy	2:35		2

Part II

2)   In cell E2, use =MINUTE(B2) to return the portion of the time after the colon, as shown in Figure 542.

Figure 542

Extract the minute.

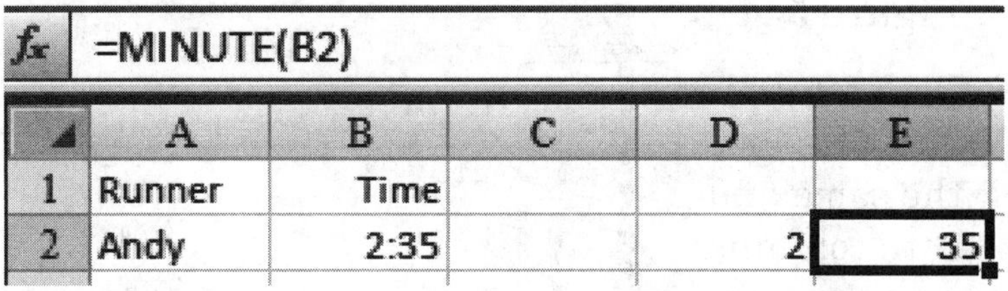

f_x	=MINUTE(B2)				
	A	B	C	D	E
1	Runner	Time			
2	Andy	2:35		2	35

3)   Use the TIME function in cell C2, as shown in Figure 543. This function requires an hour, a minute, and a second. The hour is 0. The minute is the result of the HOUR function in D2. The second is the result of the MINUTE function in E2. The complete formula is =TIME(0,D2,E2).

Figure 543

Correct formula; incorrect formatting.

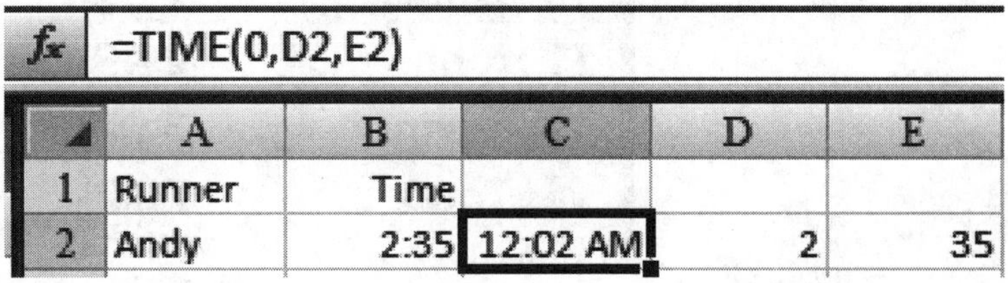

f_x	=TIME(0,D2,E2)				
	A	B	C	D	E
1	Runner	Time			
2	Andy	2:35	12:02 AM	2	35

4) Don't be immediately alarmed that the result of the formula is not what you expected. Select the cell. Press Ctrl+1 to display the Format Cells dialog. On the Number tab, select Time and then select a format such as 13:30:55. Alternatively, select the Custom category and type the custom number format M:SS.

5) Select cells C2:E2. Double-click the fill handle to copy the formulas down to row 12. Because the fill handle trick will look to the number of rows in the adjacent column, you will have the formulas copied down through the totals in row 13.

6) Delete the formulas from C13:E13.

7) Select C13 and click the AutoSum icon in the Home tab of the ribbon.

It seems funny that you've gone through all the work in this topic in order to get cell C2 to look exactly like the original cell in B2, as shown in Figure 544. However, as you can see in the totals in B13 vs. C13, the values in column C return a correct answer. This is one of the reasons that working with times in Excel is so confusing.

Figure 544

Both total formulas are the same and both columns look the same. Dealing with the subtleties of time is confusing.

	A	B	C
1	Runner	Time	
2	Andy	2:35	2:35
3	Bob	3:01	3:01
4	Carol	2:41	2:41
5	David	2:56	2:56
6	Ed	3:15	3:15
7	Frank	2:56	2:56
8	Gerry	2:32	2:32
9	Hank	3:04	3:04
10	Isabel	2:51	2:51
11	John	2:49	2:49
12	Kevin	3:02	3:02
13	Total	7:42	31:42
14			

Additional Details: Before you can delete columns B, D, and E, you need to change the times in column C from formulas to values. To do this, you highlight the cells C2:C12. Then you press Ctrl+C to copy. Then, without changing the selection, select Home – Paste dropdown – Paste Values.

Just out of curiosity, what about that value in B13? Even if Excel thought you had 31 hours, why does it show only 7 hours 42 minutes? If you select the cell, press F2 to edit the formula, and press F9 to calculate the formula, you will see that Excel thinks this total is 1.320833, as shown in Figure 545. This says that 31 hours is about 1.3 days. The default numeric format in B13 was causing Excel to show only the portion of hours in excess of whole days.

Figure 545

Cell B13 calculated 31 hours, but the built-in formatting showed only the hours in excess of a full day.

f_x	1.32083333333333	
	A	**B**	**C**
1	Runner	Time	
2	Andy	2:35	2:35
3	Bob	3:01	3:01
4	Carol	2:41	2:41
5	David	2:56	2:56
6	Ed	3:15	3:15
7	Frank	2:56	2:56
8	Gerry	2:32	2:32
9	Hank	3:04	3:04
10	Isabel	2:51	2:51
11	John	2:49	2:49
12	Kevin	3:02	3:02
13	Total	1.32083333333333	

After you press F9 to see the result of the formula, press the Esc key to return to the formula.

Using the custom number format [h]:mm in B13 would cause the cell to show 31 hours 42 minutes.

Summary: Beware: Some entries can be ambiguous. What you might interpret to mean three minutes, Excel might interpret as three hours. Always select the cell in question and look in the formula bar to see if Excel is using hours or minutes.

Commands Discussed: Home – Paste dropdown – Paste Values

Functions Discussed: =HOUR(); =MINUTE(); =TIME()

Excel 97-2003: Edit – Paste Special – Values

DISPLAY MONTHLY DATES

Problem: I have a data set that shows the actual date for each invoice (see Figure 546). When I print the invoice register, I would like to print just the month and year instead of the specific date.

Figure 546

Display daily dates as months in column A.

	A	B	C	D
1	Month	Customer	Invoice	Revenue
2	1/5/2005	Ainsworth	1101	20,992
3	1/14/2005	Air Canada	1102	72,030
4	1/16/2005	Chevron	1103	13,438
5	1/22/2005	Sun Life Financial	1104	58,901
6	1/23/2005	Verizon	1105	4,937
7	2/3/2005	Sears Canada	1106	74,173
8	2/5/2005	Bell Canada	1107	43,097

Strategy: You can use a numeric format to force dates to display the month and year instead of the specific date. Here's how:

1) Select the range of dates. If you have thousands of rows of data, you can select them all by putting the cell pointer in A2, pressing the End key, and holding down Shift while you press the Down Arrow key.

2) Select Home – Format dropdown – Format Cells (or press Ctrl+1). In the Format Cells dialog, choose the Number tab.

3) In the Category list box, choose Date.

4) In the Type list box, scroll through and select either Mar-01 or March-01 (see Figure 547). Click OK.

Figure 547

Select a number format that shows only the month and year.

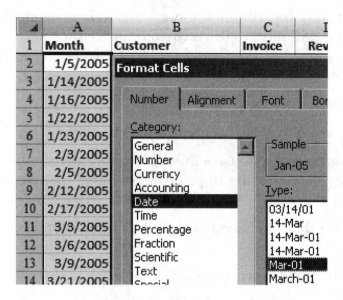

Results: The daily dates will appear as monthly dates, as shown in Figure 548.

Figure 548

Excel displays the daily dates as monthly dates.

	A	B
1	**Month**	**Customer**
2	Jan-05	Ainsworth
3	Jan-05	Air Canada
4	Jan-05	Chevron
5	Jan-05	Sun Life Financial
6	Jan-05	Verizon
7	Feb-05	Sears Canada
8	Feb-05	Bell Canada
9	Feb-05	Exxon
10	Feb-05	Texaco

This process is fine for printing and even for doing automatic subtotals. It will not work for sorting, formulas, or pivot tables. See "Group

Dates by Month" for details on actually transforming the column into months.

Additional Details: If you need to display the month and a four-digit year, you will have to use a custom number format. In the Format Cells dialog, you select the Custom category. In the Type box, you use one of these formats:

•   mmm yyyy for a date like Mar 2005

•   mmmm yyyy for a date like March 2005

Summary: You can use a number format to make daily dates appear as monthly dates if you are printing or doing automatic subtotals. Do not use it if you want to sort or use the dates in formulas.

Commands Discussed: Home – Format dropdown – Format Cells – Number

Excel 97-2003: Format – Cells – Number

See Also: "Group Dates by Month," below.

GROUP DATES BY MONTH

Problem: I have a series of invoice dates, and I need to group the data by month. In "Display Monthly Dates," I learned how to format a date to display as a month and year. However, when I format a date to look like a month, I know by looking at the formula bar that the underlying value still really includes the day as well as the month and year. If the day is still part of the date, some data analyses will not produce the desired result of one subtotal per month.

Strategy: For some tasks, simply formatting the dates to look like months will work. If you create automatic subtotals based on the date field, for example, you will get the desired results.

However, attempting to test which fields are equal will not work. A formula such as =A2=A3 will return FALSE. Similarly, a COUNTIF formula will not work. Even pivot tables will not work. If you want to sort by customer alphabetically within a month, you will not get the desired results. For example, Verizon on February 3 will appear before Air Canada on February 5.

Figure 549

Although the dates in column A are now displayed similarly, the underlying values do not match.

	A	B	C	D	E
	E3		fx	=A3=A2	
1	Date	Customer	Invoice	Revenue	Same Month?
2	Jan-08	Bell Canada	1101	20,992	
3	Jan-08	Compton Petroleum	1102	72,030	FALSE
4	Jan-08	Exxon	1103	13,438	FALSE
5	Jan-08	Sears	1104	58,901	FALSE
6	Jan-08	Texaco	1105	4,937	FALSE
7	Feb-08	Verizon	1106	74,173	FALSE
8	Feb-08	Air Canada	1107	43,097	FALSE

So, although the special case of creating subtotals does work, in almost every other case, you need to use a formula to transform the dates in column A to real months. Here's how:

1) Insert a new column A with the heading Month.

2) Format the date column (what is now column B) with the format m/d/yy.

3) As shown in Figure 550, use the formula =B2-DAY(B2)+1 in cell A2.

Figure 550

Use the formula in A2 to calculate the first of the month.

	A	B	C	D	E
	A2		fx	=B2-DAY(B2)+1	
1	Month	Date	Customer	Invoice	Reven
2	Jan-08	1/5/08	Bell Canada	1101	20,9
3	Jan-08	1/14/08	Compton Petroleum	1102	72,0
4	Jan-08	1/16/08	Exxon	1103	13,4
5	Jan-08	1/22/08	Sears	1104	58,9
6	Jan-08	1/23/08	Texaco	1105	4,9
7	Feb-08	2/3/08	Verizon	1106	74,1

4) Copy the formula down from A2 to the rest of the column and format the column with the mmm-yy format to display as months.

Part II

Here is why this works: The DAY(1/5/2008) function will return the number 5 because the date is the fifth of the month. January 5 minus 5 days will give you December 31. You add 1 to get back to the first day of this month.

Alternate Strategy: Although the formula just described is shorter and faster, you can also use the formula =DATE(Year(B2),Month(B2),1). However, this formula requires three function calls instead of one.

Summary: You can use the DAY function in a formula to convert a date to the first of the month.

Functions Discussed: =DAY(); =DATE(); =YEAR(); =MONTH()

CALCULATE THE LAST DAY OF THE MONTH

Problem: My data set shows the actual date for each invoice (see Figure 551). I want a formula to convert this to the last day of the month. Because I'm sharing this workbook with people using Excel 2003, I'm not allowed to use the =EOMONTH() function.

Figure 551

Find the last day of each month.

Date	Customer	Invoice	Revenue
1/5/2008	Ainsworth	1101	20,992
1/14/2008	Air Canada	1102	72,030
1/16/2008	Chevron	1103	13,438
1/22/2008	Sun Life Financial	1104	58,901
1/23/2008	Verizon	1105	4,937
2/3/2008	Sears Canada	1106	74,173
2/5/2008	Bell Canada	1107	43,097
2/12/2008	Exxon	1108	25,991
2/17/2008	Texaco	1109	47,662
3/2/2008	Compaq	1110	42,172

Strategy: In Excel 2007, =EOMONTH(A2,0) would return the end of the month. However, while this function is in the mainline product in Excel 2007, it was one of the 89 functions in the Analysis ToolPak in Excel 97-2003. If you share the workbook and they don't have the ToolPak installed, they will get a #NAME? error instead of the result.

Finding the last day of the month is trickier than finding the first day of the month. For the first day, you are always looking for a day of 1. For the last day, you might be looking for 31, 30, 28, or even 29 in February during leap years. Excel users have tried many different tricks for this problem. Many first attempts involve testing to see if the MONTH(A2) is equal to 1, 3, 4, 7, 8, 10, or 12 to assign a final date of 31. As you can imagine, this nested IF statement gets rather large.

One day, this was being discussed on the MrExcel board, and Aladin Akyurek chimed in with his elegant solution. Aladin pointed out that it is easy to figure out the first date of the next month. After you have figured that out, you can simply subtract one from the first of next month to get the date for the last of this month. The following table shows this logic:

Invoice Date	First of Next Month	Less 1 Day
2/17/2009	3/1/2009	2/28/2009
2/17/2008	3/1/2008	2/29/2008
3/17/2009	4/1/2009	3/31/2009
4/17/2009	5/1/2009	4/30/2009

To figure out the first day of the next month, you use the DATE function, which requires three arguments: *Year*, *Month*, and *Day*. You know that the *Day* will be 1. *Month* should be the month of the date + 1. *Year* should be the year of the date. You can see that this will work in the first row of the example in Figure 552.

Figure 552

The DATE function works in January. Will it also work in December?

E2			f_x	=DATE(YEAR(A2),MONTH(A2)+1,1)-1	
	A	B	C	D	E
1	Date	Customer	Invoice	Revenue	Last of Month
2	1/5/2008	Ainsworth	1101	20,992	1/31/2008
3	1/14/2008	Air Canada	1102	72,030	

In this example, you will have the following results:

=YEAR(A2) will return 2008.

Part II

=MONTH(A2) will return 1.

=MONTH(A2)+1 will return 2.

=DATE(2008,2,1) will return February 1, 2008.

=DATE(2008,2,1)-1 will return January 31, 2008.

=DATE(2008,2,0) will also return January 31, 2008!

However, it is not so obvious that this formula will work if *Date* in A2 is December 5, 2008. In that case, you will have the following results:

=YEAR(A2) will return 2008.

=MONTH(A2) will return 12.

=MONTH(A2)+1 will return 13.

Thus, you are asking for a date of =DATE(2008,13,1). It would seem like this would not work. What is the first day of the 13th month of 2008? Amazingly, Excel handles this with ease. As shown in Figure 553, Excel will return a value of January 1, 2009.

Figure 553

The DATE function understands that month 13 is the first month of the next year.

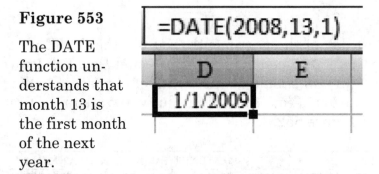

Then you subtract 1 from the result. =DATE(YEAR(A2),MONTH(A2)+1 ,1)-1 will return 12/31/2008, which is the correct last day of the month.

The fact that Microsoft allows the DATE function to correctly return the 47th day of the 18th month of 2009 is miraculous and incredibly useful. See the result in Figure 554.

Figure 554

Excel can find the 47th day of the 18th month.

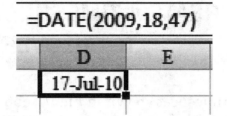

=DATE(2009,18,47)

D	E
17-Jul-10	

You can now copy the formula used in cell E2 in Figure 555 down to all rows of the data set. Column E now calculates the last day of the month for each date.

Figure 555

Column E calculates the last of the month and will work fine with Excel 2003.

E2   fx   =DATE(YEAR(A2),MONTH(A2)+1,1)-1

	A	B	C	D	E
1	Date	Customer	Invoice	Revenue	Last of Month
2	1/5/2008	Ainsworth	1101	20,992	1/31/2008
3	1/14/2008	Air Canada	1102	72,030	1/31/2008
4	1/16/2008	Chevron	1103	13,438	1/31/2008
5	1/22/2008	Sun Life Financial	1104	58,901	1/31/2008
6	1/23/2008	Verizon	1105	4,937	1/31/2008
7	2/3/2008	Sears Canada	1106	74,173	2/29/2008
8	2/5/2008	Bell Canada	1107	43,097	2/29/2008
9	2/12/2008	Exxon	1108	25,991	2/29/2008
10	2/17/2008	Texaco	1109	47,662	2/29/2008
11	3/2/2008	Compaq	1110	42,172	3/31/2008
12	3/5/2008	SBC Communications	1111	6,475	3/31/2008
13	3/8/2008	Compton Petroleum	1112	72,587	3/31/2008
14	3/20/2008	Shell Canada	1113	69,013	3/31/2008
15	3/28/2008	Ford	1114	18,244	3/31/2008
16	3/30/2008	Sears	1115	46,756	3/31/2008

Part
II

Summary: To find the last day of a month, you can use the DATE function to calculate the first of the next month and then subtract one day. This sure-fire method will find the last day, even if it falls on the 31st, 30th, 28th, or 29th.

Functions Discussed: =DATE(); =YEAR(); =MONTH()

CREATE A TIMESHEET THAT CAN TOTAL OVER 24 HOURS

Problem: I set up the timesheet shown in Figure 556. Cell D2 contains the formula C2-B2. Cell D2 is formatted with the time format h:mm. As you can see, everything works fine for this part-time employee.

Figure 556

The total works fine in this simple timesheet.

fx =SUM(D2:D8)

	A	B	C	D
1	Day	Start	End	Hours
2	Mon	8:00 AM	11:00 AM	3:00
3	Tue	8:00 AM	11:00 AM	3:00
4	Wed	8:00 AM	11:00 AM	3:00
5	Thu	8:00 AM	11:00 AM	3:00
6	Fri	9:00 AM	12:00 PM	3:00
7	Sat			0:00
8	Sun			0:00
9	Total For the Week			15:00

However, when I attempt to use the timesheet for someone who works full time, the total does not work. The person shown in Figure 557 worked 8 hours each day, plus an extra 3 hours on Saturday. This person's total should be 43 hours, yet the worksheet is reporting that she worked only 19 hours.

Figure 557

Excel reports the wrong total for 43 hours.

fx =SUM(D2:D8)

	A	B	C	D
1	Day	Start	End	Hours
2	Mon	8:00 AM	4:00 PM	8:00
3	Tue	8:00 AM	4:00 PM	8:00
4	Wed	8:00 AM	4:00 PM	8:00
5	Thu	8:00 AM	4:00 PM	8:00
6	Fri	9:00 AM	5:00 PM	8:00
7	Sat	8:00 AM	11:00 AM	3:00
8	Sun			0:00
9	Total For the Week			19:00

Strategy: Remember that Excel stores dates as the number of days elapsed since January 1, 1900. Excel stores times as a portion of a day. Excel stores 6 a.m. as 0.25 because 25% of the day is elapsed by 6 a.m.

In the scenario described here, Excel knows that the total is 43 hours. However, it thinks that 43 hours after midnight on January 1, 1900, is 7 p.m. on January 2, 1900. That cell really wants to report that it is 7 p.m. on January 2. This makes no sense in the current context. When you use the custom number format h:mm, you are basically telling Excel to ignore the date and report only the time.

The solution is to use the non-intuitive custom number format [h]:mm. The square brackets around the h allow Excel to report times in excess of 24 hours. Here's what you do:

1) Select cell D9. Press Ctrl+1 to display the Format Cells dialog. Select the Number tab. In the Category list, choose Custom. The Type box will show the current numeric format for the cell (see Figure 558).

Part II

Figure 558

h:mm tells Excel to ignore the year, month, and day.

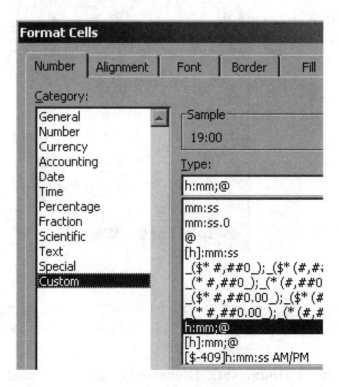

2)   Click in the Type box and type [h]:mm. As shown in Figure 559, you will see in the Sample area that the cell is now reporting 43 hours.

Figure 559

Square brackets around the h will cause Excel to report hours in excess of 24.

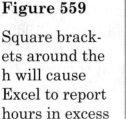
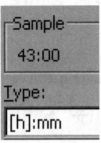

Results: The time sheet reports the correct total, as shown in Figure 560.

Figure 560

The time sheet works.

9   ▼   *fx*   =SUM(D2:D8)

◢	A	B	C	D
1	Day	Start	End	Hours
2	Mon	8:00 AM	4:00 PM	8:00
3	Tue	8:00 AM	4:00 PM	8:00
4	Wed	8:00 AM	4:00 PM	8:00
5	Thu	8:00 AM	4:00 PM	8:00
6	Fri	9:00 AM	5:00 PM	8:00
7	Sat	8:00 AM	11:00 AM	3:00
8	Sun			0:00
9	Total For the Week			43:00

Summary: Although it is not intuitive, you use square brackets around the h in a custom number format in order to display hours in excess of 24.

Commands Discussed: Home – Format – Format Cells – Number; Ctrl+1

Excel 97-2003: Format – Cells – Numeric

CAN EXCEL TRACK NEGATIVE TIME?

Problem: I keep track of comp time for employees. If employees work more than 8 hours, this time gets put into a bank so that they can work less time on another day. The company will generally let people go a few hours into the negative. But Excel completely freaks out when my formula results in a negative time (see Figure 561).

Figure 561

Cell E6 is -2 hours, but Excel refuses to display the value.

E6				f_x	=E5+(D6-TIME(8,0,0))	
	A	B	C	D	E	F
1	Date	Start	End	Total	Comp Time Balance	
2	2/18/2008	8:00 AM	4:00 PM	8:00	2:00	
3	2/19/2008	8:00 AM	6:00 PM	10:00	4:00	
4	2/20/2008	8:00 AM	6:00 PM	10:00	6:00	
5	2/21/2008	8:00 AM	12:00 PM	4:00	2:00	
6	2/22/2008	8:00 AM	12:00 PM	4:00	##############	

Part II

Strategy: The solution to this problem seems bizarre. You should make this change only on a worksheet that doesn't contain any existing date values.

Excel for Windows stores dates as the number of days elapsed since January 1, 1900. Excel for the Macintosh stores dates as the number of days since January 2, 1904. In case you are sharing files with a Mac, Excel has a setting which indicates that dates should be displayed in the 1904 system. Basically, Excel will adjust the date by 1,462 days when you choose this system.

In Figure 561, -2 hours works out to 10 p.m. on December 31, 1899. Excel simply won't display dates from 1899. But if you go 2 hours before January 2, 1904, you happen to have a date and time that Excel is willing to display!

To set up a solution to this problem, follow these steps:

1) Start with a completely blank workbook.

2) Select Office Icon – Excel Options – Advanced. Scroll down to the eighth group, When Calculating in This Workbook. Turn on the check box for Use 1904 Date System (see Figure 562).

Figure 562

Convert the workbook to the 1904 date system.

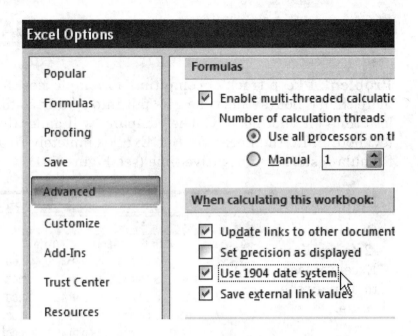

3) Enter dates in column A. For columns D and E, use the custom number format [h]:mm. See "Create a Timesheet that Can Track Over 24 Hours" on page 356.

4) Enter a starting balance for Comp Time in E2.

5) Enter the formula =E2+(D3-TIME(8,0,0)) in E3. Copy this formula down (see Figure 563).

Figure 563

Excel can display negative hours.

	E6			f_x	=E5+(D6-TIME(8,0,0))	
	A	B	C	D	E	F
1	Date	Start	End	Total	Comp Time Balance	
2	2/18/2008	8:00 AM	4:00 PM	8:00	2:00	
3	2/19/2008	8:00 AM	6:00 PM	10:00	4:00	
4	2/20/2008	8:00 AM	6:00 PM	10:00	6:00	
5	2/21/2008	8:00 AM	12:00 PM	4:00	2:00	
6	2/22/2008	8:00 AM	12:00 PM	4:00	-2:00	
7						

Result: Excel will display a negative time.

Gotcha: Use care when changing to the 1904 system. Any existing dates will instantly increase by 4 years and a day. In Figure 564, the top workbook uses the 1900 date system. The bottom workbook is the same values after being changed to the 1904 system. The value 39,495 in F4 now displays a date four years later.

Figure 564

Changing to the 1904 system will alter all existing dates.

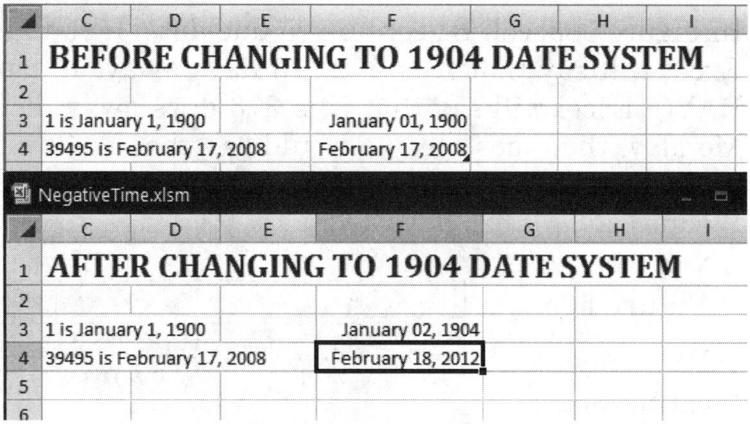

Additional Details: If someone's opening balance is negative, you enter a time of -2:00 in E2.

Summary: Changing to the 1904 system is a bizarre solution, but it will enable Excel to support negative times.

Commands Discussed: Office Icon – Excel Options

Excel 97-2003: Tools – Options – Calculation

WHAT IS THE DIFFERENCE BETWEEN NOW AND TODAY?

Problem: I see people using the NOW and TODAY functions. What is the difference between these functions?

Strategy: The NOW function will return the date and time that the workbook was last calculated. Workbooks are calculated when they are opened, when you enter a value in the worksheet, or when you press the F9 key.

If you enter NOW in a cell, it will generally show the current date and a fairly recent time.

The TODAY function is similar to NOW, except it returns only the current date. In many cases, the TODAY function is more appropriate for calculating the number of days between today and a deadline.

In Figure 565, cell B1 contains a due date. If you calculate =B1-NOW(), Excel will say that it is 372.113 days away. If you calculate =B1-TODAY(), Excel will say that it is 373 days away. If you go into work on Monday, then most people would say that Wednesday is 2 days away. If you use NOW instead of TODAY then at 9 a.m., Excel would say that Wednesday is 1.625 days away.

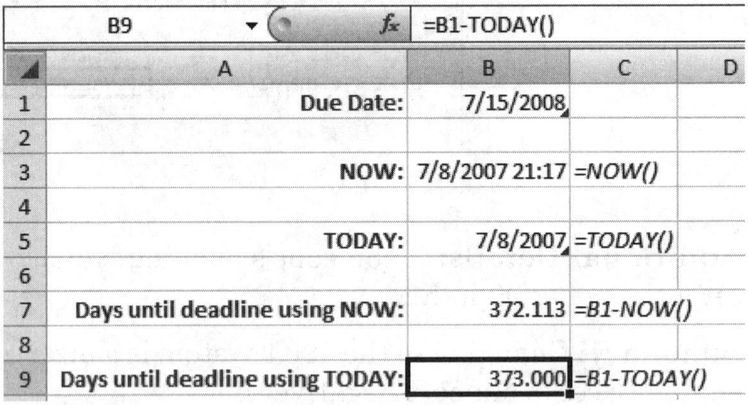

Figure 565

For many calculations, TODAY is better than NOW.

	A	B	C	D
	B9		fx	=B1-TODAY()
1	Due Date:	7/15/2008		
2				
3	NOW:	7/8/2007 21:17	=NOW()	
4				
5	TODAY:	7/8/2007	=TODAY()	
6				
7	Days until deadline using NOW:	372.113	=B1-NOW()	
8				
9	Days until deadline using TODAY:	373.000	=B1-TODAY()	

Additional Details: To calculate the current time, you could use =NOW()-TODAY() or =MOD(NOW(),1). Make sure to format the resulting cell as a time.

Summary: Excel provides two functions to calculate the current date: NOW and TODAY.

Functions Discussed: =NOW(); =TODAY(); =MOD()

CALCULATE WORK DAYS

Problem: I work in human resources. When employees start, they are on probation for 50 work days. How can I calculate the end of the probationary period?

Strategy: Excel offers two great functions you can use if your work week includes only Monday through Friday: WORKDAY and NETWORKDAYS. Both functions allow you to specify a list of company holidays and will factor the holidays into the calculation.

To solve the current problem, you use the WORKDAY function. You specify a start date, a number of workdays that must pass, and a list of company holidays. Excel will calculate the last day of the probation:

1) In a blank range in your worksheet, enter the company holidays for this year. Be sure to include the year. Instead of 12/25, enter 12/25/2008. Say that you store this list in G2:G10.

2) Enter the formula =WORKDAY(B2,50,$G$2:$G$10) in cell C2. Note that the argument containing the holidays should be an absolute reference with dollar signs.

3) Format the cell C2 formula as a date.

4) Copy the formula down for all employees (see Figure 566).

Figure 566

The WORK-DAY function will calculate a workday a certain number of days after a starting date.

C2			f_x =WORKDAY(B2,50,$G$2:$G$10)				
	A	B	C	D	E	F	G
1	EMPLOYEE	HIRE DATE	PROBATION ENDS				Holidays
2	ALBERTA WONG	3/17/2008	5/28/2008				1/1/2008
3	ALMA MADDEN	2/25/2008	5/6/2008				3/21/2008
4	AMANDA CABRERA	3/10/2008	5/20/2008				5/26/2008
5	ANTHONY WELLS	3/24/2008	6/3/2008				7/4/2008
6	BEATRICE MENDEZ	3/4/2008	5/14/2008				9/1/2008
7	BOBBIE HART	3/26/2008	6/5/2008				11/27/2008
8	CAROLINE KNIGHT	3/31/2008	6/10/2008				12/24/2008
9	CHARLOTTE MATHIS	3/17/2008	5/28/2008				12/25/2008
10	CHRISTY FINLEY	4/17/2008	6/27/2008				12/31/2008

Alternate Strategy: Excel also offers the NETWORKDAYS function, which can calculate the number of work days between two dates. If the hire date is in cell B2, you can use =NETWORKDAYS(B2,TODAY(),$G$2:$G$10) to calculate the number of workdays elapsed.

Summary: Provided that your work week is Monday through Friday, you can use the WORKDAY and NETWORKDAYS functions to calculate the number of work days between two dates.

Functions Discussed: =WORKDAY(); =NETWORKDAYS(); =TODAY()

CONVERT UNITS

Problem: I need to convert units of measure because I can never remember that there are .453 kilograms in a pound or 2.54 centimeters in an inch.

Strategy: You can use the CONVERT function to convert a certain number of one unit to another unit. The CONVERT function works with units of weight, distance, time, pressure, force, energy, power, magnetism, temperature, and liquid measure.

The syntax for this function is =CONVERT(number, from unit, to unit). It's important that you use the correct abbreviations (for example, lbm for pounds mass), so look in Excel help if you need to.

Figure 567 shows a sampling of the conversions possible with this function.

Figure 567

CONVERT handles many conversion factors.

	D10			fx	=CONVERT(A10,B10,C10)
	A	B	C	D	E
1	Number	From	To	Results	Comment
2	100	lbm	kg	45.35923	Pounds to kilograms
3	1	Nmi	mi	1.150779	Nautical miles to miles
4	1	in	ang	2.54E+08	Inches to angstroms
5	1	yr	sec	31557600	Seconds in a year
6	1	T	ga	10000	Teslas to Gauss
7	68	F	C	20	Fahrenheit to Celsius
8	1	tbs	tsp	3	Tablespoon to teaspoon
9	100	cl	oz	33.80667	Centiliters to ounces
10	1	in	cm	2.54	Inches to centimeters

Summary: You can convert from English to metric, metric to English, and more by using CONVERT.

Functions Discussed: =CONVERT()

Excel 97-2003: This function was not in the core Excel product, but you could select Tools – Add-Ins and install the Analysis Toolpak in order to use this function.

USE MATCH TO FIND WHICH CUSTOMERS ARE IN AN EXISTING LIST

Part
II

Problem: I have a list of month-to-date sales by customer, as shown in Figure 568. My co-worker just sent me a list of sales for yesterday. I need to figure out which customers are new so that I can add them to the list.

Figure 568

Which customers in D are new?

▲	A	B	C	D	E
1	XYZ Co				
2	Month to Date Sales				
3	Through 06/17/2008			Sales for 6/18/2008	
4					
5	Customer	Revenue MTD		Customer	Revenue
6	Exxon	68,200		Air Canada	1551
7	Lucent	62,744		Compaq	1963
8	Ainsworth	60,461		Compton Petroleu	1568
9	P&G	60,299		Ford	2629
10	HP	55,251		Gildan Activewea	2116
11	General Motors	54,569		IBM	1377
12	Chevron	54,048		Lucent	3137
13	Bell Canada	51,240		Molson, Inc	2273
14	Shell Canada	47,521		Nortel Networks	2355
15	Nortel Networks	47,104		Sun Life Financial	1028
16	Kroger	46,717		Wal-Mart	1327
17	Molson, Inc	45,460			
18	Gildan Activewear	42,316			
19	Compaq	39,250			
20	Verizon	35,367			
21	Compton Petroleum	31,369			
22	Air Canada	31,021			
23	IBM	27,533			
24	Wal-Mart	26,535			
25	Sun Life Financial	20,550			

Strategy: You can add a column to the new list and in this column, use the MATCH function. Any customers in the new list that don't have a match in the existing list will be assigned the value #N/A. You can then sort the #N/A values to the bottom of the list.

The supposed purpose of MATCH is to return the relative row number where a match is found. However, you don't care about the row number in this case; you only care about the items that do not have matches.

The MATCH function requires three arguments. The first argument is the customer name to be looked up. The second argument is the range of existing customers. You will want to make the range an absolute address, with dollar signs in the reference. This way, the formula can be easily copied. The third argument is a zero to indicate that you are looking for an exact match. Here's how it works:

1) Enter the formula =MATCH(D6,$A$6:$A$25,0) in cell F6. Copy the formula down to the other cells in your new list, as shown in Figure 569.

Figure 569

Items without a match return #N/A.

fx	=MATCH(D6,$A$6:$A$25,0)	

	D	E	F
5	Customer	Revenue	There?
6	Air Canada	1551	17
7	Compaq	1963	14
8	Compton Petrole	1568	16
9	Ford	2629	#N/A
10	Gildan Activewea	2116	13
11	IBM	1377	18
12	Lucent	3137	2
13	Molson, Inc	2273	12
14	Nortel Networks	2355	10
15	Sun Life Financi:	1028	20
16	Wal-Mart	1327	19

The MATCH formula is going to return an integer that represents the relative row number where the match is found. In the present case, you don't really care about the answer, unless a match is not found. If Excel cannot find a match, the answer will be the #N/A error. The #N/A errors will always sort to the end of a list.

2) Sort your new list in ascending order by column F. The new customers will sort into one spot. You can then copy and paste the new customers to the end of your existing list.

Summary: You can use the MATCH function to find customers who are not in an existing list.

Functions Discussed: =MATCH()

See Also: "Use VLOOKUP to Find Which Customers Are in an Existing List" below and "Match Customers Using VLOOKUP" on page 369.

USE VLOOKUP TO FIND WHICH CUSTOMERS ARE IN AN EXISTING LIST

Part II

Problem: My co-worker uses VLOOKUP instead of MATCH to find which values are in an existing list, as shown in Figure 570. This is different from the advice given in "Use MATCH to Find Which Customers Are in an Existing List." Which is correct?

Figure 570

Like MATCH, VLOOKUP also reports items without a match as #N/A.

f_x =VLOOKUP(D6,$A$6:$A$25,1,FALSE)

	D	E	F
5	Customer	Revenue	There?
6	Air Canada	1551	Air Canada
7	Compaq	1963	Compaq
8	Compton Petrole	1568	Compton Petroleum
9	Ford	2629	#N/A
10	Gildan Activewea	2116	Gildan Activewear
11	IBM	1377	IBM
12	Lucent	3137	Lucent
13	Molson, Inc	2273	Molson, Inc
14	Nortel Networks	2355	Nortel Networks
15	Sun Life Financi	1028	Sun Life Financial
16	Wal-Mart	1327	Wal-Mart

Strategy: Both are correct. (In "Match Customers Using VLOOKUP," you and your co-worker will see how to use VLOOKUP to get the new day's sales for each existing customer.) Most people seem to master the VLOOKUP function before they try MATCH, so it is common to see people using the VLOOKUP function to solve this problem as well. Both work fine.

As with MATCH, with VLOOKUP, you are interested in the #N/A errors. The VLOOKUP function requires four arguments. The first argument is the customer name to be looked up. The second argument is a rectangular range with existing customer numbers in the left column of the range. You will want to make the range an absolute address with dollar signs in the reference. This way, the formula can be easily copied. The third argument is the relative column number within the existing range that you want returned. In this case, you don't care which column is returned, you are merely looking for the #N/A values, so you can use 1. The fourth argument is FALSE to indicate that you are looking for an exact match. Here's how it works:

1)   Enter the formula =VLOOKUP(D6,$A$6:$A$25,1,FALSE) in cell F6. Copy the formula down to the other cells in your new list.

    The VLOOKUP formula is going to return the customer name if it is in the existing list. If Excel cannot find a match, the answer will be the #N/A error. The #N/A errors will always sort to the end of a list.

2)   Sort your new list in ascending order by column F. The new customers will sort into one spot. You can then copy and paste the new customers to the end of your existing list.

Summary: You can use a VLOOKUP function to find customers who are not in an existing list.

Functions Discussed: VLOOKUP

See Also: "Use MATCH to Find Which Customers Are in an Existing List" (p. 365) and "Match Customers Using VLOOKUP" (p. 369)

MATCH CUSTOMERS USING VLOOKUP

Problem: I have a list of month-to-date sales by customer. I have a second list with new sales from today, as shown in Figure 571. How can I add the sales from the new list to the old list?

Figure 571

Add the sales from column G to column B.

	A	B	C	D	E	F	G
1	XYZ Co						
2	Month to Date Sales						
3	Through 06/17/2008					Sales for 6/18/2008	
4							
5	Customer	Revenue MTD				Customer	Revenue
6	Ainsworth	60,461				Air Canada	1551
7	Air Canada	31,021				Compaq	1963
8	Bell Canada	51,240				Compton Petroleum	1568
9	Chevron	54,048				Ford	2629
10	Compaq	39,250				Gildan Activewear	2116
11	Compton Petroleum	31,369				IBM	1377
12	Exxon	68,200				Lucent	3137
13	Ford	0				Molson, Inc	2273
14	General Motors	54,569				Nortel Networks	2355
15	Gildan Activewear	42,316				Sun Life Financial	1028
16	HP	55,251				Wal-Mart	1327
17	IBM	27,533					
18	Kroger	46,717					
19	Lucent	62,744					
20	Molson, Inc	45,460					
21	Nortel Networks	47,104					
22	P&G	60,299					
23	Shell Canada	47,521					
24	Sun Life Financial	20,550					
25	Verizon	35,367					
26	Wal-Mart	26,535					

Part
II

Strategy: You can add a new column to the first list and then use the VLOOKUP function in the new column to grab the sales from the new list.

The VLOOKUP function requires four arguments. The first argument is the customer name to be looked up. The second argument is a rectangular range with new customer numbers in the left column of the range. In this example, the range is F4:G16. You will want to make the range an absolute address, with dollar signs in the reference: $F$4:$G$16. This way, the formula can be easily copied. The third argument is the relative column number within the existing range that you want returned. Because the sales are in column G, and G is the second column in the range

F4:G16, the third argument will be 2. The fourth argument is FALSE to indicate that you are looking for an exact match.

You need to enter the formula =VLOOKUP(A6,$F$6:$G$16,2,FALSE) in cell C6, as shown in Figure 572. Copy the formula down to the other cells in your new list.

Figure 572

VLOOKUP returns the sales from G to row C.

	C6		fx	=VLOOKUP(A6,$F$6:$G$16,2,FALSE)		
	A	B	C	D E	F	G
1	XYZ Co					
2	Month to Date Sales					
3	Through 06/17/2008				Sales for 6/18/2008	
4						
5	Customer	Revenue MTD	New		Customer	Revenue
6	Molson, Inc	45,460	2273		Air Canada	1551
7	Gildan Activewear	42,316	2116		Compaq	1963
8	Nortel Networks	47,104	2355		Compton Petroleum	1568
9	Compaq	39,250	1963		Ford	2629
10	HP	55,251	#N/A		Gildan Activewear	2116
11	General Motors	54,569	#N/A		IBM	1377
12	Ainsworth	60,461	#N/A		Lucent	3137
13	Ford	0	2629		Molson, Inc	2273
14	Exxon	68,200	#N/A		Nortel Networks	2355
15	Chevron	54,048	#N/A		Sun Life Financial	1028
16	P&G	60,299	#N/A		Wal-Mart	1327
17	Air Canada	31,021	1551			

Look at row 10 in Figure 572. Because you did not sell anything to this customer today, the result is #N/A. While the #N/A results are useful in some instances (see "Use MATCH to Find Which Customers Are in an Existing List" and "Use VLOOKUP to Find Which Customers Are in an Existing List"), they are fairly annoying here. The rule for calculation says that anything plus #N/A will return #N/A. When you add a new column to total columns B and C, the #N/A results will cause problems. One method for dealing with the #N/A cells is to simply sort by column C. All the #N/A cells will sort to the bottom. You use the formula in column D only for the customers who have sales today. In Figure 573, you would copy D6:D16 and paste the values into B6.

Figure 573

Sort customers
without new
sales to the
bottom of the
list.

	D6		f_x	=C6+B6

	A	B	C	D
1	XYZ Co			
2	Month to Date Sales			
3	Through 06/17/2008			
4				
5	Customer	Revenue MTD	New	New Total
6	Sun Life Financial	20,550	1028	21,578
7	Wal-Mart	26,535	1327	27,862
8	IBM	27,533	1377	28,910
9	Air Canada	31,021	1551	32,572
10	Compton Petroleum	31,369	1568	32,937
11	Compaq	39,250	1963	41,213
12	Gildan Activewear	42,316	2116	44,432
13	Molson, Inc	45,460	2273	47,733
14	Nortel Networks	47,104	2355	49,459
15	Ford	0	2629	2,629
16	Lucent	62,744	3137	65,881
17	HP	55,251	#N/A	
18	General Motors	54,569	#N/A	

Part
II

Alternate **Strategy:** You can also use the ISNA function to deal with
VLOOKUP results that return #N/A. The ISNA function will return
TRUE if the result of a formula is #N/A. You can then use the ISNA
function as the first part of an IF function. One solution is to use ISNA
and IF in the calculation of the new total. As shown in Figure 574, the
new total is the previous month-to-date number in B6 plus C6 if it is not
#N/A.

Figure 574

Use ISNA
inside an IF
function to
determine
which columns
to add.

	D6		f_x	=IF(ISNA(C6),B6,B6+C6)

	A	B	C	D
1	XYZ Co			
2	Month to Date Sales			
3	Through 06/17/2008			
4				
5	Customer	Revenue MTD	New	New Total
6	Ainsworth	60,461	#N/A	60,461
7	Air Canada	31,021	1551	32,572
8	Bell Canada	51,240	#N/A	51,240
9	Chevron	54,048	#N/A	54,048

Alternate **Strategy:** You can use another solution to prevent the #N/A errors in the first place. If you are using Excel 2007 and you will not share the workbook with anyone using prior versions of Excel, you can use the new IFERROR function. With IFERROR, you provide a formula as the first argument and a substitute value to use in case the formula results in an error. In this case, the first formula is the VLOOKUP. The substitute value is zero. As shown in Figure 575, you use the formula =IFERROR(VLOOKUP(A6,$F$6:$G$16,2,FALSE),0).

Figure 575

The new IF-ERROR function prevents #N/A errors from appearing.

	C6	▾	*fx*	=IFERROR(VLOOKUP(A6,$F$6:$G$16,2,FALSE),0)		
	A	B	C	D	E	F	G
1	XYZ Co						
2	Month to Date Sales						
3	Through 06/17/2008					Sales for 6/18/2008	
4							
5	Customer	Revenue MTD	New	New Total		Customer	Revenue
6	Ainsworth	60,461	0	60,461		Air Canada	1551
7	Air Canada	31,021	1551	32,572		Compaq	1963
8	Bell Canada	51,240	0	51,240		Compton Petrole	1568

Gotcha: The IFERROR function will return a NAME error in Excel 2003 and earlier. In those versions, you have to combine ISNA and IF into a long formula, and Excel must calculate the VLOOKUP twice:

=IF(ISNA(VLOOKUP(A6,$F$6:$G$16,2,FALSE)),0,VLOOKUP(A6,$F$6:$G$16,2,FALSE))

Summary: You can use a VLOOKUP function to match customers in two lists.

Functions Discussed: =VLOOKUP(); =ISNA(); =IF(), =IFERROR()

WATCH FOR DUPLICATES WHEN USING VLOOKUP

Problem: I used the VLOOKUP function to get sales from a second list into an original list, and then I received the next day's sales in a file. When I use the MATCH function to find new customers, there is one new customer: Sun Life Finc'l, as shown in Figure 576.

Figure 576

Is this really a
new customer?

=MATCH(F6,$A$6:$A$26,FALSE)

	F	G	H
1			
2			
3	Sales for 6/18/2008		
4			
5	Customer	Revenue	There?
6	Sun Life Finc'l	1,295	#N/A
7	Wal-Mart	1,950	1
8	Verizon	2,476	2
9	Sun Life Financi:	2,510	3
10	Compaq	2,885	17

Part
II

But this is not really a new customer at all. Someone in the order entry
department created a new customer instead of using the existing customer named Sun Life Financial. As a quick fix, I copy cell F9 and paste
it in cell F6. This seems like a fine solution and resolves the #N/A error
in H6.

However, when I enter the VLOOKUP formula in column C to get the
current day's sales, there are two rows that match Sun Life Financial.

Strategy: It's important that you understand how VLOOKUP handles
duplicates in the lookup list. The VLOOKUP function is not capable of
handling the situation described here. When two rows match a VLOOK-
UP, the function will return the sales from the first row in the list. As
shown in Figure 577, in cell C8, the $1,295 in sales is coming from cell
G6 only instead of cells G6 and G9.

Figure 577

VLOOKUP re-
turns only the
sales from the
first match.

=IFERROR(VLOOKUP(A8,$F$6:$G$15,2,FALSE),0)

	A	B	C	D	E	F	G	H
1	XYZ Co							
2	Month to Date Sales							
3	Through 06/17/2008					Sales for 6/18/2008		
4								
5	Customer	Revenue MTD	New			Customer	Revenue	There?
6	Wal-Mart	27,862	1,950			Sun Life Finan(	1,295	3
7	Verizon	35,367	2,476			Wal-Mart	1,950	1
8	Sun Life Financial	21,578	1,295			Verizon	2,476	2
9	Shell Canada	47,521	0			Sun Life Finan(	2,510	3
10	P&G	60,299	0			Compaq	2,885	17
11	Nortel Networks	49,459	0			Kroger	3,270	9

If you are not absolutely sure that the customers in the lookup table are unique, you should not use VLOOKUP. Instead, you should use a SUMIF formula, as shown in Figure 578. (Functions such as COUNTIF and SUMIF are explained in the next several topics.

Figure 578

Replace VLOOKUP with SUMIF.

fx	=SUMIF($F$6:$F$15,A8,$G$6:$G$15)						
	A	B	C	D E	F	G
1	XYZ Co					
2	Month to Date Sales					
3	Through 06/17/2008				Sales for 6/18/2008	
4						
5	Customer	Revenue MTD	New		Customer	Revenue
6	Wal-Mart	27,862	1,950		Sun Life Financi:	1,295
7	Verizon	35,367	2,476		Wal-Mart	1,950
8	Sun Life Financial	21,578	3,805		Verizon	2,476
9	Shell Canada	47,521	0		Sun Life Financi:	2,510

Summary: The VLOOKUP function is excellent, but you need to be aware of the unintended problems that could be caused by having duplicates in a list on which you use VLOOKUP.

Functions Discussed: =VLOOKUP(); =SUMIF()

REMOVE LEADING AND TRAILING SPACES

Problem: None of my VLOOKUP formulas are working. I can clearly see that there is a match in the lookup table in Figure 579, but Excel cannot see it.

Figure 579

None of the VLOOKUP functions work.

D2			fx	=VLOOKUP(C2,$G$1:$H$5,2,FALSE)			
	A	B	C	D	E	F	G	H
1	Date	Charge	EmpID	Name			A311	FANNIE BARR
2	6/10/2008	4.80	C912	#N/A			C912	JAN ALLEN
3	4/24/2008	2.91	C912	#N/A			U935	MICHAEL JAMES
4	10/30/2008	4.54	U935	#N/A			W121	GWENDOLYN STANTON
5	11/7/2008	2.64	U935	#N/A			W468	CHARLOTTE BURGESS
6	10/30/2008	8.02	A311	#N/A				
7	3/5/2008	4.70	U935	#N/A				

Strategy: A common problem is that either the employee ID in column C or in column G has trailing spaces. This can happen if you downloaded the data from another system.

To fix this problem, you select cell G2 and press the F2 key to put the cell in Edit mode. A flashing insertion cursor will appear at the end of the cell. Check to see if the insertion cursor appears immediately after the last character or a few spaces away.

Edit cell C2 to see if there are trailing spaces. You will likely find that either column has trailing spaces. In Figure 580, you can see that there are a couple trailing spaces after the employee ID in column C. These trailing spaces cause the VLOOKUP to not classify the cells as a match. Although you can tell that "C912 " is the same as "C912", Excel cannot.

Figure 580

Column C has trailing spaces.

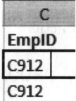

You can use the TRIM function to remove leading and trailing spaces from a value. If there are spaces between words, it will change consecutive spaces to a single space. For example, =TRIM(" Bill Jelen ") would change the cell contents to "Bill Jelen".

Additional Details: If the trailing spaces appear in column C, then you can change the VLOOKUP to use TRIM(C2) as the first argument. This will solve your problem, as shown in Figure 581.

Figure 581

Look for the TRIM of C2.

	f_x	=VLOOKUP(TRIM(C2),$G$1:$H$5,2,FALSE)

C	D	E	F	G	
EmpID	Name			A311	FANI
C912	JAN ALLEN			C912	JAN ﹡
C912	JAN ALLEN			U935	MICH
U935	MICHAEL JAMES			W121	GWE

However, if the trailing spaces appear in the lookup table, you need to add a column of TRIM functions in column F. You can either restate the VLOOKUP to use F1:H5 and return the third column, or you can use Paste Values to get the trimmed values back to column G.

Summary: You can use the TRIM function to remove leading and trailing spaces so that the VLOOKUP function works properly.

Functions Discussed: =VLOOKUP(); =TRIM()

I DON'T WANT TO USE A LOOKUP TABLE TO CHOOSE ONE OF FIVE CHOICES

Problem: I have to choose among five choices. I don't want to nest a bunch of IF functions, and I really don't want to add a lookup table off to the side of my worksheet. Is there a function that will allow me to specify the possible values in the function?

Strategy: In this situation, you can use the CHOOSE function.

The first argument of the CHOOSE function is a number from 1 to 254. You then specify the values for each possible number, entered as separate arguments. For example, =CHOOSE(2,"Red","Green","Blue") would return Green.

It is a bit frustrating that you must specify each choice as a separate argument. I always want to specify a single range such as Z1:Z30 as the list of arguments but this will not work. However, if you already have the list of arguments somewhere, you don't need to use CHOOSE; you can easily use VLOOKUP or INDEX in such a case.

In Figure 582, a CHOOSE function returns the description of the plan number chosen in cell B5.

Figure 582

CHOOSE is great for short lists that can be selected with 1, 2, 3...

	A	B	C	D	E
	=CHOOSE(B5,"All-inclusive","Super-Deluxe","Premier","Pre				
1	Name:	Jane Smith			
2	Address:	123 South Main			
3	City St Zip:	Anytown, MA 01234			
4					
5	Plan Code:	3	Premier		

Gotcha: CHOOSE works only if your plan codes are 1, 2, 3, and so on. If you have plan codes of A, B, C, and so on, you should probably use a lookup table in an out-of-the way location. Or you could use =CODE(B5)-64 to convert the A to a 1 and so on.

Gotcha: In Excel 2007, you can specify 254 arguments for the choices. In previous versions of Excel, you were limited to 30 choices. If you share your workbook with someone using Excel 2003, additional choices will be ignored.

Additional Details: If you have a list of plan names somewhere, you might be tempted to enter =CHOOSE(B5,B7,B8,B9,B10,B11). Instead, it is easier to use =INDEX(B7:B11,B5). The INDEX function will return the B5th item from the list in B7:B11 (see Figure 583).

Part II

Figure 583

Switch to INDEX if you have a list in a range.

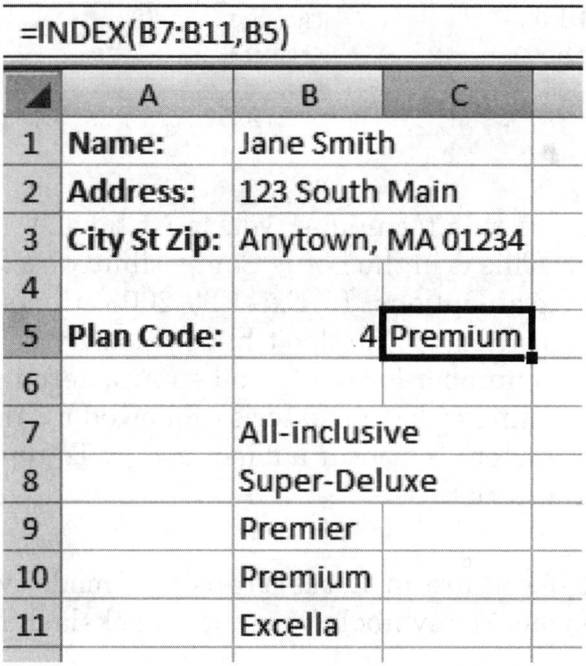

=INDEX(B7:B11,B5)

	A	B	C
1	Name:	Jane Smith	
2	Address:	123 South Main	
3	City St Zip:	Anytown, MA 01234	
4			
5	Plan Code:	4	Premium
6			
7		All-inclusive	
8		Super-Deluxe	
9		Premier	
10		Premium	
11		Excella	

Summary: You can use CHOOSE when you need to choose the nth item from a list.

Functions Discussed: =CHOOSE(); =CODE(); =INDEX()

FILL A CELL WITH REPEATING CHARACTERS

Problem: I need to fill a cell with periods. If someone makes the cell wider, I want more periods to be added, to fill the cell.

Strategy: All you have to do is type a backslash (\) followed by the symbol(s) to repeat. For example, column C in Figure 584 is filled with periods by using \. Other cells in column E are filled with other symbols. In E5, Excel repeats carets and hyphens.

Figure 584

Type a symbol after a back-slash to fill a cell with the symbol.

	A	B	C	D	E
1		Chapter 1	....	1	%%%%%
2		Chapter 2	....	15	@@@@
3		Chapter 3	....	27	########
4		Chapter 4	....	39	_ _ _ _
5		Chapter 5	....	55	^_^_^_^_^_
6		Chapter 6	....	67	

C1 f_x \.

Gotcha: To use this technique, you must have Transition Navigation Keys enabled. This is in the Lotus Compatibility section of the Advanced category of Excel Options. In Excel 97-2003, this setting is on Tools - Options - Transition. If you don't have this setting turned on, you can use the custom number format *. and enter a zero in the cell. In custom number formatting codes, an asterisk followed by any character will repeat that character. To repeat a dash, use *-. To repeat a period, use *.. To repeat an asterisk, use **.

Summary: If you are in Lotus Transition mode, you can easily fill a cell with a symbol or symbols by using a backslash followed the desired symbol(s).

MATCH WEB COLORS WITH HEX2DEC

Problem: I need my Excel document to match the colors on our website. I can tell from the HTML that the Web background is #FF9007. How can I match this in Excel?

Strategy: The colors specified in HTML are hexadecimal numbers. This numbering system has 16 digits, from 0 through 9 and A through F. Your Excel document uses RGB (Red, Green, Blue) values, which are decimal. You can use the HEX2DEC function to convert each pair of hex digits to decimal. Here's what you do:

1)   In three cells, enter each pair of digits from the color code. Enter an apostrophe before 07 to keep the leading zero.

2)   Enter a formula of =HEX2DEC(B2). Excel will convert the FF to 255. This is the red value for the color in Excel.

3)   Copy the function to the other two cells. The second value is the green value. The third value is the Blue value.

4)   Select the area to be formatted.

5)   Choose Home – Paint Bucket dropdown and choose More Colors. On the Custom tab of the Colors dialog, choose 255 for Red, 144 for Green, 7 for Blue. Click OK.

Part II

Figure 585

Use =HEX-2DEC to convert the Web colors to RGB.

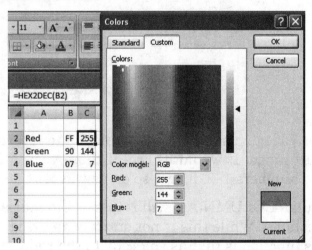

Additional Details: To convert RGB values to hexadecimal, you use DEC2HEX.

Summary: Excel can convert from numbers in various systems—binary, octal, decimal, or hexadecimal—to other number systems.

Commands Discussed: Home – Paint Bucket dropdown

Functions Discussed: =HEX2DEC(); =DEC2HEX()

SWITCHING COLUMNS INTO ROWS
USING A FORMULA

Problem: Every day, I receive a file with information going down the rows. I need to use formulas to pull this information into a horizontal table. It is not practical for me to use Paste Special – Transpose every day. In Figure 586, you can see that the first formula in B2 points to A4. If I drag this formula to the right, there is no way that it will pull values from A5, A6, A7, and so on.

Figure 586

Dragging the fill handle will fail here.

	A	B	C	D	
	=A4				
1					
2		Apples			
3					
4	Apples				
5	Banana				
6	Cherry				
7	Dill				
8	Eggplant				
9	Fish				
10	Graham Crackers				
11					

Strategy: You can use the INDEX function to return the nth item from the A4:A10 range. It would be cool if there were a function that could return the numbers 1, 2, 3, and so on as you copy across.

The formula =COLUMN(A1) will return a 1 to indicate that cell A1 is in the first column. While this is not entirely amazing, the beautiful thing about this function is that as you copy to the right, =COLUMN(A1) will change to =COLUMN(B1) and return a 2. Any time you need to fill in the numbers 1, 2, 3 as you go across a row, you can use the =COLUMN(A1) in the first cell. As you copy, Excel will take care of the rest.

Therefore, if you use the formula =INDEX($A$4:$A$10,COLUMN(A1)) in cell B2, you can easily copy it across the columns.

Gotcha: You need to use A1 as the reference for the COLUMN function no matter where you are entering the formula. In this example, the first formula is in column B. That is irrelevant. Even if the formula starts in column XFA, you will still point to A1 in order to return the number 1.

Figure 587

Copy B2 across to transpose the data.

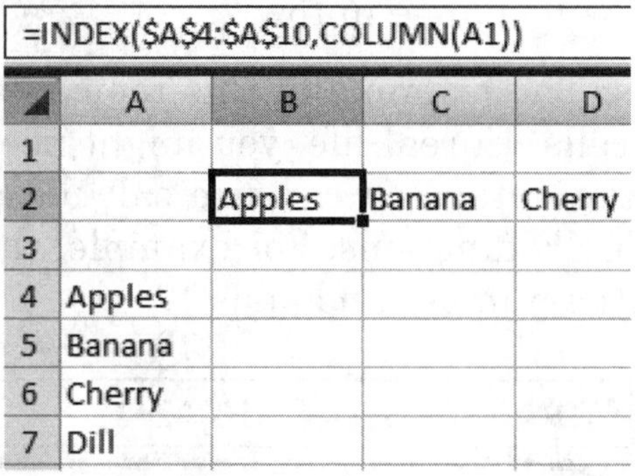

	=INDEX($A$4:$A$10,COLUMN(A1))		
	A	B	C	D
1				
2		Apples	Banana	Cherry
3				
4	Apples			
5	Banana			
6	Cherry			
7	Dill			

Alternate **Strategy:** It is slightly harder to use, but the TRANSPOSE function will perform the same task as COLUMN. The trick is that a single function has to be entered in many cells at once. Follow these steps:

1) Count the number of cells in A4:A10. In this case, it is seven cells.

2) Select seven horizontal cells. In this case, select B2:H2.

3) Type =TRANSPOSE(A4:A10). Unlike INDEX, dollar signs are not necessary in this formula. Do not press Enter.

4) Because this function will return many answers, you have to hold down Ctrl+Shift while you press Enter. Excel will add curly braces around the function, and the seven values will appear across your selection, as shown in Figure 588.

Figure 588

A single TRANSPOSE function fills in these cells.

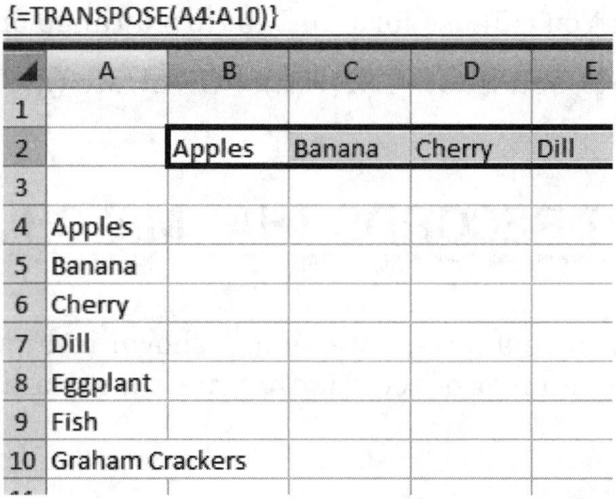

	{=TRANSPOSE(A4:A10)}			
	A	B	C	D	E
1					
2		Apples	Banana	Cherry	Dill
3					
4	Apples				
5	Banana				
6	Cherry				
7	Dill				
8	Eggplant				
9	Fish				
10	Graham Crackers				

Part II

The advantage of using TRANSPOSE over using Paste Special – Transpose is that the TRANSPOSE function is a live formula. If cells in column A change, they will change in row 2.

Additional Details: The example in this topic is a trivial example of merely copying the cells. In real life, you might need to do calculations instead of copying the data. You can use calculations with either the INDEX or TRANSPOSE functions. For example, the formula shown in Figure 589 squares the number and adds 1.

Figure 589

You can do calculations to each value whether you are using TRANSPOSE or INDEX.

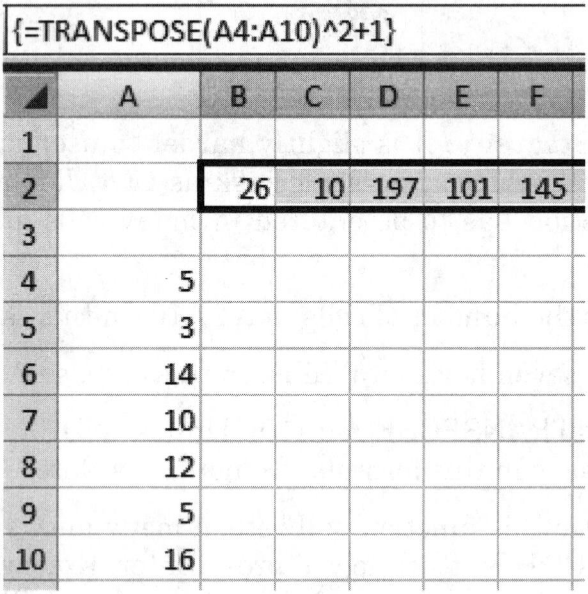

`{=TRANSPOSE(A4:A10)^2+1}`

◢	A	B	C	D	E	F
1						
2		26	10	197	101	145
3						
4	5					
5	3					
6	14					
7	10					
8	12					
9	5					
10	16					

Summary: You can use formulas to turn a range on its side.

Functions Discussed: =INDEX(); =COLUMN(); =TRANSPOSE()

COUNT RECORDS THAT MATCH A CRITERION

Problem: I have a large data set, as shown in Figure 590, and I want to count the number of records that meet a certain criterion. How do I do it?

Figure 590

Count males
and females.

	A	B	C	D
1	**Name**	**Gender**	**DOB**	**Age**
2	Zoe	F	3/2/1979	28
3	Zeke	M	11/3/1949	57
4	Zack	M	2/4/1944	63
5	Xavier	M	12/19/1939	67
6	William	M	7/10/1951	55
7	Wendy	F	10/15/1972	34
8	Victor	M	10/25/1944	62

Strategy: You use the COUNTIF function, which requires two arguments: a range of cells that you want to test and a test. To count the records where the gender is M, you use =COUNTIF(B2:B57, "M"), as shown in Figure 591.

Figure 591

The COUNTIF
function looks
through a
range, count-
ing matches.

	G2				f_x	=COUNTIF($B$2:$B$57,"M")	
	A	B	C	D	E	F	G
1	Name	Gender	DOB	Age			Count
2	Zoe	F	3/2/1979	28		Male	28
3	Zeke	M	11/3/1949	57		Female	28
4	Zack	M	2/4/1944	63			

Note that the second argument, "M", tells Excel to count records that are equal to M. Because this function is not case-sensitive, the function will count cells with values of M or m.

If you want to count the records where the age is a specific number, you can write the formula either with or without quotes around the number:

=COUNTIF(D2:D999,32)
=COUNTIF(D2:D999,"32")

You can also establish a criterion to look for items that are below or above a certain number:

=COUNTIF(D2:D999,"<40")
=COUNTIF(D2:D999,">21")

A criterion can include a wildcard character. To find any text that contains XYZ, you use the following formula:

=COUNTIF(A2:A999,"*XYZ*")

Summary: To count how many cells contain a certain criterion, you use the COUNTIF function by entering the two arguments it needs: which cells to count and what to count.

Functions Discussed: =COUNTIF()

BUILD A TABLE THAT WILL COUNT BY CRITERIA

Problem: I need to build a summary table using COUNTIF functions. How can I enter one formula that can be copied?

Strategy: It is possible to use a cell reference as the second argument in the COUNTIF function. Here's how:

1) Set up a table below your data and place all the possible values for a column, such as department, in column A, as shown in Figure 592.

Figure 592

Build a summary table with a list of all departments.

	A	B	C	D	E
1	Name	Gender	DOB	Age	Department
54	Xavier	M	12/19/1939	67	Engineering
55	Zack	M	2/4/1944	63	Mfg
56	Zeke	M	11/3/1949	57	Accounting
57	Zoe	F	3/2/1979	28	Engineering
58					
59	Employees by Department				
60					
61	Accounting				
62	Engineering				
63	Marketing				
64	Mfg				
65	Sales				

2) In column B of the first row, enter =COUNTIF($E$2:$E$57,A61), as shown in Figure 593. Note that you should press the F4 key to

make the E2:E57 range absolute. This will allow you to copy B61 to cells B62:B65.

Figure 593

Use the department in A61 as the second argument for COUNTIF.

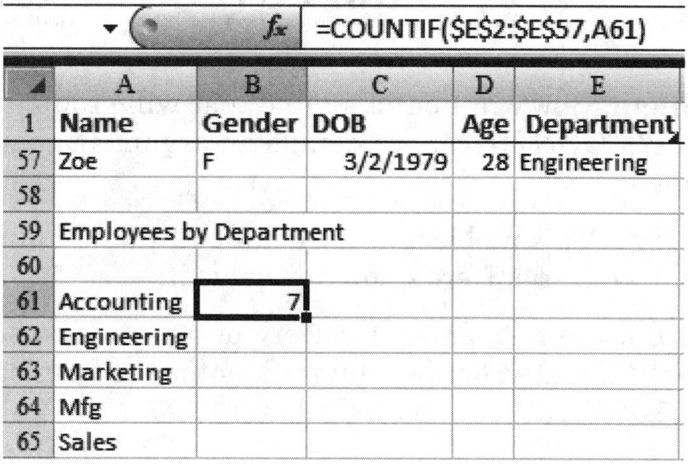

| | | f_x | =COUNTIF($E$2:$E$57,A61) |

	A	B	C	D	E
1	**Name**	**Gender**	**DOB**	**Age**	**Department**
57	Zoe	F	3/2/1979	28	Engineering
58					
59	Employees by Department				
60					
61	Accounting	7			
62	Engineering				
63	Marketing				
64	Mfg				
65	Sales				

Part
II

3)   Double-click the fill handle to copy the formula down to B62:B65.

Results: As shown in Figure 594, the table provides a summary of your data set.

Figure 594

The formula copies to all rows of the table.

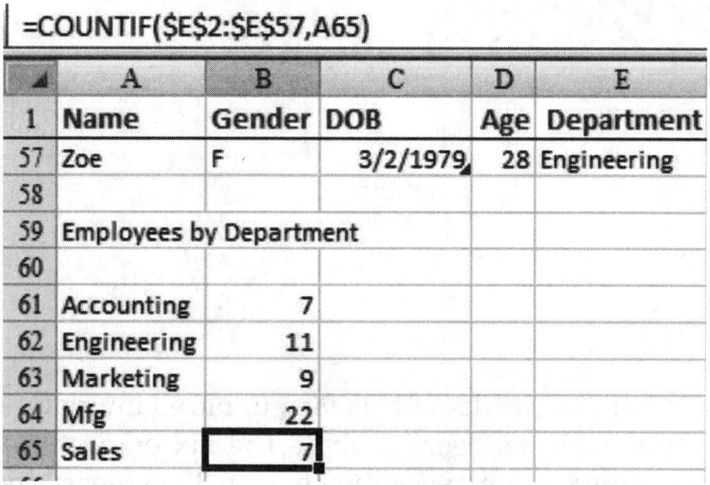

| =COUNTIF($E$2:$E$57,A65) |

	A	B	C	D	E
1	**Name**	**Gender**	**DOB**	**Age**	**Department**
57	Zoe	F	3/2/1979	28	Engineering
58					
59	Employees by Department				
60					
61	Accounting	7			
62	Engineering	11			
63	Marketing	9			
64	Mfg	22			
65	Sales	7			

Summary: Using COUNTIF with a cell reference as the second argument allows you to set up various tables to summarize your data by department, gender, or any other field.

Functions Discussed: =COUNTIF()

BUILD A SUMMARY TABLE TO PLACE EMPLOYEES IN AGE BRACKETS

Problem: How can I build a table that will group the employees in age ranges? COUNTIF cannot handle an argument that combines two conditions.

Strategy: This problem is more difficult than building a table that will count by criteria. Here's how you solve it:

1) In column A, enter a variety of age ranges, such as >=65, >=55, >=45, and so on. In column B, enter the formula =COUNTIF($D$2 :$D$57,A61), as shown in Figure 595.

Figure 595

Using a range in COUNTIF.

▲	A	B	C	D	E
			fx	=COUNTIF($D$2:$D$57,A61)	
1	Name	Gender	DOB	Age	Department
55	Zack	M	2/4/1944	63	Mfg
56	Zeke	M	11/3/1949	57	Accounting
57	Zoe	F	3/2/1979	28	Engineering
58					
59	Employees by Age				
60					
61	>=65	6			
62	>=55	20			
63	>=45	34			
64	>=35	42			
65	>=21	56			

Note that the results of this formula are cumulative. The 20 employees in the over-55 category include the six employees in the over-65 category. The 42 employees in the over-35 category include all the people in the over-45, -55, and -65 categories.

To get the real answer for any age band, you need to subtract all the previous age bands. Consider this logic:

Row 62: need to subtract row 61
Row 63: need to subtract rows 61 and 62

Row 64: need to subtract rows 61:63
Row 65: need to subtract rows 61:64

The rule, then, is that you need to subtract from row 61 to the row above the current cell.

2) Edit the formula in row 62 by adding -SUM(B$61:B64) to it (see . Figure 596). Adding this new part to the formula will subtract the sum of B$61:B64. It is important that you have a dollar sign only before the 61 to make that reference always point to row 61.

Figure 596

From the total subtract everything from row 61 to the row above the current row.

	f_x	=COUNTIF($D$2:$D$57,A65)-SUM(B$61:B64)			
◢	A	B	C	D	E
1	Name	Gender	DOB	Age	Department
57	Zoe	F	3/2/1979	28	Engineering
58					
59	Employees by Age				
60					
61	>=65	6			
62	>=55	14			
63	>=45	14			
64	>=35	8			
65	>=21	14			
66					

Part II

3) Copy the formula down to the other rows. The single dollar sign in just one portion of the reference allows the formula to be copied down. As you copy this formula down to the other rows, the portion subtracted will expand. As you look at Figure 596, note that in row 65, the formula is subtracting Rows 61 through 64.

Alternate Strategy: This solution requires two different formulas, one formula in row 61 and a different formula in rows 62 through 65. I'm not a fan of using two formulas. One workaround would be to subtract from row $60:61. By having the anchor row be the row above the first row in the table, you could use the same formula in all cells of the table.

Gotcha: At this point, the labels in column A are not technically correct. One solution would be to cut the formulas in column B and paste to column C, as shown in Figure 597. It is important to use Cut and Paste instead of Copy and Paste so that the references keep pointing to column A. You can then type correct labels in column B and hide the information in column A by making the font white.

Figure 597

Put friendly labels in B and hide the real labels in A by using a white font.

◢	A	B	C	D	E
1	Name	Gender	DOB	Age	Department
57	Zoe	F	3/2/1979	28	Engineering
58					
59		Employees by Age			
60					
61		Over 65	6		
62	>=55	55-64	14		
63	>=45	45-54	14		
64	>=35	35-44	8		
65	>=21	21-34	14		
66					

Summary: This particular use of COUNTIF is tricky. You almost need two conditions, which COUNTIF cannot handle. Luckily, the criteria in this example were adjacent to each other, so you could subtract the results of the previous formulas to get the result for a particular age band.

Functions Discussed: =COUNTIF(); =SUM()

COUNT RECORDS BASED ON
MULTIPLE CONDITIONS

Problem: The COUNTIF function described in "Build a Summary Table to Place Employees in Age Brackets" is cool. Is there a way to make it handle more conditions? For example, say that I wanted to count employees by age and gender.

Strategy: Microsoft heard your question and added a plural version of COUNTIF to Excel 2007. The new COUNTIFS function can handle up to 127 conditions.

You pass a pair of arguments to COUNTIFS for each condition. In this example, the first condition will test the gender in column B. The first argument of the pair is the range of values to check, such as $B$2:$B$57. The second argument is the value to match.

Follow these steps to build a table by age and gender:

1) In column A, enter a variety of age ranges, such as >=65, >=55, >=45, and so on.

2) In column B, enter the upper limit for each age range. For example, you might use <100, <65, and so on.

3) Above the table, enter the headings M for male and F for female.

4) As shown in Figure 598, enter the formula =COUNTIFS($B$2:$B$57,C$60,$D$2:$D$57,$A61,$D$2:$D$57,$B61) in cell C61

Figure 598

Using a range in COUNTIFS.

=COUNTIFS($B$2:$B$57,C$60,$D$2:$D$57,$A61,$D$2:$D$57,$B61)

◢	A	B	C	D	E	F
1	Name	Gender	DOB		Age	Department	
57	Zoe	F	3/2/1979		28	Engineering	
58							
59	Employees by Age & Gender						
60			M	F			
61	>=65	<100	5	1			
62	>=55	<65	7	7			
63	>=45	<55	4	10			
64	>=35	<45	5	3			
65	>=21	<35	7	7			

The first pair of arguments will look through B2:B57 to see if they match the gender in C60. You use dollar signs throughout $B$2:$B$57 to make it absolute. For C60, you only want to freeze the row number. You use C$60 to make sure the formula points to row 60 but allow the reference to change to D60 when the formula is copied to the second column of the table.

The second pair of arguments will look through $D$2:$D$57 and compare them to the lower limit in $A61. Note that you want to make sure the formula always points to A, but you want the 61 to be able to change to 62, 63, and so on.

The third pair of arguments will also look through column D but will compare it to the upper limit in $B61.

Results: Because you've used the proper combination of relative and absolute references, the formula correctly copies to C61:D65 to create the table.

Gotcha: COUNTIFS is an excellent addition to Excel 2007, but you cannot share a workbook that uses it with anyone using a prior version of Excel. In previous versions of Excel, you would have to use the SUMPRODUCT function to count records that match multiple criteria.

For example, (B2:B57=C60) will return an array of 56 TRUE or FALSE values, and (D2:D57>=A61) will also return an array of 56 TRUE or FALSE values. If you multiply the first array by the second array, only the rows where both tests are TRUE will be evaluated as a 1:

    =TRUE*TRUE is 1
    =TRUE*FALSE is 0
    =FALSE*TRUE is 0
    =FALSE*FALSE is 0

The SUMPRODUCT function can handle up to 30 such conditions. In the current example, you would multiply ($B$2:$B$57=C60) by ($D$2:$D$57>=$A61) by ($D$2:$D$57<$B61) inside a SUMPRODUCT function. Figure 599 shows the result.

Figure 599

Excel 2003 and earlier use SUMPRODUCT instead of COUNTIFS.

`=SUMPRODUCT(($B$2:$B$57=C$60)*($D$2:$D$57>=$A61)*($D$2:$D$57<$B61))`

	A	B	C	D	E	F	G
1	Name	Gender	DOB	Age	Department		
57	Zoe	F	3/2/1979	28	Engineering		
58							
59	Employees by Age & Gender						
60	>=	<	M	F			
61	65	100	5	1			
62	55	65	7	7			
63	45	55	4	10			
64	35	45	5	3			
65	21	35	7	7			
66							

Summary: The new COUNTIFS function in Excel can count based on 127 conditions and is a great extension of the COUNTIF function. If you need to do a similar task in Excel 2003 or before, you use the SUM-PRODUCT function.

Functions Discussed: =COUNTIFS(); =SUMPRODUCT()

Excel 97-2003: The COUNTIFS function was not available; use =SUM-PRODUCT().

TOTAL REVENUE FROM ROWS
THAT MATCH A CRITERION

Part
II

Problem: I want to total the sales made by Ben in the data set shown in Figure 600. How do I do it?

Figure 600

Sum sales
from column
E if column B
equals Ben.

▲	A	B	C	D	E
1	Invoice	Rep	Customer	Product	Sales
2	1010	Deb	D6287	ABC	186
3	1011	Chaz	J4769	ABC	108
4	1012	Ben	O5956	ABC	157
5	1013	Amy	H1139	DEF	166
6	1014	Ben	W6177	XYZ	157
7	1015	Deb	O2340	DEF	229
8	1016	Ben	Y1982	DEF	325

Strategy: Excel offers the SUMIF function, which is somewhat similar to the COUNTIF function. To count records for Ben, you use =COUNTIF(B2:B99,"Ben"), as shown in Figure 601.

Figure 601

The SUMIF
function is
similar to the
COUNTIF
function.

=COUNTIF(B2:B99,"Ben")

▲	A	B	C	D	E	
1	Invoice	Rep	Customer	Product	Sales	
98	1106	Ben	K5508	ABC	116	
99	1107	Ben	W9236	ABC	188	
100						
101			25			
102						

To use SUMIF, you use the same first two arguments as with COUN-TIF. The final argument is the range to be summed. This must be the same shape as the first argument: =SUMIF(B2:B99,"Ben",E2:E99). Instead of including "Ben" as a constant in the formula, you could enter Ben in a nearby cell and refer to the cell instead. You should also make the cell references in the first and third arguments be absolute. Figure 602 shows a table of sales by rep. The formula in E101 is copied down to E102:E104.

Figure 602

The third argument specifies the range to sum.

=SUMIF($B$2:$B$99,D101,$E$2:$E$99)

◢	A	B	C	D	E
1	Invoice	Rep	Customer	Product	Sales
98	1106	Ben	K5508	ABC	116
99	1107	Ben	W9236	ABC	188
100					
101				Ben	5208
102				Chaz	4684
103				Amy	5408
104				Deb	5157
105					

Additional Details: If for some reason the first and third arguments are the same range, you are allowed to drop the third argument. For example, if you need to sum all sales where sales are greater than 200, you can use the following:

=SUMIF(E2:E99,">200")

Summary: You can use SUMIF when you need to total certain rows from a data set on the basis of one condition.

Functions Discussed: =SUMIF(), =COUNTIF()

USE THE CONDITIONAL SUM WIZARD TO BUILD CONDITIONAL FORMULAS

Problem: I'm having a hard time figuring out conditional formulas such as SUMIF and COUNTIF. Is there an easier way?

Strategy: Conditional formulas that need to sum on the basis of two conditions are definitely hard to figure out. Excel offers a wizard that can walk you through building a conditional formula. Before you can use the Conditional Sum Wizard, you need to activate it. In Excel 2007, you select Office Icon – Excel Options. In the left pane of the Excel Options dialog, you choose Add-ins. At the bottom of the dialog, you select Manage dropdown – Excel Add-ins and then click Go. Finally, you click the check box next to Conditional Sum Wizard, as shown in Figure 603, and click OK.

Figure 603

Activate the add-in once, and it will be available on the Formulas tab.

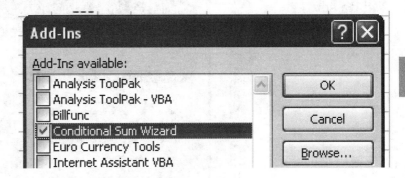

Gotcha: You may need your installation CDs in order to activate the Conditional Sum Wizard.

As shown in Figure 604, the add-in adds a new icon called Conditional Sum to the right side of the Formulas tab of the Excel 2007 ribbon or at the bottom of the Excel 2003 Tools menu.

Figure 604

The add-in is successfully installed if you see this icon.

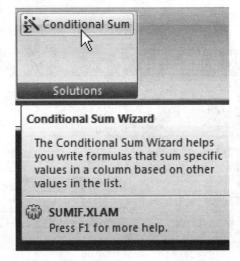

To build a formula, you select one cell in your data set, select Formulas – Conditional Sum, and follow these steps:

1) Identify the range of your data set in the Conditional Sum Wizard – Step 1 of 4 dialog, as shown in Figure 605.

Figure 605

Specify the range of your data set.

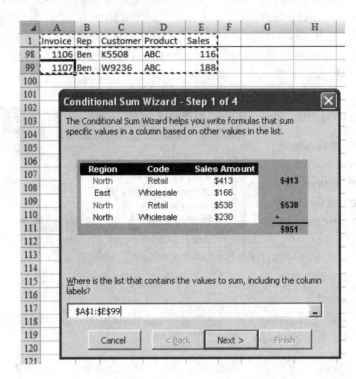

2) Select the column that you want to sum in the Step 2 dialog, as shown in Figure 606.

Figure 606

Select the column to sum.

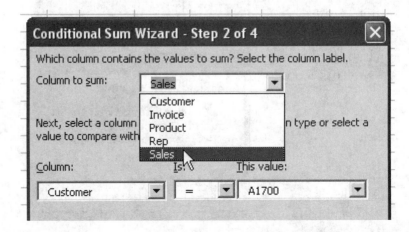

3) Still in the Step 2 dialog, build a condition using the dropdowns. When you choose Rep from the Column dropdown, the This Value dropdown changes to offer a complete list of available reps, as shown in Figure 607. Select a value from each dropdown and then click Add Condition.

Figure 607

Build the first condition.

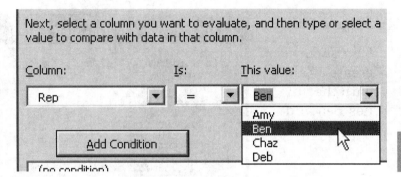

You can even add multiple conditions, as shown in Figure 608.

Figure 608

Adding multiple conditions is where the wizard excels.

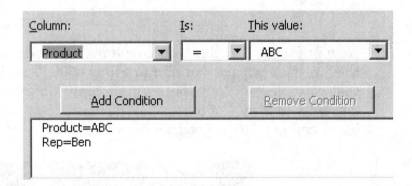

4) As shown in the Step 3 dialog in Figure 609, you can either create a single cell with the answer or you can set up a range of cells with rep name, product name, and the formula for the answer. Choose the second option. This will allow you to change Ben to Amy and have the formula update.

Figure 609

Choose to create a table with the values Ben and ABC.

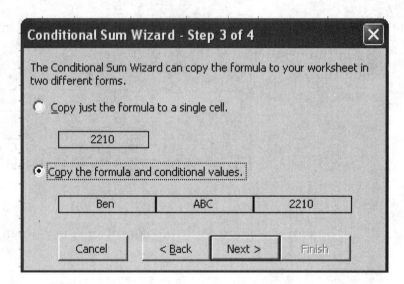

5) Note in Figure 610 that you now have a six-step wizard instead of the four-step wizard you had in Figure 609. This is due to the fact that you selected Copy the Formula and Conditional Values in the last step. In Step 4 of 6, you choose where to put the first field. The blank cell in C101 is good, so use the mouse to touch cell C101.

Figure 610

Specify a blank cell to hold the first value.

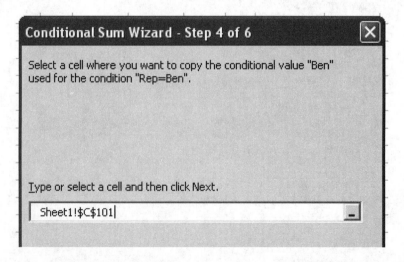

6) When the Step 5 dialog asks where the product should go, enter Sheet1!$D$101.

7) When the Step 6 dialog appears, indicate where the final formula should go, as shown in Figure 611.

Figure 611

In the last step, indicate where the formula should go.

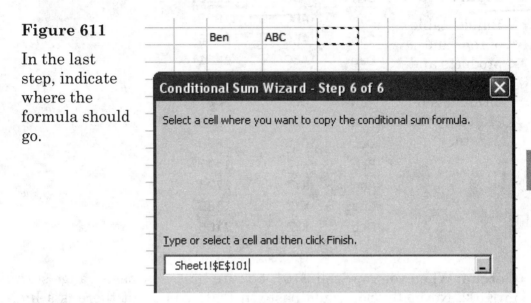

Results: The Conditional Sum Wizard has allowed you to build an incredibly complex conditional formula, as shown in Figure 612.

Figure 612

This formula sums based on two conditions.

`{=SUM(IF($B$2:$B$99=C101,IF($D$2:$D$99=D101,$E$2:$E$99,0),0))}`

CondSumWizard.xlsm

	A	B	C	D	E	F	G	H
1	Invoice	Rep	Customer	Product	Sales			
98	1106	Ben	K5508	ABC	116			
99	1107	Ben	W9236	ABC	188			
100								
101			Ben	ABC	2210			
102								

After the wizard has built the first formula, you can enter a table of reps and products and copy the formula down to the other rows, as shown in Figure 613.

Figure 613

Build a table of reps and products and then copy the formula generated by the wizard.

Ben	ABC	2210
Amy	ABC	998
Chaz	ABC	2456
Deb	ABC	1181
Ben	DEF	1551
Amy	DEF	2687
Chaz	DEF	839
Deb	DEF	1870
Ben	XYZ	1447
Amy	XYZ	1723
Chaz	XYZ	1389
Deb	XYZ	2106

Gotcha: When you copy cell E101, be sure that your paste range starts in E102. Normally, you could paste in E101:E112, but there is a limitation on array formulas. If you attempt to paste E101 on top of itself, you will get the error message "You cannot change part of an array," as shown in Figure 614.

Figure 614

Specify the range of your data set.

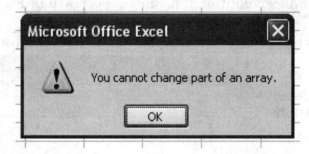

To get around this, you can copy E101 and paste to E102:E112.

Additional Details: If you edit the result of the Conditional Sum Wizard, you cannot complete the edit by using Enter. You have to hold down Ctrl+Shift while pressing Enter.

Gotcha: The Conditional Sum Wizard is a decade old. It creates a fairly complicated formula that is compatible with all recent versions of Excel.

If you will not be sharing the worksheet with anyone using Excel 2003 or previous, using the new SUMIFS function would be a simpler approach to the formula. Figure 615 shows the SUMIFS solution.

Figure 615

New in Excel 2007, the SUMIFS function easily handles multiple conditions.

`=SUMIFS($E$2:$E$99,$B$2:$B$99,C101,$D$2:$D$99,D101)`

◢	A	B	C	D	E	F	G
1	Invoice	Rep	Customer	Product	Sales		
99	1107	Ben	W9236	ABC	188		
100							
101			Ben	ABC	2210		
102			Amy	ABC	998		
103			Chaz	ABC	2456		

Part II

Summary: The Conditional Sum Wizard is a fantastic tool for building complex formulas based on one or more conditions.

Commands Discussed: Office Icon – Excel Options – Add-Ins – Manage dropdown – Excel Add-ins; Formulas – Conditional Sum

Excel 97-2003: To install the add-in, choose Tools – Add-Ins, and the new icon will be added to the bottom of the Tools menu. The SUMIFS function is not available before Excel 2007 and will return the NAME error.

CREATE A CSE FORMULA TO BUILD A SUPER-FORMULA

Problem: My data set has a column with quantity sold and another column with unit prices, as shown in Figure 616. I want one formula to figure out quantity multiplied by unit price.

Figure 616

Build one formula to total quantity times unit price.

◢	A	B	C	D	E	F
1	Region	Product	Date	Customer	Quantity	Unit Price
2	East	XYZ	1-Jan-08	Effortless Lawn Parti	1000	95
3	East	ABC	2-Jan-08	Wonderful Adhesive	500	87
4	Central	DEF	2-Jan-08	Wonderful Adhesive	100	78
5	Central	XYZ	3-Jan-08	Exclusive Yogurt Cor	500	95
6	East	DEF	4-Jan-08	Attractive Luggage Cr	800	78

Strategy: The typical strategy is to add a new column with price times quantity and add that up. However, this is not necessary if you use a type of super-formula that I call a CSE formula (and Excel calls an array formula). (I'll tell you why I call it CSE in a minute.) Here's what it would look like in this case:

=SUM(E2:E564*F2:F564)

If you've been using Excel for a while, you might think this will not work. In fact, if you enter the formula, you will get a #VALUE! error, confirming that it does not work, as shown in Figure 617.

Figure 617 f_x =SUM(E2:E564*F2:F564)

This formula seems not to work.

	D	E	F
1	Customer	Quantity	Unit Price
564	Excellent Gadget Cor	900	87
565			
566			#VALUE!

However, if you know the secret, you can still make the formula work. You need to edit the formula by pressing F2. Instead of pressing Enter to finish the formula, you hold down Ctrl+Shift and then press Enter. (Now you know why I call it the CSE formula: It requires Ctrl+Shift+Enter.)

As shown in Figure 618, miraculously, Excel does 563 multiplications and then adds them up to give you a result.

Figure 618 f_x {=SUM(E2:E564*F2:F564)}

Hold down Ctrl+Shift while pressing Enter to put Excel in super-formula mode.

	D	E	F
1	Customer	Quantity	Unit Price
564	Excellent Gadget Cor	900	87
565			
566			27,263,600
567			

Note that in the formula bar, there are curly braces around the formula. You do not enter these braces. Excel adds them when you press Ctrl+Shift+Enter.

Additional Details: Most people will only have occasion to use this type of formula once a month or maybe even less frequently. I could never remember the keystroke combination to make them work, so I began to call these formulas "CSE formulas" to help me to remember Ctrl+Shift+Enter. If you need to search Microsoft Help on the subject, check under the name "array formulas".

Summary: You can use a single CSE formula to replace hundreds or even thousands of intermediate formulas.

Commands Discussed: Ctrl+Shift+Enter

LEARN TO USE BOOLEAN LOGIC FACTS TO SIMPLIFY LOGIC

Part II

Problem: I have to enter multiple IF conditions, and I think it would help me to have a better understanding of logical operators. Can you help?

Strategy: When you are dealing with conditions, the language is full of AND, OR, NOT, NOR, TRUE, and FALSE. All these words have mathematical equivalents. Understanding them will enable you to build complex two-condition formulas.

A Boolean formula returns either TRUE or FALSE. In Figure 619, for example, the formula =A2>100 will return TRUE.

Figure 619

Logical formulas return either TRUE or FALSE.

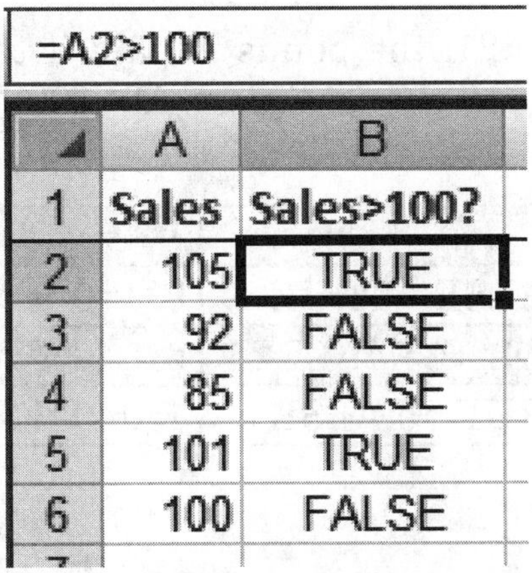

=A2>100

	A	B
1	Sales	Sales>100?
2	105	TRUE
3	92	FALSE
4	85	FALSE
5	101	TRUE
6	100	FALSE

You can have many such tests. For example, the data set in Figure 620 has columns to test whether the product is a particular product line or if the region is a particular region.

Figure 620

This work-sheet has three columns of Boolean formulas.

	E2			f_x	=B2="ABC"	
	A	B	C	D	E	F
1	Sales	Product	Region	Sales>100?	Prod=ABC?	Region=East?
2	105	ABC	East	TRUE	TRUE	TRUE
3	92	ABC	West	FALSE	TRUE	FALSE
4	85	DEF	East	FALSE	FALSE	TRUE
5	101	DEF	West	TRUE	FALSE	FALSE
6	100	DEF	East	FALSE	FALSE	TRUE

You can build a calculation from the results of multiple Boolean formulas. One popular operator in Boolean logic is the AND operator. If you want to know if D2 AND E2 is TRUE, you can state this as a formula by using the logic facts below.

In Boolean logic,

- Think of each TRUE as the number 1.

- Think of each FALSE as the number 0.

- Think of each AND as a multiplication operator

- Think of each OR as an addition operator

If the result of a calculation is 0, then the answer is FALSE. If the result of a calculation is nonzero, then the answer is TRUE.

For example, in Figure 621, the bonus is paid if the sale is >100 and the product is ABC. You use the formula =(A2>100)*(B2="ABC"), which works as follows:

A=105	B=ABC	TRUE * TRUE	1*1=1=TRUE
A=92	B=ABC	FALSE * TRUE	0*1=0=FALSE
A=85	B=DEF	FALSE * FALSE	0*0=0=FALSE
A=101	B=DEF	TRUE * FALSE	1*0=0=FALSE

Figure 621

Multiplying
two conditions
is the same as
using the AND
operator.

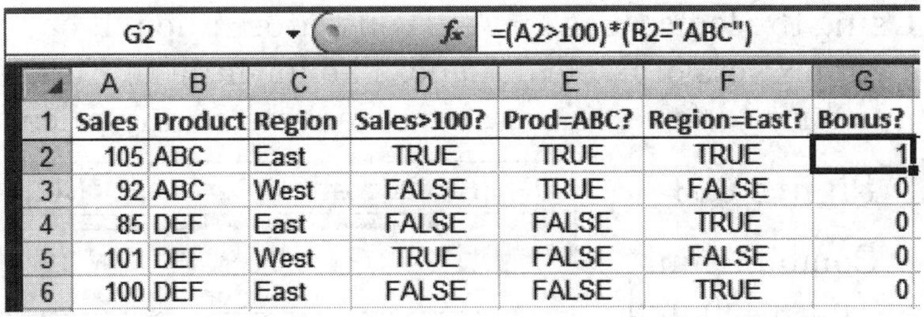

	G2				f_x	=(A2>100)*(B2="ABC")	
	A	B	C	D	E	F	G
1	Sales	Product	Region	Sales>100?	Prod=ABC?	Region=East?	Bonus?
2	105	ABC	East	TRUE	TRUE	TRUE	1
3	92	ABC	West	FALSE	TRUE	FALSE	0
4	85	DEF	East	FALSE	FALSE	TRUE	0
5	101	DEF	West	TRUE	FALSE	FALSE	0
6	100	DEF	East	FALSE	FALSE	TRUE	0

Here are the logic rules for AND operators and OR operators:

AND	OR
TRUE*TRUE=TRUE	TRUE+TRUE=TRUE
TRUE*FALSE=FALSE	TRUE+FALSE=TRUE
FALSE*TRUE=FALSE	FALSE+TRUE=TRUE
FALSE*FALSE=FALSE	FALSE+FALSE=FALSE

Let's work through another example. Say that a bonus is paid for selling any item over $100.00 or for sales of DEF product. You use the formula =(A2>100)+(B2="DEF"), as shown in Figure 622, and it works like this:

Sales	Product	Sales>100	B2=DEF	Calculation
80	DEF	FALSE	TRUE	=0+1=1=TRUE
105	DEF	TRUE	TRUE	=1+1=2=TRUE
90	ABC	FALSE	FALSE	=0+0=0=FALSE
110	ABC	TRUE	FALSE	=1+0=1=TRUE

Figure 622

Adding two
conditions is
the same as
using the OR
operator.

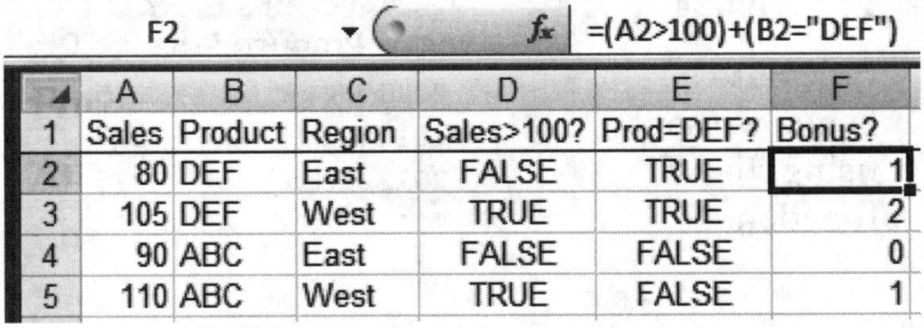

	F2				f_x	=(A2>100)+(B2="DEF")
	A	B	C	D	E	F
1	Sales	Product	Region	Sales>100?	Prod=DEF?	Bonus?
2	80	DEF	East	FALSE	TRUE	1
3	105	DEF	West	TRUE	TRUE	2
4	90	ABC	East	FALSE	FALSE	0
5	110	ABC	West	TRUE	FALSE	1

Part
II

Using the logic rules for AND operators and OR operators, you can write complex sets of Boolean logic. The formula in Figure 623 pays a $25 bonus for all West region sales of jackets at any price or caps above $50.

Figure 623

Combine multiplication and addition to mix AND and OR.

`=IF(((B2="Jacket")+((B2="Cap")*(A2>50)))*(C2="West"),25,0)`

	A	B	C	D	E	F	G
1	Price	Product	Region	Bonus?			
2	225	Jacket	East	0			
3	250	Jacket	West	25			
4	35	Cap	East	0			
5	55	Cap	West	25			
6	175	Jacket	East	0			
7	200	Jacket	West	25			
8	55	Cap	East	0			
9	35	Cap	West	0			

Summary: Excel offers the AND and OR functions. Being able to use Boolean terms as the first parameter of an IF statement allows for more complex calculations.

Functions Discussed: =IF(); =AND(); =OR()

REPLACE IF FUNCTION WITH BOOLEAN LOGIC

Problem: As shown in Figure 624, I need to calculate a 10% bonus on sales greater than $1000.00. Can I do this without using the IF function?

Figure 624

Calculate a bonus without using the IF function.

	A	B	C	D	E	F
1	Invoice	Product	Price	Qty	Total	Bonus
2	2010	Jacket	225	14	3150	
3	2011	Jacket	225	8	1800	
4	2012	Jacket	225	11	2475	

Strategy: You can use the Boolean logic facts to do this calculation without an IF function. Remember that a Boolean test that results in TRUE is treated as 1, and a FALSE statement is treated as 0. Thus, you could multiply the calculation E2*0.1 by the Boolean test (E2>1000), as shown in Figure 625.

Figure 625

Multiply the bonus calculation by the logical comparison of E2>1000.

	F2				f_x	=(E2*0.1)*(E2>1000)

	A	B	C	D	E	F
1	Invoice	Product	Price	Qty	Total	Bonus
2	2010	Jacket	225	14	3150	315
3	2011	Jacket	225	8	1800	180
4	2012	Jacket	225	11	2475	247.5
5	2013	Cap	25	6	150	0
6	2014	Jacket	225	17	3825	382.5
7	2015	Jacket	225	3	675	0

Summary: This formula combines a math calculation with a Boolean test to produce a valid result. Using these types of calculations is one key to using conditional sums with two conditions. You will learn more about these in "Test for Two Conditions in a Sum."

Part II

TEST FOR TWO CONDITIONS IN A SUM

Problem: I need to sum a data set based on two conditions, but the SUMIF function can handle only one condition. As shown in Figure 626, I want to write a formula that will total all sales by Amy of product ABC.

Figure 626

SUMIF cannot handle two conditions.

	A	B	C	D	E
1	Invoice	Rep	Customer	Product	Sales
91	1068	Chaz	Y2852	XYZ	107
92	1074	Amy	Y3129	ABC	163
93	1050	Deb	Y5668	XYZ	130
94	1063	Amy	Y7678	XYZ	270
95	1092	Chaz	Y7881	DEF	123
96	1052	Amy	Y8373	XYZ	259
97	1017	Chaz	Y8576	ABC	226
98	1020	Deb	Z2412	ABC	233
99	1069	Amy	Z9822	DEF	278
100					
101			ABC	DEF	XYZ
102		Amy	=SUMIF(		
103		Ben	SUMIF(range, criteria, [sum_		
104		Chaz			
105		Deb			

Strategy: This question comes up a lot at the MrExcel.com site. It is a very common problem, and it has a rather difficult solution. The SUMIF function will not do the trick in this situation. If you are using Excel 2007 and will not share the workbook with anyone using prior versions of Excel, you can use SUMIFS, as discussed in "Can the Results of a Formula Be Used in COUNTIF?" If you need a formula that will work in any version of Excel, you can use Boolean logic and a CSE formula. (For more on CSE formulas, see "Create a Conditional Formula to Build a Super-Formula.")

You want to test to see if each cell in B2:B99 is equal to B102. You represent this with the following formula:
=($B$2:$B$99=$B102)

You also want to test whether each cell in D2:D99 is equal to C101. You do this with the following formula:
=($D$2:$D$99=C$101)

If you multiply these two terms together, you will end up with a 1 wherever both conditions are TRUE and a 0 wherever one condition is not TRUE:
=($B$2:$B$99=$B102)*($D$2:$D$99=C$101)

Pretend that you actually entered these formulas in columns F, G, and H, as shown in Figure 627. After you have the 1 or 0 in column H, you have to multiply that result by Sales in column E and then sum up column I.

Figure 627

You could use Boolean logic in F:I to find Amy's sales of ABC.

	A	B	C	D	E	F	G	H	I
1	Invoice	Rep	Customer	Product	Sales	Amy?	ABC?	F*G	Result
2	1018	Chaz	A1700	ABC	320	FALSE	TRUE	0	0
3	1051	Amy	A3203	XYZ	309	TRUE	FALSE	0	0
4	1086	Amy	A3446	DEF	150	TRUE	FALSE	0	0
5	1049	Chaz	A4580	XYZ	228	FALSE	FALSE	0	0
6	1054	Chaz	A6969	ABC	260	FALSE	TRUE	0	0
7	1034	Amy	A7717	ABC	251	TRUE	TRUE	1	251
8	1077	Chaz	B5387	ABC	228	FALSE	TRUE	0	0

*(Cell I7 formula bar: =H7*E7)*

To multiply the Boolean terms by Sales, use this:
=($B$2:$B$99=$B102)*($D$2:$D$99=C$101)*($E$2:$E$99)

To sum the result, enter this formula in C102:
=SUM(($B$2:$B$99=$B102)*($D$2:$D$99=C$101)*($E$2:$E$99))

Instead of pressing Enter after typing the formula, use Ctrl+Shift+Enter. Excel will evaluate the formula as an array and produce the correct result, as shown in Figure 628.

Figure 628

`{=SUM(($B$2:$B$99=$B102)*($D$2:$D$99=C$101)*($E$2:$E$99))}`

This single formula replaces columns F:I in the previous figure.

▲	A	B	C	D	E	F	G
1	Invoice	Rep	Customer	Product	Sales		
94	1063	Amy	Y7678	XYZ	270		
95	1092	Chaz	Y7881	DEF	123		
96	1052	Amy	Y8373	XYZ	259		
97	1017	Chaz	Y8576	ABC	226		
98	1020	Deb	Z2412	ABC	233		
99	1069	Amy	Z9822	DEF	278		
100							
101			ABC	DEF	XYZ		
102		Amy	998				
103		Ben					
104		Chaz					
105		Deb					
106							

Note: You do not type the curly braces around the formula. Excel will add those when you press Ctrl+Shift+Enter.

Due to the careful use of the dollar signs in each reference, you've made a formula that can be copied to the rest of the table. Normally, you would copy C102 and paste it to C102:E105, but because of the limitation of CSE formulas, you cannot do this. You first have to copy C102 to C103: C105. Then you copy C102:C105 and paste it to D102:E105. The result is a summary table built from CSE formulas, as shown in Figure 629.

Figure 629

`{=SUM(($B$2:$B$99=$B105)*($D$2:$D$99=E$101)*($E$2:$E$99))}`

Copy in just two steps to build a summary table.

▲	A	B	C	D	E	F	G
1	Invoice	Rep	Customer	Product	Sales		
97	1017	Chaz	Y8576	ABC	226		
98	1020	Deb	Z2412	ABC	233		
99	1069	Amy	Z9822	DEF	278		
100							
101			ABC	DEF	XYZ		
102		Amy	998	2687	1723		
103		Ben	2210	1551	1447		
104		Chaz	2456	839	1389		
105		Deb	1181	1870	2106		
106							

Gotcha: CSE formulas, which Excel calls array formulas, are very powerful. They are also very memory intensive, so don't go overboard with them. I once tried to build a report of 800 CSE formulas with each one totaling a 50,000-row data set using three conditions. If I hadn't rebooted the computer, it would still be trying to calculate the formula.

Alternate Strategy: Aladin Akyurek has written an excellent article about this topic at www.mrexcel.com/wwwboard/messages/8961.html. Aladin notes that this problem can be solved without using a CSE formula by using the SUMPRODUCT function. If you've built the above formula, change the SUM to SUMPRODUCT and enter it as a regular formula instead of pressing Ctrl+Shift+Enter. As shown in Figure 630, the following is the equivalent formula for cell C102:

=SUMPRODUCT(($B$2:$B$99=$B102)*($D$2:$D$99=C$101)*($E$2:$E$99))

Figure 630

You can use SUMPROD-UCT instead of a CSE formula.

=SUMPRODUCT(($B$2:$B$99=$B102)*($D$2:$D$99=C$101)*($E$2:$E$99))

	A	B	C	D	E	F	G	H
1	Invoice	Rep	Customer	Product	Sales			
97	1017	Chaz	Y8576	ABC	226			
98	1020	Deb	Z2412	ABC	233			
99	1069	Amy	Z9822	DEF	278			
100								
101			ABC	DEF	XYZ			
102		Amy	998	2687	1723			
103		Ben	2210	1551	1447			
104		Chaz	2456	839	1389			
105		Deb	1181	1870	2106			
106								

Alternate Strategy: Excel 2007 now offers the SUMIFS function, which you can also use to solve this problem. This new powerful function can easily handle up to 127 conditions.

As the first argument to SUMIFS, you specify the range to be summed. In this example, you use $E$2:$E$99.

Additional arguments come in pairs; the first argument of each pair specifies a criterion range, and the second argument specifies the criterion. To check if the product is ABC, use $D$2:$D$99,C$101. Each additional criterion needs another two arguments. To check if the rep is Amy, use $B$2:$B$99,$B102. As this formula is not a CSE formula, you can easily copy it to the rest of the table, as shown in Figure 631.

Figure 631

New in Excel 2007, use SUMIFS.

`=SUMIFS($E$2:$E$99,$D$2:$D$99,C$101,$B$2:$B$99,$B102)`

◢	A	B	C	D	E	F	G
1	Invoice	Rep	Customer	Product	Sales		
97	1017	Chaz	Y8576	ABC	226		
98	1020	Deb	Z2412	ABC	233		
99	1069	Amy	Z9822	DEF	278		
100							
101			ABC	DEF	XYZ		
102		Amy	998	2687	1723		
103		Ben	2210	1551	1447		
104		Chaz	2456	839	1389		
105		Deb	1181	1870	2106		
106							

Summary: You can solve a problem in which you need to sum on the basis of two conditions by using CSE formulas and Boolean logic. This is not just a powerful extension of SUMIF. Using these types of formulas, you can write just about any conditional calculation that you can imagine.

Functions Discussed: =SUM(); =SUMPRODUCT(); SUMIFS()

Excel 97-2003: SUMIFS() will return the #NAME! error.

CAN THE RESULTS OF A FORMULA BE USED IN COUNTIF?

Problem: I'm a teacher and need to count the number of students in my class who are above average. The student grades are arranged from B2:B26, as shown in Figure 632.

Figure 632

Count students who are above average.

◢	A	B
1	Name	Score
2	Allen	92
3	Barb	72
4	Bob	60
5	Carla	82
6	Charley	72
7	Ed	64

Strategy: The second parameter of the COUNTIF can be a calculation. As shown in Figure 633, you can concatenate a text operator with a calculation, as follows:

=COUNTIF(B2:B26,">"&AVERAGE(B2:B26))

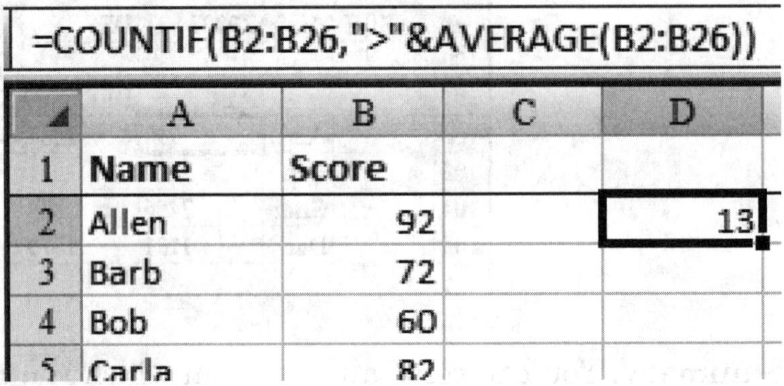

Figure 633

The criterion is built from a formula.

=COUNTIF(B2:B26,">"&AVERAGE(B2:B26))				
◢	A	B	C	D
1	Name	Score		
2	Allen	92		13
3	Barb	72		
4	Bob	60		
5	Carla	82		

Excel first calculates the average, then joins the operator with the result.

Summary: Using the result of a calculation as the criterion argument for COUNTIF opens up a number of possibilities for measurements using COUNTIF, SUMIF, and, now in Excel 2007, AVERAGEIF.

Functions Discussed: =COUNTIF(); AVERAGE(); SUMIF(); AVERAGEIF()

PART 3

WRANGLING DATA

HOW TO SET UP YOUR DATA
FOR EASY SORTING AND SUBTOTALS

Problem: I want to be able to use the powerful data commands in the spreadsheet shown in Figure 634—commands such as Sort, Filter, Subtotal, Consolidate, and PivotTable. Is there any special way I should set up the data to begin with?

Figure 634

Setting up the worksheet is the first step in successful data analysis.

	A	B	C	D	E
1	**OurCo Corporation**				
2	**Sales Report**				
3	**Fiscal Year 2008**				
4					
5	Sales Rep	Customer	Product	Quantity	Revenue
6	Joe	RST Company	GHI	624	55536
7	Mary	EFG Pty Ltd	GHI	605	53845
8	Dan	TUV Company	DEF	733	65237
9	Dan	CDE GMbH	XYZ	634	56426

Strategy: You need to follow all the rules to keep your data in list format:

Rule 1: Use only a single row of headings above your data. If you need to have a two-row heading, set it up as a single cell with two lines in the row, as shown in cell A5 (see "How to Fit a Multiline Heading into One Cell" on page 414).

Rule 2: Never leave one heading cell blank. You will find that you do this if you add a temporary column. If you forget to add a heading before you sort, this will completely throw off the IntelliSense, and Excel will sort the headings down into the data.

Rule 3: There should be no entirely blank rows or blank columns in the middle of your data. It is okay to have an occasional blank cell, but you should have no entirely blank columns.

Rule 4: If your heading row is not in row 1, be sure to have a blank row between your headings and any other filled cells. In Figure 634, for example, you have a blank row 4 between the titles in cells A1:A3 and the headings in row 5.

Rule 5: Formatting the heading cells in bold will help the Excel's IntelliSense module understand that these are headings.

Gotcha: List format won't help at all if your data is only two columns wide.

Results: If you follow the list format rules, Excel's IntelliSense will allow all the data commands to work flawlessly.

Additional Details: In Excel 2007, you can select a list and press Ctrl+T to specify that a range is a table.

Summary: You should follow the five rules presented here to set up your data before trying any of the data commands.

Excel 97-2003: In Excel 2003, a table was known as a list; therefore, use Ctrl+L instead of Ctrl+T.

See Also: "How to Fit a Multiline Heading into One Cell," below

HOW TO FIT A MULTILINE HEADING INTO ONE CELL

Problem: In "How to Set Up Your Data for Easy Sorting and Subtotals," you say that headings should occupy only one row to allow for easy sorting. My manager requires that I format a report to have the heading "Prior Year" split, with "Prior" in one row and "Year" in a second row, as shown in Figure 635. How can I make my manager happy while also following the list format rules?

Figure 635

Your manager
wants this
heading on
two rows.

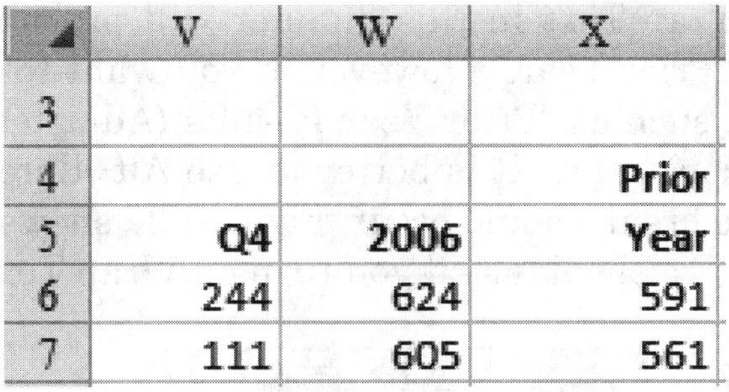

▲	V	W	X
3			
4			**Prior**
5	**Q4**	**2006**	**Year**
6	244	624	591
7	111	605	561

Strategy: This is a very real problem, where form meets function. The right thing to do in Excel is to have "Prior Year" in one cell. But some managers absolutely, positively want the formatting to be exactly as they specify. Luckily, there is a strategy that makes it possible to make the manager happy and to correctly set up the data set in Excel, too.

As shown in Figure 636, in cell X5, you type the word Prior. Then you hold down Alt while pressing Enter and type the word Year. The Alt+Enter combination adds a linefeed character in the cell. You can delete the old heading in X4 by moving the cell pointer there and pressing the Delete key.

Figure 636

Use Alt+Enter
to force Excel
to insert a
linefeed char-
acter where
you choose.

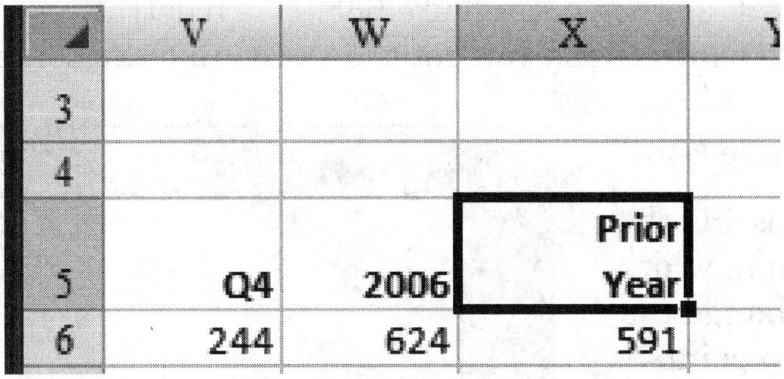

▲	V	W	X	⅄
3				
4				
5	**Q4**	**2006**	**Prior** **Year**	
6	244	624	591	

Results: You have a single cell that contains two lines of text. The cell will work as a heading in pivot tables, subtotals, sorting, and so on.

Additional Details: Using Alt+Enter automatically turns on the Wrap Text option for the cell. You could also turn on the Wrap Text option by choosing Home – Wrap Text icon.

Turning on Wrap Text in this manner will probably work for a brief heading like "Prior Year." However, if you want to have control over a long heading, such as "Prior Year Results (Adjusted for Spin-off of the Widget Division)," then it is better to use Alt+Enter to specify exactly where the line break should occur. Figure 637 shows the somewhat random splitting Excel will use if you turn on Wrap Text.

Figure 637

When you turn on Wrap Text, Excel rarely breaks the heading at logical points.

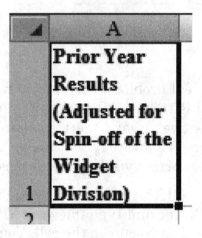

As you make this column wider, Excel changes the way the words are wrapped, as shown in Figure 638. It is frustrating to keep adjusting the column widths until you get the words to wrap correctly.

Figure 638

Adjusting the column width to change the wrap points is frustrating.

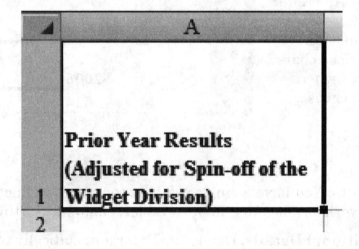

Using Alt+Enter gives you absolute control over where the heading breaks. Figure 639 shows a cell where you typed Prior Year Results<Alt +Enter>(Adjusted for the<Alt+Enter>Spin-off of the<Alt+Enter>Widget Division). You can make the column wider and center it for the perfect-looking cell.

Figure 639

Press Alt+Enter to wrap the text at logical points.

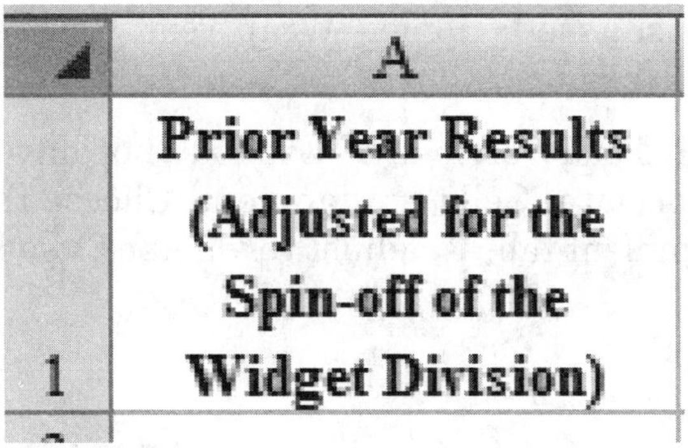

Additional Details: If you set up a cell that looks like Figure 637 and resize the column to look like Figure 638, the row height will stay tall enough to accommodate Figure 637. To correct this, you select the cell and then choose Home – Format dropdown – Autofit Row Height.

Gotcha: Sometimes you will paste some cells and frustratingly find that many of the cells have wrapped text. If you select all cells in the worksheet and globally turn off Wrap Text, Excel will remove all the wrapping, including the linefeeds you inserted using Alt+Enter. The linefeeds where you pressed Alt+Enter will show up as squares in the cells, as shown in Figure 640.

Figure 640

If you globally turn off Wrap Text, each Alt+Enter appears as an unprintable character.

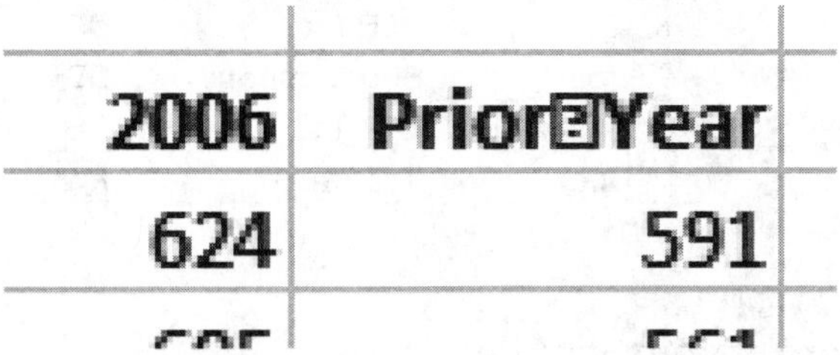

To fix this problem, you reselect these cells and select Home – Wrap Text. If necessary, choose Home – Format dropdown – AutoFit Row Height to see both lines of the cell again.

Summary: You press Alt+Enter to force a heading onto a new line within a single cell. When you do this, all the data commands work properly.

Commands Discussed: Home – Wrap Text; Home – Format dropdown – AutoFit Row Height

Excel 97-2003: Prior versions of Excel do not have a Wrap Text icon. Instead, use Format – Cells – Alignment. Choose the Wrap Text check box on the Alignment tab. To adjust row height, use Format – Row – AutoFit.

HOW TO SORT DATA

Problem: I have sales data in a worksheet, as shown in Figure 641. I would like to sort the data by product within customer.

Figure 641

Sort by product within customer.

◢	A	B	C	D	E
1	**OurCo Corporation**				
2	**Sales Report**				
3	**Fiscal Year 2008**				
4					
5	Rep	Customer	Product	Quantity	Revenue
6	Joe	EFG & Sons	ABC	357	31773
7	Bob	PQR Company	GHI	393	34977
8	Bob	DEF, Inc.	DEF	396	35244
9	Joe	BCD Company	DEF	399	35511
10	Mary	EFG, Inc.	DEF	411	36579
11	Joe	XYZ S.A.	XYZ	417	37113

Strategy: Here's what you do:

1) Select one cell within your data. The one cell can be in the heading row or any data row. Select Data – Sort. Whereas Excel 2003 only allowed sorting by three fields, Excel 2007 offers up to 64 sort lev-

els. Rather than the old dialog with the three fields, you now start with one field and add levels as necessary.

2)   Choose Sort By dropdown – Customer.

3)   Click the Add Level button. A new row will appear in the Sort dialog. Choose Then By dropdown – Product, as shown in Figure 642.

Figure 642

Build as many sort levels as necessary.

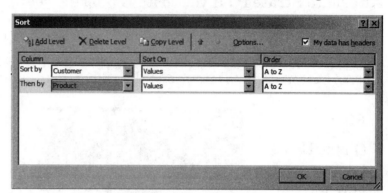

Leave the Sort On and Order dropdowns at their default values. If, for some reason, you wanted the customers sorted in descending alphabetical order, you could change A to Z to Z to A. That might make more sense if you were sorting by revenue, but it is not likely that you need the customers sorted in reverse alphabetical sequence. If your data is set up correctly as outlined in "How to Set up Your Data for Easy Sorting and Subtotals," Excel will properly guess that your list has a header row, as shown in Figure 642.

4)   Click OK to sort. Because Customer was the first sort key, all the records for "ABC Company" will sort to the top. Records for "ABC GMbH" will appear next, as shown in Figure 643.

Figure 643

Build as many sort levels as necessary.

Rep	Customer	Product	Quantity	Revenue
Dan	ABC Company	DEF	430	38270
Bob	ABC Company	DEF	529	47081
Dan	ABC GMbH	ABC	512	45568
Bob	ABC GMbH	ABC	702	62478
Joe	ABC GMbH	DEF	505	44945
Dan	ABC GMbH	GHI	553	49217
Joe	BCD Company	DEF	399	35511
Dan	BCD Corporation	ABC	575	51175
Dan	BCD Corporation	ABC	734	65326

Part III

Additional Details: When there is a tie—for example, the four records for "ABC GMbH"—those records will be sorted in ascending order by the product field. For instance, the ABC product record appears before the DEF product field. If there is still a tie, the records will remain in their original sequence from before the sort.

Alternate Strategy: If your data is properly set up in list format, you can select a single cell in the data and then select Home – Sort & Filter – Sort A to Z, as shown in Figure 644. Or, if you would like one-click access to the button as you've had in the last decade of Excel versions, click the AZ button on the Data tab of the ribbon, as shown in Figure 645.

Figure 644

On the Home tab, the AZ button is behind the Sort & Filter dropdown.

Figure 645

For one-click access to the AZ button, use the Data tab of the ribbon or add this to the QAT.

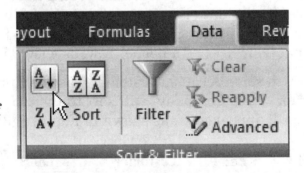

If you use either method, Excel will sort the data by the column in which the cell pointer is currently located. Because Excel resolves ties by leaving the previous sequence in place, you can sort by product within customer. First, you select a cell in the Product field and click AZ to sort by product. Next, you select a cell in the Customer field and click AZ to sort by customer. The data will be sorted by customer, with ties sorted by product.

You can click the ZA button to sort in descending order.

Gotcha: Before you try any sort operation, you must select either the entire range or a single cell in that range. If you mistakenly choose two cells in a range, Excel will sort just those selected cells, resulting in a few cells of your data being sorted within records—a disastrous result.

Summary: Sorting data is easy using either the Sort dialog or the sort buttons on the Home and Data tabs.

Commands Discussed: Data – Sort; Home – Sort & Filter – Sort A to Z; Data – AZ

Excel 97-2003: Data – Sort; In prior Excel versions, you could sort by only three levels at a time. If you needed to sort by six levels, you would have to sort by the lesser three levels first and then by the major three levels next. The AZ and ZA buttons were on the Standard toolbar

SORT DAYS OF THE WEEK

Part
III

Problem: I have a column with values such as Monday, Wednesday, and so on. When I sort this column in ascending sequence, Friday comes before Monday as shown in Figure 646. The same problem happens with month names, which sort as April, August, December, and so on.

Figure 646

Format a subset of characters in a cell.

	A	B	C
1	Day	Start	Associate
2	Friday	10:00 AM	Josh
3	Monday	10:00 AM	Bill
4	Monday	10:00 AM	Brooke
5	Monday	10:00 AM	Josh
6	Saturday	10:00 AM	Brooke

Strategy: Excel has custom lists built in for months and days. To use them, follow these steps:

1) Select a cell in your data.

2) Select Data – Sort.

3) Choose Sort by Day and Sort on Values. In the Order dropdown, choose Custom List.

4) Choose Sunday, Monday, Tuesday from the Custom List dialog. Click OK.

Excel will sort the data with Wednesday before Thursday (Figure 647).

Figure 647

Excel sorts the days into sequence.

Summary: You don't need to create a custom list to sort months or days. You can use one of Excel's custom built-in lists.

Commands Discussed: Data – Sort

Excel 97-2003: Data – Sort. In the Sort dialog, choose Days as the first sort key. Click the Options tab. Choose Sunday, Monday, Tuesday from the dropdown. You can control the sort order of only the first sort key, so you might have to do the sorts in several passes.

HOW TO SORT A REPORT INTO A CUSTOM SEQUENCE

Problem: My manager wants me to sort a report geographically (see Figure 648). My annual report typically lists results from the United States first, then Europe, and then Australia. I need to sort so that the countries appear as United States, England, France, Germany, and Australia. Within the United States, I want the regions within the United States to appear in East, Central, West sequence.

Figure 648

Sort data geographically.

Country	Region	District	Sales Rep	Customer	Product	Jan
5						
6 Germany	Germany	Germany	Joe	CDE GMbH	GHI	0
7 USA	East	MidAtlantic	Bob	STU, LLC	ABC	1
8 USA	Central	Cleveland	Mary	RST, Inc.	XYZ	3
9 Germany	Germany	Germany	Dan	GHI GMbH	ABC	5
10 USA	East	Southeast	Dan	FGH & Sons	ABC	5
11 USA	Central	Chicago	Dan	TUV Company	XYZ	8
12 USA	East	Southeast	Bob	FGH & Sons	DEF	12
13 USA	Central	Minneapolis	Dan	BCD Corporation	ABC	14

Strategy: You can use a custom list by following these steps:

1) Go to a blank section of the worksheet. As shown in Figure 649, type the countries in the order you want them to appear in a column. Select the range of cells.

Figure 649

Type the countries in their desired geographic sequence.

	A
1	USA
2	England
3	France
4	Germany
5	Australia

2) Choose Office Icon – Excel Options. In the Popular category of the Excel Options dialog, click the Edit Custom Lists button.

3) Ensure that at the bottom of the Custom Lists dialog, your range of values from step 1 is entered in the Import text box, as shown in Figure 650. Click the Import button.

Figure 650

Import your list as a new custom list.

Import list from cells: $A$1:$A$5   Import

4) The custom list is added to the Custom Lists box, as shown in Figure 651. Click OK to close the Custom Lists dialog. Click OK to close the Excel Options dialog. Repeat to create a custom list for regions.

Figure 651

Excel will remember your list as a custom list.

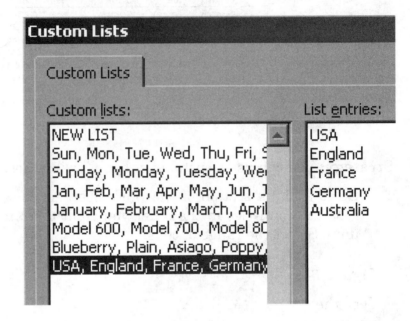

5) Select Data – Sort. In the Sort dialog, choose Country from the Sort By dropdown. In the Order dropdown, choose Custom List, as shown in Figure 652.

Figure 652

For the order, choose Custom List.

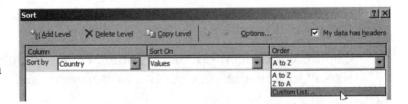

6) Excel will again display the Custom Lists dialog (refer to Figure 651). Select the USA, England, France list and click OK.

7) When Excel shows USA, England, France, Germany in the Order dropdown (see Figure 653), click OK to sort.

Figure 653

Excel specifies that the sequence of your custom list will provide the sequence for the sort.

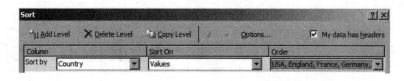

8) Click Add Level. Sort by Region. Choose Custm List as the Order. Specify East, Central, West as the region sort order.

Results: The data is sorted by country and region, in the order that you specified.

Additional Details: If there is a value in the column that is not in your custom list, it is sorted alphabetically after the entries in the list. If you sort in descending order, these unlisted entries will come first, in Z–A order.

Gotcha: In previous versions of Excel, there is no way to specify that the second sort criterion should use different custom sort criteria. In Excel 97-2003, you will have to sort on Region first, using a custom sort criterion, and then on Country in a separate sort, using a different custom sort criterion.

Gotcha: Excel remembers that the column was most recently sorted by the "USA, England…" custom list. If you click the AZ button, it will automatically sort by using this same custom list. If you need to return to alphabetical order, you will have to select Data – Sort and choose A to Z in the Order dropdown.

Summary: It is easy to add a custom list to the Excel Options dialog and then use that custom list for sorting.

Excel 97-2003: Data – Sort, specify Country as the first sort field, click the Options button in the lower-left corner of the dialog, and select First Key Sort Order dropdown – USA, England, France

Part
III

SORT ALL RED CELLS
TO THE TOP OF A REPORT

Problem: I've read through a 20-page report and marked a dozen cells in red (see Figure 654). I need to audit those records and would like to sort the red cells to the top of the report.

Figure 654

Sort the red cells to the top.

Rep	Customer	Product	Quantity	Revenue
Dan	ABC Company	DEF	430	38270
Bob	ABC Company	DEF	529	47081
Dan	ABC GMbH	ABC	512	45568
Bob	ABC GMbH	ABC	702	62478
Joe	ABC GMbH	DEF	505	44945
Dan	ABC GMbH	GHI	553	49217
Joe	BCD Company	DEF	399	35511
Dan	BCD Corporation	ABC	575	51175
Dan	BCD Corporation	ABC	734	65326
Bob	BCD Corporation	ABC	795	70755
Dan	BCD Corporation	DEF	641	57049
Bob	CDE GMbH	ABC	697	62033
Joe	CDE GMbH	GHI	612	54468
Joe	CDE GMbH	GHI	803	71467

Strategy: Excel 2007 allows you to sort by color. Follow these steps:

1) Right-click on one of the red cells.

2) From the context menu, choose Sort – Put Selected Cell Color on Top (see Figure 655).

Figure 655

Choose to sort by color.

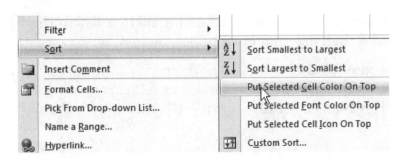

Results: Excel will sort the red cells to the top of the report, as shown in Figure 656.

Figure 656

Red cells sort to the top.

Rep	Customer	Product	Quantity	Revenue
Dan	ABC GMbH	ABC	512	45568
Dan	BCD Corporation	ABC	575	51175
Joe	CDE GMbH	GHI	612	54468
Bob	DEF, Inc.	DEF	396	35244
Dan	EFG Pty Ltd	XYZ	696	61944
Bob	FGH & Sons	GHI	522	46458
Dan	HIJ Company	XYZ	465	41385
Bob	IJK, Inc.	DEF	695	61855
Mary	KLM Company	GHI	656	58384
Joe	LMN, Inc.	DEF	787	70043
Bob	NOP GMbH	ABC	459	40851
Joe	OPQ, Inc.	GHI	664	59096
Dan	ABC Company	DEF	430	38270
Bob	ABC Company	DEF	529	47081

Part III

Additional Details: Using the context menu as described here works fine if you need to sort by only one color. If you used cells of several different colors and want to sort them in a particular order, you need to select Data – Sort to open the Sort dialog. Then, for the first sort level, you choose Quantity in the Sort By dropdown, Cell Color from the Sort On dropdown, and green from the Order dropdown.

You set the next sort level by clicking the Copy Level button and then choosing yellow from the Order dropdown. You click Copy Level for each additional color you need to specify (see Figure 657).

Figure 657

If you have many colors in a column, you might use several sort levels to specify how to sort the first column.

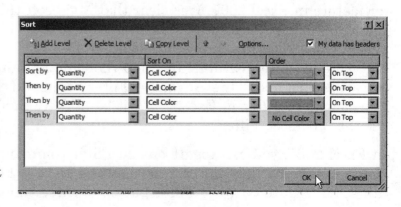

Additional Details: You can also sort by font color or cell icon. Amazingly, sorting by color will even work if your colors have been assigned through conditional formatting.

Summary: You can bring cells with a selected color to the top of a list.

Excel 97-2003: Previous versions of Excel did not allow you to sort by color.

QUICKLY FILTER A LIST TO CERTAIN RECORDS

Problem: I have 10,000 records in the worksheet shown in Figure 658. I need to be able to quickly find records that match a criterion, such as all East ABC records.

Figure 658

Find records within this data set.

	A	B	C	D	E	F
1	Region	Product	Date	Customer	Quantity	Revenue
2	Central	XYZ	Jan-08	Wal-Mart	1000	25140
3	West	XYZ	Jan-08	General Motors	1000	25080
4	Central	XYZ	Jan-08	Wal-Mart	1000	23810
5	Central	XYZ	Jan-08	Ford	1000	22680
6	East	DEF	Jan-08	Ainsworth	900	21708
7	East	XYZ	Jan-08	General Motors	900	21456
8	East	XYZ	Jan-08	Ainsworth	1000	20940
9	Central	DEF	Jan-08	Chevron	900	20610
10	East	XYZ	Jan-08	Verizon	1000	20490
11	West	ABC	Jan-08	Wal-Mart	1000	20250

Strategy: You can find records that match a criterion by using the Filter feature in Excel 2007. It is clear that Microsoft thinks highly of the Filter feature: It improved AutoFilter from Excel 2002 to Excel 2003, and in Excel 2007, it renamed the feature simply Filter, giving it more and more powerful features. In "Find the Unique Values in a Column," you will learn about the Advanced Filter command, but with the improvements to Filter in Excel 2007, it is unlikely that you will need to use the Advanced Filter.

In Excel 2007, you can toggle on the Filter command by using either Home – Sort & Filter – Filter or selecting Data – Filter icon. As you can see in Figure 659, the Filter button is three times larger than the

Advanced Filter icon, which I take as evidence that Microsoft someday hopes to add enough power to Filter to eliminate the need for the Advanced Filter.

Figure 659

Filter is the new name for what was previously known as AutoFilter.

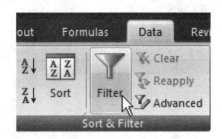

To filter your data set, follow these steps:

1) Make sure your data has a heading row. Select one cell within the data. Select Data – Filter. Excel will add a dropdown to each heading, as shown in Figure 660.

Figure 660

Excel will add a dropdown to each heading.

⊿	A	B	C	D	E	F
1	Region ▼	Produ ▼	Invoi ▼	Customer ▼	Quant ▼	Reven ▼
2	Central	XYZ	Jan-08	Wal-Mart	1000	25140
3	West	XYZ	Jan-08	General Motors	1000	25080
4	Central	XYZ	Jan-08	Wal-Mart	1000	23810

2) Select the Region dropdown, as shown in Figure 661 on the next page. You will notice several improvements. New options allow you to sort by color or filter by color. A new fly-out menu offers the ability to create fuzzy filters, such as everything that contains a certain bit of text. Whereas AutoFilter only allowed you to select one value, Excel 2007's Filter dropdown allows you to select multiple values. **Gotcha:** With all this new power, it is slightly more difficult to select a single value.

3) Click the (Select All) check box to unselect all the regions.

4) Click the East check box. Click OK. You will now see just the East records.

Part
III

Figure 661

The dropdown in Excel 2007 offers many choices.

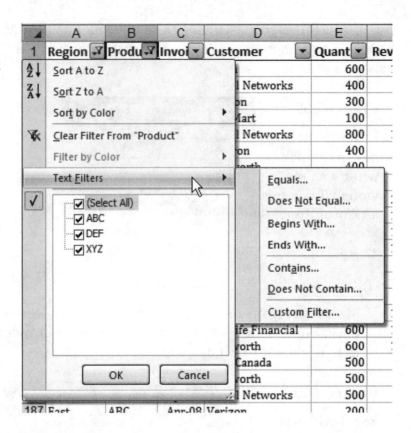

5) Select the Product dropdown and click (Select All) to unselect all products. Click the ABC check box. Click OK.

Results: You will see only sales of product ABC in the East region, as shown in Figure 662. All the other rows will be hidden.

Figure 662

A filter on sales of product ABC in the East region.

	A	B	C	D	E	F
1	Region	Produ	Invoi	Customer	Quant	Reven
27	East	ABC	Jan-08	Exxon	600	11430
34	East	ABC	Jan-08	Nortel Networks	400	7152
35	East	ABC	Jan-08	Verizon	300	6045
44	East	ABC	Jan-08	Wal-Mart	100	2066

Additional Details: You have some additional choices when filtering:

Use Clear Filter from Region to clear a filter on one column. To clear a filter from all columns, select Data – Clear icon. To turn off the filter dropdowns, choose Data – Filter icon.

If you are filtering a numeric column, you have additional options, such as to filter to all records above average, as shown in Figure 663.

Figure 663

In a numeric column, you have many new filter options.

The Top 10 Filter option allows you to specify the top or bottom "n" items or "n%" of items. The Top 10 feature was in previous versions of Excel, but all the other value filters in Figure 663 are new in Excel 2007.

After you select Top 10, the Top 10 AutoFilter dialog appears, as shown in Figure 664. You can choose whether you want the top 10% or the top 10 items, and you can also change the 10 to 5 or to any other number. You can also use this dialog to show the bottom 10 (or 5 or any other number or percentage of) records.

Figure 664

Despite the Top 10 name, you can find the top 5%, the bottom 5%, and so on.

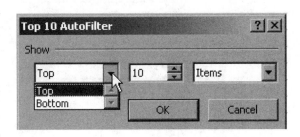

If you are filtering a column with dates, you can use select Date Filters, which offers many choices, such as last week, this month, next quarter, and so on, as shown in Figure 665.

Figure 665

The date filters are new in Excel 2007.

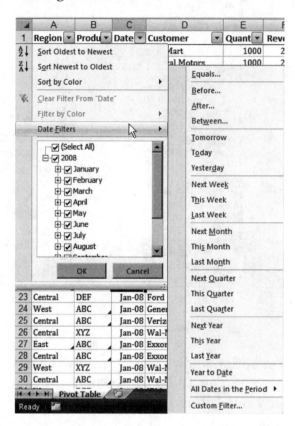

If you have used cell colors, font colors, or icon sets, you can use the Filter by Color fly-out menu to show records that have a certain color (see Figure 666.)

Figure 666

Filter by color.

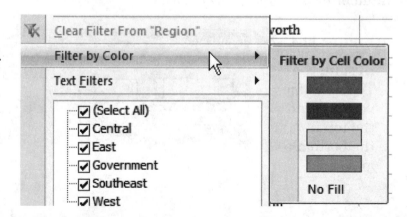

Gotcha: In order for the Date Filters or Number Filters options to appear, your data needs to be predominantly dates or numbers. If you have too many blank cells or too many text cells, Excel will treat the column as text and not offer these filter options in the dropdown.

Summary: You can use Data – Filter to have Excel show you data in a column that match certain criteria.

Commands Discussed: Data – Filter

Excel 97-2003: Data – Filter – AutoFilter. Each dropdown offered the ability to filter only on one specific item. If you needed to filter on two items, you could choose the Custom item from the dropdown and build a filter with Region equal to East or Region equal to West. There was no way in prior versions of Excel to filter on three or more items from the list.

Instead of showing a Filter icon at the top of each filtered column, previous versions of Excel used blue color for the dropdown arrow to indicate which columns had a filter applied. To clear a filter, you had to choose (All) from the dropdown.

Excel 2003 offered the ability to sort from the dropdown filter. Excel 97-2003 offered the Top 10 filter. However, none of the other features of the Excel 2007 Filter command were available in prior versions of Excel.

FIND THE UNIQUE VALUES IN A COLUMN

Problem: I have a large database, as shown in Figure 667. Before I can produce a report for each customer, I need to identify the complete list of unique customers.

Figure 667

Find the unique customers.

	A	B	C	D
1	Region	Product	Invoice	Customer
2	Central	XYZ	Jan-08	Wal-Mart
3	West	XYZ	Jan-08	General Motors
4	Central	XYZ	Jan-08	Wal-Mart
5	Central	XYZ	Jan-08	Ford
6	East	DEF	Jan-08	Ainsworth
7	East	XYZ	Jan-08	General Motors

Part
III

Strategy: There are many solutions to the unique customers problem. One is to use the Advanced Filter command on the Data tab of the ribbon. Follow these steps:

1) Copy the Customer heading from D1 to a blank area of the spreadsheet, as shown in Figure 668.

Figure 668

Copy the customer heading to an output area.

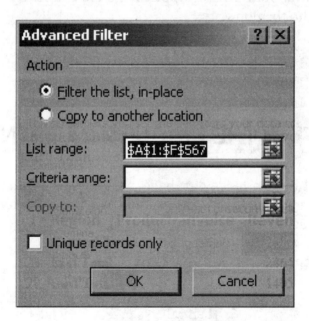

2) Select a single cell in your data range and then select Data – Advanced. The Advanced Filter dialog will appear, offering many confusing options. By default, it will look as shown in Figure 669.

Figure 669

Initially, Advanced Filter wants to filter in place.

3) Choose the Unique Records Only check box (see Figure 670). Change the Action section to Copy to Another Location. Selecting this action enables the Copy To range. Place the cell pointer in the

Copy To text box and touch the out-of-the-way copy of the Customer heading.

Figure 670

Copy unique records to the output range that you set up in step 1.

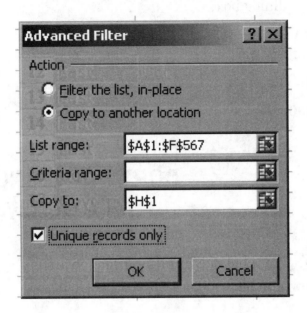

Advanced Filter

Action
- ○ Filter the list, in-place
- ● Copy to another location

List range: $A$1:$F$567

Criteria range:

Copy to: $H$1

☑ Unique records only

OK   Cancel

4) Click OK. Excel will find the unique customer numbers and copy them to the range you specified, as shown in Figure 671.

Figure 671

Excel produces a list of unique customers.

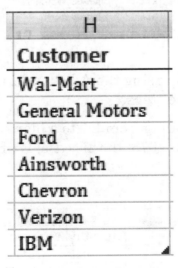

H
Customer
Wal-Mart
General Motors
Ford
Ainsworth
Chevron
Verizon
IBM

Gotcha: Any subsequent use of the Advanced Filter command during this Excel session will remember the list range you specified in the Advanced Filter dialog box.

Summary: One use of the Advanced Filter command is to generate a unique list of one particular field in a data set.

Commands Discussed: Data – Advanced

Excel 97-2003: Data – Filter – Advanced Filter

COPY MATCHING RECORDS TO A NEW WORKSHEET

Problem: I want to copy records for one particular customer from the data set shown in Figure 672 to a new worksheet.

Figure 672

Extract all records for one customer.

	A	B	C	D	E	F
1	Region	Product	Invoice	Customer	Quantity	Revenue
2	Central	XYZ	Jan-08	Wal-Mart	1000	25140
3	West	XYZ	Jan-08	General Motors	1000	25080
4	Central	XYZ	Jan-08	Wal-Mart	1000	23810
5	Central	XYZ	Jan-08	Ford	1000	22680

Strategy: You can do this by using the Advanced Filter command with a criteria range. Follow these steps:

1) Copy the Customer heading from D1 to a blank area of the spreadsheet, as shown in Figure 673. In this case, H1:H2 will be the criteria range for the filter

Figure 673

Set up a criteria range.

D	E	F	G	H
Customer	Quantity	Revenue		Customer
Wal-Mart	1000	25140		
General Motors	1000	25080		
Wal-Mart	1000	23810		

2)   In cell H2, enter the customer that you want to extract.

3)   Select a single cell in your data range. Select Data – Advanced to display the Advanced Filter dialog. Ensure that the Action setting is Filter the List, In-place. Move the cell pointer to the Criteria Range column and use your mouse to highlight the criteria range H1:H2 (see Figure 674).

Figure 674

Filter in place, with a criteria range.

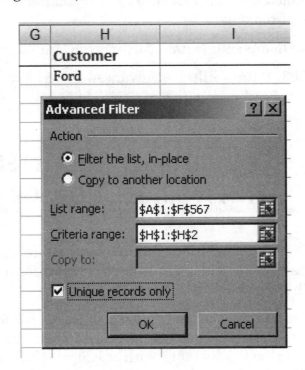

4)   Click OK to run the advanced filter.

Results: As shown in Figure 675, Excel will hide all the rows that do not match the criteria.

Figure 675

Excel hides all nonmatching rows.

	A	B	C	D	E	F
1	Region	Product	Invoice	Customer	Quantity	Revenue
5	Central	XYZ	Jan-08	Ford	1000	22680
17	Central	ABC	Jan-08	Ford	900	16209
20	East	DEF	Jan-08	Ford	600	13206
23	Central	DEF	Jan-08	Ford	600	12282

Now you can select the cells from A1:F118, click the Copy icon, and paste to a new workbook. Excel will copy only the matching rows.

Additional Details: On the original sheet, to clear the advanced filter and show all the rows again, choose Data – Clear. (The Clear icon is in the Sort & Filter group.)

Summary: One use of the Advanced Filter command is to extract a certain customer from a data set.

Commands Discussed: Data – Advanced; Data – Clear icon

Excel 97-2003: Data – Filter – Advanced Filter; Data – Filter – Show All

REPLACE MULTIPLE FILTER CRITERIA WITH A SINGLE ROW OF FORMULAS

Problem: The Advanced Filter feature can handle combinations of criteria, but I have a particular situation that requires a dizzying array of 125 rows. What can I do?

Strategy: You can replace traditional criteria with a formula-based criteria range. Excel will let you combine criteria. If you put items on the same row, Excel will join them with a logical AND. For example, the criterion in Figure 676 will return all rows where Ford ordered S112.

Figure 676

Criteria on the same row are joined with an AND.

I	J
Customer	**Product**
Ford	S112

If you put items on successive rows, Excel will join them with a logical OR. In Figure 677, the criterion will return any rows where the market is Retail or the region is East.

Figure 677

Criteria on the
different rows
are joined with
an OR.

Market	Region
Retail	
	East

The criteria fields can quickly get out of hand. What if you wanted any
records where the product is S101, S103, S105, S107, or S109; the market is Service, Financial, or Transp.; and the customer is Ford, General
Motors, Shell Canada, Exxon, or Verizon. This criteria range would cover 76 rows. You would have headings in row 1, then 15 rows of criteria
for S101 (shown in Figure 678), then 15 more rows for each additional
product.

Figure 678

When you
need to join
five customers,
five products,
and three
markets with
an OR, you
end up with 76
rows of crite-
ria.

Product	Market	Customer
S101	Service	Ford
S101	Service	General Motors
S101	Service	Shell Canada
S101	Service	Exxon
S101	Service	Verizon
S101	Financial	Ford
S101	Financial	General Motors
S101	Financial	Shell Canada
S101	Financial	Exxon
S101	Financial	Verizon
S101	Transp.	Ford
S101	Transp.	General Motors
S101	Transp.	Shell Canada
S101	Transp.	Exxon
S101	Transp.	Verizon
S103	Service	Ford

There is an obscure way to use a formula-based criterion, and it is helpful in this situation. You leave the heading in row 1 of the criteria range
blank. In row 2 of the criteria range, you enter a formula that tests the
first row of the data set and will return a TRUE or FALSE value.

In Figure 679, for example, the formula in K2 checks to see if the market in C2 is in the list of markets in M8:M10. Similar formulas in I2 and J2 test to see if the customer and products in row 2 are in lists in columns M and N.

Figure 679

Three formula-based criteria replace the 76 rows of criteria.

	H	I	J	K	L	M	N
1							
2		FALSE	FALSE	TRUE		S101	Ford
3						S103	General Motors
4						S105	Shell Canada
5						S107	Exxon
6						S109	Verizon
7							
8						Service	
9						Financial	
10						Transp.	

Formula bar: `=NOT(ISNA(MATCH(C2,$M$8:$M$10,0)))`

When you perform the Advanced Filter, specify I1:K2 as the criteria range. Excel will apply the formulas to each row of your dataset and only return the records where all three formulas evaluate to TRUE.

Additional Details: The Advanced Filter command can also copy the output to a new section of the worksheet. You can specify a subset of columns and even specify a new order for the columns. In Figure 680, the output range of P1:S1 asks for only 4 of the 7 original columns, in a new sequence.

Figure 680

Optionally include an output range in the Copy To field.

P	Q	R	S
Market	Region	Customer	Revenue

Advanced Filter

Action
- ○ Filter the list, in-place
- ● Copy to another location

List range: `$A$1:$G$567`

Criteria range: `$I$1:$K$2`

Copy to: `$P$1:$S$1`

☐ Unique records only

OK   Cancel

Results: Only records that match the desired customers, products, and markets appear in the output range, as shown in Figure 681.

Figure 681

Excel will evaluate the formula criteria and copy the data to a new range.

Market	Region	Customer	Revenue
Financial	East	General Motors	21456
Financial	East	Verizon	20490
Financial	West	Verizon	17160
Service	Central	Exxon	13314
Financial	East	General Motors	12672
Service	West	General Motors	12145
Service	Central	Verizon	11922
Transp.	East	Verizon	6045

Summary: Advanced Filter still has a few tricks that allow it to do things that the regular Filter command cannot do. For example, Advanced Filter can copy matching records to a new range and can deal with massively complex criteria.

Commands Discussed: Data – Advanced

Excel 97-2003: Data – Filter – Advanced Filter

ADD SUBTOTALS TO A DATA SET

Problem: I have a lengthy report with invoice detail by customer, as shown in Figure 682. I need to add a subtotal at each change in customer.

Figure 682

Add a subtotal to each customer.

	A	B	C	D
	Acct	Customer	Invoice	Revenue
1	Acct	Customer	Invoice	Revenue
2	A3108	Air Canada	1057	5,859
3	A3108	Air Canada	1061	2,358
4	A3108	Air Canada	1090	17,856
5	A3108	Air Canada	1108	4,948
6	A4368	Ainsworth	1014	10,445
7	A4368	Ainsworth	1015	15,544
8	A4368	Ainsworth	1030	3,922

Part III

Strategy: You can use the Subtotal feature to solve this problem in seconds instead of minutes.

Note: I designed the data set shown in Figure 682 so that the defaults in the Subtotal dialog will work. For a more complex data set, see "Subtotal Many Columns at Once" on page 455.

1)   Sort the data by customer.

2)   Select a single cell in the data set. Then select Data – Subtotal. As shown in Figure 683, the Subtotal dialog assumes that you want to subtotal by the field in the leftmost column of your data. It also assumes that you want to total the rightmost field.

Figure 683

Select by which fields to subtotal.

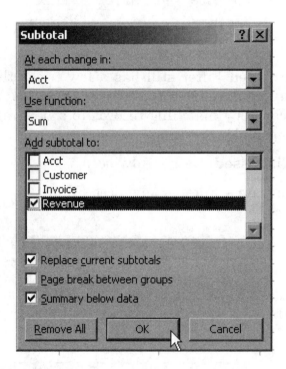

3)   Because the Subtotal dialog's assumptions are correct in this case, click OK. In just a couple seconds, Excel will insert subtotals at each change in customer, as shown in Figure 684.

Figure 684

In seconds, Excel will insert new rows with subtotals.

▲	A	B	C	D
1	Acct	Customer	Invoice	Revenue
2	A3108	Air Canada	1057	5,859
3	A3108	Air Canada	1061	2,358
4	A3108	Air Canada	1090	17,856
5	A3108	Air Canada	1108	4,948
6	**A3108 Total**			31,021
7	A4368	Ainsworth	1014	10,445
8	A4368	Ainsworth	1015	15,544
9	A4368	Ainsworth	1030	3,922
10	A4368	Ainsworth	1054	12,838
11	A4368	Ainsworth	1091	17,712
12	**A4368 Total**			60,461
13	B4504	Bell Canada	1013	15,104
14	B4504	Bell Canada	1069	18,072
15	B4504	Bell Canada	1074	14,004
16	B4504	Bell Canada	1077	4,060
17	**B4504 Total**			51,240

If you scroll to the end of the data set, you will notice that Excel added a grand total of all customers (see Figure 685). Notice that the inserted rows use the relatively new SUBTOTAL function. This function will total all the cells in the range except for cells that contain other SUBTOTAL functions.

Figure 685

The SUBTOTAL function ignores other subtotal cells.

D137	▼	f_x	=SUBTOTAL(9,D2:D135)

▲	A	B	C	D
1	Acct	Customer	Invoice	Revenue
128	**T3756 Total**			20,558
129	V6841	Verizon	1008	17,136
130	V6841	Verizon	1058	6,309
131	V6841	Verizon	1072	11,922
132	**V6841 Total**			35,367
133	W1645	Wal-Mart	1004	7,180
134	W1645	Wal-Mart	1039	10,385
135	W1645	Wal-Mart	1100	8,970
136	**W1645 Total**			26,535
137	**Grand Total**			1,235,966

Part III

Additional Details: In order to remove subtotals, you select a cell in the data set and then select Data – Subtotal. In the Subtotal dialog, you click the Remove All button, as shown in Figure 686.

Figure 686

Remove subtotals.

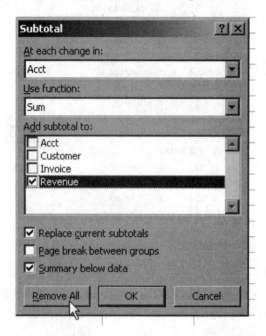

Gotcha: This example works because the data was sorted by account number. If the data were sorted by invoice number instead, the result would be fairly meaningless, as shown in Figure 687.

Figure 687

Make sure your data is sorted by the proper field, or chaos results.

	A	B	C	D
1	Acct	Customer	Invoice	Revenue
2	M3105	Molson, Inc	1001	7,520
3	M3105 Total			7,520
4	S1939	State Farm	1002	4,754
5	S1939 Total			4,754
6	M3105	Molson, Inc	1003	8,016
7	M3105 Total			8,016
8	W1645	Wal-Mart	1004	7,180
9	W1645 Total			7,180

Summary: The Subtotal command on the Data tab quickly automates the monotonous job of adding subtotals.

Commands Discussed: Data – Subtotal

Functions Discussed: =SUBTOTAL()

Excel 97-2003: Data – Subtotals

USE GROUP & OUTLINE BUTTONS TO COLLAPSE SUBTOTALED DATA

Problem: I just used the Subtotal command in "Add Subtotals to a Data Set," and now I want to print the total rows in order to create a summary report for my manager.

Strategy: If you look above and to the left of cell A1, you'll see a series of three small numbers, as shown in Figure 688. These are the Group & Outline buttons. You can use them to collapse subtotaled data in order to print the summary report you're looking for.

Part
III

Figure 688

Excel adds
Group & Out-
line buttons
when you use
the Subtotal
command.

If you click the small 2 button, you will see just the customer totals, as shown in Figure 689.

Figure 689

This is a great
summary to
print.

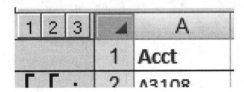

		A	B	C	D
	1	Acct	Customer	Invoice	Revenue
+	6	A3108 Total			31,021
+	12	A4368 Total			60,461
+	17	B4504 Total			51,240
+	22	C4904 Total			39,250
+	27	C8082 Total			31,369

D82   =SUBTOTAL(9,D77:D81)

As shown in Figure 690, you can click the small 1 button to see just the grand total. This view seems a bit pointless, but an attendee of one of my Power Excel classes noted that you can use the 1 button to quickly navigate to the bottom of a data set.

Figure 690

The #1 view is not as useful.

	1	2	3		A	B	C	D
				1	Acct	Customer	Invoice	Revenue
+				137	Grand Total			1,235,966
				138				

You can click the 3 button to go back to the detailed view that shows all records, as shown in Figure 691.

Figure 691

Click 3 to return to all the detail rows.

	1	2	3		A	B	C	D
				1	Acct	Customer	Invoice	Revenue
		.		2	A3108	Air Canada	1057	5,859
		.		3	A3108	Air Canada	1061	2,358
		.		4	A3108	Air Canada	1090	17,856
		.		5	A3108	Air Canada	1108	4,948
		−		6	A3108 Total			31,021
		.		7	A4368	Ainsworth	1014	10,445

Additional Details: In the 2 button view, you can collapse or expand a single customer's detail records by clicking the - or + symbols next to the customer total, as shown in Figure 692.

Figure 692

Use the + button to expand a single customer.

	1	2	3		A	B	C	D
				1	Acct	Customer	Invoice	Revenue
	+			6	A3108 Total			31,021
	+			12	A4368 Total			60,461
	+			17	B4504 Total			51,240
	+			22	C4904 Total			39,250
	+			27	C8082 Total			31,369
		.		28	C9651	Chevron	1018	8,116
		.		29	C9651	Chevron	1071	7,032
		.		30	C9651	Chevron	1084	18,290
		.		31	C9651	Chevron	1098	20,610
		−		32	C9651 Total			54,048
	+			38	E9872 Total			68,200
	+			44	F7747 Total			52,580

Additional Details: If you think the Group & Outline buttons are cool, you can manually add them without using Subtotal. You just collect a group of columns or rows to be grouped and select Data – Group. It is fairly tedious to add many groupings, but this can be easier than continually hiding and unhiding rows. In the worksheet in Figure 693, for example, you would have selected Jan, Feb, Mar and used Data – Group – By Columns. You would repeat this to group April, May, and June into Q2; July, August, September into Q3; and October, November, and December into Q4. The result is that you can quickly toggle from monthly to quarterly views, using the 1 or 2 buttons, or you can expand a single quarter.

Figure 693

Manual groupings roll months into quarters.

	A	E	F	G	H	I	M	Q
1	Account	Q1	Apr	May	Jun	Q2	Q3	Q4
2	A101	45838	16150	16312	16475	48937	51759	57088
3	A102	56174	19797	19995	20595	60387	65744	71398
4	A103	49085	17128	17813	18704	53645	58196	63600

Part III

Summary: After you use the Subtotal command, the Group & Outline buttons allow you to create multiple views of the data.

Commands Discussed: Data – Subtotal; Data – Group

COPY JUST TOTALS FROM SUBTOTALED DATA

Problem: My manager wants me to send him just the total rows in a file. I've added subtotals and then chosen the 2 Group & Outline button to see just the data he wants, as shown in Figure 694.

Figure 694

Collapse to the 2 view and copy.

	A	B	C	D
1	Acct	Customer	Invoice	Revenue
6	A3108 Total			31,021
12	A4368 Total			60,461
17	B4504 Total			51,240
22	C4904 Total			39,250

However, when I copy this view and paste to a new workbook, all the detail rows come along as well, as shown in Figure 695.

Figure 695

Disappoint- ingly, Excel brings along the detail rows as well.

	A	B	C	D
1	Acct	Customer	Invoice	Revenue
2	A3108	Air Canada	1057	5,859
3	A3108	Air Canada	1061	2,358
4	A3108	Air Canada	1090	17,856
5	A3108	Air Canada	1108	4,948
6	A3108 Total			31,021
7	A4368	Ainsworth	1014	10,445
8	A4368	Ainsworth	1015	15,544
9	A4368	Ainsworth	1030	3,922
10	A4368	Ainsworth	1054	12,838

Strategy: You can use an obscure command in the Go To Special dialog box to assist with this task. Follow these steps:

1) Choose the 2 Group & Outline button to put the data in subtotal view.

2) Select everything from the headings to the grand total by select- ing one cell with data and pressing Ctrl+*. (You can use the * key on the numeric keypad, or hold down the shift key while you press 8.) Note that if you forget to hold shift and press Ctrl+8, Excel will remove the Group & Outline symbols. Bring them back again with Ctrl+8.

3) Bring up the Go To Special dialog by choosing Home – Find & Select – Go To Special. Alternatively, you can press the F5 key and click the Special button in the lower-left corner of the Go To dialog.

4) In the Go To Special dialog, select Visible Cells Only and click OK, as shown in Figure 696. The change will be almost imperceptible. In Excel 2003's blue highlighting, you could see fine white lines above and below each subtotal. These are not perceptible in Excel 2007.

Figure 696

Select Visible Cells Only.

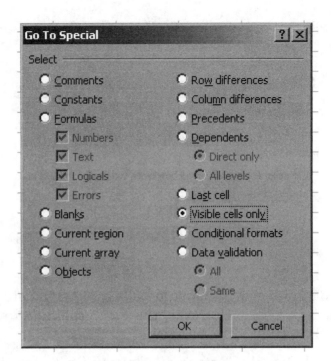

5)   Press Ctrl+C to copy. As you can see in Figure 697, Excel will indi-
       vidually select each subtotal line.

Figure 697

Copy the sub-total lines.

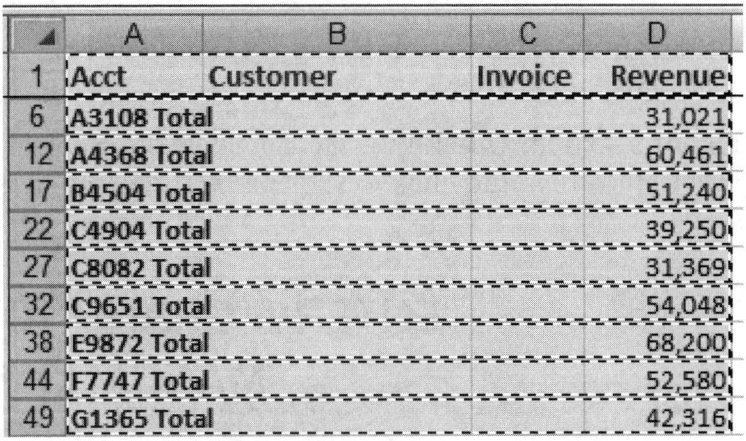

▲	A	B	C	D
1	Acct	Customer	Invoice	Revenue
6	A3108 Total			31,021
12	A4368 Total			60,461
17	B4504 Total			51,240
22	C4904 Total			39,250
27	C8082 Total			31,369
32	C9651 Total			54,048
38	E9872 Total			68,200
44	F7747 Total			52,580
49	G1365 Total			42,316

6) Switch to a new workbook. Press Ctrl+V to paste. Excel will paste just the subtotal rows (see Figure 698).

Figure 698

Paste the sub-totals only to a new workbook.

◢	A	B	C	D
1	Acct	Customer	Invoice	Revenue
2	A3108 Total			31,021
3	A4368 Total			60,461
4	B4504 Total			51,240
5	C4904 Total			39,250
6	C8082 Total			31,369

You might think that you would have to select Paste – Values instead of just doing a paste. However, the Paste command works okay. Excel converts the SUBTOTAL functions to values.

Additional Details: Instead of selecting Go To Special – Visible Cells Only, you can press Alt+; (that is, hold down the Alt key and type a semicolon).

Summary: You can use Visible Cells Only to select just the subtotal rows from the collapsed 2 Group & Outline view.

Commands Discussed: Home – Find & Select – Go To Special – Visible Cells Only; Alt+;

Excel 97-2003: Use Edit – Go To, click the Special button, choose Visible Cells Only, and click OK; or press the Alt+; shortcut.

ENTER A GRAND TOTAL OF DATA MANUALLY SUBTOTALED

Problem: My manager doesn't know the trick for doing automatic subtotals. In the example shown in Figure 699, he manually entered blank lines between each customer and entered SUM formulas for each customer. How can I produce a grand total of all customers?

Figure 699

In real life, with 25 customers, the formula for the total would add 25 different cells.

▲	A	B	C	D
1	Acct	Customer	Invoice	Revenue
2	A4368	Ainsworth	1014	10,445
3	A4368	Ainsworth	1015	15,544
4	A4368	Ainsworth	1030	3,922
5	A4368	Ainsworth	1054	12,838
6	A4368	Ainsworth	1091	17,712
7		Total Ainsworth		60,461
8				
9	A3108	Air Canada	1057	5,859
10	A3108	Air Canada	1061	2,358
11	A3108	Air Canada	1090	17,856
12	A3108	Air Canada	1108	4,948
13		Total Air Canada		31,021
14				
15	B4504	Bell Canada	1013	15,104
16	B4504	Bell Canada	1069	18,072
17	B4504	Bell Canada	1074	14,004
18	B4504	Bell Canada	1077	4,060
19		Total Bell Canada		51,240
20				
21	Grand Total			

Strategy: Sum all of the cells, including the subtotals. Divide this answer by 2 In Figure 700, the formula is =SUM(D2:D20)/2.

Figure 700

Sum the detail rows and the subtotal rows, but divide by 2.

D21			fx	=SUM(D2:D20)/2	

▲	A	B	C	D	E
1	Acct	Customer	Invoice	Revenue	
2	A4368	Ainsworth	1014	10,445	
3	A4368	Ainsworth	1015	15,544	
4	A4368	Ainsworth	1030	3,922	
5	A4368	Ainsworth	1054	12,838	
6	A4368	Ainsworth	1091	17,712	
7		Total Ainsworth		60,461	
8					
9	A3108	Air Canada	1057	5,859	
10	A3108	Air Canada	1061	2,358	
11	A3108	Air Canada	1090	17,856	
12	A3108	Air Canada	1108	4,948	
13		Total Air Canada		31,021	
14					
15	B4504	Bell Canada	1013	15,104	
16	B4504	Bell Canada	1069	18,072	
17	B4504	Bell Canada	1074	14,004	
18	B4504	Bell Canada	1077	4,060	
19		Total Bell Canada		51,240	
20					
21	Grand Total			142,722	
22					

This method works! It is an old accounting trick (taught to me by an old accountant). It is not intuitive, especially if you hated algebra. Try it for yourself a few times, comparing the results to the method of using =D19+D13+D7. You will see that you get the same result.

Gotcha: This method works only if all the customers are totaled. A manager who doesn't know how to use subtotals might be the kind of manager who doesn't total the customers with only one detail line. For example, in Figure 701, line 9 will cause the total to not work.

Figure 701

If someone is manually adding totals, he might not add a redundant total for row 9.

	D23			f_x	=SUM(D2:D22)/2	
◢	A	B	C	D	E
1	Acct	Customer	Invoice	Revenue	
2	A4368	Ainsworth	1014	10,445	
3	A4368	Ainsworth	1015	15,544	
4	A4368	Ainsworth	1030	3,922	
5	A4368	Ainsworth	1054	12,838	
6	A4368	Ainsworth	1091	17,712	
7		Total Ainsworth		60,461	
8					
9	A9875	Aironet	1040	(17,250)	
10					
11	A3108	Air Canada	1057	5,859	
12	A3108	Air Canada	1061	2,358	
13	A3108	Air Canada	1090	17,856	
14	A3108	Air Canada	1108	4,948	
15		Total Air Canada		31,021	
16					
17	B4504	Bell Canada	1013	15,104	
18	B4504	Bell Canada	1069	18,072	
19	B4504	Bell Canada	1074	14,004	
20	B4504	Bell Canada	1077	4,060	
21		Total Bell Canada		51,240	
22					
23	Grand Total			151,347	
24					

Summary: =SUM()/2 is a great method for quickly determining the totals of a data set with "manual" subtotals.

Functions Discussed: =SUM()

WHY DO SUBTOTALS COME OUT AS COUNTS?

Problem: I added automatic subtotals to the data set shown in Figure 702. The subtotals of four for Air Canada and five for Ainsworth are clearly not correct. What went wrong?

Figure 702

These totals are pretty low. Excel decided to count instead of sum.

◢	A	B	C	D	E
1	Acct	Customer	Invoice	Revenue	Rep
2	A3108	Air Canada	1057	5,859	Joe
3	A3108	Air Canada	1061	2,358	Joe
4	A3108	Air Canada	1090	17,856	Joe
5	A3108	Air Canada	1108	4,948	Joe
6	**A3108 Count**			4	
7	A4368	Ainsworth	1014	10,445	Mary
8	A4368	Ainsworth	1015	15,544	Mary
9	A4368	Ainsworth	1030	3,922	Mary
10	A4368	Ainsworth	1054	12,838	Mary
11	A4368	Ainsworth	1091	17,712	Mary
12	**A4368 Count**			5	

Strategy: The first time you subtotal a data set, Excel assumes that you want to subtotal the final column in the data set. If that column contains text data, then the Subtotal dialog will default to a COUNT function instead of a SUM function, as shown in Figure 703. (This problem will also happen even if your final column contains mostly numbers but includes one blank cell.)

Figure 703

Because the rightmost column is text, Excel chooses to count.

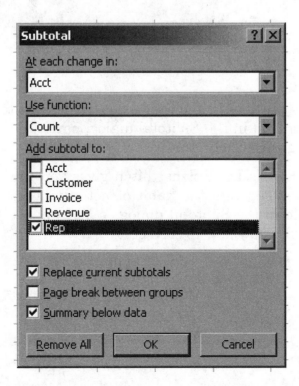

To correct this problem when it occurs, you select Data – Subtotal to open the Subtotal dialog. As shown in Figure 704, you change the Use Function dropdown from Count to Sum. Then you click OK.

Figure 704

Remember that if you are unchecking the right-most column because it is a text field that can't be totaled, you should visit the Use Function dropdown.

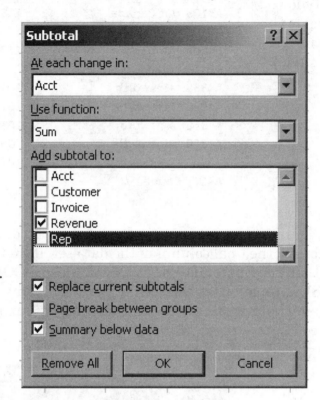

To avoid this problem in the first place, remember to double-check the Use Function field in the Subtotal dialog, particularly if your data has text in the rightmost column.

Summary: Excel's IntelliSense often gives you the correct choices, so you may get lulled into the habit of not paying attention to the Use Function field in the Subtotal dialog. When you see Counts instead of Sums, you will know how to correct it.

Commands Discussed: Data – Subtotal

SUBTOTAL MANY COLUMNS AT ONCE

Problem: As shown in Figure 705, I have data with 12 months going across the columns. I need to add subtotals to all 12 columns.

Figure 705

You want to subtotal all the monthly columns.

	A	B	C	D	E	F
1	Rep	Customer	Jan	Feb	Mar	Apr
2	Bob	Bell Canada	20,992	9,970	57,797	49,839
3	Bob	Compton Petroleum	72,030	27,714	22,737	48,059
4	Bob	Exxon	13,438	65,812	10,137	52,216
5	Bob	Sears	58,901	15,112	12,576	2,960
6	Bob	Texaco	4,937	56,399	42,673	8,706
7	Bob	Verizon	74,173	69,724	26,459	2,303
8	Joe	Air Canada	43,097	53,369	58,981	52,386

Strategy: You can subtotal all of the columns at once. Here's how:

1) In the Subtotal dialog, use the scrollbar on the Add Subtotal To box to scroll through all fields. In Excel 2007, you can see six fields at a time. In prior versions of Excel, you can see only three fields at a time. Check the final six fields, Jul through Dec, as shown in Figure 706.

Figure 706

Choose as many fields as you can see.

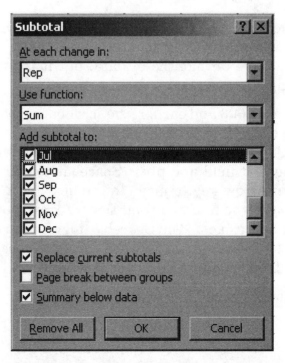

2)   Scroll up to show the fields at the top of the list, as shown in Figure 707.

Figure 707

Scroll up to see the remaining fields.

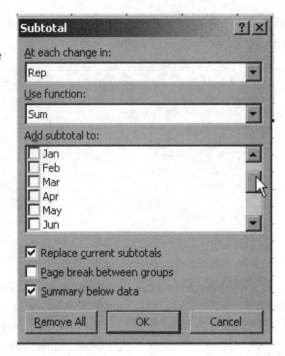

3)   Check these fields. Continue this routine, scrolling to reveal more fields and then checking them all. This gets particularly tedious when you have 36 months of data, but it is still infinitely faster than doing subtotals manually.

Gotcha: In Excel 2003 and earlier, the scrollbar is too small to be useful, so you end up clicking three fields and then clicking the up scroll arrow three times. Checking n fields requires $(n*2)-3$ clicks. A faster method is to select the first field and press Spacebar to add a check mark and then the Down Arrow key to move to the next field. If you can quickly alternate between the Spacebar and Down Arrow, you can select all the fields in $(n*2)$ keystrokes. (The Spacebar toggles the checkmark on and off. Instead, the Plus sign will always turn the checkmark on and the minus sign will always turn the checkmark off.)

Result: Subtotals are added to all the columns at once, as shown in Figure 708.

Figure 708

Subtotals are added to all the fields at once.

1 2 3		A	B	C	D	E	F
	1	Rep	Customer	Jan	Feb	Mar	Apr
	2	Bob	Bell Canada	20,992	9,970	57,797	49,839
	3	Bob	Compton Petroleum	72,030	27,714	22,737	48,059
	4	Bob	Exxon	13,438	65,812	10,137	52,216
	5	Bob	Sears	58,901	15,112	12,576	2,960
	6	Bob	Texaco	4,937	56,399	42,673	8,706
	7	Bob	Verizon	74,173	69,724	26,459	2,303
	8	**Bob Total**		244,471	244,731	172,379	164,083
	9	Joe	Air Canada	43,097	53,369	58,981	52,386
	10	Joe	Compaq	25,991	56,623	65,028	32,723
	11	Joe	Ford	47,662	30,635	58,536	29,054
	12	Joe	Sun Life Financial	42,172	43,469	30,493	17,100
	13	**Joe Total**		158,922	184,096	213,038	131,263

Alternate Strategy: In one of my power seminars, someone had a data set with 168 columns to be totaled (one column for each hour in a week). It took forever to check all the columns. I sent a note to David Gainer on the Excel team that a "Select All" button would be extremely useful in Excel 14. But, in the meantime, you can use this method:

1) Add subtotals to the final column. This should involve three clicks: Data – Subtotal – OK.

2) Use the 2 Group & Outline button to collapse to only the subtotal rows.

3) Copy the first subtotal from the first row and paste it to all the other columns. In Figure 709, this would involve clicking FN13 and pressing Ctrl+C, Left Arrow, End key, Shift+Left Arrow, Shift+Right Arrow, Shift+Right Arrow, Ctrl+V.

Figure 709

Copy the row 13 final subtotal to all the other columns.

	FN13			f_x	=SUBTOTAL(9,FN2:FN12)

1 2 3		FJ	FK	FL	FM	FN	FO
	1	Hour 164	Hour 165	Hour 166	Hour 167	Hour 168	
+	13					1589.4	
+	23					1392.5	
+	32					1145.6	
+	40					1060.2	

4) After the paste, you should have 167 subtotals selected in a contiguous range going across one row. If you are extremely lucky, there would be other subtotals that are totalling exactly 11 rows. You could then press Ctrl+C to copy the 167 subtotals and paste to

any other subtotal rows in the data that have the exact same number of detail rows. However, since it is unlikely that you will find many summary rows that work out with exactly the same number of detail rows, you will probably need to use Step 5 instead.

5) Repeat Step 3 for each of the remaining rows. This works fine with a dozen subtotal lines. It is too time consuming for hundreds of subtotal rows.

The result will be totals as shown in Figure 710.

Figure 710

This method requires a copy and paste for each subtotal row.

C23			f_x	=SUBTOTAL(9,C14:C22)		
	A	B	C	D	E	F
1	Region	Meter	Hour 1	Hour 2	Hour 3	Hour
13	**R1 Total**		1747.3	1668.4	1624.9	14
14	R10	M10695	116.1	167.2	163.9	1
15	R10	M27357	153.9	143.5	145.1	1
16	R10	M63440	194.5	106.4	105.5	1
17	R10	M46025	165.9	125.5	138.2	1
18	R10	M44668	157.9	176.1	168	1
19	R10	M83735	127.6	138.3	196	1
20	R10	M40725	184.7	103.8	137.6	
21	R10	M69320	134.2	113	164.3	1
22	R10	M31993	169.5	145.9	116.4	1
23	**R10 Total**		1404.3	1219.7	1335	13
24	R11	M37922	109	185.6	180.5	1
25	R11	M47211	102.2	132.4	185.4	1
26	R11	M13806	131.2	146.4	196.8	1
27	R11	M74194	176.9	142.5	137.5	1
28	R11	M49748	137.4	166.8	149.4	1
29	R11	M41715	125.8	150.3	103.5	
30	R11	M82887	167.4	127	102.2	1
31	R11	M20238	171	125.1	192.8	1
32	**R11 Total**		1120.9	1176.1	1248.1	9

Although it is tempting to select the visible cells from column FN and to paste those to the visible cells in C23:FM173, doing so will fail. You cannot copy a noncontiguous range and paste it to a larger set of noncontiguous cells. (see Figure 711)

Figure 711

Pasting non-contiguous cells gives this error.

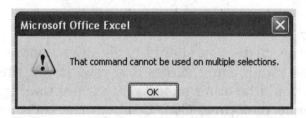

Microsoft Office Excel

⚠ That command cannot be used on multiple selections.

[OK]

Although I don't usually cover VBA macros in this book, this is a very annoying problem where the solution can be much easier by using a one-line VBA macro to perform Step 3 in a single click:

Selection.Copy Destination:=Selection.Offset(0, -167).Resize(1,167)

Summary: You can add subtotals to many columns in one pass of the Subtotal command. The downside is that the Excel Subtotal dialog lets you check only a few fields before you have to use the scrollbar. If you have an incredibly wide column to subtotal, use the technique described in the Alternate Strategy to add one subtotal and then copy across.

Commands Discussed: Data – Subtotal; Home – Find & Select – Go To Special – Visible Cells Only; Alt+;

Excel 97-2003: Edit – Go To – Special

ADD SUBTOTALS ABOVE THE DATA

Part III

Problem: My manager insists that subtotals for each rep appear above the data. There doesn't appear to be any hope of the manager being reassigned to Minsk soon.

Strategy: Luckily, someone on the Excel team at Microsoft must have worked for your manager once. There is a setting on the Subtotal dialog to move the totals to the top of the section being subtotaled.

As shown in Figure 712, in the Subtotal dialog, you uncheck the Summary Below Data box.

Figure 712

Uncheck Summary Below Data.

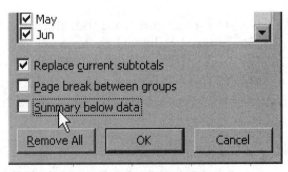

Results: As shown in Figure 713, the grand total now appears at the top of the data set, and the subtotal for each manager appears before the records for that manager.

Figure 713

Subtotals appear above the data.

C3		fx	=SUBTOTAL(9,C4:C9)	
	A	B	C	D
1	Rep	Customer	Jan	Feb
2	Grand Total		616,468	575,631
3	Bob Total		244,471	244,731
4	Bob	Bell Canada	20,992	9,970
5	Bob	Compton Petroleum	72,030	27,714
6	Bob	Exxon	13,438	65,812
7	Bob	Sears	58,901	15,112
8	Bob	Texaco	4,937	56,399
9	Bob	Verizon	74,173	69,724
10	Joe Total		158,922	184,096
11	Joe	Air Canada	43,097	53,369
12	Joe	Compaq	25,991	56,623

Summary: You can easily use the Subtotal dialog to add subtotals above each section being subtotaled.

Commands Discussed: Data – Subtotal

ADD OTHER TEXT TO THE SUBTOTAL LINES

Problem: My data set has account number in column A and a customer name in column B. When I subtotal by account and collapse using the 2 Group & Outline button, I see only the Account numbers, as shown in Figure 714. While I have memorized that B4504 is Bell Canada, my manager cannot seem to remember this, so I need to add the customer name to the subtotal lines.

Figure 714

Add customer name to the subtotal rows.

1 2 3		A	B	C	D
	1	Acct	Customer	Invoice	Revenue
+	6	A3108 Total			31,021
+	12	A4368 Total			60,461
+	17	B4504 Total			51,240
+	22	C4904 Total			39,250

Strategy: To add the customer name to the subtotal lines, you follow these steps:

1) Collapse the report by clicking the small 2 Group & Outline button above and to the left of cell A1.

2) Select all the blank cells in column B by using the mouse to drag from B6 down to the cell above the Grand Total row. In doing so, you will select all the cells in the range B6:B136.

3) Because you actually need to select just the blanks, select Home – Find & Select – Go To Special and in the Go To Special dialog, select Visible Cells Only and click OK (see Figure 715). The result will be imperceptible in Excel 2007. In prior versions, you could see narrow white bands between the dark blue highlighting. In Excel 2007, the highlighting is so light that the fine white lines are barely visible. (Note that you can use Alt+; to replace this step.)

Figure 715

Selecting Visible Cells Only will give you the cells on each total row.

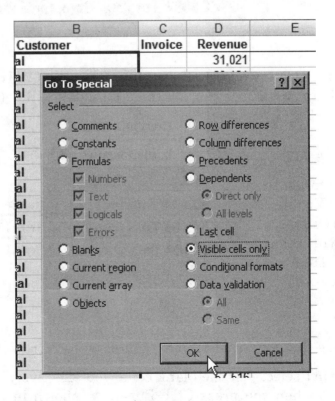

Part III

4) Note the row number of your first subtotal row. In this example, the first subtotal is row 6, and you will write a formula to copy the

total from row 5. Change the cell reference in the following formula to point to the row above the subtotal row: ="Total "&B5. To enter a similar formula in every selected cell, press Ctrl+Enter. Your worksheet should look like the one shown in Figure 716. (Note: If you use the Lotus formula technique, you can type this formula in three keystrokes: the equals sign, the Up Arrow key, and Ctrl+Enter.)

Figure 716

Add a customer name to each subtotal row.

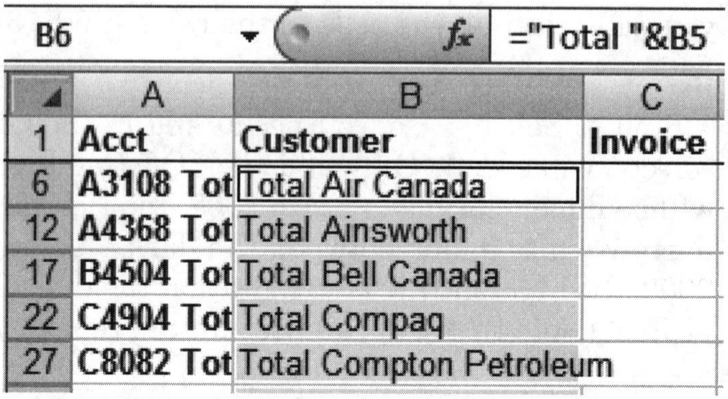

	A	B	C
1	Acct	Customer	Invoice
6	A3108 Tot	Total Air Canada	
12	A4368 Tot	Total Ainsworth	
17	B4504 Tot	Total Bell Canada	
22	C4904 Tot	Total Compaq	
27	C8082 Tot	Total Compton Petroleum	

B6   fx   ="Total "&B5

Gotcha: Selecting Visible Cells Only from the Go To Special dialog is radically important. If you fail to do this, you will get the result shown in Figure 717.

Figure 717

If you forget to select Visible Cells Only, you will see Total Total Total Total.

	A	B	C
1	Acct	Customer	Invoice
6	A3108 Tota	Total Air Canada	
12	A4368 Tota	Total Total Total Total Total Total	
17	B4504 Tota	Total Total Total Total Total Total	

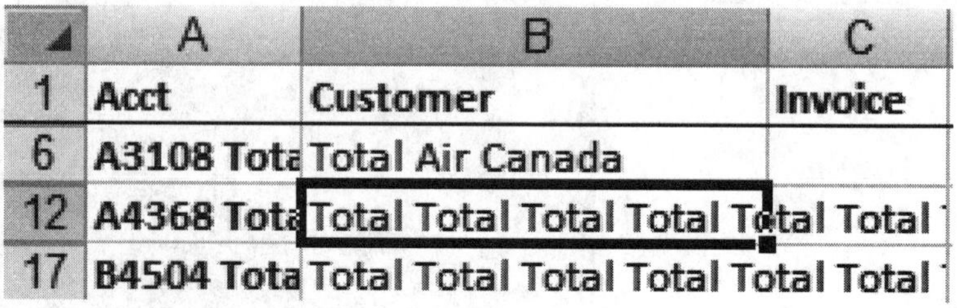

If you see this, you need to immediately press Ctrl+Z to undo.

If you don't select just the blank cells, you effectively overwrite the hidden rows when you press Ctrl+Enter. As shown in Figure 718, if you unhide the detail rows, you will see that you've accidentally entered the formula in all the detail rows and overwritten the customer names.

Figure 718

Expand the data to see that you've overwritten the customer names.

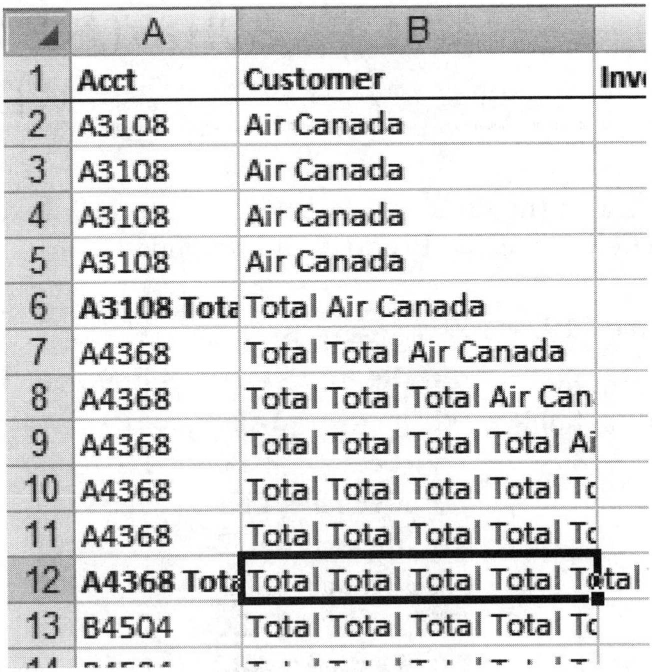

	A	B	
1	Acct	Customer	Inv
2	A3108	Air Canada	
3	A3108	Air Canada	
4	A3108	Air Canada	
5	A3108	Air Canada	
6	A3108 Tot:	Total Air Canada	
7	A4368	Total Total Air Canada	
8	A4368	Total Total Total Air Can	
9	A4368	Total Total Total Total Ai	
10	A4368	Total Total Total Total Tc	
11	A4368	Total Total Total Total Tc	
12	A4368 Tot:	Total Total Total Total Total	
13	B4504	Total Total Total Total Tc	

Part III

Summary: Selecting Visible Cells Only on the Go To Special dialog is an effective method for adding data to the subtotal rows. It would be a lot better if Excel allowed you to write an SQL-like query, such as Select First(Customer), but for now, the Visible Cells Only technique option does the trick.

Commands Discussed: Home – Find & Select – Go To Special – Visible Cells Only; Data – Subtotal

CREATE SUBTOTALS BY PRODUCT
WITHIN REGION

Problem: In the data set shown in Figure 719, I want to add subtotals by two fields, such as Product and Region.

Figure 719

Subtotal by multiple fields.

	A	B	C	D
1	Region	Product	Invoice	Revenue
2	Central	ABC	1064	67357
3	Central	ABC	1075	60248
4	Central	DEF	1067	6497
5	Central	XYZ	1052	48370
6	Central	XYZ	1070	55612
7	East	ABC	1053	65770
8	East	ABC	1056	33875
9	East	ABC	1068	21977

Strategy: Adding subtotals by two fields seems easy, but there is a trick to it. You need to add subtotals to the less detailed field first. Here's how it works:

1) Sort by product within region. You can do this with two sorts: Select cell B1. Click the AZ icon on the home ribbon tab. Select cell A1. Click the AZ icon on the home ribbon tab. The two sort method requires four mouse clicks. You could also choose Data – Sort and set up two sort levels. This method requires only one sort, but several more clicks.

2) Select Data – Subtotal and add a subtotal by region.

3) Select Data – Subtotal again. Change Region to Product. Be sure to uncheck the Replace Current Subtotals box, as shown in Figure 720.

Figure 720

Uncheck Replace Current Subtotals.

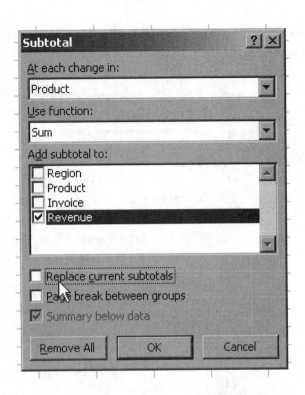

Results: You now have two sets of subtotals. As shown in Figure 721, there are now four Group & Outline buttons to the left of cell A1.

Figure 721

Excel adds two levels of subtotals.

	Region	Product	Invoice	Revenue
1	**Region**	**Product**	**Invoice**	**Revenue**
2	Central	ABC	1064	67357
3	Central	ABC	1075	60248
4		**ABC Total**		127605
5	Central	DEF	1067	6497
6		**DEF Total**		6497
7	Central	XYZ	1052	48370
8	Central	XYZ	1070	55612
9		**XYZ Total**		103982
10	**Central Total**			238084
11	East	ABC	1053	65770
12	East	ABC	1056	33875
13	East	ABC	1068	21977
14		**ABC Total**		121622

Part
III

If you choose the 3 Group & Outline button, you will have totals by region and product, as shown in Figure 722.

Figure 722

The 3 Group & Outline button shows sales by product within region.

	A	B	C	D
1	Region	Product	Invoice	Revenue
4		ABC Total		127605
6		DEF Total		6497
9		XYZ Total		103982
10	Central Total			238084
14		ABC Total		121622
18		DEF Total		32013
22		XYZ Total		92780
23	East Total			246415
28		XYZ Total		140537
29	Govt Total			140537
33		ABC Total		152667
37		DEF Total		86703
39		XYZ Total		46644
40	West Total			286014
41	Grand Total			911050

If you choose the 2 Group & Outline button, you will have totals by region, as shown in Figure 723.

Figure 723

Click the 2 Group & Outline button to hide the product totals.

	A	B	C	D
1	Region	Product	Invoice	Revenue
10	Central Total			238084
23	East Total			246415
29	Govt Total			140537
40	West Total			286014
41	Grand Total			911050

Additional Details: Here is why it is important to do the subtotals in the correct order: Say that your company sells three products. The Government region buys only product XYZ. You might have data that looks like the data in Figure 724. Note that row 15 contains an XYZ record for the East, and row 16 contains an XYZ record for the Government region.

Figure 724

Rows 15 and 16 have the same product, but they belong to different regions.

12	East	DEF	1066	2247
13	East	XYZ	1054	69552
14	East	XYZ	1055	4358
15	East	XYZ	1072	18870
16	Govt	XYZ	1063	33118
17	Govt	XYZ	1065	35401

If you subtotal by product first, the XYZ products from the East and the Government regions will be trapped in one subtotal in row 25, as shown in Figure 725. This is an absolute mess.

Figure 725

Subtotal by product first, and Excel has no idea that you will later subtotal by region.

16	East	DEF	1066	2247
17		**DEF Total**		32013
18	East	XYZ	1054	69552
19	East	XYZ	1055	4358
20	East	XYZ	1072	18870
21	Govt	XYZ	1063	33118
22	Govt	XYZ	1065	35401
23	Govt	XYZ	1071	17927
24	Govt	XYZ	1073	54091
25		**XYZ Total**		233317

Part III

If you then total by region, you will have set up groups that make no sense. Note that the XYZ total in D32 includes both Govt and East records, as shown in Figure 726.

Figure 726

Chaos ensues.

18	East	DEF	1057	20200
19	East	DEF	1059	9566
20	East	DEF	1066	2247
21	**East Total**			32013
22		**DEF Total**		32013
23	East	XYZ	1054	69552
24	East	XYZ	1055	4358
25	East	XYZ	1072	18870
26	**East Total**			92780
27	Govt	XYZ	1063	33118
28	Govt	XYZ	1065	35401
29	Govt	XYZ	1071	17927
30	Govt	XYZ	1073	54091
31	**Govt Total**			140537
32		**XYZ Total**		=SUBTOTAL(9,D23:D30)
33	West	ABC	1058	64782

Additional Details: In Excel 95, there was no workaround for this problem. In Excel 97, Microsoft added the rule that XYZ rows separated by a blank row would be handled correctly. Thus, you need to add subtotals by region first.

Summary: You can create very powerful summary reports by using two sets of subtotals. Remember to subtotal the outer grouping first and then the inner subtotals. On the second and subsequent calls to the Subtotal command, remember to uncheck the Replace Current Subtotals option.

Commands Discussed: Data – Subtotal

MY MANAGER WANTS THE SUBTOTAL LINES IN BOLD PINK CAMBRIA FONT

Problem: My manager loves my reports with automatic subtotals. Now he wants the subtotal lines formatted in bold pink Cambria 15-point font. Again, there is no hope for the manager to be transferred soon.

Strategy: Anonymously send your manager copies of job postings for other departments. In the meantime, follow these steps to please him:

1) Add subtotals to the data set.

2) Click the 2 Group & Outline button to display only the subtotals.

3) Select all data except the headings. In Figure 727, this would mean dragging the mouse from A8 to N20.

Figure 727

Select the sub-total lines.

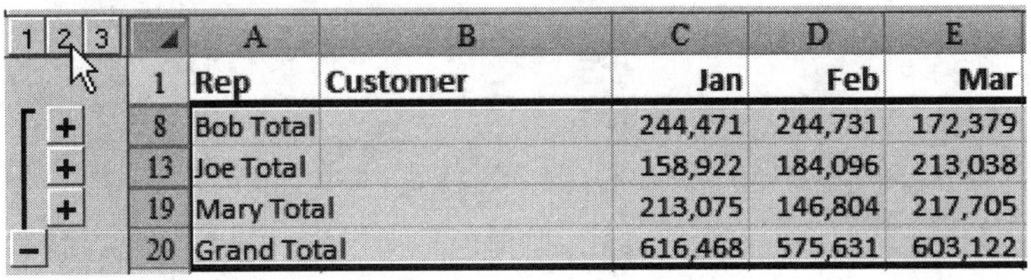

	A	B	C	D	E
	Rep	Customer	Jan	Feb	Mar
8	Bob Total		244,471	244,731	172,379
13	Joe Total		158,922	184,096	213,038
19	Mary Total		213,075	146,804	217,705
20	Grand Total		616,468	575,631	603,122

4) Select Home – Find & Select – Go To Special, and from the Go To Special dialog, select Visible Cells Only and click OK. (You can use Alt+; as the shortcut for Visible Cells Only.)

Part III

Results: You will have selected only the total rows. You can now make any formatting changes necessary to make your boss happy (see Figure 728).

Figure 728

After you select Only Visible Cells, any formatting changes affect only the visible cells.

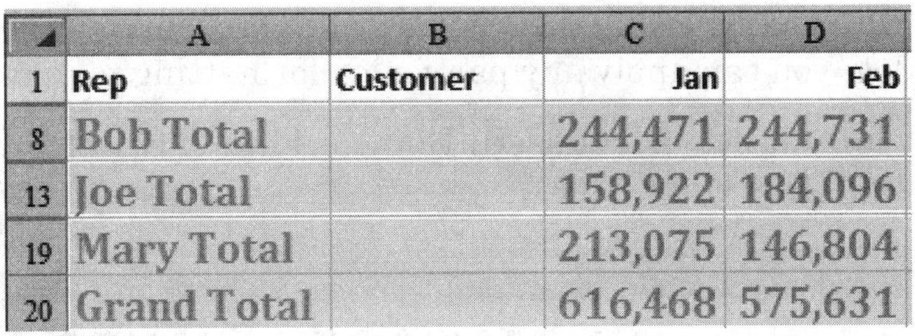

	A	B	C	D
1	Rep	Customer	Jan	Feb
8	Bob Total		244,471	244,731
13	Joe Total		158,922	184,096
19	Mary Total		213,075	146,804
20	Grand Total		616,468	575,631

When you click the 3 Group & Outline button, only the subtotal rows will have the desired formatting, as shown in Figure 729.

Figure 729

You've applied the desired effect.

Bob	Texaco	4,937
Bob	Verizon	74,173
Bob Total		**244,471**
Joe	Air Canada	43,097
Joe	Compaq	25,991
Joe	Ford	47,662
Joe	Sun Life Financi	42,172
Joe Total		**158,922**
Mary	Ainsworth	6,475
Mary	Chevron	72,587
Mary	Sears Canada	69,013
Mary	SBC Communica	18,244
Mary	Shell Canada	46,756
Mary Total		**213,075**
Grand Total		**616,468**

Summary: Using the Visible Cells Only option of the Go To Special dialog, you can apply any particular formatting to just the subtotal rows.

Commands Discussed: Home – Find & Select – Go To Special – Visible Cells Only; Alt+;

MY MANAGER WANTS A BLANK LINE AFTER EACH SUBTOTAL

Problem: My manager wants me to add a blank line between sections of a subtotal report.

Strategy: This is a fairly standard request. Quite simply, data looks better when it is formatted this way. But there is no built-in way to do this with Excel. I've tried many methods. There are two methods that will work here. One method is simpler but is really cheating; you only make it look like you added a blank row. The second method is convoluted but about 50% easier than the method I described in the previous edition of this book.

The first method is to try to fool the manager by making the total rows double height, with the totals vertically aligned to the top. This method may work if you are printing the report to give to the manager. It will give the appearance that a blank row has been inserted. Here's how you do it:

1) To do this easily, follow the steps in "My Manager Wants the Subtotal Lines in Bold Pink Cambria Font": Add subtotals, collapse to level 2, and select all subtotal rows from the first subtotal to the last subtotal. (see Figure 730)

Figure 730

Select the subtotal rows.

	1 2 3		A	B	C	D
		1	Rep	Customer	Jan	Feb
+		8	Bob Total		244,471	244,731
+		13	Joe Total		158,922	184,096
+		19	Mary Total		213,075	146,804
−		20	Grand Total		616,468	575,631

2) Select Home – Find & Select – Go To Special, and from the Go To Special dialog, select Visible Cells Only and click OK. (You can use Alt+; as the shortcut for Visible Cells Only.)

3) Select Home – Format dropdown – Row Height. Depending on your font, the row height will probably be between 12 and 14. Say that the height is 12.75. Mentally multiply by 2 and type 25.5 as the new height.

4) In the Home tab of the ribbon, click the Align Top icon.

5) Choose the 3 Group & Outline button to display the detail rows again.

Part III

Figure 731 shows the result. Although you can see that there is no blank row after the subtotals in rows 8 and 13, when you print the report for your manager, it will appear to have a blank row, as shown in Figure 732.

Figure 731

There is not a blank row between rows 8 and 9.

5	Bob	Sears
6	Bob	Texaco
7	Bob	Verizon
	Bob Total	
8		
9	Joe	Air Canada
10	Joe	Compaq
11	Joe	Ford
12	Joe	Sun Life Financial
	Joe Total	
13		
14	Mary	Ainsworth
15	Mary	Chevron

Figure 732

When you print the document, it will appear as if there is a blank row.

Rep	Customer	Jan
Bob	Bell Canada	20,992
Bob	Compton Petroleum	72,030
Bob	Exxon	13,438
Bob	Sears	58,901
Bob	Texaco	4,937
Bob	Verizon	74,173
Bob Total		244,471
Joe	Air Canada	43,097
Joe	Compaq	25,991
Joe	Ford	47,662
Joe	Sun Life Financial	42,172
Joe Total		158,922
Mary	Ainsworth	6,475

This method will not work if you have to send the data set to the manager via e-mail. The manager may be smart enough to want to stop at each subtotal by pressing the End key, and this will not work with the double-height rows.

Alternate Strategy: This method is far more complex than the one just described but creates the desired result. Follow these steps:

1) Add subtotals as described previously. Click the 2 Group & Outline button.

2) Insert a new temporary blank column A to the left of the current column A. To do this, select any cell in column A and then choose Home – Insert – Insert Sheet Columns.

3) Select the cells in column A from the first subtotal down to the last subtotal, as shown in Figure 733.

Figure 733

Select the blank cells next to the subtotal rows.

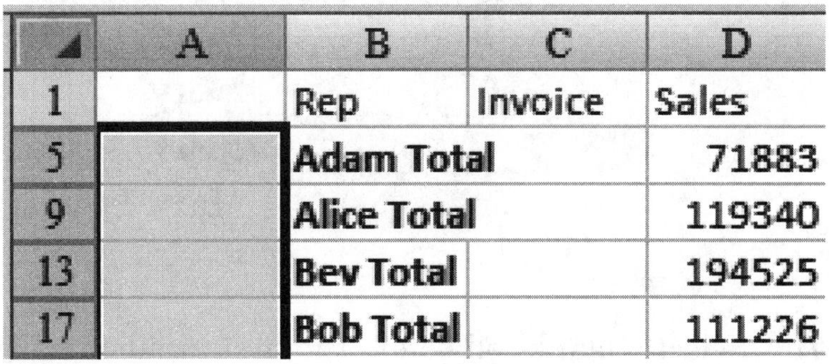

	A	B	C	D
1		Rep	Invoice	Sales
5		Adam Total		71883
9		Alice Total		119340
13		Bev Total		194525
17		Bob Total		111226

Part III

4) Select Home – Find & Select – Go To Special, and from the Go To Special dialog, select Visible Cells Only and click OK. (You can use Alt+; as the shortcut for Visible Cells Only.)

5) Type 1 and press Ctrl+Enter to put a 1 next to every subtotal.

6) Click the 3 Group & Outline button to see all the detail rows. If you did step 4 correctly, you will see a 1 on only the subtotal lines, as shown in Figure 734.

Figure 734

You've added a 1 next to each subtotal.

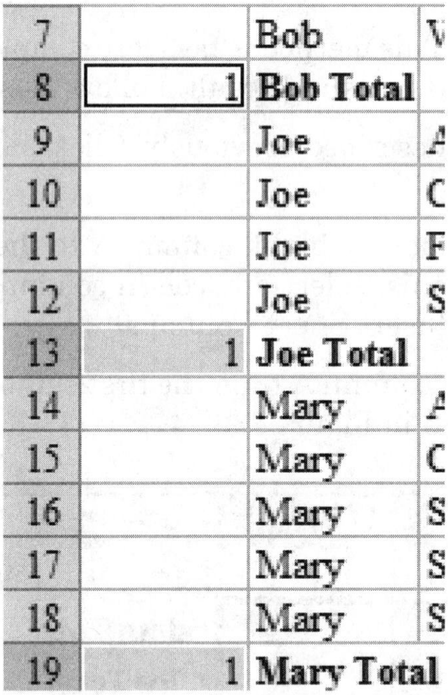

7		Bob	V
8	1	**Bob Total**	
9		Joe	A
10		Joe	C
11		Joe	F
12		Joe	S
13	1	**Joe Total**	
14		Mary	A
15		Mary	C
16		Mary	S
17		Mary	S
18		Mary	S
19	1	**Mary Total**	

7) Select a blank cell before the first number 1. This would be the cell in row 7 in Figure 734. From the Home tab, select the Insert drop-down – Insert Cells – Shift Cells Down – OK. This will move the 1's from the subtotal lines to the first row of each customer.

8) Select all of Column A. Select Home – Find & Select – Go To Special and select Constants in the Go To Special dialog, as shown in Figure 735.

Figure 735

Select just the 1s by selecting Constants on the Go To Special dialog.

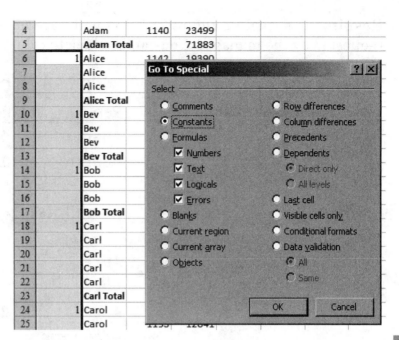

9) Select Home – Insert dropdown – Insert Sheet Rows, as shown in Figure 736. Excel will insert 1 row above each row in your selection. Through the combination of steps 7 and 8, you were able to make a selection that consisted of each cell underneath the subtotals. Inserting a new row above these cells creates the result.

Figure 736

Insert a row above each cell in the selection.

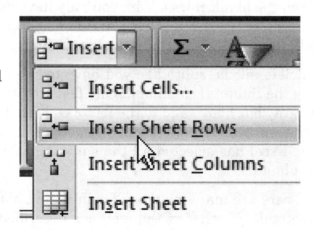

Results: As shown in Figure 737, you will have added the blank rows requested by the manager. You can now delete column A.

Figure 737

Delete column A, and you are done.

◢	A	B	C	D
1		Rep	Invoice	Sales
2		Adam	1096	14511
3		Adam	1114	33873
4		Adam	1140	23499
5		Adam Total		71883
6				
7	1	Alice	1142	19390
8		Alice	1193	53766
9		Alice	1215	46184
10		Alice Total		119340
11				
12	1	Bev	1180	69506
13		Bev	1197	71264

Gotcha: When the blank rows are in, you may have a difficult time getting rid of the subtotals. If you select cell A2 and choose Data – Subtotal – Remove All, Excel will delete only the first subtotal.

In order to delete all the subtotals, you have to select the entire range before calling the Subtotal command. One fast way to do this is to click on the blank gray box above and to the left of cell A1. This box will select all cells in the worksheet. Now when you choose Data – Subtotal, you will find that Excel has selected all the subtotals. Click Remove All to remove the subtotals.

Summary: There are many methods for inserting blank rows between groups of subtotals. Neither of the methods described here is very appealing. Though this fairly common request is relatively difficult, with practice you will find the last method can be accomplished quickly.

Commands Discussed: Home – Align Top; Home – Format – Row Height; Insert – Column; Home – Find & Select Go To Special; Home – Insert – Insert Sheet Rows; Data – Subtotal – Remove All; Home – Find & Select – Go To Special – Visible Cells Only; Alt+;

Excel 97-2003: Format – Cells – Alignment – Vertical Align – Top; Edit – Go To Special; Insert – Row

SUBTOTAL ONE COLUMN AND SUBAVERAGE ANOTHER COLUMN

Problem: In the data set in Figure 738, I want to create a subtotal of revenue. It does not make sense to subtotal the unit prices in column C. It might make sense to create an average price for each rep.

Figure 738

Total revenue and average price.

◢	A	B	C	D
1	Rep	Invoice	Price	Revenue
2	Adam	1096	4.17	14,511
3	Adam	1114	4.56	33,873
4	Adam	1140	4.83	23,499
5	Alice	1142	4.98	19,390
6	Alice	1193	4.31	53,766
7	Alice	1215	4.36	46,184
8	Bev	1180	4.56	69,506
9	Bev	1197	4.86	71,264
10	Bev	1226	4.81	53,755
11	Bob	1113	4.71	11,930

Part III

Strategy: When you add subtotals to a data set, you use the SUBTO-TAL function. In Figure 739, for example, the formula automatically added to cell D5 is =SUBTOTAL(9,D2:D4).

Figure 739

For totals, the SUBTOTAL function uses a first argument of 9.

fx	=SUBTOTAL(9,D2:D4)		

	A	B	C	D
1	Rep	Invoice	Price	Revenue
2	Adam	1096	4.17	14,511
3	Adam	1114	4.56	33,873
4	Adam	1140	4.83	23,499
5	**Adam Total**			71,883
6	Alice	1142	4.98	19,390
7	Alice	1193	4.31	53,766
8	Alice	1215	4.36	46,184
9	**Alice Total**			119,340

In this case, you need to remove that subtotal and add a subtotal that averages the Price column. You can do this by selecting Data – Subtotal to open the Subtotal dialog and changing the Use Function dropdown from Sum to Average.

Examine the formula entered in C5. Excel still uses the SUBTOTAL function, but the first parameter changes from a 9 to a 1, as shown in Figure 740.

Figure 740

For averages, the SUBTO-TAL function uses a first argument of 1.

=SUBTOTAL(1,C2:C4)			

		A	B	C	D
	1	Rep	Invoice	Price	Revenue
	2	Adam	1096	4.17	14,511
	3	Adam	1114	4.56	33,873
	4	Adam	1140	4.83	23,499
	5	**Adam Average**		4.52	
	6	Alice	1142	4.98	19,390

You can imagine that after creating the SUBTOTAL function, the team at Microsoft realized that it also needed SUBAVERAGE, SUBMIN, SUBMAX, and SUBCOUNT. Rather than create nine different functions, it created one function. The first parameter indicates whether Excel should average, sum, count, min, max, etc. This table shows the complete set of values.

Number	Function
1	AVERAGE
2	COUNT
3	COUNTA
4	MAX
5	MIN
6	PRODUCT
7	STDEV
8	STDEVP
9	SUM
10	VAR
11	VARP

You can see that Microsoft sequenced the functions alphabetically; that is why the most-often used function, SUM, is all the way at number 9.

Note: In Excel 2003 and later, Microsoft added 11 new function numbers, 101 through 111. They do the same functions as 1 through 11 but ignore hidden rows.

If you add a sum subtotal to Revenue, deselect Replace Current Subtotals and add an average subtotal to Price, the subtotals appear on two lines, as shown in Figure 741. This may not be what you want.

Figure 741

Adding subtotals twice causes each statistic to be on a different line.

	A	B	C	D
1	Rep	Invoice	Price	Revenue
2	Adam	1096	4.17	14,511
3	Adam	1114	4.56	33,873
4	Adam	1140	4.83	23,499
5	Adam Average		4.52	
6	Adam Total			71,883
7	Alice	1142	4.98	19,390
8	Alice	1193	4.31	53,766
9	Alice	1215	4.36	46,184
10	Alice Average		4.55	
11	Alice Total			119,340
12	Bev	1180	4.56	69,506

An alternate method is to add sum subtotals to both columns. The intermediate result will not make sense for the Price column. You select column C and then choose Home – Find & Select – Replace (or press Ctrl+H).

As shown in Figure 742, in the Find and Replace dialog, you specify that you want to change every occurrence of =SUBTOTAL(9, to =SUBTOTAL(1,.

Figure 742

Use Find and Replace to change the function argument in column C.

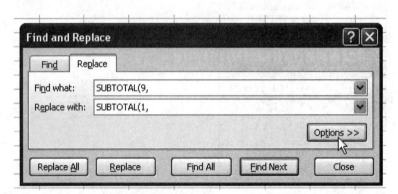

It is important that you select only column C before you replace; otherwise, you will replace the formulas in the Revenue column as well.

The Find and Replace dialog remembers settings from the last time it was used in the current Excel session. Some of the default settings in the Options button are appropriate in this case but might have been changed if you've done a Replace or a Find since you launched Excel. Therefore, you should click the Options button and make sure the Look In dropdown is set to Formulas. As shown in Figure 743, you should also make sure the Match Entire Cell Contents check box is unchecked.

Figure 743

Look In should be set to Formulas.

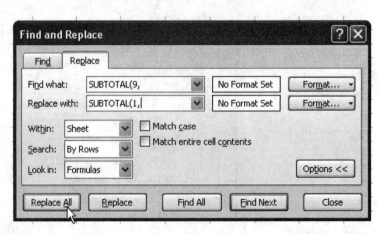

Click the Replace All button. Excel will confirm how many cells have been changed (see Figure 744). Note that in this case, a good reasonableness test is to check whether your company has 47 sales reps. (Or, 46 sales reps if you included the grand total row.)

Figure 744

Excel confirms how many changes were made.

Microsoft Office Excel ☒

ⓘ Excel has completed its search and has made 47 replacements.

OK

Results: As shown in Figure 745, Excel totals the revenue and averages the prices on the subtotal lines.

Figure 745

Average price and total revenue.

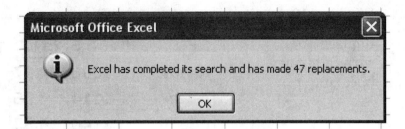

fx =SUBTOTAL(1,C2:C4)

	A	B	C	D
1	Rep	Invoice	Price	Revenue
2	Adam	1096	4.17	14,511
3	Adam	1114	4.56	33,873
4	Adam	1140	4.83	23,499
5	Adam Total		4.52	71,883
6	Alice	1142	4.98	19,390
7	Alice	1193	4.31	53,766
8	Alice	1215	4.36	46,184
9	Alice Total		4.55	119,340
10	Bev	1180	4.56	69,506

Additional Details: In Figure 745, note that the subtotal lines declare "Adam Total." This is technically incorrect because column C is an average and not a total. You could select column A and use Find & Replace to change every occurrence of Total to Summary, as shown in Figure 746.

Figure 746

Replace Total with Summary in column A.

◢	A	B	C	D
1	Rep	Invoice	Price	Revenue
2	Adam	1096	4.17	14,511
3	Adam	1114	4.56	33,873
4	Adam	1140	4.83	23,499
5	Adam Summary		4.52	71,883
6	Alice	1142	4.98	19,390
7	Alice	1193	4.31	53,766
8	Alice	1215	4.36	46,184
9	Alice Summary		4.55	119,340
10	Bev	1180	4.56	69,506

Gotcha: Be careful when using Home – Find & Select – Replace. It is unlikely that you have any sales reps with Subtotal in their names, but it is possible that you might have customers with "Sum" in their name. Be sure to select only the relevant columns or ranges before doing the Find and Replace. To avoid inadvertently changing "Summervilles" to "Averagemervilles," it helps to make sure that the text being changed is unique. You can usually do this by including the opening parenthesis in the original and changed text. Making sure to change SUM(to AVERAGE(, for example, is a simple but important step to prevent accidentally changing "summary" to "averagemary."

Summary: You can use Home – Find & Select – Replace to change the SUBTOTAL function from a sum to an average. This allows you to have one summary line per rep, with different types of subtotals.

Commands Discussed: Home – Find & Select – Replace; Data – Subtotal

Excel 97-2003: Edit – Replace; Data – Subtotals

Functions Discussed: =SUBTOTAL()

BE WARY

Problem: By using the tips in this book, I have found myself processing data faster than ever before. However, I've also begun to mess up data faster than ever before.

Strategy: It's important to save and save often. It's also a good idea to frequently check your data to make sure it's reasonable. For example, if you work for a company with $100 million in annual sales, a quarterly sales report should not show $200 billion in sales.

Try to figure out problems as soon as they happen. Excel is an incredibly logical program. Everything happens for a reason. If you can figure out the reason, you will master it in no time. Every "Gotcha" in this book represents a problem that has stung me in the past.

In 25 years of spreadsheet work, I have had only a few times when I could not find a logical explanation for something. If you are truly stumped, describe your situation on a message board such as the one at MrExcel. com. The odds are that someone else has seen the same problem and figured it out.

Part III

Summary: You need to be aware of your data processing steps and occasionally do a reasonableness test to make sure your data still looks right. You should also save frequently with different file names if you are doing something new that you are unsure of. This way, you can go back to the IncomeBeforeSubtotals.xls file if you think you have done something wrong.

SEND ERROR REPORTS

Problem: I keep getting a fatal error on a particular workbook.

Strategy: General Protection Faults (or GPFs) are the exceptions to what I said in "Be Wary" about Excel being an incredibly logical program. I can rarely figure out what is causing a GPF. Starting with Excel 2002, Excel has been much better at being able to recover from GPFs.

As shown in Figure 747, if Excel crashes and offers you the chance to report the problem, please do so: All you have to do is click Send Error Report. Millions of people are using Excel, and if everyone reports their errors, Microsoft will get a good statistical picture of the errors.

Figure 747

Send the error report to Microsoft.

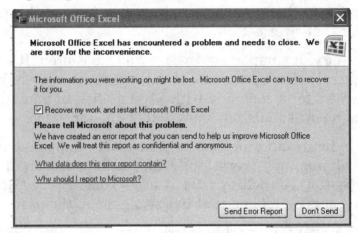

Sending an error report is particularly important if you are using a new version of the program or have recently installed a service pack.

If you keep getting a particular crash, check the Microsoft Knowledge Base. One version of Excel would crash about three steps after you had used the Edit – Find command in Excel. By the time I realized the trend, Microsoft had acknowledged the problem and offered a hotfix that was downloadable from the Knowledge Base.

After you send an error report, Excel will reopen and offer to load the last version of your workbook. You might also have the choice to open previously saved versions of the workbook.

There are certain things that I know will cause Excel to crash. For instance, in Excel 2003, I added a cell comment in the GPF.xls workbook and then ran a simple Excel macro to delete all the shapes on the worksheet. When I got the cell pointer near the red triangle in the commented cell, Excel tried to display the comment shape. Because the macro had already deleted the shape, Excel 2003 crashed with a GPF. I reported this error, and the behavior was fixed in Excel 2007, so this problem no longer causes a crash.

Sometimes, particularly in Excel 2000 and earlier versions, I would encounter spreadsheets that had simply become corrupt. I was able to open these worksheets, but if I tried to use File – Close or File – Save,

Excel would crash. I learned that the following sequence would save the data:

1)   Open the corrupt workbook.

2)   Create a new blank workbook.

3)   Copy data from the bad workbook to the new workbook.

4)   Use File – Save As to save the new workbook.

5)   Close the new workbook.

6)   Close the corrupt workbook, knowing it will crash. You can then use the saved version of the new workbook without having it crash.

Summary: Always report your crashes to Microsoft. If you keep getting a particular crash, check the Excel Knowledge Base to see if a hotfix is available.

HELP MAKE EXCEL 2009 BETTER

Part III

Problem: I have a few ideas about how I'd like Excel to operate differently. Other people must be having similar problems. How can I communicate my ideas to Microsoft?

Strategy: You actually have the ability to participate in a huge scientific study. In fact, if you have Excel 2003, you might have been participating for a while.

Say that you installed Excel 2003 on a Monday. On the third day that you used Excel, a question would appear: "Would you like to make Excel better?" If you answered yes on that day, then you are participating in the Customer Experience Improvement Program. Participants in this program allow Microsoft to track how they invoke commands. Microsoft will learn if you copy by using Ctrl+C, right-click – Copy, Home – Copy, or another method; it will track your actions, along with those of the millions of other people who signed up in Excel 2003, to create a database of 750 billion user experiences.

Before Excel 2007, Microsoft used a lot of conjecture about which commands were the most popular. In Excel 2007, it was able to query the database to find out exactly which commands are popular.

On the flip side, Microsoft can also use this data to prove that hardly anyone is using a command and can argue to take it out of a future product. But remember that with 500 million users, "hardly anyone" works out to a stadium full of people. Maybe only 0.01% of Excel 2003 customers used natural language formulas; but this works out to 50,000 people who will be angry to learn that the feature was removed from Excel 2007.

Additional Details: Did you ever use Wrap Text in Excel 2003? I did. Say that I had 10 columns of data, and 1 column had really long customer responses in column H. I would typically select this column and then select Format – Cells – Alignment – Wrap Text. However, I might then notice that all the data in A:G and I:J was set to vertical align bottom, making the data not line up with the now-wrapped text in column I. I would have to select A:G and then select Format – Cells – Alignment – Vertical – Top. In all, this process required 17 mouse clicks. In Excel 2003, there was not a Wrap Text icon that you could add to your toolbars, and the Vertical Align icons were not a part of the formatting toolbar.

Well, there must have been a million other people participating in the Customer Experience Improvement Program who had this same issue. Microsoft heard loud and clear that Wrap Text, followed by Vertical Align Top is a popular sequence of commands. In response, you now have one-click access to a Wrap Text icon on the Home tab of the ribbon. The Vertical Align Top icon is near the Wrap Text icon; it is the top-left icon in Figure 27 on Page 20.

HOW TO DO 40 DIFFERENT
WHAT-IF ANALYSES QUICKLY

Problem: I want to buy a car, and I want to compare eight price points and four loan terms to calculate the monthly payment amount.

Strategy: You can solve this problem by using a data table. As shown in Figure 748, you set up the worksheet as follows:

1) Enter one price in cell B2.

2) Enter one term in cell B3.

3) Enter the current annual interest rate in B4.

4) In cell B5, which is going to be the magic corner cell of your data table, enter this formula to calculate a monthly payment: =PMT(B4/12,B3,-B2).

Figure 748

Set up one formula in B5.

=PMT(B4/12,B3,-B2)	
◢	A	B
1		
2	**Price**	29995
3	**Term**	48
4	**Interest**	5.40%
5	**Payment**	$696.21

5) In cells B6:B9, enter the four possible terms you would like to compare. These will be your row headings. In cells C5:L5, enter the possible prices you hope to negotiate to, as shown in Figure 749.

6) Select the rectangular range B5:L9. The upper-left corner of this range contains the formula to calculate your monthly payment.

Figure 749

The headings in B6:B9 represent varying loan payback periods.

◢	A	B	C	D	E	F	(
1							
2	Price	29995					
3	Term	48					
4	Interest	5.40%					
5	Payment	$696.21	29995	28995	28495	27995	274
6		36					
7		48					
8		60					
9		72					

7) Select Data – What-If Analysis – Data Table. Excel will ask you to specify a row input cell. In other words, Excel will take each cell in the top row of the table and substitute it for the row input cell. Because these cells contain prices, choose cell B2 as the row input cell, as shown in Figure 750.

8) Next, Excel wants to know where the cells in the first column of your data table should be used. Because B6:B9 contains terms, specify cell B3, as shown in Figure 750. Click OK.

Figure 750

Specify that each cell in the top row should represent B2 in the formula.

◢	A	B	C	D	E	F	G	H
1								
2	Price	29995						
3	Term	48						
4	Interest	5.40%						
5	Payment	$696.21	29995	28995	28495	27995	27495	26999
6		36						
7		48						
8		60						
9		72						
10								
11								
12								
13								
14								

Data Table

Row input cell: $B$2

Column input cell: $B$3

OK   Cancel

Excel will enter an array formula for you, based on the original formula in the top-left cell of the table. It will show you the monthly prices for many combinations of terms and price points, as shown in Figure 751.

Figure 751

Excel will populate the values by using a TABLE array function.

f_x {=TABLE(B2,B3)}

◢	A	B	C	D	E	F	G	H	I	J	K	L
1												
2	Price	29995										
3	Term	48										
4	Interest	5.40%										
5	Payment	$696.21	29995	28995	28495	27995	27495	26995	26495	25995	25495	24995
6		36	904.37	874.22	859.15	844.07	829	813.92	798.85	783.77	768.7	753.62
7		48	696.21	673	661.4	649.79	638.18	626.58	614.97	603.37	591.76	580.16
8		60	571.56	552.5	542.97	533.45	523.92	514.39	504.86	495.3	485.81	476.28
9		72	488.7	472.36	464.22	456.07	447.92	439.78	431.63	423.49	415.34	407.2

If you are looking for a monthly payment of $495, you will have to either negotiate down to a price of $25,995 with a 60-month loan or choose a 72-month loan.

The formulas in the table are live. As shown in Figure 752, you can reenter new values in the first column and row of the table in order to zoom in on possible scenarios. By looking at loan terms of 60, 63, 66, and 69 months, you can find four price points to generate a payment near $495.

Figure 752

When you type new months in the first column, the table formula is live and updates.

$696.21	29995	29295	28795	28195	27695	27095	26595	25995	25495	24995
60	571.56	558.22	548.69	537.26	527.73	516.3	506.77	**495.3**	485.81	476.28
63	547.85	535.06	525.93	514.97	505.84	**494.9**	485.75	474.79	465.66	456.52
66	526.31	514.03	505.25	**494.7**	485.95	475.42	466.65	456.12	447.35	438.58
69	506.66	**494.8**	486.39	476.25	467.81	457.67	449.22	439.09	430.64	422.2

Part III

Additional Details: You can also change the formula in B5, and the table will update.

Summary: The Data Table command is a powerful command for comparing several what-if scenarios.

Commands Discussed: Data – What-If Analysis – Data Table

Functions Discussed: =PMT(); =TABLE()

Excel 97-2003: Data – Table

REMOVE BLANK ROWS FROM A RANGE

Problem: Someone has given me data pasted from Word. As shown in Figure 753, there are a number of blank cells in the list. I want to eliminate the blank rows.

Figure 753

Remove blank rows.

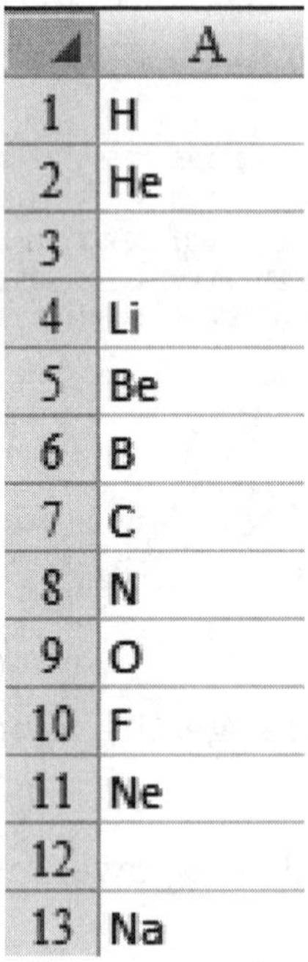

	A
1	H
2	He
3	
4	Li
5	Be
6	B
7	C
8	N
9	O
10	F
11	Ne
12	
13	Na

Strategy: If the sequence is not important, you can sort the entire data range. Excel will move all blank cells to the bottom of the sort range. Here's how you do it:

1)   Move the cell pointer to A1. While holding down the Shift key, press the End key and then the Home key. Excel will select the entire range of data in the spreadsheet.

2)   Select Data – Sort. As shown in Figure 754, in the Sort dialog, indicate that your data does not have a header row by unchecking the My Data Has Headers box. Click OK.

Figure 754

Uncheck the
My Data Has
Headers box.

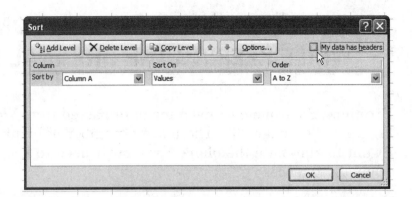

Results: The blanks will be removed from the list, as shown in Figure 755.

Figure 755

The blanks
are gone, but
the data is
resequenced.

▲	A
1	Ac
2	Ag
3	Al
4	Am
5	Ar
6	As
7	At
8	Au
9	B
10	Ba
11	Be

Part
III

Summary: Excel's Sort feature will always move blanks cells to the end of the sort. Sorting a column with blanks is a quick way to remove the blanks from the data.

Commands Discussed: Data – Sort

See Also: "Remove Blanks from a Range While Keeping the Original Sequence" on page 492

REMOVE BLANKS FROM A RANGE
WHILE KEEPING THE ORIGINAL SEQUENCE

Problem: Someone has given me data pasted from Word, as shown in Figure 753 on page 490. There are a number of blank cells in the list. I want to eliminate the blank rows, but I need to keep the data in the original sequence.

Strategy: The trick described in "Remove Blank Rows from a Range"— sorting data to move the blanks to the end—is effective, but it destroys the original sequence of the range. Before sorting, you can add a temporary column with the original sequence numbers so that the data can be sorted back. Follow these steps:

1) Insert a new row 1. Place the cell pointer in cell A1 and then select Home – Insert – Insert Sheet Rows. Because you have only one cell selected, only one row will be inserted.

2) In A1, enter a heading such as Symbol. In cell B1, enter a heading such as Sequence. Apply the cell style Heading 4 by using the Cell Styles gallery on the Home tab.

3) In cell B2, enter the number 1. Select B2. Hold down the Ctrl key while you drag the fill handle to the last row that contains data. The series 1, 2, 3 will extend down to 129 in row 130, as shown in Figure 756. **Gotcha:** If you get a series of 1s instead of 1, 2, 3, then you did not hold down the Ctrl key. Open the Auto Fill Options icon in C131 and choose Fill Series.

Figure 756

Ctrl+drag the fill handle.

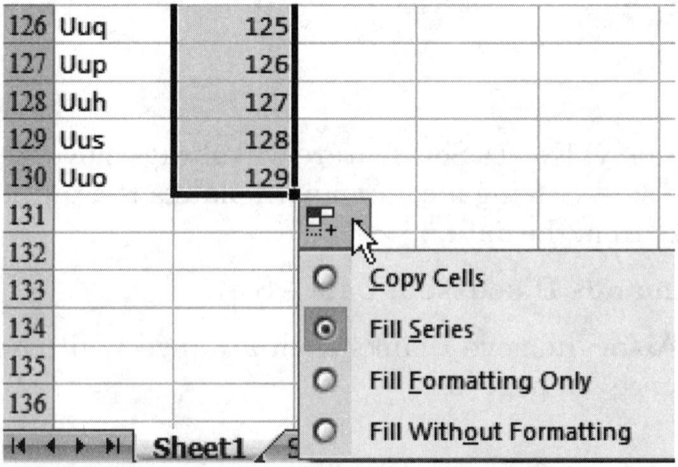

Note: If the Auto Fill Options icon is obscuring some other data, it is fairly difficult to dismiss. One method is to resize any column.

4) Next, sort the data based on column A by selecting a single cell in column A and pressing the AZ button on the Data tab.

5) Press the End key and then the Down Arrow key to ride the range down to the last cell in A that contains data. Delete the rows below this last cell by highlighting the row numbers, right-clicking, and choosing Delete, as shown in Figure 757. (These are the blank cells. It is important to delete the sequence numbers from B for the blank cells so that they do not sort back into the data in the next step.)

Figure 757

Delete the extra rows from the end.

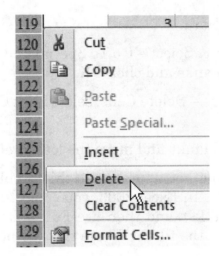

6) Move the cell pointer to any value in column B. Click the AZ button on the Data tab to sort the data into the original sequence, without the blanks, as shown in Figure 758.

Figure 758

Sort by column B to return column A to the original sequence.

	A	B
1	Symbol	Sequence
2	H	1
3	He	2
4	Li	4
5	Be	5
6	B	6

7) Delete the temporary column B by selecting Home – Delete – Delete Sheet Columns.

8) Delete the temporary row 1 by moving the cell pointer to A1 and selecting Home – Delete – Delete Sheet Rows.

Results: The blanks will be removed from the list, and the list will retain the original sequence.

Alternate Strategy: The previous steps work particularly well when your data set has many columns and you need to delete based on one column. If you truly have a data set that has a single column, try this faster method:

1) Select the range of data.

2) Select Home – Find & Select – Go To Special and in the Go To Special dialog, select Blanks and click OK.

3) Select Home – Delete – Delete Cells, select Shift Cells Up, and click OK.

Excel will delete all the blanks and move the lower cells up.

Alternate Strategy: Another approach to this problem became more convoluted in Excel 2007. In Excel 2003, you could turn on AutoFilter, filter the column to (blanks), and then use Edit – Delete to delete the rows that were visible in the filter. To use this method, in Excel 2007, follow these steps:

1) Add a heading.

2) Select the entire data set.

3) Select Data – Filter. Open the Filter dropdown for the heading. Uncheck Select All. Scroll all the way to the bottom to choose (Blanks).

4) Re-select the visible rows, excluding the heading.

5) Select Home – Delete – Delete Sheet Rows.

6) Select Clear from the Sort & Filter group on the Data ribbon tab.

Summary: To remove blanks while keeping the original sequence, you can add a temporary column with sequence numbers and then sort on that column to return the list to the original sequence.

Commands Discussed: Data – Sort; Home – Delete – Delete Sheet Columns; Home – Delete – Delete Sheet Rows; Home – Find & Select – Go To Special; Home – Delete – Delete Cells

Excel 97-2003: Data – Sort; Edit – Delete – Entire Column; Edit – Delete – Entire Row

ADD A BLANK ROW BETWEEN EVERY ROW OF YOUR DATA SET

Problem: In the report shown in Figure 759, my manager wants me to add a blank row after every row of the data.

Figure 759

Double space the report!

	A	B
1	Customer	Sales
2	Cool Faucet Supply	23986
3	Dependable Aquarium Partners	21964
4	Distinctive Briefcase Inc.	27453
5	Excellent Instrument Company	17120
6	Fine Flagpole Corporation	44172
7	Fresh Instrument Inc.	42989
8	Leading Radio Inc.	36228

Part
III

Strategy: Excel MVP Bob Umlas showed me this trick, and it has become one of my favorites. (In fact, I asked Bob to guest host episode 467 of the Learn Excel podcast to demonstrate this trick. You can watch Bob do the trick online. Find episode 467 from March 19, 2007, at http://www.mrexcel.com/podcast/2007_03_01_archive.html.)

Bob adds a new column with numbers 1, 2, 3, and so on. He then copies this range of numbers below the itself. When you sort by the new column, your report is instantly double-spaced! Follow these steps:

1)   In the blank column to the right of your data, enter the heading Sort.

2)   Fill the column with a sequence of 1, 2, 3, etc. One method is to type a 1 in the first cell, select the cell, and Ctrl+drag the fill handle to the end of the data set (see Figure 760).

Figure 760

Add a new column with record numbers.

	A	B	C
1	Customer	Sales	Sort
2	Cool Faucet Supply	23986	1
3	Dependable Aquarium Partners	21964	2
4	Distinctive Briefcase Inc.	27453	3
5	Excellent Instrument Company	17120	4
6	Fine Flagpole Corporation	44172	5
7	Fresh Instrument Inc.	42989	6
8	Leading Radio Inc.	36228	7
9	Persuasive Tackle Corporation	23999	8
10	Persuasive Treadmill Inc.	40783	9
11	Persuasive Vise Inc.	8365	10
12	Powerful Shoe Inc.	36183	11
13	Refined Bottle Company	46876	12
14	Reliable Faucet Partners	39230	13
15	Savory Necktie Supply	26335	14
16	Top-Notch Notebook Inc.	10645	15

3)   Press Ctrl+C to copy the selected numbers in the new column to the Clipboard.

4)   Select the first blank cell beneath your new column. Press Ctrl+V to paste a duplicate set of numbers (see Figure 761).

Figure 761

Copy the same numbers below.

	A	B	C
14	Reliable Faucet Partners	39230	13
15	Savory Necktie Supply	26335	14
16	Top-Notch Notebook Inc.	10645	15
17			1
18			2
19			3
20			4

5) Select one cell in the new column. Click the AZ button on the Data tab. Excel sorts by the new column. Because every number occurs twice—once in the original report and once below the report—blank rows are sorted up into your data, as shown in Figure 762.

Figure 762

Sort by column C, and the data is double-spaced.

◢	A	B	C
1	Customer	Sales	Sort
2	Cool Faucet Supply	23986	1
3			1
4	Dependable Aquarium Partners	21964	2
5			2
6	Distinctive Briefcase Inc.	27453	3
7			3
8	Excellent Instrument Company	17120	4
9			4
10	Fine Flagpole Corporation	44172	5

Part III

6) Delete the Sort column.

Additional Details: To triple space your data, you can paste two copies of the numbers below your data.

Additional Details: Check out Bob Umlas's book *This Isn't Excel, It's Magic!* (available at Amazon). It is filled with over 100 tricks like this one.

Summary: To add blank rows between rows of a report, you can add a temporary sort column with row numbers, copy the row numbers below your report, and sort by the sort column.

Commands Discussed: Ctrl+C; Ctrl+V; Data – AZ

EXCEL IS RANDOMLY PARSING PASTED DATA

Problem: Every once in a while, I paste data from a text file to Excel, and Excel will spontaneously parse my data into several columns. Check out Figure 763. I copied the names from the e-mail on the left, but when I pasted to Excel, the names appeared in one, two, or three columns. However, this may not happen tomorrow. It might happen only once every two weeks.

Figure 763

Sometimes, Excel parses pasted data.

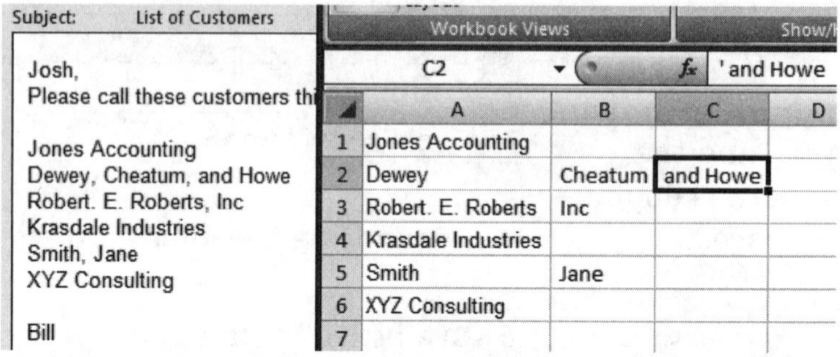

Strategy: At some point during this Excel session, you used Data – Text to Columns and specified that the data was delimited by a comma. Whatever settings are left in the Step 2 dialog of the Convert Text to Columns Wizard will be applied to external data pasted to Excel for the rest of the Excel session.

Figure 764

Excel remembers these settings for the rest of the day.

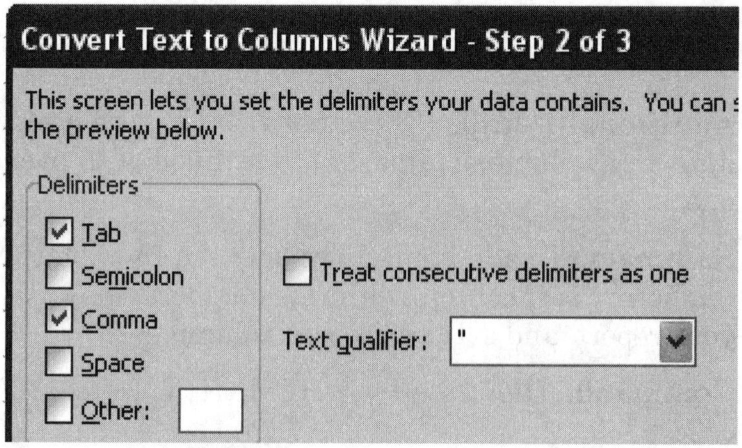

To prevent this from happening, you could close Excel when you're done working with the Convert Text to Columns Wizard. Or you could redisplay the Convert Text to Columns Wizard, go to the Step 2 dialog, and turn off the comma and tab settings. Either method will work.

On the other hand, you might want Excel to have this behavior. Perhaps you need to paste 100 documents to Excel and convert text to columns on each one. In this case, you can convert text to columns manually on the first pasted data, and the rest of the pastes will automatically be parsed using the same delimiter.

Summary: Excel remembers the setting from the Step 2 dialog in the Convert Text to Columns Wizard and applies that setting to future Paste commands.

Commands Discussed: Data – Text to Columns

INCREASE A RANGE BY TWO PERCENT

Problem: I run the repair department for a company. As shown in Figure 765, I have a spreadsheet of pricing rates. My manager tells me to increase the price on all service contracts by 2%.

Part III

Figure 765

Add 2% to every cell in column B.

◢	A	B
1	Contract	Rate
2	K3504	7.23
3	K3350	10.38
4	K10761	7.48
5	K7205	5.48
6	K8213	7.9

Strategy: In a blank cell, you enter 102%. Then you copy that cell and use Paste Special Multiply to multiply all the contract prices by this cell. Follow these steps:

1) Find a blank cell, such as D1. Enter 102% or 1.02 in that cell.

2) Select D1 and then choose Home – Copy.

3)   Select all the rates in column B (see Figure 766)

Figure 766

Copy 102% to
the Clipboard
and then select
your cells.

◢	A	B	C	D
1	Contract	Rate		102%
2	K3504	7.23		
3	K3350	10.38		
4	K10761	7.48		
5	K7205	5.48		
6	K8213	7.9		
7	K2561	7.53		

4)   Select Home – Paste dropdown – Paste Special. In the Paste Spe-
      cial dialog, choose Values and Multiply, as shown in Figure 767.
      (The Multiply setting causes Excel to multiply the value on the
      Clipboard by each cell. You need to choose Values to prevent the
      percentage formatting from cell D1 from being applied to the se-
      lected cells.) Press Esc to clear the 102% from the clipboard.

Figure 767

In the Paste
Special dialog,
indicate that
you want to
multiply the
selection by
the value on
the Clipboard.

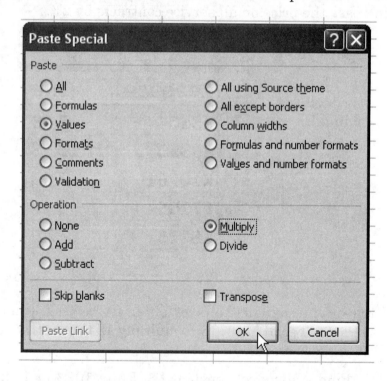

Results: All the values in column B will be increased by 2%, as shown
in Figure 768.

Figure 768

Each cell will be increased by 2%.

◢	A	B
1	**Contract**	**Rate**
2	K3504	7.3746
3	K3350	10.5876
4	K10761	7.6296
5	K7205	5.5896
6	K8213	8.058

Summary: You can multiply an entire range by a single cell by using Home – Paste dropdown – Paste Special – Multiply.

Commands Discussed: Home – Copy; Home – Paste dropdown – Paste Special – Multiply

Excel 97-2003: Edit – Copy; Edit – Paste Special – Multiply

USE FIND TO FIND AN ASTERISK

Part III

Problem: My largest customer is Wal*Mart. When I use Find or Find and Replace to search for Wal*Mart, Excel also finds Wallingsmart, as shown in Figure 769. I know this happens because Excel sees * as a wildcard character. What if I really want to search for an asterisk?

Figure 769

Ask Excel to find Wal*Mart, and Wallingsmart shows up as well.

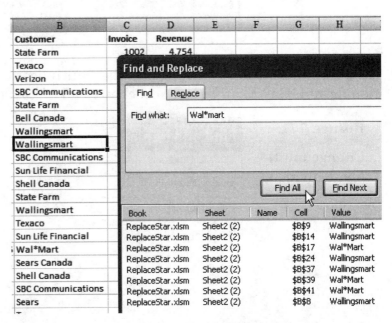

Strategy: You can use three wildcard characters in the Find and Replace dialog: *, ?, and ~.

If you include an *, Excel will search for any number of characters where the asterisk is located. For example, searching for Wal*mart will find Wal*mart and also Walton Williams is smart.

If you include a ?, Excel will search for any one character. For example, searching for ?arl will find both Carl and Karl.

To force Excel to search for an asterisk, tilde, or a question mark, you can precede the wildcard with a tilde (~). When you search for Wal~*mart, Excel will only find Wal*mart, as shown in Figure 770. If you search for Who~? Excel will only find Who? and not Whom. When you search for "Alt+~~", Excel will find "Alt+~".

Figure 770

Use ~* to really find an asterisk.

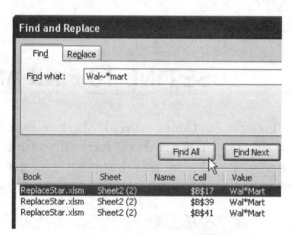

Additional Details: To change all the multiplication formulas to division formulas, you can have Excel change all ~* to /. (see Figure 771)

Figure 771

Change multiply to divide.

Gotcha: Changing a formula of =5*3 to =5/3 will work fine. Changing a math exercise sheet with 5*3 to become 5/3 might change your values to May 3rd. Use caution when changing asterisk to slashes within text.

Summary: When you need to search for an actual question mark, tilde, or asterisk, you can precede the wildcard character with a tilde.

Commands Discussed: Home – Find & Select – Find; Home – Find & Select – Replace

Excel 97-2003: Edit – Replace; Edit – Find

USE AN AMPERSAND IN A HEADER

Problem: As shown in Figure 772, I added the custom header Profit & Loss Report to my report.

Figure 772

You want to include an ampersand in the header.

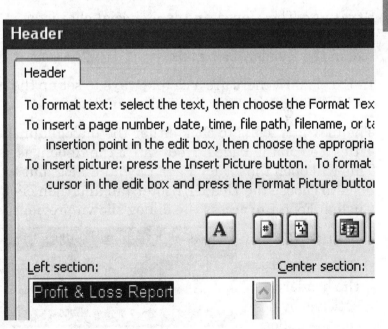

Header

Header

To format text: select the text, then choose the Format Tex

To insert a page number, date, time, file path, filename, or t:
    insertion point in the edit box, then choose the appropria

To insert picture: press the Insert Picture button. To format
    cursor in the edit box and press the Format Picture butto

Left section:

Profit & Loss Report

Center section:

When you use Print Preview on the document, the header says Profit Loss Report, as shown in Figure 773. The ampersand is missing.

Figure 773

Excel leaves out the &.

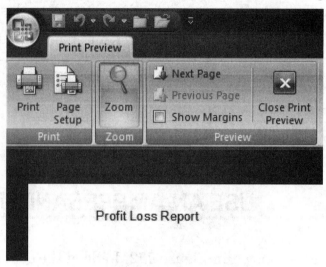

Strategy: The ampersand is a special character in the custom header and footer field. To print an ampersand in the header, you have to type && in the Header dialog box.

In Excel 2007, there are a couple ways to set up the headers and footers, and I don't particularly like either method.

The first method is to click either the dialog launcher icon or the Print Titles icon on the Page Layout tab of the ribbon, as shown in Figure 774. This will open the legacy Page Layout dialog, but to the wrong tab. You need to choose the Header/Footer tab and then click Custom Header or Custom Footer to access the dialog shown previously in Figure 772.

Figure 774

You can access the header settings by using the dialog launcher.

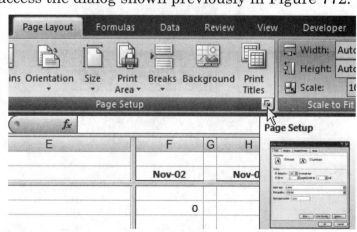

It seems strange that Excel 2007 does not have an icon for Page Setup. I suspect that Microsoft expected most people to use the new Page Layout view when creating headers and footers. The new Page Layout view is one of the great new features in Excel 2007. You can access it by using the middle icon to the left of the zoom slider in the lower-right corner of the window, as shown in Figure 775.

Figure 775

The 3 icons here are Normal, Page Layout, and Page Break Preview.

The Page Layout view shows your document as a series of pages. There are three header and footer zones. When you hover over a zone, it turns blue, as shown in Figure 776.

Part III

Figure 776

Page Layout view shows the worksheet in virtual pages. Note that I adjusted the zoom slider to 20% in this Figure. Normally, going to Page Layout view does not automatically reduce the zoom.

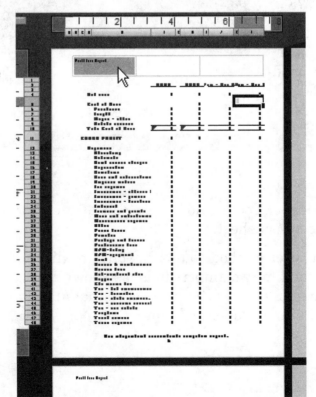

Click on one of the blue header/footer zones, and Excel will switch to a contextual tab of the ribbon: Header & Footer Tools – Design. (see Figure 777).

Figure 777

Click a header to access the Header & Footer Tools tab of the ribbon.

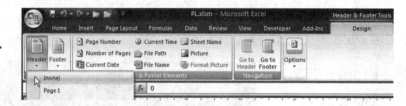

This tab gives you access to the traditional settings, as well as new settings for Excel 2007. You can use these settings to specify a different header for the first page, or for odd/even pages, as shown in Figure 778.

Figure 778

In Excel 2007, you can have different headers on odd/ even pages.

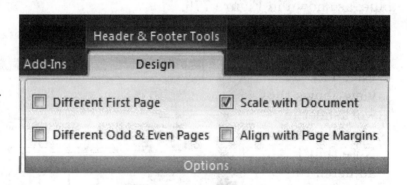

While in Header/Footer mode, you can also edit the header or footer right in the spreadsheet.

Using whichever method you wish, you can edit the header and change the ampersand to two ampersands, as shown in Figure 779. Using && in the header or footer is the secret code that allows you to print just one ampersand in the header or footer.

Figure 779

Specify &&
while editing
the header.

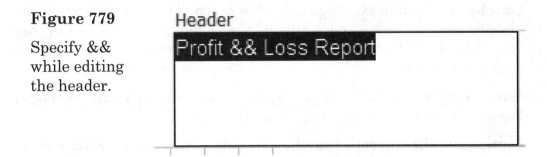

Having two ampersands will give you the desired heading Profit & Loss,
as shown in Figure 780.

Figure 780

Excel will
print the &&
as a single &.

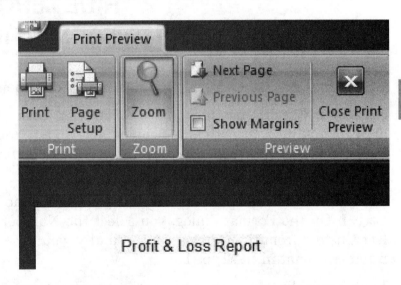

Additional Details: The ampersand doesn't print because it is used
for all sorts of custom text fields in either the header or the footer. You
can build your own custom footers by using the icons or simply typing
&[Page] or &[Pages].

Gotcha: Clearly, the Header & Footer Tools tab of the ribbon is a good
place to edit your headers. However, to reach that tab, you have to enter Page Layout mode, which requires you to turn off any Freeze Panes
settings. If you regularly use Freeze Panes, you might want to use the
dialog launcher on the Page Layout tab of the ribbon.

Gotcha: You cannot exit Page Layout view while you are editing a header or footer. You have to click outside the header to select a cell in your spreadsheet and then click the Normal icon (the leftmost icon to the left of the zoom slider).

Summary: When you want to print an ampersand in a page header or footer, you need to use two ampersands.

Commands Discussed: Page Layout view; Office Icon – Print – Print Preview; Page Layout – dialog launcher – Header/Footer

Excel 97-2003: File – Page Setup – Header/Footer

HIDE ZEROS & OTHER
CUSTOM NUMBER FORMATTING TRICKS

Problem: I don't want zeros to appear in my document.

Strategy: Excel's custom number formatting codes have an amazing array of options that not many people know about. You can specify multiple formats within one custom number code. Each format is separated by semi-colons. Read on for details.

To assign a custom number format, you select the range and press Ctrl+1. On the Format dialog, you select the Number tab and then select Custom from the Category list. Finally, you type any valid custom number format in the Type box.

You've probably run into some custom number formats, such as these:

#,##0 will display numbers with thousands separators.
$#,##0.00 will display two decimal places and a currency symbol.
#,##0,K will display numbers in thousands.
mm/dd/yyyy will display a date as 02/17/2008.
[h]:mm will display hours in excess of 24 hours.
[blue]0 will display a number in blue text.

In these simple formats, there is only one format being used. If you enter two formats separated by a semicolon, the first format is used for positive and zero value, and the second format is used for negative values.

For example, [blue]0;[red]-0 will display negative numbers in red and other numbers in blue.

If you enter three formats separated by semicolons, the first format is for positive, the second format is for negative, and the third format is for zero. For example, [blue]0;[red]-0;[green]0 will display 0 cells in green text.

If you type a second semicolon and leave out the final formatting code, Excel will suppress the display of zero values. For example, 0;-0; will show positive and negative numbers but hide zeros. Note that the final semicolon is a subtle but important difference from using 0;0. Figure 781 shows the custom number format to hide zeros.

If you specify a fourth number format, it is used for text values.

Figure 781

The zero in C2 is not displayed.

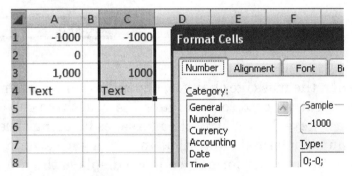

To hide all values in a cell, you can use ;;; as the custom number format.

Additional Details: The custom number formats were written long before Microsoft started using conditional formatting. You can change the formatting based on meeting certain criteria. For example, as shown in Figure 782, the following code would display numbers above 10,000 in thousands and other numbers normally:
[<10000]#,##0;[>=10000]#,##0,K,.

Figure 782

Conditional formatting replaces the need for this format, but it still works.

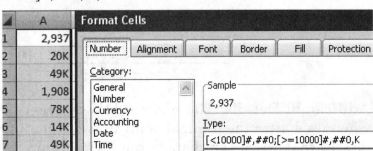

In many cases in which you might use concatenation to join text and a number, you could use a custom number format instead. In Figure 783, cell B8 contains a SUM function, yet the result is displayed with a payment message.

Figure 783

This SUM function produces a message.

	B8	▼	f_x =SUM(B2:B7)
◢	A		B
1		Amount	
2	Balance Forward		1012.34
3	Invoice 1024		473.23
4	Invoice 1036		124.56
5	Check 9874		-1610.13
6	Credit Memo		-124.56
7			
8		Credit Balance of $124.56. Do not pay.	

Further, the message changes, depending on whether the balance is positive, negative, or zero. In Figure 784, the three cells show the message for each state. You control the messages by using three zones in the custom number format. Note that in the negative zone, there is no minus sign in the number format, so Excel displays the number as positive. In the zero zone, there are no numeric characters at all, so Excel displays the No Balance Due message.

Figure 784

The message changes if the answer is positive, negative, or zero.

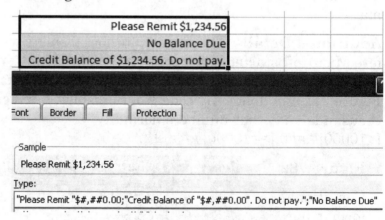

Additional Details: There is a subtle difference between the 0 and # when used after the decimal point in a custom number format. A # indicates that Excel can display the digit if there is sufficient precision in the value. A 0 indicates that Excel must display the digit. In Figure 785, the 0.000 format in D3 forces Excel to display three decimal places, even though the last two are zero. The 0.0## format ensures that there is always one decimal place, but the second and third decimal places are used only if necessary. In row 5, the number is 123.456. All of the decimals are displayed in A5, C5, and D5, but only two digits are displayed in B5 with the 0.00 numeric format.

Figure 785

In cell B5, a numeric format of 0.00 causes Excel to round 123.456 to display 123.46.

	A	B	C	D
1	General	0.00	0.0##	0.000
2	123	123.00	123.0	123.000
3	123.4	123.40	123.4	123.400
4	123.45	123.45	123.45	123.450
5	123.456	123.46	123.456	123.456

Part III

Additional Details: To fill the white space before a number, precede the number format with two asterisks. Similar to the security feature of old check printers, asterisks will appear before the number as shown in Figure 786.

Figure 786

Control places after the decimal point.

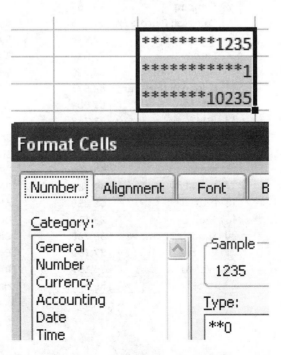

Additional Details: You can use zeros before the decimal point to force Excel to display leading zeros. The custom format 00000 will ensure that the zip code for Cambridge, Massachusetts, prints as 02142 instead of 2142. If you need a part number to appear as 4 digits, you can use the custom format 0000 to force leading zeros to appear.

Summary: Although some aspects of custom number formats are outdated, you can still achieve many useful effects with them.

USE CONSOLIDATION TO COMBINE TWO LISTS

Problem: Jerry and Tina each compiled sales figures from paper invoices, as shown in Figure 787. I need to combine Jerry and Tina's list into a single list. Some customers are in both lists.

Figure 787

Combine the lists into a single list.

	A	B	C	D	E
1	Customer	Sales		Customer	Sales
2	Ainsworth	89,357		Ainsworth	74,514
3	Air Canada	38,468		Bell Canada	63,539
4	Bell Canada	94,742		Chevron	54,857
5	Chevron	57,560		Compaq	82,488
6	Compaq	58,467		General Motors	57,840
7	Compton Petroleum	51,435		Kroger	40,896
8	Exxon Mobil	52,974		Sun Life Financial	68,674
9	Ford	75,517		Sun Life Financial	73,118
10	General Motors	36,200		Verizon	57,888
11	Gildan Activewear	88,577		Wal-Mart	69,170
12	HP	61,304		Accelent Systems	84,420
13	IBM	37,713		DigiKnow	50,924
14	Kroger	69,883		Sequoia Financial	87,895
15	Lucent	35,515		Shearer's Foods	44,510
16	Molson, Inc	53,705		Zebra Skimmers	70,996
17	Nortel Networks	49,669		3M	70,900
18	P&G	68,858		Alcoa	50,709
19	Shell Canada	83,174		Boeing	81,865
20	Sun Life Financial	86,780		Citigroup	88,839
21	Verizon	37,795		Exxon Mobil	41,736
22	Wal-Mart	35,157		Intel	88,163
23	Pfizer	39,880		Home Depot	63,528

Strategy: Excel offers a great tool for consolidating data. Here's how you use it:

1) Move the cell pointer to a blank area of the worksheet. You will need a blank area with several rows and a few columns. In Figure 788, G2 would be appropriate, so select it and then select Data – Consolidate.

Figure 788

Select a blank cell and then select Data – Consolidate.

Part
III

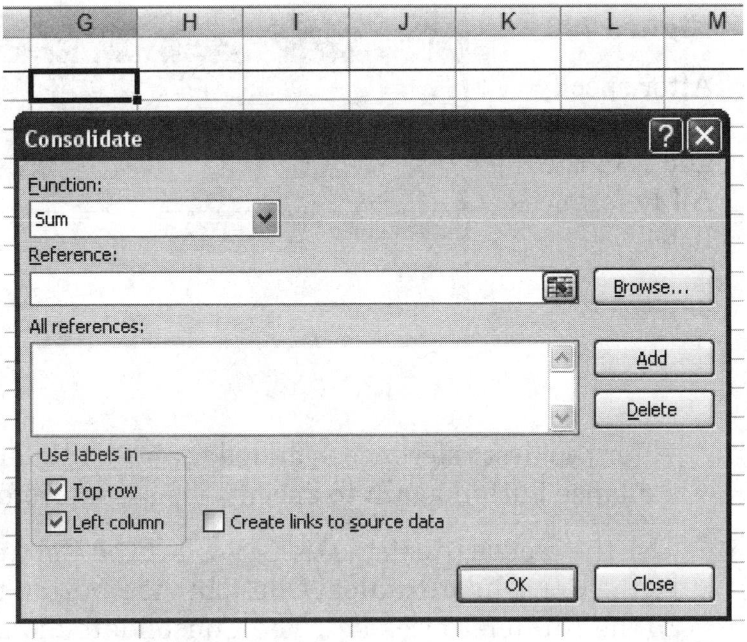

Notice in the Consolidate dialog that both boxes under Use Labels In are checked. This means that Excel relies on the headings to be the same and that the customer field is in the left column of each range.

2) Put the cell pointer in the Reference field. Click the Collapse button at the right end of the Reference field. With the mouse, select the first range: A1:B23. Click the Collapse button again to return to the Consolidate dialog (see Figure 789).

Figure 789

Specify a range to consolidate.

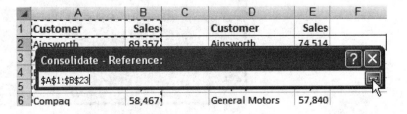

Note: There are times when you will want to consolidate just a single range of data. This would be effective if you needed to combine duplicate customers from one list. However, in this example, you need to combine two lists.

3)   Click the Add button to move the first reference from the Reference field to the All References box (see Figure 790).

Figure 790

After specifying a range, add it to the All References list.

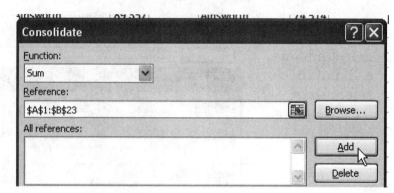

4)   After the first reference is added to the All References box, click the Collapse button again to specify the second reference.

5)   Use the mouse to select D1:E23. Click the Collapse button to return to the Consolidate dialog. Click the Add button to add the reference to the All References list. The Consolidate dialog should appear as in Figure 791.

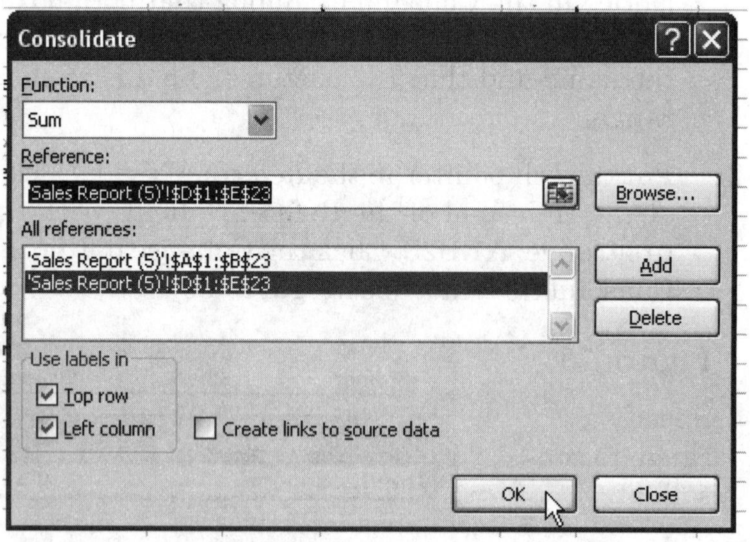

Figure 791

Make sure both ranges are in the All References box.

6)   Choose OK. In a few seconds, Excel will return a brand new list that extends down and to the right from cell G2, as shown in Figure 792. The list will contain one instance of each customer along with the total revenue from the customer.

Figure 792

Excel com-
bines the two
lists into a
single list.

	Sales
Ainsworth	163,871
Air Canada	38,468
Bell Canadi	158,281
Chevron	112,417
Compaq	140,955
Compton Pi	51,435
Accelent Sy	84,420
DigiKnow	50,924
Sequoia Fir	87,895
Shearer's F	44,510

Gotcha: The new list is not in any sequence. You can see that it kind of starts out in the sequence of the first list but then randomly inserts customers from the second list. You will probably want to sort the list alphabetically or by revenue. However, Excel always fails to fill in the label in the upper-left corner of the consolidation. If you want to sort the result, you need to type the word Customer in cell G2.

Additional Details: The Function box in the Consolidate dialog offers many functions other than SUM, as shown in Figure 793. For instance, if you want to find the largest purchase by each customer, you can use the MAX function.

Figure 793

Consolidate of-
fers more than
just SUM.

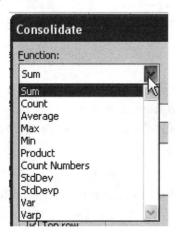

Part
III

Gotcha: The results of the consolidation shown in Figure 792 are all static values. If you change an item in the original list, the consolidation will not automatically update. This is good because it allows you to delete the original two lists and keep just the new list.

Summary: Using Consolidate is one of several methods for combining lists of data.

Commands Discussed: Data – Consolidate

FIND TOTAL SALES BY CUSTOMER
BY COMBINING DUPLICATES

Problem: I have an invoice register for the month. The report shows account, customer, invoice, sales, cost, and profit for each invoice, as shown in Figure 794. I want to combine customers in order to produce a report of sales by customer.

Figure 794

Consolidate the data to one row per customer.

	A	B	C	D	E	F
1	Acct	Customer	Invoice	Sales	COGS	Profit
2	H1247	Home Depot	1201	63,528	37,577	25,951
3	B5618	Boeing	1202	81,865	45,136	36,729
4	C2299	Compaq	1203	85,096	50,745	34,351
5	H1247	Home Depot	1204	72,410	40,704	31,706
6	Z1752	Zebra Skimmers	1205	70,996	40,925	30,071
7	D1891	DigiKnow	1206	58,784	33,431	25,353
8	K7539	Kroger	1207	40,896	23,397	17,499
9	K7539	Kroger	1208	49,463	28,145	21,318
10	A4509	Alcoa	1209	47,045	26,008	21,037

Strategy: It is possible to consolidate a single list by using the labels in the left column. This will produce a report with one line per customer and totals of each numeric field. You can use data consolidation to solve this task:

1) Select a blank section of the worksheet. Select Data – Consolidate. In the Reference field, select the complete range of your data, including the headings. Ensure that the Left Column option is checked

and that the Create Links to Source Data check box is unchecked (see Figure 795). Click OK.

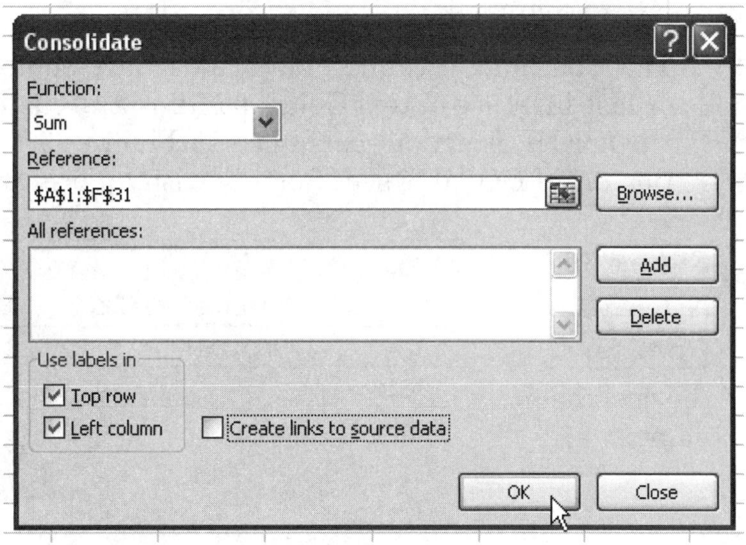

Figure 795

Specify a single range to consolidate.

As shown in Figure 796, Excel will combine all identical account numbers together. The original data did not have to be sorted by account number.

Figure 796

The new range has one line per unique account number.

H	I	J	K	L	M
	Customer	Invoice	Sales	COGS	Profit
H1247		2405	135,938	78,281	57,657
B5618		2415	141,633	78,776	62,857
C2299		2420	167,584	99,161	68,423
Z1752		2432	141,227	81,705	59,522
D1891		2428	109,708	62,994	46,714
K7539		2415	90,359	51,542	38,817
A4509		2433	97,754	55,342	42,412
G5111		2433	115,816	66,375	49,441
A5911		2441	125,222	73,009	52,213
S3647		2441	127,899	75,550	52,349
E2257		2430	91,175	51,875	39,300
S4871		2441	132,452	76,903	55,549
C5484		2438	178,422	103,219	75,203
V7797		2444	116,418	67,083	49,335
I1622		2449	128,755	74,433	54,322

Part
III

Gotcha: Note that Excel added up the invoice numbers in column J. This makes no sense.

2)   Delete column J.

3)   The Consolidate command is not smart enough to take the first or last instance of text fields, so fill in the customer name, using a VLOOKUP function, as shown in Figure 797. (For more information on VLOOKUP, see "Sorting with a Formula" on page 265.)

Figure 797

Use VLOOK-UP to fill in the customer name.

	H	I	J	K	L
		Customer	Sales	COGS	Profit
	H1247	=VLOOKUP(H2,$A$2:$B$31,2,false)			
	B5618		141,633	78,776	62,857
	C2299		167,584	99,161	68,423

4)   Copy the VLOOKUP function down by double-clicking the fill handle. Change the VLOOKUP formula to values by copying I2:I16 and then using Home – Paste dropdown – Paste Values.

5)   Excel does not fill in the label in the upper-left corner of the table, so enter Acct in H1. The resulting data set is in the same sequence as the customers in the original list.

6)   Choose a single cell in column I and click the AZ sort button to produce an alphabetical list by customer.

7)   Because the column widths are not automatically adjusted as the result of a consolidation (see Figure 798 on next page), double-click the right side of the I column heading in order to autofit the Customer column. Double-click when the cell pointer looks like an I-beam with a dual-headed arrow.

Summary: Using Consolidate is a good method for combining duplicate customers while totaling many columns of numeric data.

Commands Discussed: Data – Consolidate; Home – Paste dropdown – Paste Values

Functions Discussed: =VLOOKUP()

Excel 97-2003: Data – Consolidate; Edit – Paste Special – Values

Figure 798

Double-click to make the column wide enough for the longest customer name.

Acct	Customer	Sales	COGS	Profit
A5911	Accelent Systems	125,222	73,009	52,213
A4509	Alcoa	97,754	55,342	42,412
B5618	Boeing	141,633	78,776	62,857
C5484	Citigroup	178,422	103,219	75,203
C2299	Compaq	167,584	99,161	68,423
D1891	DigiKnow	109,708	62,994	46,714
E2257	Exxon Mobil	91,175	51,875	39,300
G5111	General Motors	115,816	66,375	49,441
H1247	Home Depot	135,938	78,281	57,657
I1622	Intel	128,755	74,433	54,322
K7539	Kroger	90,359	51,542	38,817
S3647	Sequoia Financial	127,899	75,550	52,349
S4871	Shearer's Foods	132,452	76,903	55,549
V7797	Verizon	116,418	67,083	49,335
Z1752	Zebra Skimmers	141,227	81,705	59,522

Part III

CREATE A SUMMARY OF FOUR LISTS

Problem: I have a list of Webelos scouts that shows who attended various sessions at camp (see Figure 799). I need to produce a master list of who attended which session.

Figure 799

Combine the lists into a single list.

Aquanaut	Artist	Citizen	Engineer
Joey	Rowen	Nick	Matt
Zeke	Josh	Josh	Robby
Josh	Jake	Jake	Tim
Kyle	Jordan	Kyle	Josh
Dan	Zeke	Rowen	Zeke

Strategy: You can use data consolidation to solve this task. Here's how:

1)   Find a blank section of the worksheet. Enter the headings Name and Class. Copy all the Aquanaut scouts to the list and assign a value of 1 in the Class column, as shown in Figure 800.

Figure 800

People in the first list have a value of 1.

	A	B
1	Name	Class
2	Joey	1
3	Zeke	1
4	Josh	1
5	Kyle	1
6	Dan	1

2)   Copy the Artist scouts below this list and assign a value of 10 in the Class column. Copy the Citizen scouts below those and give them each a value of 100. Copy the Engineer scouts below those and give each a value of 1000. Your list should look like the one in Figure 801.

Figure 801

Subsequent lists get values of 10, 100, and so on.

	A	B
1	Name	Class
2	Joey	1
3	Zeke	1
4	Josh	1
5	Kyle	1
6	Dan	1
7	Rowen	10
8	Josh	10
9	Jake	10
10	Jordan	10
11	Zeke	10
12	Nick	100
13	Josh	100
14	Jake	100
15	Kyle	100
16	Rowen	100
17	Matt	1000
18	Robby	1000
19	Tim	1000
20	Josh	1000
21	Zeke	1000

3) Go to a blank section of the worksheet, such as cell I1, and select Data – Consolidate. In the Consolidate dialog, choose A1:B21 as the reference. Click Add. Choose Top Row and Left Column, as shown in Figure 802. Click OK.

Figure 802

Set up the consolidation dropdown.

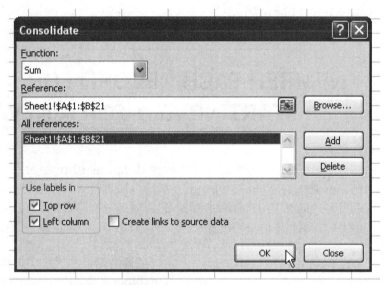

Part
III

4) Format column J with the custom number format of 0000. Select the range and press Ctrl+1 to display the Format Cells dialog. On the Number tab, choose Custom. In the Type box, type 0000. Click OK.

Results: As shown in Figure 803, any scouts with 1111 as the class attended all four sessions. Scouts with 1000 attended only the Engineer session. Scouts with 0001 attended only the Aquanaut session.

Figure 803

Each character position in column J corresponds to a session.

I	J
	Class
Joey	0001
Zeke	1011
Josh	1111
Kyle	0101
Dan	0001
Rowen	0110
Jake	0110
Jordan	0010
Nick	0100
Matt	1000
Robby	1000
Tim	1000

Summary: Consolidation is one method for identifying who is in which list when you have many lists of data.

Commands Discussed: Data – Consolidate; Ctrl+1

See Also: Use a Pivot Table to Compare Two Lists on page 612

NUMBER EACH RECORD FOR A CUSTOMER, STARTING AT 1 FOR A NEW CUSTOMER

Problem: I have a list of invoice data, as shown in Figure 804. I want to number the records in such a way that the first invoice number for Ford is 1. The next Ford invoice is 2, and so on. When I get to a new customer, I want to start over at 1.

Figure 804

You want to add sequential record numbers within each customer.

	A	B	C	D	E	F
1	Invoice	Customer	Date	Region	Product	Quantity
2	1010	Ford	1/2/08	East	XYZ	1000
3	1011	Verizon	1/2/08	Central	DEF	100
4	1012	Verizon	1/2/08	East	ABC	500
5	1013	Ainsworth	1/2/08	Central	XYZ	500
6	1014	Ainsworth	1/3/08	Central	XYZ	400
7	1015	Gildan Activewe	1/3/08	East	DEF	800

Strategy: Use a formula in a new column A to add the record number. Follow these steps.

1. Select one cell in the customer column and select Data – AZ to sort the data by customer.

2. Insert a new temporary column A and add the heading Rec #, as shown in Figure 805.

Figure 805

To sort by customer, insert a new column.

◢	A	B	C
1	Rec #	Invoice	Customer
52		1562	Ainsworth
53		1566	Ainsworth
54		1143	Air Canada
55		1169	Air Canada
56		1368	Air Canada
57		1438	Air Canada
58		1165	Bell Canada

In A2, enter the formula =IF(C2=C1,1+A1,1). In plain language, this formula says, "If the customer in C is equal to the customer above me, then add 1 to the cell above me. Otherwise, start at 1." Copy the formula down to all rows.

Excel will number each group of customer invoices from 1 to N, as shown in Figure 806.

Figure 806

The live formulas work while the data is sorted.

=IF(C54=C53,1+A53,1)

◢	A	B	C	D
1	Rec #	Invoice	Customer	Date
50	49	1538	Ainsworth	12/8/08
51	50	1541	Ainsworth	12/9/08
52	51	1562	Ainsworth	12/23/08
53	52	1566	Ainsworth	12/25/08
54	1	1143	Air Canada	3/30/08
55	2	1169	Air Canada	4/18/08
56	3	1368	Air Canada	8/23/08
57	4	1438	Air Canada	10/6/08

Part III

Now you need to copy the formulas in column A and use Home – Paste dropdown – Paste Values to change to numbers so that you can re-sort the data by invoice number, as shown in Figure 807.

Figure 807

Use Paste Values, and you can now sort by invoice.

	A	B	C	D
1	Rec #	Invoice	Customer	Date
2	1	1010	Ford	1/2/08
3	1	1011	Verizon	1/2/08
4	2	1012	Verizon	1/2/08
5	1	1013	Ainsworth	1/2/08
6	2	1014	Ainsworth	1/3/08

Alternate Strategy: You can use the formula =COUNTIF(C$2:C2,C2) without sorting.

Summary: The IF function is perfect for the task of comparing the current record to the record above it.

Commands Discussed: Data – AZ; Home – Paste dropdown – Paste Values

Functions Discussed: =IF(), =COUNTIF()

Excel 97-2003: AZ; Edit – Paste Special – Values

ADD A GROUP NUMBER TO EACH SET OF RECORDS THAT HAS A UNIQUE CUSTOMER NUMBER

Problem: I have a list of invoice data. I want to number the records in such a way that the invoices for the first customer all have a group number 1 and the invoices for the next customer all have a group number 2.

Strategy: You can do this by sorting the data by customer. You need to add a new column A, with the heading Group. In cell A2, you enter the number 1 for Group 1. In cell A3, you enter the following formula, which will be used for the rest of the records:

=IF(C3=C2,A2,1+A2)

In plain language, this formula says, "If the customer on this row equals the row above, then use the group number on the row above. Otherwise, add 1 to the group number above." You need to copy this formula down to all the other rows, as shown in Figure 808.

Figure 808

Assign each customer a group number.

f_x =IF(C54=C53,A53,1+A53)

◢	A	B	C	D
1	Group	Invoice	Customer	Date
50	1	1538	Ainsworth	12/7/08
51	1	1541	Ainsworth	12/8/08
52	1	1562	Ainsworth	12/22/08
53	1	1566	Ainsworth	12/24/08
54	2	1143	Air Canada	3/29/08
55	2	1169	Air Canada	4/17/08
56	2	1368	Air Canada	8/22/08
57	2	1438	Air Canada	10/5/08
58	3	1165	Bell Canada	4/11/08

Part III

Results: Each record will be assigned a group number. Each customer will have a unique group number.

In order to allow future sorting, you copy the formulas in column A and use Home – Paste dropdown – Paste Values to convert the formulas to numbers.

Summary: You can use the IF function to add a group number to each group of records.

Functions Discussed: =IF()

Commands Discussed: Home – Paste dropdown – Paste Values

DEAL WITH DATA IN WHICH EACH RECORD TAKES FIVE PHYSICAL ROWS

Problem: Sometime, back in the days of COBOL, a programmer was dealing with the constraints of the physical width of a page. The programmer built a report in which each record actually took up five lines of the report, as shown in Figure 809. I want to be able to analyze this data in Excel.

Figure 809

Transform this frustrating data set.

	A	B	C	D	E	F	G
1	ACCT: 12345		INVOICE: 1010			DATE: 10/21/08	
2	INVOICE TOTAL		$125.00				
3	ABC CO						
4	123 S. MAIN STREET						
5	SALEM OH 44460						
6	---------						
7	ACCT: 23456		INVOICE: 1011			DATE: 10/21/08	
8	INVOICE TOTAL		$175.00				
9	XYZ INC.						
10	456 N. BROADWAY						
11	SALEM OR 98754						
12	---------						
13	ACCT: 34567		INVOICE: 1012			DATE: 10/23/08	

Strategy: Your goal is to get the data back into one row per record. This process involves adding two new columns, Group and Sequence:

1) Add a new row 1. Insert two new columns, A and B. Add the headings Group, Seq, and Text in A1:C1 as shown in Figure 810.

Figure 810

Add two new columns.

	A	B	C
1	Group	Seq	Text
2			ACCT: 1
3			INVOICE
4			ABC CO

2) In column A, assign a group number to each logical record. One way to do this is to check to see if the first four characters of column C are ACCT. If they are, add 1 to the group number. In A2, enter the number 1. In A3, enter the formula =IF(LEFT(C3,4)="ACCT",1 +A2,A2). (This is similar to the formula from "Add a Group Number to Each Set of Records That Has a Unique Customer Number" on

page 524.) Copy it down to all the rows. Excel will assign a group number to each logical group of records, as shown in Figure 811.

Figure 811

Use the IF function.

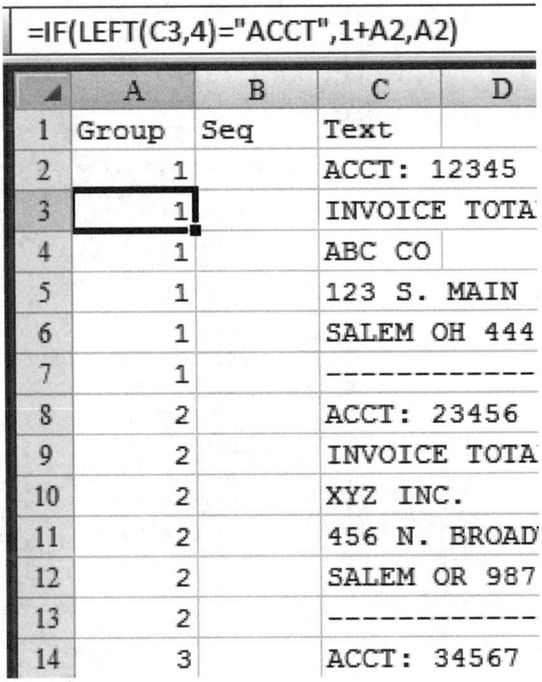

	=IF(LEFT(C3,4)="ACCT",1+A2,A2)		

◢	A	B	C	D
1	Group	Seq	Text	
2	1		ACCT: 12345	
3	1		INVOICE TOTA	
4	1		ABC CO	
5	1		123 S. MAIN	
6	1		SALEM OH 444	
7	1		------------	
8	2		ACCT: 23456	
9	2		INVOICE TOTA	
10	2		XYZ INC.	
11	2		456 N. BROAD	
12	2		SALEM OR 987	
13	2		------------	
14	3		ACCT: 34567	

3) Design a formula for a sequence number. To do this, in cell B2, enter the formula =IF(A2=A1,B1+1,1). (This formula is like the one from "Number Each Record for a Customer, Starting at 1 for a New Customer" on page 522) Copy this down. This formula will number each record in the group, as shown in Figure 812. It should ensure that all the account numbers are on a Sequence 1 record.

Figure 812

Add a sequence number using a formula.

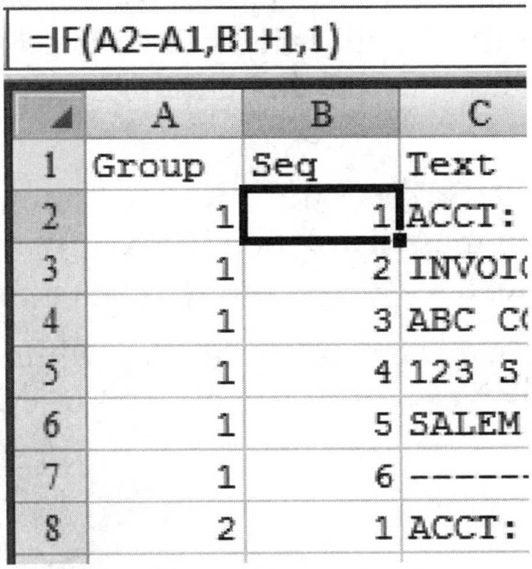

	=IF(A2=A1,B1+1,1)		

◢	A	B	C
1	Group	Seq	Text
2	1	1	ACCT:
3	1	2	INVOIC
4	1	3	ABC C(
5	1	4	123 S.
6	1	5	SALEM
7	1	6	------
8	2	1	ACCT:

Part III

4) (This step is critical.) Copy the formulas in columns A and B and paste them back, using Home – Paste dropdown – Paste Values to ensure that you can safely sort the data.

5) Sort the data by the sequence number in column B. Your data will look as shown in Figure 813.

Figure 813

Sort the data into record types.

◢	A	B	C	D	E	F	G	H
1	Group	Seq	Text					
2	1	1	ACCT: 12345	INVOICE: 1010		DATE: 10/:		
3	2	1	ACCT: 23456	INVOICE: 1011		DATE: 10/:		
4	3	1	ACCT: 34567	INVOICE: 1012		DATE: 10/:		
5	4	1	ACCT: 45678	INVOICE: 1013		DATE: 10/:		
6	5	1	ACCT: 56789	INVOICE: 1014		DATE: 10/:		
7	6	1	ACCT: 67890	INVOICE: 1015		DATE: 10/:		
8	1	2	INVOICE TOTAL	$125.00				
9	2	2	INVOICE TOTAL	$175.00				
10	3	2	INVOICE TOTAL	$225.00				
11	4	2	INVOICE TOTAL	$425.00				
12	5	2	INVOICE TOTAL	$25.00				
13	6	2	INVOICE TOTAL	$185.00				
14	1	3	ABC CO					
15	2	3	XYZ INC.					
16	3	3	BUDD & ASSOCIATES					
17	4	3	WIZARD OF OZZIE					
18	5	3	MARCINKO PUBLISHING					
19	6	3	BONNIE DOON					
20	1	4	123 S. MAIN STREET					

You have now managed to intelligently segregate the data so that all similar records are together. The contiguous range C2:C7 contains all the first rows from each record. Each of the line 1 records has three fields that really should be parsed into three separate columns. You can easily do this parsing with the Convert Text to Columns Wizard.

6) Select cells C2:C7. Select Data – Text to Columns to open the Convert Text to Columns Wizard. Select Fixed Width, as shown in Figure 814. Click Next.

7) Excel should properly guess where your columns are, as shown in Figure 815. Click Next.

Figure 814

The data is
fixed width.

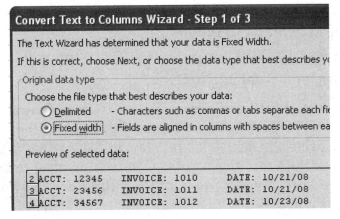

Figure 815

Excel guesses
the columns in
step 2.

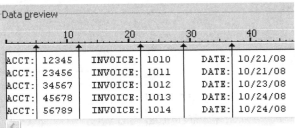

8)   Choose the heading for each column and define a data format. You
     don't really need the word ACCT each time, so choose to skip the
     first, third, and fifth fields. Make the sixth field a date. When your
     information looks as shown in Figure 816, click Finish. You will
     have data in three columns of Group 1.

Figure 816

In Step 3 of
the wizard,
skip columns
1, 3, and 5 and
change column
6 to a date.

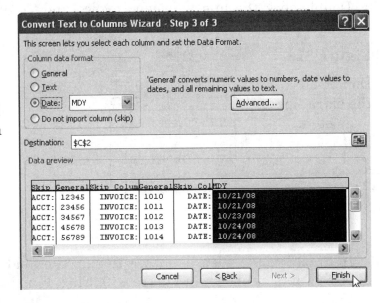

9) Change the heading in C1 to Acct, the heading in D1 to Inv, and the heading in E1 to Date.

10) Select and cut A8:C13 and paste into F2. Add the headings Group, Seq, and Total in F1:H1.

11) Select H2:H6 and choose Data – Text to Columns to open the Convert Text to Columns Wizard. In Step 1 of the wizard, select Fixed Width and click Next. In Step 2 of the wizard, Excel offers to split your data into three fields. There is no need to have one column for the word Invoice and another column for the word Total, as shown in Figure 817.

Figure 817

Excel will insert an extra column.

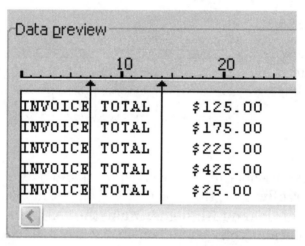

12) Double-click the line between Invoice and Total to delete it (see Figure 818).

Figure 818

Double-click the extra line to delete it.

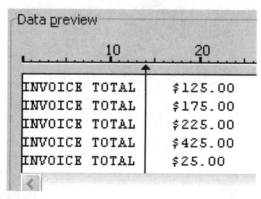

13) In Step 3 of the wizard, choose to skip the field that contains Invoice Total, as shown in Figure 819. Click Finish.

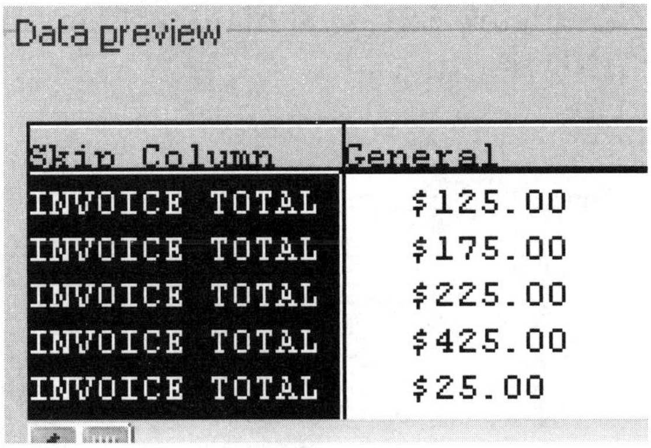

Figure 819

Skip the field label.

Data preview

Skip Column	General
INVOICE TOTAL	$125.00
INVOICE TOTAL	$175.00
INVOICE TOTAL	$225.00
INVOICE TOTAL	$425.00
INVOICE TOTAL	$25.00

14) Select the Group 3 records. Copy them to I2. Add the headings Group, Seq, and Name in I1:K1.

15) Select the Group 4 records. Cut and paste them to L2. Add headings.

16) Select the Group 5 records. Cut and paste them to O2. Add headings.

17) Because the Group 6 records have no data—they are just dashed lines (see Figure 820)—delete these rows.

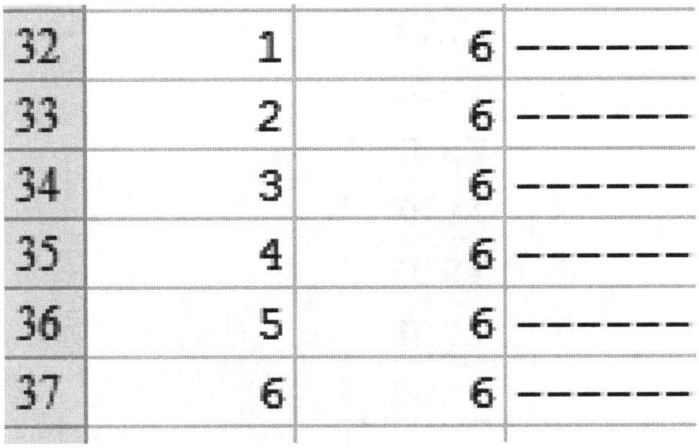

Part III

Figure 820

Group 6 has no data, so delete.

32	1	6	------
33	2	6	------
34	3	6	------
35	4	6	------
36	5	6	------
37	6	6	------

You now have all the fields, one line per record. You also have the words Group and Seq taking up about five columns each. Before you delete the Group and Seq columns, you need to make sure that everything worked correctly; the group numbers in columns A, F, I, L, and O should all match.

18) As shown in Figure 821, in a blank column at the end, enter the following AND function:

=AND(A2=F2,F2=I2,I2=L2,L2=O2)

Copy this formula down to all rows

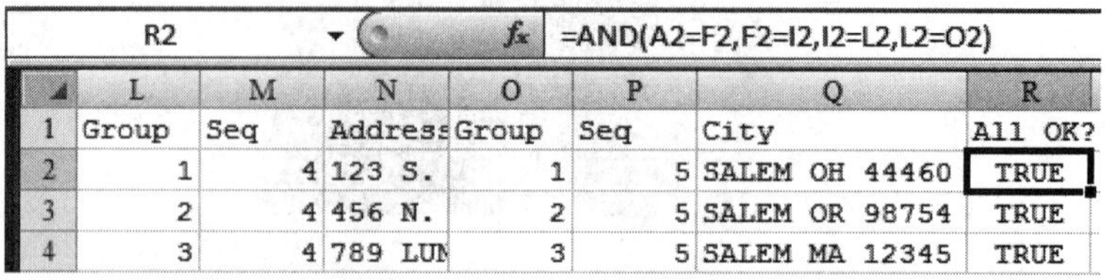

Figure 821

Check that the group numbers are equal.

	L	M	N	O	P	Q	R
1	Group	Seq	Address	Group	Seq	City	All OK?
2		1	4 123 S.	1	5	SALEM OH 44460	TRUE
3		2	4 456 N.	2	5	SALEM OR 98754	TRUE
4		3	4 789 LUN	3	5	SALEM MA 12345	TRUE

R2   fx =AND(A2=F2,F2=I2,I2=L2,L2=O2)

19) A value of TRUE means that you have successfully put all the Group 1 records back together. To test whether all the rows contain TRUE, enter the formula =AND(R2:R7) in cell R8. If this formula returns TRUE, as shown in Figure 822, you know that all the rows match up.

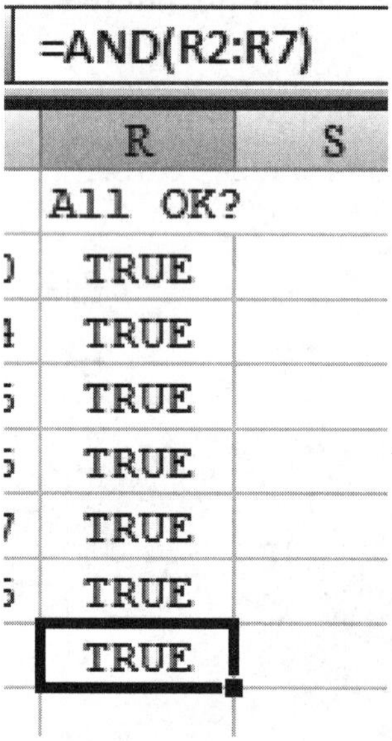

Figure 822

Cross-check that all the rows match up.

=AND(R2:R7)

	R	S
	All OK?	
)	TRUE	
ŀ	TRUE	
;	TRUE	
;	TRUE	
?	TRUE	
;	TRUE	
	TRUE	

20) Delete the columns you don't need: R, P, O, M, L, J, I, G, F, B, and A.

Results: You now have a sortable, filterable, and reportable version of the original data set. Each record consists of one row in Excel, as shown in Figure 823.

Figure 823

You can now sort and analyze this data.

	A	B	C	D	E	F	G
1	Acct	Inv	Date	Total	Name	Address	City ST ZIP
2	12345	1010	10/21/2008	$125.00	ABC CO	123 S. MAIN STREET	SALEM OH 44460
3	23456	1011	10/21/2008	$175.00	XYZ INC.	456 N. BROADWAY	SALEM OR 98754
4	34567	1012	10/23/2008	$225.00	BUDD & ASSOCIATES	789 LUNDY LANE	SALEM MA 12345
5	45678	1013	10/24/2008	$425.00	WIZARD OF OZZIE	987 KING CHURCH	SALEM WV 32145
6	56789	1014	10/24/2008	$25.00	MARCINKO PUBLISHING	654 FAIR AVE	SALEM IL 60187
7	67890	1015	10/26/2008	$185.00	BONNIE DOON	321 PERSHING	SALEM IN 46875

Summary: This process of converting data from five rows per record to one row per record is convoluted. However, if you are presented with data as shown in the original example, the only way to quickly add up figures or to produce a report is to follow steps similar to the ones shown in this topic.

Commands Discussed: Home – Paste dropdown – Paste Values; Data – Text to Columns

Functions Discussed: =IF(); =AND(); =LEFT()

ADD A CUSTOMER NUMBER TO EACH DETAIL RECORD

Part III

Problem: I've imported a data set in which the creator lists the customer number once in column A and then has any number of invoice detail records. At the end of the first customer, the next customer number is in column A and then there are detail records for that customer (see Figure 824). I cannot sort this data set, but I need to add the customer information to each record.

Figure 824

Another annoying report format.

	A	B	C	D	E
1	Invoice	Date	Quantity	Product	Revenue
2	Acct A4651 Air Canada				
3	1533	29-Mar-08	300	ABC	5859.00
4	1559	17-Apr-08	200	XYZ	4948.00
5	1756	22-Aug-08	800	XYZ	17856.00
6	1828	5-Oct-08	100	DEF	2358.00
7	Acct A8736 Ainsworth				
8	1404	1-Jan-08	500	XYZ	11240.00
9	1405	2-Jan-08	400	XYZ	9204.00
10	1414	8-Jan-08	900	XYZ	21465.00

Strategy: This is a common data format, but it is horrible in Excel. Here's how you fix the problem:

1) Insert new columns A and B. Add the headings Acct and Customer. Here is the basic logic of what you want to do: Look at the first four characters of column C. If they are equal to Acct, then you know this row has customer information, so you take data from that cell and move it to column A. If the first four characters are anything other than Acct, you use the same account information from the previous row's column A.

2) Enter the following formula into cell A2:

=IF(LEFT(C2,4)="Acct",MID(C2,6,5),A1)

Copy this formula down through column A. As shown in Figure 825, as you copy this formula down, it does the job. In cell A2, the IF condition is true and data is extracted from C2. In cell A3, the condition is not true, so the value from A2 is used. In cell A7, a new customer number is found, so the data from C7 is used in A7. Cells A8 through A59 get the customer number from A7.

Figure 825

Use an IF function to extract and copy account number infor- mation.

=IF(LEFT(C2,4)="Acct",MID(C2,6,5),A1)

	A	B	C	D	
1	Acct	Customer	Invoice	Date	Qu
2	A4651		Acct A4651 Air Canada		
3	A4651		1533	29-Mar-08	
4	A4651		1559	17-Apr-08	
5	A4651		1756	22-Aug-08	
6	A4651		1828	5-Oct-08	
7	A8736		Acct A8736 Ainsworth		
8	A8736		1404	1-Jan-08	
9	A8736		1405	2-Jan-08	

Similar logic is needed in column B. In this case, though, you need to grab the customer name. You know that the word Acct and the space that follows it take up 5 characters. You know that your account number is another 5 characters, and then there is a space before the customer name. You therefore want to ignore the first 11 characters of cell C2.

You can use the formula =MID(C2,12,50) to skip the first 11 characters and return the next 50 characters of the customer name. To avoid leading or trailing spaces, you use the =TRIM() function. You therefore use =TRIM(MID(C2,12,50)) as the formula to extract a customer name. Use this formula as the TRUE portion of the IF function.

3) As shown in Figure 826, enter the following formula into cell B2:

=IF(LEFT(C2,4)="Acct",TRIM(MID(C2,12,50)),B1)

Copy this formula down through column B.

Figure 826

Extract customer information.

=IF(LEFT(C2,4)="Acct",TRIM(MID(C2,12,50)),B1)

	A	B	C	D	
1	Acct	Customer	Invoice	Date	Qu
2	A4651	Air Canada	Acct A4651 Air Canada		
3	A4651	Air Canada	1533	29-Mar-08	
4	A4651	Air Canada	1559	17-Apr-08	
5	A4651	Air Canada	1756	22-Aug-08	
6	A4651	Air Canada	1828	5-Oct-08	
7	A8736	Ainsworth	Acct A8736 Ainsworth		
8	A8736	Ainsworth	1404	1-Jan-08	
9	A8736	Ainsworth	1405	2-Jan-08	

Part
III

You have now successfully filled in the account and customer. You need to change these formulas to values.

4) Highlight columns A and B. Press Ctrl+C to copy. Choose Home – Paste dropdown – Paste Values to convert the formulas to values. You do this to remove the customer heading rows. As you think about a method to isolate the heading rows, you will notice that heading rows are the only rows with blank cells in column D. You can move the blanks to the end of a data set by sorting the data by column D.

5) Select the heading in D1. Select Data – AZ to sort ascending by date. Any rows that have no value in column D will automatically sort to the bottom of the data set, as shown in Figure 827.

Figure 827

The extraneous heading rows sort to the bottom.

	A	B	C	D	E	
1	Acct	Customer	Invoice	Date	Quantity	Prc
561	S2328	Sun Life Financial	1960	25-Dec-08	500	AB
562	G1394	General Motors	1961	26-Dec-08	600	AB
563	G1394	General Motors	1962	26-Dec-08	600	AB
564	G1394	General Motors	1963	26-Dec-08	900	AB
565	A4651	Air Canada	Acct A4651 Air Canada			
566	A8736	Ainsworth	Acct A8736 Ainsworth			
567	B3529	Bell Canada	Acct B3529 Bell Canada			
568	C4341	Compton Petroleum	Acct C4341 Compton Petroleum			
569	C7849	Compaq	Acct C7849 Compaq			

6) With the cell pointer in D1, press the End key and then the Down Arrow key twice. The cell pointer will be located on the first customer heading. Delete all the rows below row 564.

Results: You have a clean data set with customer information on every row, as shown in Figure 828. You can sort this data and otherwise use it for data analysis.

Figure 828

Customer data has been added to each record.

	A	B	C	D	E	F
1	Acct	Customer	Invoice	Date	Quantity	Produ
2	F8417	Ford	1401	1-Jan-08	1000	XYZ
3	V8627	Verizon	1402	1-Jan-08	100	DEF
4	V8627	Verizon	1403	1-Jan-08	500	ABC
5	A8736	Ainsworth	1404	1-Jan-08	500	XYZ

Summary: A couple formulas with IF functions help to add the customer data to each record.

Commands Discussed: =IF(); =LEFT(); =TRIM(); =MID()

USE A PIVOT TABLE
TO SUMMARIZE DETAILED DATA

Problem: I have 50,000 rows of sales data, as shown in Figure 829. I want to produce a summary report that shows sales by region and product.

Figure 829

Summarize
this data set.

	A	B	C	D	E	F	G	H
1	Region	Product	Date	Customer	Quantity	Revenue	COGS	Profit
2	East	XYZ	2-Jan-08	Ford	1000	22810	10220	12590
3	Central	DEF	2-Jan-08	Verizon	100	2257	984	1273
4	East	ABC	2-Jan-08	Verizon	500	10245	4235	6010
5	Central	XYZ	2-Jan-08	Ainsworth	500	11240	5110	6130
6	Central	XYZ	2-Jan-08	Ainsworth	400	9204	4088	5116
7	East	DEF	2-Jan-08	Gildan Activewea	800	18552	7872	10680
8	East	XYZ	2-Jan-08	Texaco	400	9152	4088	5064
9	Central	ABC	3-Jan-08	IBM	400	6860	3388	3472

Strategy: To solve this problem, you can use a pivot table. As Excel's most powerful feature, pivot tables are well suited to this type of analysis. **Version Warning:** Pivot tables changed dramatically in Excel 2007. If you are using Excel 97-2003, see http://www.mrexcel.com/learnedition1.html; I've made the 90 pivot table pages from the first edition of the book available for free.

Creating a summary of revenue by region and product requires four mouse clicks and one mouse drag:

1) Ensure that your data is in list format and that every heading is unique. (For a refresher on list format, see "How to Set up Your Data for Easy Sorting and Subtotals" on page 413.)

2) Select a single cell in the database. Select Insert – Pivot Table.

3) Excel's IntelliSense will guess the range of your data. It is usually correct, as shown in Figure 830. Click OK.

Part III

Figure 830

Make sure
that Excel
guessed the
correct range.

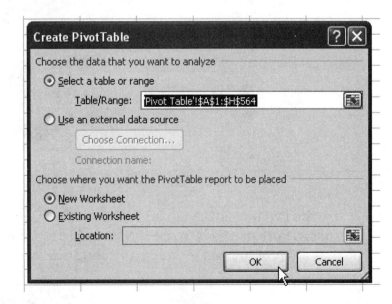

You will now see an empty pivot table icon, two new PivotTable Tools tabs on the ribbon, and the new PivotTable Field List dialog. The Excel 2007 version of the dialog includes a list of the fields at the top and four drop zones at the bottom of the dialog, as shown in Figure 831.

In previous versions of Excel, you would drag fields from the Field List dialog to the pivot table. This process was frustrating for people new to pivot tables. In Excel 2007, you drag fields from the top of the Field List dialog to the proper drop zone at the bottom of the Field List dialog. In many cases, clicking the field in the Field List dialog will move it to the correct drop zone. In this case, you want to have products going down the side of the report and regions going across the top.

Figure 831

The new PivotTable Field List dialog includes fields at the top and drop zones at the bottom.

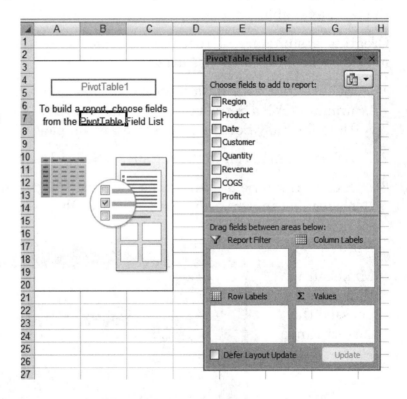

4) Click the Product check box in the top of the Field List dialog. Excel automatically moves it to the Row Labels drop zone. The pivot table shows a list of unique products in column A (see Figure 832).

Figure 832

Click a text field, and Excel moves it to the Row area.

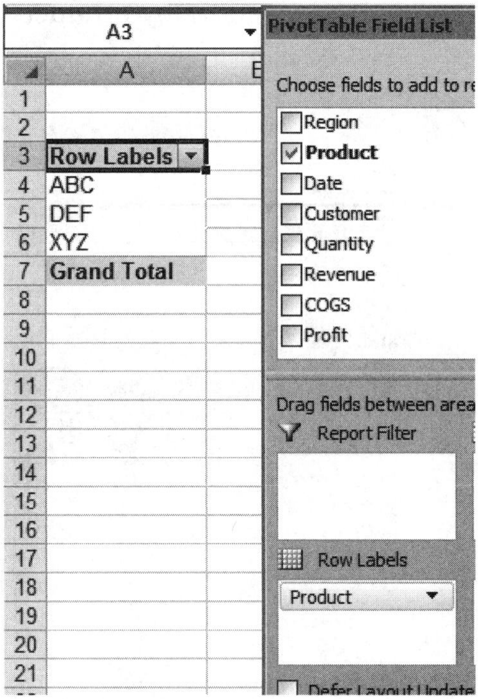

5) Click the Revenue check box in the top of the Field List dialog. Because this field is numeric, Excel will add it to the Values section of the pivot table.

6) If you click the Region check box, Excel will add it to the row area of the pivot table. Because you want regions to go across the top of your pivot table, drag the Region field from the top of the Field List dialog and drop it in the Column Labels drop zone at the bottom of the Field List dialog.

Part III

Results: Excel will summarize the data by product and region, as shown in Figure 833.

Figure 833

Pivot tables make it easy to create this summary report.

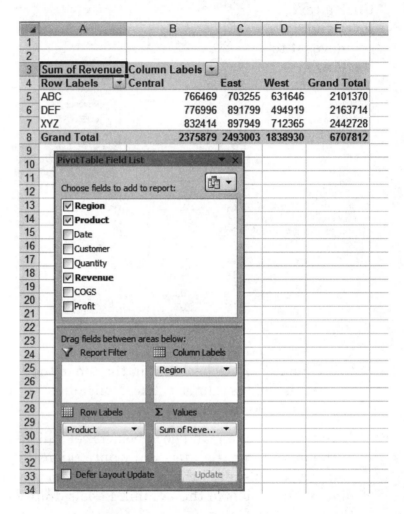

Additional Details: Pivot tables offer many powerful options. This topic describes the steps to create your first pivot table; you should read the next several topics to learn more about pivot tables.

Gotcha: If you were a pivot table pro in previous Excel versions, you can quickly adapt to Excel 2007. The drop zones have been renamed. The Row Area drop zone is now Row Labels. The Column Area drop zone is now Column Labels. The Page Field drop zone is now Report Filter. The Data Area drop zone is now $\sum$ Values (although I will call it the Values drop zone, leaving off the $\sum$ symbol).

Gotcha: Initially, the PivotTable Field List dialog is docked to the right side of the screen. You can grab the title of the dialog and drag it into the worksheet to make it float. I've done that throughout this book in order to keep the dialog in view in the screen shots.

Gotcha: It is difficult to redock the PivotTable Field List dialog. You have to grab the left side of the title bar and drag it 90% off the right edge of the Excel window.

Gotcha: A dropdown at the top of the PivotTable Field List dialog offers five different views of the dialog. Three of those views omit either the fields or the drop zones. If your dialog box is missing one section, use the dropdown to return it to Fields Section and Areas Section Stacked. There are also views where the sections are side by side. Throughout the next pages, I will refer to the drop zones at the bottom of the dialog. If you have moved them to be side by side, then mentally change those instructions to read "the drop zones on the right side of the dialog."

Summary: The Insert – Pivot Table command allows you to summarize thousands of rows of data quickly. Excel does not require you to know any formulas. You just need to be able to drag fields to a report layout.

Commands Discussed: Insert – Pivot Table

Excel 97-2003: The pivot tables process was completely different; see www.mrexcel.com/learnedition1.html.

See Also: "How to Set up Your Data for Easy Sorting" on page 413

YOUR MANAGER WANTS
YOUR REPORT CHANGED

Problem: I presented my first pivot table report, shown previously in Figure 833, to my manager. He said, "This is almost perfect, but could you have the products going across the top and the regions going down the side?"

Strategy: Pivot tables make this change easy:

1) On the worksheet, select one cell within the pivot table. Excel will display the PivotTable Field List dialog.

2) In the dialog, drag the Region field from the Column Labels drop zone to the Row Labels drop zone. In this case, it does not matter if you drop the Region field above or below the Product field. The interim result is shown in Figure 834.

Figure 834

Drag a field from one drop zone to another drop zone in the Field List dialog to rearrange the pivot table.

Row Labels ▾	Sum of Revenue
⊟ABC	2101370
Central	766469
East	703255
West	631646
⊟DEF	2163714
Central	776996
East	891799
West	494919
⊟XYZ	2442728
Central	832414
East	897949
West	712365
Grand Total	**6707812**

3) In the dialog, drag the Product field from the Row Labels drop zone to the Column Labels drop zone.

Results: With two movements of the mouse, you have created a new report for your manager, as shown in Figure 835.

Figure 835

Move two fields to create a new report.

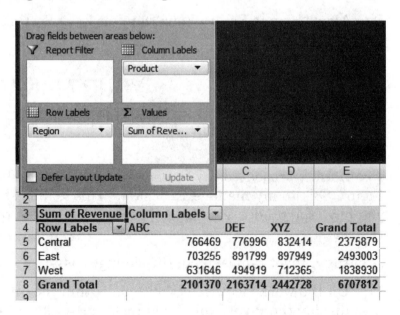

Sum of Revenue	Column Labels ▾			
Row Labels ▾	ABC	DEF	XYZ	Grand Total
Central	766469	776996	832414	2375879
East	703255	891799	897949	2493003
West	631646	494919	712365	1838930
Grand Total	2101370	2163714	2442728	6707812

Summary: The first amazing feature of pivot tables is that they can summarize massive amounts of data very quickly. This topic shows the second amazing feature: Pivot tables can be quickly changed to show another view of the data.

Commands Discussed: Insert – Pivot Table

WHY DOES THIS LOOK DIFFERENT FROM EXCEL 2003?

Problem: I'm having a panic attack. I loved pivot tables in Excel 97-2003, and they look completely different in Excel 2007.

Strategy: Relax. The new interface really is better. But if you are completely freaking out, there are a couple steps you can take to make the pivot tables look as they did before.

The first cosmetic change is that pivot tables are created in a new Compact Form view. You will see strange words like "Row Labels" and "Column Labels" where field names used to be. If you add a second field to the row area, you will notice that Excel puts both fields in column A instead of in two columns. I agree that there are times when this is completely annoying.

Figure 836

Excel 2007 uses a new view called Compact Form.

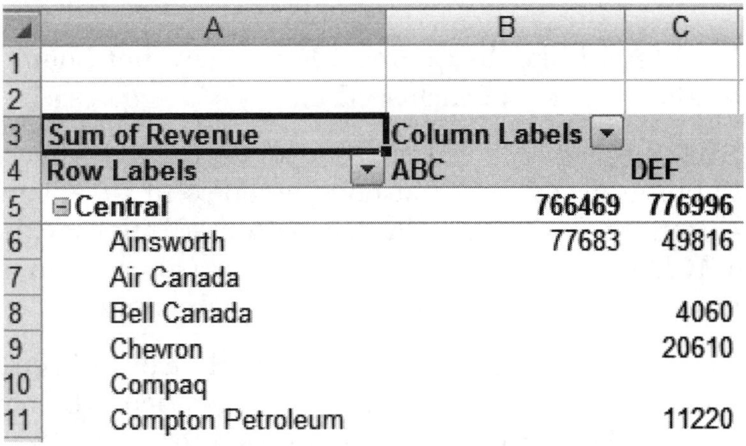

	A	B	C
1			
2			
3	Sum of Revenue	Column Labels ▾	
4	Row Labels ▾	ABC	DEF
5	⊟ Central	766469	776996
6	Ainsworth	77683	49816
7	Air Canada		
8	Bell Canada		4060
9	Chevron		20610
10	Compaq		
11	Compton Petroleum		11220

You can easily switch back to the traditional layout. When the pivot table is active, you have two new PivotTable Tools tabs on the ribbon. You need to switch to the Design tab, open the Report Layout dropdown, and choose Show in Tabular Form. As shown in Figure 837, the multiple-column fields now are each in their own columns. Field names are now Region, Product, and Customer instead of Row Labels and Column Labels.

Figure 837

Switch to Tabular Form view to arrange the fields as in Excel 2003.

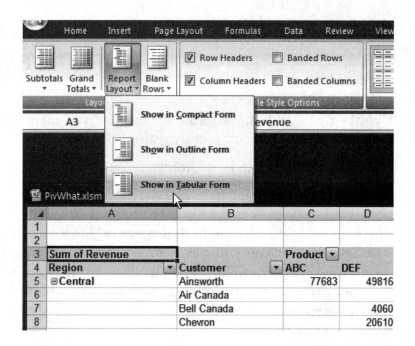

Problem: I like the Compact Form view, but I don't like how it puts the totals at the top of each section.

Strategy: Select a cell in the pivot table. On the Design ribbon, open the Subtotal dropdown. You have a choice to show subtotals at the top or bottom of each group. Choose Bottom. (Note that the Top setting works only in Compact Form or Outline Form view. Tabular Form view always has the subtotals at the bottom of each group.)

Problem: I loved the ugly borders that have been a hallmark of pivot tables for over a decade. How can I get rid of the new colors and return to the ugly formatting that I am used to?

Strategy: Go to the Design tab. Open the PivotTable Styles and choose the first thumbnail to choose the style None. Actually, if you open a file that contains an Excel 2003 pivot table, classic formatting will appear as an 86th style. You can then build a new style based on that style. But, really, that old style was horrible. Get over it.

Problem: I want to go back to dragging fields around the pivot table.

Strategy: I really don't recommend this, but there is a way to go back to the old style. Follow these steps:

1) Select one cell in the pivot table.

2) Select Options – Options.

3) Go to the Display tab within the PivotTable Options dialog.

4) Choose Classic PivotTable Layout. As shown in Figure 838, you now have drop zones within the pivot table.

Figure 838

You can go back to the old version, where fields can be dropped on the report.

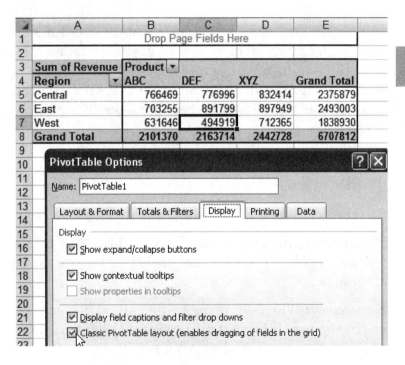

Summary: While a number of pivot table defaults have been changed in Excel 2007, you can adjust some items to operate similarly to Excel 97-2003.

Commands Discussed: Design – Layout, Options – Options

MOVE OR CHANGE PART OF A PIVOT TABLE

Problem: If I try to insert a row in a pivot table, I am greeted with a message saying that I cannot change, move, or insert cells in a pivot table, as shown in Figure 839.

Figure 839

Excel won't let you insert a row in a pivot table.

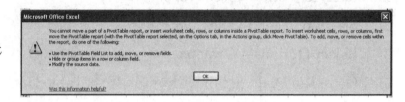

Strategy: You cannot do a lot of things to a finished pivot table. While the flexibility of pivot tables is awesome, sometimes you just want to take the results of the pivot table and turn off the pivot features. If you want to take the data and reuse it somewhere else, for example, you can convert the pivot table to regular data by using Paste Values. Follow these steps:

1)   Select the entire pivot table.

2)   Press Ctrl+C to copy.

3)   Select Home – Paste dropdown – Paste Values.

This action will change the pivot table from a live pivot table to just values in cells. You can now insert rows and columns to your heart's content.

Summary: When doing data analysis, it is common to use a pivot table to get the result but then to convert the pivot table from a live table to static values by using Paste Values.

Commands Discussed: Home – Paste dropdown – Paste Values

SEE DETAIL BEHIND
ONE NUMBER IN A PIVOT TABLE

Problem: One number in my pivot table seems to be wrong. Bell Canada does not typically buy a certain product line, yet it is shown with that product in the report in Figure 840.

Figure 840

At a summary level, you can spot apparent problems with the data.

	A	B	C	D
1				
2				
3	**Sum of Revenue**	**Product ▼**		
4	**Customer** ▼	ABC	DEF	XYZ
5	Ainsworth	177382	190533	200936
6	Air Canada	5859	2358	22804
7	Bell Canada	15104	18064	18072
8	Chevron	26406	20610	7032
9	Compaq	17250	4380	17620

Part
III

Strategy: You can see the detail behind any number in a pivot table by double-clicking on the number. If the $18,064 in sales of product DEF to Bell Canada seems unusual, you can double-click cell C7. As shown in Figure 841, a new worksheet is inserted, showing all the records that make up the $18,064.

Figure 841

Excel inserts a new sheet with the drill-down detail.

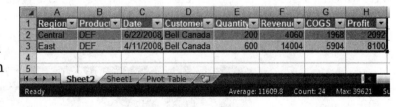

	A	B	C	D	E	F	G	H
1	Region ▼	Product ▼	Date ▼	Customer ▼	Quantity ▼	Revenue ▼	COGS ▼	Profit ▼
2	Central	DEF	6/22/2008	Bell Canada	200	4060	1968	2092
3	East	DEF	4/11/2008	Bell Canada	600	14004	5904	8100
4								
5								

Sheet2 / Sheet1 / Pivot Table

Ready   Average: 11609.8   Count: 24   Max: 39621   SU

Additional Details: If you double-click on a number in the total row or total column, you will see all the records that make up that number. You could even drill down on the Grand Total cell to get a copy of all the original records.

Gotcha: Each drill-down creates a new worksheet. The new worksheet is just a snapshot in time of what made up the original number. If you detect a wrong number in the drill-down report, you need to go back to the original data to make the correction.

Summary: Given the power to summarize data in a pivot table, you are likely to spot information that might point to a problem in the underlying data. With 50,000 rows of data, someone may miscode a region on a few of the records. Until you look at a pivot table with a quick summary, it is hard to spot obvious problems like the one shown here. When you see a number that seems suspicious in a pivot table, you can double-click the number to drill down and see the records behind the data.

UPDATE DATA BEHIND A PIVOT TABLE

Problem: I've discovered that some of the underlying data in my pivot table is wrong. After I correct a number, the pivot table does not appear to include the change.

Strategy: This is an important thing to understand about pivot tables: When you create a pivot table, all the data is loaded into memory to allow it to calculate quickly. When you change the data on the original worksheet, it does not automatically update the pivot table.

You need to select a cell in the pivot table. The PivotTable ribbon tabs will appear. On the Options tab, you click the Refresh icon (see Figure 842) to recalculate the pivot table from the worksheet data.

Figure 842

This icon makes a lot more sense than the red exclamation icon used for the last decade.

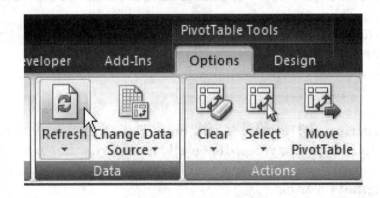

Results: The pivot table is updated.

Additional Details: Making changes to the underlying data could cause the table to grow. For example, if you re-classify some records from the East region to the Southeast region, be aware that clicking the Refresh button will cause the table to grow by one column. If there happens to be other data in that column, Excel will warn you and ask if it is okay to overwrite those cells.

Summary: Changes to the underlying data do not automatically get calculated in a pivot table. You must click the Refresh icon on the Options tab to have Excel reread the original data.

Commands Discussed: Options – Refresh

REPLACE BLANKS
IN A PIVOT TABLE WITH ZEROS

Problem: When I have no sales of a particular product in a particular region, Excel leaves those cells in the pivot table blank, as shown in Figure 843. This seems like a really bad idea. I've learned in this book that if my data has blanks instead of zeros, Excel will assume that a column is a text column. It is really ironic that Microsoft would dare to use a blank cell in the middle of numeric results.

Figure 843

It is annoying that Excel uses blanks instead of zeros.

◢	A	B	C	D	E
1					
2					
3	Sum of Revenue	Column Labels ▾			
4	Row Labels ▾	ABC	DEF	XYZ	Grand Total
5	Central		776759	776996	832414	2386169
6	East		703255	891799	882724	2477778
7	Government				24685	24685
8	Southeast	15225				15225
9	West	631646	494919	712365	1838930
10	Grand Total	2126885	2163714	2452188	6742787

Strategy: When pivot tables first came out, there was no way to correct this problem. After much outcry from accountants everywhere, Microsoft gave us a way to solve the problem. If you discover the problem after the fact in a completed pivot table, follow these steps:

1)   Select one cell in the pivot table in order to display the PivotTable ribbon tabs. On the Options tab, click the Options icon.

2)   In the PivotTable Options dialog, select the Layout & Format tab and enter 0 in the For Empty Cells Show text box, as shown in Figure 844. Click OK.

Figure 844

Add a zero to the For Empty Cells Show text box.

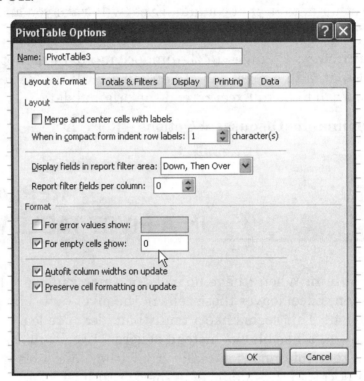

Results: As you see in Figure 845, blanks in the data section of the pivot table are shown as zeros.

Figure 845

Excel fills blanks in the values area with zeros.

Sum of Revenue	Column Labels			
Row Labels	ABC	DEF	XYZ	Grand Total
Central	776759	776996	832414	2386169
East	703255	891799	882724	2477778
Government	0	0	24685	24685
Southeast	15225	0	0	15225
West	631646	494919	712365	1838930
Grand Total	2126885	2163714	2452188	6742787

Additional Details: You can enter anything in the For Empty Cells Show text box. Some people like to use -- or n.a. in the formerly blank cells. Either works just as well as a zero.

Summary: You can use the PivotTable Options dialog to display empty cells as zeros instead of blanks.

Commands Discussed: Options – Options

ADD OR REMOVE FIELDS
FROM AN EXISTING PIVOT TABLE

Problem: I've seen how easy it is to rearrange an existing pivot table by swapping Region and Product fields. Now, what if I want to replace the Region field with the Customer field?

Strategy: In order to remove the Region field from a pivot table, you click on the Region button in the Row Labels drop zone of the PivotTable Field List dialog. Then you drag the button outside the Field List dialog. As shown in Figure 846, the cell pointer will change to include a black X, which is synonymous with Delete.

Figure 846

The X in the mouse pointer indicates you are removing the field from the pivot table.

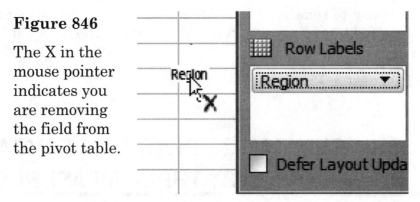

Excel will remove the Region field from the pivot table, as shown in Figure 847.

Figure 847

Excel will redraw the pivot table without the Region field.

	Product			
		ABC	DEF	XYZ Grand Total
Sum of Revenue		2101370	2163714	2442728 6707812

To add the Customer field to the Row Labels drop zone, you simply click the Customer check box in the top of the PivotTable Field List dialog. Because the field is a text field, it will automatically move to the Row Labels drop zone.

Results: The new field will be added to the pivot table, as shown in Figure 848.

Figure 848

Excel will add the Customer field.

	Sum of Revenue	Product			
	Customer	ABC	DEF	XYZ	Grand Total
5	Ainsworth	177382	190533	200936	568851
6	Air Canada	5859	2358	22804	31021
7	Bell Canada	15104	18064	18072	51240
8	Chevron	26406	20610	7032	54048
9	Compaq	17250	4380	17620	39250
10	Compton Petroleum	4158	13249	13962	31369
11	Exxon	294138	185286	224935	704359
12	Ford	191628	185675	245491	622794
13	General Motors	280967	233435	235761	750163

Summary: It is easy to remove or add fields to a pivot table by using the mouse to drag fields off or on the drop zone section of the PivotTable Field List dialog.

Commands Discussed: Pivot Table

SUMMARIZE PIVOT TABLE DATA BY THREE MEASURES

Problem: I want to summarize data by region, product, and customer. How can I use a two-dimensional report to show three dimensions of data?

Strategy: Several views of the data are possible. Say that you are starting with regions across the top and customers down the side. From the top of the PivotTable Field List dialog, you click the Product field. It is automatically added as the last row field. The view in Figure 849 shows the first customer and the products that customer bought.

Figure 849

Products with customer.

Sum of Revenue	Column Labels	
Row Labels	Central	East
⊟Ainsworth	223540	232076
ABC	77683	61660
DEF	49816	90978
XYZ	96041	79438
⊟Air Canada	4948	2358
ABC	0	0
DEF	0	2358
XYZ	4948	0
⊟Bell Canada	4060	14004

Another option is to drag the Product field heading above the Customer field heading in the bottom of the Field List dialog. There are two ways to do this. The first is to drag the Product field to the top quarter of the Customer field. A blue insertion line appears above Customer, and you can drop.

If your mouse is not accurate enough to complete this drop, you can move the Product field to the Row Labels drop zone. Then you open the dropdown arrow at the right side of the Product field in the bottom of the Field List dialog and choose Move Up or Move to Beginning, as shown in Figure 850.

Figure 850

Use the drop-down on the Product field in the bottom of the Field List dialog to access this menu.

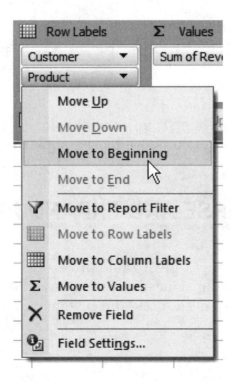

Results: You will now see a product and the customers who bought that product (see Figure 851).

Figure 851

This report focuses on each product and the customers who bought that product.

Sum of Revenue	Column Labels ▼
Row Labels ▼	Central
⊟ ABC	766469
Ainsworth	77683
Air Canada	0
Bell Canada	0
Chevron	0
Compaq	0

You can also stack fields in the Column Labels drop zone. Figure 852 shows the report that will result if you add Product after Region in the Column Labels drop zone.

Figure 852

Columns show product within region.

Sum of Revenue	Column Labels ▼			Central Total
	⊟ Central			
Row Labels ▼	ABC	DEF	XYZ	
Ainsworth	77683	49816	96041	223540
Air Canada	0	0	4948	4948
Bell Canada	0	4060	0	4060
Chevron	0	20610	0	20610
Compaq	0	0	9064	9064

Summary: You can use more than one field along either the row or column area of a pivot table to produce more complex summaries.

COLLAPSE AND EXPAND PIVOT FIELDS

Problem: I will be using a pivot table projected on a screen during a sales forecasting meeting. I need pivot tables that show products by month, but sometimes I need to see the customer detail for a product.

Strategy: You can solve this problem by building a pivot table with Product, Region, and Customer along the row area as shown in Figure 853.

Figure 853

Start with Product, Region, and Customer.

Sum of Quantity	Column Labels	
Row Labels	Jan	Feb
⊟ABC	13800	8700
⊟Central	4000	4100
Ainsworth	500	0
Exxon	0	1300
Ford	0	900

Here's how it works:

1) Select one of the customer cells. In the Options tab of the ribbon, select Collapse Entire Field. Excel will hide all the customer rows, as shown in Figure 854.

Figure 854

Collapse the Customer field.

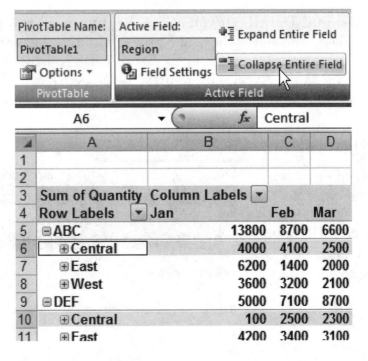

2) Select a region cell and collapse that field as well.

Notice that each product has a plus sign button to the left of the field. When the meeting agenda moves to the DEF product, you can click the plus sign in A6 to see the region totals. If you need to focus on the large January sales for the East region, click the plus sign next to East to see those customer details (see Figure 855). You can continue collapsing sections as you are finished and then expanding the next sections.

Figure 855

Expand sections as needed.

| Sum of Quantity | Column Labels ▼ | |
Row Labels ▼	Jan	Feb
⊞ ABC	13800	8700
⊟ DEF	5000	7100
⊞ Central	100	2500
⊟ East	4200	3400
Ainsworth	0	900
Air Canada	0	0
Bell Canada	0	0
Compaq	0	0

Additional Details: If you select the innermost row field (in this case, Customer) and select Expand Entire Field, Excel assumes that you must need more detail for Customer. Because there is no additional detail in the pivot table, Excel will display the Show Detail dialog, basically allowing you to add a new field as the innermost row field (see Figure 856).

Figure 856

Try to expand the innermost row field, and Excel will offer to add a new field.

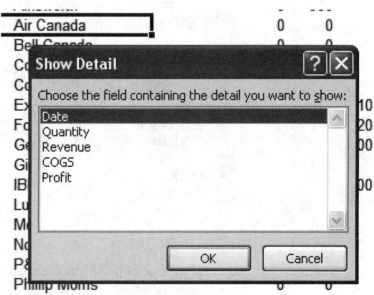

Summary: The expand and collapse buttons can make a dynamic report that is useful during review meetings.

MANUALLY RE-SEQUENCE THE ORDER OF DATA IN A PIVOT TABLE

Problem: By default, a pivot table organizes data alphabetically. For the Region field, as shown in Figure 857, this means the data is organized with Central first, East second, and West third. My manager wants the regions to appear in the order East, Central, West. After unsuccessfully lobbying to have the Central region renamed Middle, I need to find a way to have my table sequenced with the East region first.

Figure 857

Custom dictates that East should come first.

Sum of Revenue	Region			
Product	Central	East	West	Grand Total
ABC	766469	703255	631646	2101370
DEF	776996	891799	494919	2163714
XYZ	832414	897949	712365	2442728
Grand Total	2375879	2493003	1838930	6707812

Part III

Strategy: It is amazing that this trick works. Try it:

1) Select cell B4 in the pivot table (refer to Figure 857).

2) In cell B4, type the word East, as shown in Figure 858.

Figure 858

Go to the Central cell and type a new heading.

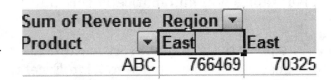

Sum of Revenue	Region	
Product	East	East
ABC	766469	70325

3)   When you press Enter, Excel senses what you are trying to do. All the data from the East region moves to Column B. Excel automatically moves the Central region heading and data to column C, as shown in Figure 859.

Figure 859

East and Central switch places. Never try this outside a pivot table.

◢	A	B	C	D	E
1					
2					
3	Sum of Revenue	Region ▼			
4	Product ▼	East	Central	West	Grand Total
5	ABC	703255	766469	631646	2101370
6	DEF	891799	776996	494919	2163714
7	XYZ	897949	832414	712365	2442728
8	Grand Total	2493003	2375879	1838930	6707812

You can easily use this trick to re-sequence the fields into any order as necessary.

Additional Details: This technique will only change the Region sequence in a single pivot table. If you would like to change the sequence in all future pivot tables, you need to create a custom list:

1)   In a blank area of the worksheet, type your regions in a column, in the desired order. Enter East in one cell, Central in the next cell, and West in the next cell. Select these three cells.

2)   Select Office Icon – Excel Options. In the Popular category of the Excel Options dialog, click the Edit Custom Lists button. The text box next to the Import button should point to the three cells in your selection from step 1. Click Import to add a custom list East, Central, West.

All future pivot tables will automatically sort into East, Central, West sequence.

Summary: The pivot table manual sort feature is astounding. You can simply type a heading in a new place to have Excel turn on manual sequencing of the data.

PRESENT A PIVOT TABLE
IN HIGH-TO-LOW ORDER BY REVENUE

Problem: A pivot table organizes data alphabetically by default, as shown in Figure 860. I want to produce a report that is sorted high to low by revenue.

Figure 860

Reports are normally sorted alphabetically.

Sum of Revenue	Column Labels	
Row Labels	Central	East
Ainsworth	223540	232076
Air Canada	4948	2358
Bell Canada	4060	14004

Strategy: Each pivot table field offers a sort option. To access the sort options for a field, follow these steps:

1) As shown in Figure 861, open the Customer field dropdown in cell A4. Note that in Compact Form view, this dropdown is called Row Labels. In Tabular Form view, it is called Customer.

Figure 861

The dropdown offers to sort in ascending or descending order.

2) Choose More Sort Options from the dropdown menu. Excel displays the Sort (Customer) dialog. Initially, the sort is set to Manual. This option lets you re-sequence items by dragging or retyping. (see "Manually Re-sequence the Order of Data in a Pivot Table.").

Figure 862

Excel offers interesting sort possibilities here.

3) Choose Descending. Excel enables the Descending dropdown.

4) Choose Sum of Revenue from the dropdown under Descending, as shown in Figure 863.

Figure 863

Choose to sort customer by descending revenue.

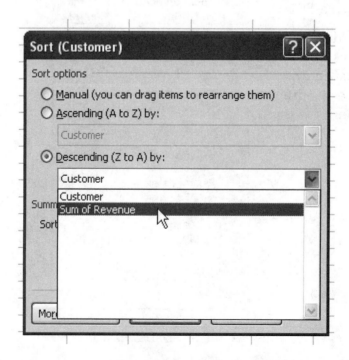

Results: The report will be sequenced with the largest customers at the top, as shown in Figure 864. Further, as you continue to pivot this report, Excel will remember that customers should always be sorted based on descending revenue.

Figure 864

Excel will sort customers by descending revenue.

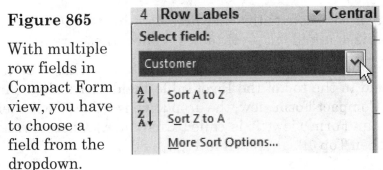

Sum of Revenue	Column Labels			
Row Labels	Central	East	West	Grand Total
Wal-Mart	327958	313454	228042	869454
General Motors	294033	260163	195967	750163
Exxon	315631	229640	159088	704359
Ford	288393	175967	158434	622794
Molson, Inc	209326	245081	159107	613514

Additional Details: If you have multiple fields in the Row Labels area and open the Row Labels dropdown, you will have to select a field from the Select Field dropdown (see Figure 865).

Figure 865

With multiple row fields in Compact Form view, you have to choose a field from the dropdown.

4	Row Labels	▼	Central

Select field:

Customer

A↓Z	Sort A to Z
Z↓A	Sort Z to A

Mo<u>r</u>e Sort Options...

An alternate method for accessing the Sort dialog is to hover over the Customer field in the top of the PivotTable Field List dialog. A dropdown appears, as shown in Figure 866. You can choose to sort or filter from this dropdown.

Figure 866

Hover over a field in the top of the Field List dialog to access a drop-down.

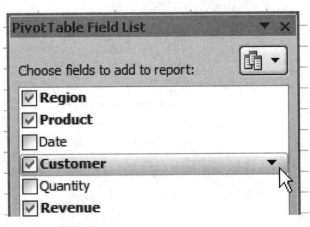

PivotTable Field List

Choose fields to add to report:

☑ **Region**
☑ **Product**
☐ Date
☑ **Customer**   ▼
☐ Quantity
☑ **Revenue**

Summary: The pivot table sort options are fairly well hidden but offer a variety of sorting options for each field in a pivot table.

Commands Discussed: PivotTable – AutoSort

LIMIT A PIVOT REPORT
TO SHOW JUST THE TOP 12 CUSTOMERS

Problem: Many times my customer reports have hundreds of customers. If I'm preparing a report for the senior vice president of sales, he may not care about the 400 customers who bought spare batteries this month. He wants to see only the top 10 or 20 customers each month.

Strategy: You can accommodate this vice president by using the Top 10 Filter feature that is available in pivot tables. Follow these steps:

1) Open the Customer dropdown in cell B4 or by hovering over the Customer field in the top of the PivotTable Field List dialog. (Annoyingly, in Compact Form view, the dropdown is titled Row Labels and in Tabular Form view, it is called Customer.) Choose Value Filters and then Top 10, as shown in Figure 867.

Figure 867

Excel offers many filters for each field.

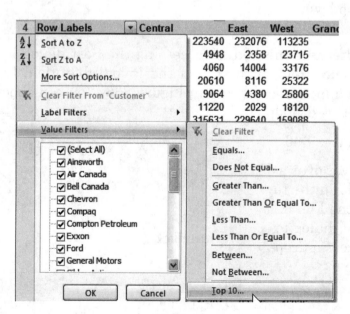

Excel displays the Top 10 Filter (Customer) dialog. By default, the dialog wants to show the top 10 items based on Sum of Revenue (see Figure 868). Although it is called the "Top 10" feature, it is far more flexible than that. The first dropdown offers to filter to the top or bottom customers. You can use the spin button to change 10 to any other number. The third field offers Items, Percent, and, new in Excel 2007, Sum.

Figure 868

Although this starts out as the top 10 items, you can change to the bottom 3 or whatever you might need.

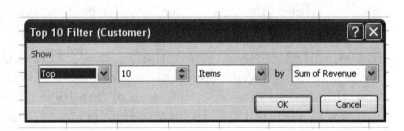

Part
III

2)   Select Top and 12. Click OK to close the dialog.

Results: The report will be filtered to show just the top 12 customers, as shown in Figure 869. Note that a Filter icon appears in cell A4 to indicate that you are not seeing all customers. You can hover over this icon to see a list of the filters applied

Figure 869

Subtle changes to the Filter icon indicate you are not seeing all customers.

Sum of Revenue	Column Labels	Central	East	West	Grand Total
Row Labels		Central	East	West	Grand Total
Ainsworth		223540	232076	113235	568851
Exxon		Value Filters (in order)		159088	704359
Ford		1. Customer: Top 12 by Sum of Revenue		158434	622794
General Motors		AutoSort		195967	750163
IBM		Customer: A to Z		103942	427349
Molson, Inc		209326	245081	159107	613514
Nortel Networks		109320	219115	77891	406326
SBC Communications		22140	38860	11680	72680
Shell Canada		20950	26571	24130	71651
Sun Life Financial		151310	199982	147645	498937
Verizon		100748	184563	105667	390978
Wal-Mart		327958	313454	228042	869454
Grand Total		2220986	2291242	1484828	5997056

Gotcha: If there is a tie for 12th place, the list may contain 13 customers. In some situations, a pivot table is limited to one obscure product that was purchased by only a few customers. This can create a huge multi-way tie at $0 for 12th place, resulting in hundreds of customers in the report.

Gotcha: The total on this report includes only the customers shown. It would be great to add one line to represent the revenue from the smaller customers. See "Build a Better Top 10 by Using Group Selection" on page 626 for an alternate strategy.

Additional Details: A new option in Excel 2007 is the Sum variety of the Top 10 Filter. With this feature, for example, you can ask Excel to show the top customers until a sum of 2 million is reached (see Figure 870). Excel will limit the filter to enough customers to just go over 2 million.

Figure 870

The new Sum feature allows you to specify that the filtered customers should reach a certain sum.

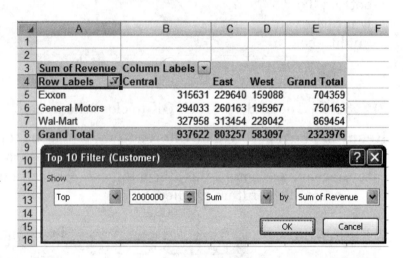

Additional Details: To clear a filter, you use the dropdown and select Value Filters – Clear Filter.

Summary: Top 10 Filter allows you to dynamically limit a report to any number of items—such as the top 5 or bottom 12—in a report.

Commands Discussed: Filter – Top 10

EXPLORE THE NEW FILTERS AVAILABLE IN EXCEL 2007 PIVOT TABLES

Problem: Microsoft added many new filters to pivot tables in Excel 2007. How do they work, and when should I use them?

Strategy: Top 10 Filter was available in previous versions of Excel, but all the other filters shown in Figure 867 on page 562 are brand new. Depending on the data type in a field, Excel will also offer label or date filters.

Open the dropdown for a text field and choose Label Filters. You can choose from any of the filters shown in Figure 871.

Figure 871

All these label filters are new.

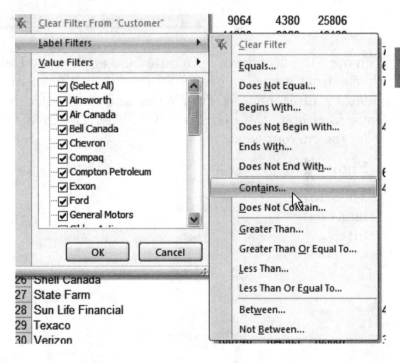

For example, you can choose to filter only customers that contain Canada in their name (see Figure 872).

Figure 872

Choose a rule for showing customers.

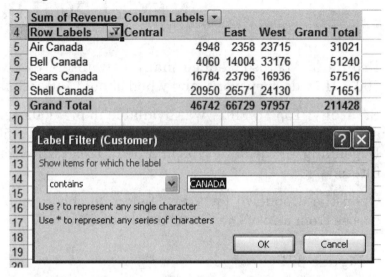

You open the dropdown for a date field and choose Date Filters. You can choose from a variety of virtual filters, as shown in Figure 873. If you choose a filter such as This Week and then refresh the pivot table 30 days from now, the information will be refreshed to show information from the current week.

Figure 873

There are many date filters.

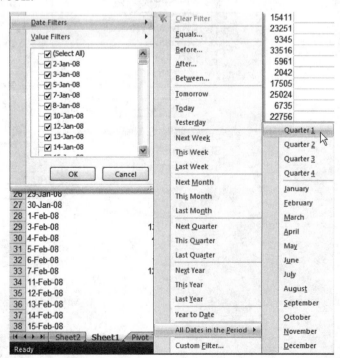

Gotcha: The filters This Week, Next Week, and Last Week assume that weeks run from Sunday through Saturday. There is no way to override this option.

Additional Details: Excel has to decide if it will offer you label filters, date filters, or just value filters. Excel examines the values in the field. If 100% of the values are dates and/or blanks, then you will have the date filter options. If just one of the values contains text, then Excel will switch to label filters instead of date filters.

Summary: Excel 2007 offers powerful new filtering options.

Commands Discussed: PivotTable – Filter

WHY AREN'T THE COOL NEW FILTERS AVAILABLE IN MY PIVOT TABLE?

Problem: I read the last topic, "Explore the New Filters Available in Excel 2007 Pivot Tables," but when I try to apply a filter, everything except Top 10 is grayed out (see Figure 874). What's the problem?

Figure 874

Most of the filters are un-available.

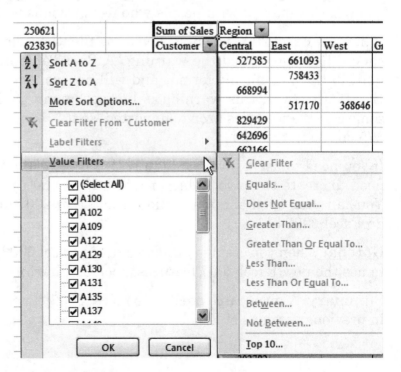

Strategy: Your pivot table was created in Excel 2003. If a pivot table was created in a legacy version, then Microsoft is afraid that you will want to open the pivot table again in the legacy version.

If you and everyone else who might open the file is now using Excel 2007, you can delete the pivot table and re-create it in Excel 2007. The new filter options will then be available.

Summary: Pivot tables created in legacy versions of Excel do not enjoy all the new functionality of pivot tables.

WHY CAN'T CO-WORKERS WITH EXCEL 2003 USE MY PIVOT TABLE?

Problem: I created a pivot table in Excel 2007. I saved the file as an Excel 97-2003 file and sent it to a co-worker. When my co-worker opens the pivot table, it opens as static values in Excel 2003.

Strategy: You have to create the pivot table in compatibility mode if you want to share it with people who use previous versions of Excel.

When the Excel 2007 machine saved the file, the Compatibility Checker should have presented the warning "A PivotTable in this workbook is built in the current file format and will not work in earlier versions of Excel." However, this warning is buried among trivial warnings that some colors and styles aren't supported, so it is easy to miss (see Figure 875 on the next page).

If you need to use a pivot table in both Excel 2003 and Excel 2007, you need to create the pivot table in Excel 2003 and save the file in 2003. You can then open and manipulate the file in 2007 and save it back as an Excel 2003 file.

Gotcha: When you create and save a file in Excel 2003, you won't be able to use the new Excel 2007 features, such as filtering on a pivot table.

Summary: A pivot table created in Excel 2007 opens with static values in previous versions of Excel.

Figure 875

There is at least one important warning among the trivial ones.

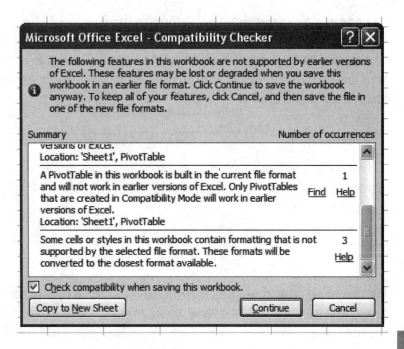

Part
III

LIMIT A REPORT TO JUST ONE REGION

Problem: I need to send a customer report such as the one in Figure 876 to each regional manager in my company. I want each manager to see only sales in his or her region.

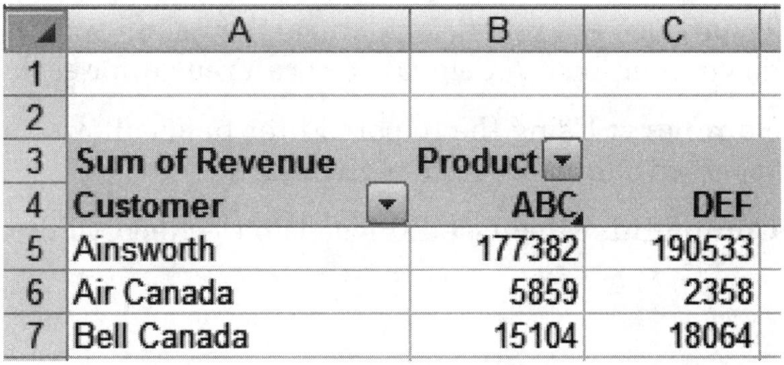

Figure 876

Limit this report to only one region.

◢	A	B	C
1			
2			
3	**Sum of Revenue**	**Product ▼**	
4	**Customer** ▼	ABC	DEF
5	Ainsworth	177382	190533
6	Air Canada	5859	2358
7	Bell Canada	15104	18064

Strategy: You can use the Report Filter area of the pivot table to create such a report. You drag the Region field to the Report Filter drop zone in the lower half of the PivotTable Field List dialog. It seems like nothing has really changed. All the numbers in the pivot table are the same, as shown in Figure 877.

Figure 877

Initially, the report still shows all regions.

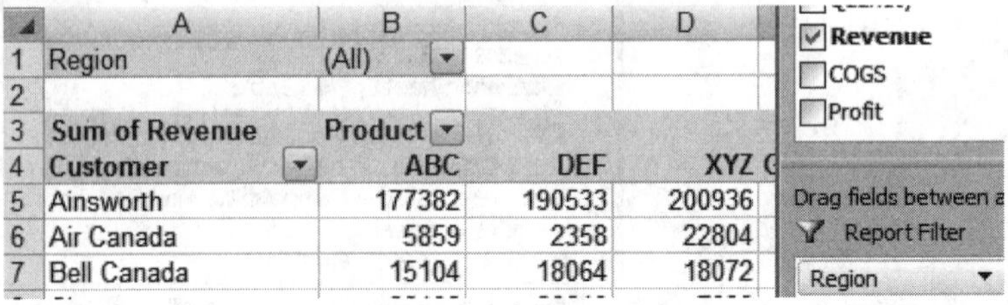

▲	A	B	C	D	
1	Region	(All) ▼			☑ **Revenue**
2					☐ COGS
3	**Sum of Revenue**	Product ▼			☐ Profit
4	Customer	ABC ▼	DEF	XYZ	
5	Ainsworth	177382	190533	200936	Drag fields between a
6	Air Canada	5859	2358	22804	▼ Report Filter
7	Bell Canada	15104	18064	18072	Region ▼

However, if you use the dropdown next to Region to select the East region, the report will update to show just the customers from the East region, as shown in Figure 878. You can print this report and send it to the regional manager for the East region.

Figure 878

Select one region from the dropdown in B1.

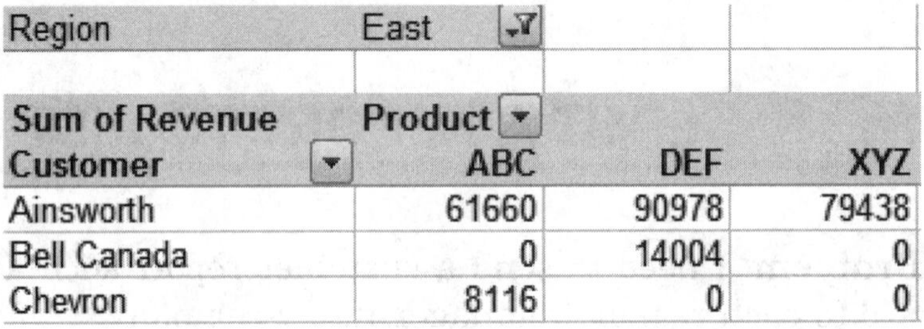

Region	East 🔽		
Sum of Revenue	Product ▼		
Customer ▼	ABC	DEF	XYZ
Ainsworth	61660	90978	79438
Bell Canada	0	14004	0
Chevron	8116	0	0

To produce the report for Central, you simply change the Region dropdown from East to Central. You can repeat for each other region.

Summary: Using the Report Filter fields allows you to quickly filter a report to one choice from a given field.

Commands Discussed: Pivot Table – Report Filter

CREATE AN AD-HOC REPORTING TOOL

Problem: I have an operations manager who is famous for asking many ad hoc questions. One day, he will want to know who bought XYZ product. The next day, he will want to know all sales to Air Canada. How can Excel help me quickly answer his questions?

Strategy: You can build a pivot table report with many fields in the Report Filter area, as shown in Figure 879. You can then use the information here to answer just about any ad hoc query your manager can dream up. For example, your operations manager can easily figure out how many ABC products were shipped to the East region on a given date.

Figure 879

Ad hoc reporting tool.

	A	B
1	Region	East
2	Product	ABC
3	Customer	(All)
4	Date	2-Jan-08
5		
6	**Values**	
7	Sum of Revenue	10245
8	Sum of Quantity	500
9	Sum of COGS	4235
10	Sum of Profit	6010

Part III

Summary: Using many Report Filter fields allows you to quickly filter a report to answer ad hoc queries.

Commands Discussed: Pivot Table – Filter Fields

CREATE A REPORT FOR EVERY CUSTOMER

Problem: I need to print a report for each of my customers. Using the Report Filter field is tedious: I spend my whole morning selecting a customer, clicking Print, selecting a customer, clicking Print, and so on.

Strategy: The feature you use to solve this problem—the Show Report Filter Pages command—is the most powerful feature of pivot tables. I don't know why Microsoft buries it so deeply in the menu system. You can use the Show Report Filter Pages command to make a report for every customer. Follow these steps:

1) Build a pivot table with the information you want to replicate for each customer.

2) Add the Customer field as one of the Report Filter fields.

3) Select PivotTable Tools Options – Options dropdown – Show Report Filter Pages, as shown in Figure 880.

Figure 880

Set up the report and select Show Report Filter Pages.

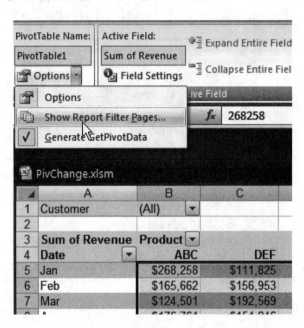

4) A dialog box will appear, asking you to show all Report Filter Pages and giving you a list of all the fields in the Report Filter. Even though this seems silly when you have only one field in the Report Filter area, choose Customer and click OK.

Results: In a matter of seconds, Excel will add a new worksheet for each customer. Each worksheet will be named after the customer, and the Customer dropdown will be changed to the particular customer. In a matter of seconds, you will have one worksheet for each customer, as shown in Figure 881.

Figure 881

Excel will replicate the pivot table for each customer.

◢	A	B	C	D	E
1	Customer	Ainsworth ▼			
2					
3	**Sum of Revenue**	**Product** ▼			
4	**Date** ▼	**ABC**	**DEF**	**XYZ**	**Grand Total**
5	Jan	$10,445		$51,053	$61,498
6	Feb		$44,492	$29,560	$74,052
7	Mar	$7,132	$34,960	$4,784	$46,876
8	Apr	$29,616	$8,776		$38,392
9	May	$25,682		$29,303	$54,985
10	Jun	$42,112		$21,960	$64,072
11	Jul		$21,555	$12,984	$34,539
12	Aug	$15,544		$11,064	$26,608
13	Sep	$19,453	$14,538	$22,014	$56,005
14	Oct	$13,397	$13,797		$27,194
15	Nov	$12,140	$24,356	$18,214	$54,710
16	Dec	$1,861	$28,059		$29,920
17	**Grand Total**	$177,382	$190,533	$200,936	$568,851
18					
19					

◄ ◄ ► ►I **Ainsworth** / Air Canada / Bell Canada / Chevron / Compaq /

You can imagine that this feature could be useful if you need one report per department, one report per product, etc.

Summary: Using Show Report Filter Pages is a fast way to make dozens of reports by using a single command.

Commands Discussed: Pivot Table Options – Options dropdown – Show Report Filter Pages

CREATE A UNIQUE LIST OF CUSTOMERS WITH A PIVOT TABLE

Problem: I need to create a unique list of customers from a large list.

Strategy: You can build a pivot table report with Customer in the Row area of the layout. Because the pivot table creates a summary report, the first column of the table will include the unique list of customers. Here's what you do:

1) Select Insert – Pivot Table. Click OK in the Create PivotTable dialog.

2)   Click the Customer field in the PivotTable Field List dialog.

That's it. You are done (see Figure 882). You can now copy the customers from column A of the new sheet and use Paste Values to put the unique list of customers wherever you need it.

Figure 882

Four clicks to create a unique list of customers.

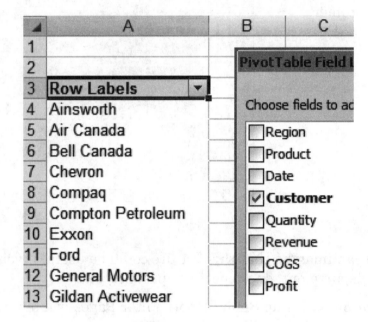

Summary: Of all the methods of getting a unique list of customers, this use of the pivot table is the fastest way.

CREATE A REPORT THAT SHOWS COUNT, MIN, MAX, AVERAGE, ETC.

Problem: All the Pivot Table examples shown thus far are for summing revenue. What if I need to find out the average sale by customer or the smallest sale?

Strategy: Pivot tables offer a variety of calculation options. To see them, you can use the dropdown on the Sum of Revenue field in the bottom portion of the PivotTable Field List dialog and choose Value Field Settings, as shown in Figure 883.

Figure 883

Choose Value Field Settings to see the possible calculations.

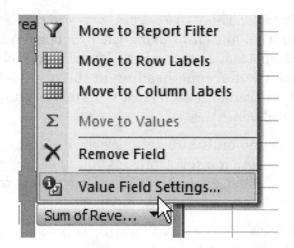

Excel displays the Value Field Settings dialog. In this dialog, you can choose Sum, Count, Average, Max, Min, Product, Count Numbers, Standard Deviation, Standard Deviation for a population, Variance, or Variance for a population. You can also change the field name from the standard Average of Revenue to Average Revenue or any other heading you would like. (Note, however, that you cannot reuse a name already in the pivot table. So, for example, Revenue would not be allowed, but Revenue_ or "Revenue." would be allowed.).

Figure 884

Change the calculation from Sum to Average.

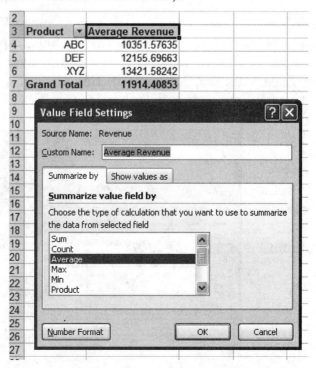

Additional Details: There are several ways to display the Value Field Settings dialog. In addition to using the dropdown on the Sum of Revenue field in the bottom portion of the PivotTable Field List dialog, you can double-click the Revenue heading in the pivot table. You can also select any revenue cell and then click the Field Settings icon in the Options tab of the ribbon.

Gotcha: There is no built-in way to create a median for a pivot table. I've heard this question a few times. If you absolutely need to create a median in a pivot table, contact MrExcel Consulting; we've custom written pivot table–like reports that do medians.

Summary: Pivot tables can create averages, find the smallest sale, find the largest sale, and find the number of sales, among many other calculations. To see the possibilities, look at the Summarize By tab of the Value Field Settings dialog.

USE MULTIPLE VALUE FIELDS AS A COLUMN FIELD

Problem: When I create a table with two or more Values fields, Excel 2007 defaults to having the various Values fields appear as a Column field, as shown in Figure 885. This is an improvement over previous versions of Excel (thanks, Microsoft!). But although this is the desired layout, is it possible to change to other layouts?

Figure 885

Choose Revenue and Profit, and Excel makes them like a column field.

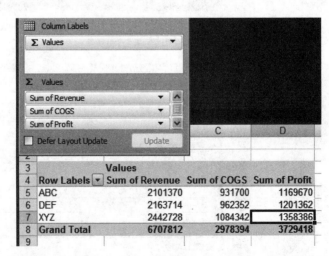

	Values		
Row Labels	Sum of Revenue	Sum of COGS	Sum of Profit
ABC	2101370	931700	1169670
DEF	2163714	962352	1201362
XYZ	2442728	1084342	1358386
Grand Total	6707812	2978394	3729418

Strategy: Yes, you can choose other layouts. Excel has a new field button called ∑ Values in the Column Labels drop zone. To rearrange the pivot table, you can drag the ∑ Values button to a new drop zone. For example, in Figure 886, the Row Labels and ∑ Values buttons have been switched.

Figure 886

Drag the Values field to the Row Labels drop zone.

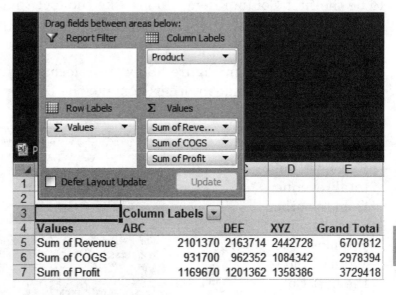

Summary: Although the default view of the pivot report for multiple Values fields is usually correct, you can easily change it by moving the ∑ Values field to the Column Labels drop zone.

COMPARE FOUR WAYS TO SHOW TWO VALUES FIELDS IN A PIVOT TABLE

Problem: When I create a pivot table with two label fields and two Values fields, Excel uses the default view of the data shown in Figure 887. How can I change this?

Figure 887

Excel adds the Values fields as the inner column field.

	Column Labels			
	Central		East	
Row Labels	Sum of Revenue	Sum of Profit	Sum of Revenue	Sum of Profit
ABC	766469	425975	703255	394100
DEF	776996	433580	891799	495247
XYZ	832414	462450	897949	493237
Grand Total	2375879	1322005	2493003	1382584

Part III

Strategy: There is really no good way to deal with this problem. Excel offers four ways to view this report, and none of them is entirely acceptable.

As shown in Figure 888, in the second view, the $\sum$ Values field is dragged to be the first Column field. I don't like the fact that it shows revenue in columns B through D, but then you have to scroll all the way over to column H for the total revenue.

Note: The numbers in Figure 888 were reformatted using the #,##0,K custom number format in order to make the columns narrower so the entire report fits in this page.

Figure 888

Excel will split total revenue from the other revenue when you move the Values field to the first Column field.

	A	B	C	D	E	F	G	H	I
1									
2									
3		Values Regi ▼							
4		Sum of Revenue			Sum of Profit			Total Sum of Revenue	Total Sum of Profit
5	Product ▼	Central	East	West	Central	East	West		
6	ABC	766K	703K	632K	426K	394K	350K	2,101K	1,170K
7	DEF	777K	892K	495K	434K	495K	273K	2,164K	1,201K
8	XYZ	832K	898K	712K	462K	493K	403K	2,443K	1,358K
9	Grand Total	2,376K	2,493K	1,839K	1,322K	1,383K	1,025K	6,708K	3,729K

In the third view, the Data field is dragged to be the second Row field, as shown in Figure 889. This view isn't bad, as the reader can probably adapt to reading Revenue Profit Revenue Profit down the rows.

Figure 889

Values as the innermost row field.

	A	B	C	D	E	F
1						
2						
3			Region ▼			
4	Product ▼	Values	Central	East	West	Grand Total
5	ABC	Sum of Revenue	766K	703K	632K	2,101K
6		Sum of Profit	426K	394K	350K	1,170K
7	DEF	Sum of Revenue	777K	892K	495K	2,164K
8		Sum of Profit	434K	495K	273K	1,201K
9	XYZ	Sum of Revenue	832K	898K	712K	2,443K
10		Sum of Profit	462K	493K	403K	1,358K
11	Total Sum of Revenue		2,376K	2,493K	1,839K	6,708K
12	Total Sum of Profit		1,322K	1,383K	1,025K	3,729K

For the final view, you drag the Data field to be the outermost Row field, as shown in Figure 890. This view is okay, although it would be preferable to have Total Sum of Revenue appear after row 7 instead of at the end.

Figure 890

Values as the first row field.

	A	B	C	D	E	F
1						
2						
3			Region ▼			
4	Values	Product ▼	Central	East	West	Grand Total
5	Sum of Revenue	ABC	766K	703K	632K	2,101K
6		DEF	777K	892K	495K	2,164K
7		XYZ	832K	898K	712K	2,443K
8	Sum of Profit	ABC	426K	394K	350K	1,170K
9		DEF	434K	495K	273K	1,201K
10		XYZ	462K	493K	403K	1,358K
11	Total Sum of Revenue		2,376K	2,493K	1,839K	6,708K
12	Total Sum of Profit		1,322K	1,383K	1,025K	3,729K

Summary: When you have two fields and two data types in a pivot table, there are four possible options for displaying the data. None of the options is perfect. It might be easier to create the report without totals and add them yourself after changing to values.

SPECIFY A NUMBER FORMAT FOR A PIVOT TABLE FIELD

Problem: In a pivot table, a Values field tends to inherit the numeric formatting assigned to the data in the original data set. This doesn't always work for me. At a detail level, sometimes I want to see invoice amounts in dollars and cents, as shown in Figure 891. However, at a summary level, I sometimes want to see numbers in thousands. If I change the number format using the settings in the Home tab of the ribbon, the number format is lost after the next pivot table refresh.

Figure 891

Change the number format.

Product ▼	Sum of Revenue
ABC	2101370.00
DEF	2163714.00
XYZ	2442728.00
Grand Total	6707812.00

Strategy:Follow these steps to specify a number format for a pivot table field:

1) Assign a numeric format to the pivot table field. Select the Sum of Revenue heading. In the Options tab of the ribbon, click the Field Settings icon to display the Value Field Settings dialog, as shown in Figure 892.

Figure 892

Access the number format here.

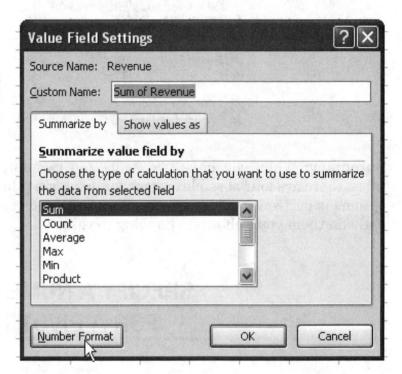

2) Click the Number Format button. Excel will display an abbreviated version of the Format Cells dialog with only the Number tab.

3) Choose an appropriate numeric format, as shown in Figure 893. Click OK to close the Format Cells dialog and then click OK to close the Value Field Settings dialog.

Figure 893

Apply a number format to the field.

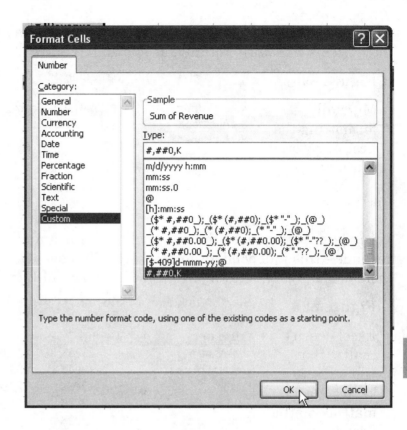

Results: As shown in Figure 894, the Revenue field will now always show the selected format, no matter how the pivot table is changed.

Figure 894

Excel remembers the number format, even after you move fields.

Sum of Revenue	Region			
Product	Central	East	West	Grand Total
ABC	766K	703K	632K	2,101K
DEF	777K	892K	495K	2,164K
XYZ	832K	898K	712K	2,443K
Grand Total	2,376K	2,493K	1,839K	6,708K

The above method formats **all rows** using the numeric formatting attached to the Sum Revenue field to assign a non-currency format.

Gotcha: One of the conventions in formatting tables says that you should include a currency symbol on only the first and total rows of a data set. There is not a built in way to do this with a pivot table. However, you can use the numeric formatting attached to the Sum of Revenue field to assign a non-currency format. Then you select the first row of cells and assign a currency format by pressing Ctrl+1 to display the Format Cells dialog. This will work initially, as shown in Figure 895.

Figure 895

Manually formatting the first row works initially.

3	Sum of Revenue	Region ▾			
4	Customer ▾	Central	East	West	Grand Total
5	Ainsworth	$224K	$232K	$113K	$569K
6	Air Canada	5K	2K	24K	31K
7	Bell Canada	4K	14K	33K	51K
8	Chevron	21K	8K	25K	54K
9	Compaq	9K	4K	26K	39K

If you later re-sequence the pivot table—for example, when you sort by revenue—this independent formatting will move within the pivot table instead of staying with the first row, as shown in Figure 896.

Figure 896

Excel doesn't realize that you want to keep your formatting on the first row.

Sum of Revenue	Region ▾			
Customer ▾	Central	East	West	Grand Total
Wal-Mart	328K	313K	228K	869K
General Motors	294K	260K	196K	750K
Exxon	316K	230K	159K	704K
Ford	288K	176K	158K	623K
Molson, Inc	209K	245K	159K	614K
Ainsworth	$224K	$232K	$113K	$569K
Sun Life Financial	151K	200K	148K	499K
IBM	158K	166K	104K	427K

Summary: You can control numeric formatting in a pivot table by using the Value Field Settings dialog.

Commands Discussed: PivotTable Options – Field Settings

GROUP DAILY DATES BY MONTH IN A PIVOT TABLE

Problem: My data set has a date on which each item was shipped. When I produce a pivot table with the date field, it provides sales by day, as shown in Figure 897. My plant manager loves sales by day, but everyone else in the company would rather see sales by month.

Figure 897

When you report by date, Excel shows daily dates.

Sum of Revenue	Product ▾			
Date ▾	ABC	DEF	XYZ	Grand Total
2-Jan-08	10245	0	41166	51411
5-Jan-08	8456	0	13806	22262
7-Jan-08	0	0	21015	21015
8-Jan-08	0	0	21438	21438
10-Jan-08	6267	0	0	6267
12-Jan-08	0	0	2401	2401
13-Jan-08	9345	0	0	9345

Strategy: You can group daily dates to show year, quarter, and month. To do so, you build a pivot table with dates in the Row area of the pivot table:

1) Select a cell that contains a date. Select Option – Group Field. Excel displays the Grouping dialog, as shown in Figure 898.

Figure 898

Choose a date field and then the Group Field icon.

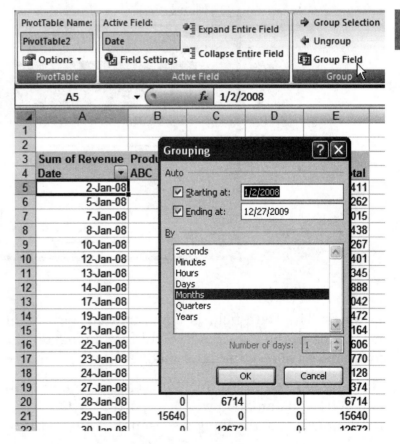

2)   The Grouping dialog defaults to selecting months. If your data
       spans more than one year, it is crucial that you also select years.
       Select Months, Quarters, and Years, as shown in Figure 899.

Figure 899

Select Months,
Quarters, and
Years.

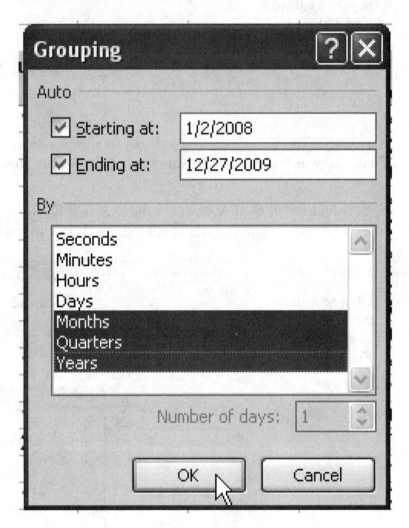

Results: The Date field is now replaced with Months. There are two
new fields in the PivotTable Field List dialog: one for quarters and one
for years, as shown in Figure 900.

Gotcha: : If you fail to include Years in the grouping, data from both
Jan 2004 and Jan 2005 will be reported as Jan. This is rarely what you
need, unless you are doing a seasonality analysis.

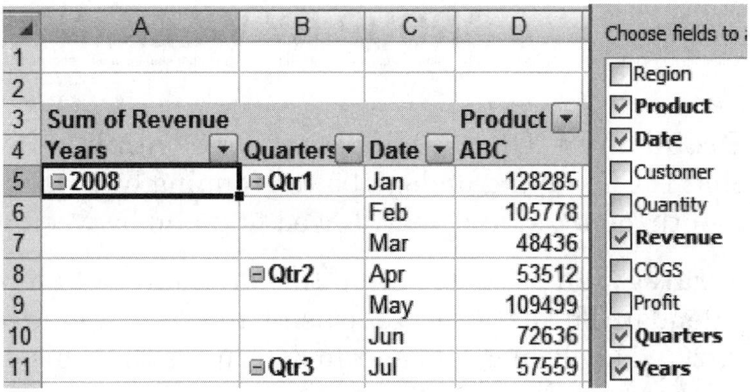

Figure 900

Excel adds new fields for quarter and year.

	A	B	C	D
1				
2				
3	Sum of Revenue			Product ▾
4	Years ▾	Quarters ▾	Date ▾	ABC
5	⊟2008	⊟Qtr1	Jan	128285
6			Feb	105778
7			Mar	48436
8		⊟Qtr2	Apr	53512
9			May	109499
10			Jun	72636
11		⊟Qtr3	Jul	57559

Choose fields to:
- ☐ Region
- ☑ **Product**
- ☑ **Date**
- ☐ Customer
- ☐ Quantity
- ☑ **Revenue**
- ☐ COGS
- ☐ Profit
- ☑ **Quarters**
- ☑ **Years**

Additional Details: Because the Year field is separate from the Date field, you can rearrange the table with dates in the row area and years in the column area to create a year vs. year analysis (see Figure 901).

Figure 901

Year vs. year analysis.

Sum of Revenue	Years ▾		
Date ▾	2008	2009	Grand Total
Jan	295609	258081	553690
Feb	285528	266190	551718
Mar	239373	250967	490340
Apr	336656	268360	605016
May	305190	309823	615013
Jun	194469	252463	446932
Jul	325954	302577	628531
Aug	314000	272259	586259
Sep	271830	209647	481477
Oct	279950	306835	586785
Nov	273057	314169	587226
Dec	268935	305890	574825
Grand Total	3390551	3317261	6707812

Part III

Summary: The Group feature is excellent for turning a daily report into a monthly or quarterly report.

Commands Discussed: PivotTable Options – Group Field

GROUP BY WEEK IN A PIVOT TABLE

Problem: In "Group Daily Dates by Month in a Pivot Table," I noticed that the Grouping dialog allows grouping by second, minute, hour, day, month, quarter, and year. I need to group by week. How do I do it?

Strategy: In order to set up this grouping option correctly, you need a calendar. The data set we're using in this example has data for January 2, 2008. Look on a calendar to determine that this date is a Wednesday, as shown in Figure 902.

Figure 902

The first date in the data set falls on a Wednesday.

Now follow these steps:

1)   If you want your week to report from Monday through Sunday, jot down that the week should start on December 31, 2007.

2)   Create a pivot table with dates in the Row area. Select any date cell and choose Options – Group Field.

3)   In the Grouping dialog, Excel defaults to showing the entire range of dates of the data set. If you left the Starting At field unchanged, your weeks would all start on Wednesday. Change the 1/2/2008 date to 12/31/2007 to have your weeks start on Monday.

4)   Unselect the Months selection by choosing it with the mouse. Select the Days choice. This will enable the Number of Days field at the

bottom of the dialog. Use the spin button to move up to 7 days (see Figure 903).

Figure 903

Group by 7 days.

Results: The report will be redrawn as a weekly report, as shown in Figure 904.

Figure 904

Excel will produce a report by week.

Date	Sum of Revenue
12/31/2007 - 1/6/2008	73673
1/7/2008 - 1/13/2008	60466
1/14/2008 - 1/20/2008	45402
1/21/2008 - 1/27/2008	81042
1/28/2008 - 2/3/2008	52186

Additional Details: Excel does not add a "Week" field to the Pivot-Table Field List dialog. Instead, the field that formerly contained dates now contains weeks but is still called Date.

Additional Details: Some manufacturing companies use a 13-month calendar. You can group by 28 days to replicate this calendar (see Figure 905).

Figure 905

Excel can handle the 13-month calendar.

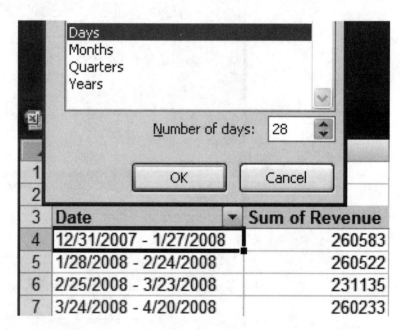

Date	Sum of Revenue
12/31/2007 - 1/27/2008	260583
1/28/2008 - 2/24/2008	260522
2/25/2008 - 3/23/2008	231135
3/24/2008 - 4/20/2008	260233

Gotcha: After you group by weeks, Excel will not allow you to group by months, quarters, years, or any other selection.

Summary: It is possible to group daily dates as weeks by using the Number of Days field in the Grouping dialog.

Commands Discussed: PivotTable Options – Group Field

PRODUCE AN ORDER LEAD-TIME REPORT

Problem: I work in a manufacturing plant, scheduling orders and material. I always appreciate it when the sales force gets orders a few months in advance so that I have enough time to get material into the plant without having to pay exorbitant prices on the gray market. As you can see in Figure 906, my data set has both an order date and a ship date.

I want to analyze what percentage of the revenue comes in two months before the order has to ship.

Figure 906

Get both order date and ship date.

Region	Product	OrdDate	ShipDate	Customer	Quantity
East	XYZ	11-Nov-07	2-Jan-08	Ford	1000
Central	DEF	5-Nov-07	2-Jan-08	Verizon	100
East	ABC	26-Oct-07	2-Jan-08	Verizon	500
Central	XYZ	1-Nov-07	2-Jan-08	Ainsworth	500

Strategy: You can build a pivot table report with OrdDate in the column area, ShipDate in the row area, and Revenue in the values area. Then you group both dates up to month and year. Follow these steps:

1) Select one cell in your data set and choose Insert – PivotTable.

2) In the PivotTable Field List dialog, choose the ShipDate and Revenue check boxes at the top of the dialog. Drag OrdDate to the Column Labels drop zone. The report is incredibly wide, but luckily, Excel 2007 no longer has the 256-column limit.

3) Select a date along column A. Select Options – Group Field. Highlight Months and Years. Click OK.

4) Select a date in row 4. Select Options – Group Field. Highlight Months and Years. Click OK.

Results: Excel will display an analysis that compares order and ship dates. In Figure 907, Cell F7 is an interesting number. It says that $60,368 of the orders that shipped in January was also ordered in January. Your manufacturing plant has to keep a lot of excess inventory on hand to be able to react to orders that come in this late. Cell E7 shows that $97,172 of orders for January was placed in December. This is still probably inside the cumulative lead time for most products.

Figure 907

Order lead-time report.

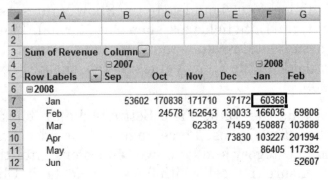

Gotcha: The order date and shipping dates have corresponding year fields. You must remember the order you grouped these fields because Excel will add the virtual Years field to the Field List dialog twice, in doing so it arbitrarily renames the second field Year2 (see Figure 908). In this example, Years is the ship date, and Years2 is the order date. It might help to write a note in the worksheet to help you remember that you grouped ShipDate first and that the Years2 field is associated with OrdDate instead of ShipDate.

Figure 908

Years2 is associated with the second field to be grouped.

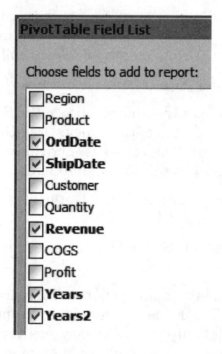

Additional Details: If you choose a Revenue cell and click Field Settings in the Options tab of the ribbon, Excel will display the Value Field Settings dialog. You should go to the Show Values As tab in this dialog. By default, the Data fields are shown as Normal. This means that Excel reports actual total revenue numbers in the report. From the many options available in the Show Values As tab, choose % of Row, as shown in Figure 909.

Before closing the Value Field Settings dialog, click the Number Format button. Then choose Percentage with one decimal place. Then click the Custom category and type two semicolons after the number format. This will ensure that cells with 0% show as blank. Click OK to close the

Format Cells dialog, and then click OK to close the Value Field Settings dialog.

Figure 909

Choose % of Row.

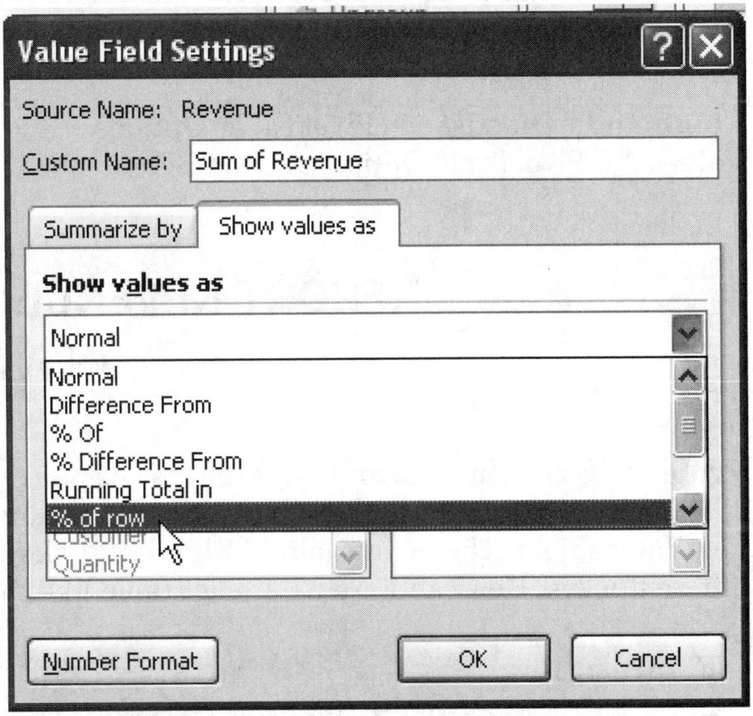

Part III

Results: The pivot table shows that 10.9% of January 2008 shipments were ordered in January. See Figure 910.

Figure 910

Use the percentage of row calculation option.

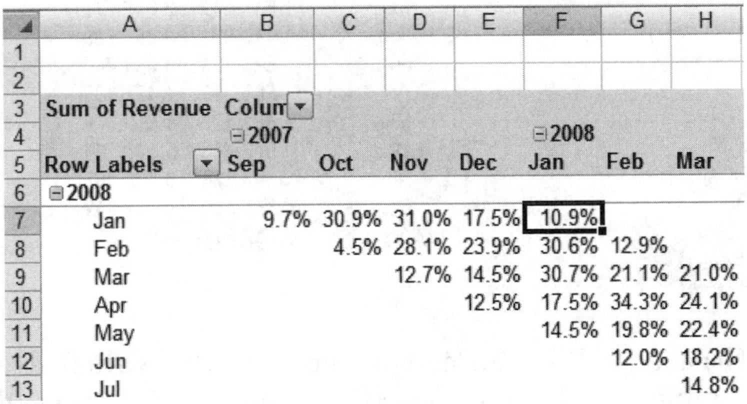

	A	B	C	D	E	F	G	H
1								
2								
3	Sum of Revenue	Colum ▾						
4		⊟2007				⊟2008		
5	Row Labels ▾	Sep	Oct	Nov	Dec	Jan	Feb	Mar
6	⊟2008							
7	Jan		9.7%	30.9%	31.0%	17.5%	10.9%	
8	Feb			4.5%	28.1%	23.9%	30.6%	12.9%
9	Mar				12.7%	14.5%	30.7%	21.1%	21.0%
10	Apr					12.5%	17.5%	34.3%	24.1%
11	May						14.5%	19.8%	22.4%
12	Jun							12.0%	18.2%
13	Jul								14.8%

Summary: Creating this report requires several techniques. You grouped two different Date fields by month and year. You also had to change the settings for the Sum of Revenue field to set the number format and to change the reporting from Normal to % of Row. This type of report will be very useful to schedulers in manufacturing plants.

Commands Discussed: PivotTable Options – Field Settings – Show Values As; PivotTable Options – Group Field

REPORT REVENUE MANY WAYS IN A PIVOT TABLE

Problem: So far, most pivot tables in this book have shown simply sum of revenue. You've said that it's possible to do many more calculations to a Values field. The pivot table in Figure 911 shows revenue in many different ways. How can I create a pivot table like this?

Figure 911

This pivot table reports revenue in five different formats.

Row Labels	Monthly Revenue	Running Total	Change from Prev Month	% of Total	Number of Orders
2008					
Jan	553,690	553,690		8.25%	48
Feb	551,718	1,105,408	-1,972	8.23%	42
Mar	490,340	1,595,748	-61,378	7.31%	46
Apr	605,016	2,200,764	114,676	9.02%	48
May	615,013	2,815,777	9,997	9.17%	55
Jun	446,932	3,262,709	-168,081	6.66%	39
Jul	628,531	3,891,240	181,599	9.37%	45
Aug	586,259	4,477,499	-42,272	8.74%	53
Sep	481,477	4,958,976	-104,782	7.18%	45
Oct	586,785	5,545,761	105,308	8.75%	46
Nov	587,226	6,132,987	441	8.75%	47
Dec	574,825	6,707,812	-12,401	8.57%	49
Grand Total	**6,707,812**			**100.00%**	**563**

Strategy: You can add Revenue to the Values area five times. After adding each field, you use the Value Field Settings dialog to change the display and name of the field. Follow these steps:

1)   Select one cell in the data set. Use Insert – PivotTable and then click OK to create a blank pivot table.

2)   Add Date to the pivot table.

3)   Choose the first date cell. Select Options – Group Field. Choose Months and Years. Click OK.

4)   Drag Revenue to the $\sum$ Values drop zone. Select the Sum of Revenue heading in B4. Choose Field Settings in the Options tab of the ribbon. In the Value Field Settings dialog, change the Custom Name box to Monthly Revenue (see Figure 912). Click OK to return to the pivot table.

Figure 912

This field is a normal Sum, but you change the name.

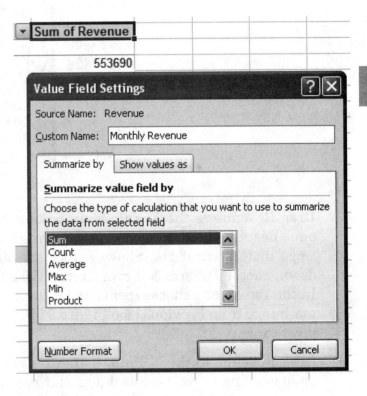

5)   Drag Revenue to the $\sum$ Values drop zone. Select the Sum of Revenue heading in C4. Choose Field Settings. In the Value Field Settings dialog, select the Show Values As tab. From the top drop-down, choose Running Total In. In the Base Field box, choose Date.

Change the Custom Name box to Running Total (see Figure 913). Click OK to return to the pivot table.

Figure 913

Running total in the Date field.

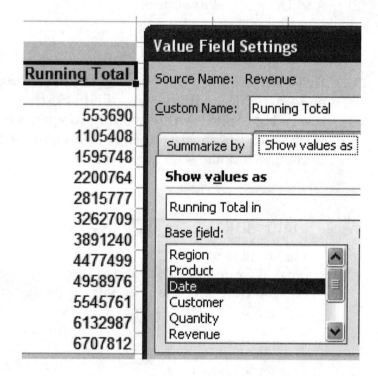

6) Drag Revenue to the ∑ Values drop zone. Select the Sum of Revenue heading in D4. Choose Field Settings. In the Value Field Settings dialog, select the Show Values As tab. From the top dropdown, choose Difference From. In the Base Field box, choose Date. In the Base Item, choose (previous). Change the Custom Name box to Change from Previous (see Figure 914). Click OK to return to the pivot table.

7) Drag Revenue to the ∑ Values drop zone. Select the Sum of Revenue heading in E4. Choose Field Settings. In the Value Field Settings dialog, select the Show Values As tab. From the top dropdown, choose % of Column. Change the Custom Name box to % of Total (see Figure 915). Click OK to return to the pivot table.

Figure 914

Use a base field and a base item for Difference From.

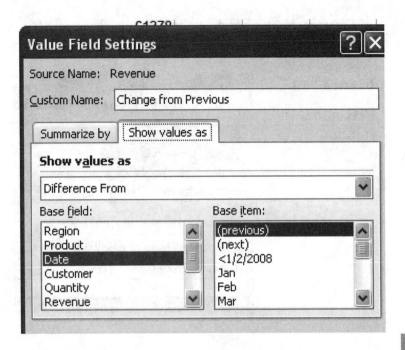

Figure 915

Percentage of column.

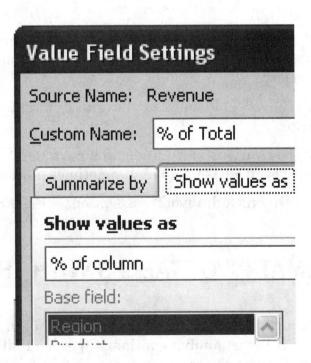

8)   Drag Revenue to the ∑ Values drop zone. Select the Sum of Revenue heading in F4. Choose Field Settings. In the Value Field Settings dialog, select the Summarize By tab and choose Count. Change the

Custom Name box to # Orders (see Figure 916). Click OK to return to the pivot table.

Figure 916

Percentage of column.

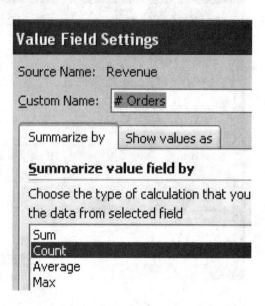

9) Select Home – Wrap Text. Adjust the column widths and row heights. Use the Format Cells dialog to make the final adjustments to the report.

Results: The pivot table will show several different calculations of the Revenue field.

Summary: The various calculations for a Values field sometimes require you to specify a base field and sometimes a base item.

Commands Discussed: PivotTable Options – Field Settings

FORMAT PIVOT TABLES WITH THE GALLERY

Problem: Due to the dynamic nature of pivot tables, it is fairly hard to format them. If I start applying formats to individual cells, the formats are lost after I rearrange the pivot table. Help!

Strategy: You can solve this problem by using the gallery on the Design tab of the ribbon. This is an amazing improvement over previous versions' AutoFormat.

The gallery offers seven color styles (grayscale and six theme colors). There are four styles each in three gradings (light, medium, and dark). There is one style with no formatting. You have (6 x 4 x 3) 72 color styles, 12 greyscale styles, and 1 plain style for a total of 85 styles.

You can modify the color and greyscale styles by using the four check boxes Row Headers, Column Headers, Banded Rows, and Banded Columns. Since each checkbox offers 2 choices, 2 x 2 x 2 x 2 = 16 variations on each of the 84 styles. 84 x 16 + 1 yields 1345 styles, (1152 color, 192 grey, 1 plain)

By choosing a new theme, you can change the 6 accent colors to any of 20 built-in sets of colors. This leads to 23,040 color styles (1152 x 20). Adding the greyscale and plain style gives you 23,233 styles.

In case one of the built-in 23.233 different styles doesn't work for you, you can create your own custom formatting. See the "None of the 23,233 Built-in Styles Do What My Manager Asks For" on page 599.

In comparison, Excel 2003 offered 22 AutoFormats, and all of them were horrible. Many of them changed the layout of your table. Microsoft did an incredible job with the formatting options in Excel 2007. Here's how you use them:

1) Select a cell in the pivot table. Open the Design tab on the ribbon.

2) Select PivotTable Style Options – Row Headers, Column Headers, Banded Rows, and/or Banded columns, as shown in Figure 917. (You should do this before opening the Styles gallery, as the thumbnails in the gallery will reflect these settings.)

Figure 917

Four check boxes to modify the styles.

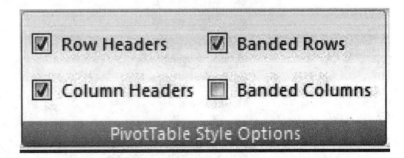

Part III

3) Open the PivotTable Styles gallery. Thanks to Live Preview, you can hover over various thumbnails and see the effect of each on the table. Figure 918 shows Pivot Style Light 24. Figure 919 shows Pivot Style Dark 3.

Figure 918

One of the light styles.

Sum of Revenue			Product ▼	
Years ▼	Quart ▼	Date ▼	ABC	DEF
⊟2008	⊟Qtr1	Jan	128285	45610
		Feb	105778	78211
		Mar	48436	81473
	⊟Qtr2	Apr	53512	96231
		May	109499	151074
		Jun	72636	37683
	⊟Qtr3	Jul	57559	120182

Figure 919

A dark style.

Sum of Revenue			Product ▼		
Years ▼	Quar ▼	Date ▼	ABC	DEF	XYZ
⊟2008	⊟Qtr1	Jan	128285	45610	12171·
		Feb	105778	78211	10153·
		Mar	48436	81473	10946·
	⊟Qtr2	Apr	53512	96231	18691·
		May	109499	151074	4461·
		Jun	72636	37683	8415·
	⊟Qtr3	Jul	57559	120182	14821·
		Aug	119372	58862	13576·
		Sep	129549	87499	5478·
	⊟Qtr4	Oct	117240	61117	10159·
		Nov	68661	139951	6444·
		Dec	87881	63961	11709·

Additional Details: On the Page Layout tab of the ribbon, you can change to any of 20 different built-in color schemes as shown in Figure 920. This will affect any of the color styles in the gallery.

Figure 920

Change theme colors and the pivot table colors will change.

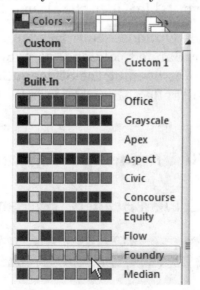

Summary: You can quickly format a pivot table by using the settings on the Design and Page Layout tabs of the ribbon.

Commands Discussed: PivotTable – Design – PivotTable Styles

NONE OF THE 23,233 BUILT-IN STYLES DO WHAT MY MANAGER ASKS FOR

Problem: My manager asks for a pivot table to be formatted with alternating stripes that are two rows high. None of the built-in styles do this.

Strategy: You can create this effect by duplicating an existing style and modifying it. Follow these steps:

1) Find a style that is close to your manager's request. In the Pivot-Table Styles gallery, right-click the style and choose Duplicate (see Figure 921).

Figure 921

Copy an existing style.

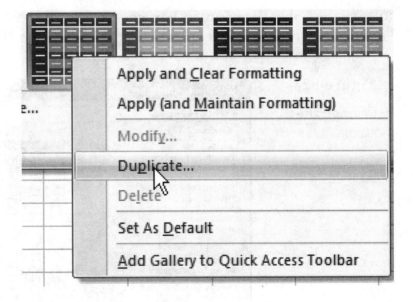

2) In the Modify PivotTable Quick Style dialog, give the style a new name. Excel initially gives the style a name by adding a 2 after the

old name. Rather than PivotStyleDark24 2, use a name like Dou-
bleRowStripe (see Figure 922).

Figure 922

Rename the
style.

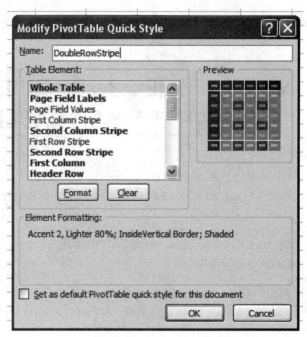

3)   In the Table Element list box, choose First Row Stripe. A new drop-
     down control appears, called Stripe Size. Open the dropdown and
     choose 2.

Figure 923

Change the
stripe size.

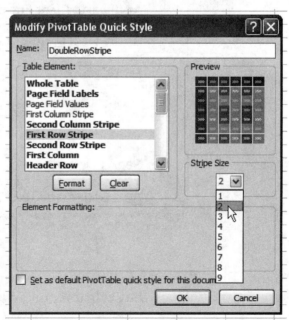

4) Repeat step 3 with Second Row Stripe.

5) Click OK to finish modifying the style. You have now created a new style, but Excel has not applied the style to your pivot table.

6) Open the PivotTable Styles gallery and find the new style at the top of the list, in the Custom section. Choose that style.

Results: As shown in Figure 924, a new style is available, with stripes that are two rows tall.

Figure 924

A new style is available.

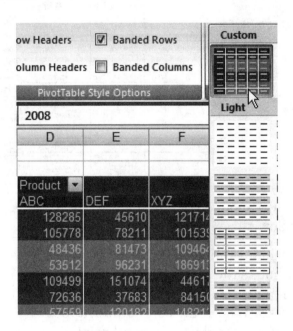

Additional Details: If you want all future pivot tables to use this format, right-click the style thumbnail and choose Set as Default.

Additional Details: While working in the Modify PivotTable Quick Style dialog, you can click the Format button to change the font, border, and fill.

Summary: You can customize pivot table styles.

Commands Discussed: PivotTables – Design – PivotTable Styles – Duplicate

SELECT PARTS OF A PIVOT TABLE

Problem: I want to manually format a pivot table. Can I select all the row subtotals? For example, in Figure 925, I'd like to select rows 8, 12, 16, and so on.

Figure 925

Select row subtotals.

3	Sum of Revenue		Region ▼			
4	Date ▼	Product ▼	Central	East	West	Grand Total
5	⊟Jan	ABC	80003	120012	68243	268258
6		DEF	2257	93759	15809	111825
7		XYZ	73814	76843	22950	173607
8	Jan Total		156074	290614	107002	553690
9	⊟Feb	ABC	77108	26693	61861	165662
10		DEF	55676	75029	26248	156953
11		XYZ	105136	88442	35525	229103
12	Feb Total		237920	190164	123634	551718
13	⊟Mar	ABC	47033	37421	40047	124501
14		DEF	52565	67683	72321	192569
15		XYZ	113544	15719	44007	173270
16	Mar Total		213142	120823	156375	490340
17	⊟Apr	ABC	48376	77337	51051	176764

Strategy: A clever mouse trick will allow you to select similar rows in a pivot table. Follow these steps:

1) Hover the mouse over cell A8. This is the January total. Slowly move the mouse toward the left edge of the cell. Eventually, the cell pointer changes to a black arrow that points to the right, as shown in Figure 926. When this cell pointer appears, click the mouse. Excel will now select all the subtotal rows.

Figure 926

Hover over the left side of cell A8 to get this cell pointer.

3	Sum of Revenue
4	Date
5	⊟Jan
6	
7	
8	J➜ Total

2) Using the formatting icons on the Home tab of the ribbon, assign a color to the subtotal rows. Figure 927 shows the result.

Figure 927

Any format-
ting is now
applied to the
subtotal rows.

Sum of Revenue		Region ▼	
Date ▼	Product ▼	Central	East
⊟Jan	ABC	80003	120012
	DEF	2257	93759
	XYZ	73814	76843
Jan Total		156074	290614
⊟Feb	ABC	77108	26693
	DEF	55676	75029
	XYZ	105136	88442
Feb Total		237920	190164
⊟Mar	ABC	47033	37421
	DEF	52565	67683
	XYZ	113544	15719
Mar Total		213142	120823
⊟Apr	ABC	48376	77337

Part
III

Additional Details: Click in the left side of cell B5, and you will select all the ABC records throughout the pivot table. In Figure 928, different colors are applied to ABC, DEF, and GHI using this method.

Figure 928

You can select
all the ABC
rows by us-
ing the same
method used
in B5.

◢	A	B	C	D
1				
2				
3	Sum of Revenue		Region ▼	
4	Date ▼	Product ▼	Central	East
5	⊟Jan	⇨ ABC	80003	120012
6		DEF	2257	93759
7		XYZ	73814	76843
8	Jan Total		156074	290614
9	⊟Feb	ABC	77108	26693
10		DEF	55676	75029
11		XYZ	105136	88442
12	Feb Total		237920	190164
13	⊟Mar	ABC	47033	37421
14		DEF	52565	67683
15		XYZ	113544	15719
16	Mar Total		213142	120823

If you have multiple column fields, you can select various columns by hovering near the top of the label for a column.

Gotcha: This feature can be turned off. To ensure that it's not turned off, enable the Enable Selection setting under the Select dropdown on the Options tab (see Figure 929).

Figure 929

Make sure En-
able Selection
is turned on.

Summary: You can use a simply mouse trick to select all subtotal rows or columns.

APPLY CONDITIONAL FORMATTING
TO A PIVOT TABLE

Problem: The new conditional formatting options in Excel 2007 are amazing, but they require special care in pivot tables. In some of my tables, such as the one shown in Figure 930, the grand totals get the largest data bars, and the detail cells have relatively meaningless bars.

Strategy: You can use the Manage Rules dialog to assign conditional formatting to only certain cells. You can initially create the "wrong" for-matting and then edit it to refer to only the selected cells. For example, follow these steps:

1)   Select cells C4:C6. Select Home – Conditional Formatting – Data
      Bars – Red. Excel applies data bars to the three cells, as shown in
      Figure 931.

Figure 930

Data bars applied to all of column C become meaningless.

	A	B	C
1			
2			
3	**Region** ▼	**Product** ▼	**Sum of Revenue**
4	⊟**Central**	ABC	766469
5		DEF	776996
6		XYZ	832414
7	**Central Total**		**2375879**
8	⊟**East**	ABC	703255
9		DEF	891799
10		XYZ	897949
11	**East Total**		**2493003**
12	⊟**West**	ABC	631646
13		DEF	494919
14		XYZ	712365
15	**West Total**		**1838930**
16	**Grand Total**		**6707812**

Part III

Figure 931

Apply the data bars to a subset of the desired cells.

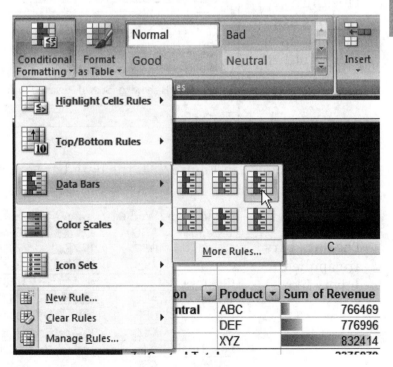

2) Select Conditional Formatting – Manage Rules. Excel will display the Conditional Formatting Rules Manager dialog.

3) Choose the Data Bar rule and click Edit Rule, as shown in Figure 932. Excel will display the Edit Formatting Rule dialog.

Figure 932

Select the proper rule and click Edit Rule.

4) In the top of the Edit Formatting Rule dialog, choose the third option; All Cells Showing "Sum of Revenue" Values for "Product" (see Figure 933).

Figure 933

This third option is available only in a pivot table.

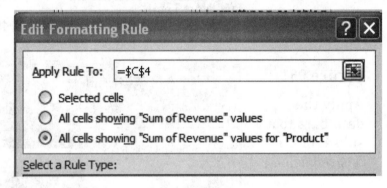

Results: As shown in Figure 934, the data bars are applied only to the detail product rows.

Figure 934

The data bars are applied only to like cells.

Region	Product	Sum of Revenue
⊟Central	ABC	766469
	DEF	776996
	XYZ	832414
Central Total		2375879
⊟East	ABC	703255
	DEF	891799
	XYZ	897949
East Total		2493003
⊟West	ABC	631646
	DEF	494919
	XYZ	712365
West Total		1838930
Grand Total		6707812

Summary: To apply a visualization to a pivot table, be sure to exclude the total cells by using the Manage Rules dialog.

Commands Discussed: Home – Conditional Formatting – Data Bars; Home – Conditional Formatting – Manage Rules

SUPPRESS TOTALS IN A PIVOT TABLE

Problem: Sometimes I use pivot tables just as an intermediate step in order to reach another result. If I'm going to be copying the data to a new workbook that will be used as a new data set, then all the totals by month, region, and year tend to get in the way, as shown in Figure 935.

Figure 935

Remove subtotals from the pivot table.

Date	Region	Product	Sum of Revenue
⊟ Jan	⊟ Central	ABC	80003
		DEF	2257
		XYZ	73814
	Central Total		**156074**
	⊟ East	ABC	120012
		DEF	93759
		XYZ	76843
	East Total		**290614**
	⊟ West	ABC	68243
		DEF	15809
		XYZ	22950
	West Total		**107002**
Jan Total			**553690**
⊟ Feb	⊟ Central	ABC	77108
		DEF	55676
		XYZ	105136

Part III

Strategy: You can turn off subtotals for any field. Follow these steps:

1) Select any cell that has a date in column A. Select Options – Field Settings. Excel will display the Field Settings dialog.

2)   Change the Subtotals setting from Automatic to None, as shown in
      Figure 936.

Figure 936

Remove subto-
tals from the
pivot table.

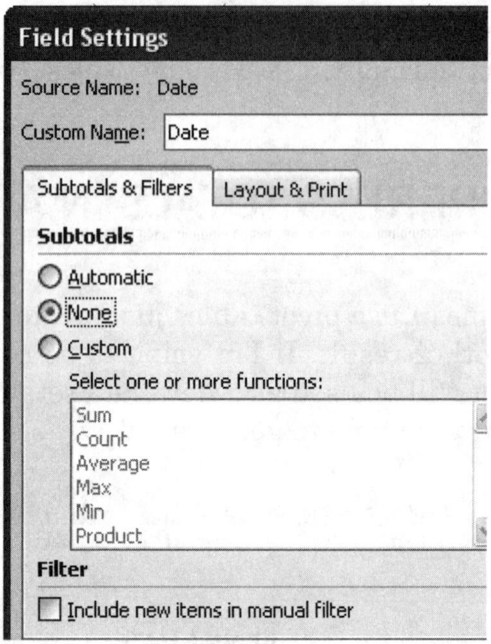

Field Settings

Source Name: Date

Custom Name: Date

| Subtotals & Filters | Layout & Print |

Subtotals

○ Automatic
◉ None
○ Custom
    Select one or more functions:

    Sum
    Count
    Average
    Max
    Min
    Product

Filter

☐ Include new items in manual filter

3)   Repeat steps 1 and 2 for a cell with a region field in column B.

Results: As shown in Figure 937, every row in the pivot table is now a
data point. If you copy and paste this table to a new workbook, you will
not have to manually delete all the total rows.

Figure 937

Every row is
now at the
same detail
level.

	A	B	C	D	E
1	Date	Region	Product	Sum of Revenue	
2	Jan	Central	ABC	80003	
3			DEF	2257	
4			XYZ	73814	
5		East	ABC	120012	
6			DEF	93759	
7			XYZ	76843	
8		West	ABC	68243	
9			DEF	15809	
10			XYZ	22950	

Summary: When you have more than one Row field, you can remove
the automatic subtotals on the outer fields in order to produce a cleaner
looking report.

Commands Discussed: PivotTable Options – Field Settings

ELIMINATE BLANKS IN THE
OUTLINE FORMAT OF A PIVOT TABLE

Problem: I have created a pivot table report and want to use this data as a database in another workbook. Excel leaves many blanks in the row area that need to be filled in. In Figure 938, for example, the Jan label from A4 needs to be copied to A5:A12. The Central label from B4 needs to be in B5 and B6.

Figure 938

Fill in the blanks in A and B.

	A	B	C	D
3	Date	Region	Product	Sum of Revenue
4	⊟Jan	⊟Central	ABC	80003
5			DEF	2257
6			XYZ	73814
7		⊟East	ABC	120012
8			DEF	93759
9			XYZ	76843
10		⊟West	ABC	68243
11			DEF	15809
12			XYZ	22950
13	⊟Feb	⊟Central	ABC	77108

Part
III

Strategy: To fill in the blank cells in the outline of the pivot table, you must make a Paste Values copy of the pivot table. To do this, you insert a new worksheet. Then you copy A3:D111 from the pivot table. On the new sheet, you select Home – Paste dropdown – Paste Values in order to convert the pivot table to static values, as shown in Figure 939.

Figure 939

Copy to static values on a new work-sheet.

	A	B	C	D	E
1	Date	Region	Product	Sum of Revenue	
2	Jan	Central	ABC	80003	
3			DEF	2257	
4			XYZ	73814	
5		East	ABC	120012	
6			DEF	93759	
7			XYZ	76843	
8		West	ABC	68243	
9			DEF	15809	
10			XYZ	22950	
11	Feb	Central	ABC	77108	
12			DEF	55676	

In this case, you need to fill in the blank cells in columns A and B with the value from the cell above. Follow these steps:

1) If A1:D109 is still selected from the previous paste, go to step 2. Otherwise, select A1:B109.

2) Choose Home – Find & Select – Go To Special. Excel displays the Go To Special dialog.

3) On the Go To Special dialog, choose Blanks from the first column, as shown in Figure 940, and then click OK.

Figure 940

Select only the blank cells.

4) (This step is confusing, but it works.) Type an equals sign and then press the Up Arrow (see Figure 941).

Figure 941

Enter the formula =cell above.

	A	B	C	D
1	Date	Region	Product	Sum of Re
2	Jan	Central	ABC	80003
3		=B2	DEF	2257
4			XYZ	73814
5		East	ABC	120012

YEARFRAC   X ✓ f× | =B2

5) Press Ctrl+Enter. Excel will fill in the formula in all the cells in the selection. Because you selected only the blank cells in step 3, you have filled in all the blanks with the value from above, as shown in Figure 942.

Figure 942

Press Ctrl+Enter to fill the blanks with a formula to copy the value from above.

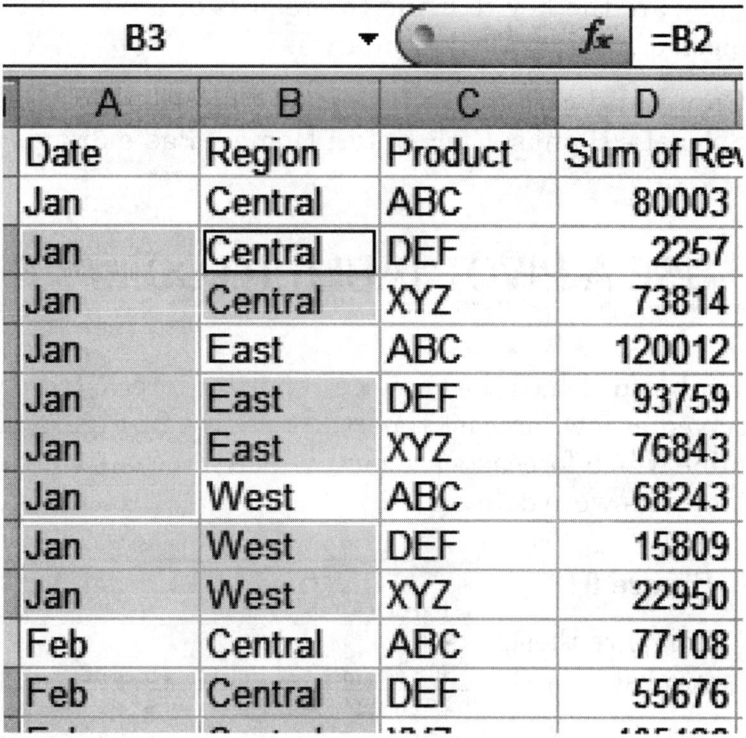

B3	▼	fx	=B2

A	B	C	D
Date	Region	Product	Sum of Rev
Jan	Central	ABC	80003
Jan	Central	DEF	2257
Jan	Central	XYZ	73814
Jan	East	ABC	120012
Jan	East	DEF	93759
Jan	East	XYZ	76843
Jan	West	ABC	68243
Jan	West	DEF	15809
Jan	West	XYZ	22950
Feb	Central	ABC	77108
Feb	Central	DEF	55676

Part
III

Here is why this works: When you press the equals sign, you are telling Excel that you are entering a formula. When you press the Up Arrow, Excel will make the formula be the cell above the current cell. When you press Ctrl+Enter, Excel will enter a similar (relative) formula in all the cells of the selection. It really doesn't matter which cell is the active cell, as log as you have successfully selected all the blank cells first.

6) Convert all the new formulas to values. (You might be tempted to use Ctrl+C and Home – Paste dropdown – Paste Values right now, but you cannot use the Copy command on multiple selections.) Re-select A3:B108. Press Ctrl+C to copy. Then select Home – Paste dropdown – Paste Values to convert the formulas to values.

Results: You have a nice solid block of data with values in all the rows for region and date. This data is now suitable for sorting and filtering.

Summary: The steps described here seem very convoluted. However, you can easily master them and carry them out in less than a minute. They are the key to using the results of a pivot table to create a useful block of data for further analysis.

Commands Discussed: Home – Copy; Home – Find & Select – Go To Special – Blanks; Ctrl+Enter; Home – Paste dropdown – Paste Values.

USE A PIVOT TABLE TO COMPARE TWO LISTS

Problem: I have last week's report of forecasted orders, and I just received a new forecast report. As shown in Figure 943, I need to determine which forecasts are new, which forecasts were changed, and which forecasts were deleted.

Figure 943

Compare these two lists.

	A	B	C	D	E
1	Forecast Last Week			Forecast This Week	
2					
3	Customer	Forecast		Customer	Forecast
4	Compton Petroleum	32,937		Ainsworth	25,450
5	Exxon	68,200		Bell Canada	32,565
6	Ford	2,629		Chevron	45,240
7	General Motors	54,569		Compaq	45,215
8	Gildan Activewear	44,432		Compton Petrole	32,937
9	HP	55,251		Exxon	68,200
10	IBM	28,910		Ford	2,629
11	Kroger	46,717		General Motors	54,569
12	Lucent	65,881		Gildan Activewea	44,432
13	Molson, Inc	47,733		HP	55,251
14	Nortel Networks	49,459		Kroger	46,717
15	P&G	60,299		Lucent	65,881
16	Shell Canada	47,521		Molson, Inc	47,733
17	Sun Life Financial	21,578		P&G	50,000
18	Verizon	35,367		Shell Canada	60,000
19	Wal-Mart	27,862		Sun Life Financial	21,578
20				Verizon	35,367
21				Wal-Mart	27,862

Strategy: You need to copy the two lists into a single list, with a third column to indicate whether the forecast is from this week or last week. Then you create a pivot table, and the new, deleted, and changed forecasts will be readily apparent. Follow these steps:

1) Add the heading Source in C3. Assign the value Last Week in C4:C19, as shown in Figure 944.

Figure 944

Add a Source column to the first list.

3	Customer	Forecast	Source
9	HP	55,251	Last Week
10	IBM	28,910	Last Week
11	Kroger	46,717	Last Week
12	Lucent	65,881	Last Week

2) Copy the data from the second list below the first list. In C20:C37, enter the value This Week, as shown in Figure 945.

Figure 945

Leave out the headings from the second list.

17	Sun Life Financial	21,578	Last Week
18	Verizon	35,367	Last Week
19	Wal-Mart	27,862	Last Week
20	Ainsworth	25,450	This Week
21	Bell Canada	32,565	This Week
22	Chevron	45,240	This Week
23	Compaq	45,215	This Week

3) Create a pivot table. Put Customer in the Row Labels drop zone, Source in the Column Labels drop zone, and Forecast in the $\sum$ Values drop zone.

4) On the Options tab, click the Options icon. On the Totals & Filters tab of the dialog, uncheck Show Grand Total for Rows. As shown in Figure 946, you will have a comparison of the two lists.

Figure 946

Excel will merge and compare the lists.

Sum of Forecast	Column Labels ▾	
Row Labels ▾	Last Week	This Week
Ainsworth		25450
Bell Canada		32565
Chevron		45240
Compaq		45215
Compton Petroleum	32937	32937
Exxon	68200	68200
Ford	2629	2629
General Motors	54569	54569
Gildan Activewear	44432	44432
HP	55251	55251
IBM	28910	
Kroger	46717	46717
Lucent	65881	65881
Molson, Inc	47733	47733
Nortel Networks	49459	
P&G	60299	50000
Shell Canada	47521	60000
Sun Life Financial	21578	21578
Verizon	35367	35367
Wal-Mart	27862	27862
Grand Total	**689345**	**761626**

Results: For any cells that don't contain a Last Week entry, the forecast is new. For any forecast without an entry in This Week, the forecast was deleted. For any forecast where the week columns do not match, the forecast was changed.

Gotcha: It would be nice to add a formula in column D that shows the difference between Last Week and This Week. However, if you use the method of highlighting a cell in the pivot table with the mouse or arrow keys while you enter the formula, Excel automatically changes the B5 reference to a GETPIVOTDATA function. Instead of getting a simple formula like =C5-B5, you get a complicated formula with GETPIVOT-DATA functions, as shown in Figure 947.

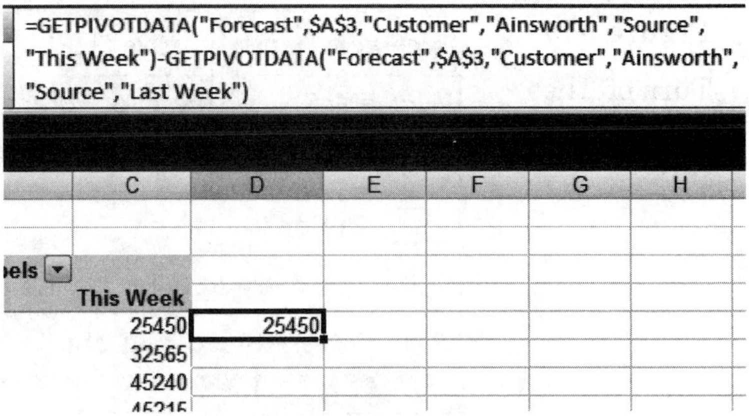

Figure 947

Excel creates
a complicated
formula...

	=GETPIVOTDATA("Forecast",$A$3,"Customer","Ainsworth","Source", "This Week")-GETPIVOTDATA("Forecast",$A$3,"Customer","Ainsworth", "Source","Last Week")					
	C	D	E	F	G	H
els ▼						
	This Week					
	25450	25450				
	32565					
	45240					
	45215					

As you copy this formula from D5 to D6, it does not have a relative reference. As shown in Figure 948, the results will be wrong in the rest of the rows.

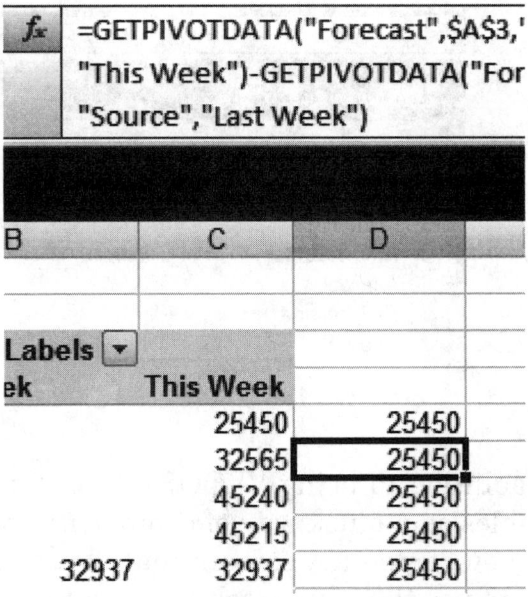

Figure 948

...that can not
be copied to
other rows.

f_x	=GETPIVOTDATA("Forecast",$A$3,' "This Week")-GETPIVOTDATA("For "Source","Last Week")	
B	C	D
Labels ▼		
ek	**This Week**	
	25450	25450
	32565	25450
	45240	25450
	45215	25450
32937	32937	25450

You have two options for entering a regular formula outside the pivot table:

- You can type =D5-C5 as the formula.

- You can select Options – Options dropdown and unselect Generate GetPivotData (see Figure 949).

Figure 949

Turn off the annoying feature.

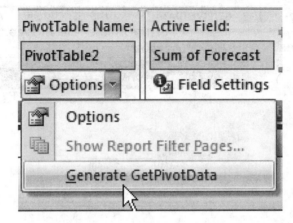

After you use either option, Excel will now generate regular formulas that can successfully be copied, as shown in Figure 950.

Figure 950

Formulas work as expected.

	D5			f_x	=C5-B5

PivCompare2.xlsm

▲	A	B	C	D
1				
2				
3	Sum of Forecast	Column Labels ▼		
4	Row Labels ▼	Last Week	This Week	
5	Ainsworth		25450	25450
6	Bell Canada		32565	32565
7	Chevron		45240	45240
8	Compag		45215	45215

Summary: In addition to using VLOOKUP or data consolidation, you can use pivot tables as a quick way of comparing two or more lists. The trick is to add a new temporary column that identifies the source of each record and then to use the Source column as a Column field.

Commands Discussed: PivotTable; Options – Options dropdown – Generate GetPivotData

CALCULATED FIELDS IN A PIVOT TABLE

Problem: I need to include in a pivot table a calculation that is not in my underlying data. My data includes quantity sold, revenue, and cost, as shown in Figure 951. I would like to report gross profit and average price.

Figure 951

You need to add some calculated fields to your pivot table.

Region	Product	Customer	Quantity	Revenue	COGS
East	XYZ	Ford	1000	22810.00	10220
Central	DEF	Verizon	100	2257.00	984
East	ABC	Verizon	500	10245.00	4235
Central	XYZ	Ainsworth	500	11240.00	5110
Central	XYZ	Ainsworth	400	9204.00	4088

Strategy: You can add a calculated field to a pivot table. Follow these steps:

1) Build a pivot table with Product and Revenue columns.

2) Select Options – Formulas dropdown – Calculated Field, as shown in Figure 952.

Figure 952

The Calculated Field option is now under the Formulas dropdown.

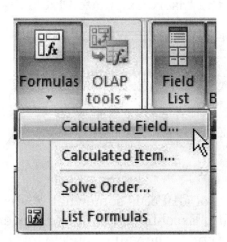

3) In the Insert Calculated Field dialog, type a field name such as Profit in the Name text box. In the Formula text box, type an equals

sign. Double-click the Revenue entry in the Fields list. Type a minus sign. Double-click the COGS entry in the Fields List. The Formula text box should say =Revenue-COGS, as shown in Figure 953.
Click the Add button to accept this formula.

Figure 953

Add a new
formula.

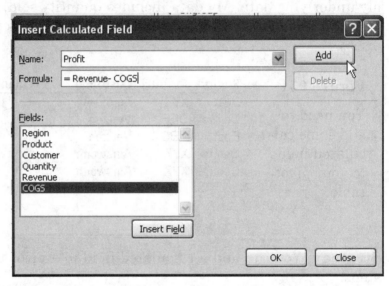

4)   Add the following formula for GPPct: =Profit/Revenue.

5)   Add the following formula for AveragePrice: =Revenue/Quantity.

6)   Click OK to close the Insert Calculated Field dialog box.

Results: The resulting pivot table will include all the fields, as shown
in Figure 954.

Figure 954

Excel adds the
new fields to
the pivot table.

Sum of Revenue	Sum of Profit	Sum of GPPct	Sum of AveragePrice
2111660	1174878.00	0.56	19.09
2163714	1201362.00	0.56	22.12
2427503	1350315.00	0.56	23.03
6702877	3726555.00	0.56	21.36

Gotcha: The label Sum of GPPct is somewhat misleading, as is Sum of
Average Price. In reality, Excel finds the sum of Revenue, finds the sum
of Quantity, and then divides the values on the total line in order to get
the average price. This makes calculated fields fine for any calculations
that follow the associative law of mathematics. Having Excel do all the
individual average prices and then sum them up would be impossible in
a pivot table.

You can rename the fields that have misleading headings. Select the Sum of AveragePrice heading. In the Options tab of the ribbon, click the Field Settings icon. You can rename the field, but you cannot use the same name that you used in the Insert Calculated Field dialog. In this case, adding a space, to make it Average Price, works perfectly.

Select the GPPct heading. Click the Field Settings icon. Change the name to Gross Profit %. In the lower-left corner of the Value Field Settings dialog, click the Number Format button. Change the number format to Percentage with one decimal place. Click OK twice to return to the pivot table.

You can use a similar method to change the revenue and profit fields so they have a numeric format with no decimal places and a thousands separator.

Figure 955 shows the final pivot table, along with the Value Field Settings dialog.

Figure 955

Visit this dialog four times to change the number formats and names of the Values fields.

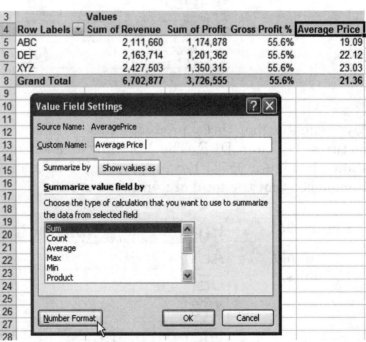

Part III

Summary: Calculated Fields add a new measure that can be reported in the ∑ Values area of a pivot table for all measures.

Commands Discussed: PivotTable – Options – Formulas – Insert Calculated Field

ADD A CALCULATED ITEM
TO GROUP ITEMS IN A PIVOT TABLE

Problem: I'm working with the small data set shown in Figure 956.

Figure 956

The initial data set.

	A	B
1	**Product**	**Quantity**
2	ABC	1
3	ABC	2
4	DEF	4
5	DEF	8
6	DEF	16
7	XYZ	32
8	XYZ	64

My company has three product lines. The Hartville division manufactures ABC and DEF. The Norwalk division manufactures XYZ. As shown in Figure 957, I have a pivot table that shows sales by product. Remember that the total of items sold is 127.

Figure 957

You've sold 127 units.

Product ▼	Sum of Quantity
ABC	3
DEF	28
XYZ	96
Grand Total	**127**

I've read that I can add a calculated item along the Product division to total ABC and DEF in order to get a total for the Hartville plant. I select Options – Formulas – Insert Calculated Item. In the Insert Calculated

Item dialog, I define an item called Hartville, which is the total of ABC + DEF, as shown in Figure 958.

Figure 958

Add a new item.

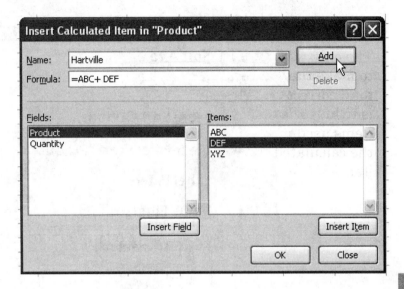

However, when I view the resulting pivot table, the total is now wrong. Instead of showing 127 items sold, the pivot table reports that the total is 158, as shown in Figure 959.

Figure 959

The total changes from 127 to 158!

Product	Sum of Quantity
ABC	3
DEF	28
XYZ	96
Hartville	31
Grand Total	158

Strategy: Your problem is that the items made in Hartville are in the list twice, once as ABC and once as Hartville. The calculated pivot item is a strange concept in Excel. It is one of the least useful items. You should use extreme caution when trying to use a calculated pivot item.

As shown in Figure 960, you could use the Product dropdown and un-check the ABC and DEF items.

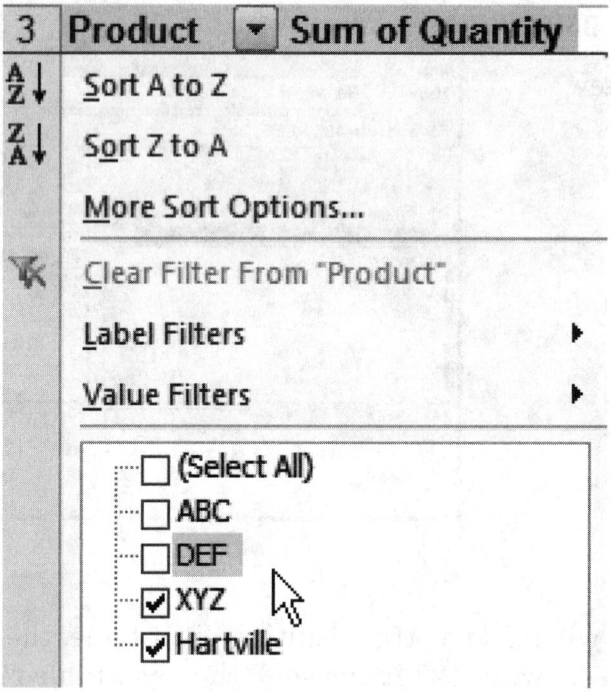

Figure 960

The only way to make the total correct is to hide the items used in the calculated item.

3	Product ▼	Sum of Quantity

- A↓Z Sort A to Z
- Z↓A Sort Z to A

More Sort Options...

✗ Clear Filter From "Product"

Label Filters ▶

Value Filters ▶

- ☐ (Select All)
- ☐ ABC
- ☐ DEF
- ☑ XYZ
- ☑ Hartville

The resulting pivot table shows the correct total of 127, as shown in Figure 961.

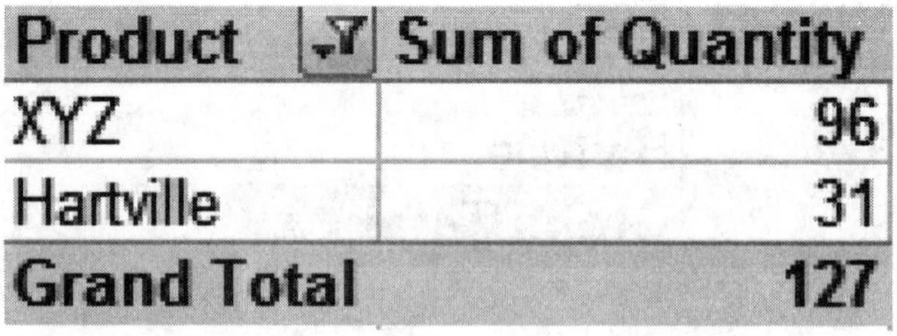

Figure 961

Sales are back to 127, but you can't see the product details.

Product 🔽	Sum of Quantity
XYZ	96
Hartville	31
Grand Total	**127**

Alternate Strategy: Instead of trying to use a calculated pivot item, you can add a Plant column to the original data. You can then produce a report that shows both the plant location and the products made at the plant, and the total will be correct (127), as shown in Figure 962.

Figure 962

Adding a plant column to the original data set solves the problem.

Row Labels ▼	Sum of Quantity
⊟Hartville	31
ABC	3
DEF	28
⊟Norwalk	96
XYZ	96
Grand Total	127

Summary: Calculated pivot items sound like they should be useful, but they are not. You should avoid using them.

Commands Discussed: Pivot Table Options – Formulas – Insert Calculated Item

Part
III

INSTEAD OF USING CALCULATED ITEMS GROUP TEXT FIELDS

Problem: As in "Add a Calculated Item to Group Items in a Pivot Table," I need to add a plant location to a pivot table. The field is not in the original data set, and I am not allowed to add a field to the original data set.

Strategy: In "Group Daily Dates by Month in a Pivot Table," you learned how to group daily dates as monthly dates. When you use a pivot table, you can also group text values along a field. Follow these steps:

1)   Create a pivot table with Product and Quantity columns.

2)   Select the cells that contain products made in the Hartville plant. When you click in those fields, click on the right half of the cell; otherwise, you will select the entire row. If the items are not in a contiguous range, hold down the Ctrl key while you select the cells.

3)   Select Options – Group Selection, as shown in Figure 963.

Figure 963

Group the se-
lected cells.

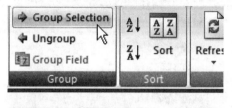

◢	A	B
1		
2		
3	Row Labels ▾	Sum of Quantity
4	H103	513
5	H104	34
6	N105	400
7	N106	1032
8	S101	64
9	S102	4
10	Grand Total	2047

The result appears to be chaos. You will be able to fix this problem, but let's take a look at what happened in Figure 964. There is a new virtual field called Product2 in the pivot table. H103 and H104 belong to a value called Group1 in Product2. Every other product in the pivot table is assigned to a Product2 equal to the product name. Note that the grand total of 2047 did not change.

Figure 964

After you
group the
first products,
chaos results.

◢	A	B	C	D
1				
2			PivotTable Field	
3	Row Labels ▾	Sum of Quantity		
4	⊟Group1		Choose fields to a	
5	H103	513	☑ **Product**	
6	H104	34	☑ **Quantity**	
7	⊟N105		☑ **Product2**	
8	N105	400		
9	⊟N106			
10	N106	1032		
11	⊟S101			
12	S101	64		
13	⊟S102			
14	S102	4		
15	Grand Total	2047		
16				

4) Select the word Group1 in A4. Group1 is a temporary name assigned by the Group Selection command. Change this name by selecting the cell and typing the new name Hartville.

5) Select products N105 and N106. To do so, click on the right half of A8 and then Ctrl+click on the right half of A10.

6) Choose Options – Group Selection. Excel will group these two products together under a Product2 heading of Group2, as shown in Figure 965.

Figure 965

Group the products for the Norwalk plant.

	A	B
1		
2		
3	**Row Labels** ▾	**Sum of Quantity**
4	⊟**Hartville**	
5	H103	513
6	H104	34
7	⊟**Group2**	
8	N105	400
9	N106	1032
10	⊟**S101**	
11	S101	64
12	⊟**S102**	
13	S102	4
14	**Grand Total**	**2047**

Part III

7) Select the Group2 label and type the new name Norwalk.

8) Select S101 and S102 in A11 and A13. Click Group Selection. Excel groups these using a temporary name of Group3. Select the Group3 label and type the new name Salem.

9) Select any of the Product2 headings. The Active Field box in the Options tab of the ribbon should say Product2. Click Field Settings. In the Field Settings dialog, change the field name from Product2 to Plant.

Results: As shown in Figure 966, you have effectively grouped product lines up to a plant location. Note that, unlike using calculated pivot items, this method does not change the total in the pivot table.

Figure 966

You've added a virtual plant field by using Group Selection.

	A	B
1		
2		
3	Row Labels ▼	Sum of Quantity
4	⊟ Hartville	
5	H103	513
6	H104	34
7	⊟ Norwalk	
8	N105	400
9	N106	1032
10	⊟ Salem	
11	S101	64
12	S102	4
13	Grand Total	2047

Summary: You can use a pivot chart to create charts for several different regions.

Commands Discussed: PivotTable – Options – Group Selection

BUILD A BETTER TOP 10
BY USING GROUP SELECTION

Problem: When I use Top 10 Filter to produce a top 10 report, the total in the report shows only the revenue from the top 10 customers. It would be much better if I could show the top 10 and then have one line called Other with the revenue from all the smaller customers.

Strategy: You should skip Top 10 Filter in this case and use Group Selection instead. Follow these steps:

1) Build a pivot table with Customer and Revenue columns. Sort the customers in descending sequence.

2) Count down 10 customer cells. In Figure 967, the top 10 will contain Wal-Mart through Verizon. Select from customer 11 through the last customer.

Figure 967

Select all the customers outside the top 10.

	Row Labels	Sum of Revenue
3	Row Labels	Sum of Revenue
4	Wal-Mart	869454
5	General Motors	750163
6	Exxon	704359
7	Ford	622794
8	Molson, Inc	613514
9	Ainsworth	568851
10	Sun Life Financial	498937
11	IBM	427349
12	Nortel Networks	406326
13	Verizon	390978
14	SBC Communications	72680
15	Shell Canada	71651
16	Lucent	62744
17	P&G	60299
18	State Farm	59881
19	Sears Canada	57516
20	HP	55251
21	Chevron	54048
22	Bell Canada	51240
23	Phillip Morris	50030
24	Kroger	46717
25	Gildan Activewear	42316
26	Compaq	39250
27	Sears	34710
28	Texaco	34364
29	Compton Petroleum	31369
30	Air Canada	31021
31	**Grand Total**	**6707812**

Part III

3) Select Options – Group Selection. Excel will add a new virtual row field called Customer2. In the new field, the smaller customers are assigned a Customer2 value of Group1. Each of the larger custom-

ers is assigned a value of its name. The interim view shown in Figure 968 looks like chaos.

Figure 968

Customers in the top 10 have a Customer2 value.

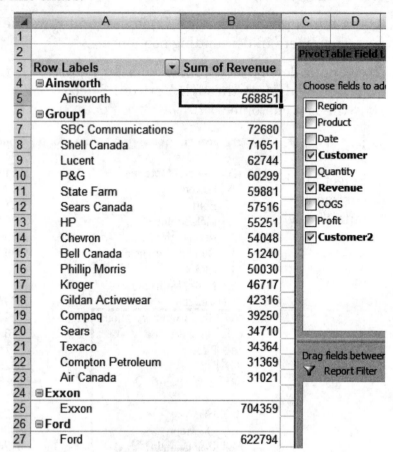

Row Labels	Sum of Revenue
⊟ Ainsworth	
Ainsworth	568851
⊟ Group1	
SBC Communications	72680
Shell Canada	71651
Lucent	62744
P&G	60299
State Farm	59881
Sears Canada	57516
HP	55251
Chevron	54048
Bell Canada	51240
Phillip Morris	50030
Kroger	46717
Gildan Activewear	42316
Compaq	39250
Sears	34710
Texaco	34364
Compton Petroleum	31369
Air Canada	31021
⊟ Exxon	
Exxon	704359
⊟ Ford	
Ford	622794

4) Select the Group1 heading in A6. Type the new name Other.

5) Uncheck Customer in the top half of the PivotTable Field List dialog. Excel will remove Customer from the Row Labels drop zone and leave only Customer2. At this point, you have a list of the top 10 customers plus Other. However, the sequence is wrong (see Figure 969).

6) Sort the Customer field in descending order, based on Sum of Revenue.

Results: You will end up with a list of the top 10 customers and all the other customers grouped into a single row called Other, as shown in Figure 970.

Figure 969

Remove Customer from the table, leaving only Customer2.

	A	B
1		
2		
3	**Row Labels** ▼	**Sum of Revenue**
4	Ainsworth	568851
5	Other	855087
6	Exxon	704359
7	Ford	622794
8	General Motors	750163
9	IBM	427349
10	Molson, Inc	613514
11	Nortel Networks	406326
12	Sun Life Financial	498937
13	Verizon	390978
14	Wal-Mart	869454
15	**Grand Total**	**6707812**

Figure 970

Top 10 customers plus Other.

Row Labels ▼	**Sum of Revenue**
Wal-Mart	869454
Other	855087
General Motors	750163
Exxon	704359
Ford	622794
Molson, Inc	613514
Ainsworth	568851
Sun Life Financial	498937
IBM	427349
Nortel Networks	406326
Verizon	390978
Grand Total	**6707812**

Part III

Additional Details: After creating Figure 970, you can copy the table and use Paste Values to change the table to static values. You can then move the Other row to the end of the data set, where it belongs.

Summary: You can group all the smaller customers into a single customer to create a better top 10 report.

Commands Discussed: Pivot Table Options – Group Selection

GROUP AGES INTO AGE RANGES

Problem: I have a data set that shows employee, age, and salary. I would like to figure out average salary by age ranges.

Strategy: You can create a pivot table and then group the Age field. To create this pivot table, you must change a series of settings from the defaults:

1) Select a single cell in your data and choose Insert – PivotTable.

2) If you select the Age field, Excel will automatically move it to the $\sum$ Values drop zone because the field is numeric. Drag the Age field back to the Row Labels drop zone.

3) Select the Salary field. Excel will move it to the Values drop zone as Sum of Salary.

4) In the $\sum$ Values drop zone, open the dropdown on the Sum of Salary field. Choose Value Field Settings. Excel will display the Value Field Settings dialog.

5) Change Sum to Average in the Value Field Settings dialog. Change the field name to Average Salary instead of Average of Salary.

6) In the lower-left corner of the dialog, choose Number Format. Change to Number, 0 decimal place, and a thousands separator. Click OK to close the Format Cells dialog. Click OK to close the Value Field Settings dialog. You will now have a report that shows every age and the average salary for that age, as shown in Figure 971.

Figure 971

Average salary by age.

AGE ▼	Average Salary
16	11,099
17	10,657
18	11,700
19	20,211
20	19,810
21	19,287

7) Select one age and click Options – Group Field. Excel suggests a default grouping, as shown in Figure 972.

Figure 972

Excel suggests a grouping.

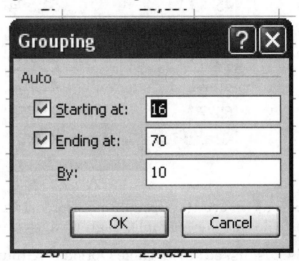

8) Change the grouping as shown in Figure 973. Click OK.

Figure 973

Override the defaults.

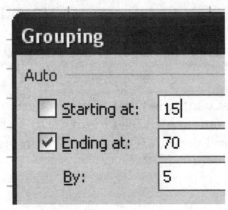

Results: Excel will show an average for each age range (see Figure 974).

Figure 974

Excel will groups the data into ranges.

AGE ▼	Average Salary
15-19	13,472
20-24	25,984
25-29	31,867
30-34	38,246
35-39	44,196
40-44	44,595
45-49	51,594
50-54	49,662
55-59	45,356
60-64	41,753
65-70	21,753
Grand Total	36,981

Summary: You can use the Group Field icon on a numeric range. You might want to do this, for example, to group ages into age ranges.

Commands Discussed: PivotTable Options – Group Field

USE A PIVOT TABLE
WHEN THERE IS NO NUMERIC DATA

Problem: My data set contains a list of manufacturing defects found in quality inspection for one month (see Figure 975). I have fields for date, manufacturing line, and defects. There are no numeric fields. Can I analyze this data with a pivot table?

Figure 975

Analyze defects with a pivot table.

◢	A	B	C
1	Date	Line	Defect
2	8/14/2008	A	Battery Failure
3	8/15/2008	C	Fit & Finish - Roof
4	8/5/2008	C	Fit & Finish - Bumper
5	8/19/2008	D	Fit & Finish - Roof
6	8/26/2008	B	Fit & Finish - Driver Sid
7	8/3/2008	D	Emissions failure
8	8/16/2008	A	Brake Failure

Strategy: You can use the COUNT function to perform a Pareto analysis. Here's how:

1) Create a pivot table. Choose the Defect field, and Excel will automatically add it to the Row Labels drop zone.

2) Drag the Defect field from the top of the Field List dialog to the ∑ Values drop zone. Excel will add the Defect field to the pivot table twice. Because Defect is a text field, Excel automatically decides to count the number of occurrences. As shown in Figure 976, you now have a list of each defect and how often it occurred.

Figure 976

Add a numeric field to the Values drop zone, and Excel will count the occurrences.

3	Defect ▼	Count of Defect
4	Air Conditioning Failure	116
5	Battery Failure	243
6	Brake Failure	381
7	Bulb Failure	241
8	Cruise Control Failure	101
9	Dome Light Failure	257
10	Emissions failure	597
11	Evaporator Coil Failure	649
12	Fan Belt Failure	248
13	Fit & Finish - Bumper	115
14	Fit & Finish - Driver Side Door	340
15	Fit & Finish - Grille	112
16	Fit & Finish - Hood	102
17	Fit & Finish - quarterpanel	117
18	Fit & Finish - Roof	1239

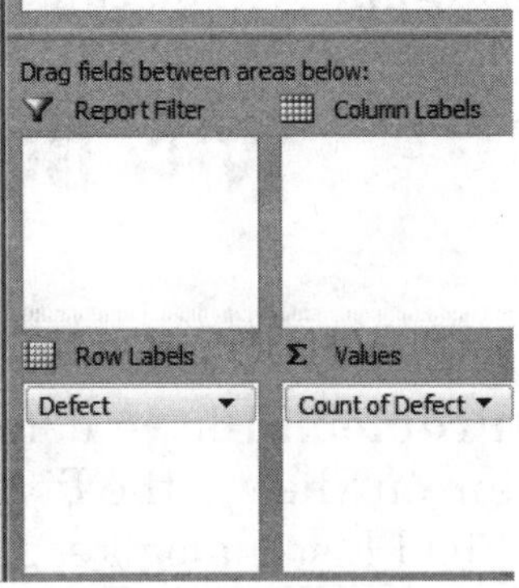

Drag fields between areas below:

▽ Report Filter   ▦ Column Labels

▦ Row Labels   ∑ Values

Defect ▼   Count of Defect ▼

3) Study the pivot table to find defects with the most problems. In the report in Figure 976, evaporator coils and the fit of the roof are causing problems.

Part III

4)   Change the pivot table to have Dates in the Row Labels drop zone and Line in the Column Labels drop zone. Move Defect from the Row Labels drop zone to the Report Filter drop zone.

5)   Choose Fit & Finish – Roof from the Report Filter dropdown in B1. This was the defect that occurred most often.

Results: As shown in Figure 977, the defect was happening a few times each day until the 28th of the month. On the 28th, line B began having problems. On the 29th, the problem began appearing in lines A, C, and D. By the 30th, all four lines were having massive problems. This doesn't look like a problem with an isolated employee, so you should probably see if a new batch of material started being used on the 28th.

Figure 977

Even without any numeric data, you can discover trends by using a pivot table.

	A	B	C	D	E	F
1	Defect	Fit & Finish - Roof				
2						
3	Count of Defect	Line				
4	Date		A	B	C	D	Grand Total
27	8/23/2008			1	3	1	5
28	8/24/2008			1		1	2
29	8/25/2008				1	1	2
30	8/26/2008		1	1	1		3
31	8/27/2008					3	3
32	8/28/2008		2	249		2	253
33	8/29/2008		15	356	19	16	406
34	8/30/2008		128	118	112	110	468
35	Grand Total		169	753	159	158	1239

Summary: You can use a pivot table to analyze text data.

WHY DOES THE PIVOT TABLE FIELD LIST DIALOG KEEP DISAPPEARING?

Problem: I have data on Sheet1 and a pivot table on Sheet2. While I am on Sheet2, the PivotTable Tools tab of the ribbon and the PivotTable Field List dialog keep disappearing. What is Microsoft's problem?

Figure 978

One second they are there, then they are gone.

Strategy: You can begin to understand what's happening here when you learn about Microsoft's rationale. At Microsoft, Jensen Harris was one of the architects of the ribbon interface. Jensen tells the story of visiting a customer who was using Excel. This customer had the Picture toolbar floating above her Excel window. There was no picture in the worksheet, and the toolbar was actually getting in the way. Jensen pointed out to this person that she could actually click the X to make the toolbar go away. The person responded that the toolbar had been driving her crazy for six months! Because of this event, Excel now has an obsessive desire to put away the contextual ribbon tabs as soon as you are not using them.

If you build a pivot table and keep the cell pointer within the pivot table, Excel will display the two new ribbon tabs and the PivotTable Field List dialog. But as soon as you click outside the pivot table, Microsoft will put away the ribbon tabs and hide the PivotTable Field List dialog. This drives me crazy. There are many reasons I might want to click outside the pivot table, including these:

- To get a better view of the pivot table

- To shoot a nice screen shot for this book

- I try to click on the PivotTable Field List dialog but miss, instead selecting a cell near the Field List dialog.

- I accidentally press the left mouse button when the mouse pointer had the audacity to not be above the pivot table.

- I type the Right Arrow key to scroll right in a wide pivot table, and I accidentally go one cell too far.

To my friends at Microsoft: There is nothing on Sheet2 except the pivot table. As long as I am looking at Sheet2, I am looking at the pivot table. Quit hiding the ribbon tabs just because I clicked out of the pivot table! The lady who lived with the picture toolbar for six months because she didn't know how to click the X to close the toolbar should not cause the other 499 million people using Excel to suffer.

To keep everyone happy, how about these rules: If your code renders a picture in the visible window of Excel, show the Picture Tools tab of the ribbon. Even if the picture is not selected, it will at least give me a clue that there are things I can do to the picture. If the ribbon is allegedly to help people discover new features in Excel, then quit hiding important tabs.

Additional Details: The new ribbon interface causes enough stress without it randomly switching to other tabs. If you are working on the PivotTable Tools Design tab and you accidentally arrow out of the pivot table, you will find yourself on the Home tab. Even if you immediately arrow back into the pivot table, you are still on the Home tab.

Maddeningly, Microsoft handled this one bizarre situation but none of the other common situations. Try this:

1) Select a cell in the pivot table.

2) Choose the Design tab of the ribbon.

3) Use the mouse to select exactly one cell outside the pivot table. Excel will hide the pivot table ribbon tabs and the PivotTable Field List dialog.

4) Using the mouse, select a cell back in the pivot table. Excel will redisplay the Design tab.

If you prefer to use the keyboard, you can instead try this:

1) Select a cell in the pivot table.

2) Choose the Design tab of the ribbon.

3) Press the Right Arrow key until you have moved exactly one cell outside the pivot table. Excel will hide the pivot table ribbon tabs and the PivotTable Field List dialog.

4) Using the Left Arrow key, move back into the pivot table. Excel will redisplay the two ribbon tabs, but it will leave you on the Home tab of the ribbon.

However, this similar scenario does not work:

1) Select a cell in the pivot table.

2) Display the Design tab of the ribbon.

3) Use the mouse to select one cell outside the pivot table. Select another cell outside the pivot table. Select a cell inside the pivot table. Excel will not return you to the Design tab.

So, Microsoft went through the incredibly convoluted task of catching when you select exactly one cell outside the pivot table with the mouse and immediately go back to the pivot table using the mouse. The whole situation frustrates me to no end.

Summary: Microsoft puts away the ribbon tabs too quickly for my taste.

CONTROL THE SHAPE OF REPORT FILTER FIELDS

Problem: I've built an ad hoc reporting tool with 24 fields in Report Filter area. There is no room to see my pivot table with all those fields at the top of the list.

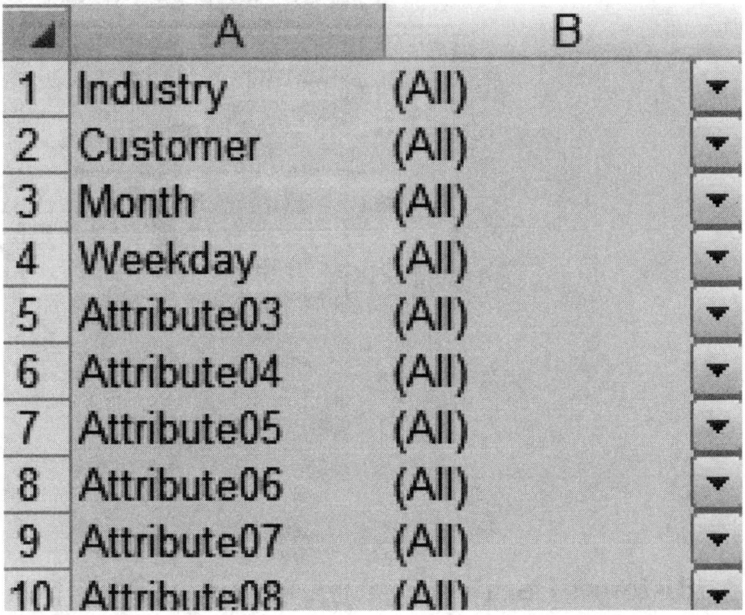

Figure 979

Too many
Report Filter
fields take up
too many rows.

	A	B	
1	Industry	(All)	▼
2	Customer	(All)	▼
3	Month	(All)	▼
4	Weekday	(All)	▼
5	Attribute03	(All)	▼
6	Attribute04	(All)	▼
7	Attribute05	(All)	▼
8	Attribute06	(All)	▼
9	Attribute07	(All)	▼
10	Attribute08	(All)	▼

Strategy: You can solve this problem by using the Layout & Format tab of the PivotTable Options dialog. Follow these steps:

1) Choose Options – Options icon.

Part
III

2)   Select the Layout & Format tab of the PivotTable Options dialog.

3)   Adjust the Report Filter Fields per Row setting. Each Filter field requires a label, a dropdown, and then a blank column. If you choose 5 for the Report Filter Fields per Row setting, the Report Filter section will be 15 columns wide (or 14, if you don't count the last blank column). However, the Report Filter section will take up only 5 rows instead of 24 rows.

4)   To control whether the filter fields progress down Column A or across row 1, use the Over, Then Down setting to have the first filters go across row 1 (see Figure 980).

Figure 980

Control the shape of the Report Filter area.

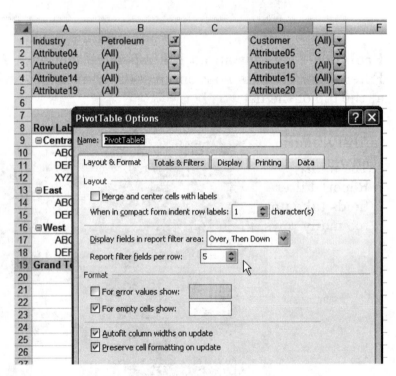

Additional Details: To have the filter fields print at the top of each page, you have to adjust Rows to Repeat at Top by using the Print Titles icon on the Page Layout tab. You would think that the Set Print Titles option on the Printing tab of the PivotTable Options dialog (Figure 981) would do this, but according to Excel Help, you still have to specify which fields to repeat at the top by using the Page Setup dialog.

Figure 981

The Set Print Titles option will not actually specify which rows should repeat.

PivotTable Options

Name: PivotTable9

Layout & Format	Totals & Filters	Display	Printing	Data

Print

☐ Print expand/collapse buttons when displayed on PivotTable

☑ Repeat row labels on each printed page

☐ Set print titles

Summary: You have control over the arrangement of Report Filter fields.

Commands Discussed: PivotTable – Options dropdown -- Options

Part III

CREATE A PIVOT TABLE FROM ACCESS DATA

Problem: I have 10 kazillion records in an Access table. I would like to create a pivot table for this data.

Strategy: You can create a connection to the Access table and build the pivot table in Excel. Follow these steps:

1) Start with a blank Excel workbook.

2) Select Data – From Access, as shown in Figure 982.

Figure 982

Choose to get data from Access.

From Access | From Web | From Text | From Other Sources ▼ | Existing Connections

Get External Data

3) Browse to your Access database and click Open.

4)   The Select Table dialog shows a list of all the tables and queries in the database. The Type column says VIEW for queries and TABLE for tables (see Figure 983). Choose the desired query or table and click OK.

Figure 983

Choose the table or query on which to base the pivot table.

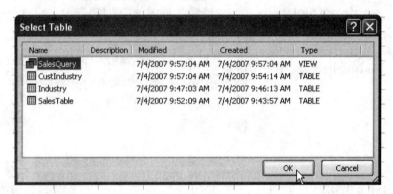

5)   In the Import Data dialog that appears, choose to create a pivot table report and click OK (see Figure 984).

Figure 984

Choose to create a pivot table report.

Results: Excel will display the PivotTable Field List dialog, with all the fields from your table or query.

Summary: Even if you have more than 1 million rows of data, you can analyze it by using a pivot table.

Commands Discussed: Data – From Access

WHATEVER HAPPENED TO MULTIPLE CONSOLIDATION RANGES IN PIVOT TABLES?

Problem: I read your book *Pivot Table Data Crunching*, which describes an awesome trick for spinning poorly formatted data into transactional data for pivot tables. The trick requires you to choose Multiple Consolidation Ranges from Step 1 of the PivotTable and PivotChart Wizard. However, Microsoft seems to have eliminated the wizard in Excel 2007, so now how can I select Multiple Consolidation Ranges?

Strategy: Although the PivotTable and PivotChart Wizard has been removed from the ribbon, you can still get to the old wizard:

1) Right-click the Quick Access toolbar and choose Customize Quick Access Toolbar.

2) In the left dropdown, choose Commands Not in the Ribbon.

3) Scroll down to and select PivotTable and PivotChart Wizard.

4) Click the Add button. Click OK.

5) Select a cell in your data set and choose the PivotTable Wizard icon on your Quick Access toolbar.

The PivotTable and PivotChart Wizard will appear, complete with new artwork, as shown in Figure 985.

Part III

Figure 985

The familiar wizard returns. Instead of adding the icon to the QAT, you could use Alt+D+P to display this dialog.

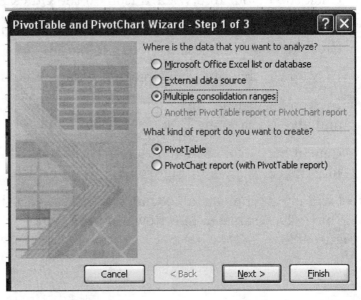

Additional Details: Using multiple consolidation ranges can help when your data is not properly formatted for pivot tables. In Figure 986, the data has been summarized with months going across the columns. Each product is on a different worksheet. To create a pivot table from this data, follow these steps:

Figure 986

You have one or more ranges with field values along the top row and left column.

	A	B	C	D
1	Account	Jan-08	Feb-08	Mar-08
2	A101	907	952	1000
3	A102	384	403	423
4	A103	463	486	510
5	A104	278	292	307
6	A105	666	699	734

Product 1 / Product 2 / Product 3

Book4:1

	A	B	C	D
1	Account	Jan-08	Feb-08	Mar-08
2	A112	907	952	1000
3	A113	384	403	423
4	A114	463	486	510
5	A115	278	292	307

Product 1 / Product 2 / Product 3

1) Click the PivotTable Wizard icon on the Quick Access toolbar.

2) In Step 1 of the wizard, choose Multiple Consolidation Ranges. Click Next.

3) In Step 2a, choose I Will Create the Page Fields. Click Next.

4) In Step 2b, choose the range on the first sheet. Choose 1 Page Field and give it the name Product 1. Click Add.

5) Repeat Step 4 for each additional worksheet. The dialog should look like the one shown in Figure 987. Click Finish.

Excel will create a pivot table that summarizes all the worksheets. The fields have the strange names Row, Column, Value, and Page1, as shown in Figure 988.

Figure 987

Specify all the areas to be consolidated.

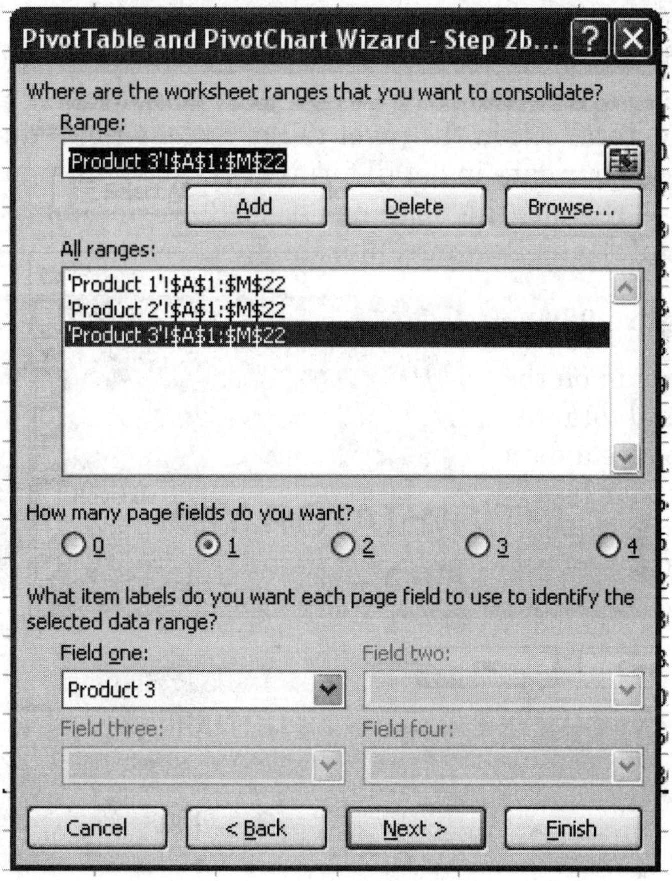

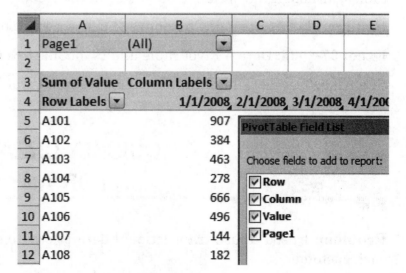

Figure 988

Excel creates a pivot table.

As you read in "See Detail Behind One Number in a Pivot Table," you can double-click any cell in a pivot table to drill down to see all the records in that cell. Here is the amazing trick: If you double-click the Grand Total cell in the pivot table, Excel will produce a new worksheet with all your data in detail format, as shown in Figure 989. All you have to do is rename the headings from Row, Column, Value, and Page1 to Account, Date, Revenue, and Product.

Figure 989

Zoom in on the grand total to produce a data set that is perfect for pivot tables.

Row	Column	Value	Page1
A101	1/1/2008	907	Product 2
A101	2/1/2008	952	Product 2
A101	3/1/2008	1000	Product 2
A101	4/1/2008	1050	Product 2
A101	5/1/2008	1103	Product 2
A101	6/1/2008	1158	Product 2
A101	7/1/2008	1216	Product 2
A101	8/1/2008	1277	Product 2
A101	9/1/2008	1341	Product 2
A101	10/1/2008	1408	Product 2
A101	11/1/2008	1478	Product 2

Summary: Excel can still use multiple consolidation ranges for pivot tables, although the option is no longer in the ribbon.

Commands Discussed: Customize Quick Access Toolbar

Excel 97-2003: Data – PivotTable and PivotChart Report

See Also: "See Detail Behind One Number in a Pivot Table" on p. 547

QUICKLY CREATE CHARTS FOR ANY CUSTOMER

Problem: I need to use transactional data to create similar charts for each customer.

Strategy: In Excel 2007, pivot charts have improved to the point where they are actually usable. Here's what you do:

1) Select a single cell in your data. Select Insert – PivotTable drop-down – PivotChart.

2) Build a pivot table by using the Field List dialog. Note that the row fields are now called axis fields. Put Region in the Axis Fields drop zone.

3) Column fields are now called legend fields. Put Product in the Legend Field drop zone.

4) Add Customer to the Report Filter drop zone. Add Revenue to the Σ Values drop zone.

Excel will show both a pivot table and a chart on the worksheet. When you select the chart, you can use the PivotChart Tools tabs on the ribbon to control the chart type and all formatting.

Figure 990

This chart is the result of a pivot table analysis.

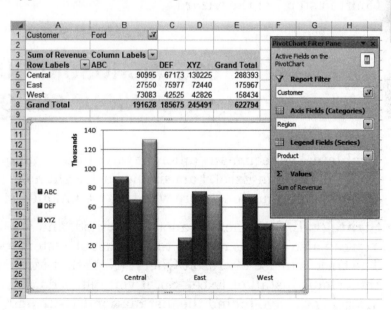

Excel shows the new PivotChart Filter Pane dialog, which you can use to sort or filter data in the chart.

Additional Details: To filter the chart to a specific customer, you can change the Customer dropdown in the pivot table.

Gotcha: The Show Report Filter Pages trick (described in "Create a Report for Every Customer") doesn't work for a pivot chart.

Note: This book contains 46 topics related to pivot tables. I think pivot tables are the best feature in Excel, and I always focus a lot of attention on them in my books. Since the first edition of this book came out, I have co-authored *Pivot Table Data Crunching* with Mike Alexander. That book is now available in editions for Excel 2007 and Excel 97-2003. I am thrilled to say that it is the best-selling book on pivot tables (out of six on the market). If you need more pivot table information, pick up that book.

Summary: Pivot charts have been dramatically improved in Excel 2007.

Commands Discussed: Insert – PivotTable dropdown – PivotChart

Excel 97-2003: Data – PivotTable and PivotChart Report; choose Pivot Chart in step 1 of the wizard.

USE MICROSOFT QUERY TO GET A UNIQUE SET OF RECORDS

Problem: I've seen many different ways to get a unique list of customers from a data set in Excel. I am sitting back right now, thinking, "Couldn't Bill Jelen offer just one more way to get a unique list of customers?"

Strategy: In fact, there is another method, and it's fast and fairly cool. You can also use this method to get a list of customers from a closed file. The trick is to use Microsoft Query. (Note that Microsoft Query is not in the default install of Excel. So, if you didn't do a complete install, you are going to have to find the installation CDs to add Microsoft Query to your installation of Excel.)

Basically, Microsoft Query lets you run some SQL against an external file. I am sure that Microsoft envisioned that this external file would be an Access table or an ODBC data source, but, of course, someone figured out that the external file could be another Excel workbook.

Let's say you have a workbook called SalesData.xlsm. It has one work-sheet called Data. The worksheet contains a bunch of records in columns A through H, as shown in Figure 991. Here is what you do:

1)   Select the data in A:H. Give this range the name MyData.

Figure 991

You have this data in a closed Excel file.

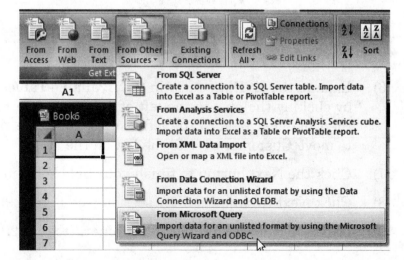

	A	B	C	D	E	F	G	H
1	Region	Product	Date	Customer	Quantity	Revenue	COGS	Profit
2	East	XYZ	2-Jan-08	Ford	1000	22810	10220	12590
3	Central	DEF	2-Jan-08	Verizon	100	2257	984	1273
4	East	ABC	2-Jan-08	Verizon	500	10245	4235	6010
5	Central	XYZ	2-Jan-08	Ainsworth	500	11240	5110	6130
6	Central	XYZ	2-Jan-08	Ainsworth	400	9204	4088	5116
7	East	DEF	2-Jan-08	Gildan Activewea	800	18552	7872	10680
8	East	XYZ	2-Jan-08	Texaco	400	9152	4088	5064
9	Central	ABC	3-Jan-08	IBM	400	6860	3388	3472
10	East	ABC	5-Jan-08	General Motors	400	8456	3388	5068
11	East	DEF	5-Jan-08	State Farm	1000	21730	9840	11890
12	West	XYZ	5-Jan-08	Texaco	600	13806	6132	7674
13	Central	ABC	7-Jan-08	General Motors	800	16416	6776	9640
14	East	XYZ	7-Jan-08	HP	900	21015	9198	11817
15	East	XYZ	8-Jan-08	Ainsworth	900	21465	9198	12267
16	Central	XYZ	8-Jan-08	Wal-Mart	900	21438	9198	12240
17	West	XYZ	10-Jan-08	Ainsworth	400	9144	4088	5056
18	Central	ABC	10-Jan-08	IBM	300	6267	2541	3726
19	Central	ABC	12-Jan-08	Sun Life Financia	100	1740	847	893

SalesData.xlsm — Data

Part III

2)   Save and close SalesData.xlsm.

3)   In a new workbook, select Data – Get External Data – From Oth-er Sources dropdown – From Microsoft Query, as shown in Figure 992.

Figure 992

Use Query.

From Access   From Web   From Text   From Other Sources ▾   Existing Connections   Refresh All ▾   Connections   Properties   Edit Links   Sort

Get Ext

A1

Book6

	A
1	
2	
3	
4	
5	
6	
7	

From SQL Server
Create a connection to a SQL Server table. Import data into Excel as a Table or PivotTable report.

From Analysis Services
Create a connection to a SQL Server Analysis Services cube. Import data into Excel as a Table or PivotTable report.

From XML Data Import
Open or map a XML file into Excel.

From Data Connection Wizard
Import data for an unlisted format by using the Data Connection Wizard and OLEDB.

From Microsoft Query
Import data for an unlisted format by using the Microsoft Query Wizard and ODBC.

4) In the Choose Data Source dialog, choose Excel Files, as shown in Figure 993. Click OK.

Figure 993

Choose Excel files.

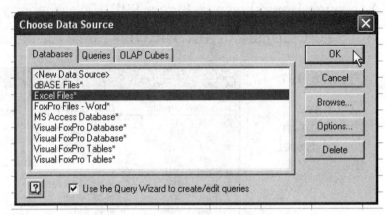

5) Laugh at the retro Select Workbook dialog. Then browse to find SalesData.xlsm, as shown in Figure 994. Click OK.

Figure 994

Browse to the Excel file.

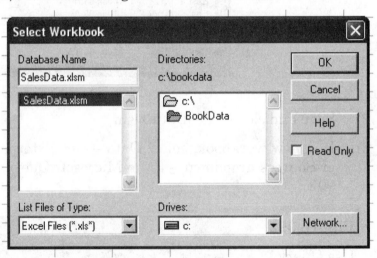

6) Expand the MyData entry in the Available Tables and Columns list by clicking the plus to the left of the entry (see Figure 995). Select the Customer field in the left list and click the right arrow button to move Customer over to the list on the right.

7) Click the Next button to finish your field selection.

8) Click Next to skip the filter section (see Figure 996).

9) Choose to sort ascending by customer. (Figure 997) Click Next.

Figure 995

Add Customer to your query.

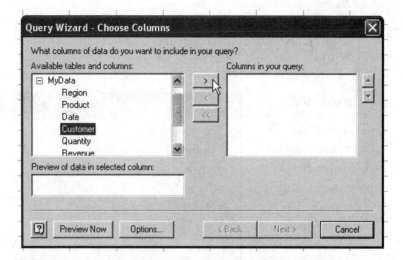

Figure 996

No filter is necessary in this example.

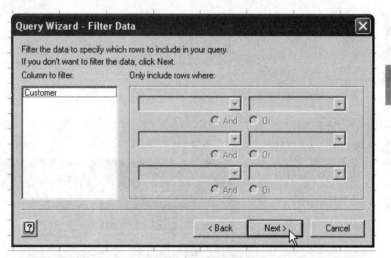

Figure 997

Add a sort.

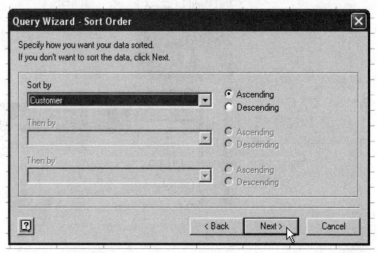

10) Because you want unique records only, edit the query in Microsoft Query. As shown in Figure 998, choose this option and then click Finish.

Figure 998

To eventually access the Unique Records setting, you need to edit in Query.

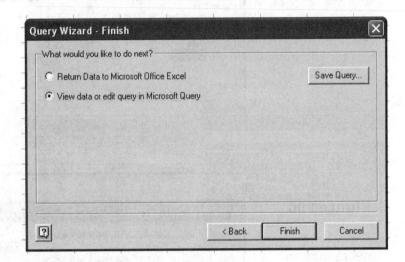

11) When the Microsoft Query window opens, select View – Query Properties, as shown in Figure 999.

Figure 999

Edit query properties.

12) As shown in Figure 1000, choose Unique Values Only and then click OK.

Figure 1000

Ensure that each customer only appears once.

13) As shown in Figure 1001, select File – Return Data to Microsoft Office Excel.

Figure 1001

Finally, take the data to Excel.

14) Choose to return the query as a table, as shown in Figure 1002. Click OK.

Figure 1002

Return the query as a table.

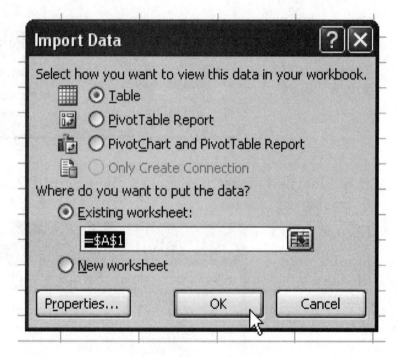

Results: You have a unique list of customers from the closed Excel file.

Additional Details: You can set up this query to update every time the workbook is opened. Select one cell in the returned table. Select Data – Refresh All dropdown – Connection Properties. Check the setting Refresh Data When Opening the File, as shown in Figure 1003.

Figure 1003

Enable refresh on file open.

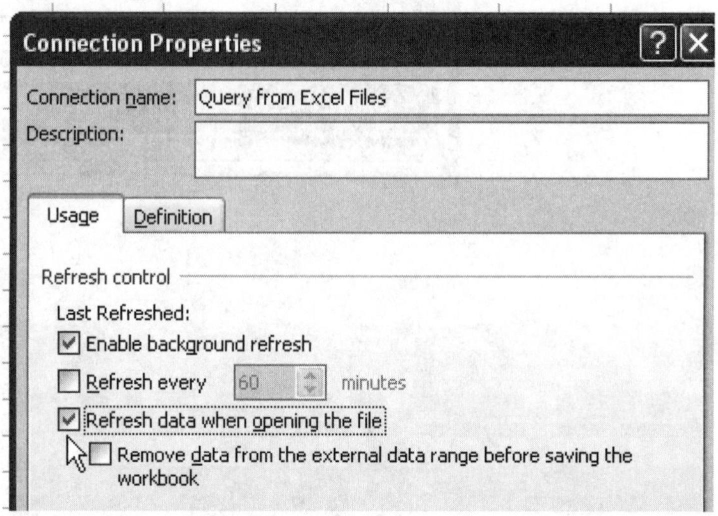

Gotcha: Unless you store SalesData.xlsm in a trusted location, Excel will still disable the query every time you open the file (see Figure 1004).

Figure 1004

Excel's new tough stance on security disables links to other data.

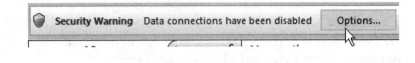

As shown in Figure 1005, you will have to choose Options – Enable This Content in order to get the updated data. To prevent these two extra clicks, use a trusted location, as discussed in "Use a Trusted Location to Prevent Excel's Constant Warnings."

Part III

Figure 1005

Use a trusted location to prevent the security hassle.

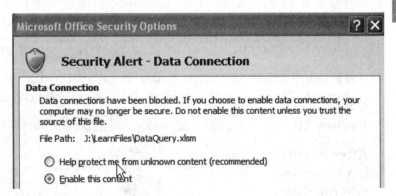

Summary: Microsoft Query provides a way to import data from Access, Excel, or ODBC data sources.

Commands Discussed: Data – Get External Data – From Other Sources dropdown – From Microsoft Query; File – Return Data to Microsoft Office Excel; Data – Refresh All

Excel 97-2003: Data – Import External Data – New Database Query

USE A TRUSTED LOCATION TO PREVENT EXCEL'S CONSTANT WARNINGS

Problem: Excel 2007 is more security-conscious than any other version. In fact, many features that I rely on are now disabled, such as links to external files, external queries, and macros.

Strategy: Microsoft will ease up if you store your files in a trusted location. Follow these steps:

1) Store all your files with macros and data for links in a folder on your hard drive. Make sure no viruses are in the folder. Delete any dragons, griffins, medusas, and Cyclops from the folder. Make sure you don't store your kid's delete-all-files-on-the hard-drive science project in that folder.

2) Select Office Icon – Excel Options. In the left pane of the Excel Options dialog, choose Trust Center. Click the Trust Center Settings button. In the left pane, choose Trusted Locations.

3) Near the bottom, click the Add New Location button.

4) In the Microsoft Office Trusted Location dialog, click the Browse button. Browse to the correct folder and click OK. (Figure 1006)

Figure 1006

After navigating the maze, add the folder.

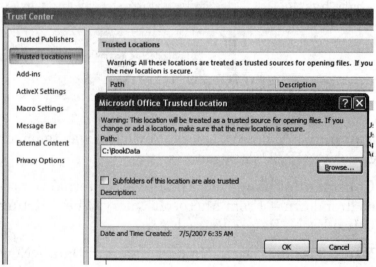

5) If you want the subfolders of the location to be trusted as well, select the Subfolders of This Location Are Also Trusted check box.

6)   Click OK to add the trusted location. Click OK to close the Trust Center. Click OK to close the Excel Options dialog.

Results: You will now be able to open files with links and external data queries without a hassle, if they are in a trusted location.

Additional Details: Microsoft is now counting on you. Please, don't randomly right-click on attachments in spam e-mails and choose to save them in the trusted location.

Summary: Excel will (sort of) return to the carefree and fun days of the Wild Wild West if you store your files in a trusted location.

Commands Discussed: Data – Office Icon – Excel Options – Trust Center

Excel 97-2003: Trusted locations were not necessary; links automatically worked.

IMPORT A TABLE FROM A WEB PAGE INTO EXCEL

Part III

Problem: Every day, I open a browser and check on the prices of my stock portfolio. I manually copy and paste this data to Excel. I know that some Web sites offer a Download to Spreadsheet option, like the one shown in Figure 1007. Is there an easier way to get this data into Excel?

Figure 1007

Downloading the data and converting to Excel is not the easiest way.

| Y! http://finance.yahoo.com/q/cq?d=v1&s=AAPl |

Columnar

Symbol	Time	Trade	Change	% Chg
AAPL	Jul 3	127.17	0.00	0.00%
MSFT	Jul 3	30.02	0.00	0.00%
INTC	Jul 3	24.59	0.00	0.00%
GOOG	Jul 3	534.34	0.00	0.00%

⬇ **Download to Spreadsheet** ✉ **Add to**

Quotes delayed, except where indicated othe

Strategy: Web queries make importing tables from Web pages easy. Follow these steps:

1) Optionally, open a browser and browse to the Web page that you want to import. In the browser shown in Figure 1007, I have already entered the four stock symbols that I want to import. The address bar in the browser contains the URL for this view of the data.

2) Start with a new workbook. Select Data – Get External Data – From Web. The New Web Query dialog box will appear, with your usual home page in the browser (see Figure 1008).

Figure 1008

A browser right in Excel.

3) If you took step 1, switch to your regular browser by pressing Alt+Tab. Highlight the correct address in the address bar and press Ctrl+C to copy this address to the Clipboard. Press Alt+Tab to return to Excel, press Ctrl+V to paste the address into the Excel browser, and click Go (see Figure 1009). Or, if you prefer, use the Excel browser to navigate to the stock quote site and enter your stock symbols.

Figure 1009

Navigate to the Website in Excel.

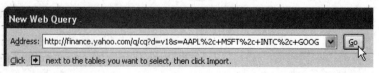

The desired Web page will appear in the dialog box. There will be a yellow box with a black arrow next to each table on the Web page. If you have ever designed Web pages, you'll be interested to see how many tables the designer used to create the page.

4) Scroll down to find the desired table. Click the yellow arrow next to that table. As you hover over the arrow, the table will be temporarily outlined. The yellow arrow changes to a green check mark, as shown in Figure 1010.

Figure 1010

Choose the table to import.

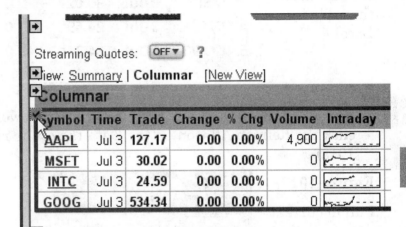

5) Click the Import button. Excel will ask where you want the data imported, as shown in Figure 1011.

Figure 1011

Choose a location for the results.

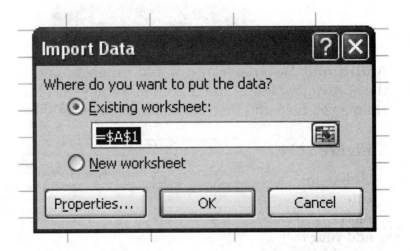

6) Click OK. The dialog box will disappear. For a few seconds, you will see a strange value in cell A1, followed by "Getting Data." In 1–10 seconds, the spreadsheet will redraw with a current version of the data from the Web page, as shown in Figure 1012.

Figure 1012

After a few moments, Excel will import the table into Excel.

	A	B	C	D	E	F	
1	Symbol	Time	Trade	Change	% Chg	Volume	I
2	AAPL	3-Jul	127.17	0	0.00%	4,900	
3	MSFT	3-Jul	30.02	0	0.00%	0	
4	INTC	3-Jul	24.59	0	0.00%	0	
5	GOOG	3-Jul	534.34	0	0.00%	0	

7) To refresh the data at any time, return to this worksheet and then click the Refresh All icon on the Data tab of the ribbon (see Figure 1013).

Figure 1013

Pull in current data from the Web site by clicking Refresh All.

Additional Details: You can add numbers and formulas adjacent to the Web query. For example, you might add a column for the number of shares you hold and then calculate a value, as shown in Figure 1014.

Figure 1014

Unlike in Internet Explorer, you can add your own calculations to Excel.

J2					fx	=I2*C2		
	C	D	E	F	G	H	I	J
1	Trade	Change	% Chg	Volume	Intraday	Related Info	My Share	Value
2	127.17	0	0.00%	4,900		Chart, Messages, Key Stats, More	100	12717
3	30.02	0	0.00%	0		Chart, Messages, Key Stats, More	100	3002
4	24.59	0	0.00%	0		Chart, Messages, Key Stats, More	100	2459
5	534.34	0	0.00%	0		Chart, Messages, Key Stats, More	10	5343.4
6							Total	23521.4

Summary: Web queries offer an easy way to regularly import data from a Web page into Excel.

Commands Discussed: Data – Get External Data – From Web; Ctrl+C; Data – Refresh All

Excel 97-2003: Data – Import External Data – New Web Query

HAVE WEB DATA UPDATE AUTOMATICALLY WHEN YOU OPEN WORKBOOK

Problem: Every day I open a spreadsheet with a Web query and use Data – Refresh All. Is there a way to have the Web query refresh automatically?

Strategy: Here's what you do:

Part
III

1) Set up a Web query, as discussed in "Import a Table from a Web Page into Excel." After you press the Import button and before you close the Import Data dialog, click the Properties button in the lower left, as shown in Figure 1015.

Figure 1015

Click Prop-
erties while
building the
query.

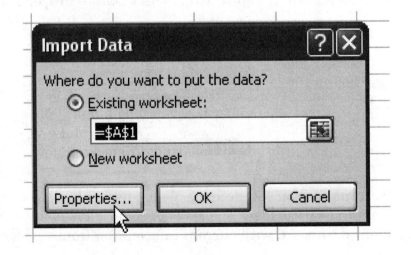

2) In the Refresh Control section of the External Data Range Properties dialog, choose the option Refresh Data When Opening the File, as shown in Figure 1016.

Figure 1016

Specify to update automatically on opening the file.

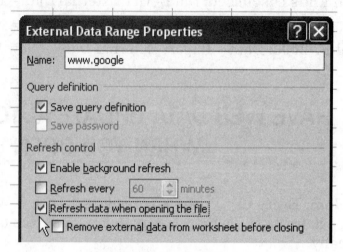

Additional Details: If you have a Web query set up and you need to access the Properties dialog to change a setting after the query has been defined, follow these steps:

1) Select one cell in the returned Web data.

2) As shown in Figure 1017, select Data – Properties.

Figure 1017

Choose Properties on the Data ribbon tab.

Summary: You can define a Web query to update automatically every time the spreadsheet opens. This could allow you to set up a management dashboard with current information from various Web pages.

Commands Discussed: Data – Get External Data – From Web; Data – Properties

Excel 97-2003: Data – Import External Data – New Web Query; Data – Import External Data – Data Range Properties

HAVE WEB DATA UPDATE AUTOMATICALLY EVERY TWO MINUTES

Problem: I have a Web query inserted in my spreadsheet that updates automatically when I open the spreadsheet. I would like the Web information to update automatically every two minutes.

Strategy:

1) Select a cell in the Web query table. Select Data – Properties.

2) From the External Data Range Properties dialog box, in the Refresh Control section, select the Refresh Every option. Change the spin button to 2 minutes, as shown in Figure 1018.

Figure 1018

Choosing to update every 2 minutes.

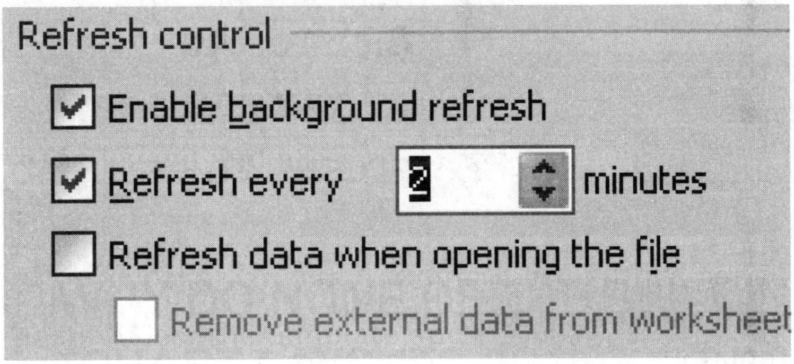

Refresh control

☑ Enable background refresh

☑ Refresh every [2] ⬍ minutes

☐ Refresh data when opening the file

☐ Remove external data from worksheet

Gotcha: A refresh cannot happen if you are in Edit mode. If you start to enter a cell in the worksheet, get a telephone call, and head off to a meeting without completing the cell, Excel cannot update the query.

You may want to open a second instance of Excel and have the query retrieved in its own instance of Excel. If you are trying to work in the same instance of Excel, the pause that occurs every two minutes while Excel refreshes is maddening.

Summary: To have a Web query automatically update periodically, use Data – Properties for the connection, to specify how often to update.

Commands Discussed: Data – Properties

Excel 97-2003: Data – Import External Data – Data Range Properties

THE SPACES IN THIS WEB DATA
WON'T GO AWAY

Problem: I imported the data shown in Figure 1019 from a Web page. After many attempts to remove the internal spaces, I am still unable do so.

Figure 1019

Those look like spaces.

◢	A
1	AK 335 986
2	AV 797 147
3	CJ 541 149
4	CR 846 746
5	CZ 137 324
6	FD 605 706

I tried highlighting column A and using Home – Find & Select – Replace to replace every occurrence of a space, but it didn't work. The blanks remain.

I tried the SUBSTITUTE function, as shown in Figure 1020. The blanks remain.

Figure 1020

This formula should have worked.

=SUBSTITUTE(A1," ","")

◢	A	B
1	AK 335 986	AK 335 986
2	AV 797 147	AV797147
3	CJ 541 149	CJ541149

If I go to cell A1 and type AK 335 986 (with spaces in the middle), the formula in column B will work, as shown in Figure 1021.

Figure 1021

If you type the data in A1, the formula in B1 works.

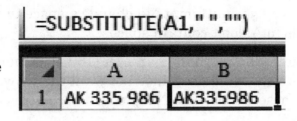

=SUBSTITUTE(A1," ","")

	A	B
1	AK 335 986	AK335986

What is going on? Why won't the formula work on numbers pasted from the Web page?

Strategy: Every character in the alphabet is assigned a number according to the ASCII character set. A capital letter A is really character code 65. Normally, a space is character code 32.

In order to find the character code for a character, you can use the CODE function. To isolate the third character in cell A1, you would use =MID(A1,3,1). To find the character code for that value, you would use =CODE(MID(A1,3,1)).

As shown in Figure 1022, this formula confirms that the value typed into cell A1 contains a space (character code 32) in the third position.

Figure 1022

A space is character code 32.

=CODE(MID(A1,3,1))

	A	B	C
1	AK 335 986	AK335986	32

Now, if you copy that formula down to the other cells, as shown in Figure 1023, you will see that all the other cells have a character code 160 in the third position!

Figure 1023

The spaces aren't really spaces.

=CODE(MID(A2,3,1))

	A	B	C
1	AK 335 986	AK335986	32
2	AV 797 147	AV 797 147	160
3	CJ 541 149	CJ 541 149	160
4	CR 846 746	CR 846 746	160
5	C7 137 324	C7 137 324	160

Part III

This explains why your attempts to change a space to nothing wouldn't work: The cells in A don't contain spaces.

A little research shows that character 160 is a non-breaking space (Nbsp). This is a space where you do not want the browser to start a new line between those words. The Nbsp character is very common on Web pages.

So, how can you use character 160 in Home – Find & Select – Replace? Here is one method:

1) Go to a blank cell in the worksheet and use the formula =CHAR(160), as shown in Figure 1024. You won't see anything in the cell, but the formula bar will show that you have a formula hidden there.

Figure 1024

Enter a character 160 in a cell.

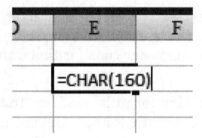

2) Copy this cell.

3) Select your range of Web data. Choose Home – Find & Select – Replace.

4) In the Find What text box in the Find and Replace dialog, press Ctrl+V to paste the non-breaking space. Again, you won't see anything that is there. Leave the Replace With box blank. Click Replace All (see Figure 1025).

Figure 1025

Replace the copied character with nothing.

Result:s As shown in Figure 1026, the unwanted spaces are removed.

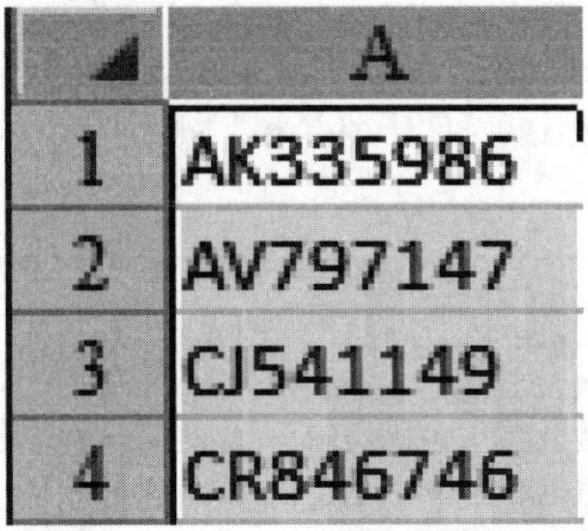

Figure 1026

The non-breaking spaces are removed.

▲	A
1	AK335986
2	AV797147
3	CJ541149
4	CR846746

Alternate Strategy: Another solution is to use the SUBSTITUTE function, as shown in Figure 1027.

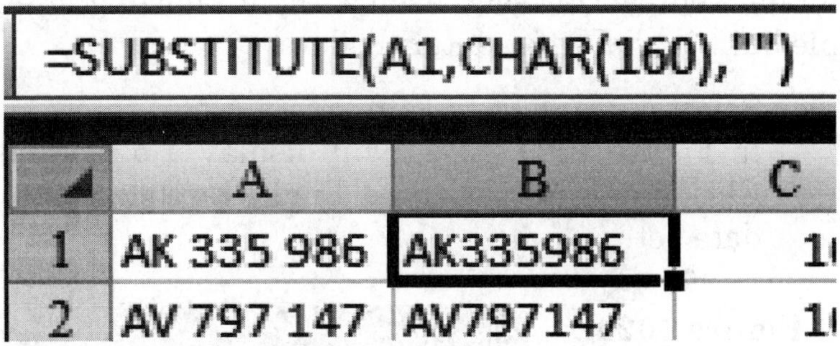

Figure 1027

Using CHAR(160) in the SUBSTITUTE function will work.

=SUBSTITUTE(A1,CHAR(160),"")

▲	A	B	C
1	AK 335 986	AK335986	1(
2	AV 797 147	AV797147	1(

Part III

Summary: Although character 160 is the usual culprit for this problem, using the CODE function will allow you to find the character code for any such offending character.

Commands Discussed: Home – Find & Select – Replace; Ctrl+V

Functions Discussed: =MID(); =CODE(); =CHAR(); =SUBSTITUTE()

USE A BUILT-IN DATA ENTRY FORM

Problem: I need to do data entry in Excel. I have a lot of records to key or to edit, as shown in Figure 1028. Can I easily create a dialog to help with this?

Figure 1028

You need to key data into this data set.

◢	A	B	C	D	E
1	Invoice	Customer	Region	Rep	Merchandise
2	1201	RST Pty Ltd.	Southern	Mary	280
3	1202	NOP Pty Ltd.	Northern Territory	Terry	237
4	1203	EFG Pty Ltd.	NSW	Joe	257
5	1204	EFG Pty Ltd.	NSW	Joe	523
6	1205	STU Pty Ltd.	Southern	Mary	266

Strategy: By using Excel VBA, you can build very complex dialog boxes for data entry. However, even without knowing VBA, you can use a simple built-in dialog for entering data:

1) Select a cell in your data. Press Alt+D then O (letter O). As shown in Figure 1029, Excel will display a dialog box with your fields. Click the Find Next and Find Prev buttons to move through the data set.

Figure 1029

The built-in data entry form.

Sheet1			[?][X]
Invoice:	1201		1 of 15
Customer:	RST Pty Ltd.		New
Region:	Southern		Delete
Rep:	Mary		Restore
Merchandise:	280		
Tax:	39.2		Find Prev
Freight:	14.95		Find Next
Total:	334.15		Criteria
			Close

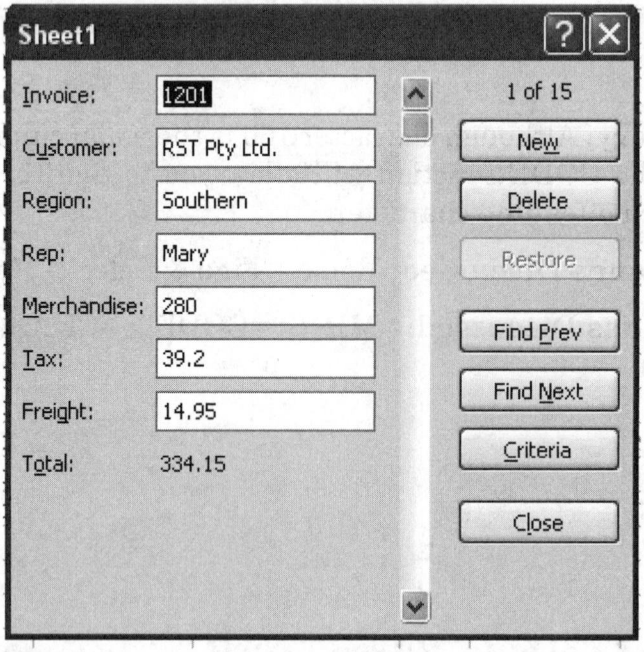

2) To add a record, click the New button. The Total field does not fill in until you click Find Next and Find Prev to enter this record. When you come back to the record, the total will be filled in.

Additional Details: As shown in Figure 1030, the Criteria button will allow you to limit the Find Next and Find Prev buttons to only contain records. For instance, click Criteria, enter Joe as the Rep, and click Next. You will see only Joe's records.

Figure 1030

Use the Criteria button to enter filter criteria.

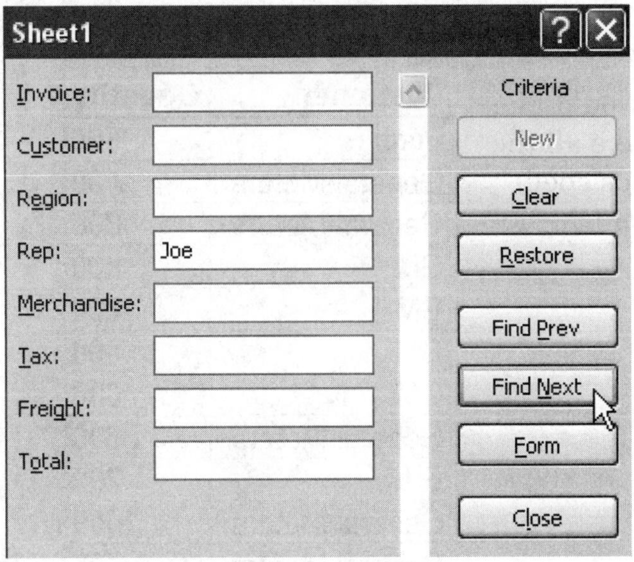

Gotcha: The Form command used to be on the Excel 2003 Data menu. Microsoft has removed this option. However, you can use the Excel 2003 access key Alt+D+O to load the data form. If you want to have an icon for Data Form, you can customize the Quick Access toolbar. In the Customize dialog, you look in the category Commands Not in the Ribbon. Having a command moved to this category is a sign that the feature might be removed from future versions of Excel.

Summary: To use a dialog box to help key records, you can select a cell in your data and press Alt+D+O.

Commands Discussed: Alt+D+O

Excel 97-2003: Data – Form

HOW DO I CLEAN UP THIS DATA?

Problem: I get data from many sources. Everyone seems to override our built-in list, and they decide to spell customer names their own way. As shown in Figure 1031, I might get GM, G.M., General Motors, and more. How can I make all the similar values in a column conform to a single standard?

Figure 1031

You would like to make all the various spellings of GM say GM.

Customer	Quantity
Ford	800
General Motors	400
General Motors	800
GM	800
GM	700
GM	800
GM	600
General Motors	300
G.M.	200
General Motors	1000
General Motors	700

Strategy: This is not an easy process, but the tools in this topic will make the process faster than anything else you might try. Follow these steps:

1) Select a cell in your original data set. Choose Insert – Pivot Table. Click OK.

2) Double-click the Customer field in the Pivot Table Field List dialog to add Customer to the row area.

3) Drag a second copy of the Customer field to the ∑ Values drop zone. When you drop the field, it will change to Count of Customer, as shown in Figure 1032.

Figure 1032

Add the Customer field as a Row field and a Values field.

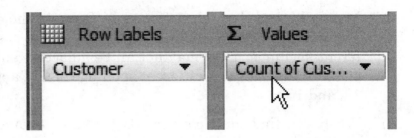

4) Select the range encompassed by the pivot table. Press Ctrl+C to copy. Select Home – Paste Values to convert the pivot table to values (see Figure 1033).

Figure 1033

Convert the pivot table to values.

5) Copy column A. Right-click column B and choose Insert Copied Cells. You will now have Customer in A, Customer in B, and Count in C (see Figure 1034).

Figure 1034

Column B will become the fixed customer column.

11	Ford	Ford	53
12	Ford Motor Co	Ford Motor Co	3
13	G.M.	G.M.	1
14	General Motors	General Motors	55
15	Gildan Activewear	Gildan Activewear	4
16	GM	GM	4
17	HP	HP	4
18	I B M	I B M	1

6)   Manually read through customer A. Because the data is sorted by customer, you will hopefully notice the same customer with different spellings. They may not all be adjacent, but they should be close. In Figure 1034, different spellings of GM appear on rows 13, 14, and 16.

7)   When you find multiple records for one customer, decide which spelling is correct. The Count column is very helpful. In Figure 1034, you can see that most of the records used General Motors, so that might be the value in the Customer dropdown. Copy the correct spelling and paste it to the second column of each GM record, as shown in Figure 1035.

Figure 1035

Later, a VLOOKUP will convert A values to B values.

11	Ford	Ford	53
12	Ford Motor Co	Ford	3
13	G.M.	General Motors	1
14	General Motors	General Motors	55
15	Gildan Activewear	Gildan Activewear	4
16	GM	General Motors	4
17	HP	HP	4
18	I B M	IBM	1
19	IBM	IBM	43

8)   Repeat steps 6 and 7 until all the customers are fixed.

9)   Return to the original data set.

10)   Insert a blank column to the right of the customer column. The heading can be Fixed Customer or Customer or something similar.

11)   Use a VLOOKUP formula in the blank customer column as shown in Figure 1036. This should look up the customer in the original data set, find the matching customer from column A of the pivot table, and return the second value from the pivot table. This will convert all the GM records to General Motors.

Figure 1036

Use a VLOOK-UP in the original data set.

| | =VLOOKUP(D2,Sheet1!$A$4:$B$38,2,FALSE) |

C	D	E	F	G
Date	Customer	Customer	Quantity	Revenue
15-Dec-08	Ford	Ford	700	13552
17-Dec-08	Ford	Ford	800	14408
5-Jan-08	General Motors	General Motors	400	8456
7-Jan-08	General Motors	General Motors	800	16416
21-Jan-08	GM	General Motors	800	14592
27-Jan-08	GM	General Motors	700	17150
29-Jan-08	GM	General Motors	800	15640
30-Jan-08	GM	General Motors	600	12672

12) Convert the new customer column from formulas to values by pressing Ctrl+C and then selecting Home – Paste dropdown – Paste Values.

Results: Misspellings and duplicate values are removed from the new customer column. You can use the new customer column for further analysis.

Summary: A pivot table's count of how many times each customer appears provides assistance in figuring out which customer name is the best spelling to keep. Also, when you use a pivot table, you need to look at only perhaps 40 customer records instead of 500 detail records.

Functions Discussed: =VLOOKUP()

Commands Discussed: Insert – PivotTable; Home – Paste dropdown – Paste Values

Excel 97-2003: Data – PivotTable & PivotChart Report, choose range and drag the Customer field to the Row area and the Data area; Edit – Paste Special.

TRANSFORM BLACK-AND-WHITE SPREADSHEETS TO COLOR BY USING A TABLE

Problem: My worksheet (see Figure 1037) is boring black and white. I want to jazz it up with color.

Figure 1037

Add color to this spread-sheet.

◢	A	B	C	D
1	SKU	Mfg Cost	Part 1	List Price
2	A409	209.03	421.06	425
3	A322	157.98	318.96	320
4	A356	18.97	40.94	45
5	A460	88.38	179.76	180
6	A976	165.08	333.16	335
7	A764	134.16	271.32	275

Strategy: Format the range as a Table. Use the Table Styles gallery to format the spreadsheet. Here's how you do it:

1) Select one cell in your range of data. Press Ctrl+T or select Insert – Table icon.

2) Excel asks to confirm the location of your table and indicate if there are headers, as shown in Figure 1038. Click OK.

Figure 1038

Specify the range of the table.

3) A new Table Tools Design ribbon tab appears. Use the Table Styles gallery, in conjunction with the Table Style Options check boxes to format your table (see Figure 1039).

Figure 1039

Choose a color scheme from the gallery.

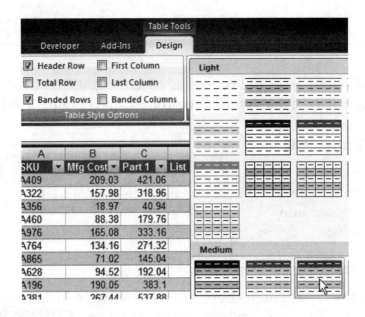

Results: Your worksheet is formatted in just a few clicks.

Additional Details: The gallery shows variations on six color schemes. To use new color schemes, you can choose a new theme from the Page Layout tab of the ribbon.

Additional Details: Creating a table enables many new and powerful features. If those features annoy you, you can use the Convert to Range button on the Design ribbon as shown in Figure 1040. Excel will convert the data from a table to a regular range, but the formatting will remain.

Figure 1040

If the table logic annoys you, convert the formatted table to a range.

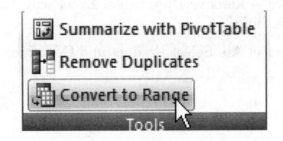

Summary: Tables offer many powerful formatting options.

Commands Discussed: Insert – Table; Ctrl+T

Excel 97-2003: Format – AutoFormat.

REMOVE DUPLICATES

Problem: I have a data set in which I would like to find every unique combination of customer and product. (see Figure 1041)

Figure 1041

Find unique occurrences of customer and product.

▲	A	B	C	D	E	F	G	H
1	Region	Product	Date	Customer	Quantity	Revenue	COGS	Profit
8	East	XYZ	2-Jan-08	Texaco	400	9152	4088	5064
9	Central	ABC	3-Jan-08	IBM	400	6860	3388	3472
10	East	ABC	5-Jan-08	General Motors	400	8456	3388	5068
11	East	DEF	5-Jan-08	State Farm	1000	21730	9840	11890

Strategy: Although there are several ways to find unique values (advanced filters, pivot tables, Microsoft Query, COUNTIF), Microsoft added a new feature to Excel 2007 called Remove Duplicates.

Remove Duplicates is a powerful feature—sometimes too powerful because it very quickly and destructively removes the duplicated rows.

To use the Remove Duplicates command, follow these steps:

1) Make a copy of your data. Copy it to a new range, a new worksheet, or a new workbook.

2) Select one cell in your data set.

3) Select Data – Remove Duplicates. Excel will display the Remove Duplicates dialog.

4) Click Unselect All. Select Product and Customer, as shown in Figure 1042.

Figure 1042

Choose which columns should be analyzed.

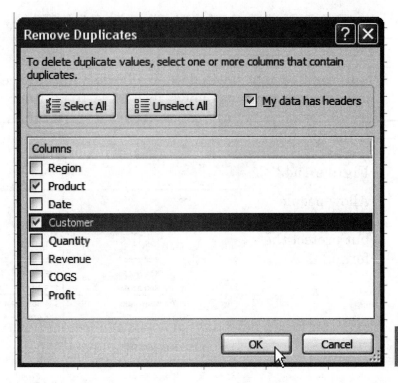

5)   Click OK. Excel will confirm how many duplicates were found and removed.

Results: Excel will delete hundreds of rows of data! If you didn't make a copy in step 1 and you need that data, press Ctrl+Z to undo.

Gotcha: Remove Duplicates is a destructive command. It's a good idea to mark the records using conditional formatting and choose which one of the duplicates to keep.

Summary: The new Remove Duplicates command will remove duplicate records.

Commands Discussed: Data – Remove Duplicates

Excel 97-2003: This command did not exist in Excel 97-2003.

PROTECT CELLS THAT CONTAIN FORMULAS

Problem: I have to key in data in a large number of cells in a month-end financial statement, as shown in Figure 1043. I don't want to accidentally key in a number in a cell that contains a formula. How can I protect just the formula cells?

Figure 1043

Allow people to enter details but protect the formulas.

A B C D E	F	G Jan	H Feb	I Mar
1				
2 Income				
3 Revenue				
4 Education		11,767.30	12,551.48	15,261.14
5 Freight		1,609.12	1,672.02	1,176.79
6 Prof Fees		151,655.17	148,880.39	159,366.05
7 Referral Fees		43,343.06	64,238.33	47,738.11
8 Retail Sales		176,287.63	221,382.87	234,778.49
9 Total Revenue		384,662.28	448,725.08	458,320.58
10 Total Income		384,662.28	448,725.08	458,320.58
11 Cost of Goods Sold				
12 Cost of Goods Sold		48,067.54	44,100.56	30,651.39
13 Cost of Sales		20.48	26.89	24.83
14 Total COGS		48,088.03	44,127.44	30,676.22

Strategy: After unlocking all cells, you can use the Go To Special dialog to select only the cells with formulas and lock just those cells.

By default, all cells in a worksheet start with their Locked property set to TRUE, but you may not realize this until you turn on protection for the first time. The first step is to unlock all the cells:

1) Select all cells by pressing Ctrl+A. Select Home – Format dropdown – Format Cells. Click on the Protection tab in the Format Cells dialog. As shown in Figure 1044, you will see that the Locked option is chosen.

Figure 1044

All cells start out locked by default.

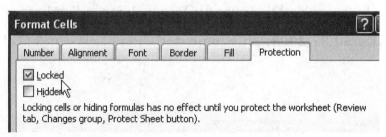

2)   Uncheck the Locked box. Click OK to close the Format Cells dialog.

3)   With all the cells still highlighted, select Home – Find & Select – Go To Special.

4)   On the Go To Special dialog box, choose the Formulas option button, as shown in Figure 1045.

Figure 1045

Select only formula cells.

5)   Click OK to close the Go To Special dialog. Excel will reduce the selection to only cells with formulas.

6)   Select Home – Format dropdown – Lock Cells. This will lock only the selected cells, which are the formula cells.

7)   Enable protection for the sheet. (Note that if you skip this final step, you can still accidentally overwrite your formulas.) Select Home – Format dropdown – Protect Sheet to display the Protect

Sheet dialog. The default settings, as shown in Figure 1046, are sufficient protection. Simply click OK.

Figure 1046

Protect the sheet.

Now, if you accidentally try to enter something in a formula cell, Excel will prevent you from entering the data.

Summary: You can use the Go To Special dialog to select only the formula cells and then protect just those cells. You also need to remember to protect the sheet from overwriting.

Commands Discussed: Home – Format dropdown – Format Cells – Protection; Home – Find & Select – Go To Special; Home – Format dropdown – Format Cells – Protect Sheet

Excel 97-2003: Format – Cells – Protection; Edit – Go To – Special; Tools – Protection – Protect Sheet

PART 4

MAKING THINGS LOOK GOOD

CHANGE THE LOOK OF YOUR WORKBOOK WITH DOCUMENT THEMES

Problem: Excel 2007 looks pretty slick at first. It uses new colors, new fonts, new chart colors. But after a while, the blue, red, green, purple, teal, and orange colors get old. Figure 1047 shows a worksheet with a table, SmartArt, a chart, a picture, shapes, and other Excel 2007 additions.

Figure 1047

Excel offers many new features that can start to look old.

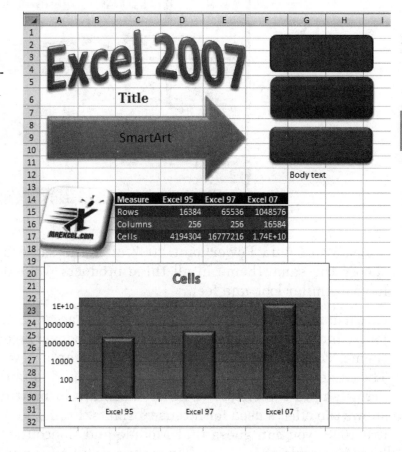

Strategy: Excel offers 20 different built-in themes. When you choose a new theme from the Page Layout ribbon tab, Excel changes the accent colors, fonts, and effects in the workbook. Figure 1048 shows some of the changes when a new theme is applied.

Figure 1048

Choose a new theme.

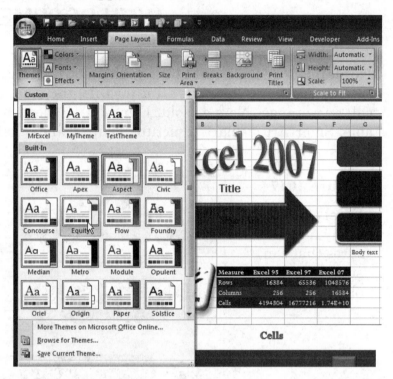

Excel, Word, and PowerPoint 2007 offer the same 20 themes. If you choose the same theme in all three products, your documents should have a similar look and feel.

Additional Details: A theme comprises six accent colors, title and body fonts, and a series of effects. The Effects dropdown is confusing. For each theme, Excel shows the effects for a circle, an arrow, and a rectangle. The circle gives an indication of the format used for simple formats. The arrow shows the effects used for moderate formatting. The rectangle shows the effects used for intense formats. From the thumbnails in Figure 1049, you can guess that Module and Concourse will offer double lines in simple effects, the Paper theme will offer muted or flat moderate effects, and the Metro theme is going to offer glass effects when you choose intense formatting.

Figure 1049

Three shapes in the Effects dropdown indicate simple, moderate, and intense formatting.

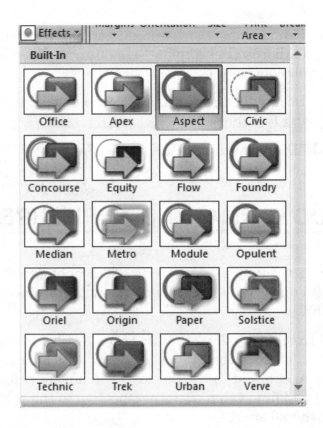

Alternate Strategy: You can add a new theme to match your company colors. Follow these steps:

1)   Select one of the 20 built-in themes from the Effects dropdown.

2)   Open the Fonts dropdown on the Page Layout tab and choose Create New Theme Fonts. Choose a font for headings and a font for body copy. Tip: If you have a stylized logo with "OurCo" and want a font to provide all 26 letters in a similar font, visit Chank.com.

3)   Open the Colors dropdown and choose Create New Theme Colors. Specify colors for light and dark text and specify six accent colors for the theme.

4)   Open the Themes dropdown and choose Save Current Theme. Give the theme a name that reflects your company name.

Results: Excel will offer the new theme in the Themes dropdown. Your custom themes will appear at the top of the dropdown.

To share a custom theme with others, you can copy the .thmx file from %AppData%\Microsoft\Templates\Document Themes\ to the same folder on other computers.

Summary: Document themes allow you to give an old workbook a new look with just a few clicks.

Commands Discussed: Page Layout – Themes

ADD FORMATTING TO PICTURES IN EXCEL

Problem: I used Insert – Picture to add a photograph at the top of my report. Excel displayed a new ribbon tab with dozens of options. What is all this stuff?

Strategy: Excel 2007 allows you to transform your photos in a number of ways. Most of the ribbon tab is a gallery that provides 28 different effects that you can add to the picture. The effects range from frames to soft edges to adding a shadow or perspective to the picture. Figure 1050 shows 6 of the 28 effects.

Figure 1050

Apply a style to a picture.

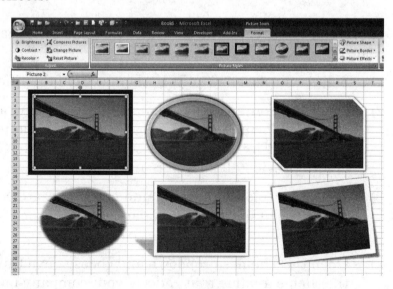

Additional Details: Beyond this gallery, there are some interesting tools. For example, you can use the Recolor icon to convert a picture to monochrome or to a sepia tone.

Frequently, with today's digital cameras, a picture will be inserted and cover the entire first window of cells. You can grab the resize handle in the lower-right corner and hold down the Shift key while you drag up and to the left to make the image appear smaller. Making the image appear smaller does not change the size of the picture, however. With a picture selected, you can choose Compress Pictures to make the image size smaller. In the Compress Pictures dialog, you click the Options button to display the Compression Settings dialog.

In the ribbon, you can also choose Print, Screen, or E-mail. Figure 1051 shows the compression dialogs.

Figure 1051

Reduce file size for all pictures in the document.

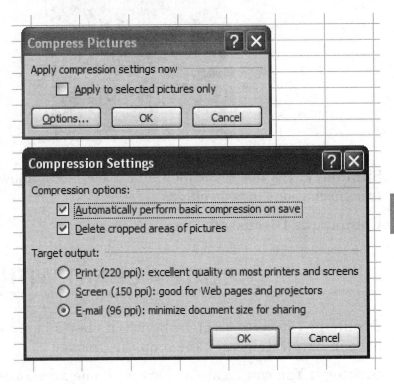

Part IV

Gotcha: Note that by default, Excel will always do a compression when you save the file. If you are producing documents that are going to be printed in a glossy annual report, change this setting to Print before you save.

Additional Details: Another tool that is very useful is the Crop tool on the right side of the ribbon. When you click Crop, Excel adds eight cropping handles around the image. You can grab a handle and drag inward to crop the photo, as shown in Figure 1052. When you are done, you click on the photo to perform the crop.

Figure 1052

Crop a photo.

Summary: It's not Photoshop, but Excel 2007 allows you to do basic transformations to your photos.

Commands Discussed: Insert - Picture

CREATE A CHART WITH ONE CLICK

Problem: I have to create a bunch of charts based on data I already have in Excel. How can I speed up the process?

Strategy: You can create a chart with one keystroke! Select the data, including the headings and row labels, as shown in Figure 1053, and press Alt+F1.

Figure 1053

Leave the top-left cell blank.

◢	A	B	C	D	E	F
1						
2		Jan-06	Feb-06	Mar-06	Apr-06	May-06
3	East	12,000	13,200	14,520	15,972	17,569
4	Central	17,000	19,550	22,483	25,855	29,733
5	West	8,000	8,400	8,820	9,261	9,724

The data will be charted as an embedded chart on the current sheet, as shown in Figure 1054.

Figure 1054

Excel creates a default chart.

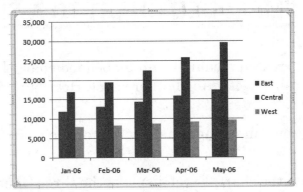

Caution: If your data includes dates as labels, the upper-left cell of the data range should be blank. Do not include a heading such as Date there.

Additional Details: You can easily change the type of chart created when you use this strategy. While a chart is active, choose Design – Change Chart Type. Select a chart type and click the Set as Default Chart button, as shown in Figure 1055. All future one-keystroke charts will be created as this type.

Figure 1055

Change the default chart type.

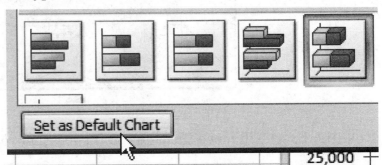

Summary: You can create a chart in a single keystroke: Alt+F1.

Commands Discussed: Alt+F1; Design – Change Chart Type – Set as Default Chart

Excel 97-2003: Instead of Alt+F1, use the F11 key to create a chart on a new chart sheet. To move the chart back to an embedded sheet, right-click the chart and choose Location. To set a default chart type, use Chart – Chart Type – Set as Default Chart.

MOVE A CHART FROM AN EMBEDDED CHART TO A CHART SHEET

Problem: I created a chart as an embedded chart. I need to move this chart to its own sheet or to another sheet. How can I change the location of the chart?

Strategy: You can change the location of the chart by following these steps:

1)   Activate the chart. Excel displays the three Chart Tools tabs in the ribbon.

2)   Select Design – Move Chart from the right side of the ribbon. Alternatively, right-click the chart border and choose Move Chart.

3)   In the Move Chart dialog, choose a new location (see Figure 1056).

Figure 1056

Specify a new location.

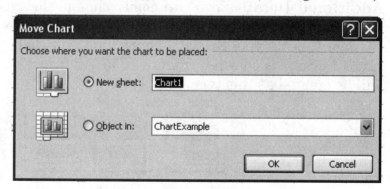

Results: Excel will move the chart to the location you specified.

Gotcha: When you move a chart from a chart sheet to an embedded object, the size and scale of the chart change. It is best to move the chart to its final location before customizing it.

Summary: You can move an embedded chart to its own chart sheet or back to an embedded chart by using the Move Chart icon.

Commands Discussed: Design – Move Chart

Excel 97-2003: Chart – Chart Location

EXCEL CREATES A CHART AT THE BOTTOM OF MY DATA; HOW CAN I MOVE IT TO THE TOP?

Problem: I have 365 data points. While in cell A1, I hold Ctrl and Shift while pressing the Down Arrow then the Right Arrow to select the data set. This leaves the Excel window showing row 350. Create the chart with Alt+F1. Excel inserts the chart in the middle of the visible window, leaving the chart around row 350, as shown in Figure 1057. It is maddeningly slow to try to drag the chart up 300 rows.

Figure 1057

If the Excel window is showing the bottom of the data when you create the chart, your chart will be placed near the bottom of the data.

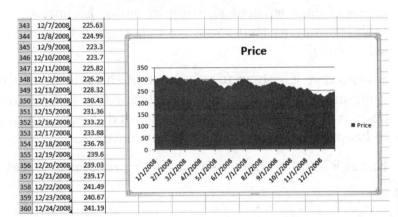

Strategy: Microsoft did not anticipate this problem. For now, you can cut and paste the chart to a new location. Follow these steps:

1) Activate the chart. Press Ctrl+X to cut the chart.

2) Press Ctrl+Home to quickly move to cell A1.

3) Select a top-left cell for the chart, such as C2.

4) Press Ctrl+V to paste the chart.

Results: Excel will place the chart where you indicated.

Alternate Strategy: Make sure that cell A1 is visible before you create the chart. After you use select the data set, press Ctrl+. (that is, Ctrl plus a period). This will move the active cell to another corner of the se-

Part
IV

lection. At most, it will take two presses of Ctrl+. to move the focus to the top of the selection, where A1 will be visible. Then you can press Alt+F1, and Excel will insert the chart in the middle of the visible window.

Alternate Strategy: After selecting the data set, press Ctrl+Backspace. The window will scroll so you can see the top of the data set. Press Alt+F1 to create the chart near the top of the data.

Alternate Strategy: Another technique is to select the entire data set from row 1. You select a cell near the top of the data set. Then you press Ctrl+* (it is easiest to use the asterisk on the numeric keypad, but Ctrl+Shift+8 will work, too). Excel will select the entire contiguous range of data without shifting focus to the bottom of the spreadsheet. Isn't it annoying that you have to become an expert in different ways to select cells?

Summary: Excel creates a chart in the middle of the visible window. Your usual method of selecting data causes the chart to appear at the bottom of a data set. You need to use a different method of selecting data to keep the focus on the top of your data set.

Excel 97-2003: This wasn't a major problem in Excel 2003.

HOW CAN I NUDGE A CHART WITHIN THE VISIBLE EXCEL WINDOW?

Problem: Thanks to "Excel Creates a Chart at the Bottom of my Data Set; How Can I Move It to the Top?" I now have a chart being created in cell H11 instead of cell H350. That is a great improvement. But I can't seem to click on the chart and move it to cell D2.

Strategy: Excel 2007 is fairly particular about where you click on a chart before dragging. To be safe, you should click on the border of the chart and drag it to a new location.

The key to successfully dragging a chart is to click inside the chart but not on any chart elements. For example, the white space above and below the legend might work. Areas to the left and right of a title might work, but not when the title is in the overlay location. If you have turned off the legend and the title, there is almost nowhere inside the chart that is safe to click and drag. If you accidentally click on a chart element, you will start dragging the element within the chart container instead of dragging the entire chart.

Additional Details: There are eight spots along the border where Excel shows resize handles. These dots appear in each corner and in the center of each edge. If you want to drag the chart, you can click on the border but avoid the resize handle area. If you want to resize the chart, you can click on the resize area and drag. As shown in Figure 1058, the mouse pointer changes if you click on the resize handle.

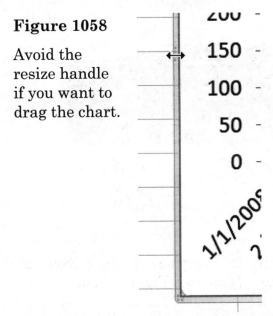

Figure 1058

Avoid the
resize handle
if you want to
drag the chart.

Additional Details: To align a chart with the top left corner of a cell, hold down the Alt key while you drag the chart to a new location. This is extremely useful if you have many charts and want to make sure they all line up.

Summary: For hassle-free chart moving, click on the border and drag.

Part
IV

WHY DOES EXCEL ADD A LEGEND TO A ONE-SERIES CHART?

Problem: I am charting one series of data. Why does Excel feel compelled to use the series heading as both the chart title and the legend? (See Figure 1059). Isn't this overkill?

Figure 1059

Do you think this chart is about price?

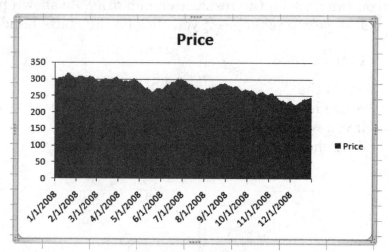

Strategy: Yes, it is overkill. Luckily, it is very easy to fix in Excel 2007. You simply select Layout – Legend – None (see Figure 1060).

Figure 1060

The Legend icon offers popular presets.

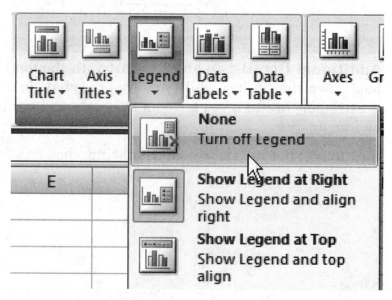

Results: Excel will remove the legend as shown in Figure 1061.

Figure 1061

Remove the legend for a single series.

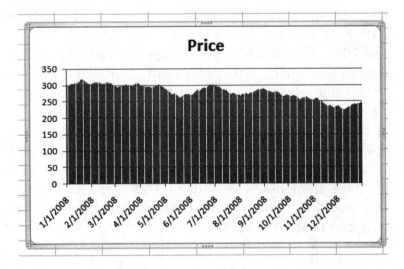

Summary: You can turn off the legend in a one-series chart.

Excel 97-2003: Click the legend and press the Delete key.

WHY DO NONE OF THE BUILT-IN CHART LAYOUTS LOOK GOOD?

Part IV

Problem: Microsoft says Excel offers professionally designed layouts that are a click away. I can see the Chart Layouts group on the Design ribbon (see Figure 1062). Why are all these layouts horrible?

Figure 1062

Microsoft promotes this gallery as a benefit.

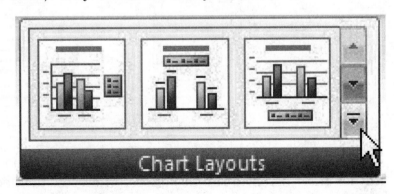

Strategy: Probability is working against you. Skip this gallery.

Depending on the chart type, you will have 4 to 12 built-in layouts in the gallery. Examine the 12 icons in the Line Chart gallery shown in Figure 1063. The various options are controlling gridlines, minor gridlines, legend placement, title placement, up/down bars, vertical gridlines, the data table, data labels, trendlines, plot area borders, and axis colors. There are probably more options that I am missing. Let's say that each of those options has an average of 3 settings. (In reality, there are some options with many more than 3 settings available.) If there were 3 settings for each element, you would have 3^10—or 59,049—combinations of these elements. The odds of 1 of these 12 matching something that you would rationally choose are 4920:1. It is just simple math that you will find that all the layouts are horrible. Skip the Layout gallery.

Figure 1063

Microsoft offers up to 12 pre-built layouts that attempt to control 10 settings.

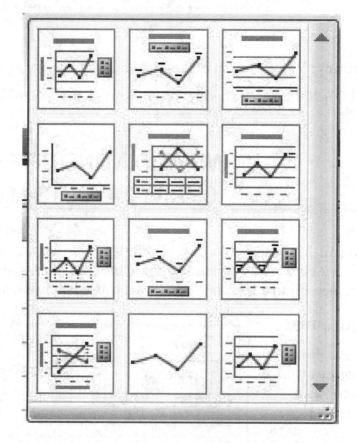

Additional Details: Within each gallery, there is one exceptional chart. Rather than listen to the designers, Microsoft tackled some incredibly complex chart problem and added this exceptional chart to the Chart

Layouts gallery. If you happen to need to create a histogram from a column chart (see Figure 1064) or a sparkline from a line chart, the Layouts gallery will enable you to create these difficult charts with only a single click.

Figure 1064

Layout 8 creates a histogram in one click.

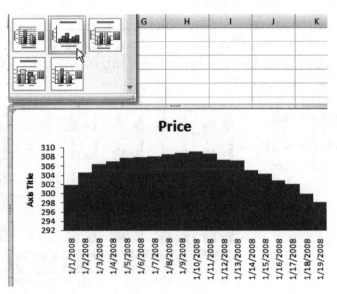

Professor Edward Tufte introduced the concept of sparklines. These are tiny word-sized line charts with a minimal amount of labeling. Microsoft added its own version of a sparkline as Layout 11 in the Line Chart gallery (see Figure 1065).

Part IV

Figure 1065

Sparkline chart.

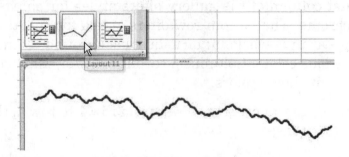

If you need to create amazing sparklines, see www.mrexcel.com/tip139.shtml for a review of the SparkMaker add-in for Excel.

Summary: Due to sheer probability, most of Excel's built-in layouts are not what you would normally select.

Excel 97-2003: This feature was not in previous versions of Excel.

THE CHART STYLES ARE COOL, BUT WHY SO FEW COLORS?

Problem: Although I don't like the Chart Layouts gallery (see "Why Do None of the Built-in Chart Layouts Look Good?"), I do like the Chart Styles gallery on the Design ribbon tab (see Figure 1066). But why does it offer so few colors?

Figure 1066

Excel offers 48 built-in chart styles.

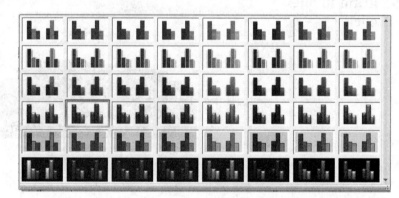

Strategy: The Chart Styles gallery on the Design tab is a great addition to Excel 2007. It offers are 48 styles, and I use this gallery for every chart I create.

The first column of the gallery offers styles for charts to be printed in monochrome. The bottom row offers styles for charts that will eventually appear in PowerPoint on a dark background. Column 2 offers styles with various colors. Columns 3 through 8 offer charts in various hues of the current theme colors.

In general, as you progress down from row 1 to row 5, the effects go from simple to intense.

Call me a sucker for a meaningless effect, but I really like the lighting accents in row 4 (see Figure 1067). Let's face it, the Excel 2003 charts had not changed in 15 years. It is nice to finally have some nice, fresh-looking charts in Excel 2007.

Additional Details: To easily get new colors, effects, and fonts, you can select Page Layout – Themes dropdown, as shown in Figure 1068. To change just the colors, select Page Layout – Colors dropdown.

Figure 1067

The built-in effects in the lower rows in the Chart Styles gallery are cool.

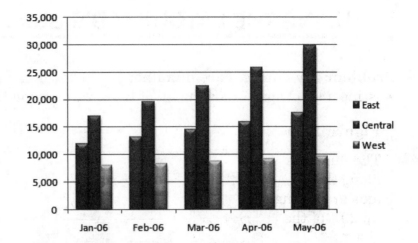

Figure 1068

Change chart colors and effects by changing the theme.

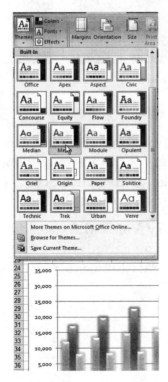

Part IV

Summary: You can use the Chart Styles gallery and the Themes gallery to find great-looking chart combinations.

Excel 97-2003: This feature was not in previous versions of Excel.

See Also: "Why Do None of the Built-in Layouts Look Good?" (p. 693)

DISPLAY AN AXIS IN MILLIONS
USING THE LAYOUT TAB'S BUILT-IN MENUS

Problem: My numbers are in millions. As shown in Figure 1069, I am wasting a lot of space showing all of those zeros along the vertical axis.

Figure 1069

The numbers along the y-axis are taking up 20% of the chart.

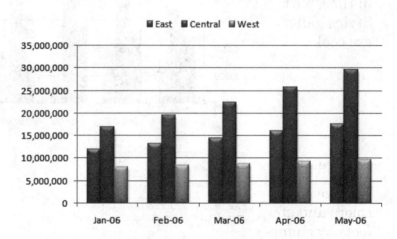

Strategy: Microsoft added many popular choices to the Labels, Axes, Background, and Analysis groups of the Layout ribbon tab. These popular settings often allow you three- to five-click access to settings without having to venture into the complex Format dialogs.

Choose Layout – Axes – Primary Vertical Axis, Show Axis in Millions. As you can see in Figure 1070, you can also choose options that handle thousands, billions, or even a logarithmic scale.

Figure 1070

The Layout tab is the home to many built-in formatting choices.

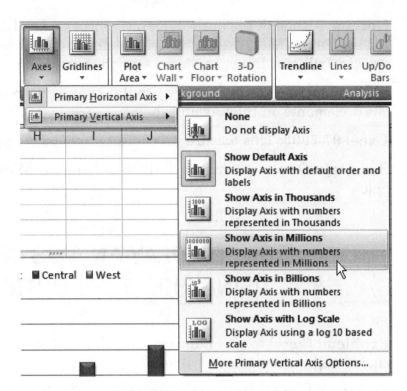

Results: Excel removes the zeros and adds a label indicating that the numbers are in millions (see Figure 1071).

Part IV

Figure 1071

It takes one menu selection to remove the zeros.

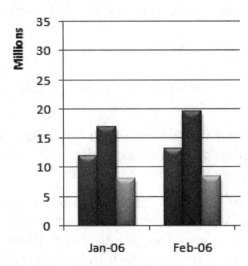

Gotcha: Although the built-in menu choices on the Layout tab are easy to use, they do not represent the complete set of choices. See "Display an Axis in Trillions, Using the More Options Choice."

Summary: You can find many popular choices for customizing various chart elements on the Layout tab.

Excel 97-2003: This feature was not in previous versions of Excel.

See Also: "Display an Axis in Trillions, Using the More Options Choice" below.

DISPLAY AN AXIS IN TRILLIONS
USING THE MORE OPTIONS CHOICE

Problem: I need to plot numbers in trillions. Why doesn't Excel offer a choice to show the axis in trillions?

Strategy: It does! Don't get complacent and believe that the choices on the Layout ribbon tab are the only choices. Every fly-out menu there ends with a "More" (More Options, More Primary Vertical Axis Options, etc.) choice. Clicking this button will lead to the appropriate tab of the Format dialog, where you can access the full range of options. Here's what you do:

1)   Select your chart.

2)   Select Layout – Axes – Primary Vertical Axis – More Primary Vertical Axis Options.

3)   From the Scaling dropdown, select Trillions. As shown in Figure 1072, the Scaling dropdown also offers the choices on the Layout tab, plus other choices, such as Hundreds.

This example is representative of the relationship between the Layout tab choices and the More choice. The Layout tab choices offer the most likely settings—in this case, thousands and millions. For obscure situations in which you want to report in hundreds or trillions, you can do so clicking the More button.

Figure 1072

The Format dialog offers a wider range of choices than the built-in menus on the Layout tab.

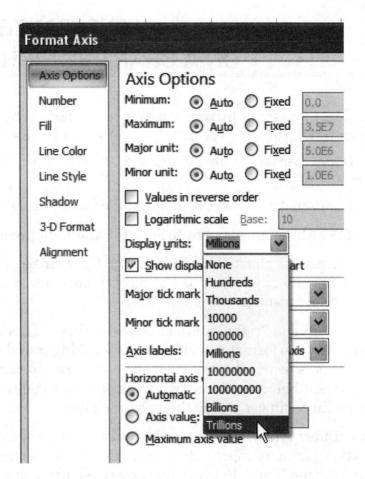

You cannot see it in Figure 1072, but the Format Axis dialog also offers a setting called Show Display Units Label on the Chart. This controls whether you see the Trillions label. The built-in menu choice for Millions always adds the label, but you can turn it off here.

Additional Details: Every menu on the Layout tab has a More button at the bottom of the list. I find that the built-in choices are sufficient about 90% of the time. However, I occasionally have to delve into the Format menu.

Summary: If the built-in menu choices don't offer what you're looking for, click the More button for more options.

Excel 97-2003: In previous versions of Excel, you use the Format dialog box to change these settings.

Part
IV

CUSTOMIZE ANYTHING
ON A CHART BY RIGHT-CLICKING

Problem: I need to further customize a chart. Why aren't there any Layout tab buttons for series? How can I change one data point?

Strategy: Everything on a chart can be customized. You can use any of these methods:

*   Right-click the chart element and choose Format

*   Click the chart element to select it and then press Ctrl+1

*   Choose the chart element from the Current Selection dropdown on either the Layout tab or Format tab and then click the Format Selection button in the same group

There is no one "right" method of these three. There are times when the only way to format something is by clicking it and other times when something is nearly invisible and the only way you can format it is from the Current Selection dropdown. So you need to be ready to use whichever method will get you to the correct element.

The leftmost group on both the Layout and Format tabs is the Current Selection group. It offers a dropdown with chart elements, a Format Selection button, and a Reset to Match Style button (see Figure 1073).

Figure 1073

Choose an element from the dropdown and then click Format Selection.

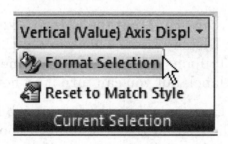

The dropdown offers an amazing array of elements, as shown in Figure 1074. (Who even thought there would be a vertical axis display units label that could be formatted?)

Figure 1074

Many chart elements are in this dropdown.

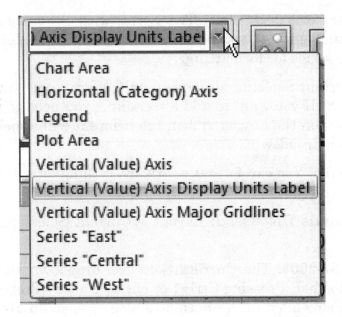

You can format additional elements, too. Say that you want to change the color of just the May central region column. The first click on the central region column will select all of the central region columns. A second single-click will select just the one column. You right-click to access Format Data Point, as shown in Figure 1075. You cannot select just the data point from the Current Selection dropdown.

Part IV

Figure 1075

You can often click on elements not in the dropdown.

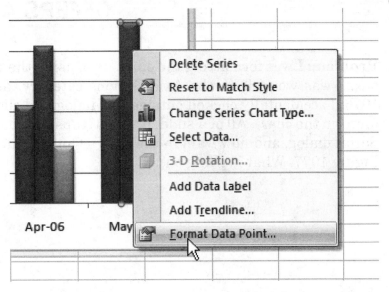

In other cases (see "Chart Two Series with Differing Orders of Magnitude" on page 714), you need to use the Current Selection dropdown to select a series for formatting.

The Current Selection dropdown only offers items that are already on the chart. If you want to add a trendline, you need to use the appropriate menu on the Layout ribbon tab before it will appear in the Current Selection dropdown.

Summary: You can format nearly everything on a chart. Different formatting methods offer different options.

Commands Discussed: Layout – Current Selection – Format Selection

Excel 97-2003: The Current Selection dropdown was on the floating Chart toolbar. Pressing Ctrl+1 or clicking a tiny Properties icon next to the dropdown led to the Format dialog. You could also right-click anything and choose Format from the right-click menu.

See Also: "Chart Series with Differing Orders of Magnitude" (p. 714)

THE FORMAT DIALOG BOX OFFERS A NEW TRICK

Problem: I was formatting the chart axis, using the Format Axis dialog box. I was working in the Axis Options category, as shown in Figure 1076. I accidentally clicked outside the dialog and clicked one of the columns in the chart. All of a sudden, I was transported to the Format Data Series dialog, and now I am in the Series Options category, as shown in Figure 1077. What is going on?

Figure 1076

You are working on the Format Axis dialog.

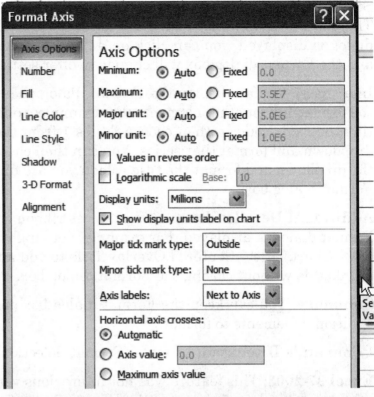

Figure 1077

Suddenly, you are in the Format Data Series dialog.

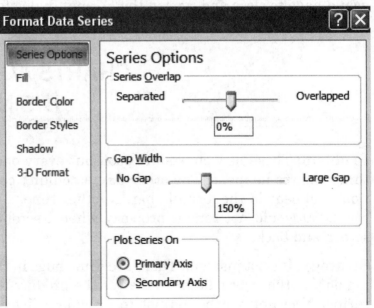

Part
IV

Strategy: You've discovered an amazing new feature in Excel 2007. There is a single Format dialog box for every drawing object. While the dialog is displayed, you can click on any new object on the worksheet, and the Format dialog box will change to offer settings for that object.

In a chart, you can display the Format dialog once and keep changing the formatting for other elements. For example, you might start formatting the axis. You can then choose Series 1 from the Current Selection dropdown and format that series. You can then choose Chart Title from the dropdown and format the title. When you are finished, you close the Format dialog box.

Additional Details: You can even access ribbon commands while the Format dialog is displayed. For example, you might need to select Layout – Chart Title – Centered Overlay Title to add a title to a chart. You can do this without closing the Format dialog box.

Summary: You can keep the Format dialog box open while you select additional elements to format.

Commands Discussed: Layout – Format Selection

Excel 97-2003: This feature was not in previous versions of Excel. You would have to close and reopen the Format dialog for each element.

CHARTS ACTING FLAKY?
IT'S NOT JUST YOU

Problem: These new charts are cool, but every once in a while, something bizarre happens. The other day, I couldn't get the SERIES function to appear in the formula bar. Another time, a chart created below row 2000 would not render properly when I scrolled the chart off the screen and back.

Strategy: It's not just you. There are some bugs in the Excel 2007 charting engine that were discovered after the product released to manufacturing. Microsoft's policy is not to provide a list of the bugs, but the items you describe are a few of the issues I've found. There are undoubtedly more.

If you are reading this book before first quarter 2008, then thank you for being one of the first to buy the book! If you are reading the book in first quarter 2008 or after, then Microsoft has probably released Service Release 1 of Office 2007. Get this version, and the known charting bugs should be resolved.

Summary: There are some bugs in Excel 2007 chart. They should be corrected in Service Release 1.

Commands Discussed: Insert – Chart

MINIMIZE OVERLAP OF PIE LABELS
BY ROTATING THE CHART

Problem: On a three-dimensional pie chart with several small pie slices, the labels for the smaller pie slices often overwrite each other, as shown in Figure 1078. How can I improve the look of the chart?

Figure 1078

Pie chart labels often overwrite each other.

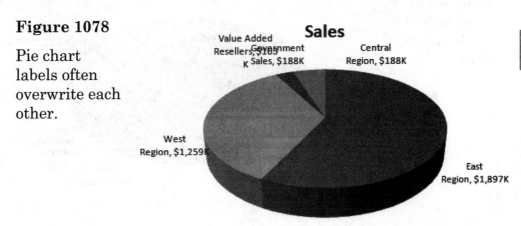

Sales

Value Added Resellers, $185 Government Sales, $188K

Central Region, $188K

West Region, $1,259K

East Region, $1,897K

Strategy: You can rotate the pie chart so that smaller slices are near the front. Follow these steps:

1) Right-click the pie chart and select Format Data Series.

2) In the Format Data Series dialog, select the Series Options pane and change the Angle of First Slice setting to about 150, as shown in Figure 1079.

Figure 1079

Change the Angle of First Slice setting.

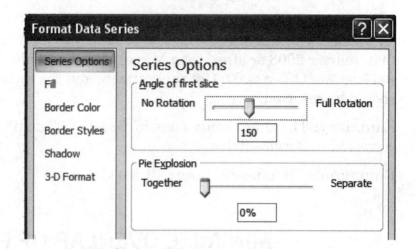

3)   Click OK to close the Format Data Series dialog.

Results: All the data labels will be visible, as shown in Figure 1080.

Figure 1080

There is now more room for labels on the chart.

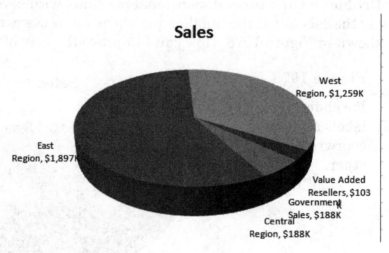

Alternate Strategy: Another method is to use the mouse to click on one of the data labels. All the labels will be selected. On the Home ribbon tab, you then choose a smaller font size.

Alternate Strategy: Yet another method is to single-click on a data label to select all data labels. Wait long enough to not qualify as a double-click, and do a second single-click on just one of the data labels that is overlapping another label. Now, only one label is selected. Then you can drag the label to a new location, as shown in Figure 1081.

Figure 1081

Drag labels into a new position.

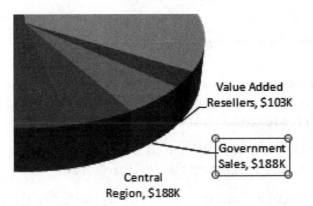

Alternate Strategy: Excel 2007 offers a new Best Fit setting for data labels. This seemingly intelligent setting finds any nook and cranny where the data label might fit. From the Layout tab, you choose Data Labels – More Data Label Options. Choose Best Fit under Label Position. As shown in Figure 1082, Excel will arrange the labels in the best manner possible

Figure 1082

Best Fit forces the labels to fit.

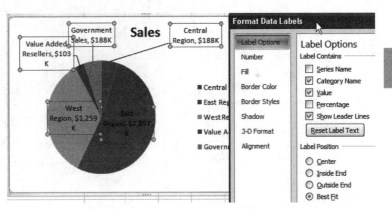

Part IV

Summary: The Angle of First Slice setting allows you to find the best angle, where the fewest labels overlap. You can also change the font size of the labels or simply move the problematic data labels out of the way.

Commands Discussed: Format Data Series; Format Data Labels

Excel 97-2003: Right-click the pie, choose Format Data Series, and find the Angle of First Slice setting on the Options tab of the dialog box; Format Data Labels

ADD NEW DATA TO A CHART

Problem: I need to create 12 charts every month. Using your previous tips, I have now created beautiful, highly customized charts. It is a real pain to re-create these charts every month.

Strategy: If your chart is located as an embedded object on a sheet, you can add data to an existing chart. Here's how:

1) Type the new data for your chart adjacent to the old data, as shown in Figure 1083.

Figure 1083

Type new data next to the old data.

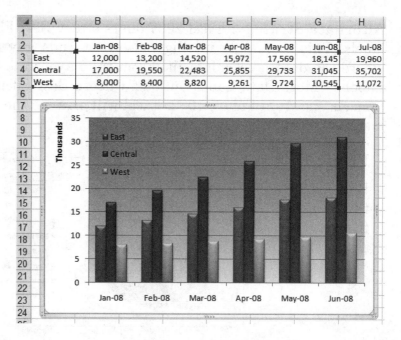

2) Click the chart to select it. You will see a blue outline in the work-sheet around the chart data. Each corner of the blue outline has a square handle.

3) Using the mouse, grab the handle in G5 and drag it to the right to include the data in column H. When you release the mouse, the chart redraws to include the new data, as shown in Figure 1084.

Figure 1084

Drag the blue handle to add new data on the chart.

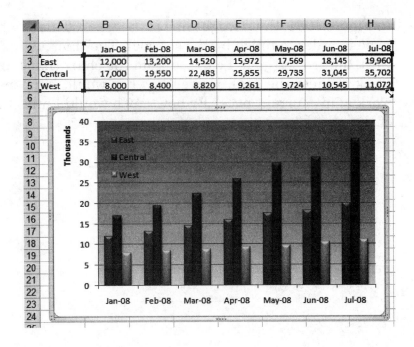

Additional Details: If you need to show a rolling six months, after adding July to the data, you can drag the blue handle from B5 to the right. You will remove January from the chart.

Gotcha: In Excel 2003, you could drag H2:H5 to the chart. The drag and drop feature for adding data to a chart was removed from Excel 2007.

Summary: You don't have to waste hours creating new charts each month. Simply type the new data adjacent to the old data and use the blue handles to add new data for the chart.

Part
IV

ADD A TRENDLINE TO A CHART

Problem: In his book Success Made Easy, retail guru Ron Martin suggests using a daily chart to track your progress toward a goal. His typical chart shows your progress toward the goal as well as where you need to be to remain on track.

In Figure 1085, the straight line is the track. This is where I would need to be in order to finish by the set goal. The thick, wavy line is my actual work toward the goal. I can see from the chart that I am not working on track to meet the goal. However, what would happen if I continued to work at my current pace? By how much would I miss the goal at the end of the month?

Figure 1085

Actuals are running just short of the track line.

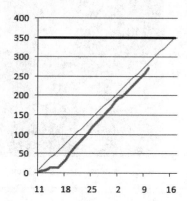

Strategy: Excel makes it easy to add a trendline to charted data.

1) Right-click the graphed line for actual results. From the menu that appears, choose Add Trendline, as shown in Figure 1086.

Figure 1086

Select the actuals line, right-click, and select Add Trendline.

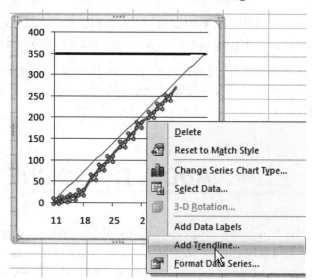

2) Excel displays the Format dialog for the trendline. Many of the defaults are appropriate. You'll usually leave the trendline as a linear regression type.

3) If you have a legend on the chart, change the trendline name to Forecast.

4) Because the trendline is only a forecast, format it with a dotted style so you know it is just a prediction. In the Line Color category, choose Solid Line. A color dropdown appears. Choose Red. In the Line Style category, choose 0.5 point width and a dash type of a square dot.

The result, as you can see in Figure 1087, is a dotted line that shows the predicted results if you continue at your current pace.

Figure 1087

Excel projects your final results based on past actuals.

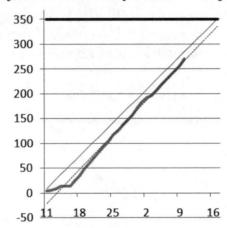

As you continue to plug in actual data, the trendline will redraw. Seeing the red forecast line predict a sizable miss usually causes me to really put it into hyperdrive for the next few days. A couple of days of above-average activity causes the actual line to go above the track line. Nevertheless, the dotted trendline is still predicting that I will miss the goal, as shown in Figure 1088. That is because the trendline sees all those days early in the month when I did practically nothing. It predicts that those days might happen again.

Figure 1088

Putting in a couple of above-average days will not fool the trendline.

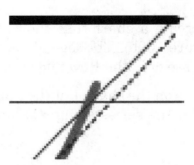

Part IV

Gotcha: I'm careful in this example to fill the Actuals column with =NA() formulas for future periods. Leaving the future periods with zeros will cause the trendline to be incorrect.

In other data sets, the chart might only show actuals, with the last actual appearing at the right edge of the chart. In that case, you can use the Format Trendline dialog to specify that the trendline should predict forward a certain number of periods.

Additional Details: Another option in the Format dialog is to include an equation on the chart. The chart will include an equation in the y=mx+b format. As you can see in Figure 1089, the y-intercept in the equation is fairly crazy because the x-axis is a date field. However, the slope of the line shows that I have been working at about 10.1 units per day.

Figure 1089

Excel can also display an equation and/ or R-squared on the chart.

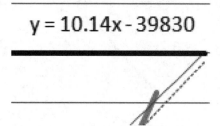

$$y = 10.14x - 39830$$

Summary: You can add a trendline to any charted series to predict the future.

Commands Discussed: Add Trendline

Functions Discussed: NA()

CHART TWO SERIES WITH DIFFERING ORDERS OF MAGNITUDE

Problem: I'm trying to create a chart that shows revenue and gross profit percentage (see Figure 1090). The legend shows that both items are in the chart, but I can see only the Revenue series on the chart.

Strategy: The GP% series is on the chart, but the numbers are too small to be seen. You need to plot the series along a secondary vertical axis. Follow these steps:

Figure 1090

The GP% series is not visible.

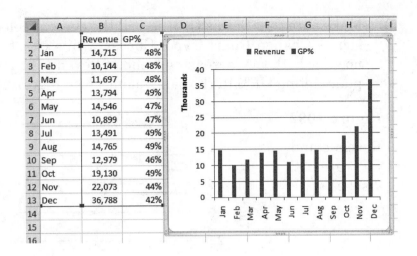

	A	B	C
1		Revenue	GP%
2	Jan	14,715	48%
3	Feb	10,144	48%
4	Mar	11,697	48%
5	Apr	13,794	49%
6	May	14,546	47%
7	Jun	10,899	47%
8	Jul	13,491	49%
9	Aug	14,765	49%
10	Sep	12,979	46%
11	Oct	19,130	49%
12	Nov	22,073	44%
13	Dec	36,788	42%
14			
15			
16			

1) Click on the chart to select it.

2) Select Layout – Current Selection dropdown – Series GP%. Excel will select the nearly invisible columns.

3) Select Layout – Format Selection. Excel displays the Format Data Series dialog.

4) In the Series Options category in the Format Data Series dialog, change the Plot Series On setting from Primary Axis to Secondary Axis. You can now see the red columns. As shown in Figure 1091, Excel will add numbers from 38% to 50% along the right axis of the chart. One problem with this setting is that Excel will now draw the red columns directly in front of the blue columns. In every month except November and December, you can't even see the blue columns. One option is to increase the gap width for the GP% series and make the columns thinner. Instead, I prefer to change the series to a line chart, as described in step 5.

Part IV

Figure 1091

The GP% series now obscures the revenue series.

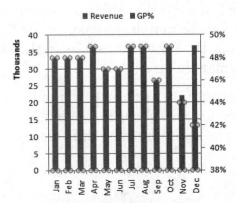

5) Make sure that Series GP% is still the current selection. Select Design – Change Chart Type. Choose a line chart. The reader can now see both the increasing trend of Revenue in December and the plummeting GP% in the same month (see Figure 1092).

Figure 1092

Revenue and GP% are both visible.

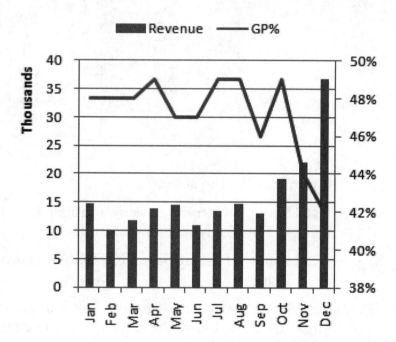

Gotcha: When the range of a series is less than 20% of the maximum value of the series, Excel automatically zooms in on the range. For GP%, the range is 42% to 49%—a 7% range. 7/49 is less than 20%, so Excel has chosen to show 38% to 50% as the range for the second vertical axis. This allows you to see more detail in the GP%, but some purists always want the axis to start at 0.

Additional Details: If the chart is going to be printed in color, I change the font for the right axis to match the color of the GP% line. This helps the reader to figure out that the right scale applies to the red line. Follow these steps to format the axis:

1) Return to the Layout tab. Click on any number along the right axis. The current selection will show Secondary Vertical (Value) Axis. If you previously closed the Format Axis dialog, click Format Selection.

2)   In the Axis Options section, Minimum and Maximum are set to automatic. In the grayed out Minimum text box, you can see 0.38. Click the Fixed option button for Minimum and type the value 0.

3)   You won't find a font color setting in the Format Axis dialog, so select the Home – Font Color dropdown – Red as shown in Figure 1093. (All the Font settings in the Home tab will work to format the numbers along the axis.).

Figure 1093

Use the Home tab to format text in the selected chart element.

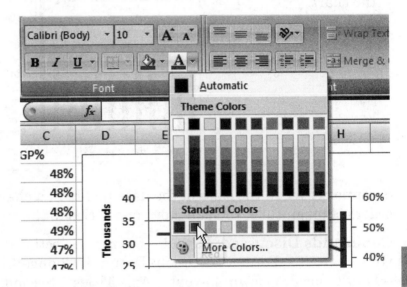

4)   Click on the numbers along the left axis. Use the Home tab to change the font color to blue.

5)   Steps 3 and 4 won't help if the chart is being printed in monochrome, so select Layout – Axis Titles – Secondary Vertical Axis Title – Rotated Title. Excel will add "Axis Title" along the right axis.

6)   While the axis title is selected, type the new title GP%. As you are typing the characters, they will appear in the formula bar. When you press Enter, these characters will replace the axis title.

Part
IV

Results: The final chart is shown in Figure 1094. After reviewing this chart, you might prefer to change the second vertical axis to have an automatic range so the reader can see more detail in the GP% line.

Figure 1094

You can see both series on the chart.

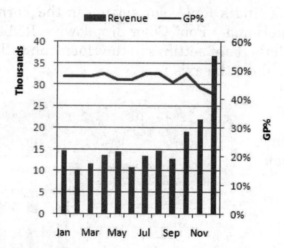

Summary: When the sizes of the data points in a chart are of different orders of magnitude, you can move one series to the secondary axis.

Commands Discussed: Layout – Current Selection dropdown – Series GP%; Layout – Format Selection; Design – Change Chart Type; Home – Font Color dropdown; Layout – Axis Titles – Secondary Vertical Axis Title – Rotated Title

USE MEANINGFUL CHART TITLES

Problem: Excel tends to add boring chart titles. A chart title such as Sales or Profit merely labels the data in the chart. The title is nothing more than a legend in a large font. How can I make my chart titles more meaningful?

Strategy: It's a good idea to add a meaningful title that guides the reader. As an analyst, you can spot trends in the data, and you can point out something interesting in the chart by using the title.

One annoying problem is that you seemingly don't have a lot of control over the chart title formatting. Follow these steps to create a long title:

1) Select Layout – Chart Title – Above Chart. Excel adds the title Chart Title in a large font above the chart (see Figure 1095).

Figure 1095

Excel chart titles are usually less than meaningful.

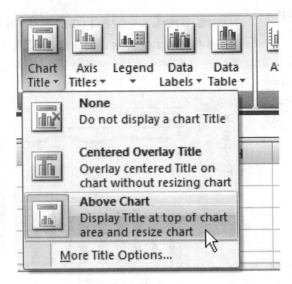

Chart Title

━━ Revenue ─── GP%

2) Using the mouse, drag to select the characters in the chart title.

3) On the Home tab of the ribbon, choose a 14-point font size. Choose the Left Align icon.

4) Type a title such as Revenue Doubled in December.

5) Press Enter. Excel will move to a second line in the title.

6) Before typing the second line, change the font to 12-point on the Home tab.

7) Type the subtitle Post-holiday sales dropped GP% to 42%.

8) Click on the border of the title to exit Edit mode.

9) Drag the border of the title to the left in order to align the title with the left edge of the chart.

Results: You've added a title to guide the reader's understanding of the chart, as shown in Figure 1096.

Figure 1096

Guide the reader with a title and sub-title.

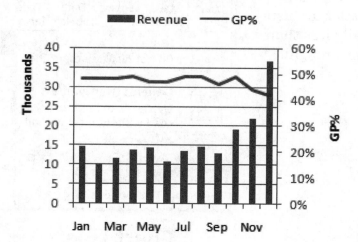

Gotcha: The border around the title has only four handles. This means you can move the title, but you cannot resize it. In step 5, you were able to force the title box to add a second line. However, Excel can have a mind of its own and may decide to add a third line. It would seem that you could correct this if you had the ability to resize the title box. Instead, you would have to select characters within the title and choose a smaller font in order to coax the title back to the correct number of lines.

Summary: You can type longer titles for charts to guide the reader, and you can use the formatting icons on the Home ribbon to format the title.

Commands Discussed: Layout – Chart Title – Above Chart; Home – Font Size; Home – Alignment

MOVE THE LEGEND TO THE LEFT OR TOP

Problem: It bothers me that Excel chart legends always start on the right side of the chart. We read left-to-right, so with Excel's setup, I tend to look at the chart data before I understand what each color or marker means.

Strategy: You can move the legend to the left or top of the chart by using Layout – Legend.

Gotcha: A legend on the right or left takes up a lot of horizontal space and leaves a lot of wasted white space above and below the legend (see Figure 1097). Compare Figure 1097 to Figure 1096. With a few series, having the legend at the top takes up less space.

Figure 1097

Legends at the side take a lot of space.

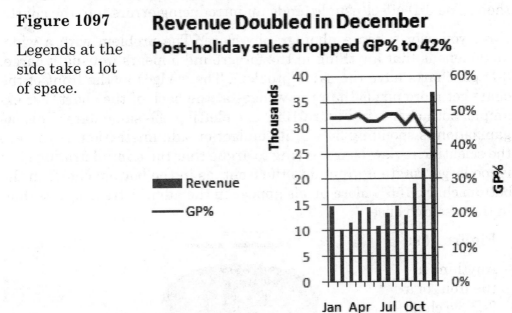

Revenue Doubled in December

Post-holiday sales dropped GP% to 42%

Additional Details: You can drag the border of a legend and drop it anywhere on the chart. New in Excel 2007, the legend starts out with a transparent fill, which will allow any underlying gradient or picture fill to show through (see Figure 1098).

Figure 1098

Float the legend above the chart.

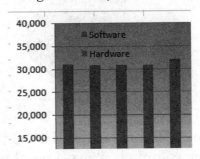

Summary: You can move the legend to the left or top of the chart.

Commands Discussed: Layout – Legend

AVOID 3-D CHART TYPES

Problem: I like the look of 3-D chart types, but they don't seem to be accurate.

Strategy: 3-D chart types are not accurate, so you should try to avoid them. The 3-D effect usually ends up introducing errors into the chart.

Have you ever taken a photography class? The problem with a wide-angle lens is that anything in the foreground appears unusually large. 3-D pie charts have the same problem. The wedges at the front of the chart get more pixels than the wedges at the back of the chart. For example, both charts in Figure 1099 are plotting the same data. This organization is spending 34% of its budget on administration. If you are the scientific review board, trying to argue that the administration slice is too large, rotate it around to the front, as in the bottom chart. In the bottom chart, 155% more pixels appear in the administration slice than in the research slice.

Figure 1099

Anything at the front of a 3-D pie chart appears un-realistically large.

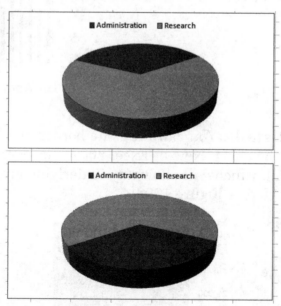

3-D column charts are not accurate, either. In the top chart in Figure 1100, you can see that each column is above a nearby gridline. The 2005 column is at 1509, which is above the 1500 gridline. Turn that chart into a 3-D column chart, and none of the columns actually extend to the neighboring gridline. People wonder if they should look at the front or the back of the column. I say it doesn't matter because neither the front nor the back reach to the gridline.

Figure 1100

The fourth column should touch the 3500 gridline, but doesn't in a 3-D chart.

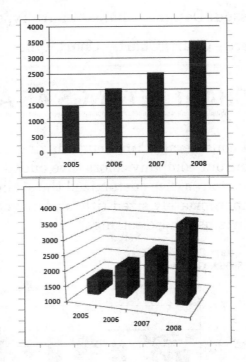

You should never use cone or pyramid charts. The categories at the top of each cone get far fewer pixels than the categories at the bottom. In Figure 1101, the 34% spent on administration seems practically nonexistent.

Figure 1101

Never use cone or pyramid charts.

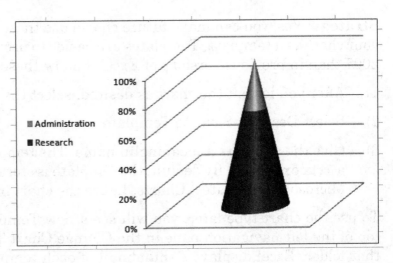

Part IV

Summary: Excel offers many charts that look cool but are simply inaccurate; you should avoid 3-D charts.

Commands Discussed: Design – Change Chart Type; Insert -- Charts

Excel 97-2003: Insert – Chart; Chart – Chart Type

SAVE YOUR CHART SETTINGS AS A TEMPLATE

Problem: I've spent considerable time customizing the chart shown in Figure 1102. I'm using our company colors. I've added the company logo as a tiled fill for the plot area. I've customized the scaling for the vertical axis. I've added an appropriately sized title and moved the legend. Can I make all future charts use these settings?

Figure 1102

Replicate these settings for future charts.

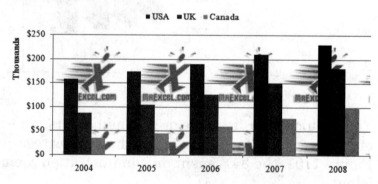

Strategy: Yes, you can make future charts use these settings by saving your chart as a template. Templates are easier to use and share in Excel 2007 than in previous versions of Excel. Follow these steps

1)   After you format the chart as desired, select the chart.

2)   Select Design – Save As Template.

3)   Give the template a meaningful name. The template is stored with a .crtx extension. By default, the template is stored in %AppData%\ Microsoft\Templates\Charts. Leave the chart in this location.

To use the chart type later, you will see a new Templates folder at the top of the left navigation pane in the Change Chart Type dialog. Select that folder. Excel displays a thumbnail of each template, but you need to hover over the thumbnail to see the file name of the template (see Figure 1103).

Figure 1103

Choose the template from the Templates category.

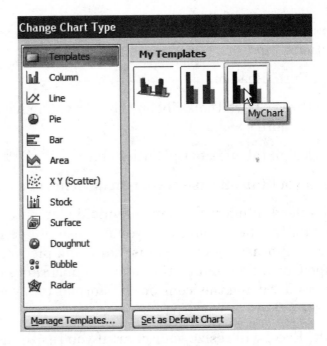

Additional Details: If you want your template to be used as the default chart for all future charts, select the template and choose Set as Default Chart from the bottom of the Change Chart Type dialog.

Gotcha: You would think that Manage Templates would lead to a nice dialog where you could specify a name for each template, but instead it simply opens Windows Explorer to the Templates folder.

Additional Details: To share your template with other people, copy the .crtx file to the Templates folder on their computers.

Summary: You can save your favorite chart settings as a template to prevent having to continually format charts.

Commands Discussed: Design – Save as Template; Design – Change Chart Type

Excel 97-2003: Select the chart, select Chart – Chart Type, select the Custom Types tab, change from Built-In to User-Defined, and click Add.

OTHER CHARTING NOTES

Problem: The charting engine has changed dramatically in Excel 2007. Any additional tips?

Strategy: Sure. Read on!

There are three Chart Tools ribbon tabs. As you move from left to right, they become more specific:

- The Design tab affects the entire chart.

- The Layout tab affects specific components of a chart.

- If you need to micro-format individual elements, move to the Format tab. On the Format tab, you can use Shape Fill to change the color or appearance of columns, bars, and pie wedges. You can use Shape Outline to change the color or appearance of line charts and borders. By using the icons on the Format tab, you can convert any text on a chart to WordArt.

By default, Excel will resize your chart if you resize the columns underneath the chart. This can wreak havoc with your chart formatting. The old trick of selecting the chart container with Ctrl+click doesn't allow you to format the container. Instead, you need to use the Format tab. You click the dialog launcher icon in the lower-right corner of the Size group to display the Size and Properties dialog. On the Properties tab, you choose Move but Don't Size with Cells.

To make several copies of a chart, you can copy and paste. To copy a chart by dragging, you click the border and start to drag. You hold down the Ctrl key before you release the mouse. (It won't work in the opposite sequence. If you try to hold down the Ctrl key before the initial click, you will not copy the chart.)

You used to be able to drag and drop data on a chart. This feature was removed.

You used to be able to change data in a table by directly dragging the height of a column in a chart. This feature has been removed.

You used to be able to change 3-D rotation by dragging in a chart. This feature has been removed.

Gradients are more difficult to apply than they used to be. You start with the Shape Fill dropdown. To apply a simple two-color gradient like the ones in Excel 2003, you use Gradient – More Gradients, choose a color for Stop 1, choose a color for Stop 2, and remove Stop 3.

Text boxes are more complicated to add than they used to be. If you need a text box on a chart, you select the chart and then select Insert – Text Box from the ribbon. In previous versions of Excel, you could just start typing.

Pattern fills have been removed. Microsoft figures that all the textures could replace patterns. This is not a popular choice for people printing charts in monochrome.

Charts created in Excel 2007 will paste perfectly to PowerPoint 2007 and Word 2007. You no longer have to worry about colors shifting after you paste.

Additional Details: I've written a book for Que Publishing that contains 425+ pages of charting tips for Excel 2007. Check out Charts and Graphs for Microsoft Excel 2007 (ISBN 978-0-7897-3610-9).

Gene Zelazny is the guru of charting for McKinsey & Company. His Say It with Charts Complete Toolkit (ISBN 978-0071474702) will teach you when to choose a particular chart type.

Part
IV

Edward Tufte's books greatly expand on how to display quantitative information. Tufte has many more examples of why 3-D charts and cone charts should be avoided. Start with The Visual Display of Quantitative Information (ISBN 978-0961392147).

Websites by Andy Pope (www.andypope.info/charts.htm) and Jon Peltier (http://peltiertech.com/Excel/Charts/index.html) will teach you how to make charts that you would never think possible with Excel.

If your job involves creating presentations and charts, consider subscribing to PowerFrameworks.com. Kathy Viella produces top-quality graphics and ideas for making presentations that stand out.

Even though Microsoft rewrote the charting engine, it did not add any new chart types. Excel 2009 might offer sparklines and a new true 3-D chart with X, Y, and Z coordinates, but there are many popular chart types that Excel will not natively produce. Mala Singh of XLSoft Consulting produces utilities to display speedometer charts (see Figure

1104) and more. If you need a utility to produce a custom chart, contact Mala. Check out www.mrexcel.com/speedometer.html and www.mrexcel.com/graphics.shtml.

Figure 1104

You can use add-ins to create unique chart types.

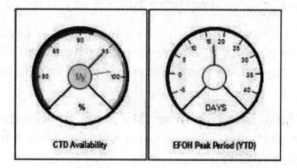

Summary: Excel 2007 charts have changed dramatically.

FOR EACH CELL IN COLUMN A, HAVE THREE ROWS IN COLUMN B

Problem: For each cell in column A, I want to have three rows in columns B and C, as shown in Figure 1105. I also want to be able to perform calculations with the values in column C.

Figure 1105

You can't easily calculate using numbers in column C.

	A	B	C
	Andy	Quota	1000
		Actual	1200
1		Variance	200
	Ben	Quota	900
		Actual	500
2		Variance	-400

Strategy: You might be tempted to use the Alt+Enter trick to enter three lines of data in columns B and C. However, this will not work well in column C. Although the numbers are displayed fine, there is no way to have the numbers in C calculate automatically.

A better option is to merge cells A1:A3 into a single cell. You can then let the data in B fill B1:B3. Here's how:

1)   Enter a value in A1. Leave cells A2:A3 blank. Select cells A1:A3.

2)   Select Home – Merge & Center dropdown. Choose Merge Cells, as shown in Figure 1106.

Figure 1106

Merge Cells is hidden behind this dropdown.

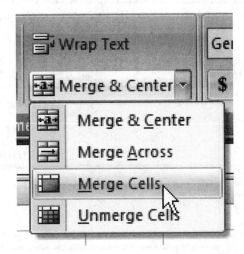

Gotcha: Notice that the vertical alignment defaults to the bottom. This looks okay in a normal-height cell, but not so good in a triple-height cell.

3)   Change the vertical alignment to top or center. Vertical alignment icons are now on the Home ribbon, as shown in Figure 1107.

Figure 1107

Align to the top of column A.

4)   If you have several rows that need this formatting, use Format Painter mode to copy the formatting. Select cells A1:A3. Double-

click the Format Painter icon in the Home ribbon tab. The double-click will put you in Format Painter mode. You can now click in A4, then A7, then A10. Each click will copy the format from A1:A3 to the clicked cell. When you are finished, you can either click the Format Painter icon or press Esc to exit Format Painter mode.

As shown in Figure 1108, some creative use of the Borders setting around each group will further enhance the illusion of three rows for each value in column A.

Figure 1108

Borders help create the illusion of three rows in columns B and C.

	A	B	C
1	Andy	Quota	1000
2		Actual	1200
3		Variance	200
4	Ben	Quota	900
5		Actual	500
6		Variance	-400
7	Charlie	Quota	900
8		Actual	875
9		Variance	-25
10	Del	Quota	850
11		Actual	875
12		Variance	25

Summary: To have three cells in columns B and C next to one cell in column A, use the Merge command on cells A1:A3.

Commands Discussed: Home – Merge & Center dropdown – Merge Cells; Home – Format Painter; Home – Align Top

Excel 97-2003: Format Cells – Alignment.

COPY FORMATTING TO A NEW RANGE

Problem: I have several similar report sections on a spreadsheet (see Figure 1109). When I get the first report nicely formatted, I would like to copy the format to the other reports.

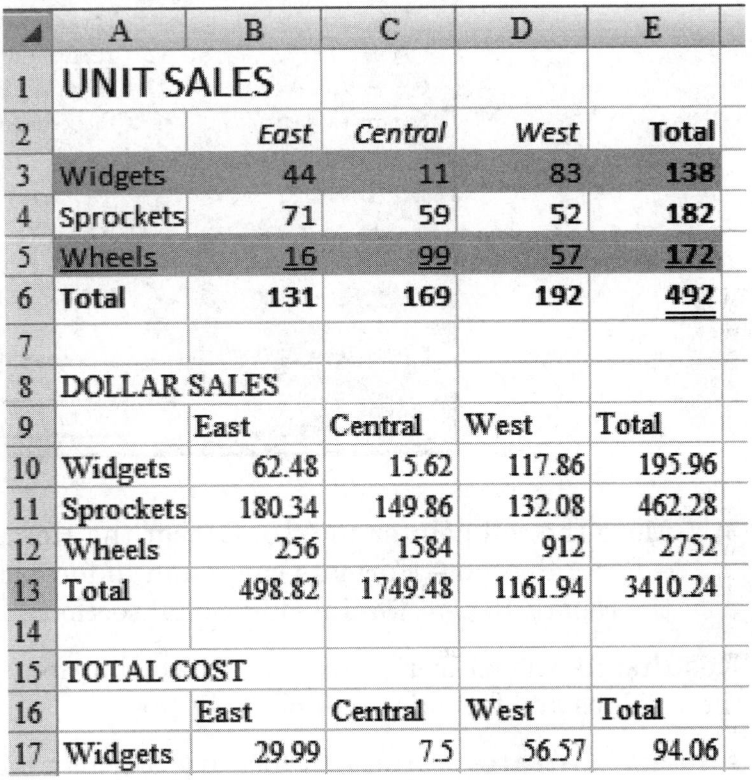

Figure 1109

Copy the formatting to other report sections.

▲	A	B	C	D	E
1	UNIT SALES				
2		East	Central	West	Total
3	Widgets	44	11	83	138
4	Sprockets	71	59	52	182
5	Wheels	16	99	57	172
6	Total	131	169	192	492
7					
8	DOLLAR SALES				
9		East	Central	West	Total
10	Widgets	62.48	15.62	117.86	195.96
11	Sprockets	180.34	149.86	132.08	462.28
12	Wheels	256	1584	912	2752
13	Total	498.82	1749.48	1161.94	3410.24
14					
15	TOTAL COST				
16		East	Central	West	Total
17	Widgets	29.99	7.5	56.57	94.06

Part IV

Strategy: You can use Paste Special Formats to copy just the formats from one range to another:

1)   Select cells A1:E6. Select Home – Copy.

Gotcha: If the target range contains any merged cells, you can not simply select the top left cell as indicated in step 2. Instead, you must select a rectangular range of the same size and shape as the range copied in step 1.

2)   Select the upper-left corner of the next section. With the cell pointer in A8, select Home – Paste dropdown – Paste Special . In the Paste Special dialog, select Formats, as shown in Figure 1110.

Figure 1110

Paste formats.

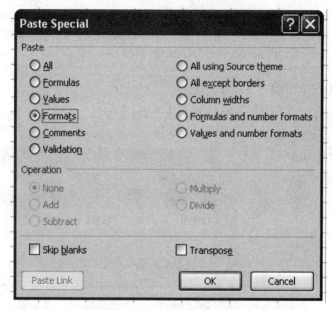

3)   Move the cell pointer to A15. Repeat the Home – Paste dropdown – Paste Special – Formats command to format the Cost section of the report. Repeat for any additional sections.

Results: As shown in Figure 1111, the cell formats will be copied, but their values and formulas will not.

Alternate Strategy: You can also use Format Painter mode to copy formats. You select A1:E6, double-click the Format Painter icon in the Home ribbon tab, and click A8 and A15. At each click, Excel will copy the formats to the new range. When you are finished, you can either click the Format Painter icon or press Esc to exit Format Painter mode.

Summary: After you've taken the time to format one range nicely, you can copy the formatting to other ranges by using the Paste Special – Formats command.

Commands Discussed: Home – Copy; Home – Paste dropdown – Paste Special – Formats

Excel 97-2003: Edit – Paste Special – Formats

Figure 1111

Copied Formats.

	A	B	C	D	E
1	UNIT SALES				
2		East	Central	West	Total
3	Widgets	44	11	83	138
4	Sprockets	71	59	52	182
5	Wheels	16	99	57	172
6	Total	131	169	192	492
7					
8	DOLLAR SALES				
9		East	Central	West	Total
10	Widgets	62.48	15.62	117.86	195.96
11	Sprockets	180.34	149.86	132.08	462.28
12	Wheels	256	1584	912	2752
13	Total	498.82	1749.48	1161.94	3410.24
14					
15	TOTAL COST				
16		East	Central	West	Total
17	Widgets	29.99	7.5	56.57	94.06
18	Sprockets	86.56	71.93	63.4	221.89
19	Wheels	122.88	760.32	437.76	1320.96
20	Total	239.43	839.75	557.73	1636.91

COPY WITHOUT CHANGING BORDERS

Problem: I have built a report in Excel and used numerous borders to outline the data, (see Figure 1112). After entering a formula to calculate profit in E3, I want to copy the formula down to E4 through E7.

Figure 1112

Copy this formula.

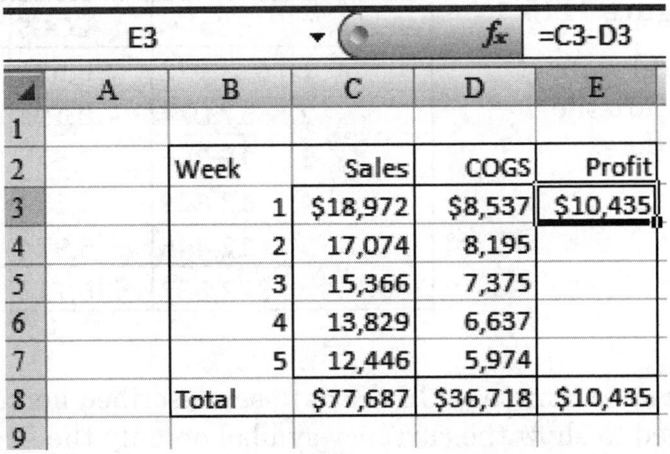

E3				f_x =C3-D3

	A	B	C	D	E
1					
2		Week	Sales	COGS	Profit
3		1	$18,972	$8,537	$10,435
4		2	17,074	8,195	
5		3	15,366	7,375	
6		4	13,829	6,637	
7		5	12,446	5,974	
8		Total	$77,687	$36,718	$10,435
9					

However, because cell E3 has a top border, copying the formula causes all the cells in E4 through E7 to also have a top border, ruining the effect of my borders, as shown in Figure 1113.

Figure 1113

Excel copies the borders, too.

Week		Sales	COGS	Profit
	1	$18,972	$8,537	$10,435
	2	17,074	8,195	$8,879
	3	15,366	7,375	$7,991
	4	13,829	6,637	$7,192
	5	12,446	5,974	$6,472
Total		$77,687	$36,718	$40,969

Strategy: You can select Home – Paste dropdown – Paste Special – All Except Borders to copy the formula and the numeric formatting but not disturb the borders (see Figure 1114).

Figure 1114

Copy all except borders.

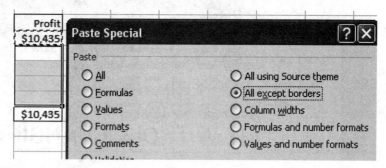

Results: As shown in Figure 1115, the formula is successfully copied, but the borders remain as they were.

Figure 1115

Excel will not disturb the borders.

Week		Sales	COGS	Profit
	1	$18,972	$8,537	$10,435
	2	17,074	8,195	$8,879
	3	15,366	7,375	$7,991
	4	13,829	6,637	$7,192
	5	12,446	5,974	$6,472
Total		$77,687	$36,718	$40,969

Alternate Strategy: In the data set described here, it appears that you decided to show the currency symbol on only the first row and the total row. In this case, it might have been more appropriate to use Paste Special – Formulas just to copy the formula as shown in Figure 1116.

Figure 1116

Copy Formulas to avoid changing any format.

COGS	Profit
$8,537	$10,435
8,195	8,879
7,375	7,991
6,637	7,192
5,974	6,472
$36,718	$40,969

Paste Special

Paste
- ○ All
- ⊙ Formulas
- ○ Values
- ○ Formats

Summary: To copy without disrupting borders, you use the Paste Special – All Except Borders option or the Paste Special – Formulas option.

Commands Discussed: Home – Paste dropdown – Paste Special – All Except Borders; Paste Special – Formulas

Excel 97-2003: Edit – Paste Special – All Except Borders; Edit – Paste Special – Formulas

GROUP COLUMNS INSTEAD OF HIDING THEM

Part
IV

Problem: I have a report with months and quarters (see Figure 1117). My manager sometimes wants the reports printed with months hidden and other times with the months showing. It is a pain to hide/unhide the four groups of monthly columns.

Figure 1117

You are constantly hiding groups of columns.

	A	E	F	G	H	I
Account	Q1	Apr	May	Jun	Q2
A101	471	101	192	160	453
A102	476	165	124	107	396
A103	409	107	188	122	417
A104	441	122	197	107	426
A105	525	114	125	110	349

Strategy: You can group the columns instead of hiding and unhiding them. Follow these steps:

1) Unhide all the columns.

2) Select the headings Jan, Feb, and Mar. Select Data – Group – Columns. Excel adds a group and outline symbol above the column headings.

3) Repeat step 2 for Apr, May, Jun; Jul, Aug, Sep; and Oct, Nov, Dec.

Excel will draw in Group & Outline buttons above the spreadsheet, as shown in Figure 1118.

Figure 1118

Click a minus to hide any quarter.

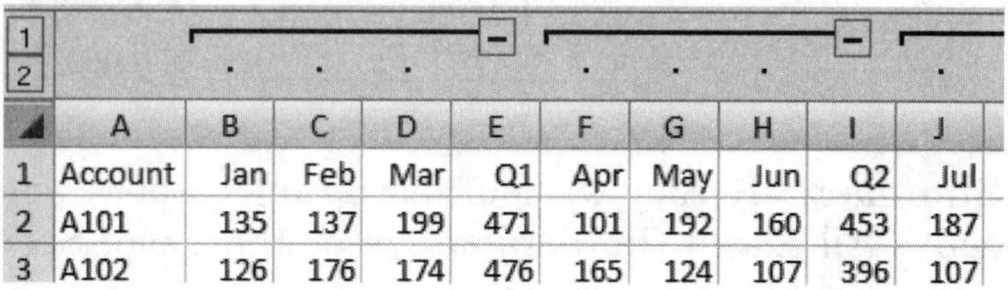

	A	B	C	D	E	F	G	H	I	J
1	Account	Jan	Feb	Mar	Q1	Apr	May	Jun	Q2	Jul
2	A101	135	137	199	471	101	192	160	453	187
3	A102	126	176	174	476	165	124	107	396	107

You can click the 1 Group & Outline button to collapse to quarters, as shown in Figure 1119. You can click the 2 button to display months.

Figure 1119

The 1 and 2 Group & Outline buttons toggle between views.

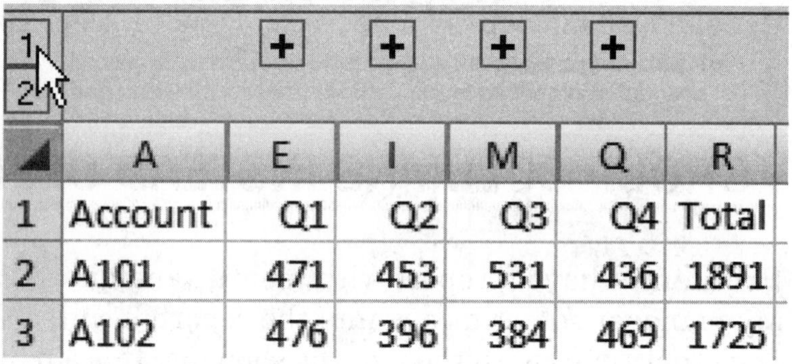

	A	E	I	M	Q	R
1	Account	Q1	Q2	Q3	Q4	Total
2	A101	471	453	531	436	1891
3	A102	476	396	384	469	1725

Summary: You can manually use groups to hide/unhide data.

Commands Discussed: Data – Group and Outline – Group

Excel 97-2003: Data – Group and Outline – Group

MOVE COLUMNS BY SORTING LEFT TO RIGHT

Problem: My IT department produces a report every day, and the columns are in the wrong sequence. It would take them two minutes to rewrite the query, but they have a six-month backlog and don't have time to get around to it. How can I rearrange the columns? (Figure 1120)

Figure 1120

The columns are not in a logical sequence.

◢	A	B	C	D	
1	City	Zip	Attn:	State	Company
2	Akron	30909	PAUL NASH	MD	Reliable Wa:
3	Andover	56116	KEVIN TURNER	AZ	Unsurpassed
4	Naperville	68522	BRANDON BURRIS	VT	Compelling I
5	Bainbridge	58587	TRACEY CHARLES	DE	Cool Doorbe

Strategy: You can sort the columns left-to-right. The quick way is to add a new row with column sequence numbers. If you really have to rearrange these every day, however, it would make sense to add a custom list with the proper sequence of the columns.

Follow these steps for the quick method:

1) Insert a new row above the headings.

2) In the new row, enter the numbers 1 through *n* to specify the desired sequence for the columns. If you want company name first, number that column 1, and so on.

3) Select the range of data to be sorted. Use Ctrl+* to select the current range. If you don't explicitly select the whole range, the Sort command tends to remove the numbered row 1 from the sort.

4) Select Data – Sort.

5) Click the Options button at the top of the Sort dialog.

6) Choose Sort Left to Right under Orientation, as shown in Figure 1121. Click OK to close the Sort Options dialog.

Part IV

Figure 1121

Steps 2, 3, 6, and 7 are all shown here.

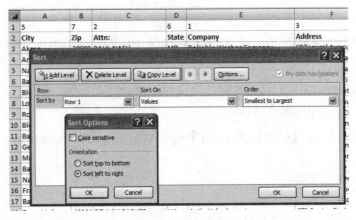

7)   In the Sort By dropdown, choose Row 1.

8)   Click OK to rearrange the columns.

9)   Because the column widths do not sort with the data, select Home
      – Format dropdown – AutoFit Column Width to fix all column
      widths.

Results: The columns are rearranged, as shown in Figure 1122.

Figure 1122

Excel sorts
the columns
into the proper
sequence.

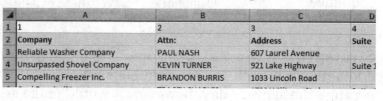

10)   You can now delete the temporary row 1.

Alternate Strategy: If you defined a custom list of Company, Attn:,
Address, Suite, City, State, Zip, you could skip the first two steps above.
When defining the sort, you would specify Company, Attn:, Address as
the sequence, as shown in Figure 1123. For information on defining
a custom sort sequence, see "How to Sort a Report into a Custom Sequence" on page 422.

Figure 1123

Skip the tem-
porary row if
you define a
custom list.

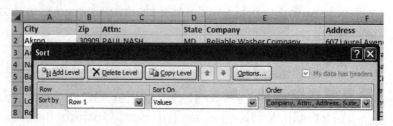

Summary: You can re-sequence many columns by using a left-to-right
sort.

Commands Discussed: Data – Sort; Home – Format dropdown – AutoFit Column Width

See Also: "How to Sort a Report into a Custom Sequence" (p. 422)

MOVE COLUMNS USING INSERT CUT CELLS

Problem: I need to rearrange two columns. The left-to-right sort trick described in "Move Columns by Sorting Left to Right" seems overly complex.

Strategy: There is a fast way to move a couple of columns. You select the entire column to be moved and use Cut. Then you right-click on the column to the right of where the data should go and choose Insert Cut Cells.

In Figure 1124, you want to move column B before column A. This will require four clicks. Follow these steps:

Figure 1124

Move column B before column A.

	A	B	
1	**Attn:**	**Company**	**Addr**
2	PAUL NASH	Reliable Washer Company	607 La
3	KEVIN TURNER	Unsurpassed Shovel Compa	921 La
4	BRANDON BURRIS	Compelling Freezer Inc.	1033
5	TRACEY CHARLES	Cool Doorbell Inc.	1793
6	NINA BRIGGS	Exclusive Shingle Supply	1396

1) Right-click the B column label. Choose Cut from the context menu.

2) Right-click the A column label. Choose Insert Cut Cells, as shown in Figure 1125.

Figure 1125

Cut B and insert cut cells before A.

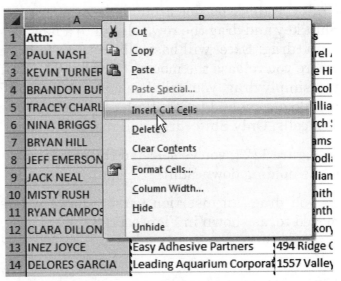

Results: The entire column will be moved, as shown in Figure 1126. This is an amazingly simple and fast process.

Figure 1126

Excel will move the column.

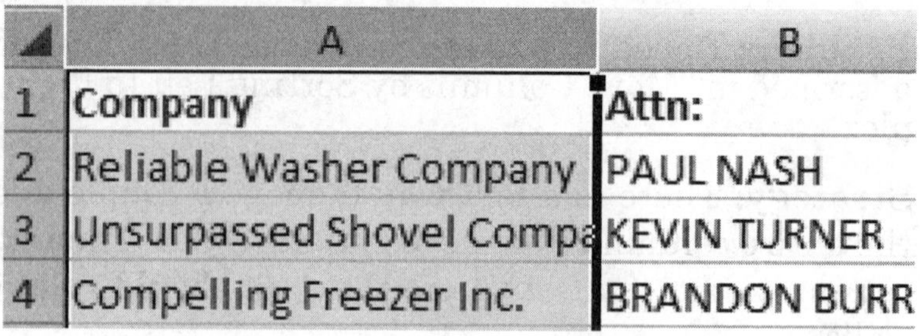

◢	A	B
1	Company	Attn:
2	Reliable Washer Company	PAUL NASH
3	Unsurpassed Shovel Compa	KEVIN TURNER
4	Compelling Freezer Inc.	BRANDON BURR

Summary: You can re-sequence two columns by using Insert Cut Cells.

Commands Discussed: Insert Cut Cells

MOVE ROWS OR COLUMNS WITH SHIFT DRAG

Problem: I need to rearrange some rows or columns. Do you have anything faster than the other methods you've described?

Strategy: You might find this method faster than the others:

1) Select an entire row by pressing Shift+Spacebar or select an entire column by pressing Ctrl+Spacebar.

2) Grab the thick border around the row or column. Hold down the Shift key and drag the row/column to a new location. When you use Shift+drag, Excel will basically cut the cells and then insert them where you release the mouse. **Gotcha:** The Shift+drag is critical. If you simply drag, you will do a cut and paste. If you Ctrl+drag, you will do a copy and paste. Both of these will overwrite the destination cells. Only Shift+drag will insert the cells.

3) In Figure 1127, you've selected the entire row. Grab the top border while holding down Shift.

As you drag, an insertion cursor shows where the row would be moved to, as shown in Figure 1128.

Figure 1127

Shift while clicking the border.

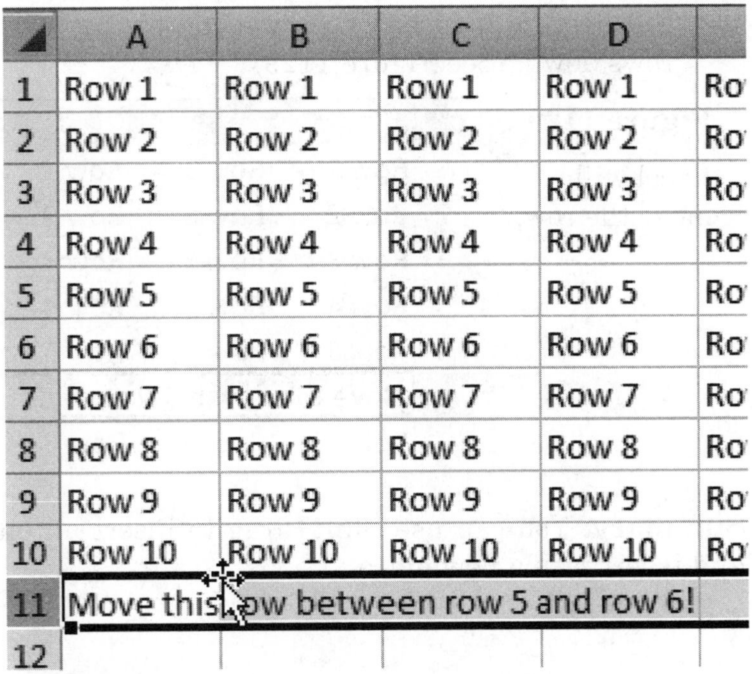

	A	B	C	D	
1	Row 1	Row 1	Row 1	Row 1	Ro
2	Row 2	Row 2	Row 2	Row 2	Ro
3	Row 3	Row 3	Row 3	Row 3	Ro
4	Row 4	Row 4	Row 4	Row 4	Ro
5	Row 5	Row 5	Row 5	Row 5	Ro
6	Row 6	Row 6	Row 6	Row 6	Ro
7	Row 7	Row 7	Row 7	Row 7	Ro
8	Row 8	Row 8	Row 8	Row 8	Ro
9	Row 9	Row 9	Row 9	Row 9	Ro
10	Row 10	Row 10	Row 10	Row 10	Ro
11	Move this row between row 5 and row 6!				
12					

Figure 1128

Notice the gray insertion character between rows 5 and 6.

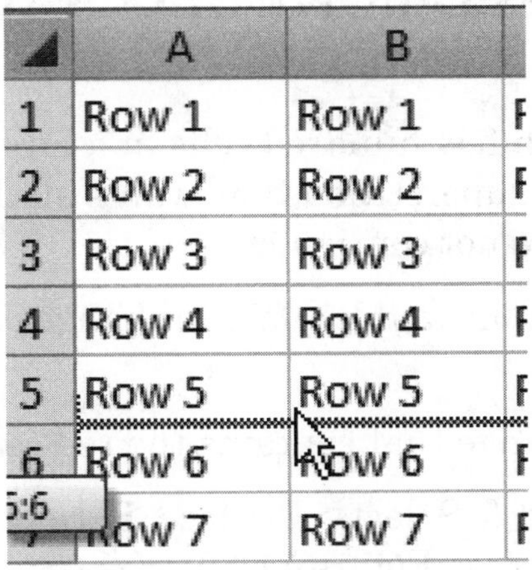

	A	B	
1	Row 1	Row 1	F
2	Row 2	Row 2	F
3	Row 3	Row 3	F
4	Row 4	Row 4	F
5	Row 5	Row 5	F
6	Row 6	Row 6	F
7	Row 7	Row 7	F

5:6

Part IV

4) Release the mouse. Excel will insert the row and shift the other rows down. (See Figure 1129).

Figure 1129

Excel will
move the row.

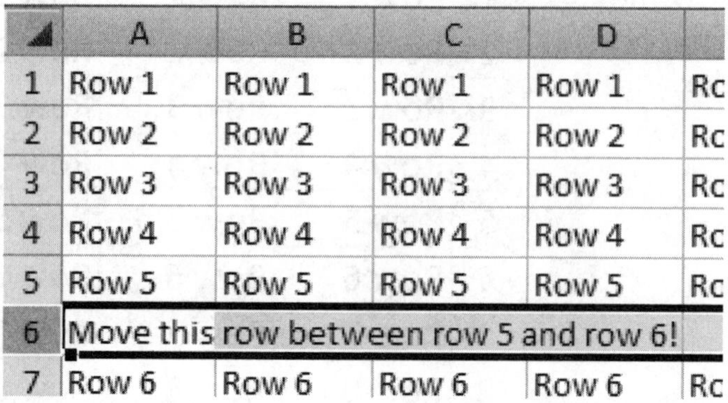

◢	A	B	C	D	
1	Row 1	Row 1	Row 1	Row 1	Rc
2	Row 2	Row 2	Row 2	Row 2	Rc
3	Row 3	Row 3	Row 3	Row 3	Rc
4	Row 4	Row 4	Row 4	Row 4	Rc
5	Row 5	Row 5	Row 5	Row 5	Rc
6	Move this row between row 5 and row 6!				
7	Row 6	Row 6	Row 6	Row 6	Rc

Summary: You can use Shift+drag to insert an entire row or column and insert it in a new place.

CHANGE ALL RED FONT CELLS TO BLUE FONT

Problem: I've marked a few hundred cells in a large workbook using a red font. My manager is superstitious and wants all the red cells changed to blue. The red cells are not contiguous.

Strategy: You can use Find and Replace to change formats. Here's what you do:

1) Select the entire range that contains the red cells.

2) Select Home – Find & Select – Replace. Excel will display the Find and Replace dialog (see Figure 1130).

3) Click the Options button to show additional options.

4) Leave the Find What and Replace With boxes blank. On the right side, choose the dropdown next to the top Format button. Excel will offer options for Format, Choose Format from Cell, and Clear Find Format. For the maximum flexibility, choose the Format option. Excel will display the Find Format dialog.

Figure 1130

Leave Find
What and
Replace With
boxes blank,
but specify a
font color.

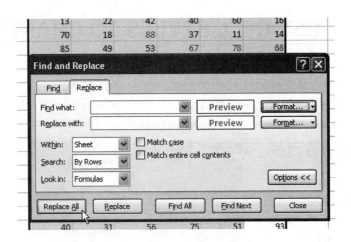

5) In the Find Format dialog, go to the Font tab. Change the Color dropdown to Red. Do not select a font. Don't make any selections on any other tab. Click OK to return to the Find and Replace dialog.

6) Click the second Format button. On the Font tab, choose blue as the Color.

7) After specifying both the original and new font colors, click the Replace All button in the Find and Replace dialog.

Results: The red fonts are changed to blue, as shown in Figure 1131.

Figure 1131

Red will
change to blue.

88	37	11	14
53	67	78	68
69	15	71	87

Alternate Strategy: When you choose the format from an existing cell, Excel picks up all the formats. When you perform the Replace, if a format does not match exactly, the cell will not be replaced. For example, if some cells were left-justified instead of right-justified, they will not be replaced.

Summary: You can use the Replace Formats command to change formats. Using cell styles, as discussed in "Use Cell Styles to Handle Changing Formats," can also solve this problem.

Commands Discussed: Home – Find & Select – Replace

Excel 97-2003: Edit – Replace; this option was not available before Excel 2002.

USE CELL STYLES TO CHANGE FORMATS

Problem: What is this huge dropdown (Figure 1132) on the Home ribbon? Who says I have to put all my calculation cells in an ugly orange font with a border? Are they insane?

Figure 1132

Calculated cells in orange? Says who?

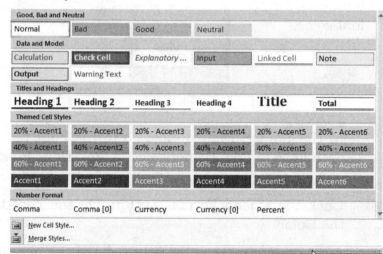

Strategy: Those cell styles are just examples. While styles are an important part of every Word guru's toolkit, I've never met anyone who used cell styles in Excel. This is partially Microsoft's fault because the Style dropdown was not on the Formatting toolbar in previous versions of Excel.

In Excel 2007, Microsoft promoted the Cell Style dropdown to the Home tab and provided a smattering of samples of how you might use cell styles. For example, Microsoft suggests that you can mark calculation cells or output cells. In another section, you can find styles for good, bad, or neutral cells. All these samples (except Normal) can be changed, deleted, or modified.

I am too set in my ways to start using orange for calculation cells and orange underlines for linked cells. However, I can imagine that someone who was brand new to spreadsheets might start using this, and it would work out fine for them.

I have started using Heading 4 for headings and Title for titles. Why not? I've never made my headings blue before, but it is an easy way to format the cells, and there is nothing particularly wrong with the blue.

Look through the settings, and if any of them seem useful to you, feel free to use them. Note that all the colors in the themed cell styles might change as you change the workbook theme on the Page Layout ribbon tab.

One cool use for cell styles is to solve the problem from "Change All Cells with Red Font to Blue Font." You know that you want to format a certain class of cells, but your manager loves to adjust the formatting. Red fonts might change to bold blue Tahoma fonts one day and then to green Cambria italic the next day. Follow these steps to set up a new style:

1) Select Home – Cell Styles dropdown – New Cell Style.

2) In the Style dialog (see Figure 1133), give the style a name, such as CheckLater.

Figure 1133

The best use is when you set up your own style.

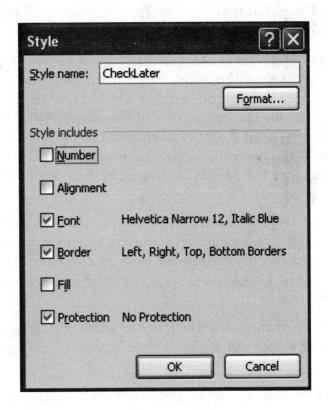

Part

IV

3) Click the Format button.

4) In the Format Cells dialog, change any settings. In this example, use the Font tab to create a blue, bold, italic 14-point font. Use the

Border tab to create a thick blue outline. Click OK to close the Format Cells dialog.

5) Look at the Style dialog's check boxes for Number, Alignment, Font, Border, Fill, and Protection. It can be useful to apply protection based on a style. But maybe you want to be able to have cells in the CheckLater style manually shaded with different colors. If so, uncheck the Fill check box. If you want the cell style to affect only the font and border but not to override the number format or alignment, uncheck the Number and Alignment check boxes as well.

6) Click OK to create the style.

If your Excel window is wide enough to show four styles in the Cell Styles gallery, your new style will appear in the gallery. Select a cell and select the CheckLater style. Excel automatically changes the font, color, and border of the cell.

Additional Details: It is frustrating to move the mouse all the way to the ribbon to select the style. Here is an amazing technique: Use the mouse to apply the style to one cell. Then, as you select other cells, press the F4 key to redo the last action. In this case, F4 will apply the cell style. (Ctrl+Y also works.) If you've performed some other command since applying the style, then the keyboard shortcut Alt+H+J+Enter will apply the first style in the gallery. If you have only one custom style, this will work fine.

Additional Details: Managers typically have no sense of style. If your manager is not impressed with your 42-point hot pink Star Trek font choice, you can easily change all cells by changing the cell style. Figure 1134 shows the CheckLater style with the Impact font. Here's how you change it:.

1) Right-click the cell style. Options allow you to apply, modify, duplicate, or delete the style. Choose Modify (see Figure 1135).

2) In the Style dialog, click the Format button. Choose a new font and a new border. Click OK to close each dialog.

Results: All the cells formatted with the CheckLater style are changed to reflect the new formatting, as shown in Figure 1136.

Figure 1134

Cells marked with Check-Later style.

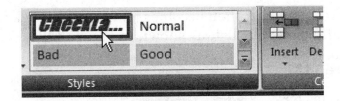

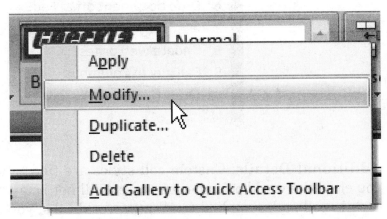

Figure 1135

Modify the existing style.

Figure 1136

All cells with the modified style change.

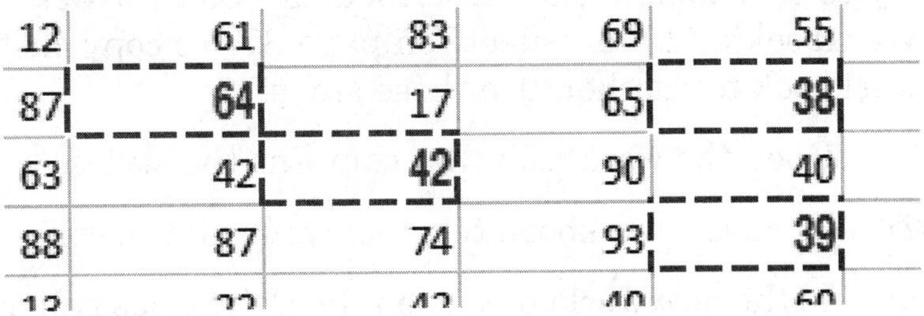

12	61	83	69	55
87	64	17	65	38
63	42	42	90	40
88	87	74	93	39
13	22	42	40	60

Additional Details: You could set up a workbook to track your to-do list and then create a Hot style in red and a Done style with gray font and strikethrough. It then becomes just a simple click in the style box to cross an item off your list, as shown in Figure 1137.

Figure 1137

Use styles for a to-do list.

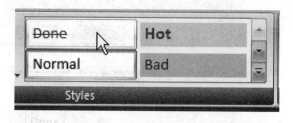

Additional Details: Custom cell styles are tied to a workbook. When you close the workbook, the cell styles will not be available. If you want certain cell styles applied to all new workbooks, you can define the cell styles in book.xltx, as described in "Control Settings for Every New Workbook and Worksheet" on page 82. To copy custom styles from one workbook to another, use these steps:

1) Open the workbook that contains the styles.

2) Open the workbook to which you want to copy the styles.

3) In the new workbook, open the Cell Styles gallery and choose Merge Styles. Excel will show a list of all open workbooks. Choose the workbook from step 1 and click OK. The styles will be copied to the new workbook.

Summary: Cell styles can make your Excel life more efficient. If you don't like the built-in sample styles, you can easily create new styles for your particular need.

Commands Discussed: Home – Cell Styles dropdown – New Cell Style

Excel 97-2003: Add a new style with Format – Style. To get the most use out of styles, right-click a toolbar and choose Customize; in the Format category, find the Style dropdown, and drag this dropdown to any toolbar

LEAVE HELPFUL NOTES
WITH CELL COMMENTS

Problem: I have figured out the confusing formula in Excel shown in Figure 1138. I want to add a note to the worksheet to remind myself how the formula works.

Figure 1138

Add a note about this formula.

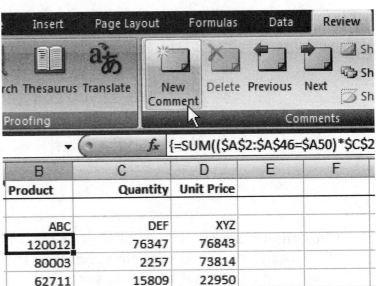

Strategy: You can use cell comment to leave notes in a worksheet. In addition to having 17 billion cells on a worksheet, you can also store a comment for each cell. Typically, a cell comment is indicated by a red

triangle in the corner of the cell. If you hover the mouse over the cell, the comment will appear. Here's how you add comments to a worksheet:

1) Select the cell where you want to add a comment. Select Review – New Comment. A comment box will appear, with your name in bold on line 1, as shown in Figure 1139.

Figure 1139

Excel will fill in your name as the comment author.

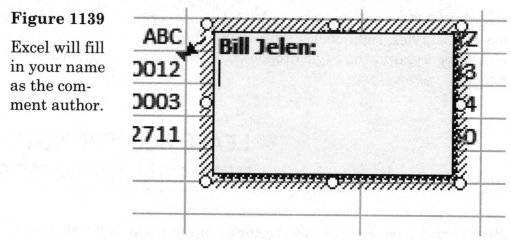

2) Type a comment, as shown in Figure 1140.

Figure 1140

Type a note.

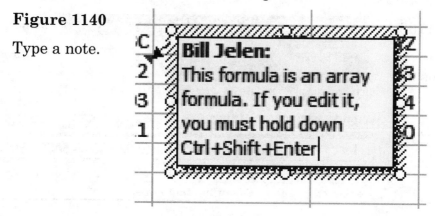

3) Click the mouse outside the comment box to complete the entry of the comment. A red triangle remains in the cell to indicate the presence of a comment there, as shown in Figure 1141.

When you hover your mouse over the cell with the red triangle, your comment box will pop up like a ToolTip, as shown in Figure 1142.

Figure 1141

A red triangle indicates a comment.

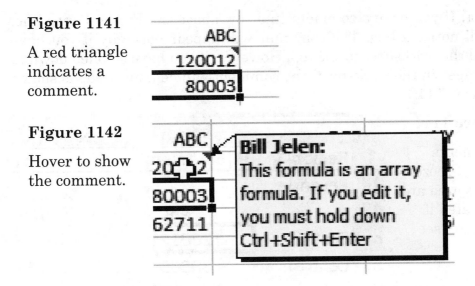

Figure 1142

Hover to show the comment.

Additional Details: To delete a comment, you select the cell and then select Review – Delete. To edit a comment, you select the cell. In the Review tab of the ribbon, the New Comment icon is now an Edit Comment icon.

The information here is based on the assumption that you are using the default settings for comments. There are additional settings available in the Advanced tab of the Excel Options dialog. On this tab, for example, you can suppress the appearance of the red comment indicator or force all comments to be shown at all times (see Figure 1143).

Part IV

Figure 1143

You can hide the red indicator or make comments always visible.

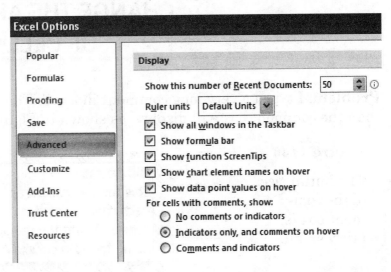

Gotcha: If you have a comment in a row above the Freeze Panes line, you will notice a bug. The comment will appear normally if you have scrolled the worksheet to the top. However, if you have scrolled down to other pages in the worksheet, the comment will be truncated, as shown in Figure 1144.

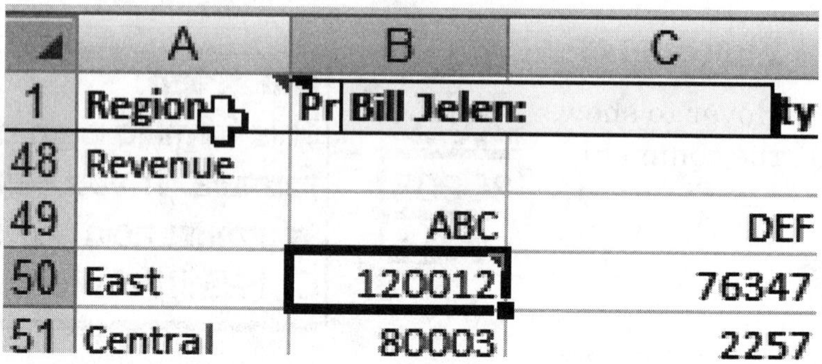

Figure 1144

Comments in the Freeze Panes area are truncated if you can't see row 2.

	A	B	C
1	Region	Pr	Bill Jelen:	ty
48	Revenue		
49		ABC	DEF
50	East	120012	76347
51	Central	80003	2257

Summary: Adding comments to cells is a great way to leave notes for yourself to help you remember something about a formula later. You can also add them to help others who are using your worksheet.

Commands Discussed: Review – New Comment; Review – Delete

Excel 97-2003: Insert – Comment. To delete or edit a comment, right-click the cell that contains the comment.

CHANGE THE APPEARANCE
OF CELL COMMENTS

Problem: I typed a very long comment in a cell. The comment is longer than the comment box will display, as shown in Figure 1145.

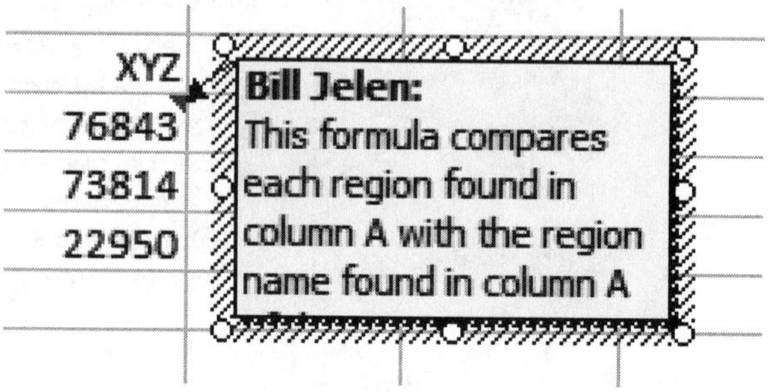

Figure 1145

The initial size of the comment box is fairly small.

XYZ	Bill Jelen:
76843	This formula compares
73814	each region found in
22950	column A with the region
	name found in column A

Strategy: Excel gives you complete control over the size and appearance of the comment box. You can right-click the border of the comment and choose Format Comment.

Gotcha: Watch for a strange behavior when formatting comments. Notice in Figure 1145 that the border around the comment comprises diagonal lines. If you right-click and choose Format Comment when the diagonal lines appear, you will get a Format Comment dialog with only the Font tab shown in Figure 1146.

Figure 1146

If you see only the Font tab, you chose to format while in Edit mode.

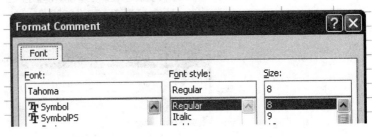

To get the complete set of formatting options, you must first left-click the diagonal lines border. This will change the diagonal lines to dots, as shown in Figure 1147. You can now right-click the dots and choose Format Comment.

Figure 1147

Click the diagonal lines border to change to dots.

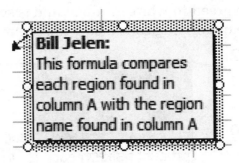

Excel will display the complete Format Comment dialog, as shown in Figure 1148.

Figure 1148

The entire Format Comment dialog box is available.

**Part
IV**

To adjust the size of the comment with precision, you use the Size tab, as shown in Figure 1149. You enter a new size that is big enough to make room for the entire comment.

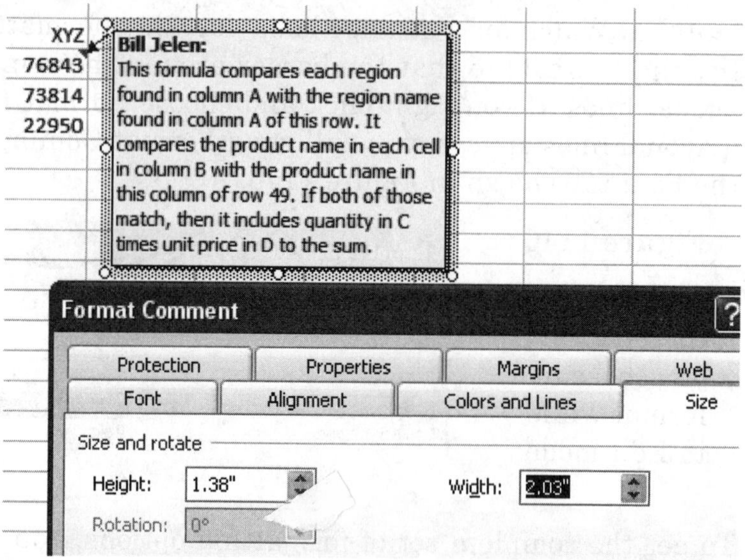

Figure 1149

Increase the comment size.

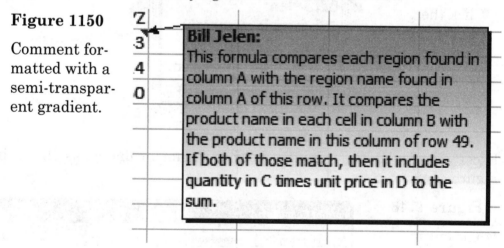

Additional Details: It is also possible to change the boring yellow comment shown earlier to a nicely formatted comment. The comment shown in Figure 1150 has a green-to-white gradient and is semi-transparent so that you can see the underlying cells below the comment.

Figure 1150

Comment formatted with a semi-transparent gradient.

Here's how you get this effect:

1) On the Format Comment dialog, select to the Colors and Lines tab.

2) In the Color dropdown in the Fill section, select Fill Effects, as shown in Figure 1151.

Figure 1151

Choose Fill Effects from the Color dropdown.

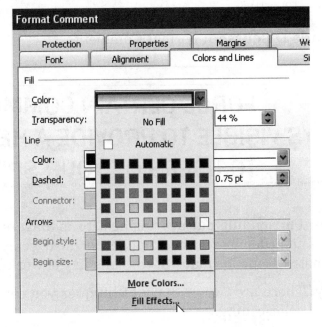

3) On the Fill Effects dialog, choose the Gradient tab. Choose the Two Colors option and select green for Color 1 and white for Color 2. You can adjust the transparency for each color independently, as shown in Figure 1152.

Part IV

Figure 1152

Set up a two-color gradient.

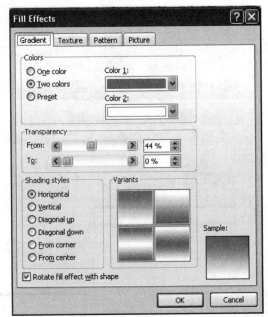

Summary: You can change the size of comments, and you can replace the default yellow comments with a variety of formats to increase interest in a workbook.

Commands Discussed: Format Comments

FORCE CERTAIN COMMENTS TO BE ALWAYS VISIBLE TO PROVIDE A HELP SYSTEM TO USERS OF YOUR SPREADSHEET

Problem: I'm sending out a worksheet to managers and division vice presidents in order to get their budget for next year. I need to include specific instructions for many of the cells in the worksheet.

Strategy: There are two primary techniques you can do this: cell comments and color-coding.

To use cell comments, for each comment you want to display 100% of the time, select the cell and choose Review – Show/Hide Comment as shown in Figure 1153. Alternatively, right-click the cell and choose Show Comment. This will force those comments to be always visible.

Figure 1153

Toggle individual comments on or off.

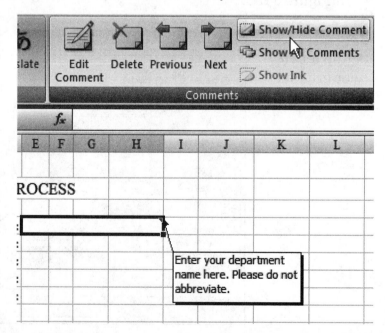

To use color coding, you can make all comments meant for managers green, and you can make the vice presidents' instructions blue. When managers and vice presidents open the file, they will have an easy-to-follow visual roadmap through their budget worksheet.

Additional Details: By default, comments will not be printed. You can choose either of two settings to control the printing of comments by following these steps:

1) From the Page Layout tab, choose the dialog launcher icon in the lower-right corner of the Page Setup group.

2) In the Page Setup dialog, go to the Sheet tab and use the Comments dropdown to control the printing of comments (see Figure 1154) .

Figure 1154

Control the printing of comments.

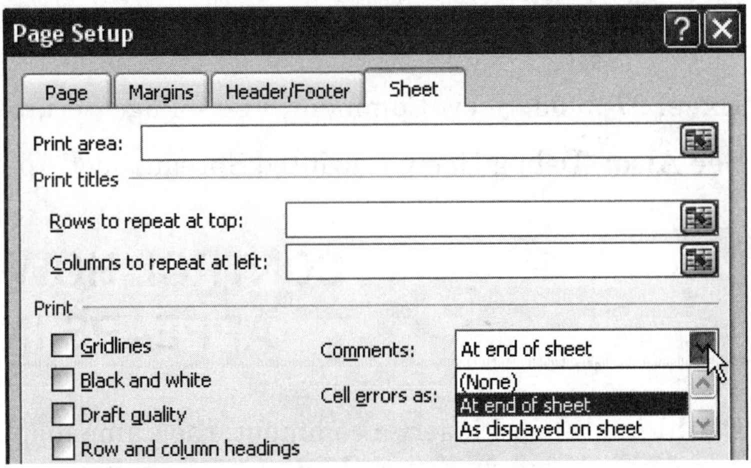

If you select As Displayed on Sheet from the Comments dropdown, the comment boxes will print in the size and format you have set up for all the displayed comments. This setting will not print comments that are hidden with only the red triangle visible. To make effective use of this setting, you would have to make a few comments visible, as described in this chapter.

If you select At End of Sheet from the Comments dropdown, the comments will print in a separate section at the end of the printout, as shown in Figure 1154. The only drawback to this method is that the comment printout indicates that a certain comment is attached to cell A50. Unless you print row and column headings (see "Debug Using a Printed

Spreadsheet" on page 848), there is no way for the reader of the printed document to know which value on the sheet is located in cell A50.

Figure 1155

Comments can print at the end of the sheet.

Cell: E4

Comment: Enter your department name here. Please do not abbreviate.

Cell: C12

Comment: Bill Jelen

Summary: You can use the Show Comments feature to keep comments visible in order to provide an onscreen guide for someone who is using your spreadsheet.

Commands Discussed: Review – Show/Hide Comment; Page Layout – Page Setup dialog launcher

Excel 97-2003: Show Comment; File – Page Setup – Sheet

See Also: "Debug Using a Printed Spreadsheet" (p. 848)

CONTROL HOW YOUR NAME APPEARS IN COMMENTS

Problem: When I insert a comment, the name displayed in bold is Customer, as shown in Figure 1156. Can I change this so everyone knows which comments I inserted?.

Figure 1156

The comment offers a generic name.

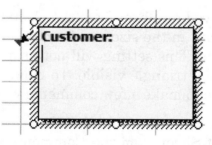

Customer:

Strategy: You can change the name that is displayed in comments. To do so, you select Office Icon – Excel Options. At the bottom of the Popular category of the Excel Options dialog is a field called User Name, as shown in Figure 1157. You can change this field to the name you would like displayed in comments.

Figure 1157

Change the name displayed in comments.

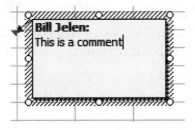

Additional Details: It is impossible to use no name in comments as the default. Even if you change the User Name field to a blank, Excel will pick up the computer user name.

If you want to remove the name from a single comment, you can select the name and press Delete or backspace through the name. Typically, the name will appear in bold, and the comment you type will appear in normal font, as shown in Figure 1158.

Figure 1158

Name in bold, comment in normal font.

When you backspace through the name and then begin to type, Excel will be in bold mode, and any comment you type will appear in bold, as shown in Figure 1159.

Figure 1159

If you backspaced to clear the comment, you are left in bold mode.

To turn off the bold mode, press Ctrl+B before you begin to type the comment.

Summary: You can change the name that appears in comments by using the Popular tab of the Excel Options dialog. You can delete the name that appears in a single comment by pressing Delete or backspacing through the name.

Commands Discussed: Office Icon – Excel Options – Popular

Excel 97-2003: Tools – Options – General

CHANGE THE COMMENT SHAPE TO A STAR

Problem: I would like to jazz up a comment by changing it to a starburst or some other shape.

Strategy: This trick has become more difficult since Excel 2003, but it is possible with a little customization of the Quick Access toolbar. The command you need is the Change Shape command. It appears on many contextual ribbon tabs, but because Microsoft puts away the tabs when you unselect an object, the command is not available to change the shape of a comment.

Instead, you have to add the icon to the Quick Access toolbar. Follow these steps:

1) Right-click the Quick Access toolbar and choose Customize Quick Access Toolbar.

2) In the top-left dropdown, choose All Commands.

3) Scroll down to the Change Shape icon. Select this item and click the Add button.

4) Click OK to close the Excel Options dialog.

When the Change Shape icon is on the Quick Access toolbar, follow these instructions to change the comment shape:

1) Add a regular comment to a cell.

2) Select the cell that contains the comment.

3) Choose Review – Edit Comment. The comment will appear, surrounded by diagonal lines.

4) Left-click the diagonal lines to change them to dots.

5) Select a new shape from the Change Shapes icon on the Quick Access toolbar (see Figure 1160).

Figure 1160

Select a new shape.

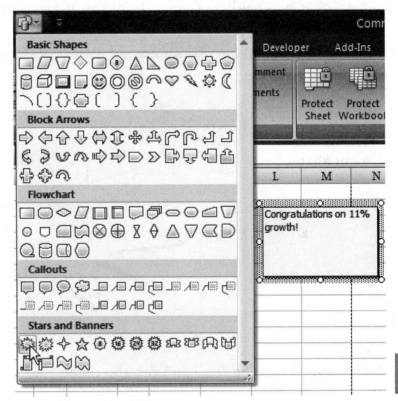

The comment will change from a rectangle to a starburst. However, the comment is not large enough to show the entire comment, as shown in Figure 1161.

Figure 1161

The shape changes, but the size is wrong.

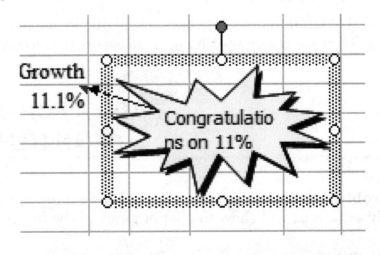

Part IV

6) Grab a corner resize handle and drag to make the shape larger.

7) On the Home tab, choose Middle Align from the vertical alignment icons. Choose Align Center from the horizontal alignment icons. Increase the font size to 10.

Results: The comment will appear as a starburst, as shown in Figure 1162.

Figure 1162

The new comment shape.

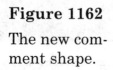

Additional Details: You can grab the green rotate handle and rotate until you have the shape that best fits the text.

Summary: After you add a Change Shape icon to the Quick Access toolbar, you can change the shape of a comment.

Commands Discussed: Review – Edit Comment; Customize Quick Access Toolbar; Change Shape

Excel 97-2003: View – Toolbars – Drawing to display the Drawing toolbar. Then select Draw – Change AutoShape to select a new shape

ADD A POP-UP PICTURE OF AN ITEM IN A CELL

Problem: As shown in Figure 1163, I have a product catalog in Excel. My sales reps will show the list of items to the buyer in a retail store.

What's New in Excel 2010 with Bill Jelen of MrExcel.com

New Perfect formatting using GetPivotData with a Shell Report

-- Recording a macro to format cells
-- Adding the macro button to the toolbar
-- Changing the picture on the button
-- Use Relative References to record a macro that moves

What's New in Excel 2010 with Bill Jelen of MrExcel.com

Advanced Data Analysis in the Afternoon

Create an Interactive Chart with AutoFilter
714 Chart Two different series with differing orders of magnitude
Chart one series with differing magnitude
XY Chart, with Trendline

Advanced Pivot Tables

Cleaning up bad data in a pivot table
Expand & Collapse
Group Numeric Fields to build a frequency chart
Fixing Customer Name problems
Group Text fields to build a true Top 10
Using a pivot table to analyze Q.A. data - Pareto Chart
Pivot Charts
Calculated Fields
Building a Report with Multiple Fields Going Across
Basing your pivot table on a List

Macro Recorder

Format Invoice Macro
Event Macros

Date Analysis   Formulas

What's New in Excel 2010 with Bill Jelen of MrExcel.com

Duplicates
Removing
Marking

New Sorting & Filtering
177 Finding total of selected cells in Status Bar
--- Filter by Selection using AutoFilter icon
Better Date Filters
Filter by Searching
Filter by Icon
Sort by Color

Pivot Table Improvements
New interface
Better Filtering with Search
Compact vs Tabular View
Repeat Item Labels
Filtering with Slicers
Multiple pivot tables, one slicer
Using GETPIVOTDATA for formatted Reports
% of Parent Row Total
Rank

What's New in Excel 2010 with Bill Jelen of MrExcel.com

Creating Charts in Excel 2010

707 Rotating Angle of Pie Chart
686 Leave upper left corner of chart data blank
686 Create a chart with one click
702 Customize anything on a chart, double-click works again
710 Copy and paste new data on a chart
710 Select a chart, use the blue handle to add new data
724 Select chart, chart type, Custom Types, User Defined, Add to save your chart type

Data Visualizations in Excel 2010

Data Bars - Now Show Negative Values
Color Scales
Icon Sets
Using Manage Rules to control where the icons change

Sparklines in Excel 2010

By Default, sparklines have different scales, which is sometimes good
Force scales to be the same when necessary
Labeling Sparklines!
Sparkbars, Win/Loss Sparklines
Merge Cells to make a single large sparkline

Better Fill Handle Double-Click, Better Formula Auto-Complete

184 Join text in one column with text in another column

The New Interface
Ribbon Customization
Protected Mode
Backstage View
Paste Options Menu
Page Layout View
Bringing Back the old Print Preview
Expanding Formula Bar
Quick Zoom
Add the Recent Files to your QAT

New Table Functionality
Ctrl+T to Define
Format
New Columns will AutoFill
New Data becomes part of table for Pivots & Charts

New Calculation Functions
IFERROR
SUMIFS, COUNTIFS, AVERAGEIFS
WORKDAY.INTL
AGGREGATE
MODE.MULT

Page #'s refer to Learn Excel 97-2007 from MrExcel

MrExcel.com

Pivot Multiple worksheets in a single table
Better DAX Functions in the grid
DAX measures in the pivot table

For a quick video of tips: http://www.mrexcel.com/preview-Northwest.com
Use the Message Board at MrExcel.com for answers to questions, or contact
Bill - pub@MrExcel.com

DATE(Y,M,D)　　　　　　MIN vs SMALL(Array,K) vs PERCENTILE(Array, 5)
EOMONTH
WORKDAY & NETWORKDAYS
Time Formulas
TIME(H,M,S)
Times in Excess of 24 hours
Converting times to hours

Advanced Subtotals
Filling in data on subtotal lines
Adding blank rows after subtotals
Subtotaling data previously sorted

Data Analysis
VLOOKUP to compare two lists
Using INDEX & MATCH instead of VLOOKUP
Pivot Table to compare two lists
Forecast Balance Example
Sorting with a Formula; RANK & COUNTIF
=MOD(ROW(),2) to highlight alternating rows
Calculating TREND with LINEST
Transposing with a Formula
SUMIF
SUMIF with two criteria
Find Vendor Changes

Page #'s refer to Learn Excel 97-2007 from MrExcel

Page #'s refer to Learn Excel 97-2007 from MrExcel

It is a pain to go back and forth between Excel and the product catalog. Can I have pictures appear on demand in Excel?

Figure 1163

Display pictures on demand?

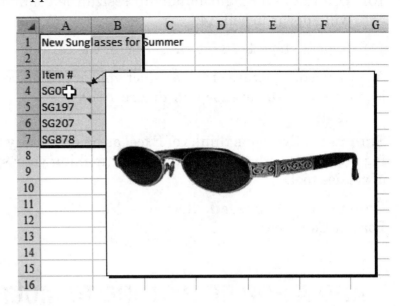

Strategy: You can add a pop-up picture to a cell. When someone hovers the mouse over an item number, the picture will appear. Follow these steps:

1) Select cell A4. Select Review – New Comment.

2) The default comment will have your name as the default text. Backspace to remove the name.

3) Using the mouse, click the diagonal-lines border in order to change the border to a series of dots.

4) Right-click the dotted border and select Format Comment.

5) In the Format Comment dialog, go to the Colors and Lines tab. In the Fill Color dropdown, choose Fill Effects.

6) In the Fill Effects dialog, choose the Picture tab and then click the Select Picture button.

7) Browse to the location where you have product pictures stored. Select a digital image of the item and click Insert.

8) On the Fill Effects tab, click OK. When you return to the Format Comment dialog, a squished version of the image will appear in the Color dropdown. Don't worry; the actual comment will look better.

Part
IV

9) Click OK to close the Format Comment dialog.

10) Use the lower-right handle to resize the comment. A red triangle will appear in cell A4.

11) Repeat steps 1–10 for each item in the catalog.

As promised, a picture of the product appears when you hover the mouse icon over the cell, as shown in Figure 1079.

Summary: Everyone thinks of Excel as being strictly for numbers. Adding pop-up pictures is a great trick for making your spreadsheets more of a sales tool.

Commands Discussed: Review – New Comment; Insert Comment; Format Comment

ADD A POP-UP PICTURE TO MULTIPLE CELLS

Problem: I gave this book to my manager for Bosses' Day. He saw "Add a Pop-up Picture of an Item in a Cell," and wants you to add pictures to dozens of cells. Adding pictures is one of the most tedious tasks in Excel. Is there an easy way?

Strategy: You can use a VBA macro to speed up a lot of jobs. I would never attempt this particular task without one, especially because this macro is so simple. This is all you do:

1) Enter these few lines of code in the VBA Editor.

```
Sub AddABunch()
For Each cell In Selection
        MyPic = "C:\Qimage\QI" & cell.Value & ".jpg"
        With cell.AddComment
                .Shape.Fill.UserPicture MyPic
                .Shape.Height = 300
                .Shape.Width = 300
        End With
Next cell
End Sub
```

2)   Select the dozens of cells where your manager wants pictures.

3)   Run the macro. Pictures will be added to all the cells in the selection.

Additional Details: For the complete guide to learning VBA, check out VBA & Macros for Microsoft Excel 2007 (ISBN 978-0789736826) from Que Publishing.

The macro described here works only if your company pictures are in the specified folder (C:\qimage\) and are named based on the values in the cells.

Summary: A few lines of VBA code can turn a horribly monotonous job into a few seconds of work.

Commands Discussed: VBA

DRAW AN ARROW TO VISUALLY ILLUSTRATE THAT TWO CELLS ARE CONNECTED

Part
IV

Problem: I have a large spreadsheet with many calculations. Results from section 1 are carried forward to cells in section 2. It would help to graphically illustrate that one cell flows to the calculation of another.

Strategy: You can use the Shapes feature to add arrows to indicate the flow of cells. The AutoShapes feature from Excel 97-2003 has been renamed Shapes in Excel 2007. (Did you notice...AutoFilter changed to Filter and AutoShapes changed to Shapes? What does Microsoft have against Auto?) Here's how you use it;

1) Select Insert ribbon – Shapes dropdown and choose an arrow, as shown in Figure 1164.

Figure 1164

Shapes are in a single drop-down instead of the multiple menus used in Excel 2003.

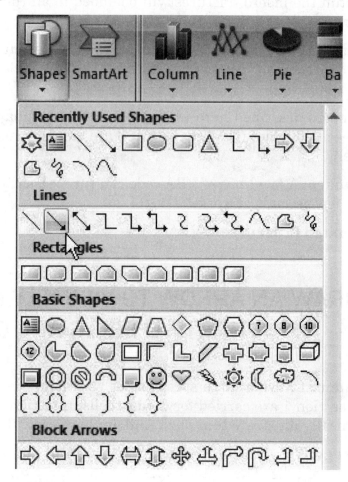

2) Click in the origin cell and drag to the final cell. When you release the mouse button, an arrow will appear, pointing from the first cell to the end cell. Annoyingly, the shape is drawn in a light shade of the first theme color, which ends up as light blue in the Office theme.

3) While the arrow is still selected, open the Shape Styles gallery on the Drawing Tools Format ribbon tab. Select one of the black styles in an appropriate thickness as shown in Figure 1165.

Figure 1165

Choose a color and thickness from the gallery.

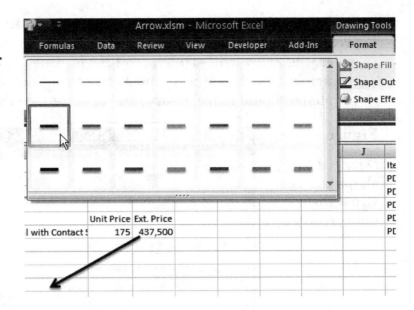

4) If you want to change any features of the arrow, select the arrow and press Ctrl+1. The Format Shape dialog appears, and you can use it to change multiple settings for the arrow (see Figure 1166).

Figure 1166

The Format dialog offers many settings.

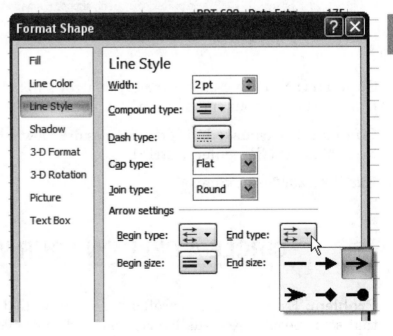

5) By default, the arrow will resize with the cells. In Figure 1167, the arrow stretches from column E to column C. If you make column D wider, the arrow will stretch. To turn off this behavior, right-click the arrow and choose Size and Properties. You can then decide if the shape should move, resize, and/or print (see Figure 1167).

Figure 1167

Decide if the shape will resize if the columns resize.

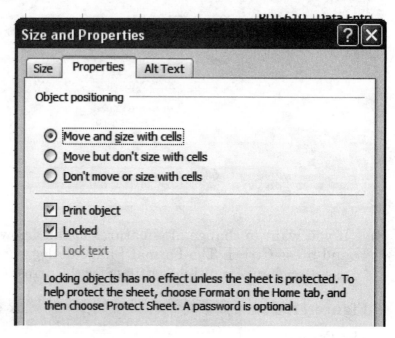

Summary: You can create a variety of arrows to help graphically illustrate the flow of your spreadsheet.

Commands Discussed: Insert – Shapes dropdown; Drawing Tools Format – Shape Styles gallery; Ctrl+1

Excel 97-2003: AutoShapes

CIRCLE A CELL ON YOUR WORKSHEET

Problem: Excel offers an excellent calculation tool. However, I know that some people are visually oriented, and their eyes glaze over when they look at a large white sheet with black numbers. I want to use graphics to call attention to certain numbers.

Strategy: You can add graphics to a worksheet by using Shapes. Follow these steps:

1) Select Insert – Shapes dropdown. Choose the oval.

2) As shown in Figure 1168, left-click fairly far above and to the left of the cell where you want to use the graphic.

Figure 1168

Start above
and to the left.

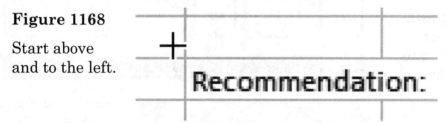

3) Drag down and to the right. in the worksheet and drag to draw an oval, as shown in Figure 1169.

Figure 1169

Drag down
and to the
right.

Gotcha: Although the shape is transparent as you drag, when you release the mouse button, the Shape is filled with theme color 1 and covers up text (see Figure 1170).

Figure 1170

Shapes are
filled by de-
fault.

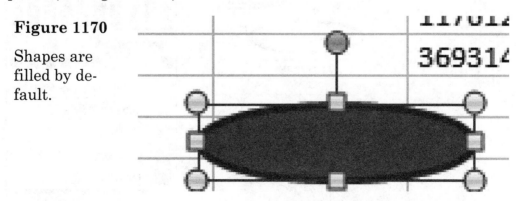

You would think that choosing from the top row in the Shape Styles gallery would solve the problem, especially since the thumbnail shows letters showing through the shape as shown in Figure 1171. However, that thumbnail refers to text box text, not cell text.

Figure 1171

The built-in styles don't allow text to show through.

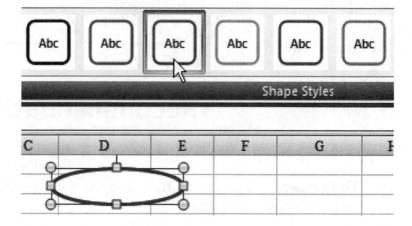

4)   Select Drawing Tools Format – Shape Fill dropdown and choose No Fill to allow the cell text to show through (see Figure 1172).

Figure 1172

Choose No Fill to create a transparent shape.

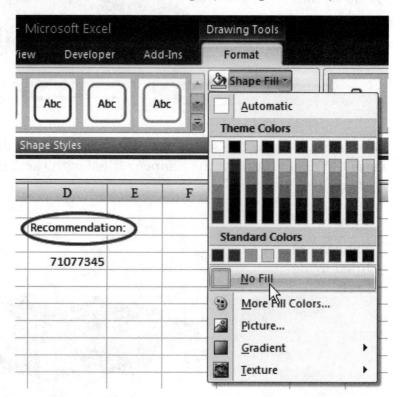

Results: Excel will add an attention-grabbing shape to the worksheet. This will draw the reader's eye to the conclusion.

Additional Details: If you will be drawing many shapes and you want them all to be transparent, right-click the first shape and choose Set as Default Shape. Any additional shapes you draw will have similar fill and line colors (see Figure 1173).

Figure 1173

Make future shapes transparent.

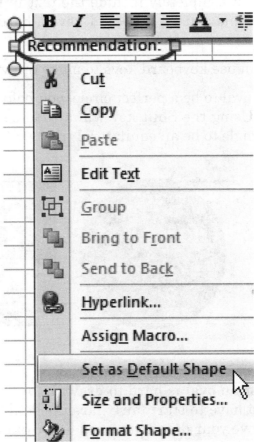

Summary: You can use Insert – Shapes dropdown to add shapes to your worksheet.

Commands Discussed: Insert – Shapes dropdown; Drawing Tools Format – Shape Fill dropdown

Excel 97-2003: AutoShapes

DRAW PERFECT CIRCLES

Problem: : The oval tool in the Drawing toolbar is hard to use. If I start drawing the rectangle in the upper-left corner of the cell, the shape will start in that corner. But if I start drawing a circle in the same spot, the oval I draw will not completely include the text in the cells. Also, why aren't there circle and square shapes? I have a hard time drawing perfectly round circles and perfectly square squares.

Strategy: You can use keyboard keys to make drawing shapes easier.

First, to force an oval to be a perfect circle, you hold down the Shift key while you draw. Using the Shift key will also force a rectangle to be a square and a triangle to be an equilateral triangle (see Figure 1174).

Figure 1174

Use Shift while drawing to make circles and squares.

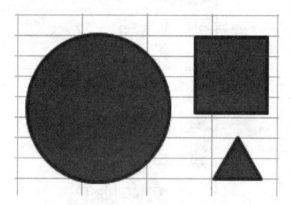

Second, a circle or an oval is hard to draw. In order to draw the circle around a cell, you have to start fairly far outside the cell. How can you know how far above your data to start in order to include all the data? One solution is to hold down the Ctrl key when you draw the oval (or Ctrl+Shift to draw a circle). Then, instead of starting in the left corner, you start directly in the middle of the circle. As you drag outward, the circle will grow.

The other modifying key is the Alt key. A rectangle drawn with the Alt key held down will snap to the cell borders. The rectangle can either be two columns wide or three columns wide, but not 2.5 columns wide when you use the Alt key (see Figure 1175).

Figure 1175

Use Alt to make the edges of the shape align with cell borders.

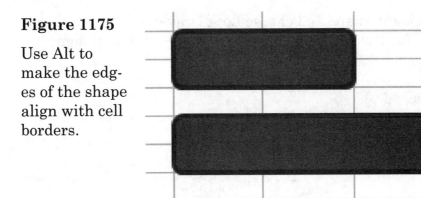

If you want to resize a square, hold down the Shift key while you drag a corner handle. This will force Excel to keep the aspect ratio the same.

Additional Details: If you need to produce many identically sized squares, Ctrl+drag the first square to make an identical copy. You can then Ctrl+click both squares and Ctrl+drag to create four squares.

Summary: Using the Shift key will cause an oval to draw as a circle. Using the Ctrl key will cause an oval to draw outward from the original point. Using the Alt key will cause a shape to fit to a range of cells.

Part
IV

CREATE DOZENS OF LIGHTNING BOLTS

Problem: I need to create multiple shapes. In the old Excel, I could double-click a shape icon and then draw multiple copies of the shape without going back to the menu. In Excel 2007, I can't seem to double-click the lightning bolt in the Shapes menu.

Strategy: Microsoft came up with a solution to this problem, although it is as subtle as the double-click trick in the old Excel.

It helps to draw one shape first, format it, and then right-click and select Set as Default Shape. This will ensure that the new shapes have the same color as this shape. Follow these steps:

1) Select Insert – Shapes dropdown.

2) Right-click any shape and choose Lock Drawing Mode, as shown in Figure 1176. The mouse pointer changes to a thin plus sign.

Figure 1176

Find a shape, right-click, and select Lock Drawing Mode.

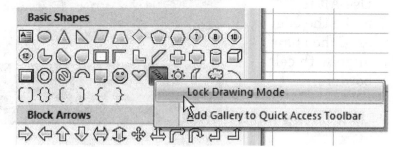

3) To draw a default size shape, click the mouse pointer anywhere on the worksheet. To draw a shape of a different size, click and drag to draw the shape.

4) When you are done drawing shapes, press the Esc key or select another worksheet to exit Drawing mode.

The lighter drawings shown in Figure 1177 are default drawings created with a single click in the upper corner of the shape. The darker drawings required a click and drag to size.

Figure 1177

Shazam!

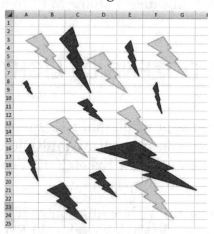

Summary: You can quickly draw many of the same shape by using Drawing mode.

Commands Discussed: Insert – Shapes dropdown

Excel 97-2003: Double-click a shape in the drawing toolbar menus to enter Draw mode.

ROTATE A SHAPE

Problem: How do I rotate a shape?

Strategy: When you select a shape, a green circle appears, as shown in Figure 1178. Grab the green circle, click, and rotate the shape. This is a free rotation; you can rotate the shape in 360 degrees.

Figure 1178

Drag the green handle to rotate the shape.

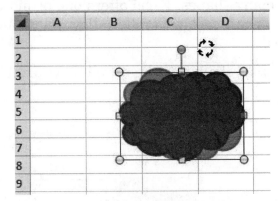

Additional Details: If you need to rotate exactly 90, 180, or 270 degrees, you can use the Rotate dropdown in the Arrange group of the Format ribbon (see Figure 1179).

Figure 1179

Rotate or flip.

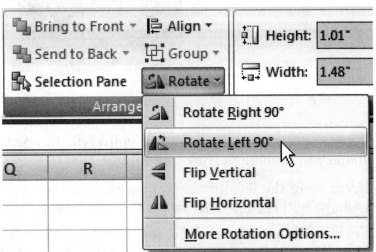

Summary: To rotate a shape, you select and use the green handle to rotate.

Commands Discussed: Format – Rotate dropdown

ALTER THE KEY
INFLECTION POINT IN A SHAPE

Problem: The Shape features a shape that is almost what I want but not quite. Can I adjust one aspect of a shape to be narrower or wider?

Strategy: For many shapes, Excel offers one or more yellow diamond-shaped handles. These yellow handles allow you to adjust the inflection points in shapes.

Figure 1180 shows a shape that has two inflection points.

Figure 1180

Grab a yellow diamond.

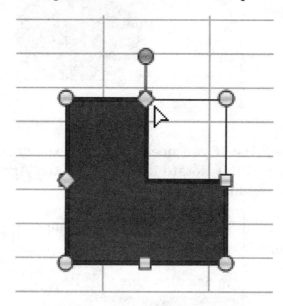

If you can drag the top inflection point left, the vertical portion of the L-shape will become narrow (see Figure 1181).

If you drag the left inflection point down, the horizontal portion of the L-shape will become narrow (see Figure 1182).

Various shapes have different numbers of inflection points. Some inflection points are limited in terms of how far they can be moved.

Summary: You can use the yellow handles on shapes to adjust the inflections and create an infinite variety of shapes.

Figure 1181

Result of moving the top handle left.

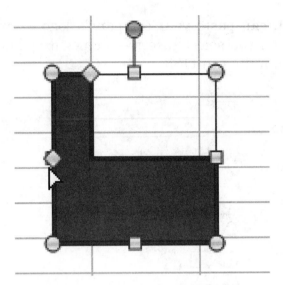

Figure 1182

Result of moving the side handle down.

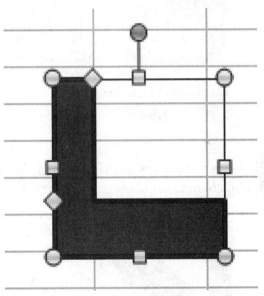

Part
IV

MAKE A LOGO INTO A SHAPE

Problem: I'm looking for a fun way to kill some time while the Internet is down. Can I make my logo into a Shape that can be formatted using the Drawing Tools?

Strategy: You can paste your company's logo or any other logo to a worksheet. Then you select Insert – Shapes dropdown – Lines – Freeform, as shown in Figure 1183.

Figure 1183

Freeform can create straight or curved lines or shapes.

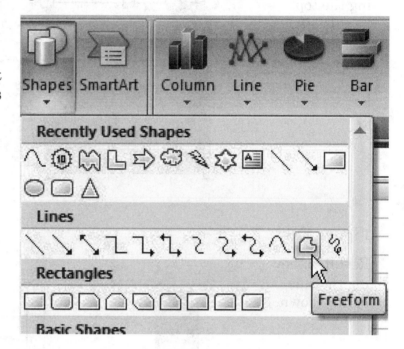

Trace the logo. It is easy to draw straight lines: You start at one corner of the logo, click the corner, as shown in Figure 1184, and then click on the other endpoint.

Figure 1184

To draw a straight line, click once on each endpoint.

If you need to follow a curved path for part of the logo, you should increase the zoom to 200% or more.

You can use the Freeform tool to create a line or a closed shape. To finish a line type drawing, you double-click on the last point. To finish a closed shape, you continue clicking at each corner. When you get back to the original corner of the logo, you click again, and the shape will appear, as shown in Figure 1185.

Figure 1185

Click the starting point again to finish a shape.

Results: You will have a custom shape of your logo that you can move, resize, rotate, or format to your heart's content. Figure 1186 shows my Max logo with a 3-D format applied.

Figure 1186

Apply formatting to the shape.

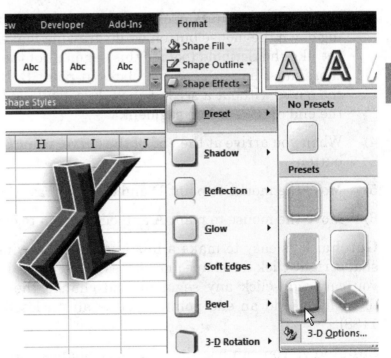

Part IV

Additional Details: To draw a curved line, you can either click frequently along the curve, basically creating a curve from a series of tiny short-line segments, or you can press the left mouse button while you carefully trace the curve. This is a little tricky. To draw the shape in Figure 1187, follow these steps:

Figure 1187

Draw three straight lines and a curve.

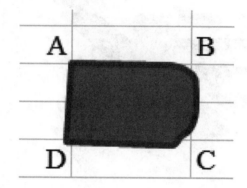

1) Click once at point A.

2) Click once at point B. This finishes the straight line along the top.

3) While still at point B, click again and start to trace the curve. Holding down the mouse button while drawing makes the Freeform tool act like the Scribble tool for this segment of the shape. Notice that there must be two separate clicks at point B. If you start drawing the curve without a second click, Excel will add a random curve to the end of the AB line segment.

4) When you arrive at the end of the curve, point C, release the mouse button.

5) Move the mouse to point D and click to draw the bottom edge.

6) Move the mouse to point A and click again to close the shape.

Gotcha: It is easy to make a mistake while drawing. To fine-tune the shape, right-click the shape and choose Edit Points. In Edit Points mode, you can right-click any segment and change the shape from curved to straight, add an end point, or close an unclosed shape (see Figure 1188).

Summary: You can use the Freeform Shapes feature tool to create a custom shape.

Commands Discussed: Insert – Shapes dropdown – Lines – Freeform

Figure 1188

You can make some rudimentary edits here.

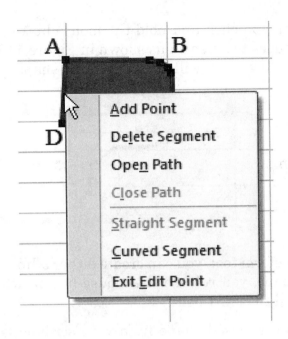

USE THE SCRIBBLE TOOL

Problem: My logo is not an angular logo, like the MrExcel logo. I'm trying to use the technique described in "Make a Logo into a Shape," but I'm having a hard time with all the curves in my logo.

Strategy: To draw a logo that's not angular, you can use the Scribble tool, shown in Figure 1189. You find it by selecting Insert – Shapes dropdown.

Figure 1189

Draw with the Scribble tool.

To use this tool, you click and hold the mouse button to start to draw. The mouse changes to a pencil, as shown in Figure 1190. As long as you hold the mouse down, you will be drawing the shape.

Figure 1190

Draw by holding down the mouse button.

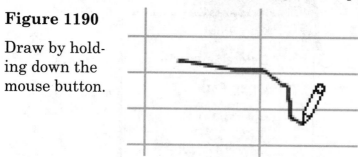

As with the Freeform tool, you can create either a line or a closed shape. To close the shape, you release the mouse button when your drawing line has rejoined the start point.

Excel will create a closed shape from your scribble (see Figure 1191). You can apply color or effects using the Drawing Tools ribbon tab.

Figure 1191

Careful tracing made this shape.

Summary: You can use the Scribble tool under Insert – Shapes dropdown to draw any shape.

Commands Discussed: Insert – Shapes dropdown – Lines – Scribble

ADD TEXT TO ANY CLOSED SHAPE

Problem: How can I add fixed text to a shape?

Strategy: All closed shapes can hold text. To add text to a shape, you simply right-click the shape and choose Edit Text, as shown in Figure 1192.

Figure 1192

Add text to any shape with the Edit Text command.

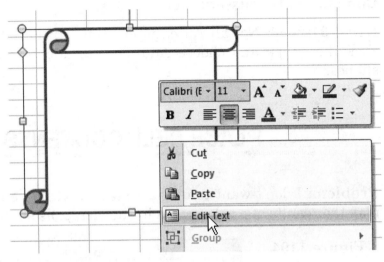

Excel will add a flashing insertion cursor inside the shape. You type your text, pressing Enter when you want to start a new line.

Additional Details: To format the text, you select the characters with the mouse and then move the mouse up and to the right to display the Mini toolbar. You can use the formatting icons on the Mini toolbar to change the font (see Figure 1193).

Part IV

Figure 1193

Select the text and move up and to the right to access the Mini toolbar.

Summary: You can add text to any shape by right-clicking and selecting Edit Text.

Commands Discussed: Edit Text

Excel 97-2003: Not all AutoShapes could initially handle text. Right-click the shape and choose Add Text to add text capability to most shapes.

PLACE CELL CONTENTS IN A SHAPE

Problem: I don't want to use just static text in a shape; I want to display the results of a calculation in the shape, as shown in Figure 1194.

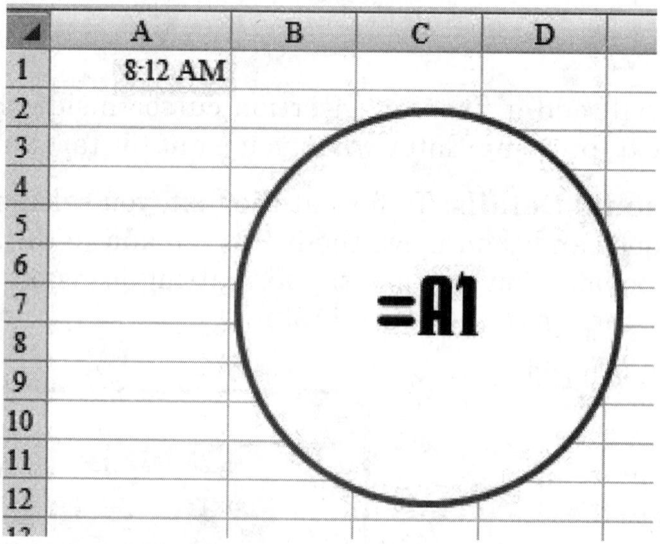

Figure 1194

Can a shape display a value from a cell?

◢	A	B	C	D
1	8:12 AM			
2				
3				
4				
5				
6				
7		=A1		
8				
9				
10				
11				
12				

Strategy: This is possible, although typing the formula in the shape is not the way to do it. Here's how you do it:

1) Select the shape.

2) Click in the formula bar and type =A1. When you press Enter, the value from A1 will appear in the shape,, as shown in Figure 1195.

Figure 1195

Type = and a cell reference in the formula bar.

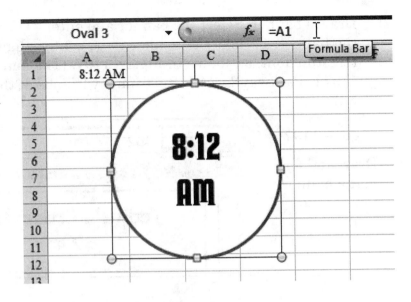

Additional Details: The formula in the formula bar can refer to only a single cell. You cannot enter a formula in the formula bar. However, there is a workaround. Say that you want to display today's order total in a banner at the top of an order entry log. The banner will appear in rows 1 through 4 of the log. Here's what you do:

Part IV

1) Move the banner out of the way and build a formula in cell D2 to hold the text for the banner. The formula might be:

="Today's Order Total:"&CHAR(10)&TEXT(SUM(C8:
C200),"$#,##0")

The CHAR(10) function will add a linefeed in the result if Wrap Text is turned on. Otherwise, you will get an unprintable character symbol, as shown in Figure 1196.

Figure 1196

Build a formula in a cell to concatenate text and a sum.

="Today's Order Total:"&CHAR(10)&TEXT(SUM(C8:C200),"$#,##0")

◢	A	B	C	D	E	F	G
1	XYZ COMPANY						
2	ORDER ENTRY LOG			Today's Order Total:◻$2,495			
3	DATE:	12/1/2008					
4							
5							
6							
7	Order #	Rep	Amount				
8	1901	Joe	174				
9	1902	Mary	244				

2) Draw a banner. Select the banner and enter =D2 as the formula for the banner. Format the banner to be center-aligned and in an interesting font, as shown in Figure 1197. (The font shown in Figure 1197 is ParkwayResortHotel from my friends at the Chank! Foundry.)

Figure 1197

Draw and format a banner.

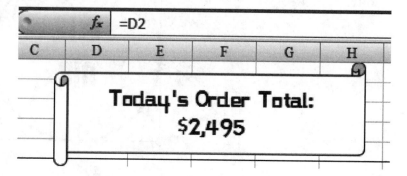

3) Move the banner so that it covers the formula in D2. As new orders are entered in the log, the total will update.

Gotcha: The text in the shape is updated only when the worksheet is calculated.

Additional Details: Say that you add a shape to a chart. If you want the text in the shape to come from a cell, you must precede the cell reference with the sheet name. For example, =Sheet2!D2 will work, but =D2 will not (see Figure 1198).

Figure 1198

When in a chart, use the sheet name in the cell reference.

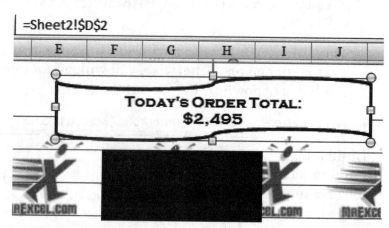

Summary: You can put the results of a formula into a shape.

Functions Discussed: =CHAR(); =TEXT(); =SUM()

ADD CONNECTORS TO JOIN SHAPES

Problem: Is there a way to join two shapes with a connector?

Strategy: In Excel 2007, all lines can be connectors. Follow these steps:

1) Select Insert – Shapes dropdown and choose any of the Lines shapes. When you click for the start or endpoint, hover over an existing shape. Red connector points will appear along each edge of the shape (see Figure 1199). If you start or end a line on a red connection handle, the line will be anchored to the shape.

Figure 1199

The triangle offers six connection points.

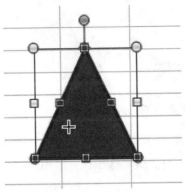

Figure 1200 shows several different types of lines being used as connectors.

Figure 1200

These shapes are joined by various lines used as connectors.

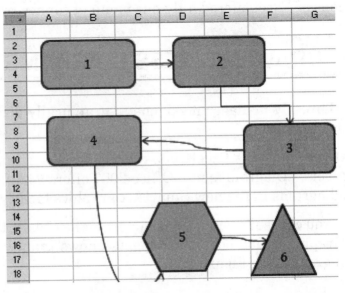

Part IV

If you rearrange the shapes, the lines will continue to connect the shapes (see Figure 1201).

Figure 1201

Rearrange the shapes, and the connectors stay in place.

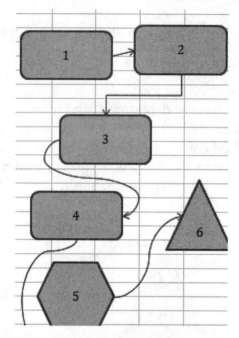

Summary: To connect two shapes, you can attach a line to one of the red connection points.

Commands Discussed: Insert – Shapes dropdown – Lines

Excel 97-2003: Normal lines could not be used as connectors. Previous versions of Excel offered a fly-out menu of connectors.

DRAW BUSINESS DIAGRAMS WITH EXCEL

Problem: My manager needs me to graphically document the steps in a project plan.

Strategy: Whereas Excel 2003 offered 5 types of business diagrams on the Insert – Diagram menu, Office 2007 offers 84 different types of business diagrams in the new SmartArt graphics facility.

When you choose Insert – SmartArt from the ribbon, the Choose a Smart-Art Graphic dialog box that appears shows graphic types arranged in seven groups (see Figure 1202):

Figure 1202

Choose a graphic type from the seven groups.

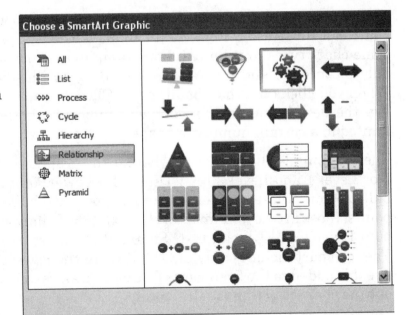

Type	Description
List	You can use these charts to illustrate a series of items. Although a list has a certain sequence, there are usually not arrows to indicate that the list contains a series of steps.
Process	Process charts are similar to list charts, but the shapes are connected by arrows or the shapes themselves are arrows.
Cycle	Cycle charts are process charts where the last step in the process has an arrow pointing back to the first step in the process. These are great for illustrating continuous improvement.
Hierarchy	Hierarchy charts are used for organizational charts and as outlines for books or projects.
Relationship	This category is a catchall for 31 different types. It offers formula diagrams, gear charts, funnel charts, balance charts, containment charts, Venn diagrams, and more. If you need to illustrate competing ideas, turn to this category.
Matrix	This category offers charts with four quadrants or four quadrants and a title.
Pyramid	This category offers shapes stacked in either an upright or an inverted pyramid.

Part
IV

Most SmartArt chart types offer an unlimited number of shapes. A list chart can illustrate 3 items or 17 items without a problem. However, some chart types are limited. For example, a gear chart can illustrate only 3 concepts, and several arrow charts can illustrate only 2 items. When you click on a thumbnail in the Choose a SmartArt Graphic dialog, the description on the right will indicate whether the graphic is limited to a certain number of shapes.

The thumbnails often indicate whether the graphic is suitable for Level 1 or Level 1 and Level 2 text. Think of a PowerPoint slide. If you have bullet points, those are Level 1 text. If you have bullets and sub-bullet points, those are Level 1 and Level 2 text. Some charts don't do well with both Level 1 and Level 2 text. Figure 1203 shows a Block Cycle chart. The top chart includes only Level 1 text. In the lower chart, some Level 2 text is added to the first point. This causes all the Level 1 text throughout the chart to get unusually small.

Figure 1203

The Block Cycle chart looks best with only Level 1 text.

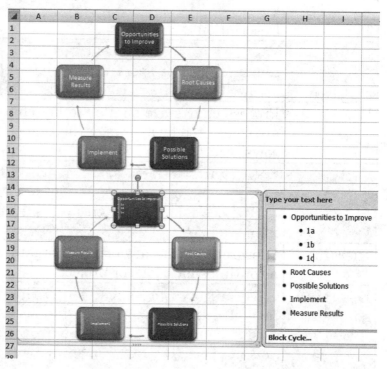

In contrast, the Vertical Box List chart is designed with accent boxes to hold long sentences of Level 2 text (see Figure 1204).

The next eleven topics discuss how to create and modify SmartArt graphics.

Figure 1204

The Vertical Box List chart offers ample room for Level 2 text.

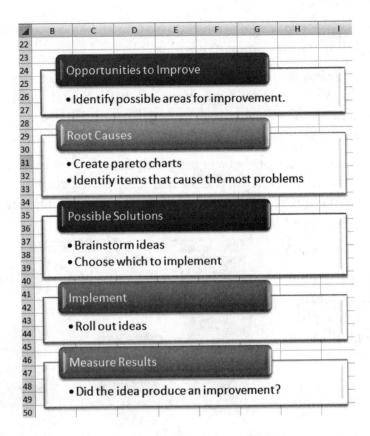

Summary: The SmartArt engine is a significant new feature in Office 2007. The previous collection of 5 business diagram types has grown into 84 different types.

Commands Discussed: Insert – SmartArt

Excel 97-2003: Insert – Diagram

CHOOSE THE RIGHT TYPE OF SMARTART

Problem: I need to illustrate a circular process in which information can flow in both directions. Which SmartArt type should I use?

Strategy: You should use the Multi-directional Cycle chart. This is the only 1 of the 84 chart types that offers bidirectional arrows between the blocks. This chart type is the sixth thumbnail in the Cycle category.

Part
IV

Some other types of charts require you to select certain SmartArt types. The following are some examples.

To accommodate extremely long sentences of Level 2 text, your choices are the Vertical Box List, Vertical Bullet List, and Vertical Chevron List charts. These are the 3rd, 4th, and 16th thumbnails in the List category.

To make a decision between two choices, use a Balance chart, which is the first thumbnail in the Relationship category. As shown in Figure 1205, this clever type will lean left or right, depending on which choice has more Level 2 items.

Figure 1205

The Balance chart leans left or right, depending on content.

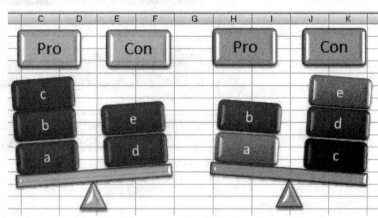

To show how parts add together to produce an output, you use an Equation chart or a Funnel chart. In Figure 1206, the Vertical Equation chart in the lower left seems unbalanced; the resulting circle is much larger than the input circles.

Figure 1206

The Funnel chart at the lower right is limited to three items and a result.

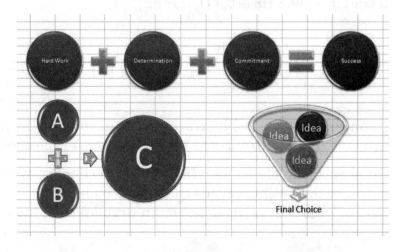

To illustrate two opposing forces, you use Diverging Arrows, Counterbalance Arrows, Opposing Arrows, Converging Arrows, and Arrow Ribbon charts. These are found in the first two rows of the Relationship category.

Many process charts can be used to illustrate a single process that progresses from left to right or top to bottom. However, to illustrate many vertical processes in the same diagram, you use the Chevron List chart, which is the 11th thumbnail in the Process category.

Some of the process charts will snake through rows and columns. If you have many shapes to fit in a small area, check out the Basic Bending Process, Circular Bending Process, Repeating Bending Process, and Vertical Bending Process charts. Figure 1207 shows 16 shapes in a Circular Bending Process chart. This chart has been rendered in the Brick Scene style.

Figure 1207

The bending layouts can fit many shapes in a small space.

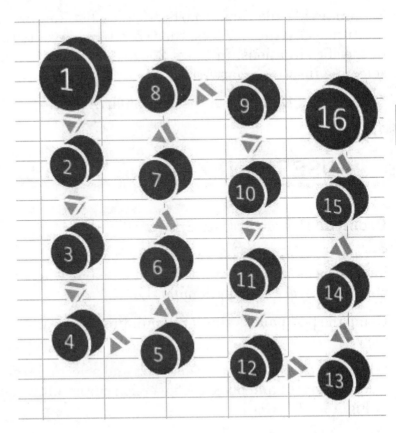

Part
IV

Microsoft attempted to allow rudimentary containment charts in Smart-Art graphics. If you need to draw a very basic containment chart, you can use either the Nested Target or Stacked Venn layouts. Figure 1208 shows a simple containment chart created from the Nested Target layout.

Figure 1208

SmartArt can handle very rudimentary containment charts.

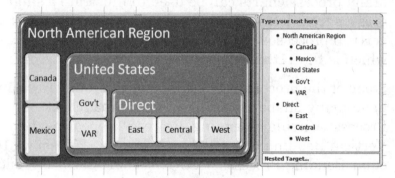

Summary: While some charts, such as list and process charts, offer a multitude of layout choices, there are some layouts that are well suited to specific situations. In Excel 2007, you can access dozens of charts by selecting Insert – SmartArt.

Commands Discussed: Insert – SmartArt

USE THE TEXT PANE TO BUILD SMARTART

Problem: How do I create SmartArt?

Strategy: Initially, you shouldn't worry about the graphics but should instead focus your attention on the text pane, where you can build bullet points of Level 1 and, optionally, Level 2 text.

Using the text pane is similar to building a slide in PowerPoint's Outline view.

When you choose Insert – SmartArt and select a layout, Excel will draw a default layout and place the insertion cursor in the text pane, as shown in Figure 1209.

Figure 1209

SmartArt starts out with bullet points that show [Text].

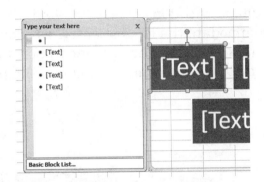

You can use these keys to navigate in the text pane:

Enter	Add a new shape at the same level as the current shape and immediately after the current shape.
Down Arrow	Move to the next shape without creating a new shape.
Tab	Demote the current shape one level. Pressing Tab on a Level 1 entry will change the entry to Level 2.
Shift+Tab	Promote the current shape one level. Pressing Shift+Tab on a Level 2 entry will change the entry to Level 1.
Delete	Pressing Delete when there is no text for a shape will delete the shape.

Initially, you should focus all your attention on the text pane. As you type in the text pane, Excel will continue to render new shapes in the SmartArt graphic.

Additional Details: In most of the SmartArt layouts, Excel will ensure that every shape is the same size and that every shape has the same font size. This works best when you have similar-length text in each shape. For example, in Figure 1210, each shape contains a single word or concept. The font sizes are fairly large.

Figure 1210

With similar length points, the fonts are fairly large.

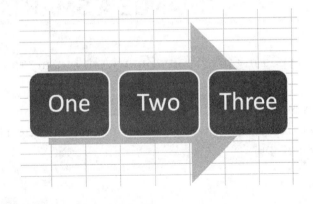

Part IV

If you add a new shape with longer text, the font size in all the shapes will reduce to accommodate the longest entry, as shown in Figure 1211. You can override this by using the Format ribbon tab as described in "Switch to the Format Tab to Format Individual Shapes" on page 803.

Figure 1211

Add a longer entry, and all the font sizes reduce.

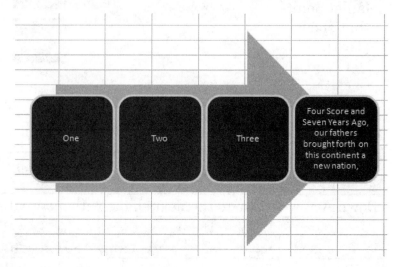

The text pane supports spell checking, formatting with the mini toolbar, and Cut and Paste.

Alternate Strategy: It is possible to edit text directly in each shape. To do so, you hide the text pane and use the Add Shape menu on the Design tab in order to build your graphic.

Summary: It is easiest to build SmartArt graphics in the text pane.

Commands Discussed: Insert – SmartArt

CHANGE A SMARTART LAYOUT

Problem: I typed my text in my SmartArt, but my manager doesn't like the layout.

Strategy: You can easily convert a SmartArt graphic from one style to any other style by using the Layouts gallery on the Design ribbon tab. Follow these steps:

1) Select the SmartArt graphic. Excel will display the SmartArt Tools ribbon tabs.

2) From the Design tab, select the Layouts gallery. It initially shows four other layouts besides the one you used, as shown in Figure 1212. Click the bottom arrow to open the gallery.

Figure 1212

Click the More arrow to open the gallery.

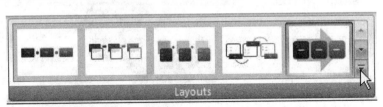

3) Initially, the Layouts gallery shows only the layouts from the same category as your existing graphic. To choose from the complete set of layouts, choose the More Layouts option. (see Figure 1213).

Figure 1213

You see more layouts, but not all 84 of them.

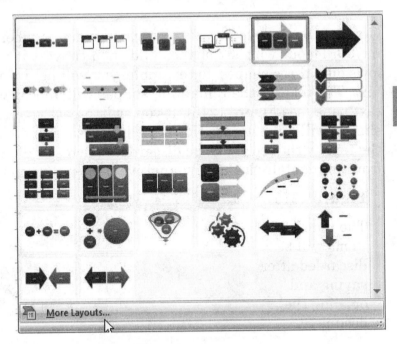

Part
IV

4) Choose the All category and then choose a new layout.

Results: Your existing message will be presented in a completely new SmartArt layout (see Figure 1214).

Figure 1214

New layout, same words.

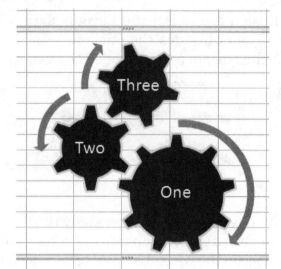

Gotcha: Some layouts allow only a certain number of shapes. If you have a layout with six shapes and then convert it to a layout that allows only three shapes, for example, you will not initially lose the extra text. The text for the remaining shapes will appear with a red X in the text pane (see Figure 1215). If you switch back to another layout, these shapes will be restored. However, if you save and close the document, the text by the red X will be discarded. Microsoft did this to prevent you from accidentally including sensitive hidden data in the graphic.

Figure 1215

The red X items will be discarded after saving and opening the document.

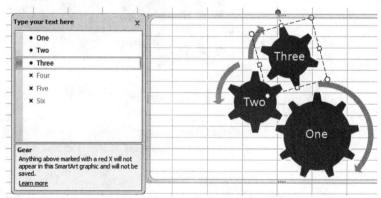

Summary: After you have written the content for a graphic, you can easily convert the SmartArt to a new layout.

Commands Discussed: Design – Layouts

FINALIZE A SMARTART LAYOUT
BEFORE ADDING PICTURES

Problem: I am using one of the SmartArt layouts that include accent photographs. When I change to a new layout, even a layout that includes picture placeholders, my pictures are lost.

Strategy: This is a bug. Or maybe a feature. But the bottom line is that pictures are lost when you change from one layout to another.

Nine SmartArt layouts offer a picture for each Level 1 item: Bending Picture Accent List, Picture Caption List, Horizontal Picture List, Picture Accent List, Continuous Picture List, Vertical Picture Accent List, Vertical Picture List, Picture Accent Process, or Radial List. When you use any of them, a picture placeholder appears for each Level 1 item as shown in Figure 1216.

Figure 1216

Nine styles offer picture placeholders.

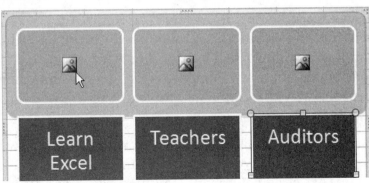

Part IV

To load a picture, you click the picture icon in the SmartArt. Excel will allow you to browse for a picture.

Figure 1217 shows the graphic with pictures loaded.

Figure 1217

The picture layouts range from small accents to larger pictures.

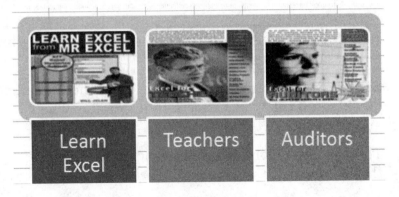

If you convert this SmartArt to a new layout, even if the new layout has pictures, your pictures are lost (see Figure 1218). If you then go back to the original layout before you save and close the document, the pictures will come back. **Gotcha:** These hidden pictures are not saved with the document, so if you save and reopen the file before returning to your original SmartArt layout, the images are lost.

Figure 1218

Switch to another layout with picture placeholders, and your pictures will be lost.

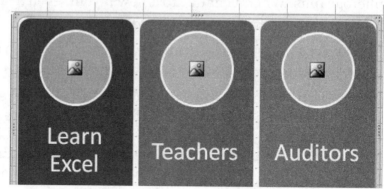

I was working on the Leveraging SmartArt e-book for Que Publishing when I discovered this problem. My technical editor was a Microsoft employee who worked on the SmartArt team. He initially thought this was a bug, but after doing research, he said that there are fairly complex reasons why this happens and that the behavior occurs by design. So it is a feature.

Summary: Excel 2007 loses picture information when you change to a new SmartArt layout. You need to make sure you are happy with the SmartArt style before you load pictures in the style.

Commands Discussed: Insert – SmartArt

FORMAT SMARTART

Problem: SmartArt always starts out as a boring blue diagram. What formatting options are available?

Strategy: You can use two galleries on the Design tab of the ribbon to quickly add color and effects to a graphic: The Change Colors gallery and the SmartArt Styles gallery.

The Change Colors dropdown, shown in Figure 1219, offers more than three dozen color styles. The Colorful row offers five combinations of the six accent colors in the current theme. The Primary Theme Colors offer two light style and one dark basic style. The remaining six rows offer variations on each of the six accent colors.

Figure 1219

Add color to SmartArt by using the Colorful row choices.

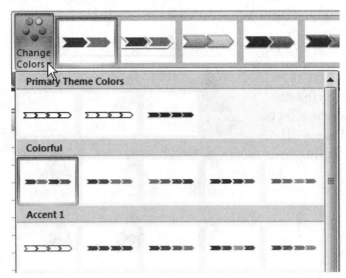

Gotcha: Each of the accent rows offer Outline, Colored Fill, Gradient Range, Gradient Loop, and Transparent Gradient Range columns. Of these five columns, only the first two seem to make any sense. For example, Figure 1220 shows five horizontal SmartArt graphics. Each row is formatted with a different accent color scheme. The Outline and Fill graphics look okay. In the third row, the Gradient Range graphic goes from dark to light, making it appear as if the company will be fading away by the final shape. In the fourth row, the Gradient Loop graphic is worse. Shapes alternate from dark to medium to light to medium to dark. This makes me think that somehow the 2006 and 2008 shapes are supposed to be related. In the fifth row, the Transparent Gradient Range graphic suffers the same problem as in row 3.

Figure 1220

In my opinion, only Outline and Colored Fill graphics look okay.

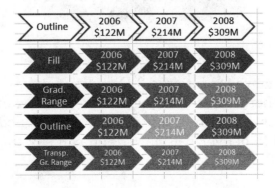

Additional Details: You can easily add effects by choosing one of the 14 styles from the SmartArt Styles gallery. As shown in Figure 1221, the first five styles are 2-D styles and labeled as "Best Match for Document." The remaining nine styles are 3-D styles.

Figure 1221

The first few 3-D styles create nice effects and are still readable.

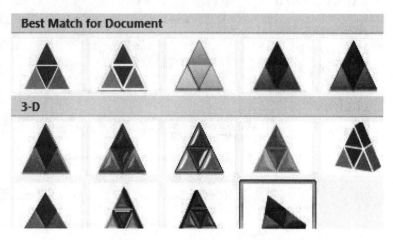

The 14 graphics in Figure 1222 demonstrate the styles available. I use the second 3-D style most of the time. It creates a nice effect but is still readable.

Figure 1222

Examples of the 14 layouts.

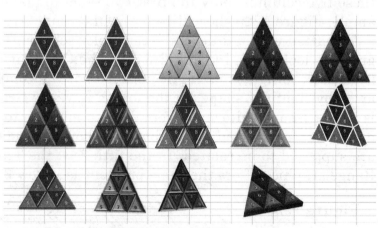

Gotcha: If you move far into the 3-D styles, many of them are unreadable. Perhaps Microsoft is doing us a favor. For example, perhaps the ninth style, known as Birds Eye Scene, is designed for messages in which you need to deliver bad news. You can say that you showed the information, but no one will really be able to read it. Figure 1223 shows the original message and the message rendered in Birds Eye Scene.

Figure 1223

Apply a little Birds Eye Scene to messages you don't want anyone to read.

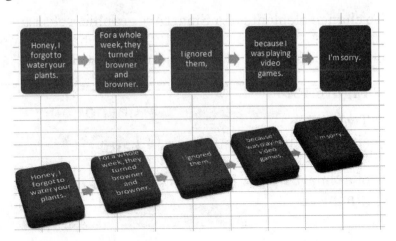

Additional Details: If you change the theme on the Page Layout tab, you will have new colors available in the Colorful row, but you will also inherit new effects that change the options available in the SmartArt Styles gallery. If you only want new colors, you can use the Colors dropdown on the Page Layout tab instead.

Summary: You can use the Change Colors and SmartArt Styles galleries on the Design tab to quickly format SmartArt graphics.

Commands Discussed: Design – Change Colors; Design – SmartArt Styles

Part
IV

SWITCH TO THE FORMAT TAB
TO FORMAT INDIVIDUAL SHAPES

Problem: Birds Eye Scene style notwithstanding (see Figure 1223 above), I've found that most SmartArt formatted using the Design ribbon looks good. Fonts remain consistent throughout. Shapes have similar effects. While giving Microsoft control over font size will usually create a suitable graphic, sometimes I need to tweak the font used within one shape.

Strategy: All the tools on the Format tab of the ribbon will allow you to change elements of a SmartArt graphic.

To change elements of a SmartArt graphic, select a single shape in your graphic. As shown in Figure 1224, the Shapes group will allow you to change the shape or size of the individual shape.

Figure 1224

Tweak the size or shape of one element of a SmartArt graphic.

With a single shape selected, you can use any of the tools in the Shape Styles group to change the shape formatting. You can use any of the tools in the WordArt Styles gallery to add effects to the text. You can use any of the formatting tools in the Home tab of the ribbon to change font or size.

Gotcha: When you change shapes on the Format tab, Microsoft will often quit updating font sizes in response to text changes. You should get your graphic as close to finished using the Design tab before moving to the Format tab.

Additional Details: If you find yourself making many changes on the Format tab, you will lose the continuity of the graphic. The graphic in Figure 1225 shows some of the many changes possible with the Format tab.

Figure 1225

If you are not careful with the Format tab, chaos results.

In this figure, each shape was changed using the Change Shape menu. The second shape was made larger, and the font size was increased on the Home tab. The Text Effects glow setting was used to apply a glow to text in the third shape. The green rotation handle was used to rotate the third shape. WordArt Styles – Text Effects – Transform was used on the text in the fourth shape, and Shape Styles – Shape Effects – Reflection was used to add a reflection. In the first shape, a preset from the Shape Effects dropdown was used.

Summary: Although it is not recommended, you can use the Format tab to tweak many aspects of an individual shape.

Commands Discussed: Format – Change Shape; Format – Larger; Format – Shape Effects; Format – Text Effects; WordArt Styles – Text Effects – Transform; Shape Styles – Shape Effects – Reflection

See Also: "Format SmartArt" (p. 800)

DON'T CONVERT ANOTHER LAYOUT
TO CREATE AN ORGANIZATION CHART

Part
IV

Problem: SmartArt offers an Organization Chart layout. This style has certain shapes that are unlike other layouts. If I convert a hierarchy chart to an org chart, I can't seem to get the assistant shape to work correctly.

Strategy: If you are creating an org chart, you should create the Smart-Art from scratch. To make the job easier, you can copy and paste text from an existing hierarchy chart to the new org chart.

Follow these steps to create an organization chart:

1) Select Insert – SmartArt. In the Hierarchy category, choose the first thumbnail. As noted in the dialog, this layout offers the assistant shape as well as left-hanging and right-hanging layouts. As shown in Figure 1226, the second entry in the text pane is an assistant. If you press Enter while the mouse pointer is on the Assistant shape, you will create a second assistant at the same level.

Figure 1226

The assistant shape is unique to organization charts.

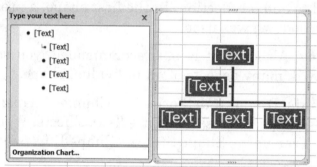

2) You will usually encounter more levels in an organization chart than in other SmartArt. It is not unusual to have Level 3 text, Level 4 text, and so on. You use the Tab key to demote an entry and the Shift+Tab key to promote an entry.

3) Build the rest of the chart and then add assistants for the lower levels. To add an assistant to the CFO, select the CFO shape and choose Add Shape – Add Assistant (see Figure 1227).

Figure 1227

Use the Add Shape menu to add assistants throughout the chart.

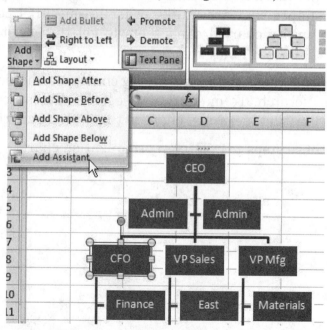

4)   For vertical layouts, choose Left Hanging, Right Hanging, or Both from the Layout dropdown on the Design tab. For example, select the CFO box and then choose Left Hanging, select the VP Sales box and choose Both, and select the VP Mfg box and choose Right Hanging (see Figure 1228).

Figure 1228

Control the shape of subordinate chains by using the Layout menu.

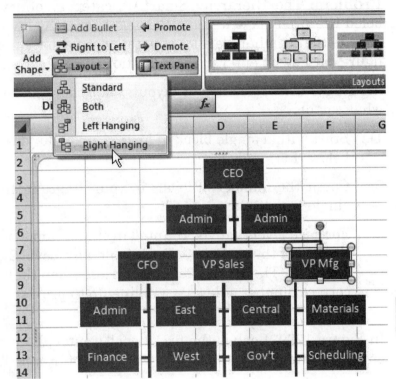

Summary: You can use SmartArt to easily create organization charts. It is better to create this layout from scratch than to convert from another layout.

Commands Discussed: Insert – SmartArt; Add Shape – Add Assistant; Design – Layout dropdown

Part
IV

HOW DO THE LABELED HIERARCHY SMARTART GRAPHICS WORK?

Problem: The Hierarchy SmartArt category offers a Horizontal Labeled Hierarchy layout and a Labeled Hierarchy layout. These look like layouts that can handle a lot of detailed information. However, I cannot figure out how to enter the information in the text pane.

Strategy: These are useful layouts, but their setup is bizarre. Here's what you do:

1) Start with a single block of Level 1 text. Build the entire hierarchy below this single block.

2) Count the number of levels in your diagram. Include the original single Level 1 as one level.

3) For each level that you counted in step 2, add a new Level 1 entry at the end of the text pane. Do not add any Level 2 text to these Level 1 entries. These final Level 1 entries, when they exactly match the correct number of levels, will line up to provide labels for each level.

In Figure 1229, Book is the first Level 1 entry. Four additional Level 1 entries create the headings Top, Part, Chapter, and Topic.

Figure 1229

Add lone Level 1 entries for each level's heading at the end of the diagram.

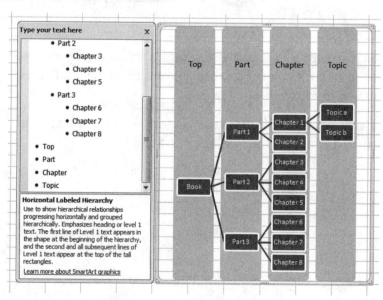

Gotcha: If you have too many Level 1 text entries at the end, the headings and color bars won't line up with the other shapes. If you add Level 2 text to any of the final Level 1 shapes, Excel will try to add it as a heading (see Figure 1230).

Figure 1230

If the level 1 text at the end of the diagram doesn't match the number of levels, the whole diagram is off kilter.

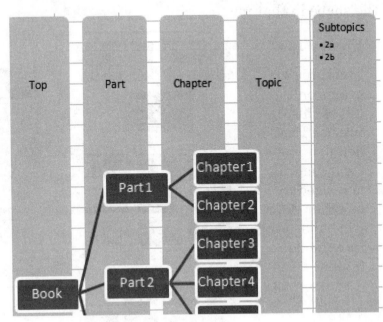

Summary: The Labeled Hierarchy charts are cool, but you have to understand how to set up the text pane in order for them to render correctly.

HOW DOES EXCEL DECIDE HOW MANY SHAPES PER ROW?

Problem: In many of the layouts, Excel seems to have a mind of its own in determining how many shapes per row. Can I force Excel to start a new row?

Strategy: Microsoft takes a simple mathematical approach (involving squares of numbers) to the layout, but you can override Microsoft's rules by changing the aspect ratio of the SmartArt.

Microsoft will try to keep SmartArt in a 4:3 aspect ratio. Because the square of 2 is 4, if you have a diagram with 2 through 4 shapes, they will be arranged with 2 shapes per row. The top of Figure 1231 shows a diagram with 3 shapes. Because the final row is incomplete, Excel centers the shape in that row.

Figure 1231

The three diagrams on the left of this figure use Excel's default. The right diagram is resized to be taller than wide to override the defaults.

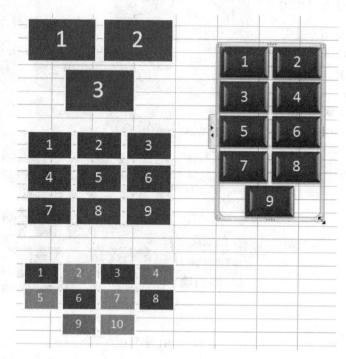

The square of 3 is 9, so if you have a diagram with 5 through 9 shapes, Excel will place 3 shapes per row.

The square of 4 is 16, so a diagram with 10 through 16 shapes will have 4 shapes per row.

This logic continues. For example, because the square of 25 is 625, a diagram with 600 shapes will have 25 shapes per row.

You can override Excel's rules: You simply use the resize handle to change the shape of the SmartArt. In the right diagram in Figure 1231, you use the lower-right corner resize handle to make the shape taller and narrower. Excel will respond by changing the diagram so it has two shapes per row.

Summary: If you change the aspect ratio of the bounding box for your SmartArt diagram, you can override the default arrangement.

ADD NEW SMARTART LAYOUTS

Problem: Excel offers 84 different SmartArt layouts, but sometimes none of them are exactly what I need. I may need circles instead of rounded rectangles, or I might want to replace the arrow connectors with dots.

Strategy: If you are willing to edit a few XML files, you can create your own SmartArt layouts. I am sure that various companies will start selling custom SmartArt layouts, although as of press time, not many have shown up on the market.

A custom SmartArt layout consists of a file with a .glox extension. To install this on your computer, you copy the file to the %AppData%\Microsoft\Templates\SmartArt Graphics\ folder. If you have Office 2007 installed, you already have the Microsoft\Templates folder available, but you might have to manually add the SmartArt Graphics folder.

After you copy the .glox file to the folder, you close and then restart Excel. When you create a SmartArt diagram, your custom layout will appear in the All category. The top-left thumbnail in Figure 1232 is for a custom layout.

Part IV

Figure 1232

By editing some XML, you can create custom layouts.

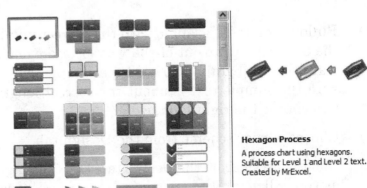

Hexagon Process

A process chart using hexagons. Suitable for Level 1 and Level 2 text. Created by MrExcel.

Additional Details: The process of building a custom layout requires several pages. If you are interested, check out Chapter 9 of Leveraging SmartArt, an e-book available from Que Publishing (ISBN 978-0-7686-6836-0; see www.quepublishing.com).

Summary: You can create new SmartArt layouts.

USE CELL VALUES AS THE SOURCE FOR SMARTART CONTENT

Problem: As discussed in "Place Cell Contents in a Shape" on page 784, Excel has been able to use values from an Excel cell as the source for text boxes on AutoShapes for over a decade. It would be obvious to anyone that the best use of SmartArt would be to populate the text pane with cell references. However, nothing I try allows me to specify cell A1 as the source in the text pane. What's going on?

Strategy: Amazingly, Microsoft did not hook up this feature in Excel 2007! It was obvious to you, and it was obvious to me, but Microsoft didn't think to include it in Excel 2007.

From Microsoft's point of view, SmartArt is primarily a PowerPoint feature that is also available in Word and Excel. Heck, in PowerPoint, Microsoft even made the Convert Any Text to SmartArt functionality. But because PowerPoint doesn't offer cells and formulas, it was not a priority to enable this feature in Excel. Luckily, I have a workaround.

Follow these steps to build a SmartArt graphic that is tied to cell values:

1) Build a SmartArt graphic with the correct number of shapes. Place the SmartArt in an out-of-the-way location; don't place it where you want the final graphic to be. Type sample text in the shapes. Make sure the sample text is about the correct length so that Microsoft will choose the right font size.

2) Choose a color scheme from the Design tab.

3) Choose a style from the Design tab. Get the diagram looking exactly as you will want it to appear, as shown in Figure 1233. (After steps 4 and 5, Excel will stop automatically formatting the SmartArt.)

4) Click on one shape within the SmartArt to select just that shape.

5) Press Ctrl+A to add all shapes to the selection.

Figure 1233

Build and format SmartArt with sample text of about the correct length.

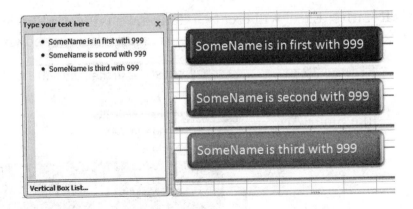

6) Press Ctrl+C to copy all of shapes to the Clipboard.

7) Click in a blank cell outside the SmartArt diagram.

8) Press Ctrl+V. Excel will paste a collection of shapes that look exactly like the original SmartArt diagram. However, this diagram is no longer SmartArt; it has been converted to shapes.

9) While the entire collection of shapes is selected, drag it into the proper location.

10) Delete the original SmartArt graphic.

11) Click on the first shape and look in the Name box to the left of the formula bar. If you see a name like Group 9, you know that Excel has grouped multiple shapes together. From the Drawing Tools Format tab, choose Group – Ungroup.

12) Click on the words in the first shape. You should see a name such as Rounded Rectangle 5.

13) Click in the formula bar. Type a formula such as =J28 and press Enter. You should see the text from J28 appear in the shape.

14) Repeat steps 11 through 13 for the additional shapes.

15) Select Home – Find & Select – Select Objects. Drag a rectangle around the collection of shapes to reselect them all. You need to exit Select Objects mode, so reselect Home – Find & Select – Select Objects.

16) From the Drawing Tools Format tab, choose Group – Group in order to group all the objects into a single unit again.

Part IV

Results: Excel will create a diagram that looks like SmartArt that will get the values from formula in cells J28:J30, as shown in Figure 1234.

Figure 1234

This looks like SmartArt but is really shapes.

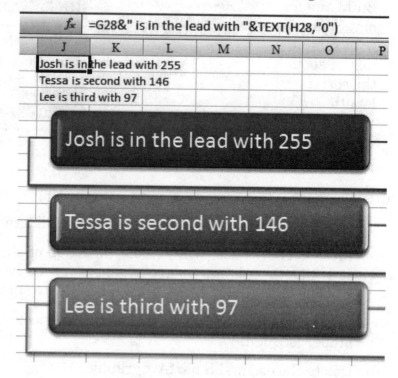

Summary: In order to use cell values in SmartArt, you need to convert the SmartArt to regular shapes.

Commands Discussed: Insert – SmartArt; Home – Find & Select – Select Objects.

CHANGE THE BACKGROUND OF A WORKSHEET

Problem: Excel looks boring. It generally has black text on a white background, with gray lines. Can I change the background of a worksheet to liven it up?

Strategy: If you have an opening menu worksheet in your workbook, you can change the background to any picture. You start by selecting

Page Layout – Background. Excel will let you browse for any image on your computer. The image will be tiled to form the background, as shown in Figure 1235.

Figure 1235

Excel will use the picture you select as a background.

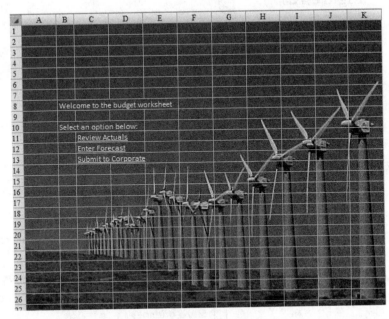

To present a cleaner view, you can turn off the gridlines for the worksheet. The Show/Hide group on the View tab allows you to turn off the gridlines, the formula bar, and the row/column headings (see Figure 1236).

Part IV

Figure 1236

Turn off gridlines and other elements on the View tab.

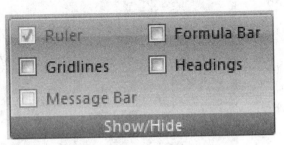

You can control other worksheet elements in the Excel Options dialog. From the Office Icon menu, you choose Excel Options. In the Advanced Category of the Excel Options dialog, you scroll down to Display

Options for This Workbook. You can turn off the display of sheet tabs and the scrollbars (see Figure 1237).

Figure 1237

Turn off scroll-
bars in the
Excel Options
dialog.

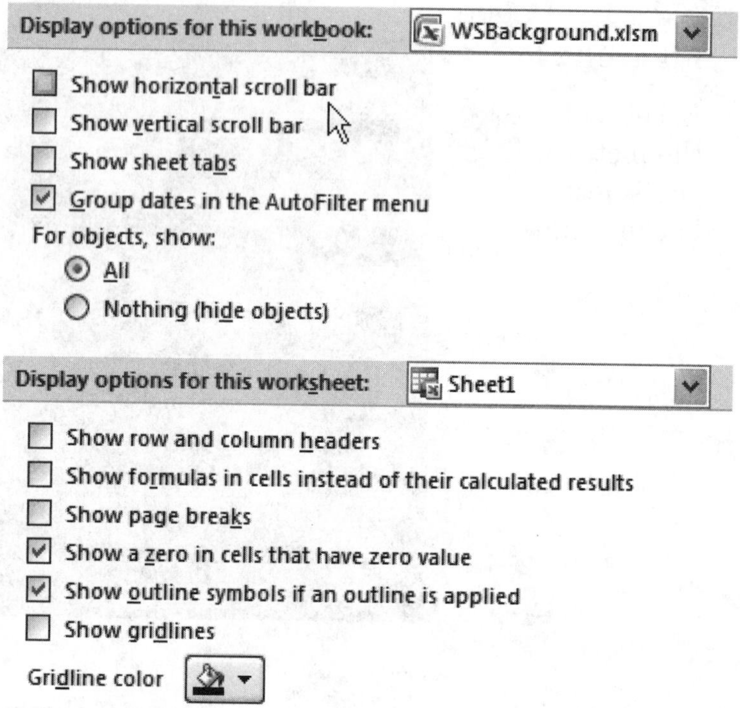

Display options for this workbook: WSBackground.xlsm

☐ Show horizontal scroll bar
☐ Show vertical scroll bar
☐ Show sheet tabs
☑ Group dates in the AutoFilter menu
For objects, show:
    ◉ All
    ○ Nothing (hide objects)

Display options for this worksheet: Sheet1

☐ Show row and column headers
☐ Show formulas in cells instead of their calculated results
☐ Show page breaks
☑ Show a zero in cells that have zero value
☑ Show outline symbols if an outline is applied
☐ Show gridlines

Gridline color

Your worksheet will now look cleaner, as shown in Figure 1238.

Figure 1238

This doesn't
appear in-
timidating to
people who
are not Excel
savvy.

Gotcha: Turning off all the scrollbar and sheet tab options will affect the entire workbook. Because someone will have to enter data on the other worksheets, this might make it difficult to actually use Excel when an Excel rookie moves on to the other worksheets in the workbook.

Gotcha: The background will never print. See "Add a Printable Background to a Worksheet" on page 817 to find out how to create a background that will print.

Additional Details: In order to change the background image on a worksheet, you must first remove the first image by selecting Page Layout – Delete Picture.

Summary: You can make Excel look less sterile by adding a background image to a worksheet.

Commands Discussed: Page Layout – Background; View – Gridlines; View – Formula Bar; View – Headings; Office Icon – Excel Options; Page Layout – Delete Background

Excel 97-2003: Format – Sheet – Background; Format – Sheet – Remove – Background; Tools – Options – View; View – Status Bar; View – Formula Bar

See Also: "Add a Printable Background to a Worksheet" below.

Part
IV

ADD A PRINTABLE BACKGROUND TO A WORKSHEET

Problem: The image I added as a background by using Page Layout – Background will not print (see "Change the Background of a Worksheet" on page 814. How do I add a background image that will print?

Strategy: You can add a shape to cover the printable area of your worksheet and then change the shape fill to be your picture. Microsoft allows you to alter the transparency of the shape. Follow these steps:

1) Choose Insert – Shapes dropdown – Rectangle. Draw a rectangle to cover your print area.

2) Select Drawing Tools Format – Shape Outline – No Outline.

3) Right-click the shape and choose Format Shape. Excel displays the Format Shape dialog.

4) In the Fill category, choose Picture or Texture Fill.

5) In the Insert From section, click the File button. Browse, select a picture, and click Insert.

6) At the bottom of the Format Picture dialog, increase the Transparency slider. You can preview the picture transparency as you slide. Around 60% seems to be appropriate. Figure 1239 shows the worksheet at 60% behind the dialog.

Figure 1239

When you use fill for a shape, you can adjust picture transparency.

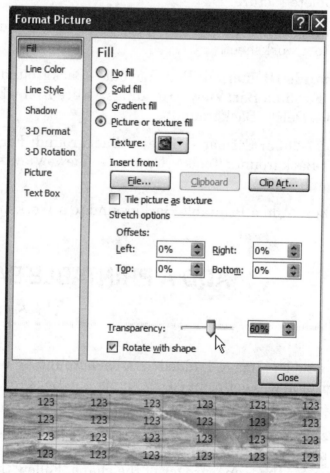

7) Click Close to dismiss the Format Picture dialog box.

Results: Excel will add a background that can be printed.

Gotcha: It is now difficult to select a cell with the mouse. If you click on a cell that is covered by the transparent picture, you will select the picture. To avoid this, you click outside the picture and then use the arrow keys to navigate to cells behind the picture.

Summary: By using a shape with a fill, you can add a semi-transparent background behind your spreadsheet that will print.

Commands Discussed: Insert – Shapes dropdown – Rectangle; Drawing Tools Format – Shape Outline – No Outline; Format Shape

Excel 97-2003: Draw an AutoShape to cover the print area. Right-click and select Format. In the Colors and Lines tab, open the Color dropdown and choose Fill Effects. Choose the Picture tab of Fill Effects. Choose a picture. In the Format AutoShape dialog, change the Transparency slider under the Color tab.

See Also: "Change the Background of a Worksheet" on page 814.

REMOVE HYPERLINKS AUTOMATICALLY INSERTED BY EXCEL

Problem: Excel has an annoying habit. Whenever you type something in a cell that looks like an e-mail address or a Web site URL, Excel will underline the value, change the font color to blue, and make it a clickable hyperlink, as shown in Figure 1240.

Figure 1240

Excel will automatically create hyperlinks.

◢	A	B	C	D	E	F
1	Submitting to Corporate					
2						
3	After you have completed both worksheets, be sure to					
4	check that the budget is within your target for the year.					
5						
6	Print this file for your records.					
7	Zip and e-mail the file to:					
8	budget@MrExcel.com					
9						
10						
11						

Strategy: To remove a hyperlink, you right-click the cell and choose Remove Hyperlink (see Figure 1241).

Figure 1241

Right-click
to remove a
hyperlink.

You can prevent Excel from adding hyperlinks in the first place, although the setting is now fairly buried. You choose Office Icon – Excel Options. In the Excel Options dialog, select the Proofing category and then click the AutoCorrect Options button. Choose the AutoFormat As You Type tab in the AutoCorrect dialog. Uncheck the Internet and Network Paths with Hyperlinks check box, as shown in Figure 1242.

Figure 1242

Prevent hy-
perlinks from
appearing.

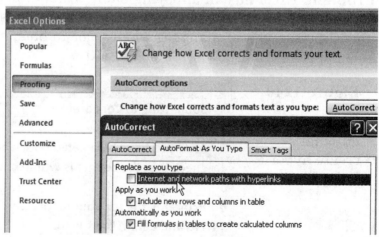

Summary: You can remove hyperlinks from a worksheet, and you can also prevent them from being inserted in the first place.

Commands Discussed: Office Icon – Excel Options – Proofing – Auto-Correct Options – AutoFormat As You Type

Excel 97-2003: Tools – AutoCorrect Options

CHANGE THE WIDTH
OF ALL COLUMNS WITH ONE COMMAND

Problem: I have a large model set up in Excel. Some of the columns are hidden. I want to globally change the width of all unhidden columns to a width of 4. If I choose all columns in the worksheet and use Home – Format dropdown – Column Width, the hidden columns will unhide.

Strategy: To solve this problem, you can use Home – Format dropdown – Default Width, as shown in Figure 1243.

Figure 1243

Change the default column width.

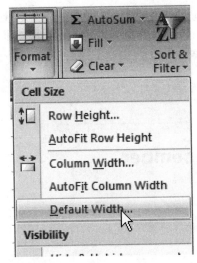

Part
IV

The Default Width dialog allows you to enter one global column width. This change will affect all columns that have not been previously resized or hidden. The result is that you can change the width of all columns without unhiding the hidden columns.

Additional Details: Changing the default width will change the width of hidden columns, but will not unhide them. When they are later unhidden, they will have the new width.

Gotcha: The Default Width command does not change the widths of columns that have previously been changed. To see this in action, open a new workbook. Manually change column C to be 20 wide. Use Home – Format dropdown and set Default Width to be 1 wide. All the columns except C will be changed.

Summary: You can use Default Width to globally adjust the width of all columns without unhiding hidden columns.

Commands Discussed: Home – Format dropdown – Default Width

Excel 97-2003: Format – Column – Standard Width

CONTROL PAGE NUMBERING IN A MULTISHEET WORKBOOK

Problem: I have a workbook that has 12 worksheets, 1 per month. Although I set the page header to print "Page 1 of 12," every sheet prints with "Page 1 of 1," as shown in Figure 1244.

Figure 1244

Page 1 of 1

You have 12 page 1s.

December

Net sales

Strategy: The key to making this work is to print the entire workbook at once. You need to organize the worksheets so that they are in the proper order for printing, with the worksheet for the first page on the left. Instead of using the Print icon, you select Office Icon – Print – Print. You will then have an option to print the entire workbook, as shown in Figure 1245.

Results: As shown in Figure 1246, the page numbers will reflect 1 of 12, 2 of 12, etc.

Figure 1245

In the Print dialog, choose Entire Workbook.

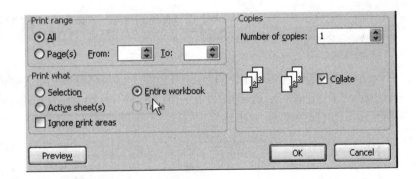

Figure 1246

Excel will properly number the pages of all worksheets in the workbook.

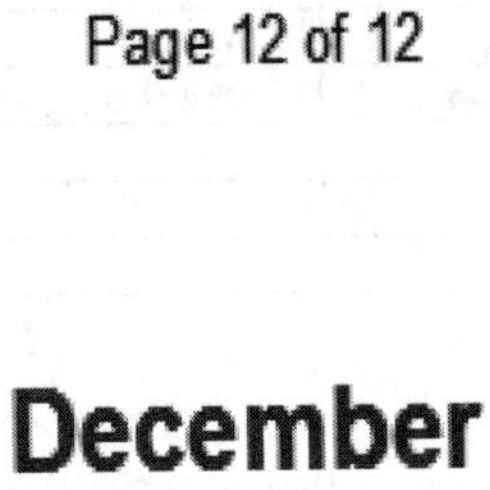

Page 12 of 12

December

Alternate Strategy: If you need to print only a few sheets, select the first sheet. Hold down Ctrl while selecting other sheets. You can now use the File – Print and choose Active Sheets in the Print dialog, or you can simply click a Quick Print icon that you've added to the Quick Access toolbar.

Gotcha: By selecting multiple sheets, you've put the workbook in Group mode. Any changes you make to the visible sheet will be made to all the selected sheets. Be sure to exit Group mode after printing by right-clicking a sheet tab and choosing Ungroup Sheets.

Summary: To ensure that your worksheet pages print with the proper page numbers, you can select the Entire Workbook option in the Print dialog.

Commands Discussed: Office Icon – Print – Print

Excel 97-2003: Excel 2003 had a Print icon on the Standard toolbar. This icon does not access the Print dialog, so you either need to select the sheets to be printed before pressing the icon or use File – Print to access the Entire Workbook selection.

Part
IV

USE WHITE TEXT TO HIDE DATA

Problem: As shown in Figure 1247, my workbook needs extra columns in order to show a graph. I'd like to hide this information from the person using the workbook.

Figure 1247

Quickly hide the data in M1:O32.

K	L	M	N	O
Food	**ACTIVITY**	To Chart	TrendLine	Actually At
	BB 1 hour	226.00	226.00	226
	Walk 20 Min	224	225.31	224
Meatloaf, sandwich, pizza	Nothing	226	224.62	226
Junk food at game; 3 skin laps	Walked at game	229	223.93	229
		224	223.24	224
		$N/A	222.55	224
		$N/A	221.86	224

Strategy: You can highlight the extra cells and choose white text color. To do this, you select Home – Font Color dropdown and choose a white font for the text, as shown in Figure 1248.

Figure 1248

Change the font to white.

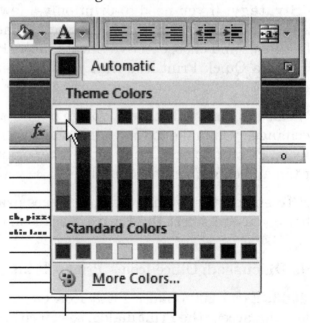

As shown in columns M and N of Figure 1249, this will prevent the cells from being seen or from printing (assuming that the cell background color is also white).

Figure 1249

The white
font prevents
the cells from
being visible
onscreen and
from printing.

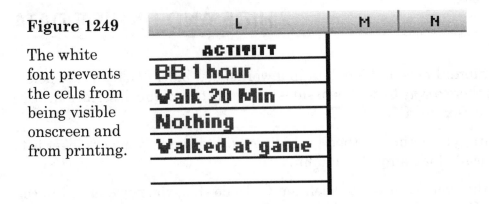

Additional Details: If you need to troubleshoot these cells, you can re-select the range and select Home – Paint Bucket dropdown. Hover over a dark color. When you use Excel 2007's Live Preview, the cell values will reappear as white text on a dark background, as shown in Figure 1250.

Figure 1250

Make the
white text vis-
ible by mak-
ing the back-
ground dark.

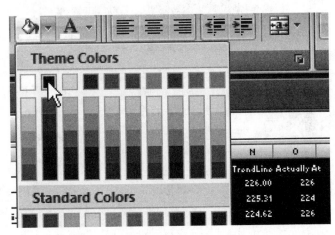

Part IV

In previous versions of Excel, you can simply select the range to add a darker selection rectangle, which is enough to see the cell values. In Excel 2007, the selection rectangle is too light for the text to be visible.

Summary: Selecting an area and making the text white will prevent the cells from printing and the user from seeing them.

Commands Discussed: Home – Font Color dropdown; Home – Paint Bucket dropdown.

HIDE AND UNHIDE DATA

Problem: I need to hide data in a worksheet, but I don't want to delete it. Is there a way to do this besides using the technique described in "Use White Text to Hide Data"?

Strategy: Another method for hiding data to simplify a worksheet is to physically hide a row or column.

Say that you want to hide column C. To do this, you select a cell in column C. Then you select Home – Format dropdown – Hide & Unhide – Hide Columns, as shown in Figure 1251.

Figure 1251

Choose to hide the column.

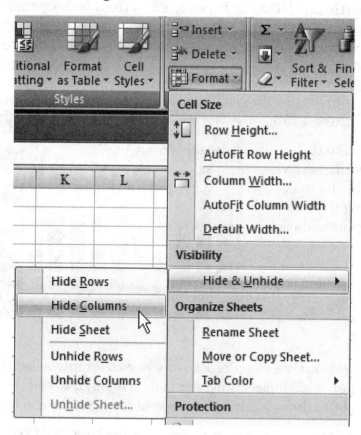

Column C will be hidden from the user. As shown in Figure 1252, it is interesting to note that the cell pointer has basically disappeared. You can see from the Name box that C9 is the active cell. You can also see in the formula bar that the value of C9 is 81. Even though the column is hidden, the active cell is still C9.

Figure 1252

Initially, the active cell is in the hidden column.

C9		▼	f_x	81

◢	A	B	D	E
7	Section 2: Number of Stores			
8				
9		Regular	30.6%	
10		BigBox		
11				

Simply press the Left Arrow key or Right Arrow key to move to a visible column to get the cell pointer back.

To unhide column C, you click the B heading and drag to the right to select the entire range B:D. Select Format – Hide & Unhide – Unhide Columns.

What happens if you need to unhide column A? You can't really select something to the left of A to use the trick just described, but you can follow these steps:

Part IV

1) Click the column letter B.

2) Drag up and to the left so that the mouse is above row 1 (see Figure 1253). The difference is subtle, but you have now selected columns B and A. Select Format – Column – Unhide.

Figure 1253

To unhide column A, drag from the B column heading up and to the left.

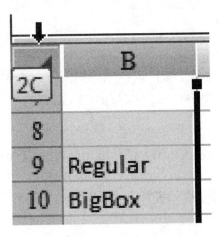

Additional Details: Immediately after you hid column C, the active cell was still in column C, so you used an arrow key to move out of the hidden column. Once you've arrowed out of the hidden column, you cannot arrow back into it. However, if you type C10 in the Name box—the area that contains the active cell address to the left of the formula bar—and press Enter, Excel will once again select a cell in the hidden column. This can be a handy trick for seeing a value in a hidden cell.

Summary: To hide data in a worksheet without deleting it, you select the column to hide and select Home – Format dropdown – Hide & Unhide – Hide Column. To unhide the column, you select and highlight the columns on either side of it before selecting Home – Format dropdown – Hide & Unhide – Unhide Column.

Commands Discussed: Home – Format dropdown – Hide & Unhide – Hide Column; Home – Format dropdown – Hide & Unhide – Unhide Column

Excel 97-2003: Format – Column – Hide; Format – Column – Unhide

TEMPORARILY SEE
A HIDDEN COLUMN WITHOUT UNHIDING

Problem: I have data hidden in column D of Figure 1254. I want to quickly view data in the hidden column without actually unhiding it.

Figure 1254

Quickly see column D without unhiding.

C	E
Date	Name
10/21/2008	ABC CO
10/21/2008	XYZ INC.
10/23/2008	BUDD & ASSOCIATES
10/24/2008	WIZARD OF OZZIE

Strategy: This trick works only if you use the Transition Navigation Keys setting. If you regularly work with hidden data, this cool trick might be enough to tip you over to turning on this setting. Here's how it works:

1) Select Office Icon – Excel Options. At the bottom of the Advanced category in the Excel Options dialog, choose Transition Navigation Keys.

2) In the image, column D is hidden, so place the cell pointer in a blank cell in column E. Type an equals sign to start entering a formula.

3) Press the Left Arrow key as if you were going to enter a formula using the arrow keys. Excel magically unhides the hidden columns, as shown in Figure 1255. You can now arrow through the worksheet to look at hidden data.

Figure 1255

When you enter a formula using the Lotus arrow key method, hidden columns unhide.

	C	D	E	Ac
	Date	Total	Name	
	10/21/2008	$125.00	ABC CO	12:
	10/21/2008	$175.00	XYZ INC.	45
	10/23/2008	$225.00	BUDD & ASSOCIATES	78
	10/24/2008	$425.00	WIZARD OF OZZIE	98
	10/24/2008	$25.00	MARCINKO PUBLISHING	65
	10/26/2008	$185.00	BONNIE DOON	32
			=D8	

Part IV

4) When you are done, press the Esc key to cancel entering the formula. The hidden ranges will be hidden again.

Gotcha: Beware. Users could employ this method to see hidden data. To avoid this behavior, you need to protect the worksheet.

Gotcha: This behavior can be incredibly annoying. If you are in cell E3 and hope to enter the formula =2*B3, you might think it would take only five keystrokes: =, 2, *, Left Arrow, Enter. However, when you actually try to do this, after the fourth keystroke, the hidden columns will open. You're likely to just catch this out of the corner of your eye, as you incorrectly enter =2*C3 in the formula.

Summary: To quickly view hidden data in a worksheet, with Transition Navigation Keys set, you select a cell in the column to the hidden data's immediate right, type an equals sign, and then press the Left Arrow key.

Commands Discussed: Office Icon – Excel Options – Advanced – Transition Navigation Keys

Excel 97-2003: Tools – Options – Transition

BUILD COMPLEX REPORTS WHERE COLUMNS IN SECTION 1 DON'T LINE UP WITH SECTION 2

Problem: I need to duplicate a fairly complex form. The form has several sections. The column widths needed for the first section do not line up with the column widths needed for the other two sections.

Strategy: This is a wildly amazing and obscure solution. It has been floating around Excel Web sites for years as a novelty. However, I recently used it in a production application to produce great-looking customer statements. Here's how it works:

1) Set up various sections of the form on individual worksheets. Make the column widths as wide as they need to be for each section of the form. In the sample, I have four different sections:

   The statement header has a logo that stretches across the page, as shown in Figure 1256.

Figure 1256

The logo fills the page.

13386 Judy Ave NW, Uniontown OH 44685 , USA

The next section has five columns, as shown in Figure 1257.

Figure 1257

The first report section has five columns.

	A	B	C	D	E
1	Section 1: Orders Shipped this Period				
2					
3	Date	Invoice #	Your Reference #	Via	Total
4	11/1/2008	1021	PO AJHOIP	FedEx Ground	225
5	11/3/2008	1027	PO KJKJLK	FedEx Ground	742
6	11/7/2008	1030	PO YUOIU	FedEx Ground	510
7	11/8/2008	1031	PO KJL DADS	FedEx Ground	241
8	11/12/2008	1034	Verbal per Marc	FedEx Next Day	185
9	11/16/2008	1038	PO 9LKJD	FedEx Ground	674
10	Total Shipments				2577

The next section has just three columns (see Figure 1258).

Figure 1258

The next section has only three columns.

▲	A	B	C	D	E
1	**Section 2: Payments Received This Period**				
2					
3	Date	Ck#	Total		
4	11/1/2008	113783	272		
5	11/3/2008	113865	161		
6	11/7/2008	113919	600		
7	11/8/2008	113990	244		
8	11/12/2008	114070	114		
9	11/16/2008	114168	485		
10	Total Payments		1876		
11					

The final section has six columns, as shown in Figure 1259.

Figure 1259

The narrow column C here doesn't line up with the wide C in Figure 1257.

▲	A	B	C	D	E	F
1	**Section 3: Outstanding Invoices from Prior Periods**					
2						
3	Date	Invoice #	Original Amount	Amt Paid	Amt Due	Your Reference #
4	1/9/2008	601	1029	929	100	PO AJHOIP
5	4/2/2008	685	393	0	393	PO YUOIU
6	4/19/2008	702	203	200	3	Verbal per Marc
7	5/17/2008	730	850	100	750	PO KJL DADS
8	9/5/2008	841	251	0	251	PO 9LKJD
9	10/9/2008	875	946	875	71	PO KJKJLK
10	Total Due from Prior Periods				1568	
11						

Part IV

To pull these parts together, you will build a printable statement on the worksheet that has the company header. On that page, you will paste three linked pictures that give a view of the back worksheets.

2) Select the cells for Section 1 and then press Ctrl+C to copy.

3) Go to cell A7 on the main worksheet. Select Home – Paste drop-down – As Picture – Paste Picture Link, as shown in Figure 1260.

Figure 1260

Paste a linked picture of the first report section.

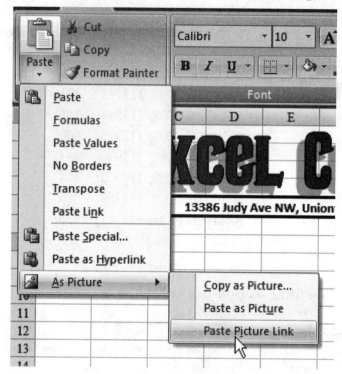

You will now have a live picture on Sheet1 of the cells on Sheet2, as shown in Figure 1261.

Figure 1261

The picture on Sheet1 shows the current value of cells on Sheet2.

	A	B	C	D	E	F	G
1							
2							
3							
4							
5				13386 Judy Ave NW, Uniontown OH 4468			
6							
7	Section 1: Orders Shipped this Period						
8							
9	Date	Invoice #	Your Reference #	Via		Total	
10	11/1/2008	1021	PO AJHOIP	FedEx Ground		225	
11	11/3/2008	1027	PO KJKJLK	FedEx Ground		183	
12	11/7/2008	1030	PO YUOIU	FedEx Ground		284	
13	11/8/2008	1031	PO KJL DADS	FedEx Ground		663	
14	11/12/2008	1034	Verbal per Marc	FedEx Next Day		738	
15	11/16/2008	1038	PO 9LKJD	FedEx Ground		274	
16	Total Shipments					2367	
17							

4)   Drag this picture so that it is centered on the page.

5)   Select A18:H18 and then select Home – Borders dropdown – Thick Bottom Border to draw a thick border along the bottom of row 18.

6)   Repeat steps 2 through 5 for Section 2: Go to Sheet3. Select the cells. Press Ctrl+C to copy. Return to Sheet1, cell A20. Select Home – Paste dropdown – As Picture – Paste Picture Link.

7)   Repeat steps 2 through 5 for Section 3.

You can resize the pictures in the new sheet so they all have the same width, or you can simply center them on the page.

Results: You can print one unified form that does not look like it came from Excel. As shown in Figure 1262, fields in Section 2 are not necessarily lined up with columns in Sheet1. Note that the pictures are live pictures. If you change values on Sheet4, the picture on Sheet1 will automatically update.

Figure 1262

Three pictures make up this report.

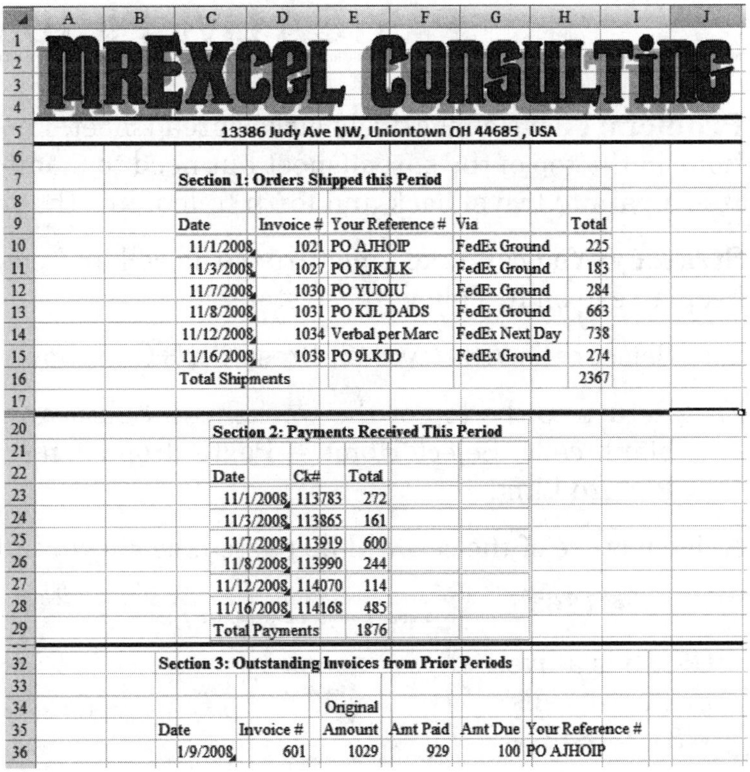

Part IV

Additional Details: In our real statement application, we used a VBA macro to put together the sections. This macro can paste a different number of rows each time.

Summary: By using the Paste Picture Link command, you can paste a live picture of cells in a new section of the workbook. For example, you can do this to avoid trying to align Section 1 column widths with Section 3 column widths.

Commands Discussed: Home – Paste dropdown – As Picture – Paste Picture Link; Home – Borders dropdown – Thick Bottom Border

Excel 97-2003: The Paste Picture Link command was hidden in previous versions of Excel. You had to hold down the Shift key before opening the Edit menu in order to see Paste Picture Link. Also, in Excel 2003, you would have to use the Border tab on the Format Cells dialog to create a thick bottom border.

PASTE A LIVE PICTURE OF A CELL

Problem: I have a massively large spreadsheet. I'm working on calculations in the top of the spreadsheet but need to monitor a result in W842. It is a pain to travel back and forth to monitor that cell.

Strategy: You can take a picture of the cell and paste it where you can keep an eye on it. Follow these steps:

1)   Select cells W841:W842. Press Ctrl+C to copy.

2)   Return to the top of the worksheet. Select an area that has a few blank cells. Select Home – Paste dropdown – As Picture – Paste Picture Link.

A live picture of the cell will be pasted, as shown in Figure 1263.

Figure 1263

G7:G8 is a live picture of cells W841:W842.

	A	B	C	D	E	F	G
1	Section 1: Historical Trends (Per Month)						
2							
3		Store Type	Size	Rent	Sales	Profit	Labor
4		Regular	1200	2400	12456	6228	6480
5		BigBox	2600	5200	36500	18250	8640
6							
7	Section 2: Number of Stores						Final Result
8							5,975,966.76
9		Regular	81				
10		BigBox	184				

As you make changes and the calculations cause the result to change, the picture will update, as shown in Figure 1264.

Figure 1264

As the pictured cell changes, the picture changes.

◢	A	B	C	D	E	F	G
1	Section 1: Historical Trends (Per Month)						
2							
3		Store Type	Size	Rent	Sales	Profit	Labor
4		Regular	1200	2400	12456	6228	6480
5		BigBox	2600	5200	36500	18250	8640
6							
7	Section 2: Number of Stores						Final Result
8							6,308,934.18
9		Regular	90				

Additional Details: The picture can be of multiple cells. Also, it is possible to move the picture by dragging it to a new location.

Summary: You can paste a live picture of distant cells by copying the cells and then pasting a picture link.

Commands Discussed: Home – Paste dropdown – As Picture – Paste Picture Link

Excel 97-2003: Shift+Edit – Paste Picture Link

Part
IV

MONITOR FAR-OFF CELLS IN EXCEL 2002 AND LATER VERSIONS

Problem: I have a massively large spreadsheet. I'm working on calculations in the top of the spreadsheet but need to monitor results in several other worksheets. It is a pain to travel back and forth to monitor those cells. Is there another way to do this besides the technique described in "Paste a Live Picture of a Cell" on page 834?

Strategy: Microsoft added the Watch Window in Excel 2002. This window is a favorite tool of VBA programmers, and Microsoft added it to the regular Excel interface. Here's how you use it:

1) Select Formulas – Watch Window, as shown in Figure 1265. The Watch Window, a floating dialog box that you can move around your screen, will appear.

Figure 1265

The Watch Window icon on the Formulas tab.

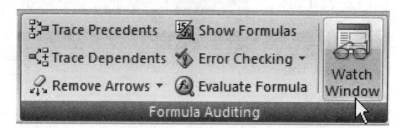

2) Click Add Watch, as shown in Figure 1266.

Figure 1266

Add a cell to be watched.

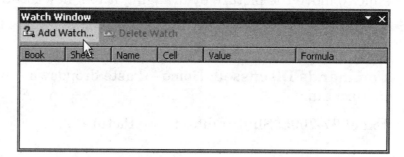

3) Using the Add Watch dialog, navigate to and touch the cell that you want to watch. Alternatively, you can first navigate to the cell, click Add Watch, and click Add.

For each cell that you add to the Add Watch dialog, you can always see the formula and the result of that formula in the Watch Window, as shown in Figure 1267. You can add cells from other sheets and even from other workbooks.

Additional Details: The cells listed in the Watch Window act as bookmarks! You can double-click a cell and jump to the cell, even if it is on another worksheet.

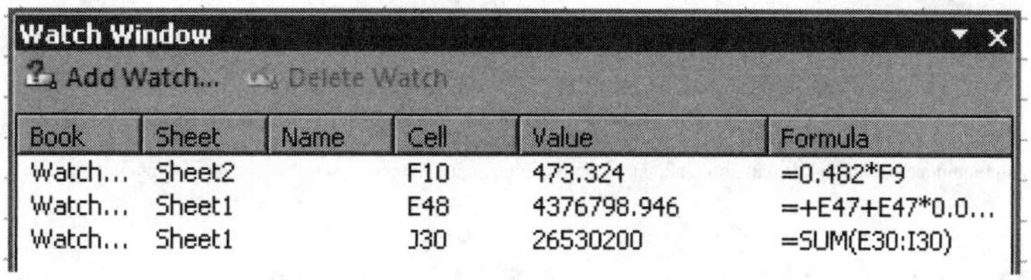

Figure 1267

The Watch Window will show the current results of the watched cells.

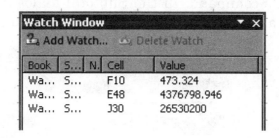

Additional Details: You can resize the column widths in the Watch Window, as necessary. Further, you can resize the entire Watch Window, and you can even dock it. To dock the Watch Window on the right side of the Excel window, you grab the title bar and drag the Watch Window off the right edge of the window. Figure 1268 shows a smaller Watch Window.

Figure 1268

By minimizing unneeded columns, you can reduce the space the Watch Window requires.

Part
IV

Summary: If you have Excel 2002 or a newer version, the Watch Window is a great tool for keeping an eye on far-off cells in your worksheet.

Commands Discussed: Formulas – Watch Window

Excel 97-2003: Tools – Formula Auditing – Watch Window; not available before Excel 2002

See Also: "Paste a Live Picture of a Cell" on page 834.

ADD A PAGE BREAK
AT EACH CHANGE IN CUSTOMER

Problem: My data is sorted by customer in column A, as shown in Figure 1269. I want to put each customer on a different page.

Figure 1269

Add page breaks at each change in customer.

	A	B	C	D	E	F
1	Customer	Region	Date	Quantity	Product	Revenue
6	Ainsworth	Central	19-Feb-08	800	DEF	18504
7	Ainsworth	East	23-Feb-08	1000	XYZ	20940
8	Ainsworth	East	1-Mar-08	400	XYZ	8620
9	Air Canada	West	30-Mar-08	300	ABC	5859
10	Air Canada	Central	18-Apr-08	200	XYZ	4948
11	Air Canada	West	23-Aug-08	800	XYZ	17856
12	Air Canada	East	6-Oct-08	100	DEF	2358

Strategy: The easiest way to do this is to add a subtotal by using the Data – Subtotals command. In the Subtotal dialog, you can choose to have a page break between groups, as shown in Figure 1270.

Figure 1270

Add page breaks by using subtotals.

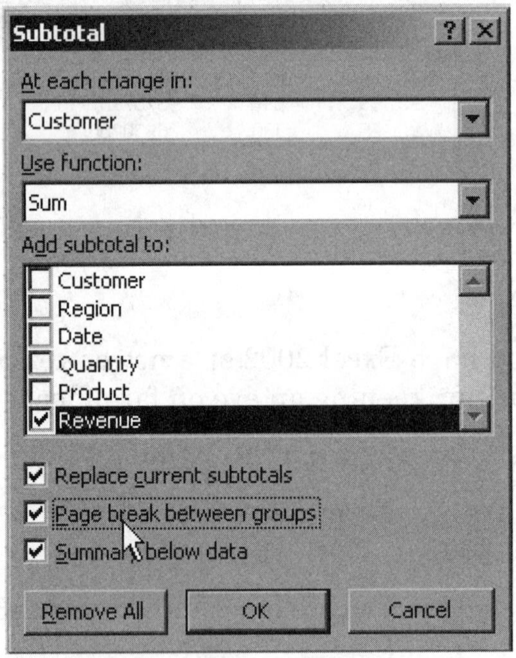

However, let's assume that you cannot use the automatic Subtotals feature for some reason. It helps to understand page breaks.

Excel page breaks can either be automatic or manual. If you use the Print Preview icon and then close the Print Preview window (by selecting Office Icon – Print – Print Preview and then selecting Close Print Preview), Excel will draw in the automatic page breaks.

In this particular report, it turns out that with these margins and print size, Excel would normally offer an automatic page break after row 46. After you do a Print Preview, Excel draws in a dashed line after row 46 to indicate that this is an automatic page break, as shown in Figure 1271.

Figure 1271

After you close Print Preview, Excel shows the page breaks.

	A	B	C	D	E	F	G
1	Customer	Region	Date	Quantity	Product	Revenue	
44	Exxon	East	8-Apr-08	500	DEF	12095	
45	Exxon	East	22-Apr-08	300	ABC	5439	
46	Exxon	Central	9-May-08	500	ABC	8785	
47	Exxon	Central	10-May-08	500	XYZ	11000	
48	Exxon	Central	20-May-08	100	XYZ	2149	

You can add a manual page break to any row. You position the cell pointer in column A on the first row for a new customer and then select Page Layout – Breaks – Insert Page Break. Excel will draw in a dotted line above the cell pointer to indicate that there is a page break after row 8, as shown in Figure 1272.

Figure 1272

This dotted line indicates a manual page break.

	A	B	C
1	Customer	Region	Date
2	Ainsworth	Central	2-Jan-08
3	Ainsworth	Central	3-Jan-08
4	Ainsworth	Central	5-Feb-08
5	Ainsworth	East	5-Feb-08
6	Ainsworth	Central	19-Feb-08
7	Ainsworth	East	23-Feb-08
8	Ainsworth	East	1-Mar-08
9	Air Canada	West	30-Mar-08
10	Air Canada	Central	18-Apr-08

Part IV

Because you've added a manual page break after row 8, Excel will automatically calculate that it can fit rows 9 through 54 on page 2. The location for the next automatic page break is now shown at row 55 instead of row 47.

Automatic page breaks will move around. Say that you change the margins for the page, using Page Layout – Margins. Excel will now calculate that the end of the second page is at another row.

Unlike automatic page breaks, manual page break will never move.

To add the rest of the page breaks, you move the cell pointer to the next cell in column A that has a new customer and select Page Layout – Breaks – Insert Page Break. Because you have 50 of these to insert, you might want to use the keyboard shortcut: Alt+I+B or Alt+P+B+I.

Additional Details: Selecting each new customer is tedious. Microsoft provides a shortcut for finding the next cell in the current column that is different from the active cell. However, it is difficult to use this shortcut. You will have to decide if it is worth the hassle. You start with the cell pointer on a customer. Then you press Ctrl+Shift+Down Arrow to select all the cells below the current cell. You press the F5 key and then click the Special button. Finally, you select Column Differences and click OK. The cell pointer will move to the first row that contains a new customer. You can then use the Breaks – Insert Page Break command. You can repeat this whole series of events by holding down the Alt key while you type EGSM. Release the Alt key and press Enter. Hold down the Alt key while you type IB. If you have hundreds of page breaks to add, mastering this keystroke might be worth the time.

Additional Details: To remove a manual page break, you should put the cell pointer in the first cell under the manual page break. When the cell pointer is in this location, the Breaks dropdown offers a Remove Page Break option.

To remove all page breaks, you select all cells by using the box to the left of column A. The Breaks dropdown will now offer the option Reset All Page Breaks.

Gotcha: To insert a row page break, you must either select the entire row or have the cell pointer in column A. If you select Insert Page Break while in cell C9, Excel will insert a horizontal page break above row 9 and also a vertical page break to the left of column C, as shown in Figure 1273. This is rarely what you want.

Figure 1273

Don't insert a page break from a column other than A.

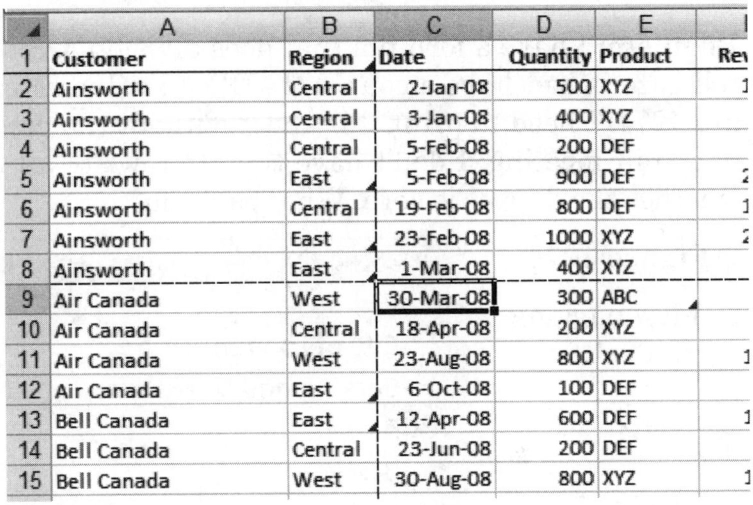

	A	B	C	D	E	
1	Customer	Region	Date	Quantity	Product	Rev
2	Ainsworth	Central	2-Jan-08	500	XYZ	1
3	Ainsworth	Central	3-Jan-08	400	XYZ	
4	Ainsworth	Central	5-Feb-08	200	DEF	
5	Ainsworth	East	5-Feb-08	900	DEF	2
6	Ainsworth	Central	19-Feb-08	800	DEF	1
7	Ainsworth	East	23-Feb-08	1000	XYZ	2
8	Ainsworth	East	1-Mar-08	400	XYZ	
9	Air Canada	West	30-Mar-08	300	ABC	
10	Air Canada	Central	18-Apr-08	200	XYZ	
11	Air Canada	West	23-Aug-08	800	XYZ	1
12	Air Canada	East	6-Oct-08	100	DEF	
13	Bell Canada	East	12-Apr-08	600	DEF	1
14	Bell Canada	Central	23-Jun-08	200	DEF	
15	Bell Canada	West	30-Aug-08	800	XYZ	1

Summary: Excel offers two kinds of page breaks. Automatic page breaks are calculated on-the-fly, based on row height and the margins of the current page. Manual page breaks that you add are permanent and will not move.

Commands Discussed: Page Layout – Breaks – Insert Page Break; Home – Find & Select – GoTo Special – Column Differences; Page Layout – Margins; Page Layout – Breaks – Remove Page Break; Page Layout – Breaks – Reset All Page Breaks.

Excel 97-2003: Insert – Page Break; Edit – Go To – Special– Column Differences; Insert – Remove Page Break; Insert – Reset All Page Breaks; File – Page Setup – Margins

Part
IV

HIDE ERROR CELLS WHEN PRINTING

Problem: I have a formula that does division. Occasionally, the divisor cell is zero, so I have a couple of #DIV/0! value errors, as shown in Figure 1274. I need to print this sheet without the errors to get the report to a staff meeting. I don't have time to rewrite all the formulas to test whether the divisor is zero. What can I do?

Figure 1274

A few nagging error cells.

	A	B	C	D
1	Region	Revenue	Units	Average
2	City of London	265.3	70	3.79
3	Barking and Dagenham	167.9	46	3.65
4	Barnet	179.01	51	3.51
5	Bexley	0	0	#DIV/0!
6	Brent	315.06	89	3.54
7	Bromley	318.75	85	3.75
8	Camden	248.88	68	3.66
9	Croydon	0	0	#DIV/0!
10	Ealing	260.13	69	3.77

Strategy: From the Page Layout tab, you can select the dialog launcher in the Page Setup group. In the Page Setup dialog, you go to the Sheet tab, select the dropdown for (Print) Cell Errors As, and select <blank>, as shown in Figure 1275.

Figure 1275

Select to print error cells as blank.

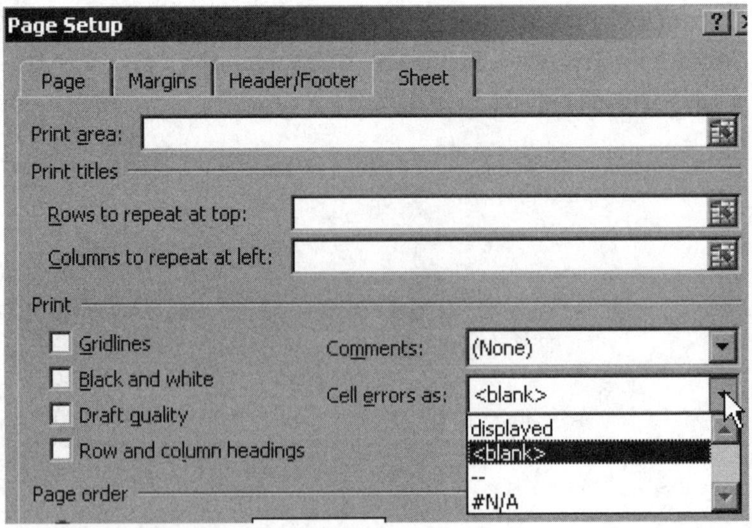

Results: Although the error will still appear in the worksheet, when you print, the error cells will print as blanks, as shown in Figure 1276.

Figure 1276

No errors will show in the printed document.

Region	Revenue	Units	Average
City of London	265.3	70	3.79
Barking and Dagenham	167.9	46	3.65
Barnet	179.01	51	3.51
Bexley	0	0	
Brent	315.06	89	3.54
Bromley	318.75	85	3.75
Camden	248.88	68	3.66
Croydon	0	0	
Ealing	260.13	69	3.77

Alternate Strategy: The ultimate way to solve this problem is to change the formula to test whether the divisor is zero. In this case, a proper formula would be =IF(C2=0,"",B2/C2). In Excel 2007, you can use =IFERROR(B2/C2,"").

Summary: To print a worksheet without errors showing, you can change a setting on the Sheet tab of the Page Setup dialog.

Commands Discussed: Page Layout – dialog launcher – Sheet

Formulas Discussed: =IF(); =IFERROR()

Excel 97-2003: File – Page Setup – Sheet in Excel 2002 or newer.

Part
IV

ORGANIZE YOUR WORKSHEET TABS WITH COLOR

Problem: I have a lot of tabs in a workbook. Can I highlight the frequently used tabs in red?

Strategy: You can right-click a tab and choose Tab Color to assign a color to a worksheet tab as shown in Figure 1277.

Figure 1277

Add color on the worksheet tabs.

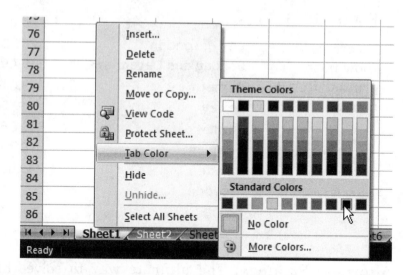

Gotcha: You can see the tab colors of all but the active sheet. The active sheet appears with a mostly white tab and only a tiny swatch of color.

Summary: You can organize your sheets visually by changing the color of the sheet tabs.

Excel 97-2003: This option was not available before Excel 2002

COPY CELL FORMATTING, INCLUDING COLUMN WIDTHS

Problem: I have one section of a report set up, including custom column widths, as shown in Figure 1278. When I copy and paste to a new section of the workbook, the column widths do not get pasted.

Figure 1278

Copying column widths is tricky.

	A	B	C	D	E	F	G
1			Manufactured in Harrow				
2							
3				Model			
4			A		B		C
5	Display		12		42		42
6	Engine		0		0		112.5
7	PCB		18		22		41
8	RAM		8		56		56
9	Other Mat'l		11.17		18.15		21.45
10	Total Matl		49.17		138.15		272.95
11							
12	Labor		8.24		12.45		15.24
13							
14	Overhead		34.608		52.29		64.008
15							
16	Total MLO		92.018		202.89		352.198
17							
18	Target Price		368.07		811.56		1408.79

Strategy: You can use the Format Painter icon. This is a cool trick, but it is hard to use. Carefully follow these steps:

1) Select the columns with the original formatted data. Select Home – Format Painter. (This icon looks like a paintbrush, as shown in Figure 1279.).

Part IV

Figure 1279

Select the original columns and choose the Format Painter icon.

2) Use the scrollbars to move so that you can see all of the new range in the window. Even if it would be more convenient to navigate using the arrow keys or Tab , you have to avoid selecting any cells or columns until the next step.

3) Click on the first new column and drag to select the same number of columns you selected in step 1. As you are dragging, the mouse pointer changes to the paintbrush icon, as shown in Figure 1280.

Figure 1280

Select the same number of columns as in step 1.

I	J	K	L	M	N		7C
		Manufactured in Trent					
		Model					
		A		B		C	
Display		12		42		42	

When you release the mouse button, the formats—including font, colors, borders, and cell height and width—will be copied, as shown in Figure 1281.

Figure 1281

The Format Painter will copy column widths.

I	J	K	L	M	N	O	
		Manufactured in Trent					
			Model				
		A		B		C	
Display		12		42		42	
Engine		0		0		112.5	
PCB		18		22		41	
RAM		8		56		56	

Additional Details: In order to copy column widths, you must select the entire column. If you don't need to copy the column widths but instead need to copy the formats, you can either use the Format Painter or select Home – Paste dropdown – Paste Special – Formats.

If you need to copy formats from one range to many ranges, you can do this cool trick with the Format Painter:

1) Select the original range and double-click the Format Painter icon. The Format Painter icon will stay lit, as shown in Figure 1282.

2) Click the top-left cell of the first destination range. As you click each top-left cell, the formats from the entire original range will

be copied to a similar-shaped area. In Figure 1283, only four clicks (in cells A6, A11, A16, and A21) were required to copy the source formatting to the other four tables.

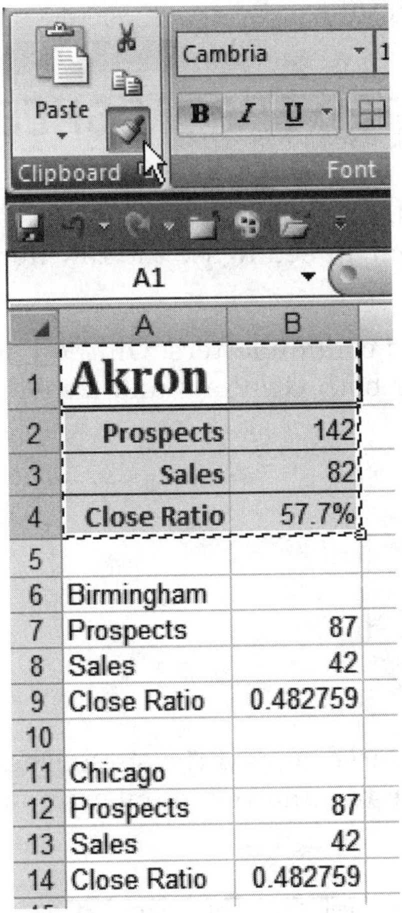

Figure 1282

Select the source range and double-click the Format Painter icon.

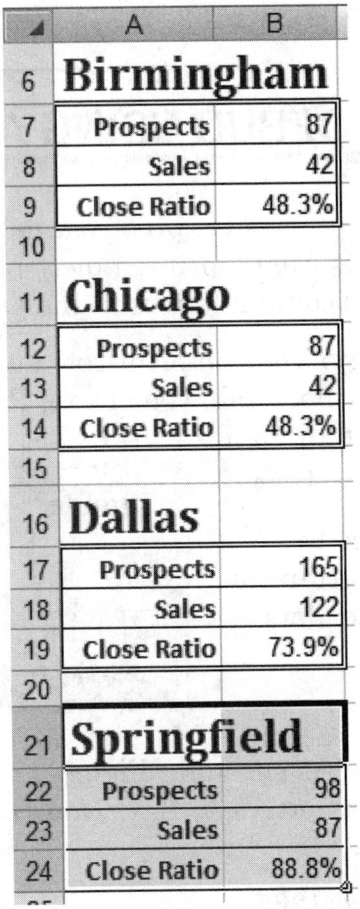

Figure 1283

Click once in A6, A11, A16, A21 to copy the formats to similar-sized ranges.

Part
IV

3) When you are done copying formats, press the Esc key to exit Format Painter mode.

Summary: You can use the Format Painter tool to copy formats, including column widths.

Commands Discussed: Home – Format Painter; Home – Paste drop-down – Paste Special – Formats

Excel 97-2003: Copying column widths did not work before Excel 2002. Edit – Paste Special – Formats; Format Painter

DEBUG USING A PRINTED SPREADSHEET

Problem: I need to proofread cells in my spreadsheet. It would be easier to do this from a printed piece of paper, but I need to see the row numbers and column letters in the printout.

Strategy: You can print row numbers and column letters. On the Page Layout ribbon tab, you choose Print under both Gridlines and Headers, as shown in Figure 1284.

Figure 1284

Choose to print gridlines and headers.

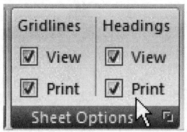

Results: As shown in Figure 1285, the printed copy of the spreadsheet will show letters A, B, C, and D across the top and row numbers down the side.

Figure 1285

You can identify cell addresses in the printout.

	A	B	C	D	E	F	G
1			Manufactured in Harrow				
2							
3					Model		
4			A		B		C
5	Display		12		42		42
6	Engine		0		0		112.5
7	PCB		18		22		41
8	RAM		8		56		56
9	Other Mat'l		11.17		18.15		21.45
10	Total Matl		49.17		138.15		272.95

Summary: Debugging printed spreadsheets is easier if you temporarily turn on the printing of row and column headings.

Commands Discussed: Page Layout – Gridlines; Page Layout – Headings

Excel 97-2003: File – Page Setup – Sheet – Row and Column Headings

COPIED FORMULA HAS STRANGE BORDERS

Problem: I copied a formula, and the borders look out of place in the paste area. In the worksheet shown in Figure 1286, I copied D4 and pasted to D5:D34. The top border from D4 was copied to every cell in the paste area.

Figure 1286

Copy the formula in column D, and the top border will get copied.

3	Date	Units	Dollars	Average
4	9/1/2006	84	312.48	3.72
5	9/2/2006	75	274.5	3.66
6	9/3/2006	0	0	0
7	9/4/2006	24	87.6	3.65
8	9/5/2006	63	236.25	3.75
9	9/6/2006	18	67.14	3.73
10	9/7/2006	18	65.52	3.64
11	9/8/2006	104	395.2	3.8
12	9/9/2006	49	175.42	3.58
13	9/10/2006	60	221.4	3.69

Strategy: After the fact, you need to clear the borders and start over again. You select the range with the unwanted formats and then select Home – Clear dropdown – Clear Formats, as shown in Figure 1287.

Figure 1287

The Clear command is behind the eraser icon.

Sort & Find &
Filter ▾ Select ▾

Clear All

Clear Formats

Clear Contents

Clear Comments

Part
IV

As shown in Figure 1288, this will clear all the borders, which is seldom what you want.

Figure 1288

Clearing for-
mats will
remove all
borders.

Dollars	Average
312.48	3.72
274.5	3.66
0	0
87.6	3.65
236.25	3.75
67.14	3.73
65.52	3.64

Additional Details: To prevent the problem in the first place, instead of pasting the cells, you can use either Home – Paste dropdown – Formulas (see Figure 1289) or Home – Paste dropdown –Paste Special – All Except Borders to copy the formulas without the top border.

Figure 1289

Paste the for-
mulas only.

Summary: It is best to use Paste Formulas to prevent borders from getting copied into your data range. If you discover too late that borders have been copied to your data range, you can use Home – Clear – Formats to get rid of them.

Commands Discussed: Home – Clear dropdown – Formats; Home – Paste dropdown – Formulas; Home – Paste dropdown – Paste Special – All Except Borders

Excel 97-2003: Edit – Clear – Formats; Edit – Paste Special – All Except Borders; Edit – Paste Special – Formulas

DOUBLE UNDERLINE A GRAND TOTAL

Problem: My boss is a Certified Accountant. He says I should double underline the grand total in a report. The Home tab of the ribbon offers a single underline icon. How can I add a double underline?

Strategy: You select the grand total cell and, instead of clicking the Underline icon, you click the dropdown arrow next to the Underline icon. Then you choose Double Underline.

Alternate Strategy: You can also press Ctrl+1 to access the Format Cells dialog. On the Font tab, from the Underline dropdown you can select Double Accounting. (see Figure 1290)

Part IV

Figure 1290

The Format Cells dialog offers more underlines.

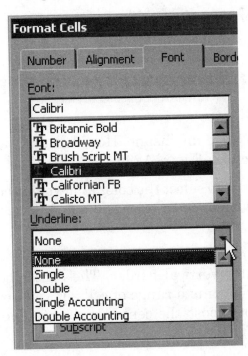

Gotcha: When you choose Double Underline from the Home tab's Underline dropdown, the Underline icon changes to a Double Underline icon (see Figure 1291). To apply a single underline, you then have to use the dropdown next to the Double Underline icon.

Figure 1291

After you choose a double underline from the dropdown, the icon changes to a Double Underline icon.

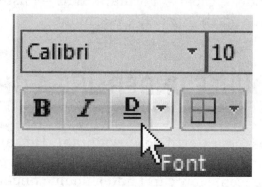

Summary: Excel offers four different types of underlines, but the accounting styles are initially only in the Format Cells dialog.

Commands Discussed: Home – Format – Format Cells – Font – Underline

Excel 97-2003: Format – Cells – Font – Underline

USE THE BORDER TAB IN FORMAT CELLS

Problem: Borders drive me insane. How do I use the Border tab of the Format Cells dialog (see Figure 1292)?

Strategy: The trick is to select the color and weight before you draw any borders. After you've selected a color and a line style, then you can begin drawing borders.

The large white area of the Border tab shows four sides plus a center horizontal and center vertical border. The center borders are enabledonly if you are formatting a range of cells. If you are formatting a single cell, you can not choose the center horizontal bar to draw a border through the center of the cell.

Figure 1292

The Border tab of the Format Cells dialog.

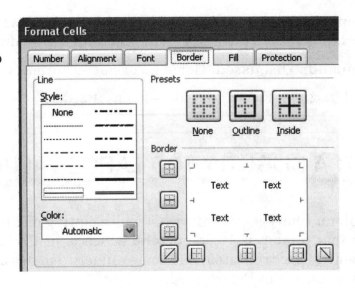

Additional Details: Here is a typical example. Say that you want a thick blue border around a selection, and you want a narrow green border around all cells inside the selection. Follow these steps:

1) Select the entire range.

2) Press Ctrl+1 to access the Format Cells dialog. Choose Borders.

3) Select Thick Border.

4) Select Blue.

5) Click the Outline button in the Presets area.

6) Select the thin border under Style and select green under Color.

7) Click the Inside button in the Presets area.

8) Click OK to apply the format to the selected range.

Additional Details: You can choose the small buttons around the outside of the white area in the Border tab to select individual border formats. This group also includes diagonal cross-through borders. The diagonal borders cross each cell, as shown in Figure 1293.

Figure 1293

Diagonal cross-through borders.

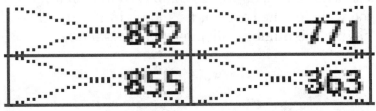

Summary: When you draw borders with the Format Cells dialog, it is important to select the line weight and color before drawing a border.

Commands Discussed: Home – Format – Format Cells – Borders

Excel 97-2003: Format – Cells – Font – Borders

FIT A SLIGHTLY TOO-LARGE VALUE IN A CELL

Problem: I have a column with a width setting of 8.5. The longest value in that column is 10 characters, which is just a bit too wide. Some text entries are truncated, and some numeric entries appear as number signs, as shown in Figure 1294.

Figure 1294

A few values are too long and are displayed as #####.

◢	A	B	C
1	Invoice	Customer	Sales
2	1901	ABC, Inc.	4,974,374
3	1902	TUVW, Inc	1,586,688
4	1903	BCD, Inc.	2,140,258
5	1904	JKLM, Inc.	#########
6	1905	FGH, Inc.	2,497,515
7	1906	STUV, Inc.	7,626,554

Strategy: To solve this problem, you can use Excel's Shrink to Fit option. To use it, you select the cells that are too large. Then you press Ctrl+1 to access the Format Cells dialog. On the Alignment tab, you choose Shrink to Fit from the Text Control section, as shown in Figure 1295.

Results: The cells will be displayed in a smaller font when they become too wide for the column, as shown in Figure 1296. This is preferable to having the numbers displayed as #####.

Figure 1295

Choose Shrink to Fit.

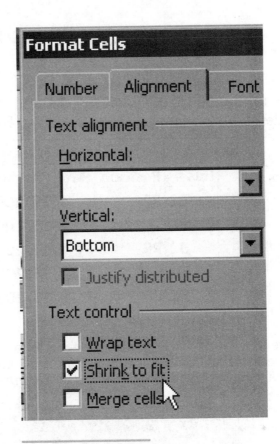

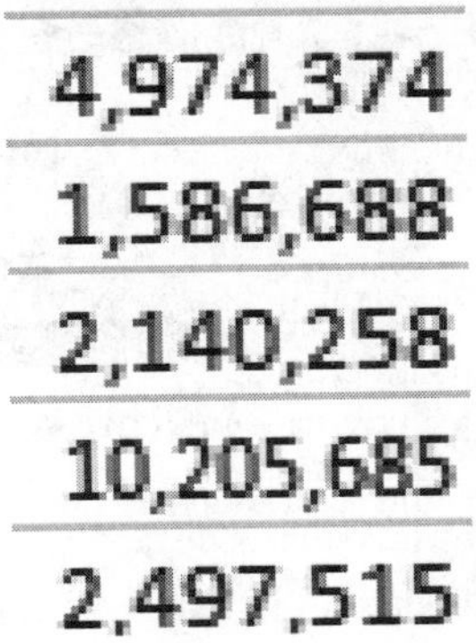

Figure 1296

The small font for 10,205,685 is preferable to #####.

> 4,974,374
>
> 1,586,688
>
> 2,140,258
>
> 10,205,685
>
> 2,497,515

Part
IV

Summary: When you have just a few cells that are too large for the column, you can use the Shrink to Fit option to allow the values to display properly instead of showing pound signs.

Commands Discussed: Format – Cells – Shrink to Fit

SHOW RESULTS AS FRACTIONS

Problem: I work in an industry that reports values in fractions. Stockbrokers are used to dealing in increments of 1/8, and tire engineers still measure tread depth in increments of 1/32 inch (see Figure 1297).

Figure 1297

Display results as fractions.

	A	B	C	D
1	**Bus #**	**Position**	**Date Checked**	**Tread Depth**
2	32	RF	8/15/2005	3/32
3	32	LF	8/15/2005	4/32
4	32	RR	8/15/2005	5/32
5	32	LR	8/15/2005	5/32
6	31	RF	8/15/2005	2/32

Strategy: There are number formats for fractions. When you press Ctrl+1 to display the Format Cells dialog, you will see that there are nine standard fraction formats available in the Number tab of the Format Cells dialog box (see Figure 1298).

Figure 1298

Excel offers built-in number formats for fractions.

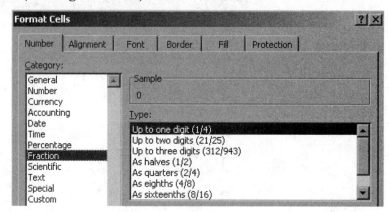

Beyond the seven shown in Figure 1298, Excel offers standard formats for 10ths and 100ths. Unfortunately, there is not a standard format for 32ths.

You can create a custom numeric format to handle 32ths:

1) Select the standard format for 16ths.

2) In the Category list on the Number tab of the Format Cells dialog, scroll down and select Custom. As you can see in Figure 1299, the

custom number format code for 16ths is # ??/16. From this, you can deduce that # ??/32 might be a valid number format.

Figure 1299

By clicking Custom, you can learn the code for 16ths.

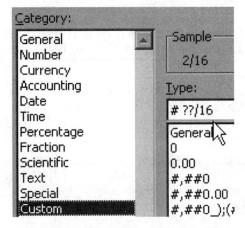

3)   Click in the Type box and change the 16 to 32. The Sample area will immediately confirm that you have hit upon the correct format for 32ths.

You can use this a custom numeric format to build fractions in any format you need.

Summary: Excel can display numbers as fractions.

Commands Discussed: Format Cells – Numeric – Fractions; Format Cells – Numeric – Custom

Part
IV

CONVERT A TABLE OF NUMBERS
TO A VISUALIZATION

Problem: My manager's eyes glaze over when he sees a table of numbers like the one in Figure 1300. Is there anything I can do to help him spot trends in the data?

Figure 1300

Help your manager to understand this data.

	A	Monday	Tuesday	Wednesday	Thursday	Friday
1		Monday	Tuesday	Wednesday	Thursday	Friday
2	Allen	38	22	57	20	28
3	Betty	25	64	57	59	33
4	Charley	43	32	51	23	37
5	Missy	63	59	60	64	69

Strategy: You can use one of the three new data visualization tools on the Excel 2007 Conditional Formatting menu: data bars, color scales, and icon sets.

Adding a data bar to a range adds an in-cell bar chart to each cell. You can see which cells have the largest values by seeing which cells have the most color.

To add data bars, you select a range of numbers and then select Home – Conditional Formatting – Data Bars – Blue as shown in Figure 1301. Excel offers 6 built-in colors, but you can choose More Rules to add any of 16 million colors.

Figure 1301

Choose a color for the data bars.

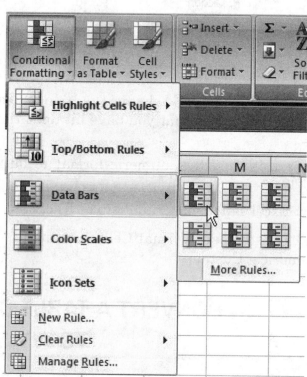

As shown in Figure 1302, with the data bars visualization added, you can see that Wednesday is the busiest day. Calls fall of on Friday for everyone except Missy. Missy is consistently the strongest performer.

Figure 1302

Easily spot trends in the data.

◢	A	B	C	D	E	F
1		Monday	Tuesday	Wednesday	Thursday	Friday
2	Allen	38	22	57	20	28
3	Betty	25	64	57	59	33
4	Charley	43	32	51	23	37
5	Missy	63	59	60	64	69

Gotcha: You should not include any total cells in your selection when applying conditional formatting. The relative size of the totals would make all the detail numbers receive small bars, as shown in Figure 1303. The 904 in cell G6 makes all the cells in B2:F5 look relatively the same.

Figure 1303

Don't include totals in a visualization.

◢	A	B	C	D	E	F	G
1		Monday	Tuesday	Wednesday	Thursday	Friday	Total
2	Allen	38	22	57	20	28	165
3	Betty	25	64	57	59	33	238
4	Charley	43	32	51	23	37	186
5	Missy	63	59	60	64	69	315
6	Total	169	177	225	166	167	904

Additional Details: You can use color scales to apply a mix of colors to a range. Excel offers built-in three-color scales such as red-yellow-green as well as two-color scales. The two-color scales look better than three-color scales when printed in monochrome. You can also use More Rules to design your own color scheme. In Figure 1304, the largest numbers are in the darker green, and the smallest numbers are in the lighter yellow.

Figure 1304

Color scales assign a color based on the cell's position within the sorted range of values.

◢	A	B	C	D	E	F
1		Monday	Tuesday	Wednesday	Thursday	Friday
2	Allen	38	22	57	20	28
3	Betty	25	64	57	59	33
4	Charley	43	32	51	23	37
5	Missy	63	59	60	64	69

Part IV

The final new visualization is icon sets. Due to the way that Microsoft has chosen to align icon sets, I don't like the icon sets as well as the other two visualizations.

As shown in Figure 1305, there are 17 sets of icons, running from three traffic lights to five cell-phone power bar symbols. Note that for many of these sets you need to print in color in order for the reader to differentiate the symbols. If you are printing in monochrome, the arrows or power bars are good choices.

Figure 1305

Choose an icon set.

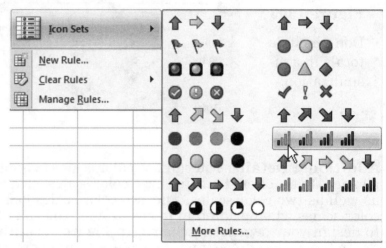

After you choose an icon set, Microsoft will display the icon at the left of each cell. To me, this is really confusing. For example, in Figure 1306, the 22 in cell C2 seems to correspond to the four-bar symbol in cell D2.

Figure 1306

The icons are too far away from their corresponding numbers.

◢	A	B	C	D	E	F
1		Monday	Tuesday	Wednesday	Thursday	Friday
2	Allen	38	22	57	20	28
3	Betty	25	64	57	59	33
4	Charley	43	32	51	23	37
5	Missy	63	59	60	64	69

Excel won't let you specify that the icon should be aligned next to the number. One feeble solution is to center the numbers, but centering numbers doesn't completely solve the problem as, shown in Figure 1307.

There is one interesting alternative. You can select the range of numbers and choose Home – Conditional Formatting – Manage Rules. Then you select the rule and click Edit. Excel will display a dialog with the settings shown in Figure 1308. For icon sets, you can choose to hide the number and display the icon only. Ironically, when you use this setting, the icon responds to the Left, Center, and Right Align buttons in the Home ribbon!

Figure 1307

If you click
Center Align,
you move the
numbers closer
to the icons.

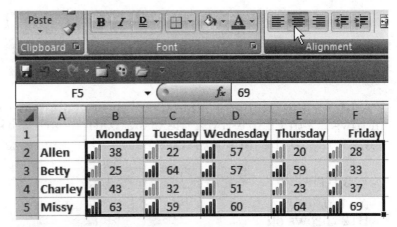

Figure 1308

Display icons
only.

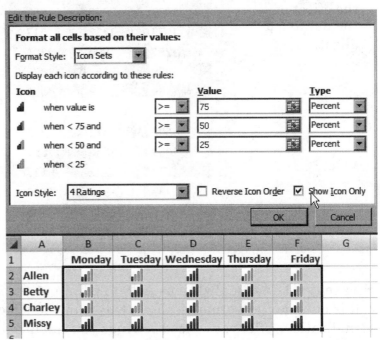

Part
IV

Summary: The new data visualizations in Excel 2007 can help you to
spots trends in your data.

Commands Discussed: Home – Conditional Formatting – Data Bars;
Home – Conditional Formatting – Manage Rules

Excel 97-2003: This feature is new in Excel 2007.

PREVENT OUTLIERS FROM
SKEWING THE VISUALIZATIONS

Problem: I'm having trouble using data visualizations. As you can see in rows 2:7 in Figure 1309, the visualizations are working fairly well. In rows 9:14, all the numbers have nearly the same size bar.

Figure 1309

An outlier in B12 throws off the effect of the data visualization.

◢	A	B	C
1			
2	506	616	811
3	1089	866	851
4	1073	1222	517
5	1257	800	1104
6	1068	1485	1429
7	1369	1339	1425
8			
9	506	616	811
10	1089	866	851
11	1073	1222	517
12	1257	-900	1104
13	1068	1485	1429
14	1369	1339	1425

Strategy: Data visualizations help to point out trends. However, if one cell is outside the normal scale, it will ruin the effect. Each of the data visualizations offers advanced settings you can use to tweak the display. To access the settings, you select the cells that contain the visualization and choose Home – Conditional Formatting – Manage Rules.

Excel will show a list of all rules applied to the range. You select the appropriate rule and click Edit Rule, as shown in Figure 1310.

Figure 1310

Select a rule and click Edit Rule.

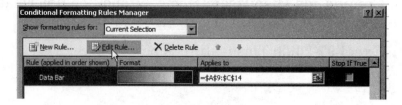

By default, Excel will use the shortest bar for the lowest value, as shown in Figure 1311.

Figure 1311

Excel will calculate a range based on the smallest and largest numbers.

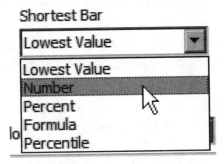

Edit the Rule Description:

Format all cells based on their values:

Format Style: [Data Bar ▼]   ☐ Show Bar Only

Shortest Bar   Longest Bar

Type: [Lowest Value ▼]   [Highest Value ▼]

Value: [(Lowest value) 📊]   [(Highest value) 📊]

Bar Color: [_____ ▼]   **Preview:** [_____]

[OK]   [Cancel]

When you open the dropdown for shortest bar, you can specify that the shortest bar should be assigned to a specific number, a percentile, and so on. In this case, you should choose Number, as shown in Figure 1312.

Figure 1312

Change from Lowest Value to Number.

Shortest Bar

[Lowest Value ▼]

| Lowest Value |
| Number |
| Percent |
| Formula |
| Percentile |

After you choose Number, you can select the value to receive the smallest bar. As shown in Figure 1313, you can define numbers of 500 and lower get the smallest bar and numbers of 1500 and larger get the largest bar.

Figure 1313

Specify a new range.

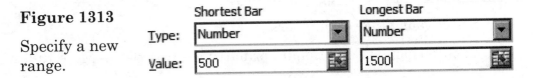

Shortest Bar   Longest Bar

Type: [Number ▼]   [Number ▼]

Value: [500 📊]   [1500| 📊]

Results: The data bars will show a relative size from 500 to 1500, as shown in Figure 1314.

Figure 1314

You can now see variability.

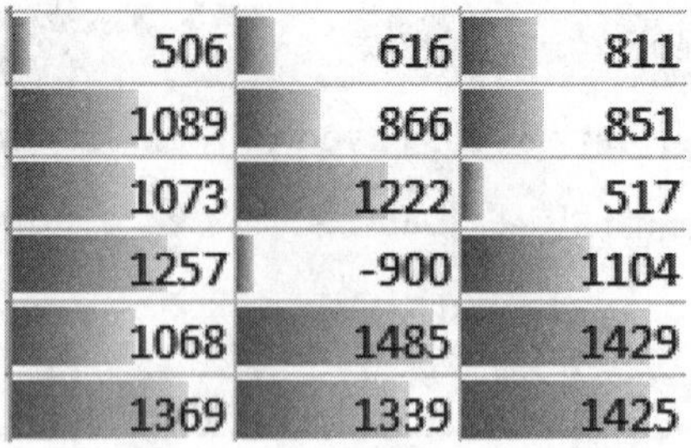

506	616	811
1089	866	851
1073	1222	517
1257	-900	1104
1068	1485	1429
1369	1339	1425

Summary: Although you can create a visualization in a few clicks, you sometimes need to edit the rule behind a visualization to ensure that you get the expected results in the display.

Commands Discussed: Home – Conditional Formatting – Manage Rules

ADD ICONS TO ONLY THE GOOD CELLS

Problem: I monitor product quality, and I need to mark any cells where the total quality is 99.1% or higher. I don't want to mark any other cells.

Strategy: Microsoft added a new check box called Stop if True to the conditional formatting rules in Excel 2007. This check box allows you to achieve the effect you're looking for.

First, you set up a three-icon set and make sure the green check marks display for 99.1 and above. Next, you set up a conditional formatting rule that says do nothing if the value is less than 99.1. Because Excel evaluates the most recent rule first, you can tell Excel to stop evaluating more rules if the less-than-99.1 rule is true. This prevents Excel from ever drawing in other icons from the set.

Follow these steps to set up the display:

1)   Select your range of numbers.

2)   Choose Home – Conditional Formatting – Icon Sets – More Rules.

3)   Change the Icon Style dropdown to 3 Symbols (uncircled). Because this is a three-icon set, the default settings are to display the green check mark for values above the 67th percentile. (Figure 1315)

Figure 1315

Change the default values.

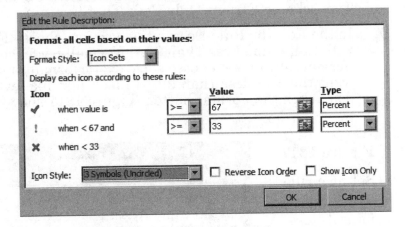

4)   Change the Type dropdown for the green check mark from Percent to Number.

5)   Enter 99.1 as the limit for the green check mark. There is no need to go further. You do not have to change any settings for the yellow check mark or the red X because they will ultimately never be shown.

6)   Click OK. Excel will show a mix of icons, as shown in Figure 1316.

Figure 1316

Excel will display all the icons.

Date	Icon	Value
5/1/2008	✖	98.2
5/2/2008	✔	99.2
5/5/2008	✔	99.3
5/6/2008	✔	99.4
5/7/2008	❗	98.6
5/8/2008	✔	99.4
5/9/2008	✔	99.2
5/12/2008	✔	99.2
5/13/2008	✖	98.2

Part IV

7) With the same range selected, choose Home – Conditional Formatting – New Rule.

8) In the top of the New Formatting Rule dialog, under Select a Rule Type, choose Format Only Cells That Contain.

9) In the Edit the Rule Description section, choose Format Only Cells with Cell Value Less Than 99.1. Normally, you would then click the Format button and choose some exotic format, but in this case, you want the cells less than 99.1 to look just like every other cell, so, don't click the Format button. Figure 1317 shows the dialog defining this rule.

Figure 1317

Set up a rule to do nothing for cells less than 99.1.

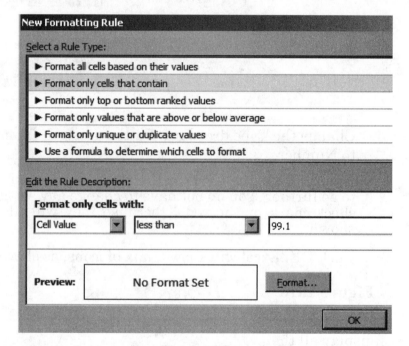

10) Click OK. Absolutely nothing will change. The screen will still look as shown in Figure 1316.

11) Select Home – Conditional Formatting – Manage Rules. The Conditional Formatting Rules Manager dialog shows the most recent rule at the top. Click the Stop if True check box for the first rule, as shown in Figure 1318. This tells Excel that if the value is less than 99.1, it should apply no special formatting and not proceed to the icon rule.

Figure 1318

In the Conditional Formatting Rules Manager dialog, indicate to stop if the first rule is true.

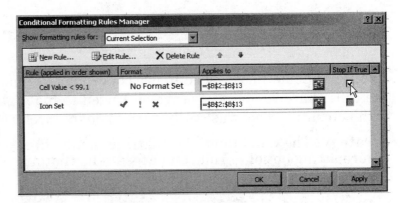

Results: Excel displays only the green check marks, as shown in Figure 1319.

Figure 1319

An icon set with only one icon.

5/1/2008		98.2
5/2/2008	✔	99.2
5/5/2008	✔	99.3
5/6/2008	✔	99.4
5/7/2008		98.6
5/8/2008	✔	99.4
5/9/2008	✔	99.2
5/12/2008	✔	99.2
5/13/2008		98.2
5/14/2008		98.7
5/15/2008		98.2
5/16/2008		98.8

Part IV

Summary: Although it requires many extra steps, the new Stop if True setting allows for some interesting conditional formatting.

Commands Discussed: Home – Conditional Formatting – New Rule; Home – Conditional Formatting – Manage Rules; Home – Conditional Formatting – Icon Sets – More Rules

SELECT EVERY KID IN LAKE WOBEGON

Problem: Sometimes I need to use conditional formatting to choose all the cells that are above average or I need to highlight cells in the top fifth percentile. This was really hard to do in Excel 97-2003.

Strategy: The Conditional Formatting menu offers a whole new range of formatting options. You can choose cells that are above average, below average, and so on, as shown in Figure 1320.

Figure 1320

The top/bottom rules are new.

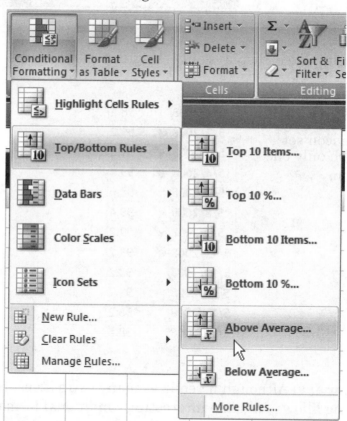

Additional Details: You can actually adjust the options with "10" to show the top or bottom 5, 2, 20, or any number. When you choose one of the "10" options, a new Top 10 Items dialog box will appear, where you can choose how many items or what percentage to show (Figure 1321).

Note: Lake Wobegon is a fictional city on the Prairie Home Companion radio show. The inside joke is that all the kids in Lake Wobegon are above average.

Figure 1321

Adjust top 10 to show any number.

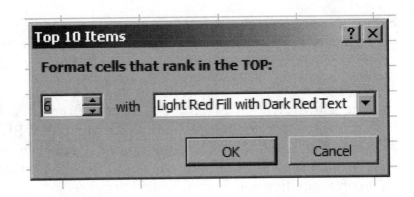

Summary: The new top/bottom rules simplify complex conditional formatting.

Commands Discussed: Home – Conditional Formatting – Top/Bottom Rules

COLOR ALL SALES GREEN
FOR A DAY IF TOTAL SALES EXCEED $1,000

Part IV

Problem: My company offers a bonus pool on any day when the total sales exceed $1,000. I have invoice data by date, as shown in Figure 1322. I would like to highlight all records for the days that exceed $1,000 in sales.

Figure 1322

Highlight if total sales for day is more than $1,000.

	A	B	C
1	Date	Invoice	Sales $
2	12/1/2008	1506	82
3	12/1/2008	1507	172
4	12/1/2008	1508	202
5	12/1/2008	1509	155
6	12/2/2008	1510	107
7	12/2/2008	1511	249
8	12/2/2008	1512	156
9	12/2/2008	1513	450
10	12/2/2008	1514	227
11	12/3/2008	1515	125

Strategy: You can use a formula version of conditional formatting to perform a complex task such as this. But first, before getting into conditional formatting, you should develop the formula you need:

1) The first task is to add a column that will total all sales for this day. As shown in Figure 1323, the SUMIF function can do this. There are three arguments in the SUMIF function: =SUMIF($A$2:$A$30,$A2,$C$2:$C$30). This function tells Excel to examine each cell in A2:A30. If the cell value is equal to cell A2, then it adds up the corresponding cell from C2:C30.

Figure 1323

Create a temporary formula in the worksheet to make sure it works.

	fx	=SUMIF($A$2:$A$30,$C$2:$C$30)		
	A	B	C	D	E
1	Date	Invoice	Sales $	Temp	
2	12/1/2008	1506	82	611	
3	12/1/2008	1507	172	611	
4	12/1/2008	1508	202	611	

Enter the formula in D2. Double-click the fill handle to copy the formula down. In Figure 1323, you can see that every row contains the total sales for that day. There are a lot of dollar signs in the formula. As you copy the formula down in your temporary column D, you want the ranges in the first and third parameters to be frozen. In the temporary formula in column D, there is no reason to freeze the A2 in the second parameter. However, in the New Formatting Rule dialog, this formula will be applied to cells in A, B, and C, so it is important to freeze the second parameter to column A.

2) As a reasonableness test, highlight the sales for the December 2. As shown in Figure 1324, the status bar at the bottom of the Excel window confirms that the total of these cells is $1,189.

3) The formula for conditional formatting requires a formula that evaluates to either TRUE or FALSE. To convert the current formula, edit the formula and add >1000 to the end. The temporary formula will now show either TRUE or FALSE (see Figure 1325). The formula in D correctly identifies all of the individual records where total sales for the day exceed $1000.

Figure 1324

Use the Status Bar quick sum area to add cells for one date.

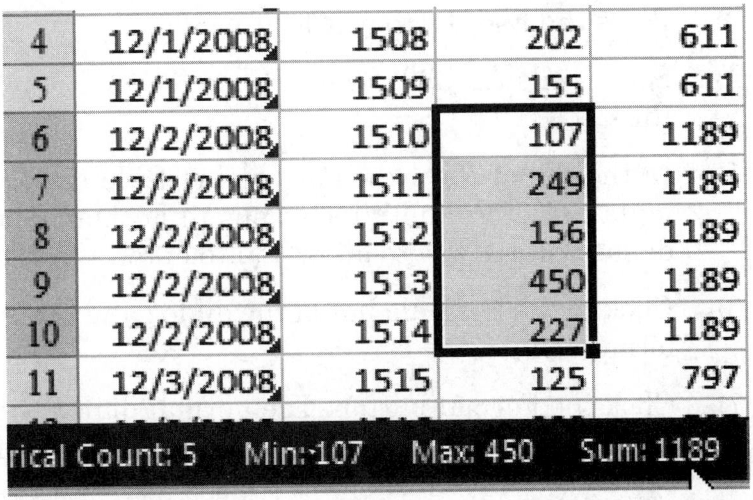

4	12/1/2008	1508	202	611
5	12/1/2008	1509	155	611
6	12/2/2008	1510	107	1189
7	12/2/2008	1511	249	1189
8	12/2/2008	1512	156	1189
9	12/2/2008	1513	450	1189
10	12/2/2008	1514	227	1189
11	12/3/2008	1515	125	797

rical Count: 5   Min: 107   Max: 450   Sum: 1189

Figure 1325

Add >1000 to the formula to return a TRUE/FALSE value.

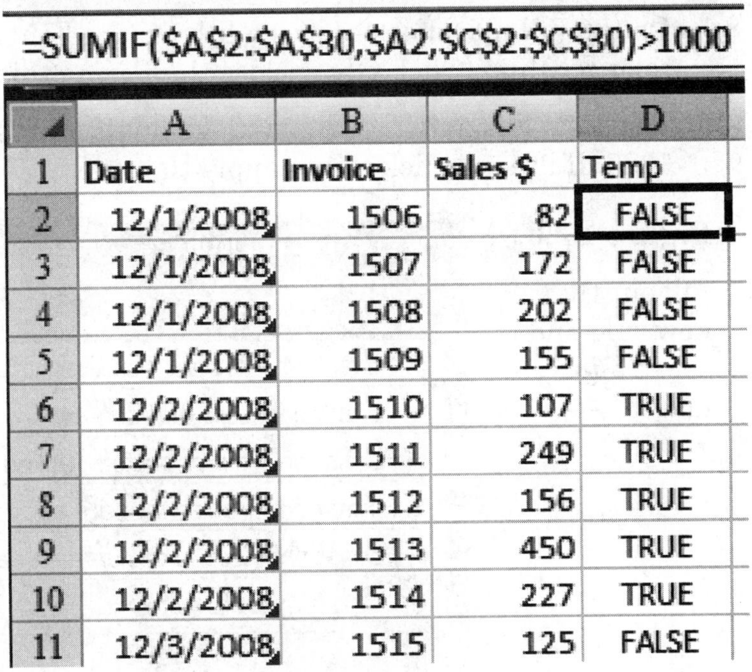

=SUMIF($A$2:$A$30,$A2,$C$2:$C$30)>1000

◢	A	B	C	D
1	Date	Invoice	Sales $	Temp
2	12/1/2008	1506	82	FALSE
3	12/1/2008	1507	172	FALSE
4	12/1/2008	1508	202	FALSE
5	12/1/2008	1509	155	FALSE
6	12/2/2008	1510	107	TRUE
7	12/2/2008	1511	249	TRUE
8	12/2/2008	1512	156	TRUE
9	12/2/2008	1513	450	TRUE
10	12/2/2008	1514	227	TRUE
11	12/3/2008	1515	125	FALSE

Part IV

To set up the conditional format, you follow these steps.

1) Copy the formula that is working by going to cell D2 and pressing the F2 key to put the formula in Edit mode. In the formula bar, drag to highlight the entire formula.

2) Press Ctrl+C to copy the formula from the formula bar. Copying from the formula bar allows the text of the formula to stay on the Clipboard after you press the Esc key.

3)   Press the Esc key to exit Edit mode.

4)   Select cells A2:C30. Select Home – Conditional Formatting – New Rule.

5)   In the top of the New Formatting Rule dialog, choose Use a Formula to Determine Which Cells to Format. The bottom half of the dialog will redraw to allow you to enter a formula.

6)   Click in the Formula box of the dialog and press Ctrl+V to paste the formula.

7)   Click the Format button. The Format dialog will appear. If desired, specify a border, fill, and/or font color. New in Excel 2007, you can specify a number format as well.

8)   On the Fill tab, choose a green fill. On the Font tab, change the font color to white. Click OK to close the Format dialog.

9)   The New Formatting Rule dialog should appear similar to Figure 1326. If it does, click OK to apply the rule.

Figure 1326

Fill out the new rule and select a format.

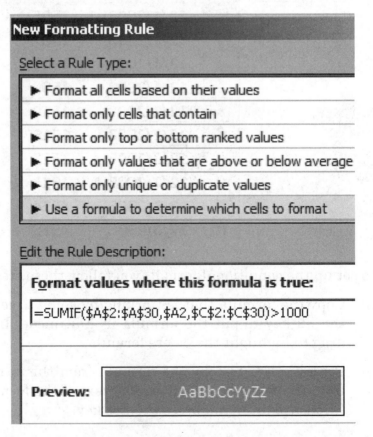

New Formatting Rule

Select a Rule Type:

► Format all cells based on their values

► Format only cells that contain

► Format only top or bottom ranked values

► Format only values that are above or below average

► Format only unique or duplicate values

► Use a formula to determine which cells to format

Edit the Rule Description:

Format values where this formula is true:

=SUMIF($A$2:$A$30,$A2,$C$2:$C$30)>1000

Preview: AaBbCcYyZz

If everything worked okay, all the rows for the December 2, 4, and 6 will be highlighted in green, as shown in Figure 1327.

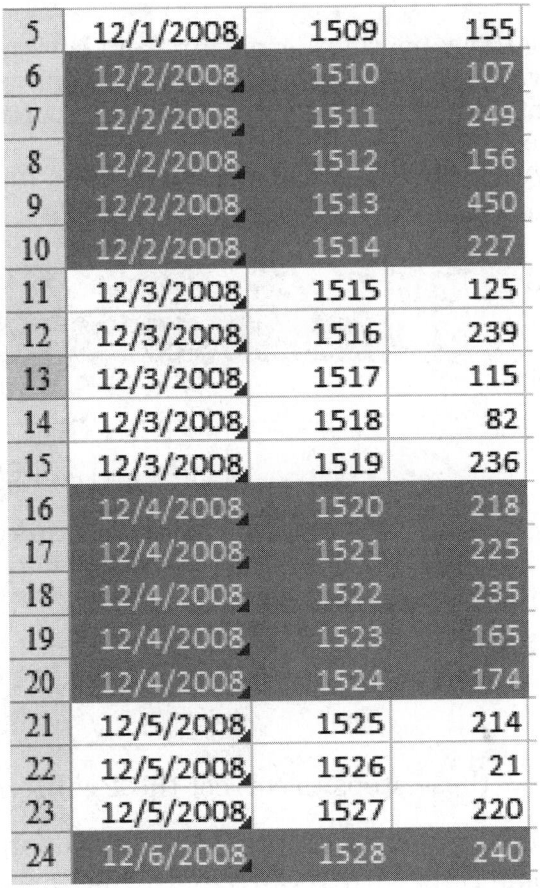

Figure 1327

Excel will highlight all records for a day when the sales exceed 1,000.

5	12/1/2008	1509	155
6	12/2/2008	1510	107
7	12/2/2008	1511	249
8	12/2/2008	1512	156
9	12/2/2008	1513	450
10	12/2/2008	1514	227
11	12/3/2008	1515	125
12	12/3/2008	1516	239
13	12/3/2008	1517	115
14	12/3/2008	1518	82
15	12/3/2008	1519	236
16	12/4/2008	1520	218
17	12/4/2008	1521	225
18	12/4/2008	1522	235
19	12/4/2008	1523	165
20	12/4/2008	1524	174
21	12/5/2008	1525	214
22	12/5/2008	1526	21
23	12/5/2008	1527	220
24	12/6/2008	1528	240

You can now safely delete your temporary formula in column D.

Summary: By using the formula version of the Conditional Formatting command, you can create amazingly powerful formulas to highlight entire rows if some condition is true.

Commands Discussed: Home – Conditional Formatting

Functions Discussed: =SUMIF()

Excel 97-2003: Format – Conditional Format, and change the first dropdown from Cell Value Is to Formula Is

TURN OFF WRAP TEXT IN PASTED DATA

Problem: I regularly paste information from Web pages, and I am frustrated by the way Excel wraps text in cells. In Figure 1328, for example, column A is not wide enough for the date, and column B is wrapped so that you can see only a few rows on the screen. Using AutoFit to make the columns wider will not work when the cells have their Wrap Text property turned on.

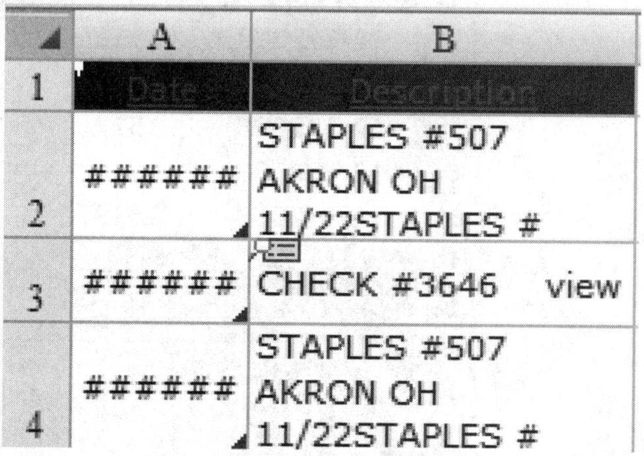

Figure 1328

Data pasted from the Web often has Wrap Text turned on.

	A	B
1	Date	Description
2	######	STAPLES #507 AKRON OH 11/22STAPLES #
3	######	CHECK #3646 view
4	######	STAPLES #507 AKRON OH 11/22STAPLES #

Strategy: Follow these steps to correct the **Problem:**

1) Select all cells by pressing Ctrl+A. The cells in your selection will contain some cells with Wrap Text turned on and some cells with Wrap Text turned off. Click Wrap Text on the Home tab to turn on Wrap Text cell for all cells. Click Wrap Text again to turn off the property for all cells. Each row will now be a normal height, and you can see more cells, but you still need to make the columns wider.

2) Select Home – Format dropdown – AutoFit Column Width.

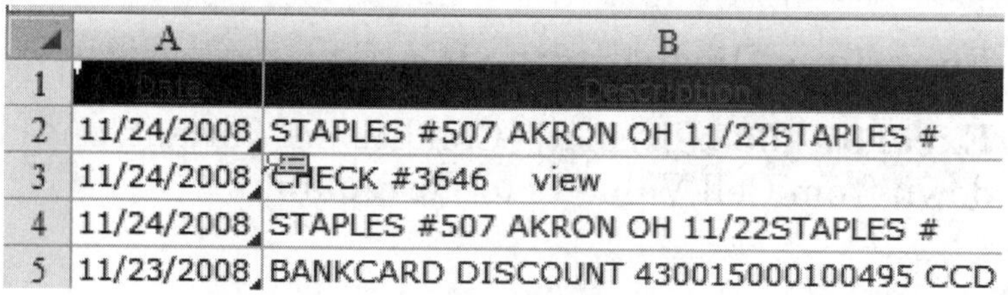

Figure 1329

The pasted data now has normal formatting.

	A	B
1	Date	Description
2	11/24/2008	STAPLES #507 AKRON OH 11/22STAPLES #
3	11/24/2008	CHECK #3646 view
4	11/24/2008	STAPLES #507 AKRON OH 11/22STAPLES #
5	11/23/2008	BANKCARD DISCOUNT 430015000100495 CCD

The pasted data will no longer be wrapped within cells.

Summary: Data pasted from Web pages often has the Wrap Text property turned on. This prevents the AutoFit command from working.

Commands Discussed: Home – Wrap Text; Home – Format dropdown – AutoFit Column Width

Excel 97-2003: Format – Cells – Alignment – Wrap Text; Format – Column – AutoFit

DELETE ALL PICTURES IN PASTED DATA

Problem: I copy data from my bank's Web page into Excel. On the Web page, the bank has little check icons that let me view a physical copy of a check. As you can see in Figure 1330, these check icons show up as annoying images in my Excel workbook. How can I delete all these images in one step?

Figure 1330

Delete all images.

Strategy: Excel offers a tool, Select Objects, that allows you to select all images in a rectangular area. In Excel 2007, the tool moved from the

Drawing toolbar to be a choice in the Find & Select dropdown on the Home ribbon tab. Here's how you use it:

1) Turn on Select Objects mode by selecting Home – Find & Select – Select Objects.

2) Using the mouse, start highlighting above and to the left of the first cell that contains a check icon. Drag down and to the right to encompass all the cells that contain check icons. As shown in Figure 1331, all the drawing objects in the rectangle will be selected.

Figure 1331

Drag a rectangle around the objects.

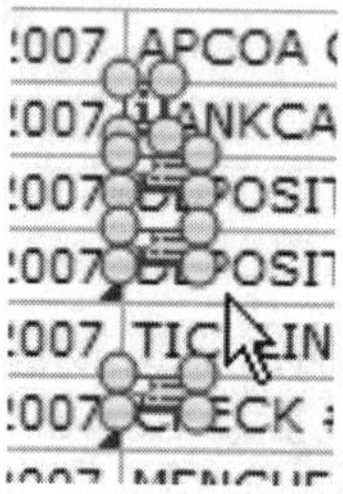

3) Press the Delete key to delete all the selected objects at once.

Gotcha: You have to remember to turn off Select Objects mode, or you will no longer be able to select any cells. It is very annoying to try to select cells and have the mouse not respond to clicking. To exit Select Objects mode, you simply press the Esc key.

Summary: You can use Select Objects mode to select all images in a rectangular range.

Commands Discussed: Home – Find & Select – Select Objects

Excel 97-2003: View – Toolbars – Drawing and select the white arrow.

ADD WORDART TO A WORKSHEET

Problem: My spreadsheets are blah. How can I make them more eye-catching?

Strategy: You can create attractive spreadsheets by adding WordArt. WordArt has become more complex in Excel 2007. This means that you can create far more effects, but it also means it is harder to create the effects you want.

Figure 1332 shows three different WordArt samples. The top sample is typical of Excel 2003. The text is filled with a radial gradient. The text is outlined. A transform is applied to the text to make it bend up.

The second example shows off some regular effects and also some of the new effects available in Excel 2007. For the regular effects, the text has a red fill and a yellow outline. The text is transformed into a shield shape. New Excel 2007 effects include adding a blue glow around the shape and then using 3-D Rotation for the text.

The third example fills the text with a picture. A full reflection is added below the text.

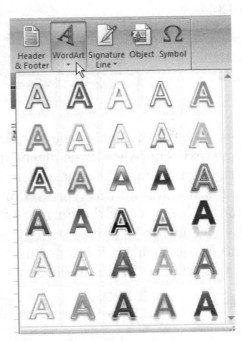

Figure 1332

Samples of WordArt in Excel 2007

Figure 1333

There are about 1.78E+53 possible combinations of WordArt. Microsoft can only fit 30 of them here, so don't feel bad if your favorite is not here.

Part IV

To create WordArt, you select Insert – WordArt. The initial dropdown asks you to choose from among the 30 choices shown in Figure 1333. This is a bit perplexing to WordArt veterans. Unlike in Excel 2003, this gallery offers no twisting effects. But you can easily change every effect in the gallery after you create the WordArt. Do you want to fill the inside of the letters or leave it white and use the outline to define the letters. If you want no fill, then choose one of the white letters. Hover first to read the descriptions: Some have Fill – White, some have Fill – None, and some have Fill – Transparent

Choose one of the types, and Excel will insert new WordArt in the center of the visible range. The WordArt starts with a value YOUR TEXT HERE. In Figure 1334, notice that the WordArt is surrounded by a dashed box, which indicates that the WordArt is in Text Edit mode. You can start typing the text you want to appear as the WordArt.

Figure 1334

WordArt starts with this default text.

Of course, as you finish typing, the flashing insertion point will be at the end of the text. There are three places that you can begin formatting WordArt. You can change the font on the Home tab of the ribbon; you can add an outline around the WordArt or add a fill by using the tools in the Shape Styles group of the Format tab (see Figure 1335); and you can actually format the letters by using the tools in the WordArt Styles group of the Format ribbon. Changes on the Home ribbon tab require you to select all the text in the WordArt before applying the change.

Figure 1335

The Shape Styles group will add a box around the WordArt.

Figure 1336 shows some effects that you can apply using the Shape Styles group. While these few limited examples work in the Shape Styles group, most settings here will frustrate you. I will explain why.

In the top example, a gradient is applied from Shape Fill. You'll notice that the gradient is applied to the area inside the bounding box for the shape. In the next example, a black border is applied using the Shape Outline dropdown. In the third example, Preset 8 is chosen from the Shape Effects dropdown. While this formats the bounding box, it also applies an effect to the letters. In the final example, 3-D Rotation affects all the letters.

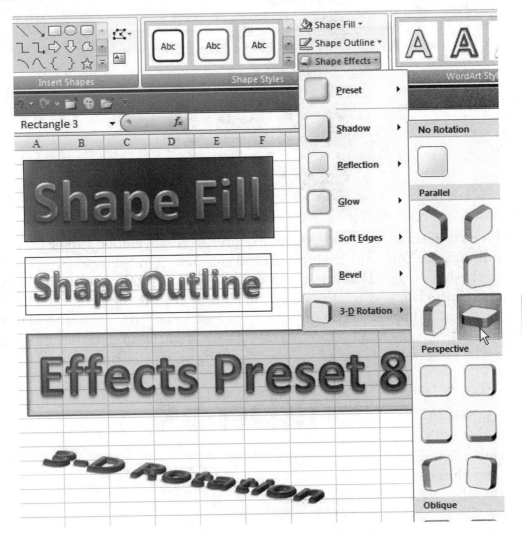

Figure 1336

A few shape style settings work well with WordArt.

Other settings in the Shape Styles group work well only when you've applied a fill or an outline to the WordArt bounding box. If you try to apply a glow or soft edges to WordArt without a border or fill, you would not see any changes. Figure 1337 shows that the remaining options in the Shape Effects menu basically format the gradient fill and not the letters.

Figure 1337

Other shape style settings affect only the bounding box.

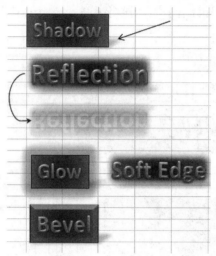

The next settings you can change are on the Home ribbon tab or on the mini toolbar. You have to select all the characters in the WordArt to apply these settings. If you plan on using the Home tab, you can simply press Shift+Home when the insertion character is at the end of the text. To get the mini toolbar to appear, it is best to use the mouse to select from left to right and then move the mouse slightly up and to the right. Figure 1338 shows a variety of font changes using the Home tab.

Figure 1338

Calibri 54 point is the default font. You can change it to other fonts.

When most people think of WordArt, they think of the effects available in the WordArt Styles – Effects – Transform menu, which you can use to twist or bend the type to fill a wide variety of shapes. Figure 1339 shows some of the available shapes. You do not have to select all the text in the shape to apply a Transform effect.

Figure 1339

Transforms apply the classic WordArt look.

The Text Fill menu in the WordArt Styles group will apply an effect to the letters in the WordArt. Figure 1340 shows a gradient, a picture, and a texture fill.

Part IV

Figure 1340

Fill the letters with an effect.

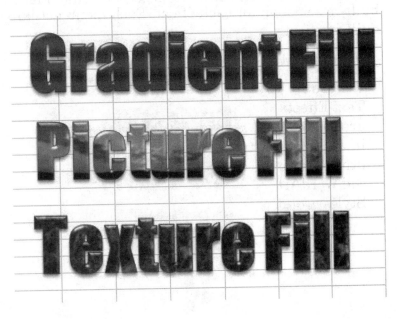

The Text Outline menu in the WordArt Styles group controls the color, weight, and style of the outline around the letters, as shown in Figure 1341. Using a white fill and a thick outline for the letters creates an interesting effect. Note how using the Outline menu in WordArt Styles affects the outline of the letters. Using the Outline menu in Shape Styles (a short distance away on the ribbon) affects the square outline around the entire shape.

Figure 1341

WordArt outline effects.

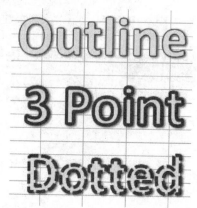

Settings in the WordArt Styles Text Effects menus affect Shadow, Reflection, Glow, and Bevel. These settings can be applied to a portion of the characters in the WordArt. In Figure 1342, a small glow and a larger glow are applied to the individual words in the Glow Glow WordArt. To apply the effect to all characters in the WordArt, you either select all characters or click on the dotted bounding box around the WordArt to change it to a solid bounding box. Note that Figure 1342 shows just 1 built-in selection for each effect. Each menu actually offers from 9 to 44 built-in effects.

Figure 1342

WordArt Text Effects are located in the third dropdown in the WordArt Styles group.

The settings on the fly-out menus are often a small subset of the vast range of settings. If you choose the More option at the bottom of each menu, you will be presented with the Format dialog, where you can access all settings. In the 3-D Format category, you can change the Material dropdown to a variety of materials, including wire frame or translucent. In the 3-D Rotation settings, you can rotate the WordArt around three different axes. Figure 1343 shows just a few of the custom settings.

Figure 1343

Access the Format dialog box for more settings.

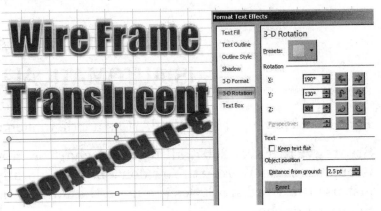

Earlier in this topic, I estimated that there were 1.78E+53 different varieties of WordArt possible. That estimate does not include the various options available if you change the inflection points in some of the transforms. Figure 1344 shows WordArt with a left slant transform applied. Look for a pink diamond handle when the WordArt is selected. By dragging this handle up or down, you can control the amount of slant applied. The top WordArt in Figure 1344 has the maximum slant, and the second WordArt has a moderate slant. As you drag the handle, Excel will draw in guidelines to show the amount of slant you are about to apply.

Part IV

Figure 1344

Drag the pink handle to adjust many transforms.

Summary: By using WordArt and its various options, you can make your worksheets and charts really eye-catching.

Commands Discussed: Insert – WordArt

Excel 97-2003: Insert – WordArt. The WordArt toolbar in previous versions of Excel offered about 73 million variations, which is actually a tiny fraction of the variations available in Excel 2007.

CHART AND SMARTART TEXT IS AUTOMATICALLY WORDART

Problem: How can I add WordArt as a title in a chart?

Strategy: In Excel 2007, all text in a chart or in a SmartArt graphic is eligible to be WordArt. You don't have to do anything special: You just use the WordArt Styles group on the Format tab while editing the SmartArt or chart.

In SmartArt, you have full access to all the WordArt styles, including reflection and transforms. The SmartArt at the top of Figure 1345 shows three different styles of WordArt in each shape.

Unlike in SmartArt, in charts, the settings Bevel, 3-D Rotation, and Transform are grayed out. You can only change the fill, outline, shadow, and glow.

Figure 1345

Text in Smart-Art and charts is WordArt.

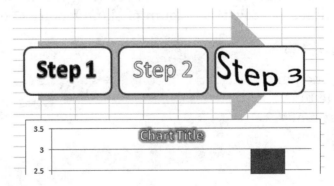

Alternate Strategy: Rather than formatting a chart title as WordArt, you can leave out the chart title and add WordArt as the chart. Follow these steps:

1)   Select Layout – Chart Title – None.

2)   Keep the chart selected. Select Insert – WordArt. Excel will embed the WordArt in the chart.

3)   Resize the WordArt so that it's title sized.

4)   Use any of the full range of WordArt effects, including 3-D rotation and transforms. Figure 1346 shows a chart with a WordArt title.

Figure 1346

Create bending WordArt titles.

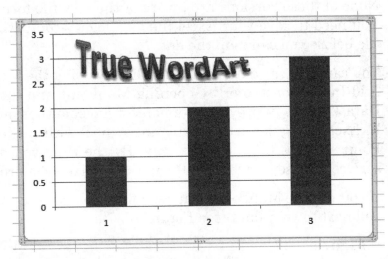

Part IV

Summary: All text in shapes, charts, and SmartArt can be WordArt.

Commands Discussed: Format – WordArt Styles; Layout – Chart Title – None; Insert – WordArt

Excel 97-2003: In previous Excel versions, you would have to select the chart and use Insert – WordArt. You could not automatically format chart titles as WordArt.

USE MAPPOINT TO PLOT DATA ON A MAP

Problem: I have a retail store and keep a mailing list of everyone who shops in my store. The data contains street address, city, state, and zip code. How can I view my customers on a map so I can easily see where they're concentrated.

Strategy: Microsoft MapPoint is an extra program that you can buy from Microsoft, in either a North American version or a European version. With a US$299 list price, it is fairly expensive. However, Microsoft often gives it away for attending its seminars. You also might be able to pick up a copy on eBay for far less than the list price. MapPoint allows you to do some very cool geographic analysis of data.

There are versions of MapPoint labeled 2000, 2002, 2004, and 2006. None of these versions are aware of the new file formats in Excel 2007. You need to save your Excel file as a legacy-compatible Excel 2003 .xls file before you can map the data.

You can map the data in Excel either by using the MapPoint icon on the Add-Ins ribbon tab or by opening MapPoint and using Data – Import Data Wizard. In previous versions of Excel, either method worked fine. In Excel 2007, using the MapPoint symbol with earlier versions of Map-Point appears to be fairly buggy. By the time you are reading this, a service release for Office 2007 may have fixed the problem.

If you use the MapPoint Map icon in Excel, you will have a map embedded next to your data (see Figure 1347).

Figure 1347

Embedding a map in Excel was cool in Excel 2003. It is somewhat broken in Excel 2007.

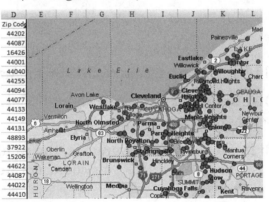

If the feature is fixed, you will be able to select the data, including the headings, and click the MapPoint Map icon on the Add-Ins tab, as shown in Figure 1348.

Figure 1348

MapPoint adds icons to Excel.

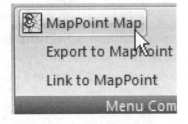

MapPoint will match your addresses to its database. Soon, you will have a map in Excel that shows your customers (see Figure 1349). Your store had one customer from Alaska and several from Florida, so the map initially zooms out to show those customers.

Figure 1349

The initial map is zoomed out to show all customers.

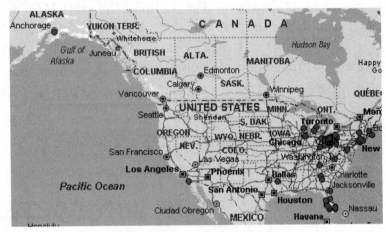

To get a better view of the majority of your clients, you can click and drag to zoom in to the region around your store. You can see that you get a lot of customers from the local area, and you also get people who travel the interstate. As shown in Figure 1350, your store in Cleveland gets a fair amount of traffic from people who live along I-90, I-80, I-77, and I-76.

Figure 1350

Zoom in for a regional view.

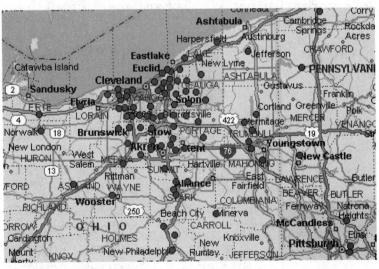

If your original data included street addresses, you can zoom in further. You can now see from which sections of your city your customers generally come. This information can help you to target newspaper or billboard advertising.

Gotcha: In several previous versions of Excel, Microsoft had a license to bundle a MapInfo product called Microsoft Map with Excel. Microsoft Map was taken out of the default install in Excel 2000 and removed from the product entirely in Excel 2002. The MapPoint product offers far more flexibility than Microsoft Map.

Summary: Plotting geographic data in MapPoint is a great way to get a visual of your customer base.

Commands Discussed: Add-Ins – MapPoint Map

WHY DOES EXCEL MARK CELLS WITH A PURPLE INDICATOR?

Problem: I'm starting to see crazy cells being marked with a purple indicator. Why are cells with values like COST and ALL being flagged? I've become used to red indicators for cell comments and green indicators for Excel errors. Why is Excel marking all these seemingly innocent values?

Strategy: Purple triangles are SmartTag indicators. If you enter a stock market ticker symbol in a cell, for example, Excel adds a SmartTag indicator, as shown in Figure 1351.

Figure 1351

Why are ALL, DIRECT, and COST marked?

	A	B	C	D	E
1	PROGRAM	START	END	COST	APPLIES TO
2	P101	1/1/2008	12/31/2008	49768	DIRECT
3	P102	2/18/2008	3/19/2008	74024	ALL
4	P103	12/31/2008	1/30/2009	63487	INDIRECT
5	P104	8/17/2008	9/16/2008	74020	DIRECT
6	P105	5/15/2008	6/14/2008	43601	ALL
7	P106	1/23/2008	2/22/2008	63504	ALL
8	P107	12/31/2008	1/30/2009	89412	ALL

A SmartTag lets you insert the stock price for the symbol, as shown in Figure 1352.

Figure 1352

SmartTag options.

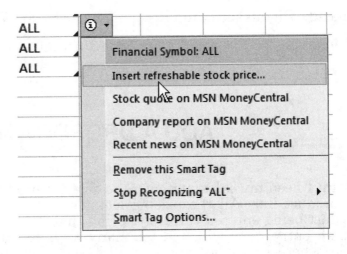

This is fine, but even cells that just look like ticker symbols are marked. For example, ALL is Allstate. COST is Costco. In previous versions of Excel, TRUE was recognized at the TrueTime company. Thankfully, Symmetricon bought out TrueTime in 2002, so we no longer have all TRUE cells marked.

In Excel 2002, your only choice was to turn off the Financial SmartTag by using Tools – AutoCorrect Options – SmartTags and unchecking the MSN MoneyCentral Financial Symbols.

In Excel 2003, a SmartTag itself now has an option to stop recognizing ALL as a SmartTag, as shown in Figure 1353.

Part IV

Figure 1353

Turn off the SmartTag for this value.

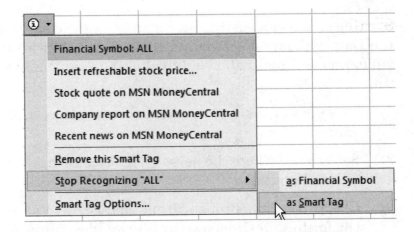

Summary: In Excel 2003 and later versions, you can turn off Smart-Tags for specific values.

Commands Discussed: Stop Recognizing as Smart Tag

Excel 97-2003: In Excel 2002, you can turn off the Financial Smart-Tag.

ADD A DROPDOWN TO A CELL

Problem: I need my sales managers to select a product from our company's product line. All the pricing lookups in the worksheet rely on the product being entered correctly. I find that if I allow my managers to type an entry, they will find too many ways to misspell items. For example, where I may be expecting PDT-960, they are likely to enter PDT 960, 960, and many other variations, as shown in Figure 1354. If I could offer them a list to select from, they would automatically select the correct spelling of the product.

Figure 1354

If the product name is not entered exactly as it needs to be entered, lookups fail.

=IF(ISBLANK($B8),"",VLOOKUP($B8,$K$2:$M$6,2,FALSE))

▲	A	B	C	D	E
1	XYZ Company Sales Order				
2					
3	Customer:				
4					
5	Qty	Item	Description	Unit Price	Ext. Price
6	25	PDT-960	Data Entry Terminal with Scanner	795	19,875
7	10	PDT-710	Data Entry Terminal - 512K	250	2,500
8	125	PDT 960	#N/A	#N/A	#N/A

Strategy: You can easily allow managers to select from a list by using the Data Validation command. It turns out that every cell has a data validation setting to allow any value. You can change this default setting:

1) In an out-of-the-way section of the worksheet, type a valid list of values.

2) Select a cell where the person will be entering data and choose Data – Data Validation.

3) Choose the Allow dropdown and change Any Value to List. The check box for In-Cell Dropdown appears and is automatically checked.

4)   Point to the range in the Source field. Alternatively, if the list is short, you can skip step 1 and type the list items, separated by commas, in this box. This particular worksheet already has the valid products as the first column of a lookup table used to get prices. (see Figure 1355)

Figure 1355

Specify the location for the list.

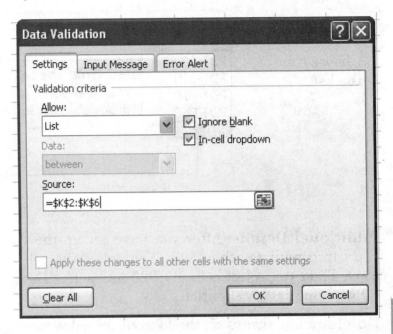

Part
IV

5)   Optionally, use the Input Message tab of the Data Validation dialog to provide instructions to the sales managers (see Figure 1356). You can also use the Error Alert tab to display custom text when the sales managers do not select from your list.

Figure 1356

Optionally, provide a ToolTip with a note.

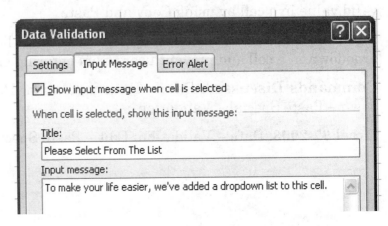

6) Click OK to apply the validation.

7) When someone selects the cell, a dropdown will appear, along with your input message. Choose the dropdown arrow, and the managers will be able to select from a list of products, as shown in Figure 1357.

Figure 1357

Choose from the list.

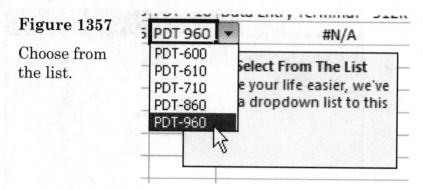

Additional Details: After you have set up the validation in one cell, you can copy it to other cells. You select the cell and press Ctrl+C to copy. Then you select cells B7:B20 and select Home – Paste dropdown – Paste Special – Validation.

Gotcha: I am always on the lookout for sales managers who know just a little too much about Excel. If a manager were smart enough to delete row 5, he could also delete row 5 of the lookup table off to the right. See "Store Lists for Dropdowns on a Hidden Sheet" on page 893.

Gotcha: If someone copies a bunch of cells and pastes them over your validated cells in B, the validation will not work. Anyone can get an invalid value in a cell by using Copy and Paste.

Summary: You can use the List option with data validation to provide a dropdown in a cell and prevent users from entering erroneous values.

Commands Discussed: Data – Data Validation; Home – Paste dropdown – Paste Special – Validation

Excel 97-2003: Data – Validation; Edit – Paste Special – Validation

STORE LISTS
FOR DROPDOWNS ON A HIDDEN SHEET

Problem: The Data Validation dialog will not allow me to reference lists stored on another worksheet. Is there a workaround?

Strategy: Starting in Excel 2007, you are free to store your validation lists on another worksheet. You can store your validation lists on a worksheet and even hide the worksheet. In Excel 2003 and earlier, you need to follow the steps in the Alternate Strategy instead. For Excel 2007, follow these steps:

1) Insert a blank worksheet in the workbook.

2) Give the sheet a name such as Lists.

3) Type your list on the new Lists worksheet. Note the range of the list.

4) When you set up the Data Validation dialog, you cannot use the Reference icon to point to another sheet. Instead, type an equals sign, the sheet name, an exclamation point, and the range of the list. Figure 1358 shows the proper syntax for a worksheet without any spaces in the name. If the worksheet you're referencing has a space in the name, you need to use apostrophes around the name, as in ='Validation Lists'!A2:A9.

Part IV

Figure 1358

Specify a list on another worksheet.

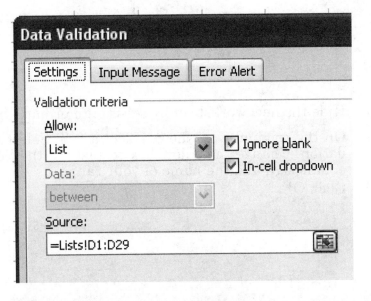

Results: Excel 2007 will allow the validation to work properly.

Gotcha: You can save this workbook as an Excel 97-2003 workbook and the validation will work in Excel 2003. However, you will not be able to edit the validation in previous versions of Excel.

Alternate Strategy: If you need to set up validation in previous versions of Excel, you should make the list a named range on another worksheet. Follow these steps.

1) Insert a blank sheet in the workbook. Type your list on this sheet.

2) Highlight the list. Click in the Name box to the left of the formula bar. Type a name, such as ItemList, and press Enter (see Figure 1359). This action sets up a workbook-level named range.

Figure 1359

Name the list.

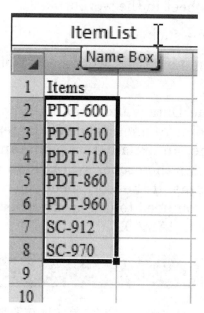

3) Hide the new worksheet by selecting Format – Sheet – Hide.

4) On the original worksheet, select a cell. Select Data – Data Validation. Change the Allow box to List. In the Source box, type an equals sign and the name of your range, as shown in Figure 1360. Click OK.

Figure 1360

Excel 2003 would accept the named range.

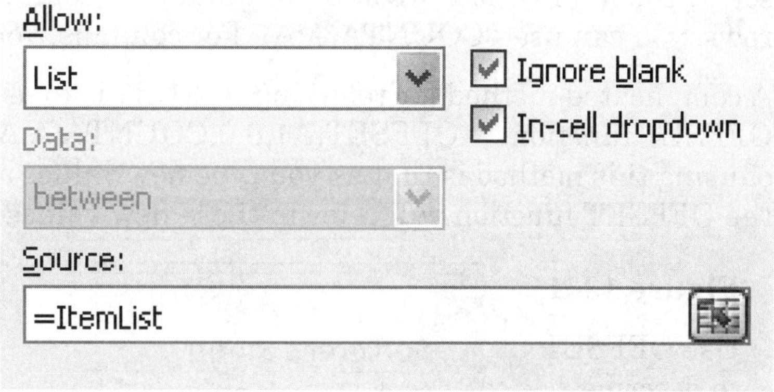

Results: The cell will have validation based on a range on another worksheet.

Summary: Excel 2007 will allow you to store validation lists on another worksheet. In Excel 2003 and earlier, you have to set up a workbook-level named range in order to use a list on another worksheet.

Commands Discussed: Data – Validation

ALLOW VALIDATION LISTS TO AUTOMATICALLY REDEFINE AS THEY GROW

Part IV

Problem: I'm storing a number of validation lists on a hidden Lists worksheet. Every time I add new values to the list, I have to redefine all the range names.

Strategy: You can create a dynamic named range by using the OFFSET function. This is a flexible function that allows you to describe a rectangular range. This function can have up to five arguments.

Let's say that you want to describe the list shown in Figure 1361. The first argument in OFFSET is a starting cell reference. This would be A1. The next two arguments say that the top-left cell should move down a certain number of rows and over a certain number of columns. In this example, both of those arguments are zero. The next two arguments describe the number of rows and the number of columns in the range. For rows, you can use =COUNTA(A:A). For columns, you use 1.

A complicated method for referring to A1:A7 is to use the COUNTA and OFFSET functions: =OFFSET(A1,0,0,COUNTA(A:A),1). The advantage of using this method is that as you type new values at the end of the list, the OFFSET function will refer to those new values.

Figure 1361

Use OFFSET to describe this list.

◢	A
1	Sorcerer's Stone
2	Chamber of Secrets
3	Prisoner of Azkaban
4	Goblet of Fire
5	Order of the Phoenix
6	Half-Blood Prince
7	Deathly Hallows
8	

To build validation lists that will automatically grow, follow these steps:

1) Insert a new worksheet in the workbook. Give the sheet a one-word name, such as Lists.

2) Type the first list starting in cell A1. Do not add a heading.

3) Type additional lists (if necessary) starting in B1, C1, and so on.

4) Select Formulas – Name Manager. Click Add.

5) Give the list a name. Set the scope to Workbook. In the Refers To box, carefully type the entire OFFSET function, making sure to use absolute references and the worksheet name before all references: =OFFSET(Lists!$A$1,0,0,COUNTA(Lists!$A:$A),1). Click OK. Excel will return you to the Name Manager, which should look as shown Figure 1362.

6) Repeat steps 4 and 5 for each additional list.

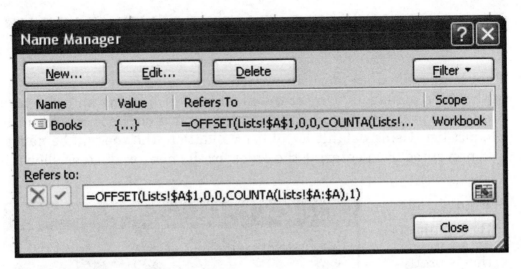

Figure 1362

The name Books will grow as necessary.

7) When you set up validation on another worksheet, use =Books as the list.

Results: As you add new items to the bottom of the list, the dropdowns will automatically reflect the new items.

Gotcha: For this process to work, you must make sure there are no blank cells in the middle of a list. You cannot randomly type other data below your lists. It is best to use a dedicated Lists sheet that is hidden so no one will accidentally add temporary calculations below your lists.

Additional Details: Depending on the circumstances, you can allow the people using the spreadsheet to add new values to the bottom of these lists. Finish each list with an entry of *** Enter New Values Below ***. Then, when the workbooks are sent back in, you merely need to look to see if any new values were added in that section of the list worksheet.

Summary: Using the Input Message tab of the Data Validation dialog allows you to create helpful ToolTips that can appear in any cell.

Commands Discussed: Formulas – Name Manager

Functions Discussed: =OFFSET(), =COUNTA()

Excel 97-2003: Insert – Name – Define

Part
IV

CONFIGURE VALIDATION TO "EASE UP"

Problem: I set up a worksheet with data validation to ease the job of the sales managers. One of the managers is entering an order for a brand new product. The product is so new that it does not appear in the product list. Using default Excel list validation, the rep will be nagged and prevented from entering the order for the new product, as shown in Figure 1363.

Figure 1363

By default, data validation is pretty strict.

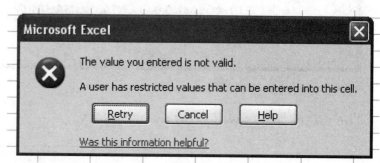

You can tell what will happen here. At the next sales conference call, the sales manager will say that he couldn't enter his $4.5 million order because the lousy spreadsheet wouldn't let him. As the spreadsheet designer, you will be demoted to manager of the "revenue prevention" department.

Strategy: There are three different settings on the Error Alert tab of the Data Validation dialog. The default is the hard-line version of the message, shown in Figure 1363. This is known as the Stop style of Validation.

On the Error Alert tab of the Validation dropdown, you can change Stop to Warning, as shown in Figure 1364. With a warning, the person using the spreadsheet is greeted with a dialog box with Yes, No, Cancel, and Help buttons. The default button is No, but people can override and allow the value if they are absolutely sure. You should type a message to indicate this, as shown in Figure 1364.

When a sales rep enters incorrect data, he will see the message in Figure 1365. Of course, because the message is longer than five words, he will press Enter without reading the message. Because the default button is No, he will then need to choose from the list.

Figure 1364

Warning is probably the best setting.

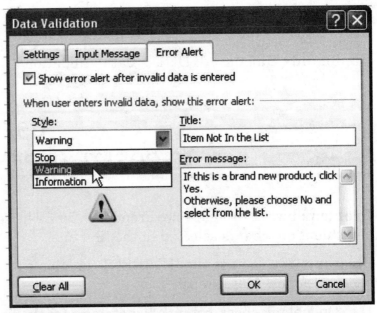

Figure 1365

Note that No is the default button.

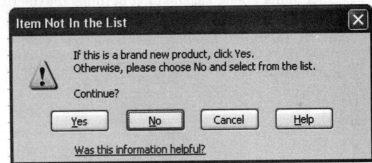

Part
IV

The final choice is to set the Error Alert style to Information. This choice is the "ease up" king. The error message defaults to having the OK button selected, as shown in Figure 1366. You will certainly end up with a lot of invalid data if you use this setting.

Figure 1366

With the Information setting, the OK box is default.

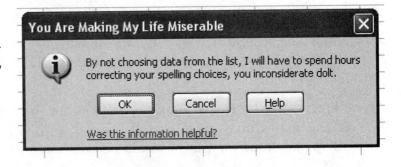

Summary: You can decide how strict to make data validation by using the Error Alert tab on the Data Validation dialog.

Commands Discussed: Data – Data Validation

USE VALIDATION
TO CREATE DEPENDENT LISTS

Problem: I want to create two dropdown lists. The second list should be dependent on what is selected in the first one.

Strategy: You can use the INDIRECT function as the source of the second list. Follow these steps:

1) On a blank sheet, set up a list of items for the first dropdown: Writing, Science, Math, and Geography. Name the range Subjects, as shown in Figure 1367.

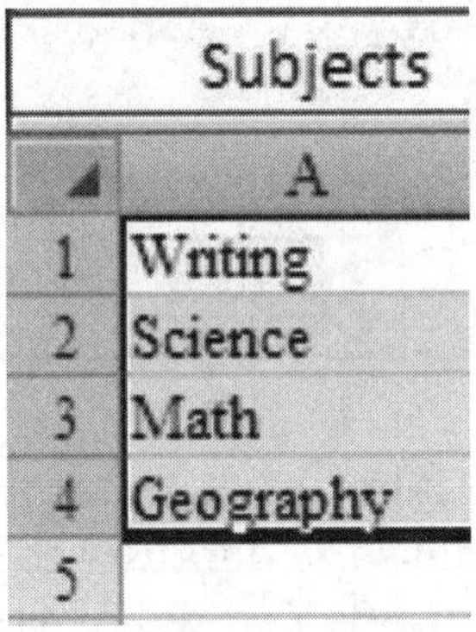

Figure 1367

Define the
first list.

2) In other columns, set up a list of choices available for each subject.

3) Name the second list Writing, as shown in Figure 1368. It is critical that the range name for this list match the value in the original list.

4) Repeat step 3 for each item in the first list. In each case, the name of the new range must match the value in column A. In Figure 1368, the name for C1:C4 would be Science, and so on.

Figure 1368

Set up depen-
dent lists, each
with a name
from the first
list.

Writing	▾	(	●	f_x	Creative Writing

◢	A	B	C	
1	Writing	Creative Writing	Physical Science	Patten
2	Science	Narrative Writing	Chemistry	Proble
3	Math	Poetry	Biology	Numbe
4	Geography		Earth Science	Geome
5				Algeb
6				Estima
7				

5) To select the subject from cell D2, select cell D2 and then select Data – Data Validation. Change the Allow box to List; in the Source box, type =Subjects.

6) Click OK. Cell D2 will have a dropdown list of subjects.

7) To set up the second dropdown, select cell D4 and then select Data – Data Validation. Change the Allow dropdown under Validation Criteria from Any Value to List. In the Source box, enter =INDIRECT(D2), as shown in Figure 1369.

Figure 1369

The second
dropdown uses
the INDIRECT
function to
grab a range
name from cell
D2.

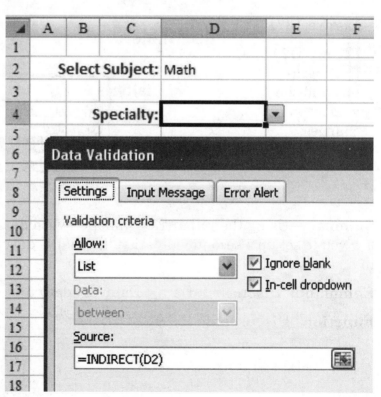

Part
IV

Results: When you select a value in D2, the formula for the second dropdown list will automatically update, as shown in Figure 1370. The INDIRECT function looks in D2 and hopes to find a formula there. When you select Writing in D2, the validation formula becomes =Writing. Because you cleverly set up a named range called Writing, Excel is able to populate the list.

Figure 1370

Choose Reading in D2, and the list in D4 reflects the Reading list.

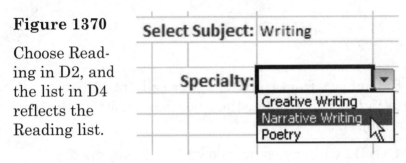

When you change D2 to Geography, =INDIRECT(D2) will become =Geography. Again, because you have a named range called Geography, Excel is able to fill in the second dropdown with geography subjects, as shown in Figure 1371.

Figure 1371

Change D2 to Geography and the validation list changes.

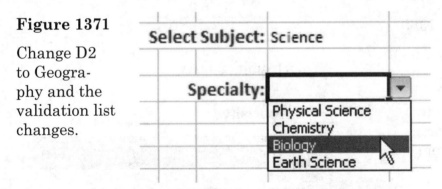

Summary: Using the INDIRECT function with data validation will allow you to set up a second validation list that is dependent on the choice in an earlier list.

Commands Discussed: Data – Data Validation

Functions Discussed: =INDIRECT()

ADD A TOOLTIP TO A CELL TO GUIDE THE PERSON USING THE WORKBOOK

Problem: Excel offers all sorts of ToolTips to help understand the tool-bars, as shown in Figure 1372. It would be cool if I could add a ToolTip to a cell.

Figure 1372

ToolTips provide instant help.

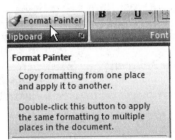

Strategy: You can easily add an informative ToolTip to any cell. The ToolTip will appear when someone selects the cell. Follow these steps:

1) Move the cell pointer to the cell. From the ribbon, choose Data – Data Validation. In the Data Validation dialog, select the Input Message tab.

2) On the Input Message tab, type a title for the ToolTip. In the Input Message area, type instructions for the person filling out the worksheet, as shown in Figure 1373.

Part IV

Figure 1373

Write the cell ToolTip on the Input Message tab.

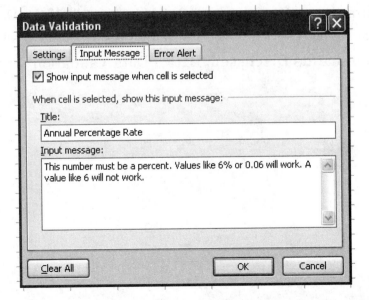

Results: When you move the cell pointer to that cell, an informative ToolTip will appear, as shown in Figure 1374.

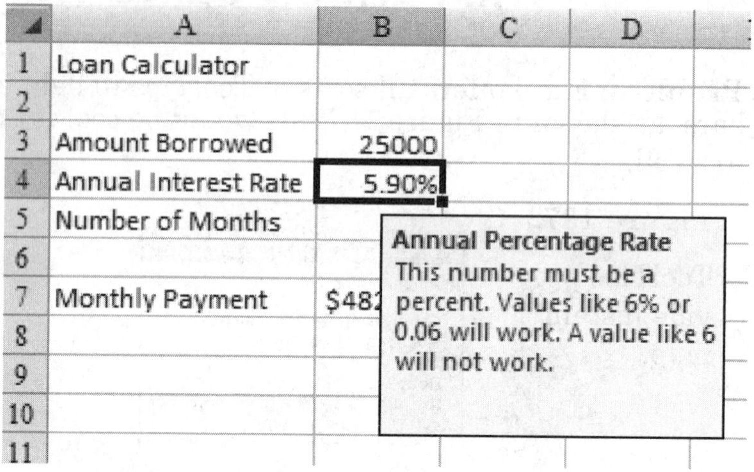

Figure 1374

Help appears for an input cell.

◢	A	B	C	D	
1	Loan Calculator				
2					
3	Amount Borrowed	25000			
4	Annual Interest Rate	5.90%			
5	Number of Months				
6					
7	Monthly Payment	$48			
8					
9					
10					
11					

Annual Percentage Rate
This number must be a percent. Values like 6% or 0.06 will work. A value like 6 will not work.

Additional Details: This is an innovative use for the Validation command. You are not actually specifying anything in particular in Allow dropdown, but merely using one of the auxilary settings in order to have the tool tip display. The validation input message only appears when the cell is selected and might be slightly preferable to cell comments since they will not litter the spreadsheet with tiny red triangles. For information on cell comments, see "Leave Helpful Notes with Cell Comments" on page 749.

Summary: By using the Input Message tab of the Data Validation dialog, you can create helpful ToolTips that can appear in any cell.

Commands Discussed: Data – Data Validation

AFTERWORD

There you have it: 377 problems and their solutions. Hopefully, you have found many that will make your experience with Excel far more efficient. When I am teaching Power Excel class, every new class brings new people with new problems, and you will undoubtedly run into problems that are not in this book. I invite you to send your problems to NotInTheBook@MrExcel.com. I'll try to get an answer to you, and your question might end up in the next edition of this book!

Any time I am in a room full of 100 accountants for a morning, I learn a few new tips. Do you know of a cool technique that is not in the book? Send your tips to BetterWay@MrExcel.com. If your tip is one I haven't heard before, I will reward you with one of my Excel Master pins that you can wear to show off your Excel mastery.

Part
IV

THE PRINT VERSION OF THIS BOOK IS HEAVY

Problem: I travel frequently. I want to carry my copy of Learn Excel, but it is too bulky.

Strategy: Use the e-book version. If you are holding the print version of this book, I will propose a trade; if you can give me a bit of information about your location, I will offer you a free high-resolution copy of the e-book version. The version is completely searchable and fits on your hard drive.

I would like to get a sense of where in the world my distributor manages to get the print book sold. If you visit http://www.mrexcel.com/ibought-theprintbook.php, I'll ask you for a city and country so we can add the data to our map. You can then download a personalized version of the e-book. It is 20-30MB, so a fast internet connection is a plus.

Gotcha: When you visit the page, I will ask you for a few random numbers from this matrix, so have the print book nearby.

Figure 1375

Matrix of numbers.

	A	B	C	D	E	F	G	H	I	J
1	25	86	48	92	57	02	35	40	06	70
2	01	59	55	20	30	26	29	09	76	18
3	38	63	51	24	04	05	22	61	80	52
4	82	87	96	39	41	67	68	42	31	10
5	07	75	73	62	94	46	23	78	89	13
6	32	79	93	11	83	37	56	85	08	95
7	64	72	12	91	45	00	33	81	98	90
8	58	97	19	50	03	65	36	15	88	43
9	21	17	28	54	60	14	77	69	84	74
10	99	66	16	47	71	34	44	53	49	27

Summary: Thanks for buying the book!

E

F

K

Kapor, Mitch, 160
Keep Text Only, 41
Keyboard Shortcuts
　Legacy, 16
　New, 18
Knowledge Base, 484
Krams, Howard, 326

L

Landscape, 68
Large Grid, 30
Large Values in a Column, Fitting, 854
Laser Printer, 96
Last day of Month, 352
Last Name, First Name, 209
Last Week, 567
Layouts, Chart, 693
LCM, 308
Leading Zeroes, Imported Data, 203
Leadtime Report, 588
Least Common Multiples, 308
Least-Squares Method, 274
LEFT function, 189, 193
Legacy Dialogs, 12
Legacy Keyboard Shortcuts, 16
Legend Location, 720
Legends, Needless, 692
LEN function, 196
Length of Text, 196
Lies, Charts, 722
Lightning Bolts, 773
Line Feed, 417
Line Thickness, 767
Linefeed in Formula, 784

LINEST Function, 274, 280
Linked Pictures, 830
Links, Suppressing, 86
List, 258
List Diagram, 788
List Format, 413
List in Excel 2003, 414
Lists
　Add two, 369
　Compare, 365, 367
　Compare Using Pivot Table, 612
Live Preview, 36
Loan Payment, 224
Lock heading rows, 57
Locked Cells, 676
Locked Cells Can be Edited, 676
Locked Reference in Formula, 148
Logic Rules, Boolean, 401
Logo as Shape, 777
Lookup, 369
Lottery Probability, 306
Lotus 1-2-3, 162
Lotus Arrow Keys, 237
Lotus Transition Mode, 828

M

Macro Editor, 80
Macro to Customize Startup, 79
Macros, Accessing, 28
Manage Add-Ins, 393
Manual Calculation, 319
Manually Format Pivot Table, 602
Mapping Data, 885
MapPoint, 885
Margin, Footer, 66
Margins, 68
Martin, Ron, 711

N

S

CHARTS AND GRAPHS FOR MICROSOFT OFFICE EXCEL 2007

This book shows you how to coax Excel to create many charts you might not have believed were possible. You'll learn techniques that allow you to ditch the Microsoft defaults and actually create charts that communicate your point. Learn how to create charts right in Excel cells using the new Excel 2007 data bars–or even the decades-old REPT function! In no time, this book will have you creating charts that wow your audience and effectively communicate your message.

PIVOT TABLE DATA CRUNCHING

Pivot tables are Excel's most powerful feature. This book will show you how to master pivot tables to produce powerful summaries of reams of data with just a few mouse clicks. You will learn techniques to quickly highlight your top 10 customers, compare sales from this period to last period, summarize transactional data by month, quarter, or year -- all without writing a single formula. Available in a first edition covering Excel 97-2003 and a second edition covering Excel 2007.

VBA AND MACROS FOR MICROSOFT OFFICE EXCEL 2007

You are an expert in Excel, but the macro recorder doesn't work and you can't make heads or tails out of the recorded code. Macros might work today but not tomorrow. These are all common problems that unfortunately cause too many Excel gurus to turn away from writing macros. This book shows you why the macro recorder fails and the steps needed to convert recorded code into code that will work every day with every dataset.

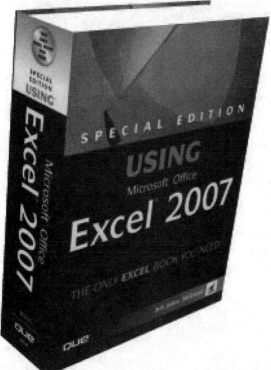

SPECIAL EDITION USING MICROSOFT OFFICE EXCEL 2007

Does your life play out in a spreadsheet? Do numbers in columns and rows make or break you in the work world? Tired of having numbers kicked in your face by other Excel power users who make your modest spreadsheets look paltry compared to their fancy charts and pivot tables? This book is the ultimate guide to every feature and function in Excel 2007. Contains 1080 pages, including a 300-page function reference.

TRAIN YOUR STAFF

Liven up your next annual conference by having MrExcel perform tricks from this book live for your audience. Whether you need a 2-hour breakout session at your controllers conference or a half-day training session for the accounting department, Bill Jelen will entertain and inform your audience, from 25 to 2000.

To book a seminar, visit speaking.html at MrExcel.com. For a list of upcoming seminars, visit pressapearances.shtml at MrExcel.com.

Poster © 2007 Hatch Show Print
Reprinted with permission.

DAILY VIDEO PODCAST

Learn a new trick every weekday with a 2-minute video from MrExcel.

No iPod required - you can download and watch the free video on your Windows PC.

To get started, search for Learn Excel in the iTunes Podcast Directory, or visit www.MrExcel.com/podcast.shtml for instructions.